Gloryhunting

Alan Porteous

authorHOUSE®

AuthorHouse™ UK Ltd.
500 Avebury Boulevard
Central Milton Keynes, MK9 2BE
www.authorhouse.co.uk
Phone: 08001974150

First published by AuthorHouse 2/23/2010

ISBN: 978-1-4490-6802-8 (sc)

This book is printed on acid-free paper.

Thanks to Mike and Iain for keeping me going, Brian for the Dumferline trip, Niamh, and everyone else who helped me get this done.

Contents

We sing when we're winnin'
We cry when we're no.
Our fear keeps us goin'
When there's nothin' tae show.
'Cos we cannae miss oot
When the big win goes doon,
We're huntin for glory,
An' we hope it comes soon.

Anon. 1907

Chapter 1 Pre – season

1.

I'm scared of dying on the toilet.

Not something I'd admit to in polite conversation but a fact nonetheless. Imagine pegging it; the victim of a sneaky stroke or a heart attack you never saw coming - Sitting there...... *on the pan*.

Dead.

One minute alive, focussing on the job in hand. The next minute gone, forever. And then being *found*, Lord preserve us, slumped with trousers at your ankles, by family , friends or worse, an axe wielding fireman or some green clad, 'doesn't give a toss' ambulance driver! The ignominy of it, to my mind, is paralysing.

I can see it now. A row of nose wrinkled witnesses, standing, staring, wondering how they are going to tell everyone down the pub the wonderfully embellished yarn about Craig the Crapping Corpse and his terminal deposit. All except my mother that is who is racking her brains to remember if she's put the green loo cleaner round the rim recently. After all, you know how the neighbours talk.

Then there's my adoring public gathered outside, mobilised by the arrival of an emergency vehicle in their locality.

"How did he die?", shouts Mrs Riley, the neighbourhood watch from Number 43.

"Don't know", shrugs the ambulance-man, "but he wasn't getting enough roughage that's for sure!"

Just as the triumphant revelation that "He died-on-the-pan!" ripples through the expectant throng of gathered wifeys, I am transported in a state of galloping rigor mortis to the awaiting ambulance. At the vital moment a gust of wind pulls the cover sheet off me and with a magician's flourish I am revealed as a colourless downhill skier inexplicably bereft of his strides, skis and those pointy pole things they use for balance.

"Oooooooooaaaaaahhhhh", the crowd gasp appreciatively.

"Check the Ys!" snickers a wee boy with a cone and a face rash.

And as my Quasimodo form disappears into the shadows, a final nail is pushed painfully into my coffin when someone stage whispers to the world, "He's that nutter that supported The Rovers you know".

Such is my nightmare.

So you may find it strange for me to say that contrary to my usual SAS operation of 'in-shit-n-out', I am, and have been for some fifteen minutes now, perched on the ceramic seat reading a dog-eared, seven week old copy of the Daily Record dated Monday the 17th of May, 2007. I'm looking at the football league tables. No that's wrong, I'm not just looking. For about the hundredth time I'm absorbing, enjoying, contemplating and reflecting on all the glory that this 6cm square of newsprint represents. My eyes are lingering lovingly on the top line of one league in particular;

Scottish First Division

	Pld	W	D	L	GF	GA	PTS
Arthurston Rovers	36	24	7	5	83	37	79

Impressive numbers yes, but more importantly than that , *much* more importantly, is the single, thin, black line drawn deliberately under my team's statistics. A line that separates the great from the good, the victorious from the also rans, from us and them. A line that has confirmed again and again, all summer long that we are champions and will be playing our football next year in the Scottish Premier League.

So 'see ya St Mirren! ','adios Ayr!' and 'bye bye Brechin!' It's on to bigger and better things; The opulent splendour of Ibrox, the intimidating grandeur of Celtic Park, Firhill. This is sailing on a different sea altogether. A sea with bigger boats, stronger winds, higher waves and pizza slices as well as pies at the snack bar.

What makes it doubly satisfying is that we're not supposed to be there. The powers at be don't like it one bit. We are salmon steaks passed their sell-by date under the aristocratic noses of 'The Big Teams'. Arthurston have a barely acceptable stadium, a home support of around 2000 that dwindles to 1950 for away games, no star players and a PA system that pronounces " substitute for Inverness – McFadyen!" as "muffmamoof aw imfermeff – McMuffin!" (Wilmot Park, our home ground, has seen more McMuffins over the years than a McDonalds stock-taker).

The upper echelon of Scottish football in this new millennium is not designed for, or accommodating to clubs like Arthurston. Trying to hurdle, side-step, or sneak under the stringent requirements allowing entry to the SPL is like being the hero in an Indian Jones movie. Owning your own all-seater stadium, having adequate parking facilities etc. are all just the early obstacles. They are however large enough and insurmountable enough to kneecap ninety percent of the teams making up the Scottish league, whether they are good enough or not. Should any unsavoury elements daringly tip-toe by these initial mantraps then surely they'll fall down the other deep, branch covered holes dug to thwart any ambitious but ultimately unsuitable adventurer. Indeed I have spent most of the summer agonising whether The Rovers have the pre-requisite number of tea-ladies, enough variety of wine for corporate hospitality or the regulation number of carpet tiles in the players' lounge. With three weeks left before the start of the season I still have the vision of getting up one morning and being met with the newspaper headline 'Arthurston refused SPL entry shocker – Grass wrong shade of green!'

So far so good though. The Scottish press have, as usual, contented themselves with suggesting every player in The Rothmans Football Yearbook (and the Panini Korea/Japan World Cup '02 sticker album) as potential Old Firm signing targets. That way when Rangers or Celtic actually do sign someone, the rag that guessed correctly can proudly cry "You heard it here first!"- kind of like tabloid-speak for 'House!' really .

Yes indeed. It's fair to say that it is with unbridled, almost childish excitement that I am looking forward to the new season and all the activity that comes along on tow. Before all that, however, comes pre-season and I have to admit, I LOVE pre-season! In many ways it's the best bit. Not for another twelve months will I be as hopeful, expectant, optimistic, and motivated to the cause as I am now. Right now I'm untouched by all those upcoming games, the games where we will be ; woeful, gubbed, lucky, unlucky, cheated, done by the ref, or possibly all of the aforementioned. And knowing the way I usually feel by about six or seven weeks into the season, it's a good place to be.

The game is afoot though, so to speak. By midday tomorrow myself and my two good friends, Dave and Jonesy, will be winging our way northwards, heading for the Huntly Hotel in, strangely enough, Huntly, Aberdeenshire. This will be our sightseeing base for three days and two nights allowing us to visit with relative ease the tourist hotspots of Kynoch Park, Christie Park and Allen Park, the stately homes of Keith, Huntly and Cove Rangers respectively.

You see, while the elite of Scottish Football go gallivanting to foreign climbs like Spain, Holland and Norway to get some pre-season action, (and play some football as well) the likes of Arthurston have to make do with tours of the Highlands, the Borders, Yorkshire and the like. That said I wouldn't have it any other way. The pleasure to be derived from seeing your team fight out nil-nil draws with Buckie Thistle and Forres Mechanics in the thin summer rain, whilst heavily under the influence of alcohol, believe me, knows no bounds.

One more squint at the old league table and suddenly I'm acutely aware that I'm lingering unnecessarily on the throne. An odd disquiet has settled in the vicinity and an intangible rising panic suggests I've pushed my luck. It's time to vacate. With accustomed precision the trousers are up, the shirt is tucked, belt buckled and I've swooped through the bathroom door, all within a nano-second. I've lived to fight another day and the only sign of my recent presence is a dog-eared sports page from the Daily Record and a sheet of pink two-ply gently floating to the floor.

2.

"Quick, get in the car!"

"What? Why? What's goin….."

"JUST DO IT! I'll tell you later"

With that I'm scooped up and sucked into the back seat of Dave Gorman's black Golf Gti, the wheels screech and we're off up the street like that scene from 'Back to the future'.

"What the *hell* is going on?" I ask removing the Magic Tree from my ear and un-entwining the seatbelt from one ankle and the crack in my ass.

"It's Linda", Dave replies with the hint of a smile curling one side of his mouth. "She found out I was doing the tour."

"You didn't tell her?" I ask incredulously.

"I was going to get round to it but the opportunity never really presented itself. You see I made a bit of a song and dance a couple of weeks ago about not going away for a long-weekend with the in-laws and I laid it on thick about tightening the purse strings and prioritising things a bit more. Then I remembered the tour and it occurred to that being a woman she would go ballistic, apply 'Linda's Consistency Theory' and tell me I couldn't go.

"So where is she now?"

"Not sure", shrugs Dave then with a quick glance in the mirror adds "I think I lost her round Beechwood Crescent."

"She was *following* you?" I exclaim wide eyed.

"You know Linda, she likes the last word."

"What are you going to do?"

"I'm going to pick up Jonesy."

"No, about Linda."

"Well if I keep up a steady 50 she'll never catch up, she's quite tentative about the town."

"You know fine well I mean about the … situation"

5

"Look mate it's not your worry, I'll deal with it."

"But…."

"LEAVE IT – I said I'd deal with it!" Dave runs his hands through his thick black hair and tilts the rear view mirror to an angle, running an appraising hand down a shadowy square jaw-line.

So I leave it and instead stare sightlessly out the side window.

I frequently wonder what's going on in Dave's mind. I've known him since Primary School and I'm now 35, but I'm no closer to understanding the guy. Personally, if I was Linda, I wouldn't put up with him. That said, if I were him I wouldn't put up with her either - I could tell you some stories about Linda Gorman that would make your toes curl. So maybe they're just one of those enigmatic couples destined to stick together come what may. Arthurston's answer to Alex Totten and Falkirk if you will. It doesn't stop me thinking though that if it were my other half, you wouldn't see her for dust as a result of such treatment. Not a pressing issue it's fair to say. Me with a woman is like Pierluigi Collina with a bottle of Wash'n'Go these days.

"Will you phone her?" I mutter after a hollow minute's silence.

"Yes."

"Promise? I push.

"Promise."

A warm gust of wind blows through the car, ruffles our hair and flits out through my open window taking with it, seemingly, any hint of lingering tension.

"When are we picking up Jonesy?"

"Quarter of an hour ago" replies Dave lightly. "How many clothes do you think he'll bring this time?"

"Quite a few I should think, we *are* going for three days. Have you planned the route? I think maybe we should stagger the journey, what do you think?"

"Yes, I suggest stopping at The Little Chef near Auchenmauchen" says Dave and we dissolve into fits of laughter.

A private joke - Jonesy is obsessed with 'staggering' journeys. Any time we venture further north of Perth or more southerly than Hamilton he insists that we must set up Camp Number One at any over-priced roadside eatery, pub or petrol station along the way. That way we can toilet, consult the maps, take on water and rest the tired mules. I presume.

"I bet you he's done another one of those route-finder things on his computer at work." suggests Dave.

"Well if he has please ignore it this time."

Anyone ever having tried to navigate the roads of Britain with the aid of a computer generated route suggestion will bear testament to this. They are, undoubtedly, full of shit. Plug into the system the engine size of your car, the types of road you prefer, the average speed at which you intend to travel, the number of pen lids and Toffee Crisp wrappers down the side of the driver's door and this wonder of modern technology will send you on the mystery tour of your life. It will invent roads that don't exist, instruct you to take left turns that aren't there, plough you into major road-works EVERY TIME and generally create enough confusion to prompt a nervous breakdown in the most patient of drivers. Throw into the equation a full family stuck together in hot car on a long journey and what we have, ladies and gentleman is a potential bloodbath. Bill Gates, you are an evil man.

"Its ok, I remember the way", says Dave.

"Are you sure? It must be, what, ten years ago since we were last there."

"Twelve actually. I remember it well. Linda and I had our first date on the Friday night before the game."

"Really, its been that long?"

Dave glances quizzically at me then continues "yeah it was a third round cup tie wasn't it?"

"Uhuh. Stevie Graham scored the only goal with a couple of minutes to go. He hit it with his left foot if I remember rightly. And Stevie's left foot was just for balance, wasn't it?"

Now there's a thing. I easily forget who starred in movies I saw last week, who won Wimbledon last year, which country America invaded last, in fact it happens so regularly now I'm getting a bit worried. Yet I could tell you that Jimmy Swan scored the worst own goal you've ever seen in the snow against Morton in December '92, that a border collie ran on to the park during a home game against Motherwell in the last game of season '94/'95 and that I had to go to my cousin's wedding in September '87 and missed Kevin Payne's debut goal for the club (a 'sublime half-volley from the edge of the box, through a ruck of players' as Jonesy excitedly described it during a hasty 'between speeches' phone conversation). The wonders of selective memory. If evidence were needed of the real impact football has made on my life so far, I guess this would have to be Exhibit A.

"And remember the wee guy who sprinted on to the park at the end with the bag of chips and offered one to big Frank Rogers", Dave laughs, "To this day I don't know where he got th ..... oh Jesus will you look at that!"

"What is it?", I ask but as I follow Dave's gaze towards the fast approaching street corner I see what he's talking about.

Standing at the side of the road, tilting forward in expectation is Chris Milne, the thinnest man in the world. Except to call Jonesy thin is like calling The Chuckle Brothers mildly irritating. Voted 'pupil most likely to attract foreign aid' in high school he is the human version of a stork on Slimfast.

Today he got dressed in the dark and is sporting shorts. Baggy green ones to be exact. Well when I say baggy I mean skin hugging cycle shorts to the rest of the nourished world. To Jonesy though we're talking Flap City, Arizona. In combo with these are an old black and white striped cotton Juventus shirt (too long), a navy hooded sweat-top with GAP emblazoned across the front (too short), white ankle socks (too ankley) and a slightly scuffed pair of Adidas Samba trainers. Its like Hurricane Jumble just hit and Jonesy saved the world.

"Fine pair of legs!" I shout, hanging out of the car window," any finer and they'd snap!"

"Yeah, very funny", he smiles and strokes his long pointed chin. "They're nicely tanned too don't you think?"

"Baywatch style mate. What have you got in the bag – a dead body?"

The bag in question is sitting at is feet and does indeed look like a prop from CSI.

"Need a hand?" Dave offers lamely.

"No, I've got it, just spring open the boot and I'll be right with you."

Five grunts, three "ooofs" and a tight lipped "fuckin' hell" later, Jonesy's dearly departed luggage is aboard and we're off. After a quick but heated debate I have won the cherished front seat with Jonesy glowering in the back like a kid that's just been told he's too old for the swings.

"Can I choose the music?" asks a small voice in my ear.

"Yes you can son", I reply, "just as long as you promise to behave yourself 'til we get there – is it a deal?"

"It's a deal!"

"Good, now put that rap shit that I can see you hovering with back in its box and pick us something good.

3.

There's something about driving through the Scottish scenery in the sunshine that makes you feel glad to be alive. I get quite proud and patriotic gazing out at the rolling hills and the tree lined rivers. You don't get that in England you know (except in the scenic, hilly areas with rivers obviously) and as we sweep northwards, joining up with the A90 raceway, it occurs to me, not for the first time, how supporting a football team, home and away, gives you the opportunity to see so many places that otherwise you simply would have no call to visit.

In these days of affordable foreign holidays and centralised shopping there isn't nearly as much scope for spending time in places like Arbroath , Forfar, Ayr or Dingwall. Yet these are all nice places and its not just flowery romanticism to say that my life *does* feel all the richer for visiting them.

Communities should foster their football teams a lot better. For most of the smaller towns their representative football team will be easily their most visible feature. With all due respect to the good people of Dumbarton, for example, the only national exposure their town is likely to get outside of a local mass genocide or a plane landing on it will be on a Saturday at 5.45pm via Grandstand's vidi-printer. *Even then*, when you say it out loud- 'Gun-wielding lunatic runs through Dumbarton' – not something terribly unusual that's necessarily going to raise the proverbial media eyebrow is it ?

People should, in these days of self-interest, find a common bonding in their local team. Shop-keepers in particular should see the economic potential in a successful football team. Hundreds of marauding hooligans raiding down the main street have spending power after all and it shouldn't be forgotten. A shop selling King Billy lunch boxes and competitively priced elastic-waisted trousers would make a packet when Rangers were in town. Fortunes could be made punting Federico Fellinni DVDs to Partick Thistle fans, FM radio reception boosters to St Johnstone fans and so on. Iceland or Farmfoods could base a whole marketing campaign around a home tie with Hibs for God's sake! - 'Take out their eye with a frozen Scotch pie!' Kind of catchy isn't it. For the more market conscious retailer the potential is almost limitless.

My Grampa, a lifelong Rovers fan himself, tells a good story of when he owned his shop on Gulliver Street. To let you get your bearings, Gulliver Street sits at the bottom of The Brew, a small but steep hill that many of the older locals consider to be the spiritual heart of Arthurston. Follow the gently curving, still cobbled, Brew Road up its less gentle incline and you'll find yourself standing (breathless no doubt) with a brilliant, panoramic view of the town below you and to your left - the main stand of Wilmot Park – The Home of Football.

Anyway, as Grampa tells it, it was about 7.15 on a baltic Wednesday night. Snow was starting to fall and he was rushing to shut up his ailing gents outfitters business in time for a rearranged league game with Queen of the South. You know the kind of shop, there's one in every town in Britain I reckon. The sort of place that has a window bedecked with lemon and black polo shirts and insipid pale blue diamond patterned pullovers with socks to match. Where there's more Farah on display than Lee Major's honeymoon night and tweed jackets come with a repayment plan. Well, Grampa was about to put the light out and lock up when a rusty old single-decker pulled up. Two bare-chested heavy-set men jumped out and hopped the couple of pavement yards into the now open shop doorway.

"Nasty night isn't it?" stated the plumper of the two, a waft of alcohol filling the air around him.

"Indeed," replied Grampa politely "coldest of the year I reckon."

"Aye we're just up for the football ye know, Queen O' the South game eh?"

"Em...yes" replied grampa struggling a little for an answer, " So what can I help you with gentlemen, I'm about to go up to the game myself"

"Oh aye, a Rovers man are ye, how are yiz playin? We're struggling wi' injuries at the moment"

"Aye?"

"Oh aye! But the lads are up for it tonight, we've got a full bus load out there ye know."

"First time this season the supporters bus been full " belched his slightly-less-plump sidekick, beaming.

"Naw Tam, we filled her fur the Stranraer game, ye know!" said Plumper

"Never did Sam! We ....." started Plump but was hijacked by a monumental rift that sucked so much control out his body that he inadvertently let out a mini, economical fart at the end. "Never did." he repeated sullenly looking floorward for comfort.

"So….. em, what can I do for you gents?" Grampa eventually ventured, breaking the tension.

"We'll be in the market for tops." said Plumper matter-of-factly.

"Is it for yourselves?" Grampa asked immediately regretting the question. Plumper looked at Grampa like he'd just asked him if he wanted to buy a tartan parrot.

"For the moment aye, but we'll be needing more"

"More?"

"Aye," said Plumper slightly irritated," there's thirty-eight of us out there"

"Of course" injected Grampa nodding his head ridiculously," will they want measuring?"

"Naw, if ye could sort them into small, mediums and larges I'll get them to come through and pick."

"Are we talking shirts, pullovers or what, sir?"

"Aye whatever, just stick them on the counter" and before Grampa could ask any more Plumper disappeared back out into the cold, rifting another rotten beer smell into the air as he goes.

Less than a minute later the shop resembled an Icelandic whale cull with pale blubbery flesh as far as the eye could see. One by one the bus boys filtered sheepishly and silently through the small shop not uttering a word, pausing only to pick up large pale green polo shirts or medium beige crested v-necks and the like.

It took less than five self-conscious minutes for Hell's Titty Bar to clear the majority of Grampa's 'above the waist' stock. Not a word was spoken asides from the odd "Keep moving" and a "Just fuckin' pick one Tommy!" uttered in a deep warning monotone by a rapidly sobering Plumper who was, all the while, casting a critical eye to and from his watch.

As the last hairy belly murmured thanks on his way out the door, Plumper swayed over to the counter, scooped up a particularly fowl red 'Gabicci' polo shirt with cream pockets, buttons and what appeared to be epaulets, and asked loudly "So what's the damage chief?"

List at the ready, Grampa announced "Eighteen mens' casual shirts, twelve v-necked sweaters, seven turtle-necks and a gent's formal dress shirt with ruffed front – that comes to six hundred and fourteen pounds and fifty pee, just round it to six hundred.

"Good of you mate" said plumper scrawling the details onto a scraggy looking cheque book, "What time have you got?"

"Twenty-five past seven"

"Aye, we'll make kick-off alright!" and with that Plumper shoved the cheque into Grampa's hand, scratched his ample breast and made for the shop door, Plump trailing sullenly two steps behind. Holding the door open to let Plump trundle past he finally turned his head and fixed Grampa a steely gaze. With gruff foreboding he slowly uttered ' Always , and I mean *always,* check that a bus door is properly closed when yer on it!" And with that gem of passenger transport safety advice he slipped out into the darkness amidst a waft of confetti snow and the icy, whistling wind.

Grampa's inexplicable brush with 'The men from Dumfries' is a family legend now and the old boy rolls out the story at every opportunity, usually at my prompting. I hoot with laughter while predictably my Dad snorts in disbelief, eyes raised to the ceiling. Okay, the bus gets bigger and the fat boys fatter as the years go on but Grampa's eyes glint and he chuckles away happily when he tells it. After all it's a good memory for an old man.

A few years back I was sitting in the social club up at the ground killing time with an old bloke called Janny Turnbull . His real name was Frank but he used to be the Janitor at Arthurston Primary and the name stuck. Janny was a bit of a hero to me in my formative years. He was there the day I went to 'The Primary' for the first time, he was there when I left for the 'big' school and he was there, jumping up and down behind the goals like a dafty the day I saw my first Rovers goal. Janny never missed a game. He had a little room, I remember, down in the depths of the old school where he kept all his janny stuff and sometimes I'd wander in with wee Johnny Mackie and pass the time of day. Johnny said he wanted to be a janny when he grew up and was always in there asking questions. "Janny, whit does this button dae?" and "whit's that brush fur?" I was more interested in Janny's box of programmes. He had hundreds of them in a musty brown cardboard box with 'Property of Her Majesty's Navy' stamped on the lid. He let me rummage through them any time I wanted and sometimes he would stop whatever it was he was doing and tell me about the games themselves. Always they would be tense and dramatic with fantastic last minute goals, feats of goalkeeping bravery or vile acts of brutality (usually by 'their big bastard centre-hauf'). I visited places like Love Street, Fir Park, Cappielow and Pittodrie in Janny's room long before I ever saw them in person. I liked going there. It was always warm in that wee room, even on the coldest day in January.

Anyway, it was the same week that the aeroplane crashed at Lockerbie and we're in the club talking about how terrible it all was and imagine a plane landing on your back garden. Inevitably we get round to debating if our match, next week, against Queen of the South would get cancelled and then naturally on to discussing past games with the 'Doonhamers'

"… it's a great wee ground Palmerston" Janny's saying, " Aye a good atmosphere, 'specially under the lights. They've got a good big stand there an' all, shouldn'ae be a wee team really. Mind you they're a funny bunch whit supports them. Comin' from aw they wee toons roonaboot the Boarders - too much marryin' yer cousin if ye ask me. They're no the full shilling, no?" He taps a single finger against the side of head and looks genuinely discomforted.

"Ah mind a night a while back. Freezin' it wiz...." he continues and suddenly I know what's coming.

"Aye, it wiz as cold as a Witch's tit. We're playin' Queen O' the South up here and aw these bawheids fae Dumfies turn up like it wiz summer dressed like Lee Trevino on a night oot. No a colour in sight. They 'casuals' ye hear about these days hud nuthin' on those boys. Whit a pastin' they got an aw, huddlin' under that old shed kiddin' on they wurny cauld."

I don't think I've laughed as much in years as Janny ranted on about the badly dressed 'golf-types'. Maybe it was Janny's words and actions that made me laugh a little longer and harder but I tend to think I was just pleased that Grampa hadn't made the whole thing up after all.

My round-about point is this. Grampa probably made more in that one night than in a month of normal trading. And all because of the 'fitba'. So you see, people should value their home town team more. The local businesses, the residents and particularly the sketchy town councils who, when they're not away on 'jollys' to research public toilet provisions in Cancun's beach areas, seem more and more frequently determined to banish teams to characterless retail parks on the outskirts of town. These clubs, *their* clubs, should be encouraged in all that they do to ensure that they are, and remain, standard bearers for the people they represent. And if they're not encouraged, if they come up against resistance of any sorts, well then they should appeal to the EU, march on Westminster, write to the Judge in the Daily Record or Esther Rantzen or *something*. SOMETHING HAS TO BE DONE! And here you just thought it was all just a dubious seventeen quid's worth of entertainment on a Saturday afternoon. How wrong ... how very wrong.

4.

"Here we are" says Dave triumphantly like he'd just found America.

"Uh?"

"Come on, waken up we're here!"

I don't normally sleep in the car but a post-midnight series of 'Buffy The Vampire Slayer' re-runs is beginning to take its toll.

"Uh, whatsit…?" I crawl up my seat and peer out the window. We are indeed 'here'.

And 'here' actually looks quite nice. Dave has brought the car to a stop midway down the left hand side of a pleasant market square. A proud looking statue and a fountain memorial are islands in the stream of traffic to our right. Despite being surrounded by encroaching buildings jostling for position around the town centre there doesn't seem to be much in the way of shops. The obligatory WH Smith in one corner and a rather imposing 'stocks everything' sprawl called 'Cruikshanks' diagonally opposite are the highlights. If window shoppers went to hell, they'd end up here, no doubt. Looking back in the direction we've come I can make out a dingy looking pub and the aptly named Gordon Rhind 'The Family Butcher'.

A glance at the dashboard clock says its half past one. The sun is still beaming down and a few bare-armed townsfolk are sedately strolling along Huntly's uneven pavements or meandering across the heat shimmering square. A small bird-like women with a tweed skirt farts by on a shiny red moped and a road digger rhythmically dunts his heavy-weight pick onto the dry, cracked ground. Beside him three work-mates sit on a low wall pointing pink, perspiring faces skyward, eyes scrunched up avoiding the sun's glare. On our left, casting an imposing shadow is an inviting, traditional looking sand-stoned hotel bearing 'The Gordon Arms' in golden letters across its dark canopied entrance.

"Is that where we're staying?" asks Jonesy coming alive in the back seat.

"Nope," I reply, "We're in the Huntly Hotel which I think is… yes.... over there at the end on the left, see it?"

"Oh yeah,. It looks shit" mumbles Dave, "Lets try and get rooms at the Gordon Arms"

"Can't , they're full. I tried to book in there originally but they've got a convention of pony trekkers staying."

"Well lets get tents or a log cabin, I'm not staying anywhere bugsy !"

"Dave, just chill out will you, it won't be bugsy, I promise."

"Will there be en- suite facilities" asks Jonesy's nose at my right ear.

"Jesus, I don't know! I only spoke to them on the phone and the toilet provision was not at the top of my list. Anyway, after last year's 'pissing in the wardrobe' incident I'd hardly think you're in the position to get particular about the facilities!"

"I was disorientated, right! and you said you wouldn't mention it again."

"I lied!" I reply sternly," Can we get on or are we going to sit here all day whinging?"

Situations like this get right on my goat. You take responsibility for making all the arrangements, spend ridiculous amounts of time (usually in work hours) to drop things conveniently in their laps and yet they *always* find something to complain about. Dave huffs and puffs and 'never has the time' when you ask him to sort things out while Jonesy is a dead loss at anything involving responsibility. He hates speaking to people on the phone as a rule and consequently won't get involved in the planning of anything. It's just one of Jonesy's many confidence issues that undoubtedly stem (*I* think) from his dad leaving home when he was fourteen. Mr Milne, in the summer of '84, ran off with the woman from meat counter at the Co-Op by all accounts leaving Mrs Milne an empty bank book and Jonesy without anything resembling guidance and encouragement at an important stage in his life. Jonesy's confidence took a hell of a beating and although he just about gets by on his own wit and outlook, I think he's struggled one way or another ever since.

"I'm not whinging" says Jonesy indignantly.

"Who's whinging?" adds Dave starting the car back up."

And slowly we drive towards the Huntly Hotel.

5.

Huntly has more than a whiff of history about it. In the 1400s it was the stronghold of the powerful Gordon clan and was considered to be the headquarters of the Catholic faith in Scotland (this has subsequently moved to Coatbridge). Walk north-east from the main square along a tree lined avenue and you'll pass the elegant Gordon schools and eventually arrive at the impressive ruins of Huntly Castle which is the dominating feature of the town. Originally called Strathbogie Castle, it welcomed such famous lodgers as King Robert the Bruce, James IV and Mary of Guise – mother of Mary Queen of Scots. The Fourth Earl of Huntly, known infamously as 'The Cock of The North, eventually renamed Strathbogie Castle as it is said that the original name 'got up his nose' .'The Cock' was a fearsome 'bon viveur' who liked nothing better that meeting up with 'The Knob of the East', 'The Schlong of the South', and 'Wang of the West' for a few holes of golf and some flagrant womanising. The Gordon flag still flies proudly in Huntly displaying the traditional clan coat of arms and brandishing its fearsome motto 'Bydand! 'which means 'Standing ready for action!'. Always the traditionalist The Fourth Earl was determined and proud to uphold this standard, sometimes several times in the one night.

On closer inspection the Huntly Hotel (not to be confused with the Huntly Castle Hotel which is much posher) presents itself as a three storey, mishmash of Victorian Sandstone, slated roofs and dormer windows. The top corner room, shaped a lot like an upside down ice-cream cone gives the building a certain Adams Family quality and the main mosaic-tiled entrance and reception echoes finer days long gone. Definitely not The Waldorf but not bad for under £25 per head.

6.

"Rooms aren't bad ,eh?" says Jonesy surveying the town square below from our bedroom window. Coins have been tossed and Dave has won the right to a room of his very own.

"Yeah, pretty good." I reply, "Better than you'd imagine from the outside. The place looks like its just been refurbished doesn't it?"

"Yup, I thought we were in for one of those musty old dives that hasn't seen a lick of paint since decimalisation."

I smile and look round the room which is indeed surprisingly well appointed. The walls actually match the new-smelling carpets. A portable TV has been stylishly mounted on the wall, and the furniture is light wooded and modern. There's not a heavy net curtain in sight and brown and beige are wonderfully absent in the decoration. Also I am pleased to report that there is nothing of a fungal nature growing out of the walls or the carpet under the bed. (an ever present feature of hotels found in the Scottish Tourist Board's 'Small But Moth-eaten' brochure.)

"So, how's things with you? "Jonesy says casually, his gaze remaining fixed on the languid proceedings outside.

"Fine mate, looking forward to the weekend. Its just nice to get away for a bit, don't you think?'

"Oh aye' Jonesy replies vaguely.

"What tops have you brought?'

"Last years home, the '92 pin-stripy thing and cup-semi final away one', he answers, eyes anchored on the window view.

I didn't need to ask which semi-final he was on about. When you support a team like ours there aren't too many to talk of. The one in question, the furthest we've ever got in the Scottish Cup, was a dour encounter with Aberdeen that failed in every way to live up to the massive expectation we all had of it. Speak to everyone and they'll swear 'our name was on the cup' that year. However a solitary Dons goal two minutes from the end put paid to all of that. Any dreams of Lee Simpson, our captain of the time, lifting the famous trophy went up in smoke the instant that ball rolled inexorably over the line, our keeper agonisingly diving the other way due to a cruel deflection. I had pre-empted my reaction as Lee held the cup aloft so often that it had become almost real and for my dream not to be realised was, quite literally, a criminal act. I hardly spoke to anyone for a week after that. I felt the world had dealt me a bum deal.

"So what else is in that monster bag you brought' I ventured

"Huh?….sorry , I'm just watching a big-headed alien bloke in a long purple dress walking across the square.'

I laugh. 'Funny, I spoke to Big Jammy the other day and he said he wasn't coming up'

"No seriously, there's a dome headed alien out there – quick come here and look!'

"Settle down, I'm not in the mood for any of your weird shit'

"No really, come here quickly!'

"Mate, if I abandon my annual toe-nail pick to come over to the window and I don't have a close encounter you're a deadman, I ..."

"QUICK!"

I slide off the end of the bed, get to the window and stare into the square. The scene is singularly unremarkable.

"Well?...what am I looking for?"

"Aaaawww man you missed him, or it, or whatever" Jonesy mutters sheepishly fingering the curtain in a nervous manner.

"Really? What a surprise. Maybe it beamed up to the Mothership"

"It went into that pub beside the other hotel. I swear!" says Jonesy almost squealing.

"Don't take a tone with me young man," I say, trying to keep a straight face, "Obviously it went to the pub"

"Of course it did. Wait - Why obviously?"

"Well there'll definitely be a public phone won't there?"

Jonesy looks a little mystified "Yeh –so?"

"Well it obviously wants to phone home doesn't it?"

"Oh ha-ha, the King of Comedy is among us. I swear I saw .... what I saw.'

"Relax Jonesy, I believe you" I say trying hard to sound reassuring, "By the way have you seen my wallet?"

"Oh Christ not again!" It's Jonesy's turn to sound consternated.

And he's right to be so. I'm murder to spend any time with. I lose everything. My wallet' four times a week, my car keys double that, and my current favourite, my mobile phone. Friends and family must be sick rigid with me calling up at odd hours on my land-line and asking them to call my mobile so I can follow the ringing. Even then its not a done deal that I'll find the bloody thing. It once took me two days to find a phone that I *knew* was somewhere in my room. I could hear it *ringing* for God's sake! But I couldn't for the life of me find it. I reckon it was a special ventriloquist model with the built in ability to throw its ring sneakily to other areas of the room. I swear every time I dug to the bottom of a pile of dirty y-fronts or old magazines where the sound was *definitely* coming from, the location of the ringing changed to different part of the room. I was about certifiable by the time I found it under my bed. A place I might add that the ringing never, *ever* came from. Sometimes I think strange, unseen forces are at work.

"Try in the drawer at the side of your bed, I saw you empty your bag there"

"I wouldn't have put it in there." I say dismissively. It must be in my clothes. I'm now feverishly wading through the same jacket and trouser pockets for the third time like the wallet will suddenly appear if I wish hard enough.

"Try in that drawer" Jonesy suggests again quietly

"I've not even been in that drawer… hey look I've found a tenner in this pocket!"

"Jesus" sighs Jonesy padding over to my bedside cabinet, "There! I told you" he says as the drawer gives up its prize.

"Did you put that there?" I ask accusingly.

"Don't be stupid" comes the reply

"Well I'm sure I didn't" I continue steadfastly.

"Mate, I watched you do it. You sat down, started to unpack, got your toothbrush out and put your wallet into that drawer. Then you began messing around with the alarm clock on the bedside cabinet.

"Shit, really?"

"Yup, your problem is you've got too much on your mind. Your mind is never focussed"

"Hmmm. What's the story with hotel alarm clocks any way?"

"How do you mean? " asks Jonesy distractedly, back at the window intent on the square below.

"Well they're never set are they. Every hotel room has one but when you lie down on the bed the clock is sitting there blinking at you with four red eyes – zero zero - zero zero. Flashing on and off, on and off. I mean why should *I* have to set it, can hoteliers not tell the time, what is it?"

"Can't say I'd thought about it. You know, *you* need to calm down more. No , really you do! Think 'cool blue sea' or something. I've never known anyone that gets more uptight about meaningless things than you."

Point taken, I get irrationally annoyed about the strangest, most inconsequential things. Shoppers in front of me in the 'ten items or less' queue with more shopping than that (I count them too - always), hesitant drivers, songs sung in a cockney accent, luke-warm soup, families with bus-sized people carriers' because they've now got two kids.... I could go on and on forever. And yet perversely the 'big' things in life like money, work and good-health aren't big worries for me. My lack of perspective when it comes to worry is, well, worrying I guess. Then again because I *am* worrying about my lack of perspective does that mean it is inconsequential and not worthy of the worry in the first place? Shit.

"Craig, are you ok?" asks Jonesy

"Huh, sorry I was a mile away, did you say something?"

"I said I'm definitely losing my hair, don't you think?"

"What? Oh don't start that again." I mutter, slightly irritated.

"Well its all right for you, these things don't bother you, do they?"

"Nope, and do you know why? Because you can't do anything about it. Yes, you *are* beginning to lose your hair, a *bit*, but so are loads of folk and you don't hear them complaining." I'm beginning to raise my voice and I know it, "There are plenty worse things that could happen don't you think? You've got your health and a roof over your head. There are lots of people out there with real problems that don't complain as much! This is typical of you Jonesy…"- I'm becoming whiney- "….getting all tied up and self-absorbed. I mean god forbid if one day you do have a problem, a *real* problem "

"That's not fair, I …."

"No!" I continue "you've been going on about this hair thing for ages now!" – Getting screechy - "You've got no worries at all. You couldn't come up with a real problem if we sat here all day, could you? I mean try it, tell me something that matters – one real problem that you're struggling with just now."

Jonesy is looking away from the window now and straight at me. I know I've gone too far but I'm here now and there's no way back.

"Go on, just one thing! One thing that really matters!"

Jonesy turns his face back to the window and mutters something undistinguishable.

"Sorry?" I push pointedly.

At which Jonesy wheels round, eyes flaming and speaking in a low even tone says,

"I SAID YESTERDAY I LOST MY JOB".

7.

I'm wounded by the silence. Its painful on my furrowed brow. After an eternity I pull myself together and racking my brains to say the right thing I finally plump intelligently for;

"What?"

"I'm being made redundant." The tightness and anger induced by me, apparently gone as quick as it came.

"But you work in a bank, you just got promoted, how can they do that?

Jonesy shrugs, "I ……"

A knock at the door and Dave's face is peering in.

"Alright boys ready to …Jesus you look cheery, what's the deal?"

I look at Jonesy who gives me a wide-eyed look and a barely discernable head-shake.

"Em, nothing, I just thought I'd lost my wallet." I reply quickly"

"Oh what a surprise! – there it is there, look!"

"I know I just found it"

"Right are we ready for some lunch and a couple of jars?" continues Dave enthusiastically.

"Absolutely!" pipes in Jonesy with equal enthusiasm, "I don't have to carry the key do I?"

A good point indeed as the room key in question is attached to what can only be described as a shiny silver coffee table. This is presumably to prevent the erstwhile traveller losing, stealing or indeed moving the thing.

"I'll take it" I offer helpfully

"Indeed you will not" Jonesy replies quickly." I want the luxury of thinking I'll get back in again, no, on second thoughts I'll take it."

"Suit yourself, better get a supermarket trolley to transport it though" I sniff.

"Girls, girls, will you stop bickering and get a move on . I'm gasping", Dave, the voice of reason, injects," we'll go to that pub on the corner beside the good hotel"

"What do you mean, this *is* the good hotel, isn't this nice... isn't it?... eh?"

But no one is listening. The door has clicked shut and guys are off down the corridor, laughs and muffled chattering fading fast.

I'd quickly run after them and join in the banter except I seem to have lost my wallet again. I think I need therapy.

8.

It's the bar scene from Star Wars. Standing as we are just inside the door of the imaginatively named 'Cheers' Bar, the scene facing us consists mostly of strange coloured faces, big heads, pointy ears and enough ray guns to start the War of The Worlds. My initial thought is that there's a bus trip from Lanark in.

A large friendly banner on the far wall explains otherwise, 'Trekkers Welcome To Huntly- Where no man has gone before'

"Full of pony trekkers eh!" Dave comments from the side of his mouth as we both hesitate at the door. Unabashed, Jonesy is purposefully fighting his way to a heavily populated, small but well stocked bar stuck half way along the left wall of the rectangular shaped room. An overweight chap with heavy foundation makeup, severe eye-brows and an alarmingly ridged forehead catches my gaze as he rolls toward the toilet door. He nods briefly and I strangely feel the need to acknowledge him in some way.

"May the force be with you!" I venture tentatively.

Ridgehead scowls then disappears into the gents.

"So much for being friendly, eh Dave" I suggest

"May the force be with you?" he replies " If you'd said that to me I'd have punched your lights out?"

"Well, when on Mars..."

"Pints or bottles?" Jonesy interrupts shouting over his shoulder.

"Eh? Oh pints, definitely"

Crossing to the bar we join Jonesy who has surprisingly been served.

"Crisps or nuts?" he says jauntily.

"No thanks" we reply in unison.

"Hey Jonesy" Dave starts "that was quick service for you, surely"

And he's right. We don't usually ask Jonesy to go to the bar anymore.

Even when its quiet. He suffers badly from BIS and the whole drink ordering experience can be very traumatic for him. I once read a pamphlet in the doctor's surgery all about it. BIS or Bar Invisibility Syndrome is apparently ' something many of us will suffer from at some point in our lives to a certain degree'. Indeed medical research figures show that 92% of us will display some mild form of BIS at some time, usually in our late teens or early twenties. However for a small number, these extreme debilitating episodes will last well into later life. A sobering thought indeed. Before his diagnosis, Jonesy could disappear in a pub for anything up to twenty minutes at a time, returning to the company in a depressed, irritable and confused state (sometimes with the wrong drinks).

Matters came to a head for Jonesy four years ago at a mutual friend's wedding- in a hotel somewhere near Bristol if I remember rightly. I watched Jonesy stand alone at the deserted bar for twelve and a half minutes directly in front of two bar-staff without being served. The two girls washed forty two glasses through that revolving brushy whirlpool thing in that time without looking up and it was only when Jonesy missed his footing on the bar and stumbled into a basket of complimentary pork scratchings that one girl noticed him and asked, in a slightly surprised tone, "Oh, are you not being served?" When I eventually challenged him he broke down and admitted there was a problem. Thankfully that was the first positive step on his road to recovery and he has since integrated himself back into the 'ordering fraternity' reasonably successfully. Others haven't been so lucky. According to The Lancet one man reportedly waited over four hours at a 'Brewers Fayre' in Cumbernauld, for two pints of Boddingtons and a Bacardi Breezer before going completely mad. This case has since been challenged after an independent investigation discovered that this was, in fact, nothing unusual for such establishments 'particularly around lunchtimes'.

"Yeh well done Jonesy" I chip in. supportively.

Jonesy smiles, "Well to be honest the boy next to me farted and cleared a bit of a space. A couple actually sat back down, the smell was that fowl"

As if to validate Jonesy's claim, a smell of death wafts up my nostrils.

"Aww bloody hell is there a farm animal under the bar? Pick up your beers and lets sit down . If we can that is."

"There's a table over there, take mine over with you. I need to visit the little boys room" announces Dave and disappears through a melee of pallid pointy- eared folk.

9.

Jonesy and I sit down at a small, well worn wooden table that has more rings than a naked wrestling championship.

"Sorry about earlier, I don't know what got into me. I think I was just pissed at myself for losing stuff again."

"That's ok," replies Jonesy, "I wanted to tell you anyway but couldn't work out how to fit it into the conversation. Listen you won't tell Dave just now will you. You know how aggressive he can get and he'll sure as hell give me a lecture on how I could have avoided this, what to do now and how to reek vile retribution and revenge upon the guilty parties that did this. I don't need that just now"

"Fair enough, in your own time. So what happened?"

"No major mystery. They've been threatening to cut staff in my area for ages and they finally got round to it. It was either me or another guy and he had a BBC accent and a low golf handicap – I didn't stand a chance."

"Have you sent away to the other banks yet?"

"A few but they're all in the same boat. Centralise this, outsource that. Pretty soon there'll be only one guy, working in one room working an awful lot of buttons."

"When do you finish?" I ask.

"I'm done." he replies," They frog-marched me out of the office yesterday. Apparently I'm a security risk. I quite enjoyed that actually. It made me feel ... important." A wry smile appears on his face.

A hearty cheer and raucous laughter from the Federation officers at the back of the pub suggests the beer is beginning to flow.

" There's a group of our boys over there in the corner" says Jonesy," I can see that guy who stole the mascot's head at Scarborough last year"

"Oh yeah ", I snort," Remember that. What a laugh!"

"Those two fat cops chasing him up the side of the park" continues Jonesy smirking.

" I heard the guy spent the night in the slammer for that"

"Wouldn't be surprised. Just another day at the office for these boys though. He's had more prison meals than hot dinners I'll bet"

"What?"

"Huh?"

"Does that mean prisons tend to opt for cold buffets?" I ask

"What?"

"You said he had more prison meals than hot ....Oh never mind. Where's Dave got to, he's been away for ages"

" Here he is now" replies Jonesy as Dave weaves his way through the even more crowded room.

"Sorry boys, got a bit of the squirts." Dave announces sitting down gingerly," What's happening then?"

"We were just talking about Scarborough last year and ..ehhh, our first ever match "

"First match , eh! I'll never forget mine. Arthurston home to Rangers. It was a Scottish cup tie and we got gubbed"

"February 1977, 5-1" injects Jonesy.

"Yeh that's right" Dave continues," I went with my Uncle Jock who was a dyed-in-the-wool Rangers man. He'd been on at my old man for ages to let him take me to the footy. I think he was on a recruitment drive- got me a red, white and blue scarf and everything. Anyway I was keen and my dad was never going to give up a Saturday's fishing to take me so he eventually gave in to Uncle Jock "

"Did your dad ever like football?" I ask

"Not ever" replies Dave "He never even watched the World Cup when it was on."

"What a freak! "says Jonesy looking mystified, " You know I don't trust blokes who don't like football"

A flicker of annoyance passes over Dave's face but he continues anyway. " A bit narrow but yeah I kinda know what you mean. Its guys that don't like sport at all that I worry about."

I find myself nodding my head too.

Guys who don't like sport have, undoubtedly, to be watched. Apart from the obvious questions needing answered like what do they actually do on Saturdays and where do they buy those tweed jackets with the burgundy leather elbow patches? You have to wonder what's left to make them tick. I think its sex. Their socio-cultural void is filled with unnatural practices performed in garden sheds - outwardly normal but painted red inside, fully fitted with S&M gear with porno movies being projected at slanty angles across tight timber ceilings – possibly with The Nolans, 'I'm in the mood for dancing' as background music. They are the sort of men who are familiar with drill bit diameters, buy National geographic *and* actually read it, and put knives through kiddies' footballs in their twilight years.

"So do you remember the game much?" I ask

"Funnily enough, no. I remember being petrified but excited at the same time and it was *really* noisy, at times deafening. Oh, and I couldn't see a thing when anything exciting happened. It's mostly smells I remember. Lager and urine, liniment and sweat ..... and that was just Uncle Jock!"

We laugh.

"He took me to the pub before the game and let me have a sip of his beer. It was Tartan Special out a black can, remember that ? "

We nod.

"Absolutely boggin' it was. I drank cider 'til I was twenty because of that one mouthful and its funny because all the way through my teens that smell and taste became my association with alcohol. Even now when I go into a 'spit and sawdust' pub, that ever-present stale lager and piss smell takes me back to that day." Dave pauses for a thirsty draw on his pint

"Then there was Uncle Jock's heart attack.", he continues, " Right in the middle of the away end of Wilmot Park"

"Bloody hell what happened? Jonesy asks

"He got over excited and keeled over when Rangers were awarded a penalty."

"What's exciting about that, it happens frequently enough" I inject sourly.

"Yeh well he'd had a weak ticker for a while apparently but hadn't told anyone about it."

"Was he ok?" Jonesy ventures.

"Oh yeh. And he's still alive and well. Saw him last month in fact. I had to leave the game and go with him in the ambulance though. I remember him holding my hand and asking me if I thought he'd be ok. Pretty frightening. It was the first time I think I'd seen a grown up scared and vulnerable that way. At that age you think your family and friends are invincible don't you." Dave takes another long draw on his pint, "You have to hand it to him though. There he was, teetering on the brink, all hooked up to drips and strapped to a stretcher, and the first thing he asked the doctor in the emergency room in a thin wavering voice was if Rangers scored the penalty."

We all laugh in appreciation of Uncle Jock's priorities in life .Like Dave though I can't remember many of the finer points of my first game. I know it was a home game against Arbroath that ended in a one each draw and it was raining. That's about it. We scored from a free kick. I've no idea how we lost one but I shouted loudly for off-side with all the big people around me despite the fact I didn't have a clue what off-side was. In fairness I was only a wee kid at his first game, there are plenty officials who have made a fair career in the game without really getting to grips with the nuances of the off-side rule.

When I think back its more general things particular to that era that stick out in my mind. It may only have been twenty-odd years ago but the crowds seemed bigger and more enthusiastic, strips were plainer but more outstanding because of it and they seemed to contrast better with the opposition. At cup finals people still wore rosettes unashamedly without realising how stupid they looked. It was a harder, more honest game too. This sounds like the sort of spiel that would come from your semi-incontinent, mind-wandering Great-Grampa but it was *true* I swear. A yellow card back then had to be earned and red cards were infrequent and only came as the result of some form of grizzly, carnage inducing incident. Cheating only happened during the afternoon card schools where players betted their families and possessions for laughs, and to miss a game through suspension meant the player in question was still hanging by his toe from the nearest lamp-post in punishment on account of him 'no howfin the ba oot the grund tae waste time when he was telt' during the previous week's encounter.

Slip back a little further in time and it was really a man's game, if the definition of 'man' happened to be 'homicidal maniac with a penchant for mindless thuggery' that is. In those days (according to the flickery old newscasts and RAF pilot commentators) you could legally melt the goalie with a crow-bar at corners and if they fell into the back of the net with the ball it was a goal and they were branded 'a poof'. 'Tanner- ba'' players , the tricky, skilful artists of their day, were such because they had to be. It was survival.

Amidst the fading spectacle that is Scottish football for the new millennium we should maybe cast an eye back to the halcyon days of Hughie Gallacher and Jimmy McGrory and understand why they had such finely honed skills allied to their commitment and determination. It was self-preservation, pure and simple. Failure to develop the required level of skill and tenaciousness meant one thing only; a size twelve, steel-toed boot so far up your back passage that the offender had squatter's rights.

I miss other things about the Scottish game I watched as a child. Like the way crowds changed ends at half-time in the hope that all the action would be down their end in the second half (Scuffles walking through the old tunnel under the stand at Starks Park were legendary). Like the old bloke who walked the length of Wilmot Park to hang the half time scores on a board built in to the wall behind the goals. Like Arthur Montford's jackets.

10.

"All I asked her was how long she'd been Ahoora!" cries Dave indignantly, holding his jaw and rotating it in what seemed a pain-racked process.

"Really?" I ask in mock surprise, "seems a bit off that she hit you then."

"I know!" Dave continues oblivious to my flippancy. "She didn't like me touching her badge either"

"Considering where she's wearing it I can see her point" I offer.

"Who's side are you on anyway?"

"The side of lecherous ogling and macho privacy invasion of course." I reply convincingly.

"Good boy. What's happened to Mr Milne then?"

"He's over there talking to the other Arthurston boys"

"Good for him, ready for another pint?"chuckles Dave jovially.

"Slow down a bit that's our fourth and we've only been here an hour"

"Another pint?"

"Please."

As Dave fights the good fight towards the bar I look round to see Jonesy weaving his way back in my direction. Flopping onto the chair he rests his head in his hands and looks at me with a serious expression engraining his face.

"Craig, I have two pieces of news …." He starts deliberately.

Of course he's drunk. He never calls me Craig until he's had a few and four pints of an afternoon unfortunately constitutes 'a few'.

"…First up," he continues," There's a Star Trek conference on, here in Huntly!"

"Really?"

"Yup. can you believe it? I'm not a big fan myself but, well, it's a bit unusual isn't it?" Resisting the urge to take the conversation down the obvious route I simply agree.

"Oh yeah, that'll account for the weird looking folk then. What else?"

"You're not going to like it" says Jonesy biting the side of his lip.

"Go on try me"

"Well it seems we've missed the Keith match."

"How do you mean missed it, its this evening."

"We've missed it. Its been and gone. They played it this morning. Didn't think many folk would be up and the Keith manager had to go for a vasectomy this afternoon – apparently."

"Who told you this?"

"What – that the Keith boss was having a vasectomy?"

"No, that the game was this morning"

"It was the same bloke."

"And?"

"And what?"

"And what was his name?"

"I don't know", Jonesy shrugs.

SS Interrogation Officers during the war must have had easier shifts than this.

" But…." He continues, "…I know his face, he goes around with that guy Stan"

"Stan – The guy who looks like a young Burt Baccarach?"

"Huh?, I suppose – Yeahhhh now that you mention it ,he does doesn't he" Jonesy starts sniggering like a little kid.

"Do you think he knows the way to San Jose?" he continues, spluttering a mouthful of Lager over the table in front of him. Laughing uncontrollably he misses his elbow on the edge of the table and further soaks his knee with half of the remaining contents of his pint glass.

"Ahh Bollocks…" he begins still smiling inanely. His eyes light up as Dave appears awkwardly brandishing three more pints and about ten bags of crisps held between his teeth.

"What's so funny then?" Dave asks as he collapses back into his seat and takes a healthy draw on his pint.

"Jonesy says we've missed the Keith game." I spout.

"I know, I was speaking to Danny Swinburn's brother at the bar. They were at the game. They happened to phone the Keith office this morning to check the kick-off time and were told it had changed to 11-o-clock. Soddin' typical, eh!"

Sodding typical? Absolutely! Somewhere down the line the clubs and their regulators have completely lost sight of the point of football. Funnily enough it was *not* invented as a vehicle for young men to earn good money prior to becoming middle-aged publicans. Nor is it a staged excuse for loosely termed 'businessmen' to cut around publicly in club crested suits and ties. At professional level football is, purely and simply, one amongst many forms of entertainment to keep us, the discerning general public, amused. Take the supporters out of the Scottish League cake-mix and all your left with is a little dough and a group of individuals with an unsustainable hobby. All football clubs would do well to remember that.

The one thing the game has in its favour though compared to the likes of the cinema, theatre and other competitive entertainment is the loyalty factor. The ongoing identity with the team and its supporters is an attraction that is as compulsive as it is addictive. And boy do *they* play on it. Increasingly the Scottish Football Fan is the wronged spouse in a case of sporting infidelity. They will be the last to know if the game is cancelled, delayed or re-arranged. The last to be considered in game scheduling yet the first to be called on to foot the overwhelming financial burden placed on clubs today.

I mean, how many times in a season does the loyal fan continue to fall victim to the last minute postponement either outside the venue, or en- route to the game. They say its getting better but I see little evidence. How often are travelling supporters stuck en-mass in traffic without the kick-offs being delayed? Or herded unnecessarily into limited view areas of half empty stadiums.

How often do the clubs actually bother to ask their fans before decisions effecting them are made?

Arthurston are probably more guilty than most when it comes to supporter disregard. Last year alone two midweek games kicked-off fifteen minutes earlier that the time the club published via the national press. Not even an apology! Then they re-scheduled a match to coincide *exactly* with a Saturday international fixture. If you support the national team, as many Arthurston fans do, TOUGH! A bad year was crowned by the postponement of a March home fixture due to flooding of the pitch. Bad enough that it was the groundsman's fault for leaving the sprinkler system (a big hose) unattended for almost an hour on the morning of the match. But the fact that the club then told nobody beggars belief. The result – Hundreds and hundreds of people milling around the car parks wondering why the gates weren't open. Of course the club pointed fingers at the press and the press returned the accusations accordingly but the only real losers were, well, you know who.

The Rovers aren't alone by any means. You do not have to go searching far to find accomplices. Take last winter for example. Now professional integrity dictates that I cannot mention the club involved. It would be grossly unfair, I feel, to cite an isolated incident which may not be representative of this club's normal administration. As such its only proper that they remain anonymous. Anyway, we're half way to Kirkcaldy and its around two o-clock. The patter is flowing and we're looking forward to another solid performance from the boys. Imagine our surprise when the eloquent Richard Gordon of Radio Scotland calmly announces that they'll now go over to the Arthurston game for a half-time report. A HALF-TIME REPORT! What the hell is that all about? Surely he's got it wrong, fluffed his lines or something. Except no, "It was a dour first half with no real goal-mouth opportunities…" the reporter cheerily announces and then goes on to describe 45 minutes of football we have undoubtedly missed. Twenty minutes of swearing, blame apportionment and debate and we're at the ground. Having established that there was no mention of an early kick-off in Dave's Daily Express we approach the ticket office with gritted teeth and attitude. Hoping for some sort of reasoning or apologetic concern towards our situation we were ready for pacification. Alas we met Ms Shrug.

Ms Shrug: Yes, can I help you?

Dave: Yes , could you tell us when the match was rescheduled?

Ms Shrug: (shrugs)

Dave: Because it didn't seem to be in the papers and we've now missed the first half.

Ms Shrug: We informed the press

Dave: Not the Express you didn't, Nor was it our local paper.

Ms Shrug (shrugs)

Dave: Do you think this is acceptable?

Ms Shrug: (shrugs)

Dave: Well what are you going to do about it?

Ms Shrug: (shrugs, thinks, then shrugs again)

Dave: Will we have to pay to get in?

Ms Shrug: Of course

Jonesy: You couldn't give us complimentaries for the second half, we *have* come a long way.

Ms Shrug: I have no authority to do that.

Dave: So what do we do now?

Ms Shrug: (shrugs)

Dave: This is absolutely ridiculous. Not only was this game badly advertised leaving us out of pocket and inconvenienced but you have been singularly unhelpful and unaccommodating (or words to that effect)

Ms Shrug: (shrugs) Complain to the League then. Its not our fault. Sandra, is that Hello' magazine you've got over there? Pass us it over for look will you.

And with that our consideration is over and we're left to decide our own fate for the day. Of course we retreat quietly, pay the full price and see a disjointed half of poor quality fayre just as they knew we would. We lost one- nil as well. Oh happy days.

Lack of consideration isn't confined to the traditional Central Belt teams either, as a matter of fact in my experience the more northerly you go the less hospitable league clubs become. You'd have thought that our Highland friends would roll out the red carpet to the travel weary fanatic who, due to the long journey, arrives dishevelled and in need of sustenance and a warm welcome. 'Fraid not. Its like we've all done them a big favour by embarking on a six hour round trip in the numbing cold (six and a half if you get stopped by the traffic cops) to expose ourselves to two hours of the elements, poor quality football, cheeky bastard stewards and overpriced Mars Bars. Really we should be paying them *much, much* more for the deep-seated joy of it all, surely.

11.

"How long have we been in here Craig?" Jonesy slurs.

"Dunno", I reply giving my watch painful scrutiny, "Bloody hell its after eleven o-clock. Is that right? It can't be. Is it?"

"It must be about that.- its dark outside"

"How can you tell, the curtains are shut."

Jonesy looks mysterious and taps his nose three times with his left index finger..

"In-built awareness mate. Some of us have that little bit extra, others don't. It's a simple fact."

Before I can make any comment he hauls himself out of his chair and stumbles off in the direction of gent's toilet. A quick glance tells me that his fly is gaping open and he has a beer mat stuck to his ass.

Looking around, the pub is doing a blinding trade. A quick estimate suggests that there are upwards of eighty people crammed into the tight little boozer, all, it would appear, drinking like we were on the verge of prohibition.

Dave has been up and down to the toilet all evening and thinks he has food poisoning. Hard to believe as we haven't actually had anything to eat except for some crisps and the little individually packed digestives from the hotel room. I'm feeling a little light headed and detached from my surroundings. I look down at the metallic yellow bottle in my hand then defiantly take a swig. Not unpleasant I'm thinking, a mixture of Creamola Foam and Windoleen by the taste of it, with just a twist of lime if I'm not mistaken. 'Hawaiian Night ' is etched cheerfully in bold red letters around the bottle and a smaller green-coloured proclamation suggests I'm drinking 'an explosion of exotic fruits blended with the finest rum and gin the islands have to offer'. I'm sold. The fact that it's 'brewed in Surrey' cannot shatter my illusion.

Tina Turner is belting out 'Nutbush City Limits', a sleeper hit in these parts no doubt, and under its beat is a constant, vibrant chatter mixed with laughter and the intermittent click and clatter of pool balls. The incessant noise is busily sweeping over me and I'm beginning to feel disoriented.

The music seems to growing. Its beat deeper and more insistent. A group of blue-shirted 'officers' clap in unison throwing their heads back in loose humour. The crowd directly in front of me parts slightly and I can just make out Dave lurking beside the girl with the left hook. Through the mist I see it all. A mouthed comment followed by a sharp look. An angry glance from the big bloke beside her. More words. Hand movements. Then SWOOOOSH. Almost in slow motion Dave and Captain Kirk are at each other and the pub ignites.

Shouts fly and a glass smashes in the vicinity of the pool table and suddenly its a wild west bar brawl. All that's missing is a honky-tonk piano accompaniment and the screaming can-can dancers running for safety.

I'm pished but resolute. I need to get to Dave and Jonesy (wherever he may be). Everyone is hitting everyone else. A group of Klingons have gathered together and are getting weighed into 'The Federation' table in the corner. Some old scores being settled there by the look of it. Intermittent flashes of red and white suggest that the Arthurston contingent are dealing out their own brand of Star Wars. Deftly, as only a drunk man can do, I weave my way through a ruck of 'Big Heads' who are battling with each other. I let out a yell as I come face to face with one of the Domes who unfortunately has had his fake forehead pulled down over the bridge of his nose. Grotesquely he now looks like an everyday baldy bloke but with no eyes. I turn him round and push him into a welcoming couple of red shirted 'science officers' who lose no time in jumping on his not inconsiderable head. I continue onwards aiming roughly in the direction I reckon I saw Dave last. Miraculously I avoid being hit in any way. Tina Turner has given way to The Prodigy's Firestarter which serves only to intensify the mayhem.

The sounds and movements are merging around me and I'm losing my bearings and worse my balance. A heave, a sway and a stumble later and I'm on my back having fallen over someone taking refuge from the fracas by, it would appear 'making like a tortoise' on the floor below punch-level.

Turning myself the right way up I end up virtually nose to nose with Dave.

"I've lost my watch" whispers Dave smiling inanely and starts shuffling around on his hands and knees.

"Never mind that, you started this didn't you?"

"I am a Firestarter" he replies slowly and confidentially, the same grin remaining fixed on his face.

"Well, collect your matches and lets go!" I suggest sounding more together than I surely am..

A pint glass drops between us and miraculously does not smash. Dave raises an eyebrow, grabs the glass, then catapults it back into the air.

"My watch" he says vaguely.

"Was it expensive?"

"Nah, Rip-off-Rolex"

"Bugger that then, let's get Jonesy and go"

"Not without a final word from Boyfriend Bill I fear"

"Who?"

Dave answers by looking up beyond my left shoulder and tilting his head.

I wheel round, still on my backside and follow his gaze.

"Oh." I say blankly.

Staring down at us with a savage grin not unlike Jack Nicholson's in The Shining is the wildest, maddest, most insane looking gorilla I've seen since my Aunty Phoebe before her HRT.

He looks at the empty Budweiser bottle in his hand as if suddenly aware of its presence.

We in turn look at the empty Budweiser bottle in his hand and the three of us unquestionably understand where the receptacle is about to go.

Our eyes meet momentarily, the mental grin widens slightly then the bottle is raised deliberately above our assailant's left ear. Absently I note that he has a dark thatch of protruding hair sprouting from that very ear.

"He wants to get some scissors onto that" I float.

The mayhem is building around us and the base is rumbling out of control and yet it has all faded into the background as the Incredible Hulk slowly points at Dave and in action-replay slow motion mouths inaudibly in his direction. I'm no expert in lip-reading but even Deef Donnie, who hangs around Arthurston Library all day, every day would be left in little doubt as to the Hulk's assertions on Dave's doubtful parentage.

The light gets dimmer as the bottled hand reaches the apex of its swing.

Prepare for pain I think then TONK. A hollow dunt of a noise and the beast above us hits the deck like the original King Kong.

Standing unsteadily in his place is Jonesy with a broad, cheesy smile on his face. Hanging from his left hand like the lethal oriental weaponry it isn't is our room key and its magnificent attachment.

"Weyheyyy!" he shouts meaninglessly, still grinning. Then we're stumbling to the door, ducking and diving bluntly but somehow holding together in a human chain. Dave is two steps ahead of me and is about to burst out of the beckoning door when his path is suddenly blocked by a tall, pale man clearly fancying himself as a Spock lookalike. We halt and there is a brief moment of sizing. Deciding he's the man, he stumbles forward aggressively. Dave's beer soaked reactions are sluggish and Spock manages to lift his arm unopposed. However instead of landing a good blow to Dave's defenceless face he deliberately grabs him midway between his neck and shoulder and comically gives Dave a tweak. Dave, standing rooted to the spot looks down at his shoulder then back up, his face a picture of confusion. The faux-Spock returns his gaze looking equally bemused and a strange, momentary impasse is reached. Recognisable growls reach from behind and Dave is yanked into action. With a shrug and a smile he almost apologetically pulls the big tumshie from the doorway, turns him round and propels him back towards the still ensuing fracas. Still looking perplexed at his lack of disabling power, Spock stumbles back into the darkness and is instantly lost to sight.

And we're running down through the blackness. Running and laughing. In contrast to the smoky, tightly populated pub, the square outside is fresh and exhilarating. We run and run. A war memorial flashes by and we speed under a decorative archway. Despite having the collective lung capacity of a garden pea we are, tonight, Olympic sprinters. And as I pump my arms and force my legs it becomes clear all at once. All these athletes wasting their time experimenting with performance enhancing drugs have got it all wrong. Ten pints of mixed stouts, ales and lagers is what champions are made of. The elixir of invincibility that sports stars the world over strive for. Forget all that steroids nonsense and drugs malarkey. Get down the pub, drain them dry and excel physically in your chosen field.

I'm just thinking Alan Wells must have been a real bevvy merchant when Jonesy yells from just behind me.

"Stop!" he gasps, "In the name of God…. Stop will you."

Uniformly we pull up and look at each other. We're standing in the middle of a pathway beside the black, reaching shadow of imposing castle ruins. The full moon above us is illuminating our surroundings casting a silvery shroud over the silent countryside.

"What the hell are we running for?....... there's no one chasing us " wheezes Jonesy barely coherent.

Looking back up the tree lined hill we've just marauded down he's right. All is quiet.

We look at each other, there's a moments silence, then we burst out laughing.

"What was that all about, eh?" rasps Jonesy

"Ask your pal here." I reply with a snigger, motioning towards Dave who has fallen backwards onto the grassy verge behind us.

Dave looks up at us with rolling eyes, clearly still the worse for wear and deliberately announces that he 'may well have been, inadvertently, responsible for that stooshy, yes '

"People are so touchy though, don't you think. Incapable of accepting compliment "

"Oh yes I can imagine your type of compliment," I snigger" not one from the Cary Grant Book of Schmooz I'll wager"

"No," Dave agrees reluctantly "but, you know, she *had* great…." He cups his hands to his chest..

"Oh well then, that's ok"

We fall silent, each of us staring sightlessly up at the splatter of stars above us. For a minute or ten we're lost in our own thoughts. I personally am wallowing in the random wonder of how Pele could have ended up advertising male impotency treatments. Maybe they never actually told him and he thought he was punting flu capsules or something. 'How the mighty have fallen' I speculate then snigger at my own comic genius. I glance over at Dave who unwittingly has a sublimely contented smile on his face.

"Thinking of your ample-chested friend?" I venture.

"Don't be ridiculous," he replies barely audibly, still gazing upwards. "Tomorrow we're going to see the boys play again, how good is that"

How good indeed.

Chapter 2 Christie Park

1.

The day is too bright for anyone's needs and the temperature is already approaching the fabled mid-seventies. I say 'already' but its actually gone two o-clock in the afternoon. An early rise was never on the cards even with the lure of a bought and paid for 'Full English' waiting for us downstairs. Jonesy had made a bold, if misguided, effort to seize the day by waking me at 7.30 to announce that Hong Kong Phooey was on the television.

"Haven't seen this in years" he twittered excitedly, sitting at the bottom of my bed pointing his remote controlled dagger menacingly towards the wall-mounted portable. In the cold light of day it may have been wrong of me to hit him on the side of the head with the 'thoughtfully provided' bedside Bible and I must admit to two or three intriguing seconds contemplating how many concurrent sins I had committed by doing so, however the end justifies the means and the Arthurston branch of the Hannah Barbera Fan Club was sent scuttling quickly back to bed for a few more hours of enforced kip.

We've decided to give lunch a body swerve and are instead heading straight to the game. No one has said anything so far but I think we are all a bit worried about the potential repercussions of last night's activities.

The first thing I did when I woke up was to scan the square for anything resembling police activity, peeping out furtively from behind the cover of the pastel green curtains in our room. Seeing a couple of cops casually walking down the square I found myself instinctively gripping the fabric in my hands just a little tighter and shrinking further back behind the drape. The sight of the constabulary moseying away in the opposite direction caused me to expel a little laugh. Talk about paranoia. In saying that I caught Jonesy twice performing the same look-out duty as he got dressed. I didn't mention it.

2.

The football ground is tucked away at the East end of the town. Had we been more observant (and less inebriated) the night before we might have caught a glimpse of the Main Stand roof off to our right as we made our sprint for freedom towards the castle. We didn't, however, and the grey granite turnstile entrance proudly proclaiming 'Christie Park' is our first, welcoming greeting. Despite the distinct absence of sporting occasion a familiar surge of anticipation rises in my stomach as we head across what is not illogically signposted East Park Street. Why should I fell like this? Who knows? Dogs circle their beds before lying down, spiders eat their mates and grown men get in a lather going to the football – It's the natural law.

Six pounds lighter of wallet we purposefully enter the arena to be immediately confronted by two red faced, tweed adorned old blokes sitting at a strategically positioned table. They should by rights be selling homemade tablet and old fashioned lemonade at 20p a cup. They are in fact enthusiastically foisting raffle tickets upon unsuspecting supporters still brandishing their wallets having just paid their entrance. Caught in this Venus Cash-trap we each buy a couple of tickets then continue on to survey the scene.

Its still half an hour before kick-off but already the pitch is full of activity with players going through pre-match warm-ups. My eyesight's not the best but I can make out a few familiar faces. Ray Stark, the lankiest forward in Scottish football is unmistakeable His long oily black hair is marginally more distinctive than his prominent hooked nose and as he absently taps the ball from foot to foot I can't help wondering if today will be the day his twig-like legs finally snap under the pressure. Our German manager, Wilf Schnabbel, has his tracksuit on today and is out on the turf stroking his long drooping moustache, thoughtfully assessing the goings on around him. Beside him stands Jim Storrie our 'baldy man at the back' and Robert Crush a six foot two evil-monster of a defender. Jim, in his late thirties now, reads the game like a scholar. Robert on the other hand acts like he never quite mastered the vowels. Like good partnerships though, both compliment each other perfectly and are undoubtedly one of the major reasons we got promoted last year.

"Is that Ally Fairful playing keepy-uppy on the centre spot?" asks Jonesy, squinting into the sunlight.

"I hope not," I answer, "It doesn't look like him though."

"It is." Injects Dave in a level tone, "He's just got a tan and a haircut that's all."

We sigh collectively.

Ally Fairful, God bless him, is shit. All the supporters know it and in fairness I think he has suspicions himself. The only one who doesn't see the guy's fundamental lack of ability is the manager. It is however a footballing tradition for every 'Gaffer' in charge of every team to have a blind spot about one member of the first team squad. I don't think I've seen an Arthurston team this side of the eighties that didn't have an out and out duffer knocking around somewhere. Yet this 'duffer' would always seem, to all intents and purposes, to be mysteriously intrinsic to the Boss's plans. In this respect an inexorable cycle repeated itself over and over again with the hapless mutt getting his game week in - week out, never getting injured (the diddies are always un-breakable), slowly getting worse *and worse,* incurring the wrath of The Faithful in the process until the hallowed day when the manager cannot ignore reality any further and the boy gets dropped. We rejoice and slap each other on the backs for we understand and know about football, perhaps even a little more than the gaffer himself. After all we watch lots of football don't we, on Sportscene as well - have done for years. Its not that difficult. And we look forward to the future accordingly.

Except three weeks later he's back.

Tripping over the ball with his shorts at his ankles, he's back.

The team has a couple of injuries in key positions or the young winger with genuine talent and flair has had a quiet game the previous week (only one mind you!) and our anti-hero is back to proudly claim his place and so the cycle starts over.

It *is* Ally Fairful. A painful stare with screwed up eyes confirms it. He does look fit and well though. Almost, dare I say it, *athletic*. Maybe somehow things have changed and this will be his year. Maybe he's been working on his game and he'll score sixteen goals from left-midfield, staking his claim for international recognition along the way. Maybe - but no chance. It's the tan you see. Guaranteed to make any player look that little bit fitter and slicker, more 'show-biz' if you will. Only just because your skin is temporarily the same shade as Christian Ronaldo doesn't mean that the tools have been sharpened over the close season to a similar standard. As if to underline this Ally manfully keeps the ball up for three, dunks the fourth touch off his boot at ninety degrees and looks round guiltily as the ball squirts off coming to rest some fifteen feet away.

Oh well.

Sporting red training tops, white shorts and white socks, the rest of the team are combing their way across the far end of the field, concluding some unified training session. I can't make any of them out clearly so I instead turn my attention to my surroundings.

Christie Park has a nice feel to it. On the face of it, it is made up of the usual constituent parts found in most lower league grounds, yet it all seems to hang together better. A Subbuteo stand no more than a third of the length of the park bisects the half way line and the obligatory 'cow-shed' faces on the other touchline. Behind the goals nearest to the turnstile we've just entered stretches a small terraced area. This area is bereft of supporters at the moment although a green Portaloo and a couple of sizeable blue bins can barely contain their enthusiasm. The small terracing continues to travel round the pitch, pushing past the cow-shed enclosure and grinding to a halt three quarters of the way up the touchline. An unpopulated, tree backed area of grassland behind the far goals completes the picture nicely. Not the Amsterdam Arena by any stretch but vital all the same.

What is instantly noticeable is the amount of advertising on view. Every available hoarding is taken by what must be every business in Huntly. Hats off to the commercial manager. Reading round the adverts, the ones I can see that is, it's the usual mix of local hotels, shops and small businesses. I particularly like the emphasis on the board proclaiming 'J & I Smith Bakers and Confectioners – One of Grampian's better bakers!'. Ram that message home boys! This approach obviously coming from the advertising company that brought us 'Nike, Just do it - tomorrow', 'Glasgow's miles better…than Beirut' and 'Marks & Spencer- You can always take it back.'

I also ponder a vague sign for 'Love Limited'. A small town dating agency perhaps? Wedging together the lonely hearts of Huntly with the proviso that all liaisons end before the ten o-clock news and that the clients leave separately?

A deep rumbling in my stomach pulls me back to reality reminding me I've not eaten anything today.

"Anyone fancy a pie?" I suggest.

"Aye, go on" replies Jonesy enthusiastically.

"Dave?"

"Ehhh, no. I'll leave it just now thanks".

Dave's face has taken on a green hue since we reached the ground and dark shadows that definitely weren't there before have appeared under his eyes.

"Feeling a bit rough?" I ask Dave gently.

"A bit." he replies with the air of a wee boy with toothache.

"Fair enough. That's the pie-stand over there isn't it" I offer lightly and without waiting for an answer head off to our left in the direction of a welcoming snack bar sitting expectantly between the entrance and the Main Stand.

3.

By the time I return, the boys have moved round under the roof of the cow-shed where about fifty or so Arthurston supporters have congregated. Looking round I find I know, if not the names, most of the faces of those present. These are the hardcore. The little, ill-defined 'club within a club' that remain constant and loyal, travel long and weary, and always, always deserve better.

Nodding to a number of folk in the passing I find Jonesy and Dave lending their weight to a barrier. Its five to three, the players are imminent and glances are expectantly being laid on the door in the stand leading to the dressing rooms.

The pies are hitting the mark. More of a mince and gravy pie than a spicy Scotch Pie but tasty all the same. I wonder absently if the meat came from Mr Rhind the butcher and more importantly if the pastry was from one of Grampian's better bakers. No matter, I'm hungry and have bought two.

A tribal yell explodes and I'm there too. "COME ON THE ARTHURSTONNNNN!"

And there they are. If not the finest sight in the sporting world not a damned kick in the backside off it. Gods in red and white stripes? In the grand scheme of things maybe not but in the grander scheme of things, just maybe.

"Here's the team." says Dave thrusting a single sheet into my hand. A photocopied sheet with Huntly FC's emblem on the top. Under the typed heading 'Arthurston Rivers' (Joan's brother presumably) is the following;

1. **Andrew Thomson**
2. **Paul Marker**
3. **James Storrie**
4. **Robert Crush**
5. **Alistair Fairful**
6. **Jacob McDonald**
7. **Scott McLean (Capt.)**
8. **Trialist**
9. **Michael Hedge**

10. **Raymond Stark**
11. **Trialist**

Substitutes:

12. **Trialist**
13. **Russell Dinsmore**
14. **Francis Boyle**
15. **William Burgoigne**
16. **Trialist**

"Where did you get this?" I ask sideways.

"Guy down there was in the social club before the game. Got it from one of the players. I didn't know Jay McDonald's real name was Jacob did you?"

For the first time today Dave has a smile on his face.

"No I didn't. Michael Hedge seems a bit grand for wee Mickey too eh?"

Its quite funny, though, listening to the official team sheets being read out by the match announcer. I bet the players just love the weekly airing of their Sunday names. In days gone by it was well known that stadium announcers could earn 'a little extra' by *not* divulging birth-certificated Christian names. Players like Leroy Aitken, Franklin McGarvey and Algernon McCoist reputedly paid out fortunes in bribes over the years. If only Eugene Daddi's wages at Aberdeen had been a little better.

The best one I heard a while back was our own Jimmy Bently's enthusiastic announcement of the former Arsenal and Airdrieonians stopper, 'Augustus Caesar!'. Big Gus visibly flinched when that one was read out. And there was me thinking all the while his name was Angus!

Another 'roar' and Huntly are there too. Black and gold stripes, black shorts and socks. A mixed bag of unfriendly giants and nippy looking young lads wearing shorts that look a size too big. Huntly as a team are no slouches it must be said. In the late nineties they enjoyed Old Firm style dominance up North winning the Highland league no fewer than five times while regularly giving senior sides awkward passages in the Scottish Cup. Teams like Cove Rangers, Keith and Deveronvale have done well to break the Huntly stranglehold in recent years but they are still nevertheless a club to be reckoned with as their most recent title win in 2005 proves.

Despite displaying the sort of irritating dominance that must have hacked off every other Highland team supporter for a long, long time, I still like their style. Their fans show the same rural cantankerousness as the Emmerdale extras that populate Station Park, Forfar, only they don't hang their crooks over the barriers and they actually give the referee *more* of a hard time, if that is possible. I think I *especially* like them because they don't like the men in black. It's a healthy pursuit that no-one should be ashamed of. Anyone that pathetically whines, "Poor guys- they do a hard job" should bugger off and content themselves watching old episodes of Songs Of Praise if you ask me. They are *not* poor guys. They are pedantic control freaks put on this earth for the sole purpose of propelling me and my kind towards a state of extreme hyper-tension, known only by the likes of John McVeigh and parents who mistakenly bought their kids a Furbie for Christmas a few years back.

But yes - Respect to Huntly. They have taken referee harassment into uncharted territory. When Christie Park was forcibly closed down for two months in 1975 after a referee was assaulted on the park by marauding supporters, Huntly fans sent out a clear message that shoddy decision-making simply would not be tolerated. The whistler in question, a Mr George Macrae by all accounts, had outrageously booked three Huntly players for dissent in a tousy clash with fellow Highland Leaguers, Rothes. Following the final whistle that saw the visitors run out 2-1 winners, Macrae called Huntly defender Ian Chalmers back in order to administer a second booking to the stopper. While in the process of sending him off spectators crossing the pitch, heading for the far corner exit, surrounded the referee and in the ensuing melee, unceremoniously dispatched him face down in the turf.

Huntly had neglected to arrange any police that day and suffered in consequence. The referee's report stated that he had been struck on the head and had fallen unconscious and while Huntly maintained that it was an innocuous incident and that Macrae had merely been 'tripped from behind' , the SFA and the Referees' Committee saw it differently and ordered the ground to be closed down. Chalmers, for his part, suffered a six week suspension for being in the wrong place at the wrong time (allegedly) and spent the majority of his 'freed up Saturdays' stripping wallpaper and visiting home furnishing warehouses with his wife and his three restless kids. Punishment indeed.

The club's problems didn't end with the temporary closure though. The SFA ban fanned the flames of major financial instability and with the club teetering on the brink of ruin, the board seriously contemplated voluntary liquidation. Thankfully the decision was unanimously made to stagger forward and a good job too. Familiar names like Joe 'Wide-Load' Harper, Steve 'Betting Slip' Paterson and Doug 'My Head Is Slightly Too Small For My Big Long Body' Rougvie have all subsequently had the opportunity to manage the club into better times with Paterson's contribution being particularly influential. It was under his guidance that the foundations were laid for that successful team of the nineties and it is testament to his ...... *resolve* if nothing else, that he went on to successfully manage at a higher level with Inverness and Aberdeen. And resolve is probably exactly the right word for it- Huntly, Inverness *and* Aberdeen? The man must either be made from the hardiest of stock or be a complete loon[1]. One can only assume he owned a big tartan Thermos, a portable fan heater *and* an excellent set of thermals.

---

[1]   According to Walton's 'Where are they now?' (12th Edition) Paterson now resides at The Windy Pines Home For The Slightly Jaded in Pe-terhead where he can be seen most days staggering round the corridors shouting for penalties and incoherently muttering 'Shut the door after you Son- there's a draft!'

4.

I'd like to say that it was all worth waiting for but like a million other times it wasn't. After losing an goal in the first five minutes we huffed and puffed and only equalised when Russ Dinsmore, on as a substitute, sclaffed a header in with a couple minutes to go, notably at a time when their big, imposing central defender was off the park getting treatment.

I can't think of any other decent goalmouth action in the whole game, in fact the most memorable incident of the match came courtesy of Jonesy. Midway through the second half he dropped a pound coin out his pocket and it landed on the terrace in front of him. In a strained effort to retrieve the said coin he dangled himself precariously over the barrier, reaching closer and closer to his money until, hilariously, with his feet fully off the ground, his balance gave way and he fell on his head in a crumpled heap with his arse in the air. My how we laughed.

So a one each draw it was. The trialists were poor and the 'usuals' were poorer. I should have been prepared but somehow I thought this time it would be different after all were in the Premier now. It just goes to show you though, diddies aren't scared of heights.

5.

Deciding a beer is required to drown our post match indifference, we head for the Huntly FC Social Club which we are economically informed is 'oot the gate - right an' right again - beside the stand — yecannaemissit!'. Following these able directions we find ourselves outside an inauspicious entrance debating whether we will, in fact, be allowed in. Another tweedy old boy appears mysteriously from the shadows of some nearby trees and assures us that we *are* allowed and indeed are *welcomed* into the club. By way of afterthought he does cock his head and mutter 'aye, should be ok, it's a match day, aye' then scuttles off back into the foliage.

I wonder what happens on non-match days that precludes visitors' entrance. Virgin sacrifices perhaps? Masonic rituals? farm implement auctions? who knows? Anyway, with no fuss we're through the tight little door and have successfully negotiated an equally compact entrance area to find ourselves in a large, bustling function room. A room I might add that seems impossibly larger than any outside view had implied. Kind of like Dr Who's TARDIS if it was sponsored by Tennents.

Its a long thin room with a sizeable bar running down the right hand wall. Somewhat bizarrely the far end is taken up by an empty dance floor area where a large DJ unit is spewing out flashing coloured lights in tempo with booming, hard-core 'garage' music. Four woolly tweed suits are huddled round a small table, guarding pints of heavy, with their backs to the dancerless rave, seemingly oblivious to the inappropriate beat. Perhaps they're more into 'trance', I don't know.

Directly in front of us stands the obligatory pool table. Attached proudly on the wall is an impressively stocked trophy cabinet suggesting that Huntly FC are right up there with Barcelona in terms of achievement. A closer look shows that the twenty or so trophies are all in fact for pool, that sport of Kings and athletes alike. The décor has, predictably, black and orangey gold at its base and the furniture is from the standard working mens' club 'highly flammable' range. Hesitantly, for constitutions are still fragile, we opt for three bottles of beer at the bar and sit down at a free table on the left hand wall away from the noise. The tables all generously have plates of complimentary sandwiches on.

"Just help yourself boys" smiles a woman nodding at the plates whilst collecting empty glasses from the next table. God love her.

A number of Arthurston supporters have had the same idea as us for their post-match beveraging and have commandeered the pool table area. A cheer goes up as someone finishes off his opponent in fine style. The sandwiches, although best intentioned, have failed to live up to initial expectations. Although the Jolly Green Giant would have been proud as Punch with the selection, there is, unfortunately, only so much you can do with sweet-corn.

One of the pool players wanders over. I know his face but can't readily come up with a name to match. He's grinning like the man who kicked the Cheshire cat.

"Bollocks of a game eh? We'll get humped every week if play like that."

We agree in unison.

"Never mind", he continues," Its been a good weekend so far. You boys stay here last night?

"We did indeed" replies Dave becoming the self-appointed spokesman.

" Me and a couple of others stayed in Aberdeen then drove over this morning. What a night!"

A misty hue of wonderment fills his eyes causing him to pause mid-flow. I get the feeling he's not kidding.

"Aye." he sighs, regretfully being drawn back to the here and now. "Mind you according to my brother it was a bit tasty here last night. Apparently there was a massive barney in the pub on the square"

"Really? " responds Dave rubbing the back of his neck while shifting in his seat slightly.

"Absolutely. It gets funnier though, it was a bunch of weirdoes up for a Star-Trek convention that were battering lumps out each other. What a sight that must have been, a bunch of Spocks beating the crap out each other."

Dave makes a strangled sound from his back of his throat that is somewhere between a laugh and a gag.

"Sounds mental" he manages.

"You boys weren't there then I take it"

"Nah" I pitch in," we had a quiet one in the bar at our hotel. Never heard a thing. Did we boys?"

"Nah" repeat Dave and Jonesy shaking their heads regretfully.

"Aw, unlucky. Mind you its probably as well. The police here are bastards and are diggin' their heels into it. Don't think they get much excitement up here normally. They've been doing the rounds asking lots of questions. Wanting to know who started it, who was all involved. They interviewed everyone in my brother's hotel, so they did."

"Did they, em, get their man then" croaked Dave sounding suddenly dry and throaty.

" Nah, whoever it was must have been staying at a different place. They took loads of statements and banged on about crime and punishment then buggered off to make more inquiries"

Dave has his mouth open ready to ask some more when a yell flies across the room from the direction of the pool table.

"Joe, your up again!"

Our informant, obviously called Joe, throws up his hand and shouts that he'll be right there.

"Alright boys, nice talking to you. See you at the Cove game no doubt?"

"Oh aye" we murmur as the bold Joe disappears off towards his expectant mates.

The walk back to the hotel is a tense affair. Dave is worried. By implication its fair to say that Jonesy and I are too. Sitting on hard, condemning steps, backs rigid against the old war memorial we talk of excuses and denials as well as the police, court cases, fines and worse prison. The sun is lower in the still blue sky but the air is heavy. An inviting smell of home cooking is hanging comfortingly, except we are far from comfortable. The one conclusion being we are no heroes. Okay, its not the crime of the century we're talking about here but there is no anti-establishment bravado about us. There's none of the cocky disrespect for an impotent justice system that reeks from every pore of your average Sheriff Court Ned. You see we're just saft lads with reasonable standards that should have known better.

We unanimously agree the level-headed thing to do is stay cool, keep our heads down and we'll never hear any more about the 'Huntly Riot'. After all the chances of any blame finding its way to our feet, or Dave's to be more exact, are probably negligible.

Suffice to say that approximately twenty minutes later the three of us are scuttling our way furtively away from the hotel, packed bags over our shoulders heading towards the car park. If I hadn't lost my phone we'd have done it in fifteen.

6.

I've learned three things this weekend. One, I need an eye test. Two, always pay hotel bills in cash - no personal details involved, and three, clubs like Huntly remain at the heart and soul of the Scottish game. Amidst the monitory madness that infects Scottish football today, £1 transfers to the stand, scant floodlights facing random directions and beer drenched social club puggies are what its all about. There's an honesty and understanding about our game and its origins that frequently gets lost in the suspiciously questionable 'professionalism' demonstrated by our more senior teams. The names may not be famous and the ability may be sadly lacking but everything's relative. Given the option of watching Huntly v Cove or Aberdeen v Dundee I know which one I'd choose. And it doesn't make me a fruitcake either.

"We've definitely done the right thing- DEFINITELY" twitters Jonesy from the back of the car as we turn onto the duel carriageway and head towards Aberdeen.

"Yeah, well, we'll miss the Cove game, won't we" I mention ruefully.

"Fuck the Cove game!" Dave injects , "Better this than sharing a cell in Barlinnie with a mental psychopath that wears eyeliner and likes to be called Marjory!"

"You're over- reacting" I persist half- heartedly. I must admit though, I'm not too unhappy at leaving Huntly behind.

"What if they trace us?" Jonesy

"Won't happen" replies Dave

"You're probably right" I suggest "Our only problem might be that the room is under my name. It was booked under Donald"

"Oh don't worry about it, I changed it", Dave says lightly

"What do you mean you changed it?" asks Jonesy leaning through the gap in the head-rests.

"I changed it. When I went down to pay the bills the register was just lying there, open at this weekend's bookings. There was no one about so I added 'Mac' to your name Craig, so the rooms are under MacDonald and not Donald. Good eh!"

Dave breaks into a smug smile and pops a Softmint into his mouth.

"So its next stop Arthurston, reckon we'll be home by eight."

"Just one thing", Jonesy looks worried.

"Yes, What is it?"

"It's a long way, maybe we should stagger the journey."

7.

The house seems quiet and I feel slightly at odds with its confined surroundings. Despite the brightness of the early evening outside the hallway is dark and uninviting.

"I'm home!" I shout, resting my bag gently on the faded blue carpet.

No answer.

Walking through to the kitchen I deftly turn on the kettle with my left hand, without looking or breaking stride, and continue to the back window.

My mother, Jean, is sitting on a Wimbledon-green garden chair, plum in the middle of the lawn reading a thick paperback novel. My father, George to the friends he never sees anymore, is standing hands on hips, staring downwards, looking as if he just dug the Glasgow Underground single handed. The object of his attention is a frail looking sapling all of two feet high. He wipes his brow and, as if drawn by something extra-sensory, looks over to the house. I manage a thin smile and a small wave. He hesitates slightly then lifts his hand in the air with all the enthusiasm of someone admitting they were next in line for circumcision. Satisfied that sufficient bonding has occurred, his appraising stare returns to the newly planted tree in front of him. Shadows are lengthening and his new-arrival pushes dark veins along the ground towards the back wall and the outside world beyond.

The sun is still strong but the light is softer and sweeter. Midges cloud around the overbearing apple-blossom tree and somewhere not far off, an electric gardener monotonously drones. Over burdened with the oppressive 'nature' of it all, I turn around and slip back into the cool darkness of the house.

Chapter 3
The shopping will have to wait

1.

Main Street is alive. A throng of excited men of all ages mill around purposefully and expectant chatter and smiles are the order of the day. Four large buses chunter deeply and rhythmically while last minute sorties to the bookies and the off-licence are arranged. New strips are modelled and compared to last year's design and the air is charged with backslapping, handshaking and enthusiastic cries of 'Awright Andy-Boyyy!' and 'Here we go (by the way)!'.

"Bastards" I mutter under my breath as I weave my way through the assembled group of Rangers and Celtic fans. As they prepare to jump ship and head off to their respective bright lights, I'm heading in the direction of 'The Barrel' for our traditional pub-lunch. Normally I'm really, really pissed off at the legions of 'Shallowmen', as I call them, leaving the town to see their Old Firm favourites, taking their vocal and financial support with them. Today I'm only pissed-off. That argument I've decided, is for another day. In three hours we'll be playing our first home game ever in the Premier league against Dundee United so for one day only I say 'live and let live' and walk on in a carefree manner. I must be getting old.

The Barrel sits at the far end of Stirling Street and is not the best pub in the town. It does however allow Rovers only football colours and serves a mean steak pie and chips (no peas). For these things alone it has become the favourite haunt of Rovers punters on match days.

As I approach, I see the landlord has optimistically placed on the wide pavement outside two rickety tables and a scattering of equally unstable chairs. There is, however, no feasibility that anyone will actually sit there. Firstly, sunshine hours have been as frequent as a Scotland away goal recently and secondly, Arthurston is the sort of place where people walking by would steal your chips.

A sign on the door says 'Children welcome!'. This is only a matter of opinion. If children were welcome in pubs they would be the main course. Let drinking establishments cater more for the saddled parent by all means. Provision of a 'Kiddie-cloakroom would be fine. An enclosed area by the door where the young'uns, god bless them, could be hung on a hook by the lapels and collected on the way out would be a forward thinking gesture that I, for one, would applaud. Everything in its place I say. After all I don't turn up at playgroup or in the primary school bus queue swilling lager and pestering the kids volubly for advice on my fixed odds coupon do I? No, I don't - everything in its place.

The first thing that strikes you about The Barrel is the feint odour of cheese that immediately slides under your nose as you set foot in its confines. It is as constant as the sea and few newcomers to the pub manage to get from the door to the bar without giving a quick nostril twitch followed by a slightly uncomfortable glance around. One Saturday a while back having had a few I asked old Charlie, the proprietor, what the smell was. To which he looked surreptitiously at me and almost challengingly asked "What smell's that son?" As I pointed out the dairy undertones of his pub, however, he simply shrugged at me and stalked off up the bar to serve someone else. I've never mentioned it again.

A quick glance around the oak panelled, stone floored room tells me I'm the first one here. Here is another of my phobias. Standing in the middle of a pub on your own like Johnny Nae-Pals with everyone looking at you (except they're not). I'd rather stand in the classic fiction section of Waterstones wearing a beige, crimplene tank top with 'I am a dick' knitted into the back, inquiring loudly if they've got Jordan's autobiography. The challenge is how to kill the time in a casual manner thus it is important to have a few techniques up your sleeve to avoid those uncomfortable moments. I use the following ten 'dos and don'ts' of time filling and you are welcome to use them too.

1. On establishing you're on your own, scowl deeply, tut loudly and perform an accentuated, wide sweeping arm motion bringing your watch up to within four inches of your eyes. (make sure you have a watch on as this can look stupid otherwise)
2. Don't sit down. It limits your options.
3. Buy your pint. Even if you're a lager drinker order Guinness. It takes longer to pour. Ideally there's a queue and if there's any dubiety that its your turn to be served, be polite and gently say 'No, on you go'. Not only do you waste more time but people become envious of your laid back attitude.
4. Find a spot with a view of the TV. 99% chance it will be on and showing Sky's Soccer Saturday. If so, your quid's in. Pull a crumpled fixed odds coupon from your pocket and alternately scrutinize the coupon and the TV screen. (omit the screen option if some weirdo has subsequently changed the channel to some mad cooking programme or the Formula One)
5. Look at the door and repeat 1 above.
6. DO NOT play the machine. You'll subsequently need to remain there for a little while or you'll look skittish and if it isn't paying you'll lose a fortune and won't be able to afford lunch. Win and you'll piss off the psycho in the corner who's just heaved his gyro in without as much as nudge in return.
7. Don't go to the toilet. People will think you're only in the pub for condoms.
8. Don't speak to anyone. Guaranteed within three sentences you will self- justify by explaining your late friends. Casualness will be lost.
9. Return to the fixed odds coupon, turn to the back and see if you can understand how they accumulate the odds

with that strange multi-numeric table. Succeed and you may have identified a possible career alternative.

10. Don't drink quickly or you'll be a couple of pints ahead for the rest of the day. No problem to you but you will annoy the hell out of your companions with your out of context remarks that only make sense when everyone is smashed. (You will never be given credit for the un-witnessed pints anyway and will be accused of 'drinking like a girl')

Having working my way through points 1 to 3 of the system, I'm standing, pint in hand watching Thunderbirds with the assembled clientele who mainly consist of the type of regulars you would swear a) are welded to their barstools, b) have never seen a happy day in their life and c) own a racing dog of some variety. An old boy who has been hunched at the bar quietly nursing a half of heavy and a wee whiskey leans over and taps me on the arm.

"What's the matter with them chaps on the telly, son? Have they got rickets or sumthin?"

"I think they're puppets" I offer pleasantly.

"MUPPETS?" he exclaims loud enough that people look in our direction, "like the ones that steal out your fridge?"

"Eh?"

"Aye!" the old boy continues, "watch out for they wee bastards!-eat yer eggs so they do"

"Muppets?" I ask almost meaninglessly.

" Whassat....CALLIN' ME A MUPPET! ....WHASSAT?"

"Wait, I nev..." I begin but I've suddenly been invaded by a swarthy bloke, smelling of stale digestives with a tattoo of a pneumatic drill on his left arm.

"Are you takin' the piss out of ma Da? He rasps

"Absolutely not" I reply sounding more confident than I feel.

"Well it fuckin' sounded like you were. Callin' ma Da a whippet!

"Whuh?.......Look mate", (mate?) " I'm sorry if you or your dad have mis-understood but I think he just misheard me." I push my glance back to the TV hoping that my feigned indifference has been enough to dampen Rambo's aggression. In my mind I see him shrug his shoulders, grin and say "My mistake, sorry for bothering you". A sideways glance confirms this foolishness. The bloke is staring at me fiery eyed full of confrontation. You can almost hear his brain chugging in an effort to justify his continuation of the conversation. A light flickers dimly in his lifeless eyes and almost triumphantly he growls,

"Did you call me a dick?"

"Sorry?"

"Ahh sez.... DID YOU CALL ME A DICK?"

(It would have been a justifiable comment but ...) " No I didn't!"

"Ye fuckin' did!" he menaces.

My heart is thumping and I'm thinking rapidly of something benign to say to diffuse the situation. The pub seems to have quietened around me and pint glasses have been downed in anticipation. But instead of taking the path of least resistance something deep inside snaps and suddenly words are spilling out my mouth that I can't control. An overspill of years of pent up frustration towards thugs like this guy. Narky neds who force their violent nature on normal people simply because they can. Because they're bigger, angrier with life or are just too stupid to know fear the way people with a decent upbringing seem to.

"What's your problem!" I cry," I didn't call you a dick and I didn't insult your dad in any way so WHAT THE FUCK IS YOUR PROBLEM!". And I'm off and running, pointing a shaky finger under the big bloke's chin.

"Guys like you make me sick. Forcing yourself on people and threatening them because its all you can do AND you know you probably wont get hit back. Not because people like me can't hit you back, because we can, oh *yes*, we just don't want to. Now just give it a rest will you and go back to what you were doing and leave me in peace!"

I am the champion of wimps the world over. I've made my stand and proved my point. A flicker of confidence twitches on my face and I feel myself gain an inch in height.

"And another thing….."

And then he punches me.

"Fuckin' weirdo", the guy mutters heading for the door .

Picking myself up from the floor, for that is where I am having stumbled backwards over an inopportunely placed mushroom bar stool, I catch a final silhouetted glimpse of the white Tyson with his wee Da trailing behind. And then they're gone. At least he didn't accuse me of spilling his pint.

I know I'm shaking visibly and people are still staring but the area of my cheek where he hit isn't so painful that I think I'll be spending the first day of the season in A& E. I'm more embarrassed than anything and somehow manage to smile weekly , shrug at the room and take a tentative sip at my pint.

2.

"What happened to you ? You look like you saw a ghost" says Dave appearing beside me, pint in hand.

"A mental guy punched me"

"Ah well, you must have deserved it, - Some day outside eh ?

"Thanks for your concern, but, yeah, magic weather. An advert for summer football what do you think?"

Of course my tongue is firmly in my rather tender cheek by suggesting such an evil. No self-respecting anorak would *ever* agree to the idea of regularly sitting in shirt-sleeves, mild breezes and, God forbid, sweet bronzing sunshine.

Give me rain, sleet and snow anytime. Throw in a biting wind and the sight of your breath in front of your face and we're in business. This may seem a slightly bewildering stance to the casual observer but it serves only to reinforce my belief that being a follower of Scottish football really is a form of penance; a punishment self-inflicted to serve us right for eating the wean's sweets or for taping Scotsport over the wife's 'Titanic' video when she wasn't looking. While I freely admit that I trot along each week full of optimism and expectation of a fine day's entertainment, there is always the pestering tug on my shirt hinting that we're not here to enjoy ourselves, not really. Not that, deep down, we really *do* want to enjoy ourselves anyway.

Summer football then. An age old debate that visits as regularly as your Christmas cousins and funnily enough, usually around the same time of year. In fairness there are some faintly understandable pros to playing from February to September:

1. It's the summer – it should be warm and pleasant. The pitches will be in good condition and be conducive to accurate, skilful football. Postponements due to inclement weather should be infrequent thus allowing fans a better degree of certainty when making plans for the weekend. Agreed.

2. We would get to wear our short-sleeved replica jerseys a little more often. £40 a throw is not good value when your prized, plastic based, fire-risk of a home top is limited to being worn on the first and last games of the season, and a couple of dubious outings on the 5-aside pitch when a boy from work couldn't get his usual ten bodies and asked you to fill in. Question – As it is usually miserably cold in Scotland, why is there *never* , unless you're Rangers, Celtic or one of those dubious Scottish Man Utd fans, the option of buying a long sleeved version of your team's strip ?

3. The ball will be lighter. I don't think I can prove this physically but watch any non-Scottish game and the players seem able to ping the ball about the park with relative ease. Shots hit the top corner of the net and crosses float majestically through the air with apparently little or no effort. Cut to our boys and it seems like they're playing with one of the Elgin Marbles at their feet. One man's strength alone would not appear to be nearly enough to successfully lift these Mitre medicine-balls off the deck. The cause - It's the weather I tell you.

4. Games will finish in daylight so less need for floodlights. Not only would this save the clubs on their 'leccy bill but the fans would be spared the eye strain at grounds where the 'dark band effect' is most prevalent. Remember how the lantern light at Brockville never quite made it to the centre of the park? The ball would appear periodically out of the murk chased by its willing followers only to disappear back into the void leaving all but those supporters equipped with heat-seeking night vision goggles oblivious to what was going on.

5. Fans would get to wear more fashionable gear than snorkel parkas, balaclavas and North Pole-friendly army surplus gear.

6. No more would we be subject to the TV and radio pundits whinging about the relative merits of Summer football because, of course, it would be here. In fairness these guys whinge for the sake of filling air time and column inches, not because they have a good point and genuine concern for what is best for the game and its supporters. Most of them don't even have to go out in the winter's cold anyway and come early December will no doubt be found comfortably ensconced in a cosy TV studio or press room somewhere, drinking mulled wine and hot toddies. I assume.

Fairly compelling stuff then. But come on, Summer football? Football - *In the summer*? Consider the following six points for the prosecution, the sadistic bastards amongst us that genuinely embrace the miseries that tradition hands us, showing nothing but a thin lip, a clenched fist and a slight eye twitch ;

1. Better weather conditions would deprive us of the elation of having those God sent 'free' Saturdays when your match has been postponed. The ones that grant us a cosy afternoon in the pub or a relaxing lounge around the house just when the common sense was kicking in and we were wondering what the hell we were doing spending 'quality' time watching duff football in the pissing rain. Give us that one week off and nutmeg me if

we're not champing at the bit for a dose of footy, our enthusiasm and tolerance batteries charged to bursting once again. Without these enforced breaks supporters would get well tetchy and crowd violence would spread like wild fire, especially amongst the senior citizens and DIY enthusiasts, mark my words.

2. The cup final would be in October. Hampden in the sleet kind of dampens the showpiece vibe a little don't you think.

3. In the absence of cold weather, Bovril companies would go out of business leaving gangs of factory workers with beefy smelling fingers out of work. By way of replacement, pie stands would foist upon us new flavours of luke-warm Merry-Mate 'juice' guaranteed not only to rot your teeth but have you subconsciously clearing your throat for a good fifteen minutes into the second half of the game.

4. Going head to head against the relative thrills of traditional summer pastimes like cricket, pike fishing and punting could potentially prove fatal to our beloved game. The non Old Firm fans are rightly fed up of the predictability of the SPL and thousands could well be enticed towards the 'Nonce' Sports in their weariness and disillusionment.

5. No more Boxing Day or New Year football. Ergo at least two more invitations to attend ritual family get-togethers punctuated by stale aunties and After-Eight mints. Yeuugh!

6. Fat boys in Hawaiian shirts

"Summer football? – Bugger that! ", chips in Jonesy appearing at Dave's shoulder with a pint of orange juice in one hand and an assortment of different coloured football coupons in the other. "You're not alive until you can't feel your feet, eh?"

Dave lowers the fold up menu he's been scrutinising and looks faintly perplexed . Deciding not be drawn further he shakes his head and disappears under his fringe, returning his attention to the main course section whilst muttering under his breath something about there 'still being a fuckin' smell of cheese in here.'

"Sit down Jonesy and tell me a bit about this new signing of ours" I ask, smiling.

Jonesy drags a nearby stool over and sprays his coupon collection over most of the table and begins, bright eyed, what is in effect a thorough but typically well researched tale.

"Tony Bunton? Midfielder. Got him on a free from Reading but he's been about a bit, Started twenty three games last year and………."

3.

Two pints of lager and one steak-pie meal heavier and we've joined the flowing hoards of fans snaking their way towards the ground. When I say hoards I mean two other guys about our age wearing red and white scarves, a middle aged man wearing a tweed jacket with burgundy leather elbow patches, and an old lady pulling a Black Watch tartan bag on wheels. The tweed jacket disappears up a beckoning driveway and I catch a glimpse of a magazine hanging out of his right side pocket. My eyesight as we know is not great but the title 'Shed Shaggers Monthly' jumps out. I bloody knew it!

I could walk this road blindfolded, in complete darkness, and still end up directly outside the main stand at Wilmot Park. Along Stirling Street, past the court building. Up the slight incline that takes us into Main Street with the sand-stoned town hall on our left and a row of bargain basement shops to the right. Two rows of cars parked at jaunty angles act as a central divide to the cluttered town-square type thoroughfare which continues for a few hundred yards before the road splits either side of the innocent white walls and the stout oak doors of St Jude's Church. Choose left and your heading out the town on the Old Wet Road- The 'road not taken' as I like to think of it. Go right and you saunter past 'The Last Supper' our somewhat dubiously titled local chip shop. Then onwards by Jessie's Shoes, stockists of the most extensive range of snide slip-ons this side of Kilmarnock, foul gold lame sling-backs, and men's shoes a shade of grey not seen since the Ark Royal got scrapped. Up The Brew hill, past the small leafy swing park bereft of swings on your left, skip on fifty yards or so until you have on your left shoulder Turnstile 4; a coffin sized gap in the brickwork with 'Section C, k – n' boarded above in flaky painted writing.

We complete this march in less than ten minutes and although we have lost tartan trolley lady we have picked up a fair crowd of Rovers fans and a smattering of black and tangerine Dundee United lads to boot.

A cunningly positioned, lank-haired lad with a running nose and a faraway look is selling match programmes, yanking each successful sale roughly from a see-through poly-poke and thrusting the offending literature haphazardly towards the buyer. Despite costing a fearsome £2, I buy one anyway, setting my face into a well worn scowl as I do so. Poor value I think without even opening a page.

Content-wise The Rovers Review strictly follows the Scottish Football 'Division 1 downwards' programme template. For make no mistake these programmes are, and always have been, all grown from the same garden. And what an arid, creatively barren garden it tends to be at that. Generally speaking we have the inside page devoted to the manager's column, usually under the headline of some naff alliteration like Boss's Banter, Ally's Angle, Frank's Flannel ,Gaffer's Guff, you get the idea. Ours is called Schnabbel's Babble – Eiyaah!. This spiel involves the manger in question making a number of stock comments about last week's performance, probably from a multiple choice set of adjectives and adverbs to be inserted into a standard pre-written sentence thrust into his hand by the club secretary at a quiet moment. A welcome to players, officials and fans of today's enemy comes next, then a brief comment relative to the form of the away team (usually 'looking to get back on track' or 'building from last week's result').

With creative juices running dry, the manager opts typically for the somewhat dubious claim that games between these clubs are always exiting, hard-fought affairs before culminating in a cheery call to arms for today's clash. Riveting stuff.

Next up comes 'Pen-pics'. A double page of bland detail (sometimes without the 'pics' even) describing the members of the visiting team of the day. It's difficult to work out just who this section is designed for. The information imparted is too basic for the visiting supporter and is of no interest to the average home fan who understandably has little interest in which junior club John Naebody was signed from in 1983. Guaranteed though is the sight of away fans scratching their heads over at least a couple of their featured 'stalwarts' who in reality no one has ever heard of, or at best are vaguely remembered as once playing the last five minutes of a midweek B&Q Cup tie against Alloa at Recreation Park in 1989.

Bringing us close to stimulation overload, the ever present 'player interview' jauntily regales us with interesting insights into the mind of a professional footballer such as Favourite food? – Lasagne, Married to ? – Chantelle, Favourite post-lunchtime location instead of being on the training pitch ? – The bookies. Oh, and of course the burning question on everyone's lips, a question right up there with -'Did the Americans land on the moon and was there a really a conspiracy in the assassination of John F Kennedy?' Nickname? – Chic.

Completing these junk journals are a statistics page plastered with names typed too small for the visually challenged amongst us to make out, the current league table (maybe), and a small quiz compiled by some mentalist anorak asking 'teasers' like 'What was odd about Jock McGiver's left sock in the 1975 reserve league cup quarter-final against Falkirk?' or 'Name ten African club sides with the letter Z in their title'. I don't even look at them now. They make me feel like the Football Philistine I probably am. From there on in its 'Welcome to the Wonderful World of Adverts!'. Pages and pages of them. From the local Interflora supplier to the guy who built the stadium (badly). In forty years time when we're sitting in our bubble-homes, fed up with our Sony Orgasmatrons, rummaging through our old programme collection, we'll not be reminiscing over the state of Scottish Football in days gone by. More likely we'll be wondering whatever happened to Woodward's Cars on High Street or remembering the great pies you used to get from Shanks 'The Family Butcher' up beside the bus stop.

Surely it wouldn't take too much extra time and effort to produce a programme that was actually worth reading. I would even pay *more* if it had some creative content that engaged me longer than a cursory half time flip through. What about an article on 'This week in the world of Football' or giving last week's opposing fans a chance to voice *their* opinion on the previous game, a spotlight on other clubs maybe, 'Ask the manager' questions and answers page, a general letters page and so on. Sure, the editor will complain that it would take a few late nights to write something like this but I'm willing to bet plenty of able fans would be delighted to submit an article or two for the cause. Who knows, maybe this year there will be some better quality reading matter on offer what with us being in the Premier an' all but I'm not holding my breath.

A quick search for Jonesy and Dave picks them out amidst the now bustling crowd about to slip into the turnstyle. An economic saunter with my rolled up programme in hand and I'm with them. A sharp rip of voucher number one of my bright red season ticket book, a mechanic click of the barrier in front of me and I'm in.

4.

I can see from within the dusty blackness a glow of sunlight above me. Leaping up a short flight of flaky wooden stairs three at a time, a cool breeze strokes my face and the outside world once again appears in front of me.

Rising up to meet me is the hallowed Wilmot Park turf, a green chequered rug spread neatly between red and white netted goals.

Sitting round expectantly, like hungry pic-nickers waiting for the rolls to be buttered, are the other old wooden stands that make up our 8,328 capacity 'all-seater' ,'not-quite-state-of-the art' stadium. The virgin white centre circle and half-way line are etched into the grass with careful precision and once again that first glimpse of the pitch enthrals me, causing an involuntary intake of breath. I can't put my finger on what's so stimulating about walking into a football ground high above the pitch but it consistently remains a nerve-tingler every time I do it, at every ground I go to. Even after all these years.

The T.P. Hughes Stand across to our left is just about full for the first time in living memory. It usually contains a small smattering of home fans harbouring the preference of watching the game from behind the goals but today they've obviously brought their inquisitive friends. The corrugated roof above them, boldly painted in three sections - red, white, red, is like a lid for the growing excitement underneath. The club emblem, three black and white patched footballs hovering serenely above a brown beer barrel with A.R.F.C scripted below in fine italics, sits defiantly in the sunshine stamped boldly on the middle white section of roofing with the slightly tenuous words 'Play it the Rovers way!' etched in black below.

Behind the goals to our right 'The Benches', as we know them, are open also. Twenty or so United fans are draped over the sixteen straight rows of wooden planks like they were contemplating a dip in the pool. There's no cover whatsoever over there barring the ground's most unique feature, a mature Maple tree which stands a short distance diagonally up from the corner flag. For a few months of the season its hanging leafy branches offer token protection from the prevailing elements but all in all it's a bit of a cheek claiming our all-seated status considering the overall *basicness* of facility. But hey, the letter rather than the spirit of the stupidest law ever devised is being followed. Just don't go out there in a storm.

We sit in the main stand, just left of half-way, four rows from the back. The best way to describe this structure would be a slightly smaller version of the old main stand at Aberdeen's Pittodrie Stadium complete with its risen walled frontage and large advertising hoardings.

Edging our way along a tight row of legs I nod tiny acknowledgements to the familiar faces down the line to our season ticket seats. I don't know everyone's name and yet they all feel like family, not the sort you'd invite round all that often, but family all the same. We've been through some hard times together you see. We've shivered and sweated together. And we've rejoiced together in a way none of us would dream of doing out there in the real world. Eighteen years sitting in these seats, the majority of our company probably even more, I feel I'm justified in that little nod and a wry smile.

5.

Like two vultures, Ray Stark and fellow striker, Russ Dinsmore hang over the ball expectantly. Stark's boney , knobbly frame almost trembling with anticipation. Dinsmore, mindlessly running tanned hands through heavy, blond tipped lion hair.

Someone a couple of rows behind bellows 'Come on the Rovers! ' like a Braveheart-esque battle cry to everyone around us. A roar surges upwards from somewhere in the bowels of the stand pushing everyone to their feet like the first half of a Mexican wave.

"COME ON THE BREWERS!" I yell as the whistle shrills , Stark knocks the ball two feet forward – And we're away.

Captain, Scott McLean has lost the toss and we're kicking right to left, not that that matters any today. I allow myself a sweeping panoramic view of the scene working hard to take it all in. I want to savour this history, this fervour. Its been a long time coming and I want to drink it down.

Dinsmore has trundled the ball out, far right, to wide-man Mickey Hedge who collects it on the touch-line. His diminutive stature is on the verge of being swallowed up by the bright orange beast that *is* the baying United crowd pulsating along the length the away stand, fuelled, seemingly, by the powerful sunlight. A couple of unsure steps, then a shimmy and he's wriggled by his marker. Two more paces and the ball is launched skywards towards the penalty area. Seven thousand faces point upwards as the ball soars, slows then begins to fall.

'Keeper's ball' I think. 'My ball' the keeper thinks and ploughs forward. Except in Hollywood slow motion it *isn't* his ball. A mistimed flail, the slightest of stumbles and the ball floats tantalisingly over outstretched padded gloves and Stark is swan diving. The ball strikes Ray square on the forehead and the ball is in the net with the striker spread-eagled on the turf face down.

A short vacuuming silence then YYEEEESSSSSSS!!!. Jonesy has grabbed me by my shoulders and is shaking me. Dave pushes in and joins an ungainly three-way-hug-and-jump movement. Grown men are jigging up and down and a field of arms are held aloft jubilantly clapping or punching the air feverishly. Time is suspended as the celebration dance plays out. Breathlessly we untwine from each other and sink heavily to our seats.

"Shorer ur Arfurfun, Haaayy Haaaaarf!" the PA crows and the ground shakes again with a rousing cheer. Across in the other stand, things have turned distinctly one dimensional. What a start! I find myself looking around nervously thinking what's the catch? Where's the payback coming from? Life isn't this good really

"What happened?" whispers Jonesy out of the side of his mouth.

"What do you mean?" I reply." I missed the goal. I was watching a bloke carry a tray of Bovrils up the stairs wasn't I" continues Jonesy exasperatedly.

"Ahh it was quality from start to finish….." and as I ramble a drawn out account of the goal the skill is 'sublime', the cross 'pinpointed' , the finish 'world class'. Any matters of fortune are quite rightly banished for the moment.

The match is tense and the pace is blistering. There's a cutting edge intensity to the game that just isn't there in the lower leagues and as the whistle blows for half-time I catch young winger, Jay McDonald, looking skyward blowing deeply into the air.

"Not bad eh!", chirps Jonesy as we stand hands in pockets watching the subs doing their half time 'routine', "Held them to a couple of long range efforts and that header past the post."

"Yeah, and we could even have got a second if their players had got out of the way for a moment ." I add.

Dave leans over confidentially and smirks, " Look at this."

Following his stare onto the park, Ally Fairful is lining up an arse-winder of a shot from about thirty yards out. Standing, straight backed, like he was about to hit a rugby conversion he lightly toe taps the grass twice with his left foot then hares forward. Mis-timing his stride he gets there just too early and the ball quirts off left missing the target by a good twenty feet. Our reserve keeper Chris Barlow, to his credit, hasn't bothered to face the shot anyway and looks round, startled, as the ball crashes off an advertising hoarding to his right.

"I remember when that used to be funny" Dave says flatly. "Mind you the others aren't much better. There doesn't seem to be much in the way of organisation out there, is there?"

Random chaos more like. The two sets of substitutes are a straggling bunch who seem content in milling around chatting to each other, doing the odd stretch and periodically unleashing an torrid avalanche of shots at the hapless reserve keeper who is clearly unable to stop four balls at the one time. It's a strange phenomenon this half time training 'show-piece' . I would have thought that in these days of finely tuned fitness regimes and in-depth tactical analysis we would see a coach out there directing the players in stretching exercises, co-ordinated ball-work and the like. As it is - and every team seems to have the same attitude - I wouldn't be surprised if any one of the subs sat down on the ball, pulled a fag out and lit up. I can see it now. The manager nodding to the subs bench just as the ref blows the half-time whistle, growling in a guttural tone, " Right boys, I want to see plenty of lay offs finishing up with a shot into the street outside, as many reminisces of auld nights oot ye can manage... and

Boaby, son, see if you can trap the ball wi' the back of your neck and haud it there for ten seconds – awright, back here in fifteen minutes, on yiz go!".

The pace of the first half seems to have carried over into the second. I just wish someone would stop and think about it a bit more instead of expending all energy and brainpower into hustling and bustling around. A midfield pinball game has developed with nothing close to a goalmouth opportunity. Not that it isn't exciting mind you. I'm kicking every ball. During the last fracas in the centre circle I even managed to do an old man's leg jerk like I was making the tackle myself. No one noticed.

"Five minutes to go." Jonesy announces, "Keep it tight Rovers!"

But things are getting slacker by the second. There's an air of desperation about Dundee United who are getting a grip on midfield and pushing men forward more purposefully. A good save by Andy Thomson down at his left hand post and then a low, cut back cross narrowly missing two sliding United forwards has the away support on its feet urging their team forward.

"Come on Rovers, DON'T PANIC!" yells Jonesy in a shrill tone.

Dave and I both lean ever so slightly forward and look at each other with a flicker of amusement in our eyes.

For the immortal words have been spoken.

Ask Jonesy where he inherited his somewhat inappropriate nickname from and he'll no doubt regale you with a florid tale of a five a side football session steeped in mysticism and wonderment. In this fairy story Jonesy plays a blinding defensive role full of poise, passion and with no small amount of physical intimidation and hard tackling incorporated. So much so that as we left the court (allegedly) the onlooking hall caretaker whistled under his breath as Jonesy walked by, grabbed him by terri-towelling sweat top and growled in everyone's ear shot "Good, hard game son, Vinnie Jones would've been proud of that!" From that moment on, plain old Chris Milne became 'Jonesy'; defender extraordinaire, all round sportsman and Thug of the People.

Now anyone having seen Jonesy play football will realise this explanation is about as plausible a concept as the Cranhill Symphony Orchestra. Indeed the real story about the nickname is much simpler and infinitely more believable. In short Jonesy is unstable. He gets easily excited. Especially at the football (and selected James Bond movies). Now it didn't take either Dave or myself very long into our first season sitting together to realise that his favourite instructive yell to the team when the going got a bit spicy was 'Don't Panic!". Being a bit of a fan of the old wartime sitcom Dads' Army as I am, the similarity to Corporal Jones was totally unmistakeable. Although Clive Dunn could never have matched Jonesy in the anxiety stakes without physically having a cardiac arrest, the comparison was, as Dave readily agreed, 'spot on'.

At which point the name was introduced and our two stories diverged I can't be sure. I rather think the pivotal moment came on a drunken night out, the smudging of details leaving Jonesy, thankfully and quite amusingly, oblivious to the ongoing joke.

"They're panicking at the back aren't they!" bursts the now screeching Jonesy grasping his bare left arm with his right hand so tightly that it is going a reddish blue colour. "Look at Marker and Storrie. They're just kicking the ball the way they are looking!"

I glance at my watch. Ten to five. Really its just before a quarter to - One of my lateness saving ploys.

"How long to go?" asks Dave quietly without taking his eyes off the pitch.

"I make it about a minute to go with little or nothing extra to play" I reply.

Dave raises an eyebrow, exhales like he'd been storing air up to sell, but says no more . All around tight, drawn faces look upwards then wristwards then feetwards. Dundee United have the ball right in front of us , just inside the Rovers half. Their tall, blond sub who I don't recognise has it and has begun to move forward into the space vacated by the whole Arthurston midfield who have recoiled to the edge of their penalty box.

He strides forward, seemingly in slow motion. "Shut him down!" someone shouts anxiously in front of us. But that can't happen as we're so much on the back foot. Scott Mclean is the only midfielder to react as he realises like the rest of us what is about to happen. Checking out of his backward retreat he makes a mad lunge for the advancing man in possession but its too little too late. The sub has had plenty time to decide what to do and has drawn back his right foot for a shot. McLean's valiant slide comes up a few feet short and the ball is unleashed with a venom and ferocity not seen since Hot Shot Hamish hung up his boots.

Nothing is getting in the way of the hardest shot I've ever seen. Andy Thomson in goal doesn't even move. Nor do any of the players except to turn their heads sharply to follow the missile's rapier flight.

The ball hammers the bar about a foot in from the right post and flies high into the air.

HAMMERS THE BAR!

THE BAR..... NOT THE NET!

The United fans, on their feet to celebrate what looked the certain equaliser cave in as Thomson reacts quickest and jumps unopposed to clasp the ball as it falls to earth.

There's barely a whimper from the home support who are busy trying to catch their breaths. That is until the keeper, through with his 'calm down' hand actions, hoists the ball high over half way and three resonating whistles indicate time up and cue a tumultuous, pressure releasing victory yell. Everyone is on their feet, arms stretched to the heavens. We are here. This is the Premier league and its going to be ok!

6.

"Had a nice day dear:" my mum asks as I float into the kitchen.

"Great!" I reply grabbing an apple out the fruit basket and taking a huge bite right into the seeds.

"Who won then?" she continues absently, the focus of her attention moving to a pile of unpeeled potatoes on the unit in front of her.

"We did" I splutter, juice and a bit of apple making a bid for freedom out of my too full mouth. "Beat Dundee United one nil"

"Is that good?"

"Yeh, of course. We're in the Premier league now and......" but I cut myself short. Its wasted breath attempting any kind of football related conversation with my mother. I've tried on numerous occasions but invariably her eyes glaze over after the second comment and she develops a far away look akin to the one worn by the poor souls forced to judge the 'Women's Dirge' section of the annual Highland Mod.

"Where's dad?" I ask

"Oh, he's outside tending his root" is the slightly terse reply.

"Really, is that allowed? " I smile.

My mother looks up with an irritated scowl and I decide to take my wit outside into the fresh air

7.

Its still noticeably warm outside. Not Scottish warm though, more of a 'holiday' warm with the air heavy and fragrant. The trees are hanging limp and tired after a hard shift in the heat and all that's missing is the up tempo hissing of cicadas in the background to complete the foreign feel. The inevitable smell of smouldering barbeque has kindly visited our garden from somewhere up the street and my stomach involuntarily gurgles in appreciation.

I stop at the bottom of the stairs at the edge of the immaculate lawn. My father is oblivious to my presence planted, as he is, in the muck bed surrounding his baby tree. It is obviously a 'serious' gardening session as he is wearing his brown cords and green Wellingtons combo. A hint of white paunch is poking out from under an open necked white office shirt, his sleeves rolled up circulation threateningly high. Standing stroking his wispy white hair in full contemplation, his strong facial resemblance to Inspector Morse is uncanny.

Humming tunelessly under his breath and carelessly flicking small secateurs open and closed in a continuous motion with two fingers of his right hand , he has an enviable look of contentment spread over his tanned face.

"Hi." I venture tentatively.

"OH- JESUS CHRIST-IN-A-SIDE-CAR! " yelps the old boy jumping round wildly and dropping the scissors. "What are doing creeping up on folk like that for!"

I smirk at his terminology. Jesus Christ in, or on, various methods of transport has long been my father's favourite curse, much to my mother's annoyance. Over the years our Saviour has been on a bike, on a moped, in a taxi, on an ocean liner and on one memorable occasion when Mr Bibby from next door accidentally reversed his disabled buggy through the lattice fence, on a combine harvester.

"Its not funny . What if I had a heart attack or something? Where would you be then, eh?

Before I can form even the simplest of lists he continues.

"Well, what about the football?" he says gaining a level of composure.

"We won 1-0!" I announce triumphantly.

My eyes alight , ready for a full account.

"No son, The Rangers, How did they do?"

Stopped in my tracks.

"They won 2-0 " I reply unable to keep a flat, irritated tone from my voice"

"Oh aye" he continues visibly cheered, "Who were they playing then?"

"Falkirk away, but surely you knew that being a devoted fan an' all."

"Now don't start that, I ...."

But I've been down this road before and knowing where it will all lead I head him off at the pass. "How's the tree then?"

"Aye, so far so good." he says, returning his gaze to the small tree in front of him. "Its taken root fine."

An uneasy silence falls as we both stand and look at the sapling, Dad running his hands through his hair again feverishly, me tracing a figure eight in the dirt with my toe. A small dusty bee hums aimlessly round, senses nothing attractive and flies off to another corner of the garden.

The tree is only small and it stands uncomfortably, fragilely in its surroundings. The other plants and flowers around it have seen other summers, survived hard winters, they are comfortable and established in comparison . It's small green leaves and pencil thin stalk have a Tiny-Tim frailty about them yet at the same time seem so alive and full of promise. In a detached way I wonder what the fate of this little plant in front of me is going to be. Will it have enough strength to survive the wind, rain , frost and snow that will surely attack over the coming months or is it already doomed by its vulnerability. Either way I cannot avoid a sweeping sense of empathy towards the tree and, faced with the unnerving notion that I am bonding with a twig, it seems an appropriate time to investigate the savoury smell of steak and onions which has just wafted out from the direction of the kitchen.

Chapter 4 'Away we go'

1.

If only I could open my eyes.

If only I could open my eyes I'd lead a better life .... I swear. I'd do charitable work, speak to old people, offer myself for medical research. I'd even buy the Big Issue from the guy with the big dog and better trainers than me. EVERY MONTH! If only I could open my eyes.

Its part blinding headache, part eye-gunk that's holding them shut. The headache is the direct result of a Friday night visit to the pub for 'one pint only'. The eye-gunk? I've never been offered any satisfactory explanation for the overnight appearance of semi-crustaceous yellow puss that seems intent on matting up my eyelashes. My mum called it stardust when I was younger. STARDUST! All I can say is don't buy a 'nice little runner' or bet on a 'dead cert' from the person who thought up that terminology!

The swamp-like state of my eyes is marginally less disgusting than the staleness of my breath. I smack my lips, trying desperately for any level of salivic action that will carry the taste of rotting lager away. No joy. Another effort at lifting my eyelids however and BINGO we have openness. Except there's no jackpot prize only the arrival of more pain. Not a big pain, just a jabby, irritating one. The sort you get when watching Cilla Black on the telly. Slowly my room comes into focus. In the dark all rooms are grey except mine which is a kaleidoscope of colourful, shimmering stars. A couple of long, unpleasant minutes pass with the contemplation that I may have a brain tumour, however, by the time I've debated it fully the Aurora Borealis has subsided and by God's miracle I can see.

My room is pretty much the junk coffin you would expect of a 35 year old guy still staying with his parents. All my worldly possessions are squeezed into this magnolia-walled shoe box. Clothes and shoes defiantly overspill from the pencil thin wardrobe in the right hand corner of the room where a TV-bearing, self- assembly unit sits adjacent. Piles of CDs and DVDs lie on the floor longing for a permanent home and at the other side of my bed beside the door a small family of cardboard boxes have found a corner to call their own.

It wasn't always like this. In a previous life I was a man of substance with a mortgage, a nice car and my own small business. A couple of financial decisions that I like to think of as 'unlucky' put paid to all that though, and in the absence of a job, income or, indeed, savings I found myself back in the family nest. (The twigs are familiar but my arse now seems to be constantly hanging over the edges)

Dimly illuminated by a ray of invading light that has penetrated my intricately devised defence system (a £6.99 roller blind from B&Q), the floor looks uncharacteristically Spartan and free of clutter. Asides from the hanging dead body of coats on the door facing me, I can see a carpet absent of clothing. 'Unusually tidy getting to bed', I think. A swift check under the covers shows I've still got my gear on. Hoping against hope its not time to get up I twist my neck painfully round to my bedside cabinet where my radio alarm clock resides. I blink and it blinks back. 00:00 then black. Off, then on, then off, then on in luminous red defiance.

"Bollocks" I mutter and turn over to my right side. Ear wedged deeply into my pillow, I'm facing a long pine shelved unit crammed with books, magazines and assorted debris. Vaguely I wonder if my motor insurance policy is in there somewhere as I'm pretty sure my tax is due for renewal. Sideways reading with a hang-over is not my forte but I begin to work my way along the middle shelf thinking absently that I should really read some of these again. 'Serious' names like Steinbeck, Fitzgerald, Du Maurier and Salinger are hopelessly outnumbered by a stretching series of Ian Rankins, some Grishams and around ten or so football related paperbacks, all pressed intimately together in mutual disorder. Wedged somewhere in the middle I see the almost obligatory copy of 'Feverpitch'. 'Part-time supporter' I mutter to myself , my attention turning to the large paper pile precariously slouched like a drunken concertina on the end of the top shelf. 'I need to clear through that' I decide for the hundredth time. Typically though, this train of thought misses its stop and disappears further up the line. It's a dangerous business leafing through old documents in any case and should not be entered into lightly. There may be bank statements in there for God's sake! Worse still there could be unpaid bills, un-replied letters or old photographs showing you younger, fitter and happier than you are now. Let the tidier beware!

The TV starts whispering to me. Quietly at first but I can hear it. "Turn me on." it alluringly suggests. "Turn me on and I'll show you foxy blondes presenting mindless Saturday morning kiddies programmes"

"Leave me alone" I murmur.

"Nooo, you know you want tooo". Taunting.

"I don't- its kiddies TV, I'm not interested ". Defiant.

"Ah but they're luscious aren't they. ...., yon buurrd from Toonattick, or Caa…"

"Don't say it"

"Caaaa…."

"NO ! I beseech thee"

"CAT DEELEY!"Triumphant.

Sod it. Ignoring all new pains I'm shuffling limply over to the Deeley, I MEAN THE TELLY, and sliding my finger along its smooth plastic frontage, I eventually finger the right button that kicks things into life. The screen effortlessly bathes the room in a ghostly hue and I stumble back to bed. The TV is silent as the pre-set sound level is sensibly set to mute. No nasty loud shocks to the system for me. To my disappointment a recently made, more modern looking Tom and Jerry cartoon is starting. I can tell it's a new one since Fred Quimby isn't the producer, the animation is of inferior quality and Jerry has a Gay Rights T-shirt on. Why must they tinker with the classics?

Never mind. My thoughts, blurry though they are, turn to the day ahead. We're off to Rugby Park this afternoon to play Kilmarnock in what will be our first 'Premier' away game ever and this is exciting for a couple of reasons. We haven't played Kilmarnock since I was in my teens so it will be good to make the trip again. Also, for fear of stating the obvious, it is... well.... an away game, which is enough to give it that little edge that home matches somehow fail to conjure. Our travelling support always seem to be that bit louder and more excitable during these games. Probably its got as much to do with getting away from Arthurston for a while as the promise of an exciting day's football though. Staring up at the ceiling above me, hands behind my head, sketchy memories of past Killie encounters sneak into my mind. When I first saw Kilmarnock I remember them as a team of giants. They had an unnatural number of guys called Clarke playing for them and a big evil ogre called Derek McDicken who was clearly on commission by the local Accident and Emergency Unit. I remember their pitch was so wide that the far corner flag was in a different post-code and that games were never postponed in the cold weather due to Kilmarnock being eight and a half miles nearer to the sun than anywhere else in Scotland at any particular time. ... or something like that.

Oh, and in those pre- stadium development days at Rugby Park, who could forget the big shed roof painted red with 'Johnnie Walker' etched on it in large white letters, and the gargantuan megaphone that hung from the terrace roof spreading the word to the assembled masses below. Grampa told me that during the war they used the outsized PA system to shout instructions miles into the air to trainee parachutists as they fell to earth. 'The audible range required meant that the equipment had to be as massive as possible' he explained. He said it without a smile on his face and I believed him - Old Git. Funnily enough, I later found out that Rugby Park *was* actually used during the war, although for the more mundane purpose of fuel and military vehicle storage and not as Grampa had suggested.

Groping blindly under my bed I successfully lay my hands on my mobile phone which on closer inspection tells me that it is 10.58 and I have 2 text-messages. One is from Dave saying he will take his car today despite it not being his turn. Good news. The other is from the telephone network telling me I am 'a valued customer' and there will be a 'new scale of charges' coming soon. All in the one sentence. Wonderful.

I should really get up, take off my clothes and put some clothes on. Meet the day head on so to speak. A glass of fresh orange and a roll and sausage and I'll be brand new. And I nearly make it too. My right leg is slung out the bed to the point that the sole of my foot is flat on the floor, and I've managed a semi-upright position propped up ungainly by my right elbow. The carpet feels crusty between my toes, the direct result of an untreated tea spillage from a couple of days back if I'm not mistaken. I'm about to hoist myself up when I catch a glance of the TV which is silently glowing away in the corner. A blond mop and a whiter than white smile is bobbing around cheerfully on the screen. Without taking my eyes from the screen I grasp the remote and edge the volume upwards. A little grin of appreciation curls the corners of my lips and a warm sense of well-being settles on my pain-wracked soul.

"Hi, I'm Cat Deeley and this is the ITV weekly chart show!" the sunshine voice begins.

Ah well, I guess another half hour in bed probably wouldn't hurt.

2.

"Where the hell are we?"

"Jonesy mate, I swear if you ask that one more time I'll put Radio Clyde on!" snaps Dave.

"Well," Jonesy persists indignantly, "the first away game of the season and you've got us on a wild goose chase looking for a garage that doesn't exist."

"It does exist. I just can't find it, alright! I must have taken the wrong turn-off at that big roundabout."

"Which one, there's been hundreds of the bloody things. We're lost aren't we? We're going round and round in some parallel dimension with no hope of breaking out the loop. Admit it Dave we're going to die in East Kilbride!"

And it seems entirely feasible that we will. I'm not getting involved though. I despise fannying around in the car needlessly and I'm climbing the irritometer nicely. Whether its being stuck in traffic jams, crawling round car parks looking for the space that doesn't exist or getting lost on avoidable trips like this, that simmering feeling of aggravation remains the same. We were not put on this earth to spend our lives sitting inside little boxes of metal mindlessly pootling around new town Scalextrics tracks like this. If we were we'd all be called Jeremy Clarkeston and wear too- dark denim. We left Arthurston really early because Dave wanted to check out a car he'd seen advertised in the newspaper. "Don't worry boys, its on the way to the game." He calmly assured us. Yeah on the way if the game was in Peebles! Anyway as I said, I'm not getting involved. Instead I'm lost in the passing urban sprawl and the hundreds of commuters straggling their way along roadside pathways or scooting by in their motorised jail-cells.

I feel sorry for the people who learn to drive in East Kilbride. Six months of extensive training, whirling around roundabouts, always remembering to look right, slowly growing more confident at pushing into the merry-go-round of tetchy travellers then HAZZAR! The test is sat, licence got, and off they go. You can see it all. Young Miss Newdriver on a quick hurl to Hamilton or Blantyre, sorry 'Blanturr'. The family are tightly packed in making supportive noises whenever the gears crunch. "Don't worry dear, they often make that noise." encourages dad looking diagonally upwards. "Took that roundabout well though" chips in Granny pleasantly. Things are going like clockwork as East Kilbride is left behind. Then WHAM! A JUNCTION! "What the hell is that?" asks our young driver incredulously. "Wait I remember this ....hold on...ehh" stammers Dad but too late. Panic sets in and BANG! the brakes are thumped and the air-bags are out to say hello. The cousins are crying in the back and Granny's teeth have shot out her mouth and are gripping the headrest behind a half strangled father who is grasping madly at the safety-belt coiled round his neck. His eyes are now protruding so far from his head that the betting man would have a swift fiver on them exploding within the next ten seconds. Time passes, tears flow and a traffic cop shakes his head as he once again completes his road traffic accident form. The accident description box is filled with 'FEKE 4/13 incident'. Three sardonic letters that the boys back at the station recognise only too well as yet another Failed East Kilbride Emigration.

"I'm beginning to wish I hadn't read your bloody newspaper," says Dave shooting me a sideways glance.

"*My* Paper? Where do I fit into this?" I reply surprised.

"It was your paper I saw the advert in. I read it last night when I was waiting for you to get ready."

"Couldn't have been, we don't get a paper delivered anymore. Haven't done since the folks stopped them when they went to Tenerife last November. The old boy thinks they only report scandal and bad news. 'All tits and terror' he says."

"Well he must have got one yesterday 'cause I read the motor ads and found this garage in East Kilbride that sells all kinds of classic cars from the seventy's and eighties. Look I even wrote down the address!" Dave struggles around awkwardly in his tight jeans pocket and pulls out the crumpled evidence.

"Dave, I swear you couldn't have read a newspaper in my house during the week. I sometimes get the Sunday paper for the football but I take them to work with me. I haven't seen one for ...... hold on, where exactly did you find this paper?"

"In the kitchen."

"Where *exactly* in the kitchen?"

"I made myself a cup of tea and sat down at the kitchen table with it - You're out of chocolate biscuits by the way. Anyway, the paper was lying on the floor beside that hideous garden gnome thing that your dad made."

"Beside the dog's basket?"

" Aye, I suppose"

"Awww for God's sake Dave, that's the dog's paper!"

"What ... your dog likes to keep up with current affairs?"

"No, Sparkey's been lying on that paper for well over seventeen years. And I don't think it was even an up to date newspaper then. It usually lies under her blanket - according to mum it keeps the cold from seeping up from the floor tiles through her basket."

Strange looks pass amongst us.

"Yeah I know. That's my mother for you. She must have been doing one of her clearouts and tidied up the dog's basket."

"What kind of car was it?" asks Jonesy smirking

" A Triumph TR7" Dave mutters dolefully.

"Yeah and they don't make them any more do they?"

"Of course they don't. I thought it was one of those places specialising in classic models didn't I. It was a really good deal as well."

"Of course it was you divot! That was the 'on the road' price in 1982!" Jonesy persists, clearly enjoying not being the butt of the Mickey-take for once.

"Didn't you think the paper looked sort of old and tatty?" I inquire, the corners of my mouth quivering.

"I thought you had dropped tea or something on it, that's all."

"That wasn't tea mate!", sniggers Jonesy, "Sparkey was never one for holding back eh Craig?" And we explode with laughter.

"Alright, let's leave it shall we. It wasn't that funny."

"I'm sorry Dave but it absolutely is. Its right up there with the time you went over the Erskine Bridge the wrong way to get to Dumbarton's ground?"

"Oooo yeh," chimes in Jonesy, "Weren't you just outside Dumbarton when you decided to jump to the other side of the Clyde Estuary and head for Greenock instead?

Dave looks ready to burst.

"And not only did you argue with a petrol station assistant that Boghead WAS on this side of the river, despite the fact she was pointing over to Dumbarton Rock showing you its actual location, but you had a stand up fight with the bridge's toll collector when you refused to pay to go back over due to their ...... what exactly...?"

"Their shit-awful signposting." Dave murmurs, his brow drawn down to his chin in a deep, resentful scowl, " Anyway, it wouldn't have happened if you two pussies hadn't been going to the rugby though, would it?"

It's our turn to look embarrassed and Jonesy clears his throat nervously, a cardinal sin exposed once again.

We've spent a good ten minutes rounding more round-abouts and skipping down more connecting roads, all the while pasting Dave for his misunderstanding naturally. Things are on the up though. He seems to have found his directional focus again and having located a sign for Hairmyers Hospital and Eaglesham, we're thankfully heading for open country leaving the circular man-trap from Hades behind.

It's a strange road of contrasting scenery that points to Ayrshire coming as we are from the new-town urban sprawl of East Kilbride. Passing the outpost that is the relatively modern Strathclyde Police Training Facility at Jackton, the surroundings immediately have a more rural bent to them. Eaglesham has a picture postcard quaintness about it with its meandering uphill thoroughfare, past sturdy oaks and low whitewashed shoppes and dwellings. It is the sort of place that still holds public floggings for people caught dropping sweetie papers in the street. Slip through the village's leafy haven and its onwards and upwards to the Fenwick Moor, a place so weather-beaten and desolate that the inhabiting sheep stand hopefully by the side of the road trying to hitch a lift to 'Anywhere but here'. No one picks them up though – they have no thumbs.

The first thing that grabs you is its rugged expansiveness. You can almost see Richard Hannay in 'The 39 Steps', being pursued by foreign despots, stumbling his way over its windswept barrenness. The full spectacle of the Lanarkshire Valley is now behind you, and the panoramic sight of Glasgow snuggling in to the West leaves you with a clear understanding of how high you actually are. Perfect-white wind generators, a small reservoir configuration and some radio masts are the only man-made attempts at taming the territory. As the narrow, two lane road hugs the rolling contours of heather and gorse for miles ahead it is clear that the elements are in control here and we will always be uneasy travellers just passing through.

The Fenwick Moor is nothing if not inspirational. Morose '70s singer/songwriter Leonard Cohen, on crossing the moor was moved to pen the obscure title 'Sleet in August'. The song never appeared on any subsequent album as, by his own admission, it was 'just too depressing.' For most others hardy enough to attempt its crossing, inspiration comes in the more instant form of nudging the speedometer 10 mph or so faster in an effort to clear its desolate expanse in as short a duration as is humanly possible. Just in case.

From there it's a matter of negotiating what must be one of the most hazardous stretches of roadway ever constructed. The A77 is 20 miles or so of tormenting two and four lane carriageway bisecting frugal, tumbling farmland. Hardly any of it has a central reservation and throw into the mix that it is always, always raining or worse, shrouded in fog, and the ride becomes a terrifying roller-coaster ride that Alton Towers could never hope to match. Drivers completing this section of carriageway without a brow-pulsing head-ache just aren't human.

"What do you think the team will be?" asks Dave as we take the Kilmarnock slip road which is happily also displaying a yellow 'Football traffic' road-sign.

" Hmm, not sure, probably similar to last week's with a couple of changes . Isn't Jay McDonald injured anyway? Aye ....Thomson in goals. Defence of , emm.... Storrie and Bird and err, no wait a minute, McLean in, em ... midfield and ....

Meanwhile, as I stab at the selection of possibilities with all the precision of an Amoruso free kick (remember them) Jonesy is busying himself in the back seat, frantic rustling and scribbling noises emanating from his general direction.

"Here!" he interjects thrusting a piece of scrap paper through the divide in the seats, "Life's too short – ever thought about being a pundit?"

I take the scrap of paper and look at the barely discernable scrawl of names scratched, in formation, onto the page in front of me..

A Thomson

Paul Marker   *Jim Storrie*   *Robert Crush*   *Mark Bird*

Mickey Hedge   *Scott McLean*   *Tony Bunton*   *Ally Fairful*

Russ Dinsmore   *Ray Stark*

Subbies ; Chris Barlow, Wille Burgoyne, Frankie Boyle, Dougie McKenna

"You know when you look at it we don't have much of a squad do we - I mean Frankie's ok, brilliant on his day even, but Willie's nothing more than a veteran hatchet-man, Dougie McKenna has only started one game that I can think of and even you can't think of the last sub Jonesy"

"We've got those two young guys, Smith and Hamilton, that played at Huntly and Jerry Kidd should be back in the frame soon as well." Jonesy suggests.

"Jerry Kidd?" splutters Dave , "Jerry Kidd is about as much use as a rubber spanner and you know it!"

"I don't think he's that bad actually." Jonesy replies haughtily, "If he could stay fit and get a run in the team ...."

"Yeh, yeh, IF he could stay fit he would STILL be feckless. Face it Jonesy the guy's a wreck. He's the sort of weed you send into the Swiss mountains to recuperate from a strength sapping illness. Give him a wheel chair and a tartan rug for his knees. Get him to breathe the air, take the spa waters, that sort of thing. "

I wish I had a pound for every time we've had this argument. Jonesy has a soft spot for Jerry who, in fairness, *isn't* the worst player that ever pulled on a Rovers shirt. Dave on the other hand despises the guy. When it comes to the erratic wingback he's like a battle hardened military general sensing weakness in a disappointing son. Scorn and disdain don't really cover Dave's attitude towards the guy. And yet they never settle it and agree to disagree. They poke away at each other with their Kidd sticks, Dave's zero tolerance scratching irritatingly against Jonesy's gentle accommodation. And here is the thing. Barring some major change in Mr Kidd's contribution and demeanour, neither will ever be converted to the other's way of thinking. Excellent! Little inflexible opinions like this are what supporting football is all about.

3.

Dave brings the car to a halt at the edge of an expansive road beside the entrance to a tree-lined park. Across the way a line of large Victorian houses begins with a particularly grand and affluent looking structure. A small sign proclaims 'Dundonald Road' to the passing world.

According to Grampa this is a good place to park and his directions through the straggling outskirts of Kilmarnock have been spot on. Rugby Park is apparently just a walk down the road and round the corner from here. The other option he suggested was a little further on in a Morrison's car park on Westshaw Street (wherever that may be) but this seems as good a place as any. Despite our wayward travels its still only one-o-clock so we have plenty time to look around.

"Right then!" exclaims Dave clambering out the car, stretching and pulling on his brown corded jacket awkwardly, "its time for a pint and some steak pie. Which way do we go?"

"Well there's a couple of pubs if we walk down this road and turn left at the lights. I've been here on a night out with a guy from work.... Ex-work that is" he adds self-consciously. "One of them is a strong Killie supporters' pub though, the Howard Arms I think its called."

"Oh aye, I remember it. I think that was the pub that was painted with blue and white stripes when Kilmarnock were in the cup final wasn't it?" says Dave to no one in particular.

"Well we don't have colours on so we should be ok." I suggest.

"Yeh, and then we can get ourselves up to the ground and have a couple of beers at the hotel in the car park." continues Jonesy our newly appointed Kilmarnock expert.

"Oh yeh, I had forgotten about that. Can you handle all that beer before the match though?" I ask, half smiling half serious.

I love having a beer before the game but it's a fine line you tread when deciding how much to have. One or two pre-match pints are good for getting a wee buzz of enthusiasm going, especially for that mid-table home game against Forfar in the February rain. Years ago I used to have youthful excitement and anticipation escaping from every pore to the extent that my natural exuberance saw me through. Nowadays however I need a lager jumpstart to approach anything like the eagerness and raw emotion I cultivated in my formative years. But you have to be careful. One over the eight and your afternoon is easily lost in a misty blend of detached thoughts, echoed swear words, and vague recollections that only come back to you in dribs and drabs, more specifically at the next match when your mates point out just how loud and annoying you were the week before. Its also worth remembering that a lunchtime drinking session during the day is a different beast altogether from your standard night on the sauce.

This theory is not without scientific basis either. Indeed primary research has indicated that an alcoholic drink at lunchtime can be over twice as effective as one drunk after six in the evening. This was the dramatic claim made by Dr Leo Weinstein of Southern California University who in 2003 researched the differing effects of alcohol on bodily reactions at differing times of the day. Experimenting on an assortment of dogs, small monkeys and chinchillas, Weinstein's findings were, for many, somewhat inconclusive. Despite establishing a complicated formula featuring the Weinstein Daylight Drinking Multiplier (WDDM), *and* creating a useable conversion scale allowing the comparison between levels of drunkenness at different times of day, his work failed to gain widespread recognition amongst his piers. Unabashed, Weinstein fiercely defended his research claiming that his results would in time be celebrated and almost certainly would go on to have a profound effect on the drinks and leisure industry for years to come. "In any case," he triumphantly concluded in his final report, "the sight of those little furry dudes staggering round the lab bumping into things was totally hilarious." [2]

Jonesy at any rate feels more than confident of his daylight drinking capacity and is off up the road muttering inaudible directions over his shoulder. Dave and I look at each other, back to Jonesy, then scuttle off in pursuit.

A left turn at a bustling crossroads and we're heading away from where we reckon the ground is and down a busy, thoroughfare called McLelland Drive. Red sand-stoned houses line the way and a steady flow of traffic journeys down the wide roadway.

"Is it far?" I gasp, struggling to keep up with the power-walking pace set by Jonesy. "Its alright for you, you've got your Ichabod Crane inside-leg measurement to deal with this."

"Just down here!" he replies, puffing also." Hey look! The Morrison's that your Grampa was talking about. I wish we'd parked in there."

Empty spaces lie dotted around the car park on our right hand side mocking us as we walk by.

---

[2]   Source- National Geographic Oct '05, article - 'If I could drink with the animals.'

" Well at least we'll be nearer the ground for a quick getaway" says Dave defensively, "Bloody hell Jonesy where is this pub then?

"There!" he shouts triumphantly, " On the corner of the crossroads ahead there."

"That doesn't say Howard Arms on the sign" I venture screwing up my eyes.

"That's not it. That's another pub across the road but hey, we'll just have to go there too." replies Jonesy cheerily.

"Yes ... well .... we'll see" mutters Dave in a low tone, the conclusion no doubt dawning on him that a drinking opportunity has presented itself and he, unfortunately, has his driving gloves on.

A hundred yards skip and we arrive in front of a pastel green pub perched on the corner of yet another crossroads. Hanging from the wall next to the entrance is Kilmarnock FC emblem. No illusions here as to where their allegiances lie. The theme is continued in the tiled doorway with the emblem once again, proudly displayed. I have no problem with this, we are in Kilmarnock after all. We dive in full of expectation however in short The Howard Arms proves to be a bit of a disappointment and one swiftly drained pint later we're scuttling our way across a maze of pedestrian fences and crossings towards the handily placed alternative.

"That was a bit dark and soulless didn't you think" I suggest

"Absolutely," agrees Jonesy. "I suppose its ok if you're a Killie fan but from the look of the outside I expected a bit more than a big room with a pool area stuck on the side."

"Yeh ," chips in Dave his tone laced with irritation " Open and sterile - No ambience whatsoever.

"Ooooooaa - *ambience*!" Jonesy and I both coo together laughing.

"Alright , shut it! You know what I mean". He's about to grump some more but we've reached a black and white mock Tudor establishment with 'The Hunting Lodge' emblazoned above the door.

"This is more like it, " I exclaim enthusiastically. Having squeezed through the stain- glazed, double-door entrance three abreast we've fallen into a snug and inviting interior. The Malty Hop Lounge, as it is advertised on the wall, is pleasantly filled with a scatter of small tables and a clutter of bric-a-brac hanging from the walls and ceiling in contrived disarray. Walking across the rich green carpet we nuzzle in beside the bar-flies who are perched on stools at the tight, curved bar. A sign hanging from above our heads suggests that 'Unattended children will be sold as slaves.' This is definitely my kind of place. The Lodge is evidently a 'free house' and sprouting from the bar are a generous selection of draught beer, lager and ale taps. Faced with the opportunity of drinking 'Thumping Farter' or 'Dingle's Wattery' or whatever, Jonesy and I unadventurously plump for pints of Stella. As we settle down at a table in the middle of the room, Dave joins us caressing a fearsome looking pint of what he informs us is 'Reverend James'.

"This'll be my one and only today boys" he says, his tone laced with regret. "Here's to our first away win of the season."

Lifting our glasses , they chink together in solidarity .

"Bit of a strange place this." offers Jonesy.

"Hmmm yes," I agree, "but I quite like it."

Casting my eye around, there seems to be a talking point in every nook and cranny. Beside the door stands a six foot signpost indicating the roads to Rome, London and The Ladies. Over Dave's shoulder, it's partner is kindly showing the way to Oban, Glasgow and The Gents. A statue of what looks like Einstein holding a pile of books guards the womens' toilet door and behind Jonesy a blackened stone fireplace waits patiently for winter. Looking upwards a squad of painted wooden soldiers guard various junk items sitting on the ledge running above our heads.

"My mum suggested we do a bit of sightseeing when I said we were going to Kilmarnock." I smile, leaning over taking a sip out my pint

The lads snigger. "Really?" asks Dave

"Oh aye. She's pretty tuned in is my mum. She suggested we visit the Dick Institute. Very interesting apparently."

"What's that then," asks Dave "A training college for referees?"

"Apparently it's a museum-come-art gallery thingy. She particularly recommends viewing the embroidery exhibits" I conclude doing a vague impression of my mother in a high falsetto voice with half closed eyes.

"Excellent! Sod the game and let's go there instead. I'm quite partial to viewing a tapestry of an afternoon"

Jonesy looks like he's going to reply to this but holds his peace and instead picks up a menu from the table. Looking at it momentarily he ventures, " I think I might have a burger for lunch. Errr.... Yup. With cheese and bacon. Definitely!" and with that he wraps up the laminated card and places it back on he table, folding his arms in Superman style as if to say 'My work here is done!'

"I think I'll have lasagne. I've not had that in ages." I add.

"Well I'm having steak pie and chips. No messing about. Give us some money and I'll go up to the bar and order."

We both lean back and dig into too tight pockets. I find my wallet surprisingly easily and Jonesy yanks out a crumpled mess of fivers and tenners.

"What kind of burger do you want again?" asks Dave looking at Jonesy's ball of cash disparagingly.

"Well .... Now I think on it I think I might have steak pie as well."

"Please yourself, " says Dave sighing in full resignation, "And it was lasagne for you Craig, wasn't it?"

"Em, maybe I'll just have steak pie too"

"For God's sake, its like having lunch with Indecisive Igbert's toddler twins. Right, anything else?"

"Yeh, no veg for me with that if that's ok?"I appear with screwed up eyes.

Dave snorts, grabs our money and stalks over to the bar leaving us gazing up at a TV which has conveniently been mounted on the ledge above our table and is showing Celtic v Sacrificial Lamb United on Sky.

4.

I'm in a quandary about the food. While it certainly was tasty enough and, in line with my cunning plan, I got a bigger portion of chips than the others to replace the absent vegetables from my plate, the first Steak-Pie Commandment was surely broken.

Thou shalt not unceremoniously dump a separate piece of puff pastry on top of stewed meat and gravy and call it a pie.

In the Holy Book of Pub Grub everyone knows this to be true.

Yes, our plates were overflowing with big chunks of succulent Ayrshire beef, Yes, the gravy was thick and beefy with a delicious hint of Guinness if I'm not mistaken. And at £5.95, not the worst value for money I've ever experienced. But all this counts for nothing when presented with a dod of pastry perched fraudulently on your plate like the food equivalent of an introductory time-share offer. That said I still leave my plate cleaner than the speeches at a Baptist wedding.

The walk back towards the ground is a welcome one given our straining waistbands and we discuss, amongst other things, possible amendments to the off-side rule, the 'as seen on TV' shirt abominations of Dougie Donnelly 1998-2007, and just to show we are equally capable of talking about things other than football, the current state of the Wales international team.

5.

They're an old club Kilmarnock. One of the League's oldest in fact. Back in the pre Old Firm days of 1869 when Queen Victoria was just getting into her stride and Graham Bell was having trouble communicating with his friends, a group of local cricketers decided they needed a winter pursuit to keep them in trim. Looking for another suitably pointless sport requiring little or no skill, they naturally set about learning the 'intricate' rules of rugby. A slightly confusing start for a football team admittedly but pretty soon everyone saw sense, got the ball on the deck where it belongs, and Kilmarnock FC as we know them were formed.

After initially making use of a number of local parks, the oldest professional team in Scottish football eventually settled in their own ground. Their roots showing, they called it Rugby Park. They played their inaugural 'home' match in 1878 , a full five years after they had made history by participating in the first ever Scottish Cup tie. The record shows that they went down 2-0 to Renton that fateful day and asides from a 'blip' in 1997 when they spectacularly won the competition, they have done precious little in modern times to reverse this trend of premature cup exits.

Recent Scottish Cup exits aside (some of them painfully at the hands of Ayr United too) the League Cup has possibly been even *crueller* to Kilmarnock. For the Scottish Cup, for its sins, at least stood firm, and gave the Ayrshire club little or no encouragement. The League Cup however has frequently been a wicked, teasing temptress enticing the boys in blue and white towards its final triumphant climax on no fewer than five occasions. Five times though Killie have reached the final, and five times they have frustratingly come up a buck short.

The last one – a five one drubbing at the hands of Celtic – was probably the most painful. And not just for the score-line either. Something much worse made it so. Something, dare I say it ..... from hell.

You see someone, somewhere had a great idea that since Killie's luck was finally going to change it would be nice to have a commemorative song to remember the occasion by. Obviously it would have to be a dance track- no question. It also went without saying that Rolf Harris would *have* to sing it. Add into the pot (the same pot everyone involved must have smoking to come up with idea in the first place clearly) a mad church choir and an intriguing character called Steve Lima and what you end up with is 'Fine Day' a song to move mountains, a song to work miracles, a song to make Jim Jeffries sound interesting.

Steve Lima (real name Steve Lima) is a strange one. Look on the home(y) page of his website and his face glares out at you with all the attitude he can muster. Except he really looks too old to be hanging on to all that Grand Master Mixer nonsense. He's your dad in a beanie hat. Famed for his 'wickedly unlikely mash-ups', Steve's 'thing' is to take two startlingly unrelated, reasonably famous tracks, 'mash' them together in the one mix then rename the monster by fusing parts of both titles together in a 'clever and urbane' manner. His more popular mashes include Madonna/Bronski Beat doing 'Beautiful Small-town Stranger', Nirvana/Ultra Nate with 'Smells Like Free Spirit', and U2/Patrick Hernandez giving us 'Born to Vertigo'. Get the picture? .... Of course you do. I for one am off to order all his records so I can learn his dark secret too and create my own masterpieces. I can see it now, hundreds of mad-eyed revellers jigging around to Travis and Madonna singing 'Why does it always rain on holiday?', Queen and the Beatles doing ' Crazy little thing called Yoko' and the instant club classic; Dusty Springfield/Chuck Berry with 'I just don't know what to do with my ding-a-ling.'

6.

So...... undoubtedly luckless in the cup, Kilmarnock also found little fortune in their initial league exploits. An early Malky McCormick cartoon depicts Killie celebrating winning the 1898 second division championship in style only to be told that Clyde, who had only won one game all season, would in fact be promoted in their stead. There was no automatic promotion at that time and the Bully Wee, unfortunately for Kilmarnock, had a ground in Glasgow. How crudely unsporting Scottish football was in those days - Imagine the injustice of being the best team in your league and not being allowed promotion simply because your stadium isn't the best. Thank heavens we've moved on from that brand of thinking.

Never mind. The football club was to take this on the chin and in local hero, McCormick, their supporters had a new artistic champion to stride forward with towards the twentieth century. Within no time national newspapers and cheap barbershops were filled with cartoons chock full of chisel chins and bitingly satirical graffiti proclaiming 'Disraeli Rools!' and 'David Livingston luvs Irn Bru!' Kilmarnock was, both in a cultural and a sporting sense, well and truly on the map.

It was an era when the heroic, gentlemanly image was popular and much sought after, and for a while it seemed you could only get a game for Kilmarnock if you had a cracking good, traditional, 'Boys Own' football name. Stalwarts like 'Bummer' Campbell, Jocky Johnstone, Peerie Cunningham and 'Handy' Andy Kerr undoubtedly all benefited from this unwritten policy over the years. It didn't stop with a guaranteed first team place either. A good quality spiffing nickname won these sporting idols the right to sport damnably fine droopy moustaches and to regularly use the phrase 'Isn't it a bully day! It also allowed them to pose majestically on local street corners, arms folded, one foot on a laced up brown leather football, while wearing a defiant facial expression that said to all and sundry "These tweeds may be chaffing my crotch to buggery but I'm more the man for it!"- Status symbols every young lad could only dream of and aspire to.

Surprisingly for a team their age they have only been Scottish league champions once. In 1965 to be exact under the expert managerial guidance of Willie Waddell. Unfortunately the history books will never reflect truly what a talented squad of players Killie had in the early '60s. In that period the team had lost two cup finals and had been runners up in the league for four seasons before their eventual defeat of Hearts in the '65 final game cliffhanger. The likes of Tommy McLean, David Sneddon, Bertie Black , Brien McIlroy and Jackie McInally all donned the traditional blue and white strip in that period and it was their commitment allied to Waddell's supreme man-management skills that ultimately lead Kilmarnock to the title, perhaps their greatest achievement in their long, unpredictable history.

Kilmarnock's muscle flexing wasn't confined to the domestic stage however. Having won the league in such dramatic style their reward was a European draw with the Spanish giants Real Madrid. An impressive 2-2 draw at Rugby Park unfortunately couldn't be built upon and Killie eventually succumbed 7-3 on aggregate. Intent had been shown though and in their Fairs Cup campaign the following year they really got into their stride. After dispatching Antwerp, Gent and Locomotive Leipzig they only came a cropper in the semi-final against the burgeoning talent of Leeds United, Bremner, Lorimer, Hunter and all. In a bizarre turn of events Soviet Leader, Aleksei Kosygin, stirred no doubt by Killie's fine European run, chose to attend a Kilmarnock league match at Rugby Park where he reputedly 'enjoyed the competition very much', commenting graciously as he did on the 'pleasant climate' and the 'extra peppery Bovril'. He also reportedly quizzed three of the ball boys on missile placements and was last seen loitering on Rugby Crescent, holding what looked like an early prototype cam-corder, asking for directions to the Holy Loch.

Nowadays Kilmarnock are much like all the other non Old Firm Premier clubs in Scotland in the sense that under the current set up they will never win the league. That is no criticism on the team, its just the harshest fact in Scottish football today that no club has the financial clout to compete over the course of a whole season against the Twisted Sisters of Glasgow. Killie however enjoy things as best they can. They seem almost perennially safe from relegation, have seen their fair share of qualifications for European football and Rugby Park is periodically used by the SFA for international matches. Not the worst predicament for a team that as recent as 1988 were languishing in the second division going nowhere further than Arbroath for a Smokie, a charmless defeat and a stiff neck from the blustering east coast wind.

7.

Underneath the main stand beside the obligatory merchandise shop is The Killie Club, a large square bar area crammed full of excitable Kilmarnock fans bedecked in blue and white. There's little in the way of away support in here and having swooped past a well turned out young lad at the door guarding a signing in register, we come to the conclusion that it's probably members only.

Dave has already ordered at the bar so Jonesy and I agree that we'll stay for one then move on to the 'hotel in the car-park'. The walls are covered with framed pictures and photographs of Kilmarnock players past and present. Predictably, the cup win against Falkirk in '97 is extensively featured and it really brings home how important such an achievement is to a provincial team like Kilmarnock. It was undoubtedly a wonderful, memorable day for everyone associated with the club and the smiling faces of the men, women and children pictured at Ibrox that day enforces how much effort Kilmarnock have made in fostering a family atmosphere at Rugby Park.

Jonesy is looking at a photograph of an open top bus surrounded by an ocean of blue and white.

"They called that 'The Friendly Final' or something didn't they?' he asks moving closer to the photograph.

" I can't remember," I reply truthfully, " but it figures. *Any* non Old Firm final gets a tag like that doesn't it.. The 'Family' Final or the 'Warm and Snugly' Final …"

" Yeh, why don't they give the Rangers - Celtic games a homely title as well. What about the 'Spitting Venom Final or 'The Wife's Getting A Beating After This Depending On The Score' Final. What do you think?"

I'm forced to agree but before I can add to the conversation Dave returns with yet another two pints of the golden stuff. Absently I take my glass as I find myself drawn to a striking photograph of a recent squad of players who are individually modelling all the Kilmarnock strips down through the ages. What an excellent idea. I make a mental note to write to Jeff Winter, Arthurston's current chairman, to suggest we do something similar. A good Christmas present I'm thinking.

We drink quickly, for despite not wearing anything to identify us as Rovers fans, we all feel strangely conspicuous. Edging our way through the crowd and past a large wooden table offering a variety of football coupons we nod and smile to the Keeper of the Guestbook and make our escape.

Outside in the sunshine the Park Hotel beckons. A modern looking building sitting separate from the main stadium complex, it looks from a distance like one of those fancy, high tech Mercedes or BMW garages you see nowadays. Ambitiously owned by the club themselves, the hotel was optimistically built in the summer of 2002 as overspill accommodation for the Korea/Japan World Cup. Attracting a disappointing number of guests willing to make the lengthy transfer between the hotel and match venues, the directors reluctantly settled on offering its 50 bedrooms, conference facilities, cafe bar and restaurant to local patrons on the understanding that they accepted the extortionate mini-bar prices, avoided peak-time showering (usually around 5.45 pm) and didn't steal the towels. They also relented in other areas and allowed the local Rotary club to hold their monthly meetings in the small and draughty 'Somerset Suite' providing they paid in advance and promised not to act 'too Smart-Alecy'.

As we slide along the main stand and approach its airy entrance I can make out a large group of revellers through the extensive glass frontage. Encouragingly I can see they are wearing the colours of both teams.

Sidestepping the pale young whippersnapper trying to flog us a 50/50 halftime draw ticket at the door we dive full tilt into what I can only describe as *not* your average fitba boozer. Its like Tam Cowan's 'Offside' meets the Ideal Home exhibition. Crowds of supporters from both teams are either draped on the light wood banister connecting a split level grey marble floor or are lurking around large potted plants, pint-handed and cheery for it. Others are reclining on bright blue, leather effect, circular chairs around low, modern designed, glass tables. To our right a long reception desk is acting as a rest home for old, empty pint glasses and running the full length of the wall beyond is a massive window flooding light into the room and offering an exceptional view of the Moffat Stand and its entrance. The open feel of the area is further enhanced by the surrounding balcony above us which is supporting a panoramic dining area.

"Well this is certainly different." says Dave admiringly as he slowly scans the scene around him.

And its hard not to be impressed at the stylish but relaxed atmosphere that 'The Park' boasts. Kids are scooting around excitedly while the dads peer over their beers contentedly and the less encumbered are in happy conversation or staring at the ultra modern wall mounted flat screen TV that is well positioned for all to see .

Its my round and while I attempt to get the beers in from a small overflow bar on the lower level near the entrance, Jonesy is dispatched to the main bar up at the top of the foyer in case he can get served first.

As if.

I'm attended to pretty quickly and give a wave to signal the success. Transporting what will undoubtedly be the last alcoholic drinks of the day I catch Jonesy out of the corner in my eye forgetting the step down to ground level and falling his length on the floor. While those in the immediate vicinity take a concerned step back I glance at Dave who is standing shaking his head with a resigned look upon his face.

"Bloody hell that's an awkward wee step" mumps a red-faced Jonesy, shuffling up to us, brushing his back side with one hand and reaching for his pint with the other

"Not for anyone else though." states Dave curtly, his sobriety clearly wearing him thin. He's about to add something acidic when a stumbling noise comes from over Jonesy's shoulder this time accompanied by a wholesome cheer. A young guy in his mid-twenties wearing a blue and white striped Killie top under a black leather jacket is in the process of getting up from the floor, his mates laughing and ruffling his hair teasingly.

Jonesy sniffs.

Seeing a 'moment' looming I seize the conversation. "So how's the job hunting going then?"

"Not great." Jonesy replies disconsolately with the hint of a slur ," I've applied for a few things but those forms they send you take so long to fill out that it takes me all day just to do one. Then…", his finger now wagging threateningly, " …. THEN ,they just ignore you anyway!"

Unfortunately I seem to have put out one fire and lit another.

"I'm thinking about only applying for jobs that ask for a CV now." he continues his eyes rolling strangely around in his head."

"Well I can't believe you didn't tell me about this sooner", growls Dave.

"And what would that have achieved. I was getting kicked anyway."

" I could have suggested a few things,. Told you how to play things a bit better"

"I appreciate that but unfortunately I don't think my bosses would have responded to a dose of Teakwando."

" Yeh well, you can't let these bastards walk over you!"

" I DIDN'T let anyone walk all over me."

"No, you let them manhandle you out the premises though. In full view of everyone too!"

"They didn't ……" but Jonesy stops dead and looks out the large window towards the stadium. He is shaking ever so slightly and I hear him muttering a string of words under his breath . "... thinks I'm Jackie 'fuckin' Chan" is all I can make out.

"Look …. sorry Jonesy." continues Dave softly," its just this thing with you has got me riled. You're a good guy and you were good at your job. You didn't deserve this. I'll bet that guy that sacked you hadn't a clue who you were or what you did."

Jonesy turns back slowly, a weak smile on his face. "Of course he didn't. I think he spoke to me directly twice in the space of a year, and the second time he called me Ken." He falls silent and gazes into the distance." I was really good at that job."

"We know." continues Dave patting Jonesy on the shoulder.. "Something will turn up. No doubt about it" he concludes.

An uneasy silence falls over us and lingers for what seems an age. Dave breaks the hush with a sigh and an exaggerated stretch of his arm, purposefully revealing what looks like a shiny new watch. "Well boys , a quarter to three. What do you think, time to get over to the game?"

We both agree and drain the remnants of our drinks purposefully. The crowd at reception has thinned and as we stroll out, I dive over to the desk and dump our glasses. Catching up quickly, Dave and Jonesy are chatting away as if 'words' had never been spoken earlier

"What do think then, predictions for the game?

" I've a nasty feeling that we'll lose one nil." I offer gravely.

Jonesy pitches in immediately, "No way Craig. We're on a roll . Two-one to the Rovers!".

Dave looks at me challengingly then turns to Jonesy smiling, "That's what I like about you Ken. Its your optimism."

And with that we head to the game.

8.

The Chadwick Stand is the designated 'away' end of the ground and having squeezed through the inevitable brick walled turnstile, two things immediately spring to mind. Firstly, TWENTY QUID FOR A FOOTBALL MATCH ! Woahh, that put a shiver down my spine as I handed over the equivalent of three trips to the pictures. Secondly, looking upwards as I am, how much of a temporary, unfinished quality the structure above us has. The three 'newly' developed stands around Rugby Park are all of the 'shell' variety. This means they have no real enclosed capacity under the seated areas for office space, bar facilities or club rooms. Implemented no doubt as a cost cutting exercise, you have, in fairness, to hand it Kilmarnock for building like this. After all the design does the job amply well and presumably when you're inside, the lack of any 'encasing' structure is lost upon you anyway.

Rovers fans are mingling under the Meccano-like building around them. Some are queuing for pies and other exorbitantly priced eats while others are climbing the exposed stairs towards the raised entrance and their seats. To the side of us a middle aged gentleman is standing ashen faced with two kids. At first I think he is having a heart attack but as I look closer I catch him give a barely discernable shake of the head and silently mouth the words 'Forty-eight pounds', a faraway look resting in his eyes. Safe in the knowledge that the chap is not about to breathe his last I leave him to his woes and start to climb the white cement staircase.

Emerging as I am from an entrance half way up the sizeable Chadwick Stand, I can't help thinking that Rugby Park looks too big for Kilmarnock's needs. It's only five minutes to kick off and while the centre areas of the main stand and directly opposite are well filled, elsewhere is populated by only a smattering of people (possibly sufferers from claustrophobia or individuals who frequently and mysteriously smell of fish). With a capacity of 18,000 and an average home gate of around a third of that you have to think that Killie, much like those ' two-kid parents' who own that muckle jeep with the big wheels and the cow-bar, could have made do with something a little smaller.

We find seats a few rows up from the central walkway that runs the length of the stand. Mrs Chadwick, whom this wonderful erection is in tribute to, must have been a midget as leg room is definitely not at a premium. Looking around, the number of 'normal' sized blokes sitting with their knees around their ears or else pushed together effeminately to one side would be quite amusing were it not for the acute pain resonating from the top of my own shin bones. Jonesy by the look of him will need outside help if he is ever to leave.

I'm taking some quiet time to get my bearings. A small, pale blue building wedged between the stands in the far left corner has attracted my attention. It has the outward appearance of a wartime control centre or a shelter of some sort and I imagine a group of code crackers and radio operators working feverishly within its secret confines. Down to our left a row of flag poles neatly fills a gap in the stadium although we are still afforded a nice view of the sun-drenched residential area outside. I'm dragged back to life when a wave of noise rises up around the ground and Kilmarnock, in their dark and light blue 'away' shirts take the field. A quick glance around shows me around five or six hundred expectant bodies in red and white looking towards the thin grey portable tunnel jutting from the main stand.

"How many do you think we've got here today?" I ask Jonesy not taking my eyes from the tunnel.

"It's a good support. Must be over a thousand" he replies excitely. "We haven't had this many since...."

But his words are lost in the eruption as Scott Mclean sprints onto the field closely followed by the rest of his team. Ripped up programmes fly into the air giving the effect of a potted version of the Argentina '78 confetti spectacular and as the tiny paper snow flakes fall to earth, the faithful singularly belt out 'There's only one Arthurston!"

"The park looks nice" I comment as the first round of singing subsides.

"They used to get a sheep to eat it" says Jonesy absently

"What's that you're saying?" asks Dave leaning over

"Yeh, back in the 50's they had sheep called Angus that they let graze on the park and behind the goals."

"How do you know that?" Dave asks suspiciously.

"I was at the library on the internet yesterday checking the recruitment sites and I got sidetracked into looking up stuff about Kilmarnock. Quite interesting really. The sheep got huckled out of the way for first team games of course but sometimes it was allowed to stay for reserve games." Jonesy chuckles.

"Are you making this up?" I ask.

"Absolutely not. I found lots of good stuff. They have a Dutch supporters club formed by a group of Ajax fans. Did you know that? ..... Eh?"

"Nope, how's that then?"

"A group of guys came over here for a Champions League game at Ibrox, took in a game here too, got the grand tour , really enjoyed themselves and it kind of developed from there. The guy that writes their web-site calls Kilmarnock The Greatest Club on Earth and beyond!"

Jonesy says the last bit in the style of Buzz Lightyear and we laugh.

"Oh and one more thing!" he continues happily on a roll, " There's this one site that has a page completely devoted to Ayr United honours...."

"Eh? But I thought they didn't like Ayr." Dave butts in.

"My thoughts exactly" Jonesy chuckles,"but when I opened the page it read – League wins .... none Scottish Cup wins .... none, League Cup wins .... none and so on. Did you know Ayr had as miserable a record as that? – Not *one* major honour?

"Can't say I had thought about it but, hey, excellent anyway! I like a bit of bitter twistedness now and again."

"Aye but even funnier than that, for *added* dig the page was sponsored by a company that had developed the world's number one penis enlargement system, isn't that great!"

This immediately starts off a heated debate as to what the number one penis enlargement system could possibly consist of and we spend a pleasant couple of minutes striving in turn to be the least knowledgeable on the subject.

9.

Fifteen minutes in and things are looking promising. Both teams seem keen to have a go and a flurry of chances at both ends has kept our fans singing, shouting and kicking every ball along with the boys on the park. This is more than can be said for the home support who seem, at present, to be as stirred as a pot of bad soup.

The team is exactly as Jonesy predicted right down to the four-four-two formation. New boy Tony Bunton is looking like a bit of class in the midfield. He cuts an imposing figure standing a few inches over six feet in his boots. Had he a different hairstyle from the grey sandpaper skinhead he sports, he would be even taller. From a distance there is a touch of the Roy Keane about him and the way he's getting torn in , physical appearance isn't the only similarity.

We all jump to our feet, dragged upwards simultaneously by invisible pulleys slung from the roof. Fingers are pointing and bitter and violent screams of derision are slung in the direction of the Kilmarnock winger who has gone down (in our eyes) rather softly as a result of a typically half-hearted tackle by Ally Fairful. He then rolls around in something approaching final death throes, bites on a bullet whilst being administered his last rites by the Killie physio, drags himself to his feet like someone getting out of bed for the first time after a hip replacement and then, AND THEN! sprints lithely into the box to await the impending free kick being crossed from what is undoubtedly a dangerous position. The crowd howl abuse and the physio runs towards the dug out pausing only to produce some loaves and fishes from the bucket he is grasping divinely. Fairful takes his yellow card with a rueful shake of the head as the ball is placed two yards in from the touch-line, wide to our left.

In the penalty box pushing and jostling commences. The ball is slung over with a vicious out-swinging bend. One head rises above all the others and bang, the ball is in the net with Arthurston, to a man, rooted to the spot. Our peaceful hosts come alive with surprising ferocity as the Kilmarnock players fly over to the main stand in order to celebrate en-mass in front of their newly enthused fans.

By half-time we're a little deflated to say the least. Kilmarnock have skilfully taken the earlier sting out of the game and we haven't had a single shot since the goal. To make matters worse a herd of teenie cheerleaders have appeared from nowhere and are bouncing along on the vacated pitch slightly out of sync with an excessively grating Britney Spears number.

An old boy in the row in front catches my eye and shakes his head. "Bonking to music, that's what that is." he mutters disapprovingly. Without waiting for a reaction he pulls out a family bag of Werthers Originals, turns back round and settles down for the rest of the show.

The large computerised scoreboard hanging from the roof of the faraway stand is doing an impression of a migraine at its peak, an explosion of colours rippling and blinking painfully. In combination with those five pints from earlier I have developed a blinding headache. I'm about to get truly irritated when Dave saves the day. I didn't notice him disappear off but he has returned armed with pies and Bovril. And not just any pies mind but *Killie Pies*! These delicacies have the reputation as being the best in Scotland and I'm in need of sustenance.

Now I'm not prone to exaggeration but this is undoubtedly the best halftime combination of meat and pastry I have ever tasted. Huge hunks of steak in rich gravy are crammed inside light buttery pastry. We're talking cow en-croute here. All in all a culinary delight for any Scottish football fan. By the time I've finished I feel pleasantly stuffed and certainly more amenable that before. Irritation returns instantly when the club mascot makes an appearance. A big furry squirrel that the programme informs me is called 'Nuts', has flounced into view and is waving limply to the disinterested crowd. 'Total entertainment' I think returning to my programme in search of something more stimulating.

10.

Rovers have come out for the second half minus Ally Fairful who's had his usual low impact game. Frankie Boyle is on in his place and the crowd are expectant. Frankie is unreliable but on his game he'll make good defenders look bad. Were it not for a dubious temperament and his propensity for finishing a bottle of vodka in the time it takes most folk to unscrew the top, few are in doubt that Boyle could have played at a much higher level.

From the whistle we're at them and the previously unruffled Kilmarnock defence is soon looking stretched. A Stark lob drops tantalising over the bar then Rovers come closer still with Storrie of all people hammering the bar with a baldy header. The Arthurston contingent are sensing something in the air and the singing and encouragement is constant. On thirty five minutes, just when I'm thinking its not going to happen, Boyle gets the ball wide left. His pace is geriatric as he edges towards the waiting right back. Showing him way too much of the ball, inviting the challenge, he looks vulnerable. The tall defender takes the bait and dives in. Frankie is past him in an instant and the crowd rises to its feet. Stark is steaming towards the penalty spot and Dinsmore is free at the back post.

"Cross it !" yells Jonesy madly as both strikers raise their arm screaming for the ball. Boyle looks up then swerves left looking to take on the next defender at the edge of the box. The crowd groan.

"Wrong option!" shouts Dave in exasperation.

Then it happens. Boyle takes one more touch and just before the final defender arrives he opens his body and chips the ball across the goal to the back post. We're back in slow motion and for an instant there is silence. The goalie stands rooted then looks upwards, helpless as the ball drops over his head.

As the ball delicately falls in the net we're wide eyed and open mouthed and when Dinsmore and Stark simultaneously raise their arms in the air it is the sign to go mad.

One each then and the game has kicked off again before I've settled back in my seat. Scott McLean has the ball in the centre circle and throws a speculative through ball at Stark who is sprinting along side Killie's centre half. They're both in the box but Ray is never winning this one. Inexplicably, incredibly even, the Killie boy throws his arm up and the ball deflects off it as sure as death and taxes. Stark wheels round to the referee and the crowd shout as one "PENALTY!"

No doubt. And the referee is running to the spot pointing as he goes. In an instance the ball is on the spot and Ray Stark is shaping to hit the ball. I hold my breath. Ray takes three steps back and dispatches the ball high into the roof of the net, the goalie slumping in the other direction.

Cue the celebration! Bodies falling over each other. Bouncy hugging. Meaningless yelling. You'd think we'd won the cup.

Steeling ourselves for the inevitable panic stricken last ten we sit awaiting the charge. But it never comes. Kilmarnock have been shell-shocked and cannot find any rhythm to their game. The time ticks by with a series of throw ins, bad passes and fouls and when the final whistle blows proclaiming us 2-1 winners we stand jubilantly as the players group in front of us and applaud our effort, for after all it was us who kicked every ball.

11.

I'm back on the pan and its hard to believe what I'm looking at. No I've not been eating anything funny nor have I succumbed to any kind of excessive scrutiny of my bodily parts. Its just that the Rovers are top of the league. TOP OF THE SCOTTISH PREMIER LEAGUE! I can't believe it. Ok there's only been two games played and we're only there in alphabetical order (God bless the 'H' in Hearts!) but that's not important right now. Also, by some quirk, Rangers and Celtic have both drawn a game and are languishing mid-table. Ha, how mediocrity must hurt. So there we are, in pole position, the Champions League beckoning.

I'm so delighted that my fear of impending death has taken a back seat. Proof positive, I feel, that love conquers all. I thought this year would be good but never like this. The whole 'Kilmarnock experience' made for a great day out. Rugby Park is a fine facility and Kilmarnock have such a healthy 'feel good', family orientated set up going on there. And ok, they are financially challenged much like the rest of Scottish football but *unlike* so many of the other clubs there seems to exist a real will to be maximising their potential off the park as well as on. Oh and of course there's those pies; Ooohh yesss.... I'm still picking strands of meat from between my teeth as we speak.

But never mind all that. Its all about us tonight. We're top of the league and no one can touch us.

Role on the next match, we're invincible.

Roll on the next match, WE ARE INVINCIBLE!

Chapter 5 A history lesson

1.

'Arthurston – Haste ye back' the sign sincerely demands. Nothing unusual in that except for the fact that is the first sign you see on the way *in* to the town. I like to think it sums the town up quite well both in terms of the 'keep on driving' mentality Arthurston induces on commuters and the general lack of order that surrounds the place. Continue heading west along the Old Wet Road back towards the town by-pass and another sign displays the town coat of arms and amiably proclaims 'Welcome to Arthurston!'. This mindbender is the result of a council balls-u.... I mean 'initiative' back in 1983 where some unworthy was mistakenly given total responsibility for erecting the two signs at their respectively designated locations. A job too far I fear. Laughably these two signs had been the sole recommendation of a council steering committee formed at that time to encourage tourism in the area. A stroke of marketing genius unquestionably. Such was, and indeed still is, the prevailing apathy, that no-one has ever complained nor has anyone at the council ever sought to swap them over. 'Well you see we don't strictly have a budget for that and it's not my department anyway.' - I can hear it now.

For those who have never had the pleasure of visiting Arthurston, I commend you. Those who linger very quickly develop a look that can only be described as 'Arthurstonian'. Indeed the Oxford English Diction officially defines 'Arthurstonian' as;

Adjective), **Descriptive attitude of mild irritation due to the feeling that one should be elsewhere as time is getting on.**

Go on check it.

Don't get me wrong, I am very fond of the place and I've lots of good memories here. Friends and family have lived, died, loved and cried here for generations with a resoluteness of belief that this is a fine town to be a part of. But familiarity breeds myopia. When I meet up with friends who have settled away from Arthurston (usually up the local at Christmas) their comments bring matters home somewhat. 'Dead end' and 'Decrepit' are a trifle harsh but nonetheless well worn. In these situations I unwillingly find myself casting an outsiders eye on my surroundings and realistically it doesn't bear up to too much scrutiny. Its not that Arthurston is a particularly ugly town, it isn't. The town centre is quite attractive in the sunshine, there are some nice parks and our neighbour, two-down, won the Sunday Post Rockery of The Year Award a few years back. Its just that it could all be so much better. I don't know when it happened exactly but Arthurston has recoiled into the sort of place you can't buy anything up the street for over 99p and the best appointed building on show is the Job-centre. Vitality, civic pride and community seem intent on escaping down the town's frequently blocked drains while unkempt street corners, spray painted walls and litter-bin pavements act as a constant tug on your jumper nagging on and on that standards, collectively and individually, are slipping fast. Maybe this is a problem plaguing Scottish society in general and you'll meet it wherever you go these days but when its in your own backyard and you can remember better times, its bloody depressing.

Arthurston as a town never really got going until the Brewery was built in 1865.Before then it was merely a collection of small weavers cottages and a couple of farmhouses that were, by chance, placed in close vicinity to one another or more exactly to the main muddy track that connected Stirling to the West Coast.

Pop into 'Johnston's Gifts' on the Main Street and its proprietor and self appointed 'local historian' will spin you a wonderful story of how the town was named after King Arthur somewhere around the sixteenth century. 'Auld Ronnie Johnston' will have you believe that on his way home from a hunting weekend the King spent an uncomfortable night sheltered under a local rocky cragg, now known as the Arthur Stone. Historically this doesn't bear up to much scrutiny though, and Johnston's assertions, according to my Grampa, had more to do with a large consignment of King Arthur paperweights and Camelot chess sets that Auld Ronnie had bought 'fur the Yank tourists' and couldn't get rid of, than any commitment to historical accuracy.

The other, more compelling argument suggests that the town was named after an unscrupulous character called Wade Arthur, a landowner who was no more remarkable than he was meaner and richer than any of his contemporaries around the time the town collectively began to prosper. Detailed archives describing the area begin in the 1650's and although in these early descriptions the town inexplicably remained nameless, geographical details leave us in no doubt that it is the present Arthurston limits being considered.

Local historical accounts are littered with references to Wade and his plentiful (usually drunken) exploits. The aptly named Old Wet Road for example undoubtedly bears testament to Wade's love of ale and his particularly small bladder capacity. It was said he habitually urinated his way home from the local hostelry sometimes stopping seven or eight times along the main, muddied route to his sizeable farmhouse at the edge of town.

Born of Yorkshire origin, Wade Arthur arrived overnight in the town annuls with 'a wife, two cows and a full purse'. Rumours of theft, infidelity and corruption wafted around this sudden new arrival although none were ever proven as being the reason for Arthur's hasty southerly relocation. Explanations were limited to his own admissions via some sketchy, unreliable memoirs, claiming he was 'victim' to a number of 'financial misunderstandings' resulting in the enforced leave of 'his dour beloved homeland'.

Whether he was remembered for his virtue or his depravity is debateable. It was probably a little of both. Early local constabulary documents list Arthur's misdemeanours as assault (3 cases), assault with a 'blunten' object (2 cases), Drunk and disorderly (13 cases), urination in a public place (123 cases) and, intriguingly, 'interference of a dead chicken'. Wade Arthur was clearly no saint, yet even his detractors were forced to admit he had been an effective driving force in the progression of the town towards the organised collective it is today. Arthur was a major benefactor in many worthy local causes of the time including the construction of the original Variety Theatre, the first of its kind in the area, and the rebuilding of St Jude's Church after it was raised to the ground by fire in the summer of 1662 (many suspected that Arthur had been responsible for the incident in the first place with an eyewitness account attesting to Arthur's presence "the worse for wear.... amongst the gravestones.... footering with a candle.... and what looked like some agitated poultry".

Within two years of settling in 'the town with no name', Wade Arthur had established himself as the richest landowner in the area trading in quality livestock, timber from the plentiful forest surrounding his dwelling, and retailing in dairy produce from a mobile wagon-cart which toured the town daily. Of the latter a scribe of the time was moved to write " .... *alang they'd come, two of Arthur's lackies, atop the Evening Cream Cart. 'Pigeon' Jim driving, flogging fresh cream and wafers, an' all the while 'Mangey' Bill McGovern gittin' oor attention up wi' the playin o' Greensleeves on his bagpipes !*" By all accounts Arthur made a fortune from this enterprise until 'The Wagon Wars' of 1674 resulted in the injection of much needed consumer choice for the townsfolk and some unwelcome competition for Wade (although not before Doo Dougal's cart had been torched twice and 'Hawnless Wullie's mules had suspiciously come down with multiple bouts of explosive diarrhoea.)

Being, in his own words, 'the most worthy of all men this side of The Ochils' its perhaps understandable that Wade was the man to ultimately share his name with the town. How that occurred seems no more complicated than he offered more money than anyone else for the privilege. At his own suggestion an auction was arranged whereby locals were asked to put forward a suitable name and bid accordingly, the winner to be announced at the approaching annual livestock festival held in the town square each August. Unsurprisingly Arthur's 'not unsubstantial' monetary bid was enough to secure his name in Scottish history, the closest rival being fellow farmer, Jack McTeer, who offered two ducks and a turnip for the town to be called 'Dennis'. From that historic day Arthur's Town (shortened colloquially to Arthurston) strode bravely forward, proud of a new name and identity that it was hoped would become, in Wade's own words, 'synonymous with all things cultural, civilised and progressive.' Whether that hope has ever been realised is debateable but for the early inhabitants of a young Arthurston , they could rejoice in their newly found identity, sense of place and the confidence in ordering from mail order catalogues without fear of the goods going astray.

2.

Arthurston always was 'The Brewery'. Even decades after its decline and eventual closure, the ghost of The Wilmot Brewery undoubtedly lingers. Its in the street names and landmarks and its etched in the faces of the old town Worthies many of whom haven't worked a day since James Wilmot Jnr locked the doors for the last time; At quarter past three on November 4th 1974 for the historians amongst you.

The brewery was founded in 1865 by a Frederick Charles Wilmot, originally of Ottawa, Canada. Predominantly dealing in Scottish fabrics, he had made a million before his fortieth birthday by a willingness to diversify and through the exporting of essentially anything he could get his Midas hands on. Realising the potential market for Scottish branded alcohol in such far flung locations as India, The Africas and Central America, Wilmot chose Arthurston as the base for a brewery producing a small range of beers and lagers – it had been his original wish to produce a new concept in fruit based alcoholic beverages, 'Alco-ades' as he christened them, but was persuaded by a few close advisers that such 'frivolous ranges' would never catch on. The same advisers also suggested that the whiskey market was too competitive and that 'wine was for girls'. Beer was naturally the next best alternative. So it was that Wilmot enthusiastically and aggressively set about producing a small but varied range of beverages from what was to be, right from the outset, one of the biggest independent breweries in Scotland. Ask your average working Jock about brands such as Wilmot's Best, Curious Cream and Old Oxter and they'll undoubtedly slur 'never drank it and never heard of it' and this would be true as the produce of The Wilmot Brewery rarely saw the light of day on these shores. The proprietor preferred to dispatch thousands of casks every month to foreign climbs where, as Wilmot would often be heard to claim, "those bastards will drink anything"

The original 'old brewery' was built precariously on the top of a steep, Easterly positioned , windy hill known as Sheep's Look. Within a short space of time the rise became more familiarly known as 'The Brew' and it was up a newly cobbled track that more or less two hundred bent-backed workers hauled their way to work every day for the fifty seven years that the brewery remained 'up yonder'.

There were many dark days on that hill. Wilmot, after becoming a widower for the second time, became a cynical, bitter man and an unbending taskmaster when it came to brewery business. In his final years shifts were long and sackings frequent. By the mid 1880's worker moral was lower than a Gretna home gate and it took the initiative of one man, a certain Thomas Painter Hughes, to inject some much needed humanity and community back into a disillusioned workforce. He may have worked on The Brew but his head certainly wasn't in the clouds. As the brewery floor manager Hughes realised that if he couldn't ignite some unification in the workers and do it pretty quickly the business would flounder and many livelihoods would be lost.

His answer - a football team. A team that the workers would aspire to play for and bond together supporting. Hughes was a doer not a talker and within a two week period had cajoled a reluctant, unenthused Wilmot, publicly announced his proposition, had found fifteen keen players of varying ability, an agreement with a local farmer to utilise a fallow field and (luckily enough) a ball. According to one of the original squad, "We didn't have no real goalposts at first and had to practice into two of McStruthers pigs. We found if we filled 'em wi' the barrel dregs they'd lie still for up to an hour at a time"

Three months later Hughes had negotiated admittance into the Stirling and Ayrshire Plough and Anvil League. Such speedy entry was more to do with the monthly lager 'tribute' accepted 'under duress' by the League Committee than any great need on the league's part for a new member. Meanwhile great debate raged over the team name with Arthurston United and Arthurston Central being mooted. Hughes, however, felt that a brewery reference would curry favour with Wilmot and obtain team members shift concessions when training commitments dictated. At the club's first general meeting on the 18th of February 1884 the name Arthurston Brewers was motioned and unanimously adopted by resolution.

Hughes proved to be an early pioneer of work psychology as his football team had the desired effect of galvanising the workforce. 'The Brewers' were the talk of the town and a crowd of two hundred and fifty three turned out on a wet Saturday afternoon in June of '84 to see the club's first game against a rough Ayrshire outfit called Kilwinning Blades. It was to be a tough baptism for the league's new boys. Kitted out in heavy, dull red woollen jumpers knitted by Painter's wife and sister, and grey working trousers cut-off at the knees, they were lambs to the slaughter against a fearsome collection of 'sluggers, muggers and cheats' as Hughes described the men from Ayrshire. The aptly named Blades returned to Kilwinning with a 6-1 victory leaving a battered and bruised Brewers team licking their wounds, of which there were many. As the following excerpt from the Brewery's monthly newsletter suggests, injuries were many and varied. '*Wee Scotty Mcgovern suffered a broken nose when ..... pushed onto the post by the Blades number 4........ Tam Rankin, centre forward... scythed down....carried aff with a bloody gash in his left calf....... Frank McDougall .....grotesque mauling at the hand s of their big erse of a left back......ripped ear and dislocated shooder... Tricky winger, Wee Will Franks..... grizzly forehead gash......battered*

over the heid with a bucket by Blades manager on the sideline.' Not
encouraging. However the Brewery workers were a sturdy lot
and the experience only served to intensify their enthusiasm and
support. The team was to improve and games were to be won
and if the newsletter references were to be believed, those early
days of the Arthurston Brewers were to be the most effective and
harmonious period in the company's history.

It was in the spring of 1922 that practicalities finally caught
up with the brewery. Frederick's son Renton was now chairman
of the board and it was he who took the decision to relocate to
a more easily accessible site at the edge the town, specifically,
closer to sea-level. The winter of '21 had been a particularly
harsh one with heavy snow and ice resulting in the Brewery being
closed for eight consecutive days. The reason was pure and simple.
No-one could make it up the slope in one piece due to the wild
gusting winds, driving snow and sleet and treacherous underfoot
conditions. In that eight day period there were reports of seven
broken arms, three legs, six ankles and a collar bone fracture. Add
to that numerous cases of hypothermia and the heart attack of Rab
Wishart the caretaker, and the ensuing carnage was beginning to
resemble an all-Ayrshire Junior Cup semi-final. Slapstick comedy
though it was watching the efforts of those committed workers
valiantly trying to get to work, Renton Wilmot wasn't laughing.
Orders were lost and production was down. Time was money and
the only solution was apparent - Get off the hill.

Although no longer involved in the management of the team,
Hughes' initiative was to be influential to an extent that even he
couldn't have foreseen. Renton Wilmot, unlike his father, had
embraced the team totally from the beginning. As a teenager,
he was an ever present at 'The Brewers' games, standing, as he
always did, on his own at the 'tree end' of McStruthers field. A
shy boy, no doubt unsure of his social standing, Renton would
cut a lone, silent figure under the imposing oak that stood directly
behind the goals. His in-animation belied his enthusiasm though
and Hughes recognised this. Never one to miss an opportunity
to sow a seed and cultivate it, he gently encouraged Renton to

be more involved in team matters. Frequently Hughes would wander round to the tree and casually ask 'Young Wilmot' if he was enjoying the game and what he thought of *this* tactic or *that* formation. Next he was invited to attend training whenever he wanted and quickly became a regular participant in the sessions. Renton was found to be unassuming and likeable and there was never any question as to the validity of his involvement. Indeed no one gave it a second thought when, due to a dearth of available players on a cold afternoon one December, his name appeared on the team sheet. Hughes' decision to include the boss's son in the line up ensured a vital league fixture was played that day without the points being surrendered. He also ensured that Renton, an average player at best, was made to feel a genuine part of the team, giving him a treasured memory that served only to fuel his growing compulsion.

It was an older, more worldly-wise Renton Wilmot that took that historic decision to relocate the brewery, and it was then that the club hit pay-dirt. Jaws 'visibly dropped' when, during an uninspired speech at the official opening of the new Couper Road site, Wilmot proudly announced he would be gifting the land on which the original brewery stood to a newly named Arthurston Rovers Football Club " creating the foundations of a football ground the whole town of Arthurston could be proud of!" He also pledged to meet the costs of bulldozing the existing building and offered an interest free loan with no fixed term of repayment to finance the construction of any new development necessary. At the edge of the crowded, marble-floored entrance hall that day, Thomas Painter Hughes must have stood quietly and reflected on the reasoning behind life's bounteous harvests and unquestionably must have smiled inwardly to himself.

The ground was completed in the spring of 1924 and was, according to the Arthurston Gazette 'unaminously nomed Gilmot Park'. The good people of Arthurston knew what they meant and began to attend Wilmot Park in droves. League membership followed one year later and on the 28th August 1925, Scottish senior football first witnessed the now traditional red and white stripes of Arthurston Rovers.

Changed days brought changed methods and to carry them boldly into a new era, the club appointed their first 'non-brewery' manager. The historic appointment went to a certain Billy McLung whose previous experience in football remains, to this day, somewhat unclear. The grainy black and white team photo of the time shows McClung as a gaunt, snidey looking fellow with a pencil moustache and a greasy black, left to right, comb-over. Standing at least a foot shorter than any team member photographed that day, the bold Billy holds an immortal pose of defiance, seemingly on the very precipice of asking 'What the fuck are you lookin' at?' Unfortunately for Arthurston's footballing public McLung's reputation was to be made off the pitch and not on it. In the local hostelries and dance halls to be exact. A conspicuous stranger in town with a penchant for thick cigars and fake crocodile shoes, Billy successfully did the rounds. Coming, as was alleged, from Motherwell, his 'big city ways' were irresistible to the more impressionable of the town's womenfolk and it became well known, and accepted, that Billy would stand the lucky lady a pickled onion *as well as* a bag of chips before the inevitable 'knee-trembler' behind 'McCracken's Liniments' on the Main Street. He was James Bond in whippet form. For all that though, he couldn't manage for toffee. Things had got off to a shaky start when during a pre-season practice match, Billy reportedly berated the entire team for fully ten minutes for being unnecessarily defensive. Once it was pointed out to him that the teams had, in fact, changed ends at half time, McClung simply shrugged and instead turned his venomous tongue on the hapless 'keeper who was apparently wearing his cap 'like a fuckin' Golf Larry!'

Then the money from Mrs Nelson's jar went missing. Mrs Nelson (no-one knew her first name) was the club secretary and a severe woman of system and habit. A small bird-like creature with a constant air of disapproval, she positively prided herself on her organisational skills. Every day was one of routine for Mrs Nelson who contented herself by doing each little chore or duty in its own particular order, at the correct time of day, and on the appropriate day of the week. If a document was needed Mrs Nelson could locate it immediately and without fuss from her elaborate filing system. If cash was required, two forms had to be completed and signed in duplicate with a verified entry being made in the petty cashbook . Then, and only then, would she contemplate opening the small mottled grey safe with the silver key that hung on a chain around her neck. "Any one wanting to steal from this club will need to take my head off below the ears to do it!" she was often heard to bark. Plenty vowed to do just that, albeit quietly, under their breath and with no intentions of stealing any money.

This methodical nature also carried over into her personal affairs. Each day she would wear a particular blouse and tweed skirt combination, the same order being repeated from week to week. She always went to the toilet at twenty past one each afternoon - her one and only visit of the day - and on the way back would brew herself a cup of tea and wash her lunch plate whilst she was on her feet. Monday evenings, Mrs Nelson caught the Number 42 bus, straight from work, to visit her sister in Stirling and on Thursday afternoons, without fail, she would allocate herself ten minutes to compiling the weekly shopping list allowing her an efficient, methodical uplift of all her provisions from the Co-Op first thing on Saturday morning. She even had a system for paying her hairdresser. In order to ensure she could afford her monthly shampoo and set at 'Deirdre's' on Collection Road she would religiously place a fraction of her weekly pay in an old, rather large jam jar that sat prominently on the left hand side of her desk.

Scandal hit when, one afternoon in late November, Mrs Nelson returned from completing her banking duties only to find her pristine desk disturbed and the three weeks worth of deposits she had put in her jam jar gone. The possibility that Mrs Nelson had misplaced the money was, under the circumstances, not even considered and everyone associated with the club was immediately questioned by Chairman, Jack Samuels. The only things to become clear, however, were that the money had definitely been stolen and no one had seen a thing. Just as it seemed that any clues had gone with the wind, Mrs Nelson herself took one last look around her desk. She was about to give up when her eyes were drawn to dark substance speckled at the bottom of the jar. Looking around she found a little more on the carpet beside her seat. A rub through her fingers and a careful run under her nose was enough to detect a familiar aroma. Cigar Ash.

All things considered, Samuels reluctantly decided that Mrs Nelson's find wasn't substantial enough to accuse McLung directly, however among certain individuals at the club, 'The Wiry Wanderer's' card was well and truly marked.

A six month spree of drinking, dancing and pickled onions came to an end in typically scandalous style. On the Monday morning after the Rovers' tenth consecutive defeat, a record that stands today incidentally, players and officials alike arrived at the ground to be greeted by a crowd of locals including Jim Starling from the Gazette, standing at the main stand entrance staring upwards at the flagpole perched on the roof directly overhead. Instead of the blue and white Saltire which had flown proudly and constantly since the stand itself was built, the assembled crowd was treated to the sight of McLung's leopard-skin pants waving resplendently in the breeze. That such exotically designed briefs were the property of Mr McLung was never in doubt. On the one hand pants like that were not readily available in a town like Arthurston in those days and details of McLung's nether regions were scarcely a state secret. On the other, his name was embroidered into the inner waistband. It was too much for the already patience-stretched board of directors and in those halcyon days without formal contracts McLung was sacked on the spot without as much as an explanation being sought.

And so a historic chapter of the club's development inauspiciously came to an end with the image of a hung-over, undernourished, slip of a man stumbling ungainly down the Brew's cobblestones; A vision in cheap-skinned loafers clutching personalised underwear under one arm and pausing every ten steps or so to gob on the pavement, throw a 'Git it right up ye!' over one shoulder and take a deep draw on a thick, brown, turd-like cigar.

McLung was undoubtedly a trailblazer. Since his demise, a stream of managers have come and gone and although none have ever emulated his level of incompetence on the park, its fair to say the club has had more than its share of questionable appointments. Sure, we've had hardworking, knowledgeable gaffers over the years. Eddie Fisher spent ten successful years at the club gaining promotion to the First Division – twice and taking Arthurston to the'84 Scottish Cup semi. Bill Martin, 'The Canny Yorkshireman' steered a safe, if unspectacular course for the club through the mid seventies. He knew a player when he saw one and sold many a prospect on to the big teams, for good money too. But for every stalwart that has sat in the manager's chair it is undeniable that there has been an equally unsuitable character chosen to steer the good ship Rovers.

Arthurston's managerial problems have in many ways been borne out of an ongoing boardroom policy that opportunity should be given to new young talent with potential rather than employing members of the merry-go-round brigade. Those 'same old faces' that mysteriously build reputations on predictable non-achievement yet are always in line for the next vacant post after their most recent sacking. For that the Rovers are no doubt to be commended however it has opened the door from some rather strange individuals over the years. In fact looking down the list, it would be no exaggeration to describe Arthurston's managers as a bewildering array of wackos, wasters and crooks, the likes of whom wouldn't have looked out of place on The Best of Judge Judy.

1938/39- Jim Bland. Sacked for stealing approximately twenty gallons of lawnmower fuel from the groundsman's shed.

1946/47 – Albert Reynolds. Exposed as a nazi sympathiser by The Sunday Mail after two reserve team players, whilst attending a New Years' party, inadvertently discovered his secret basement shrine to Hermann Goering.

1953/54 – Jim Dempsey. Sacked for shagging the chairman's wife.

1955/56 – Fred Wallace. Sacked for shagging the chairman's wife and daughter.

1965/67 – Ralph MacDonald. Had an imaginary friend called 'Danny Lad' who he would reputedly consult with during team talks. Sacked after post match press comments blaming Danny Lad's dodgy off-side tactics for the early cup exit suffered (To Whitehill Welfare for reference).

1973/74 – Gordon Whitelake. Sacked for shagging the chairman.

1980/81 – Ben Jeffries. Sacked for misrepresenting the credentials that lead to his appointment. The Sunday Mail again coming to the club's aid revealing that there was, in fact, no such Frankfurt based training establishment as The Horst Rubesch Academy of Footballing Excellence.

1992/95 – Sandy Hepburn. Gave up football to join a religious cult called The Martinarians. He now lives in a converted barn near Newcastle-Under-Lyme. He believes plastic is inherently evil and in 1998, for no apparent reason changed his Christian name by Deed pole to Audrey.

It's a curse.'The Curse of the Gaffers Bench'. All that's missing is Peter Cushing, a low movie budget and some creepy background music. Thankfully the last few years have been relatively loon-free. That's not to say the men in charge weren't worthy of criticism. Each of them in their own special way showed an all round inability to advance the club in any way, shape of form and as a result bought themselves a one way ticket down The Brew much as Billy McLung had done all those years before.

Which brings us nicely to Wilf Schnabbel, the current man. In his two years at the Rovers there can be no denying he has transformed an average team of journeymen into a force to challenge the lower reaches of the Premiership. Yet once again, like so many of his forbears, one can't help feeling he is one draw short of a coupon win.

46 years old, born and raised East Berlin, Schnabbel arrived in Arthurston fresh from a successful stint as assistant manager at FC Groenigan, of Holland, Norway, or possibly Belgium? One of them anyway. Asides from the loopy grey handlebar moustache over-running his upper lip, the immediate concern of most supporters was how little English he could speak. At a press conference arranged, for reasons obscure, in Arthurston swimming baths, Schnabbel was presented to the assembled press and supporters. Seated at a short table at the far end of the pool, flanked by Chairman Jim Acre and director Gordon Miller, smiling and winking at the assembled media, Schnabbel rolled out such familiar, colloquial phrases as 'Please, yes I have the company car', ' I still play with myself', and interestingly'The tree leafs are falling, and I am Scotland!'. With directors and press alike nodding their heads knowledgeably as if they were listening to one of the great orators of our time, Schnabbel went on to conclude proceedings with a spontaneous list of things about Scotland that he 'much admired'. Included in this stuttering roll of honour, in no particular order of importance ; Robert Burns, Doug Rougvie, 'Riverdance'(???) and Glasgow Airport.

There was a certain irony in the placement of that press conference table and the local paper was not slow to highlight this. 'Schnabbel in at the deep end!' it forcefully suggested across its Wednesday night sports page. And it was fair comment. The Rovers squad inherited by the vocal German was in the doldrums, languishing second bottom of the first division with only five points from their first eight games played. There was little to suggest that things would improve either with the club boasting an aging rear-guard and no youth policy to speak of. Those in between were either disillusioned, off-form, suspended or unfit.

After his first month in charge little had changed save for a couple of minor personnel changes through swap deals and the arrival of Russ Dinsmore, an unproven striker of dubious temperament signed on a 'free' from Rochdale. Just as the local and national press were sharpening their collective knives suggesting that Arthurston had bought a single fare to Division

Two, 'Schnabbel's Rabble' flickered into life. Suspensions were served and the queue for the treatment room dwindled. Suddenly there was stability. A couple of scraped away- draws and the first home win of the season had local eyebrows raised. Then came 'cautious hope' closely followed by its big brother -'blatant expectation'. For the team was winning and playing well to boot . Ultimately though the poor start was to haunt the club and the Rovers eventually ran out of games finishing third behind promoted Falkirk and perennial challengers, St Johnstone.

There were inevitably those who belittled Schnabbel's achievement arguing that it had been a weakened league and team form had been a flash in the pan built on short term enthusiasm but Schnabbel was defiant. " I have radios in my oven that say we will go Premier next year" he had said sagely on STV's 'Football First' after a mid season victory against Ayr United and with reasoning like that, it was difficult argue.

Indeed by the following December it seemed things had fallen into place. Veteran striker, Ray Stark had returned to the club for a second stint and was banging in the goals, Young midfielder, Jay McDonald, the cream of a budding youth policy, had successfully broken into the first team, attracting the attention of big name scouts along the way, and wayward winger Frankie Boyle was off the booze and turning defences inside-out 'for fun' as Big Ron would say. And as the team got better so did Schnabbel's English – sort of. In an early interview with The Arthurston Gazette he reluctantly admitted that his English 'wasn't so good' but he was learning every night by watching our 'excellent television' for hours on end. A good idea on the face of it. Until, that is, keen observers became more than a little suspicious that Wilf was really only watching the adverts. Initially it was scarcely noticeable with Schnabbel introducing little phrases like 'Pure Genius' and 'Va Va Voom' into his answers with only slightly more frequency than was acceptable. Then all of a sudden Boyle was putting over 'exceedingly good' crosses, numerous issues arose that Schnabbel 'didn't give a four-ex about', and accounting for Arthurston scoring three last minute goals in consecutive matches to keep their promotion bid on track, he cryptically put it down to 'The Lynx Effect'. The national press of course hadn't really cottoned on due to their limited coverage of the team but we knew what was happening. 'Slogan Bingo' became the local pastime and many a hilarious pub conversation arose from the likes of Wilf describing a Russ Dinsmore free kick on Radio Scotland as 'finger lickin good', and The Rovers being 'probably the best team in the world.'

Schnabbel particularly excelled himself on TV as the studio guest on Scotsport. Leaving the assembled pundits confused and bewildered and a good proportion of Arthurston in hysterics, he came out with a couple of blinders. When asked to justify why he had quite vocally demanded an immediate three year extension to his contract he looked tantalisingly at the camera and calmly stated in a soft accented voice "Because I'm worth it." He then outdid himself by suggesting that Teams like Dundee and Motherwell could have avoided financial trouble by "consolidating all their existing debts into one affordable monthly repayment."

Six points clear by New Year, the Rovers were to lose only two more league games in the run in gaining promotion as champions with games to spare. The only sore point on this historic run of form was a shock Scottish Cup exit at the hands of perennial strugglers East Stirling.

The dismal 2-1 defeat was further aggravated by an embarrassing misunderstanding between club officials and the team bus-driver on their way to the game. Due to what The Scotland on Sunday described the next day as 'a laughable breakdown in communication', the full squad plus management and directors arrived at 1.30 pm outside Forthbank Stadium, supposedly in plenty of time for kick-off. The only problem being, as every self-respecting Scottish football fan knows, that Forthbank is the home of Stirling Albion Football Club and not East Stirling.

Why nobody on the bus noticed they were going the wrong way remains a mystery and according to all sources, Arthurston actually made it into the dressing rooms before the mistake was realised. Arriving, as they did, some minutes before Albion's *actual* cup opponents of the day, Morton, Forthbank officials simply assumed that Arthurston were, in fact, the Greenock side and ushered the party through to the players' area. It was only when the 'real' Morton showed up that the error was discovered and the 'red necks' commenced.

Arthurston arrived at Firs Park, the majestic home of East Stirling, with minutes to spare although in hindsight they probably shouldn't have bothered. Of course Schnabbel, in true managerial fashion, wasn't slow to blame the lack of preparation time for the shock defeat. Will McVicar of Rovers fanzine 'Lager Louts' was more pragmatic when he described the performance " as entertaining as watching 'Last of The Summer Wine' dubbed into Japanese."

Anyway, Arthurston were promoted and when the players and supporters danced on the Somerset Park turf after the final whistle of the season had sounded, it seemed like the end of a journey. A long journey jammed full of drama and unpredictability stretching back a long time. Longer than anyone on the park that day could ever remember.

Schnabbel's final comment of the season was one of defiant optimism. Leaning precariously out of the elevated main stand at Ayr he waved jubilantly and spread a toothy smile under his distinctive 'tash. "We have won! We will win again! And next year we will stay up like we are on Viagra!" he shouted down a hastily organised loudhailer and the mass of fans bathing in the seaside sunshine roared back, a field of fists clenched in the air.

And the dancing began again only now the crowd had swelled. Look closer and you saw they were all there. Craig Donald, Dave Gorman and Chris Milne, at the front, arms around each other's necks, bouncing up and down. Jimmy Bently the PA man hugging old Janny Turnbull who was crying. Look closer still.... Jack Samuels, hopping round a rigid looking Mrs Nelson, and a man called Renton Wilmot doing a strange kind of jig to himself. A group of straggly young men with red woollen jerseys and grey cut offs are there too slapping each other on the back, and around them all jumping, cheering and crying are hundreds of people, men and women, in old fashioned black and grey working clothes. Each one of them smiling and waving, strong and proud. At the edge, leaning on a goalpost, Thomas Painter Hughes, smiling gently with an old man beside him, still looking stern of face, but unable to resist tapping his walking stick rhythmically up and down in the grass.

Chapter 6 'Grampa'

1.

The car door slams shut behind me, only instead of closing cleanly it makes a thick, clunky noise and bounces back open defiantly.

'Shit' I mutter under my breath gathering up the snake-like safety belt that is making a successful bid for freedom from the side of my red, dusty 'K reg' Ford Fiesta. Second time of asking the door whirls on its hinges and crashes shut. Half way up the red stone driveway I realise I've forgotten Grampa's bag of messages.

"Fuck!" I curse out loud, eyes skyward. Turning round I take a flying kick at a pile of stones scattering them like machine-gun fire onto the street ahead of me. Stalking back to the car, head down, it flashes into my mind again.

Six – Nil.!

- And again.

SIX …. NIL!

At home into the bargain!

Ok Aberdeen are a solid Premier side, a much improved one at that this year but SIX BUGGERIN' NIL! I feel a sudden urge to drop-kick a basketful of sad-eyed puppies or pull the legs off a gang of Barbie Dolls.

We started pretty effectively as well. A Mickey Hedge chip bounced off the bar and we had a solid penalty claim turned down, both within the first ten minutes. Then it all just fell to pieces. Three goals in five minutes mid-way through the first half and the game was as dead as your granny's granny. Mind you in retrospect, losing only the six goals was a blessing as we could have easily lost a bucket-load more. After the fourth went in the whole team seemed to shut down in a state of shock. Storrie, Crush and Marker were collectively like rabbits stuck in red

Aberdonian headlights, unable, in the face of danger, to move in any worthwhile direction whatsoever. Two wonder saves, the post and some horrendous finishing were all that stood between Arthurston and total annihilation.

It was painful but at least we stayed right until the final whistle. More than a few of our 'loyal' fans headed for the exits as the last couple of goals went in but we stood firm.

I'm proud to say I have never succumbed to leaving early from a Rovers match, EVER. Even in our darkest hours. I witnessed every foul and desperate minute of our defeat last season at East Stirling and I sat for the duration, face burning, the day we lost eight-one at home to Dunfermline in a second division promotion clash . Their fans gave us so much stick over the ninety minutes I wanted to die. Adding insult to injury that day, the Pars stuck their reserve goalie on for the last ten minutes - as an OUTFIELD player! (I can hear strains of 'We shall overcome' rising in the background)

I just don't get it. I simply *cannot* understand or sympathise with the mentality that leads people to leave the game early - for *any* reason. For long and weary the pre-final whistle 'Ibrox exodus' has been held up to ridicule amongst non-old firm fans (although half time *is* a bit early to be scooting off home for your dinner) but singling 'The Berrs' out is unfair as every team has their premature leavers. Why do they do it though? You wouldn't get up and leave the cinema ten minutes before the final credits just because the storyline wasn't going the way you'd hoped, or leave the theatre during the second last scene just to make sure you didn't get stuck in the car-park So why do it at the football?

The problem lies predominantly with the folk who are only there to see their team win. I know that sounds a strange thing to say as we're all there to see our team win. But for the success seekers, I think they go to the games to see a victory at the exclusion of everything else. They are insecure you see. They *have* to align themselves with success at all costs for, in their minds, failure of their team is somehow a reflective failure on themselves. After all it's an unsettling and uncomfortable thing losing and it makes us feel bad. The answer – don't put yourself in the position. Bigotry aside, this is clearly why so many people outwith the Glasgow area support the Old Firm. They haven't the shoulders to carry the oh-so-frequent disappointment and failure that supporting your local team predictably brings. How many Monday morning workplace ribbings for example, does your average East Stirlingshire supporter take about the latest Shire loss - Hundreds. And do you know it doesn't matter, for these people can take it. They are all back-bone, people of impenetrable moral fibre, people to be respected.

'What team do you support ?' – Without doubt one of life's more illuminating questions. On the face of it a simple ice breaker in unfamiliar company. In reality though a heavily loaded inquiry into the perseverance, depth and faithfulness possessed by the targeted individual.

If I was interviewing prospective employees for a job vacancy 'What team do you support?' would unequivocally be in my top three vital questions to be asked (along with 'Would you interrupt a meeting to answer your mobile phone?' and 'Have you ever laughed at Paul O'Grady?') This is a sound recommendation and any HR managers out there should take heed. Face it, the resulting answer will probably say a lot more about the person's character than a thousand role-plays, presentations, and psychometric testing ever could. My consultancy fee is in the post.

More inexplicable than the bad losers, however, must be the group who leave five minutes before the end of almost every game *irrespective* of what is happening on the pitch. Its 5-4, the quality is brilliant with the game flowing backwards and forwards irresistibly. Old boys are keeling over in the excitement and the most experienced pundit couldn't predict the outcome. Watches collectively say twenty to five, the tension is building ….

AND THERE THEY GO!

Muttering 'excuse me' apologetically to everyone in their row. People who are now tutting, bobbing and weaving left and right in an irritated fashion in a mad effort to see round the offenders.

There they go - scurrying to the exits without as much as a backwards glance.

What is so important that forces these men (for it is usually men) to abandon this excitement, this Holy Grail of footballing scenarios that, as dedicated football fans, we persistently yearn for. You would like to think it was sex. Diving home, unable to be contained any longer, for a quick steak and chips then rampant rumpy-pumpy all night with the wife who looks as luscious and alluring now as she did on her wedding day. Looking at them though, their dull lifeless eyes suggest early evening supermarket queues, dinner with the in-laws, tea-time telly not to be missed, assorted 'wife related' situations too numerous to mention here.

Either that or it's a control thing. 'I'd better make a start for home in case a) I get stuck in the car park with the other twenty cars out there b) I fall down a hole and miss the start of 'Ant and Dec' or c) the sky falls down.

To these people I say stick with it. Relax and enjoy. BE... AT ....PEACE. And while they are there maybe they should think about running that amber streetlight once in a while, going out without a wristwatch on or God forbid, having that second pint of shandy. It wouldn't do any harm.

2.

"Hello? Anybody in?" I sing, peeking my head round Grampa's frosted glass front door, which, as always, is unlocked.

"Aye Son – In the living room – Come on in!"

"Ok, I'll just put these messages away", I reply, already making my way down the shadowy passage towards the kitchen . On the way past I give my usual glance at the three old black and white photographs hanging with dignity on the magnolia wall. Framed in rich oak they show Wilmot Park in days gone by. Players, all big boots and thick socks, sporting damn fine haircuts and cutting strange contorted poses, and in the background unfeasibly large crowds crammed into familiar surroundings . I take a little time to unpack the groceries and fit them into Grampa's strict fridge and cupboard storage system. Happy that everything is in its place I make my way through the downstairs flat and into the relative light of the front room.

"Well?" says Grampa leaning forward, hands on his knees, "Was it painful?"

"We were piss poor." I grunt, " We lost some bad goals."

"Aye son, six of them. When did we last lose a good goal , eh?"

"Hmm," I mutter, not really in the mood for being philosophical about it. I kick off my shoes and slump into a huge jobby brown armchair.

"You're not going to bring your bad mood in here with are you? If you are you can just turn around again."

"Not at all." I reply with a thin, forced smile. "Well, how are you then?"

"Not too bad son, plugging away."

Always the trooper; Eighty two years old next month and still fighting the Battle of Independence. In his head he's winning. Physically though, the wagons are burning and he's calling in the reinforcements. Since his hip replacement a couple of years back he's barely made it past the end of the driveway and he needs his zimmer-frame, the 'Devil's Clothes Horse' as he calls it, just to make it to the kitchen and back. He talks the talk though and bubbles away cheerfully, cajoling you into believing he's as contented as ever. Deep down, however, his resentment towards his galloping frailty is smouldering away and every so often his mood sinks like a stone down a well and you can't get a word out of him. Take the day that dad turned up to power-drill the handrails onto the bathroom wall. Hardly spoke to anyone for weeks after that. And when he did he was so short you couldn't have a sensible conversation with him.

"How's your dad?"

"Ok…" I reply, " …. I suppose. I've not really spoken to him this week."

Grampa grunts and flips through the match programme I've handed him. "And what about Chris? Has he got a new job yet?"

"Nothing firm. He muttered something mysteriously about an 'opportunity in the pipeline' but he wouldn't embroider any further."

"Aye, its terrible days we live in. Used to be a job in bank was for life. Nothing's safe now. How's your job anyway, you've not mentioned it in ages."

"Nothing to say. I get up, go in , get irritated with Sandy and come home again."

Poor Sandy - This is ungracious of me. When my picture framing business went down the tubes and I was stuck for a job, and I mean *really* stuck, Grampa's long standing friend, Sandy Bonefield (of Bonefield Hardware Supplies – 'DIY Advice you can trust! 'as it proclaims boldly over the door.) kindly offered me a position. He said he needed an assistant in the shop as he couldn't run the place 'like in the old days'. What he really meant was he quite fancied a bit of company and needed someone to go up ladders to reach the 'hard to get to' boxes from the rickety, death-trap wall shelves at the back of the shop.

And Sandy talks.

Incessantly.

About anything and everything. Everything except, unfortunately, football. Sandy's favoured topics range from models of cordless drills to the universal existence of black holes. The superior design in Greek oil tankers, wasp populations in the new millennium to the frailties of the British justice system. Oh and the politics – God save us, the politics.

Sandy got satellite TV some time ago and unlike almost the whole rational thinking population of Scotland, he swerved past The Simpsons, the sports and the movies channels, choosing instead to anchor his system on the 'Parliament Live' channel. Now he spends a torturous proportion of his day regaling me with the ins and outs of Land Act amendments and the varying idiosyncrasies of Liberal back benchers. I've nothing against current affairs but half an hour with Sandy when he's on a roll is the conversational equivalent of picking out weeds in the rain.

"Now don't be down on Sandy," starts Grampa half-heartedly with the traces of a knowing smile, " He was kind enough to give you that job when you needed it and I'm sure he can't really afford to pay you as much as he does"

"Oh I don't know. We've had a real run on two-inch rawlplugs recently, Old Sandy's doing ok"

"You know." Insists Grampa lightly.

"Yeh, I know" I admit laughing.

The end of the conversation leaves me thoughtful and a little uncomfortable.

"Why don't you go and make us a cup of tea Son," suggests Grampa, wincing as he changes position in his chair, "and then tell me more about the game"

Seizing the opportunity to escape the world of Sandy and all things hardware I bounce to my feet and skitter off to the kitchen.

3.

When I come back into the cluttered little living room awkwardly brandishing two lopsided mugs of tea and two Kit-Kats, Grampa is over at the mantelpiece fingering the various objects decorating the dark wooded ledge.

"Are those new photos you've put up? I ask, gritting my teeth as the heat from the mugs of tea becomes exquisite"

"Grampa is pulled back from some far away place. "Eh?– Oh aye. Some pictures of your Grandma. I found them in a box under the stairs the other night. They're good aren't they?"

He hands me over a couple of silver framed snaps gently like he was handing over the Crown Jewels. One shows a young couple cheerfully peering out from faded, tea stained surroundings which by the look of it is somewhere by the sea.

"That's your Grandma and I at St Andrews. Summer of 1953."

Grampa smiles and catches my eye.

"I remember that because it was when we were … you know… thinking about your father"

I must have looked bemused.

Grampa looked momentarily floorward

"Ahhh, *thinking* about my dad. I see"

"Oh aye." He continued, "We thought quite seriously about him that weekend if truth be told. In fact we did so much thinking…"

"Alright that's enough." I interjected. The conversation was not, to my mind, heading in a particularly palatable direction. "What about that one?" I continued, holding the second frame up. It showed a group of about ten middle aged men and women standing on someone's back lawn. They were smiling and shouting excitedly as a couple, my grandparents on closer examination, shook a bottle of Champagne into the air.

"Is that you celebrating dad's arrival then?" I ask with a smile on my face.

"Lord no" replies Grampa sharply, "That was the day the case was won"

"The case?"

"Aye, the big court case between the club and the young Wilmots. Have I never told you all about that'"

He had. Numerous times.

"I think so but tell me again anyway" I said, sitting down, taking a sip of tea.

"It was a big day for the club and the town," he began, licking his lips slightly. " You see Wilmot Park was getting gye run down and the board wanted the Wilmots to pay for reconstruction work to be done."

"Which they would have been quite happy to do surely." I suggested'

"Well no. Renton Wilmot's son and daughter, Gerard and … oh what was her name… Janine? Naw that wasn't it ….Jasmine! aye Jasmine. Well they didn't give a monkey's about the club and with Renton being a good number of years in the ground, they were more than ready to sever any family connections with the club. They were certainly not about to commit part of the family fortune to developing Wilmot Park that's for sure"

"But it wouldn't have cost much to do the place up " I offered, enjoying the part I was playing in the scene.

"Ah but the directors weren't suggesting a lick of paint here and there. They were ambitious and saw the next step in Arthurston's development as something that would put them up there with the big boys. That's when they got their hearts set on an all-seated stadium. Not a bad idea nowadays with the Taylor Report an' all but back then we thought they were mad. Not that the thought of it didn't excite us all mind. Anyway, to cut a long drawn out story short, the board dug around the club's old archived paperwork and dredged up old Renton's pledge to the Rovers , the one he had made when he gifted the land in the first place"

"And what did that achieve?"

"Well, they picked their way through yon document like vultures on a carcass and found the bit where Renton promised ....how was it he worded it?..... to ' offer an interest free loan with no fixed term of repayment to finance the construction of *any* new development necessary'. It went something like that anyway. Well, the directors were delighted at the inference and presented their case to the living Wilmots assuming they would understand that they had no choice but to follow their father's ''wishes'

"But they didn't roll over did they?"

"They certainly didn't and the whole affair ended up in court. That's when things got difficult for the club. 'Fast' Eddie Bateman was the chairman at the time and what an objectionable character full of his own self-worth he was. He felt, in his ultimate wisdom, we had a cast iron case to make and ignored all advice to the contrary. Indeed strong rumour had it that The Family offered him fifty thousand pounds at the eleventh hour to help put up one new stand behind the goals but Bateman refused. Once it ended up in court we all began to realise just what was on the line. That fool of a man Bateman had been so sure of his own council that it didn't occur to him what would happen to the club if we lost the case. The legal fees would have crippled us. No doubt about it. "

"But we won the case then, didn't we" I suggest enthusiastically.

"Aye, but only just. It took them over a week to side in our favour. The worst week of my life it was. We nearly didn't have a football team."

"And all because of a small group of naïve, stubborn men"

"Well that's right. It all played out alright in the long run though. Benefited us actually when you think on those stupid SPL rules about six thousand seater stadium requirements. More by luck than good judgement though. Anyway that photo was taken out Jamesy Buchan's back garden the day we were awarded the money."

Grampa laughed. "I remember that soor-faced daughter's picture in the papers afterwards. She wasn't a happy woman I can tell you."

"Nor would you be if you'd just been stung for a fortune to pay for a stadium housing a team you don't like, in a town you've no allegiance to, for a sport you have no interest in."

"Ach, the money didn't scratch the surface of that family's wealth." says Grampa taking the photos back and placing them carefully back on the mantelpiece.

"They were just plain greedy. More tea?" he says looking over at my empty cup.

" Don't mind if I do" I reply making a move to get up.

Grampa pushes his hand out, collects my mug muttering something awfully like "sit on yer arse, I'm not useless" then shuffles his way slowly out into the hall.

4.

The time flies by when I'm at Grampa's. We always have something to talk about. Granted it's usually something to do with football but we connect nonetheless. It's a connection I've never made with my father strangely and I often wonder if it's the football alone that has fostered this and other personal links whilst at the same time possibly cutting off others. Maybe if my father had been a Rovers man, or at least kidded on a bit that he was then things might have been different.

Maybe.....

"There you go"

"Huh" I grunt waking from a dream.

"There's your tea".

"Oh ... cheers."

As Grampa eases himself gingerly into his chair I take a small sip of the piping hot tea. As always it tastes better than anything I could ever make .

"I saw June McDonald at the game today. She looked old I thought"

"Aye none of us are getting younger. She's a poor lass isn't she, did you speak to her?"

"Didn't get a chance. She left before the end"

Grampa pursed his lips together, made a sucking noise and slowly shook his head. "Left before the end eh? That won't have gone down with you then would it?"

"Aye well...I suppose not." I smile. "Its good she still goes. When you think on it there can't have been many women going to the football when she first started."

"Not many, but a few. Of course I met your Grandma at the Rovers if you think on it"

This was news to me.

"I thought you met in the Forces at the end of the war"

"Aye we did but only briefly. We got re-acquainted over on the long terracing under the old shed. I can't believe I've never told you this. She showed up one game with some sharp looking bloke with slick black hair and a long herring-bone coat right down to his toes - a right spiv he was. They stood three or four rows down from me and I must have stared at her for the whole of the first half. I 'mind there was a big crowd in that day, it was the Hearts we were playing, and I kept catching glances of her through the big ugly nappers bobbing around directly in front of me. I couldnae take my eyes off her. She looked like an angel."

Grampa paused and took a mouthful of tea. Looking pleased with himself he went on" Aye, so we're into the second half and just when I'm beginning to go off my mind trying to think of ways to speak to her, the Lord above stepped in."

"What happened?"

Grampa starts laughing, "Devine intervention my lad. As I said it was a tight squeeze under the shed. Not much room for manoeuvre. So when the big pigeon from the rafters let go with the largest fried-egg bird-shit I ever saw and hit Spiv square on the shoulders, it started an almighty stramash. He tried to duck out of the line of fire but caught his foot in yon big coat he had on. He pulled at least three others on the way down and all hell broke loose. People pushed and pulled , fell over, got up and fell back down again. It was mayhem. The last thing I saw was him ducking out of sight and reappearing legs in the air down at the fence about ten steps in front of us. Once all the mouthing and jostling died down I turned to my right and there she was with a wee cheeky grin on her face. Well, my heart did all the points of the compass in under a second!"

"And your big opening line was what then?"

"Didnae get a chance son, She was as sharp as a tack your Grandmother. She looked me in the eye and said to me in a scolding voice ' Well Johnnie Donald , that was lucky – you can get a closer look at my earrings now!'" And with that Grampa dissolves into fits of laughter giving way to a furious onslaught of coughing drawn, by the look of things, from somewhere around his big-toe region.

Red faced and watery eyed he pulls himself together and looks out of the window. " That was the quickest half of football I've ever been at. I missed the Rovers winner too but you know it didnae matter.

"What about Spiv though?" I venture. "Surely he didn't take you muscling in on his date lying down"

"For a while he did though", and that set Grampa off again hee-hawing and spluttering away to himself.

"Sorry," he says eventually pulling himself together. Dabbing his eyes with a greying hanky he goes on, " I talked Jenny into leaving a wee bit early and we disappeared through the crowd without him seeing a thing. She wisnae interested anyway. She said he smelled of fish oil and talked incessantly about gas-boilers. Not your Grandmother's type at all."

Pausing for breath Grampa stretches painfully over to a little side table. I make the slightest of moves but he's ready for me.

"Leave me" he growls and successfully grabs the mahogany pipe he's aiming for.

"Naw, not many women back then , but more than enough for me to contend with." He falls silent momentarily lost in an evidently better place. "Still, it's a bit different now isn't it. Lots more of them go to the games. Playing it too. I saw a game on the TV and it wasn't half bad. Arsenal against someone or other."

I have to agree. Female interest in the game is undoubtedly on the up. I can also state confidentially that during the odd Rovers game I too have caught myself staring at the odd pretty young thing in the crowd and wondered what it would be like to have her licking chocolate buttons from my belly, wearing a little something from the La Sensa Autumn collection, and all the while her debating the wisdom of the manager's decision to go 'four-four-two' for the last ten minutes of that day's game. It sounds a combination made in heaven.

I like women's football too. Much like the gents' game some of the players look quite feminine. The standard of play at the top level is really good and the understandable reduction in physical emphasis compared to the guys isn't detrimental to the spectacle, indeed if anything it seems to force a more skilful approach to proceedings.

Except for the goal keepers that is. With all due respect to any female custodians out there, they are, in the words of TV witch, Anne Robinson, 'The Weakest Link.' Almost every womens' game I've ever seen has been fiercely competitive and skill-laden up until, that is, a good cross or a reasonable shot has asked questions of the keeper. What happens next is fairly consistent both in club and international competition. We're treated to a wild concoction of flapping, flailing, rolling and/or collapsing all done in a tentative nervous manner more befitting a naked barbeque chef than a professional sportsperson.

Why should this be so? Its obvious surely;

It's a breast thing.

Think about it. What could possibly be more worrying to a woman footballer than having a heavy ball hurtling towards your wheechlers at top speed or having them crushed under the body after a full length diving save. Take the pain for the team? – I don't think so. The guys may snigger but think on this. How good at heading the ball would blokes be if their 'nads were to be found attached to their forehead, somewhere around the hairline vicinity? Not very. Joe Jordan and Alex McLeish would certainly never have played for Scotland that's for sure.

Despite these 'up front' issues womens' football in Scotland is flourishing. Women are playing the game and playing it in numbers. This year, their twelve club Premier league is propped up ably by three subordinate leagues comprising a further *thirty-eight* teams and a healthy youth scene bodes well for the future of the woman's game. Recognisable club affiliations predictably exist such as Hibernian, Kilmarnock, Celtic , Aberdeen , Raith Rovers and Hamilton Accies, but its nice to see new teams like Vale of Clyde represented and even nicer to see one single team from Glasgow playing under the banner of Glasgow City Ladies.

As I crunch down Grampa's driveway a cool wind suddenly gusts by causing me to shudder and sink my neck deep into my jacket collar. I wave over my shoulder and hear the front door click shut behind me. Scurrying to the car I heave myself into the drivers seat where without warning a strong wave of depression sweeps over me. I pause and stare ahead of me out the wind-screen which now has tiny pin-points of rain speckling the outside view. Its Saturday night and once again I have nothing much to do. The clock is ticking loudly on my life and I should be out there meeting new people and doing interesting things. In reality all I have on the agenda is a Chinese takeaway and a DVD to watch in my room, killing the time before Match Of The Day and the inevitable 'lights out' and another restless sleep.

I don't much care for these thoughts and force them out the back of my mind. Turning the ignition, I crunch the gears badly and set off up the road. Within seconds my mind is clearer and focussing on the road I feel a little better, But there's a nagging doubt. I sense my worries are chasing me. Subconsciously or otherwise, I switch on the stereo, turn the volume up and push down on the accelerator making the car go just a little bit faster. The race is on.

5.

Sunday morning and here I am, sitting on the toilet again, as always, praying for a safe and speedy 'bombing run' if you know what I mean. Staring hypnotically at the 'Rovers Hit for 6!' headline emblazoned on the page between my feet I can't help contemplating the idea of getting old. Being me, I'm not thinking on the benefits of maturity, the knowledge and wisdom that the years will undoubtedly have brought me. In my eyes it seems to be all about illness, immobility, smelling of pee and all my pals being dead.

Which scares the hell out of me. I want my golden years to be …well…. Golden. I want to be free to do all the stuff I can't be bothered doing now. I want to be independent and contented and consistently capable of sexy thoughts when watching the female newsreaders on the News at Ten.

I want to have done stuff too. Written a book maybe, been successful in my chosen field, married a nice girl, starred in a porno movie (possibly titled 'Big Chris and the lonely Beach Volleyball Nymphos'). However given all these things I think I would walk past them all for one thing; to see Arthurston win the cup with my Grampa at my side.

The days are short and the chances are slim but it doesn't hurt to dream. I can see his face. We are hanging on to each other smiling , cheering and maybe even crying a bit. The others are there too but they are slightly apart. We, however, are one family standing together not just enjoying the moment for ourselves but taking something from each other's happiness. In my deepest moments of self criticism I get to thinking that underneath I'm quite a selfish person. Right now that doesn't feel the case and the thought of Grampa in raptures is a warming one.

The thought is powerful and real and fulfilling. Also it has unquestionably given me an idea.

Chapter 7   Capital Punishment

1.

"Christ on a bike son - You're going to do what?"

"I said I'm going to take Grampa to the Rovers for his birthday. And don't try and stop me!"And so begins a verbal fight to the death. Me the reckless and irresponsible optimist advocating life on the edge. My Dad the voice of negativity, the voice of limitation - the voice of reason actually.

But some things defy reason. Sometimes you've got to toss away the practicalities and meet things head on and have faith that it'll all work out alright in the long run. This is one of those times.

Its left us not talking though. Again. Another series of dining-room meals with self-conscious chewing and the guilty clinking of cutlery on ceramic. Soul destroying stuff.

I'm not going to bend though. At the very least Grampa gets the final word on it. If he feels he's up to it then I don't care if Dad boots me in the nuts and hands me a roadmap. If Grampa thinks it's a bridge too far then fair dos, I'll get him socks again.

2.

Sometimes jumping in the car and heading for an away game acts as 'The Great Escape'. A chance to leave life's trials behind. For me, its been a bad week and the trip to Edinburgh to play Hibernian has the feeling of a diver splashing out the water just before his air runs out. For the first ten minutes or so of the journey I cannot speak. I'm just trying to get my breath back.

Dave is driving again as my car has developed a grotesque rattle around the undercarriage and we don't want to tempt fate.

Jonesy is installed in the front seat footering with one of his infamous tapes.

"What are we going to listen to then?" I ask peering between the head-rests .

"Oh, are you alive back there?" replies Jonesy," Well boys, I have a treat in store. I thought to myself this morning 'What kind of music would suit the trip . Something new that we've never really done before."

"*Good* music?" Dave injects sharply, his gaze fixed firmly ahead.

"Country and Western my friends!" announces Jonesy triumphantly as if this would make our day in some meaningful way.

Dave shakes his head and although I can't see his face I know he is looking skyward for inspiration.

"There you are" Jonesy says handing me over an empty CD box, "The Yellowbellies , they're a Glasgow band."

I must have looked blankly.

" I'm surprised you haven't heard of them." He went on.

"Seriously?" I ask.

After a short moment of contemplation he mutters quietly "No , I suppose not. "

Looking at the song list printed neatly on the back of the box the selection is enthralling;

My widespread eyes are crying
Twangy Love Song
Punch yer wife goodmornin'
Sittin' in the outhouse (with my dead dawg and ma banjo)
My cousin's mom's ma sister (but i still can count to 10!)
Say goodbye to Dollywood
Man on the Moonshine
A bride for 7 brothers
My well done gone dry
The gallows took poor Gummy Tate
Fakey, Snakey Boots
Cleetus's new spitoon

We make it to the second verse of 'Sittin' in the outhouse', a particularly morbid drone containing the memorable line ' ah cried ma self to sleep for a week, when ah pulled ma soggy doggy from the creek', before Dave, with ninja-like reflexes, pops the disc out and flips it into Jonesy's face, not once taking his eyes off the road ahead.

"Don't bring that back" he growls in a low threatening manner indicating that the local Country & Western revival is well and truly at an end.

Jonesy, clearly well used to such damning musical criticism, sighs, switches the radio off and turns his attention to liberating a singular block of sherbet lemons which seem to be industrially glued to a tattered paper poke he's produced from his anorak pocket.

3.

Away to Hibernian is not my favourite trip. Probably because we never win. In fact I'm not sure I've even seen the Rovers score a goal at Easter Road. There's more to it though. It has also been a fixture plagued over the years with more than its fair share of incidents and irritancies. I can remember being attacked by a swarm of wasps while sitting on the old uncovered seats behind the goals. I've been drenched by torrential rain in the same uncovered area on a cold cup-replay night in February, a soaking that resulted in my worst bout of flu in living memory. On one memorable occasion Jonesy fell up some stairs in the old main stand and tore ligaments in his ankle. Not only did we spend most of that game in a small room with the St John's ambulance folk but Jonesy dropped the pies and Bovril into the bargain.

Then there was the time our car overheated and broke down in heavy traffic on the way through Corstorphine. For those unfamiliar with the area, Corstorphine is the affluent West End suburb of Edinburgh that in the pre city-bypass 1980's was the main motor route from the Glasgow side of the city and thus a real traffic bottleneck. In order to negotiate Corstorphine in those days you had to set off a good two weeks in advance of your target arrival time, packing the car full of necessary supplies like water, bread, rope, tinned meat and a BIG bag of midget-gems. Despite being well prepared for this particular expedition we omitted to pack a car mechanic and consequently never made it to the game, spending most of the afternoon consuming all day breakfasts in a street-side greasy spoon café waiting on the kindly gents of the AA for a tow back home.

Despite everything I kind of miss the old road into Edinburgh. I know it was a bit of a long haul but it was definitely more interesting than the new by-pass alternative which seems to be permanently under roadworks and, in reality, not even that much shorter an option. The old way had style, passing, as it did, the airport, the big inflatable gorilla at Ingliston Market , the speed trap at the zoo and of course, the Victorian refinement of Corstorphine, culminating in your first sneaky glimpses of the Castle through old town roofs and chimneys.

On the left hand side of West Coates just before Haymarket Terrace sits an imposing, almost stately, school building that had my nose pressed to the window every time I crawled by in the car. Lush, green playing fields clamber up to the magnificent sandstone structure that my mother reliably informed me was (en-route to one of many childhood holidays in North Berwick) the School for the Blind. For years I was mesmerised and perplexed in equal measures by the two white football goal-posts sitting expectantly in front of the school's grand entrance. I never saw anyone playing on that park but fostered a perverse longing to witness 22 blind boys, arms stretched out in front of themselves, chasing after a big ball with bells attached. I held that thought fondly until a couple of years back when I inadvertently discovered that the building in question was none other than the Donaldsons School for the *Deaf.*

THE DEAF.

Talk about a disappointment.

Dave, Jonesy and I once did a drunken, post pub re-enactment of Arthurston's top 10 goals of all time, in our boxers, on local music teacher- Mrs Daislie's front lawn and the level of footballing mayhem and disarray was nothing, I repeat NOTHING, compared to my vision of those imaginary games on the hallowed Donaldsons turf.

And then there were the chases .... Dear Lord the chases.

Occurring mainly in the vicinity of Easter Road itself, these were terrifying confrontations with Hibs 'affiliated' militia the likes of whom would not have appeared out of place on the 1987 'Evil gangs of Beirut' fundraising calendar. It didn't matter what time you left the stadium, they were always there waiting for you. Emerging with dark menace out from the drab brick-worked side streets and street- corner pubs. Some with green and white scarves pulled up to nose level in mask effect, the majority painfully 'casual', colourless and difficult to spot.

Hibernian's flirtation with the First Division together with a couple of unfortunate cup draws saw us become regular cannon fodder for the East coast's answer to Al Qaida. Mounted police escorts back to our cars and buses became the standard rather than the exception. Scuttling for safety into brightly lit, highly stocked, licensed grocers became so frequent and predictable that the cynics amongst the Rovers faithful began to suspect that the reign of terror was the carefully masterminded, joint-marketing plan of Easter Road shop-owners as we would invariably feel obliged to make a purchase or two in return for five minutes refuge in their premises until the orchestrated violence outside had died down . My own personal acquisitions from these Easter Road skirmishes amounted to four cartons of Kia-Ora (all out of date), a six-pack of Swan 100-watt lightbulbs, six boxes of matches, issue 143 of Spiderman magazine and a second hand three-bar fire. You cannot put a price on personal safety but if I had to make a stab at it, it would be £12.73.

4.

Scholars out there will immediately point out that Hibernian is a derivation of the Roman word for Ireland. A strange choice of name as I can't for the life of me remember any Romans ever playing for the club. Founded back in the days of brown teeth and scurvy, Hibs began their days as a group of local lads from the Catholic Young Mens Society of St Patrick's Church, Cowgate. Under the watchful eye of Canon Edward Hannan, a man with possibly religious undertones, the team quickly became the focal point of the large Irish contingent living in Edinburgh at the time. By 1887 the team had become a major force in Scottish football winning the Scottish Cup and defeating then FA Cup holders Preston North End to become 'World Champions' (If your 'world' happens to encompass the bottom part of the M74 that is.) Then, just as things were looking rosy for the club someone over in the West thought it would be a good idea to play, in a football sense, the Catholic card in Glasgow. In 1888 Glasgow Celtic were founded and it all began to go pear-shaped for the Edinburgh 'Irishmen'.

With a bigger fan base and more cash at their disposal, Celtic sportingly went about signing all Hibs' best players and pretty soon it was Glasgow's East end that became home to the premier catholic team in Scotland. Things down Leith way quickly went from bad to worse and no amount of frantic candle-lighting and bead-rattling could stop Hibs slipping closer and closer towards oblivion. In 1891 the original Hibernian Football Club folded for good.....

If your definition of 'for good' means for a few months over the holiday period that is - Later that same year the club was to professionally reform, this time free from any religious ties and affiliation. Spliced from any chapel influences the new Hibernian FC championed themselves as a club 'for all people of all religions' (although they firmly drew the line at Hare Krishnas and those 'out-there' people with the headscarves who were, even then, considered to be 'no fun at all') and gradually they fought their way back to their rightful place as a major force in Scottish football.

Hibernian will rightly take credit for quite a number of 'firsts' in the Scottish game. They were the first Scottish team to play in Europe, the first to install under-soil heating. The first to attract jersey sponsorship - Remember the stramash when TV companies insisted on Hibs wearing a third strip *without* the Bukta name on the front? They had the first female director in Sheila Ronald and were the first football club to have the area surrounding their ground declared an official war zone by the United Nations. The club were pioneers in every sense.

The first time I saw Hibs in person two things stuck out in my mind. How 'hard as nails' Jackie MacNamara (Snr) was and how outstanding that green jersey with the white sleeves was. It was a sunny day (wasn't it always) and Hibs looked resplendent running onto the Wilmot Park turf in those brilliantly plain cotton, logo and pattern-free strips. I was standing with Grampa and I recall like it was yesterday; me chowin' on a McGowan's penny caramel, him manfully explaining how until the late thirties Hibs used to wear all green shirts. It was then the club chairman of the time, a great admirer of the successful Arsenal team of that era, decided that the club would change to the famous red and white design of The Gunners. Traditionalists were rightly horrified at the idea however after much gnashing of teeth a compromise was reached. The green shirt would be kept but with the introduction of the white sleeves, The chairman wasn't fully convinced but was finally persuaded that in a certain light with the aid of five double brandy's and a noseful of snuff, the team could easily be mistaken for the London giants.

The second time I saw them, some time later I might add, only one thing stood out – a purple away strip the likes of which had seldom been seen outside The Edinburgh Playhouse at Christmas-time. It was like watching Hibs on TV wearing their home kit, only with the channel not quite tuned in properly. All that was missing from the scene was blue grass underfoot and the constant hiss of static. Adorned with hundreds of that strange Bukta emblem down the sleeves (the one that looked like a crude farming implement in silhouette) and hints of green in inappropriate places, the strip was a monstrosity comparable in its 'yukkyness' with Coventry's oft-remembered chocolate coloured away strip and Hull City's infamous tiger skin number. Little kids left the ground crying that day - I remember it well.

5.

For one reason or another certain players from other teams stick in your mind. Maybe its because they're fast, or cumbersome, tall or bald. Whatever it may be, every team ends up with a player or three who is outstanding and synonymous with that one club in particular. Consequently you remember them well, sometimes for the rest of your life. For me, Hibs has loads of them spanning my time as a fan. John Blackley with his apt nickname – Sloop, Mickey Weir whose strip was always too damn big for him, John Burridge with his stick-to-the-ball goalie jersey, and Mixu Paatelainen, undeniably the spooky love-child of Shrek and that mental bird Jade from Big Brother.

I also strongly recollect Ally Brazil. His bad perm and big nose made for one of the worst stickers ever to grace my Panini album. Typically, his was the one sticker that summer that I kept 'getting' with the most frequency – at one point I must have had seven 'Ally Brazils' for swapping. Unfortunately the older kids and more casual collectors were chasing the bigger names of the day and the little kids were scared of the photograph so I couldn't get rid of any of them. Jeff Somers, the strange boy in my class, eventually took them all with a disconcerting level of enthusiasm and I remember them turning up on the cover of his 'Modern Mathematics For Schools' textbook as part of a mutilated team of freaks, each face comprising carefully cut features from a host of different other footballers from the collection. His prize creation was his grizzly centre-half made up of Hibs' goalie Jim McArthur, Davy Dodds, Danny McGrain and of course numerous bits of

Ally Brazil. When I saw it I felt a strange urge to shriek ' It's Alive!' and look to the heavens with arms aloft.

Des Bremner is another one indelibly etched on my memory. The right- sided midfielder possessed the gentlemanly air of a bygone era I thought, looking, as he did, like a moustachioed relation of David Niven. I held the vision of him, after a hard day's training with the Hibees, retiring to the officers' mess in full neck-strangling uniform for a spot of tiffin and a moan about the 'bloody Zulus' and the 'damnable raging heat!'.

And so to George Best, God rest his soul. Damn if I wasn't just a bit jealous when Hibs signed him. En-route to the San Jose Earthquakes in the bankrolled North American Soccer League, he played 22 games for Hibernian scoring 3 goals in what was undeniably the last orders of his career. It was a shrewd signing though by chairman Tom Hart that had everyone talking. So much so that Best's first home game against Partick Thistle attracted 21,000 people to a fixture that would ordinarily have been seen by around 5,000. The Scottish press loved it and I can still picture the contrived photograph of George sitting in the 'Jinglin Geordie' at a table completely covered by empty beer glasses. Of course George and the other Hibs players in his company had just sat down and were waiting for the table to be cleared but that just wasn't a story now was it?

However Hart will probably be the first to admit he got a bit of mixed bag for his money. By all accounts when Best turned up for training he trained well and his performances showed tantalising glimpses of the natural ability the man still possessed. He also reportedly remained tea-total at the club's Christmas night out – a level of restraint that no doubt earned him numerous requests by team mates to 'Jist drop ush off at the nearesht kebab shop Chief!' But then he went AWOL on a sojourn down south and proceeded to miss a Sunday cup tie against Ayr United having spent the Saturday night in the North British Hotel celebrating with the Grand Slam winning French rugby team. Such was the enigma.

Except, I suppose, its not really anyone's place to judge is it? The Hibs fans were exultant and honoured that he wore their strip, the players around him had nothing but compliments to offer, and it sounds like the man enjoyed himself. All in all another small yet outstanding chapter in the history of a club where colour and incident is never far away.

Then, of course, there was the Easter Road Slope. Not a dance step from the 1940's but the significant gradient at which the Easter Road turf used to slip down (Right to left if your were sitting in the main stand). I say 'used to' because its gone now. Lifted and levelled, the pitch would now satisfy a snooker referee armed with a spirit level. Ex-Hibs hero and one-time Rangers reserve Kenny Miller once commented ' The only time I ever noticed the Easter Road slope was when I had to run up it'. An analogy for life if ever there was one. Fittingly though it was a young Miller who scored the final goal down the slope, the subsequent pitch alterations leaving Berwick Rangers the proud custodians of the most remarkably slopey playing surface in the Scottish game (if you discount the crampon-requiring hillside played on by Inverurie Locomotives that is). Perversely I miss the concept of the Easter Road slope. I see its demise as a further sanitation of the Scottish game, another small unit of individualism lost to history. Playing up and down slopes added something to the drama, tactic and intrigue of the sport. As did playing on snow covered pitches with an orange ball, on big, wide open surfaces like Boghead, Dumbarton or within the tight claustrophobia of Broomfield Park, Airdrie. All these things have been lost to our game in favour of the pursuit of standardisation. I had the same feeling when I bought my last car. Deep down I knew it looked better and worked better yet for some hard to pinpoint reason it wasn't as good and I still kind of missed the old one.

6.

It wouldn't be the done thing to avoid a couple of pre-match beers. Having parked down at the bottom of the expansive Leith

Walk, we call in on 'Robbies', a traditional looking establishment on the left hand side of the street as you walk up towards the city. Sometimes you have to watch yourself down in these parts on match-days, especially with colours on, however this fine August afternoon, the atmosphere in Robbies seems relaxed and friendly.

Decorated with old advertising banners for products like Lyons Tea, Capstan and Players cigarettes, and Firestone Tyres (Most miles per shilling!) the pub has nailed that 'comfortable clutter' look perfectly. As I stand at the crowded bar waiting to be served I gaze at a number of nautical looking emblems hanging from the roof behind me. Each one has its own proclamation but I can't for the life of me work out the link. I am just pondering inscriptions on the first three 'Orkney', 'Torquay' and 'Formidable' when I am interrupted by the bartender looking for my order. Plumping for two pints of Wildcat Scottish Ale and a Diet Coke I pay up clumsily then weave my way awkwardly back to the boys who have remained tentatively over by the door. I say awkwardly because due to the relative sizes of the glasses involved, two pints and a softy is unquestionably the hardest round to carry across a crowded pub without dropping or spilling[3]. Supplement the round with another soft drink and the handful strangely becomes easier and better balanced but with that three drink combination I always feel on the verge of losing the whole shebang over the floor and everyone around me.

Jonesy and I sink our sooty tasting beverages thirstily with Dave again left looking on enviously.

"I'll drive next time, honestly." I mutter self-consciously.

Despite the pub's acceptable air we agree to move on and a five minute skip though a mix of grey tenements and modern new-builds finds us standing in front of the black double-door of Middleton's on Easter Road itself. Football fans are flowing by, mostly in green and white, towards the stadium which is now only a stone's throw away.

---

[3]   Known now as the 'Fleeting Combination' after Frank Fleeting, Head of Spurious Market Research Division – Alloa Breweries 1977-79

We dive in agreeing we've time for 'just the one'. Despite its close proximity to the stadium Middletons is not the exclusive property of Hibs fans and today there is a healthy smattering of red and white shirts on show. Although the furnishings are predominantly traditional dark wood, the pub is light and airy. There are numerous TV screens of varying sizes strategically positioned around the room and, as if to reinforce its non-Hibs alignment, the walls are covered with old black and white Scotland international photos, veteran players and even, rather daringly, a Hearts team picture from days gone by. Behind the bar in a prominent position are a group of three pennants. One is the green and white of Hibs, another belongs to Bohemians, the most striking though is that commemorating the Cup Winners Cup tie between Raith Rovers and Bayern Munich which after initial confusion I remembered had been played at Easter Road , a choice of venue that gave the men from Kirkcaldy admittedly bigger gate receipts but ultimately poorer romance. A bad deal I reckon. Walking under a roof beam sporting one of Bill Shankley's many legendary quotes we find a cosy corner complete with fireplace and leather couch. Beer in hand, friends together, we spend a good half hour discussing days of old and the game ahead. Yet again there never has been a better moment of abject contentment. Looking into the eyes of Jonesy and Dave I don't need a psychology degree to know they feel the same. Perfect.

7.

One of our retired regulars at the hardware store is a Hibee from way back. Mr McCracken, for that is his name, was ' born and raised on Ferry Road in Leith – just up from the library' A fact he constantly reminds anyone in the shop within ear shot at least once a visit. In between slagging people from Glasgow in his low East coast lilt and complaining bitterly about the unavailability of 'Salt 'n Sauce' with one's bag of chips 'anywhere West of Penicuik!', he likes to wax lyrical about the games of old. I seemingly, have become a kindred football spirit to

Mr McCracken and if I've heard once, I've heard a hundred times about the glorious European nights where Napoli were humbled 5-0, Real Madrid were chased out of Easter Road 2-0 and Sporting Lisbon lost by six to one. He chuckles at that one recounting every time on how the Portuguese 'gave oor players nice commemorative watches and we gave them tartan rugs!'.

His favourite, most well worn, euro- tale though concerns an epic encounter with Barcelona in the old Inter City Fairs Cup of the early sixties. Having drawn the first leg in the Nou-Camp 4-4 (that opened my eyes alone) the tie was balanced perfectly for a dramatic return leg in Edinburgh. 1-1 with five minutes to go and Mr McCracken licking his lips as he describes it, Hibs were awarded a penalty. Despite being 'a stonewaller' according to Mr McCracken the Barca keeper blew a fuse and attacked the referee for making the decision. The first time I heard this story the goalie merely shouted madly at the ref, now it sounds more like he pulled a cleaver from under his shirt, chased the poor man round the ground and then lopped his ear off on the penalty spot. Anyway Hibs duly converted the spot kick and the Spanish bulls were let loose. The game was delayed almost ten minutes as the referee was pursued about the park by the 'rabid Catalonian dogs' as Mr McCracken poetically described them. It took police intervention to get the game restarted and the Hibs players were forced, for the last five minutes , to play 'kick and jump' for fear of losing a leg or at the very least, being maimed for life. When the referee finally blew the final whistle he was standing right beside the main stand and legged it down the tunnel leaving the unfortunate far side linesman to be impaled, in his stead, on the corner flag with his boots set on fire. To cap things off the incensed Spaniards tried to break down the referee's door to get at the man in black and would surely have succeeded had they not been deterred by a keen young reporter by the name of Archibald McPherson who was on hand looking for a few post match comments. Juan Calera the Barcelona right-back that night was later quoted in Spanish paper 'La Vanguardia' saying ' We would have got the foreign scum-dog were we not confused by the pink man with the fuzzy hair and the big, long words we could not comprehend!'

When Mr McCracken's eyes really start to shine though is when he starts on about the derbies. Those glorious days when local rivals Hearts, weren't fit to lace the boots of the best team in Edinburgh - the boys in green and white. He goes on about two in particular. The 1975 Ne'er Day game when Hibs 'tanked 'em seven tae nothin' (like) 'and the more recent 6-2 victory which apparently welcomed the new millennium to Easter Road 'like Sweet Helen Jamieson', a woman whose relevance to Mr McCracken I have never inquired into.

His stories have become many and varied over the time I've known him and although they stretch from obscure pre-season friendlies in the borders to cup replays in the highlands, he has a stock selection of pet favourites that, worryingly now, I too can rhyme off with relative ease. Most discussions tend to, at some point ,tend to touch on;

- The 2 league Derby wins (obviously). The 7-0 game particularly seems to resonate with Mr McCracken. For him it was a pinnacle for the aptly named 'Turnbull's Tornadoes' with Messrs Stanton, O'Rourke, Cropley, Duncan, Gordon and co. irresistible in their quality and flair.
- Beating Hearts 2-1 in the '78/'79 Scottish Cup quarter final at Easter Road. 'A great looper of a heeder from 'Big Dode' Stewart and a 30 yard screamer of a winner by Gordon Rae' so says Mr McCracken, spitting slightly as he tells it.
- The frankly 'perfect' Season of '80/81 when Hibs were promoted, Hearts were relegated and "the parque flooring got laid in the kitchen".
- His favourite player, Pat Stanton. Mr McCracken worshipped the 'Quiet Man' and constantly bangs on about Stanton's days as a player and manager of the club. Judging by Mr M's exaltations the man is as legendary as

it gets out Leith way.

- The 'non- Scottishness' of Joe Baker. Baker was one of the most talented strikers to grace the Scottish league and it was no surprise that he would move on from Hibs and play for the likes of Torino in Italy, Arsenal, Nottingham Forest and Sunderland. What yanked Mr McCracken's chain however, together with the rest of Scottish footy fans of the day I assume, was that Joe was born in Liverpool and lived in England for a whole six weeks after that, thus making him ineligible under fusty old pre-1967 rules for a Scotland call up. To make matters worse he would eventually be capped by England, a terrible cross to bear for a young man brought up in Lanarkshire and reared on the Scottish game. As Mr McCracken frequently rants, " He scored four in the one game against Hearts for God's sake! – the man's more Scottish than a haggis lyin' on the beach at Ayr ! "

- His irrational hatred of a striker called Joe Ward. Part of a swap deal that took Des Bremner to Aston Villa, waiting for him to score a goal was like 'waiting for summer' apparently.

Mr McCracken is one of life's Gentlemen. Always politely asks if I have time to talk a bit about Saturday's game. Never fails to thank me 'kindly' for the smallest screw set I wrap for him, wouldn't utter a profanity if you nailed his hands to the wall– A man of quiet dignity and decorum .Until, that is, two words come up in conversation. Two words that ignite a Jeckyll-and-Hyde-like reaction, turning mild mannered Mr McCracken into a slavering, wild-eyed beast. Those two words;

Wallace Mercer.

First up, this man had a surname as a Christian name. Never a good attribute to sit comfortably within the working class world of Scottish football. More pertinent to Hibs fans though, he was the Hearts chairman of the mid-nineties who wiped his nose with a page from an accounts book once and decided it would be a financial masterstroke to merge the two Edinburgh clubs. His previous two ideas of bringing prohibition to Scotland and funding 'The Krankies – The Movie' hadn't taken off so he had turned his attention to infuriating the Edinburgh sporting faithful in a way that showed possibly *the* most spectacular misunderstanding of what Scottish Football is all about.

He had a vision you see. A grand vision to spawn a Super-club that would harness the potential of the nation's capital and create a team capable of finishing the league within twenty points of the old firm. It would have been a fair merger though. One that would have sat well with both sets of fans. Rumour had it that Mercer would equitably have taken the first part of Hibs name together with the last part of Hearts to give the club its new title – Hearts. This was never confirmed.

What made matters worse was Mercer's overall demeanour. To my mind, and Mr McCracken agrees with me on this, the man was probably the sort of person nobody liked at school. The sort who covered his answers during class tests even though no-one was looking, boasted about toys he didn'ae really have, and sneakily told tales on his classmates in his irritatingly rounded accent. Probably.

Of course the history books tell that the merger never happened. Hibernian were ultimately saved by Sir Tom Farmer of Kwik-Fit fame leaving poor Wallace to concentrate on his two newest campaigns ; a sex tax and the reintroduction of scratchy toilet paper in public conveniences.

8.

There's a bustling flow of bodies squeezing over the little foot-bridge at Bothwell Street. Within a stone's throw of the ground this is another historic ambush location. Perhaps the most infamous. Crushed and easily outflanked on both sides, away fans are cannon fodder to any organised assault whilst positioned on or around this; Edinburgh's answer to the Bridge at Remagen. Old memories have me skittish but today we pass over the thin walkway without incident. Possibly.... probably, those days are gone now, consigned to history's waste-bin like old bloodstained newspapers.

We are a couple of minutes late and standing at the South Stand entrance I can hear the echoing chants from inside as well as intermittent high pitched peeps of the referee's whistle. Tension rises in my stomach as I rock on my toes and heels, willing the turnstile to click that little bit faster. Second in the queue and the guy in front does not have the exact money. Evidently the turnstile operator has no change and a serious amount of huffing and puffing is going on. I'm about to whinge when suddenly thunder breaks from above my head. The rumble continues then slips into clattering applause dying eventually to a mild murmur . The guy in front and I both look at each other, our shoulders simultaneously fall. The footballing paradox has been struck – Arthurston have surely scored.

I say a paradox because this situation leaves me in the same mixed up frame of mind – every time. I mean you're delighted that your team has obviously scored and yet at the same time you are experiencing a gut wrenching exasperation at having missed the thing. In many ways, mostly selfish ones, it would almost have been better if they hadn't scored at all.

"Come on – what's the hold up!" shouts Dave fiercely right in my ear.

A muffled exclamation of indignation emanates from the operator's booth

"Jesus! " Dave yells to the air, " if we don't get in soon we'll miss another…"

BOOM ! The thunder bursts again. From the same place.

"…. Goal." Dave finishes flatly

AWWWWWWW groans the small group around us collectively.

A guy a few places back in the still substantial queue is standing with a radio welded to his ear.

"What's the script mate?" someone shouts to him, "Was that us scoring?"

"Wait a minute," the guy replies holding one finger up listening hard.

We all stand bated breath.

"Well, What is it ?" another impatient voice.

The guy drops the radio from his ear.. "Its one nil at Ibrox ! "

"Whaaaat?" Shouts of anger. "Who the hell cares about that !" the impatient boy cries.

" I do" replies the radio guy indignantly, "I've got Rangers on my coupon."

Just as it appears that the radio guy is going to get more trouble than he bargained for, the cheering subsides and the singing cranks up inside the ground to the tune of The Village People's 'Go West'- TWO NIL, TO THE ARTHURSTON !…..

Confirmation then.

And the queue is moving. Muttered apologies from the tweed capped turnstile man and the three of us are skipping up the white cemented stairs four at a time. Upwards with our fellow band of itching latecomers. Upwards into the action.

9.

"Two nil then?", Dave asks collapsing into his bright green plastic 'bucket' seat. The middle aged, ginger haired chap to his left turns round and smiles.

"Miss them did you?"There is an air of smugness about the guy's tone that by the look on Dave's face he has sensed too. Fortunately Dave just nods, smiles politely and adjusts his position on his seat.

The Ginger leans over ever so slightly."The first one was a cracker. Straight from kick off. Two passes, they were sleeping and Ray Stark pinged it in from the edge of the box."

"The second was a farce" the guy went on, " The goalie punted an easy clearance off his own defender's back and the ball

looped over him into the net. You'll not see a goal like that again."
The smug tone was accentuated.

"Not until Scotsport tomorrow at any rate" said Dave with his most pleasant air.

"Ah well, I suppose" said the Ginger looking back to the game faintly disappointed.

We are behind the goals and the Easter Road Stadium is laid out before us. The main stand to our left is only partially filled unlike the shallow-banked seated area to our right, the old East terrace which is almost full. Over in the distance with a distinctive nibble taken out its top left seated area is the delightfully named 'Famous Five' stand. Respect indeed to Hibs for laying tribute to one of Britain's best loved children's authors, Enid Blyton. Hopefully this will not be the end of it and I look forward to hearing good things of their ' Secret Seven Suite' and the 'Tales of Binkle and Flip' Lounge.

"You're not going make another Enid Blyton comment about the Famous Five are you?" asks Jonesy settling into his seat.

"Me?", I reply with mock indignation. "Would I dare to trivialise the great Famous Five, collectively the best forward line ever to grace Scottish Football?"

"Its never stopped you before.

Predictably Jonesy rattles their names off immediately, together with a brief yet informative description of each. God love him! For the record The Famous Five from right to left were:

Outside right - Gordon Smith

Not the dapper, debatably-haired .... and ex-football pundit but nevertheless the best looking of the bunch. Five league championship medals to his name and none of them with the old firm (three with Hibs, then Hearts and Dundee) make Smith nothing short of a legend. Strangely though he won nothing in his short spell at Morton. A player of electrifying pace on the ball and a fearsome scoring record - in his twenty-three year career he scored seventeen hatricks or better! A Scotland internationalist who despite attaining the honour of captaining his country, collected only eighteen caps in total. Undoubtedly a scandalously unfair haul in comparison to some players of the modern era – look to your toes Messrs Aitken, Booth and McKimmie.

Gordon Smith died in 2004, aged 80

Inside right – Bobby Johnstone
Slightly built creative genius, Johnstone was very much the unsung hero of the 'five'. By all accounts once the ball was at his feet, 'a gang of armed roughnecks couldn't dispossess him' Promoted from the 'Hibees' reserve team Bobby was an excellent example of an astute 'grow your own' policy. Another internationalist, (thirteen caps) he went on to play with great effect down South for Manchester City and Oldham Athletic.

Centre forward – Lawrie Reilly
Started his career as a replacement outside left for the injured Willie Ormond but moved into a more central role to become one of the most feared Strikers in Scottish Football history. Nicknamed 'Last minute' Reilly owing to his propensity for scoring goals right at the death (figures show he did it nineteen times), he was top scorer for seven consecutive years at Easter Road and three years on the trot with Scotland. Reilly was so prolific that he retired from international football with a better 'goals per game' average than both Kenny Dalglish and Dennis Law. Lawrie would undoubtedly have gained more adulation from the terraces had his name been easier to sing by supporters mangled with the bevvy.

Inside Left – Eddie Turnbull
The Famous Five's answer to Hotshot Hamish. 'Ned' Turnbull was physically domineering, powerful, and like a Duracell battery he would go on and on and on…. A born leader, he naturally became Hibs' captain as well as another respected internationalist. A master tactician of the game he inevitably evolved into management holding the reigns at Aberdeen and Hibernian from 1965 - 1980. Renowned for a furious temper

when provoked, Turnbull seldom missed the mark when asked his opinion on football matters and has consistently aimed honest swipes at amongst other things the structure of the Scottish Premier League, the lack of quality in the Scotland international team, the unsporting antics of Sir Alex Ferguson, poor quality coaching and dubious management styles in the modern game. Although frequently gruff and confrontational , few who played under his charge would argue that they weren't better players for the experience.

And finally;

Outside left – Willie Ormond

The only one of the 'Five' to cost Hibs a transfer fee (£1,200 according to Jonesy). Willie was as 'wan fitted' as they came. He was pacey and direct though and with 15 years of service at Hibs showed a level of loyalty that clubs can only dream of these days. Unfortunately his playing days were dogged with injury and Hibs, Scotland and laterally Falkirk fans didn't see as much of the winger as they would have liked. It was at Falkirk that he started a journey into coaching that would see him manage St Johnstone in Europe and claim the premier (yes, the *Premier*) job in Scottish football.- that of manager of the Scottish national team. He would ultimately return to the capital to manage both Hibs *and* Hearts, further endearing himself to the Hibees faithful by doing 'nothing much' with the Jam Tarts during his time there. In deference to bringing Scotland back from the 1974 World cup as the only undefeated side in the tournament, he had a street and a Children's Hospital named after him.

By all accounts Willie was a likeable man held in great esteem by all those involved in Scottish football. He sadly died pre-maturely in 1984 aged 57.

The Famous Five were widely considered to be the greatest forward line ever to grace the one club. That Hibernian, in the late forties and early fifties, won the league three times in a six year period with this strike force as the tip of their arrow surely bares testament to their individual and collective ability.

10.

Half time has arrived and we've yet to see the Rovers have a shot at goal. Worse still Hibs skipped up the park just before the break and buried a low shot through legs of Andy Thomson. Its times like this I often wonder if I'm a jinx. Had I not turned up and disrupted the molecules around the ground in question would things have ran more smoothly and favourably? I'm not sure I want to know the answer to this.

Sitting down reading my programme I feel enclosed by the traditionally upstanding bodies around me. Like a fox in a hole. Habitually people can't wait to stand up at half time. Some are so expectant that in the time the referee's elongated peep has taken to fade, they have jumped to their feet, stretched, unwrapped a minty sweetie, had a quick, reassuring look at their fixed odds coupon and commenced a serious conversation with their pal about the next-door neighbour who had apparently been seen around Saturday lunchtimes erecting a garden shed in his back garden. All this in a matter of seconds mind. These folk have the reactions of a mongoose

I look up from my shadowy world. Dave is standing above me waving a pie in my general direction which I happily relieve him of. Joining the Tall Tribe I get to my feet and gaze sightlessly round in much the same manner as everyone else. Casting around for something to say I turn to Jonesy.

"So, eh ... any news on the job front?"

"Well since you ask ,yes." says Jonesy coming out of the trance-like state he had sunk into, " Had interviews with a couple of the banks but I haven't heard anything back yet."

" Good," I reply, "Maybe one them will be interested, what do you think?"

"I'm not really much worried if the are." His eyes are glinting. " I am seriously considering going into self-employment." he continues deliberately, ending the statement with a winning smile.

"Really?" I ask faintly gobsmacked, " What are you thinking about doing?"

"Lets just say I'm thinking of going up in the world!"

"What are you going to be Jonesy, a freelance guide at the Wallace Monument?" says Dave leaning into the conversation

"Ha ha Smart-arse."

"Well what then?" we both cry simultaneously.

Jonesy is clearly enjoying the interest he has created. " Look I don't want to talk about it anymore, just in case things don't work out. I'll let you know if anything happens. OK?"

Dave and I are about to protest when a cheer goes up and the teams run back on to park. Glancing at Jonesy, satisfied that by the look on his face the conversation is well and truly over , I look back to the pitch and start clapping my hands furiously finishing the action with a fierce "COME ON THE BREWERS!"

11.

So Hibs run up the park and score, don't they – almost straight from the restart. The home fans applaud and the players congratulate each other casually like it was all expected. A slipped pass out wide from the midfield, a swift cross from the wing ending in an unmarked header and its 2-2.

Credit where credit is due though. For ten minutes or so we rally and create a few scuffled half chances. The Arthurston contingent , around 1,500 of them by rough estimate, noisily get behind the team enthusiastically cheering throw ins and hefty clearances. But to no avail. As the game progresses The Rovers look less and less likely to score with the home team growing in confidence and stature by the minute.

We ride our luck a couple of times with an acrobatic header off the line by Paul Marker and then a shot that cannons off the bar with Thomson missing in action. We stagger on though and just as it looks like we're going to weather the storm disaster hits.

Young Jay McDonald, too far back in defence for his own good gets caught in possession in the penalty box and rashly hauls the Hibs boy down with a girlie rugby tackle just as he is about to shoot. Jay gets a red card for his trouble and the penalty is converted without fuss, the 'keeper doing an impression of a street statue as the ball trundles into the bottom right of his goal.

"What was Jay thinking about?" Jonesy cries in despair. "If only he'd just booted it out the park instead of trying to beat the man there!"

But he didn't, we're getting beaten and we're down to ten men as well. Schnabbel reacts from the bench by sticking hard-man Willie Burgoyne on for a limping Tony Bunton in midfield and Frankie Boyle for a struggling Mickey Hedge out wide right. Ally Fairful who hasn't kicked the ball in 25 minutes somehow manages to avoid substitution - again.

The Arthurston fans cheer in expectation as Boyle's name is announced and Burgoyne makes an immediate impact by cleaving his opposite number at the half way line leaving him corpse-like on the ground. A yellow card is flourished, charitable punishment for the butchering that has just occurred.

There's just too much to do now and for all our encouragement it comes as no surprise when, with five minutes to go, Hibs score again. The goal again coming from slack marking in the heart of our defence allowing the ball to be prodded in, unopposed, from five yards out. When the whistle blows to put the game out its misery its not a moment too soon and as the Hibernian faithful salute their heroes off the park, the fans in red and white shuffle, cowed and thoughtful, to the exits licking collective wounds and dwelling apprehensively no doubt, on how difficult the season is rapidly becoming.

12.

The journey back home in the car was a trifle subdued to say the least. Not only had we been soundly beaten but the thought of missing our goals, the only high point in the match, was festering in all of us. In a bid to lighten proceedings I mentioned my thoughts on sloping pitches becoming a thing of the past. One thing lead to another and we ended up compiling our top ten other things you don't see at the games anymore. In no particular order we came up with:

1. Rosettes – The big, round, flowery silk badges in the colours of your chosen team. There were enough pins and sharp, bendy tin shapes attached to these things to give a Trading Standards Officer a nervous breakdown and contrary to belief at the time, they succeeded only in making the wearer look like 'Best in Breed' at the local dog show.

2. Old men selling chewing gum and macaroon bars - This somewhat limited range of confectionery was sold by old men who spent their weekdays blowing into mouth organs for loose change on Sauchiehall Street. Possibly it was good market research that indicated that the demand was there. Probably chewing gum and macaroon bars were easier to 'knock off' than proper sweets.

3. Big square goal posts – Proud and solid, their sharp edges caused many an unpredictable rebound and grotesque goalkeeping lacerations. The last example of which, by my reckoning, was to be seen at Firhill a good number of years after disappearing from every other ground in Scotland.

4. Space in the programme to write the half time scores – Fixtures of the day were printed, usually alphabetically from A to M or N. A space was left for the programme owner to write the half time score in the box beside the game. This service was obviously targeted at Rainman-like 'anoraks' and supporters suffering short term memory loss.

5. Flags at the half way line – It's difficult to pinpoint when exactly these flags, identical in size and design to the corner flags, disappeared from the game. Why they disappeared is another mystery. Perhaps they were impeding subbies from getting on the park. More likely a linesman in Uruguay or Columbia was stabbed by one after one poor decision too many.

6. Blue invalid cars – The little plastic bath coloured three-wheelers that sat mysteriously around the edges of football grounds. No one ever saw them drive in or out nor, much to my disappointment, were they ever hit by the ball. Dave's Uncle Jack, a man of stout physical fitness even today, once spectacularly blagged his way into Wilmot Park as an 'invalid'. There he sat in his metallic gold Ford Granada at the side of the park, amidst the little blue cars, puffing on a huge cigar and listening to Frank Sinatra on the radio. Jack maintains he couldn't find anywhere to park his car and took a wrong turning into the ground, no one at the club, it seemed, had the guts to question his presence.

7. Players wearing socks at their ankles – A la Paul Sturrock and Davie Provan. Exposed calves and shins were like bait to knuckle dragging defenders and the gesture by trickier more skilful players always seemed to taunt 'I'm so good, you'll never get near enough to hurt me'.

8. The 'Magic' sponge – A standard sponge from ASDA with the secret ingredient – water. It worked every time.

9. The Pink Times – The hastily printed Saturday evening edition that you would pick up on the way home from the game, particularly when your team had won. Inexplicably printed on pink paper, the match reports only went to half time or if you were lucky you got a score update in dark red writing on the back page. Never , *ever*, did you get details of your game beyond the 61 minutes mark. Completely pointless.

10. Two points for a win – It was argued that replacing two points for a win with the now accepted three would encourage teams to be more positive and attack minded. It was never considered that teams might, after taking the lead, hang on defensively to protect their potential 3 points rather than drawing and getting only one point . Who's right ? The one that gets to argue last I suppose.

If we were ten years older we agreed we could probably have come up with twenty more of these things. In the course of the journey the boys also pledged themselves to my 'Take Grampa to the Game' campaign adding, for good measure, that if we could talk him into playing centre half when he's there it would be better for all of us.

13.

The league tables tend to flip by sharply on Sky TV's Sports News Channel. OK so they come around again pretty quickly but you just don't get time to properly absorb the information presented. Just as you're projecting the effect of next week's win on the teams around you, you've been cruelly replaced by Falkirk in the First Division. Blink, and its East Fife in the second. In no time you are left staring blankly at English Division 4, or whatever its called this season, casually wondering how all these non-league teams sneaked into the Football League without you noticing.

That's why I tape it. I'm probably the only sad case in history to tape Sky Sports news but I do and it means I can rewind back to the SPL, pause it, and scrutinise the frozen frame at my leisure.

So I'm sitting in front of the TV, too close, like a six year old. The screen is a clutter of information with the blue sectioned leagues sitting to the right and individual results and scorers running across the bottom of the screen like a Reuters news-printer. Highlights of some English games are rattling away in the top left but I am poised, ready to stop the flow as soon as our league comes up.

Steady.....Steeaadddyyyyyy........And there it is! A quick push on the remote and picture is paused on the correct part of the show with tonight's league sitting shocked and stunned as if caught on film by the paparazzi doing something wrong.

Scottish Premier League

	Pld	W	L	D	GF	GA	PTS
Celtic	4	3	0	1	8	1	10
Rangers	4	3	0	1	8	2	10
Hearts	4	3	0	1	6	3	10
Dunfermline	4	2	2	0	5	4	6
Arthurston R.	4	2	2	0	5	11	6
Aberdeen	4	1	1	2	7	3	5
Hibs	4	1	2	1	6	7	4
Kilmarnock	4	1	2	1	3	5	4
Dundee Utd.	4	1	2	1	4	7	4
Motherwell	4	0	1	3	6	7	3
Falkirk	4	0	2	2	5	8	2
Patrick Th.	4	0	3	1	1	6	1

Already the top of the league has a predictable look to it although all credit to Hearts for their good start to the season. Despite coming off the rails in the last couple of weeks we are still nicely settled in fifth place, however a glance at the credit card sized fixture list I've pulled from my back pocket shows that we play Motherwell next Sunday at Fir Park, another ground we have a hellish record at.

My attention is pulled away from the telly as our local Radio's voice of Sport which has been gently babbling away to itself in the background announces that "We'll now go to Jim Smith who is with Arthurston manager Wilf Schnabbel.

Despite the lack of any visual supplement I stare at the radio intently.

" So Wilf, are you disappointed with the way the game finished today?"

"For sure Jean, I think today we had probably the best start in the world….Emmm… But we lose four sickly goals and that's it. Pwooof!"

"The team is leaking quite a few goals at the moment are you happy with the current playing staff?"

"Yes and no, Jean. Yes the squad is there but no I'm not so happy with it.

" Will there be new faces at Wilmot Park soon then?"

" I …emmm… cant be saying so much about that … emmm… it would not be fair on my players …emmm"

"OK well … "

"But I will buy a defender within the month ! A tall horse for the middle defence!"

"I see….. Sooo… err..have you any last message for the Arthurston fans out there listening?"

"Yes I do. I like to thank them all for keeping the clap going in this town and even more with the cheers. They must keep faith and I promise them good times. The team in front is the Rovers!"

"Ok thanks Wilf"

"Thanks Jean."

And with that the legend is gone. I have already clicked the radio off, turned off the video via the remote still in my hand and am lunging to the telephone in the hall spoiled for choice as to which part of that interview I'm going to discuss with Jonesy first.

Chapter 8
The smell of Firs in Autumn

1.

Dave Gorman and I first met in the dinner hall of Arthurston Primary. At the far corner table beside the toilet door to be exact. I was skulking round the shadows of my first day at a new school, Dave was stabbing to death what looked like a crusty steamed pudding with a spoon and a maniacal stare. He was at the table on his own and as I sat down beside him he continued to hack at his dessert in Psycho fashion, muttering under his breath, seemingly oblivious to my presence.

Faced with my own overpriced, free school dinner, a mangled road-kill cutlet befriended by a semi-sphere of grey, stodged potato, I had opted for the carton of milk on my tray instead. I can see that carton even now; white and pyramid shaped with a variety of small red pictures down the side. My particular one unaccountably featured a telephone and a fire engine although by rights it should also have had a no entry sign on it because I could not open it by any obvious means. I pulled the top back, yanked it forward, twisted and turned it but to no avail. Giving it one final all or nothing, red-faced stretch which made my eyes bulge and brought beads of sweat onto my forehead, I remember collapsing back in my chair with the carton stubbornly still in tact.

Having caught my breath I looked up to see Dave smiling at me waving a small straw in his hand. "There's a small hole in the top you moron, give it here!" And so it began.

Our first meeting kind of sums Dave up. Irritable, boorish and insular one moment, full of kindness and consideration the next. Irrespective of how Dave conducts himself, I've always admired his steadfastness in being himself. Whereas I am always uptight about saying the right thing and concerned about what people think about me, Dave neither cares nor compromises. He tells life the way he sees it, whether he is a mile off or otherwise, because he has a burning, inner self-confidence to do it. Going back to our school days he was the only kid I knew that ever shouted back at a teacher (and remembering the incident with adult eyes, he could have been forgiven for doing so) and even though it resulted in a two day suspension Dave was defiant, he refused to apologise and was genuinely unaffected by the whole affair. Throughout his school days he always seemed to have one girl or another hanging around. It was something I was always jealous of. Jonesy, on the other hand, never seemed to notice or if he did, he never mentioned it. Dave's 'Chickolitas' as he liked to call them when they were out of ear-shot, never lasted long though. I think the record was Mandy Timmins, a thin, pale faced brunette from fourth year who survived for almost a month. This was due in the main to Dave being on holiday for two of those weeks and then contacting a vicious strain of Glandular Fever which landed him in the infectious diseases ward of Arthurston General for another. It wasn't that Dave was mean or dismissive to any of his girlfriends, he wasn't. Its just that they expected too much of him. One by one each girl would quickly become suckered by whatever mysterious charm Dave wafted in their direction then would invariably, predictably look for more commitment than was on offer. When pressed as to why he would rather spend his Saturday afternoons at the 'stupid football' and the majority of his evenings talking about the said footballery with his 'boring mates', Dave would shrug his shoulders and reply ' Its me, Its what I choose to do. Cue then the miffed expressions, the condemnation of his fierce loyalty to us his friends and the Rovers, his passion, and cue Dave walking the other way.

Five years ago he eventually married Linda whom he met at a hypnotist evening in the student union of Caledonian University - Glasgow Tech. as it was then. They both ended up on the stage eating onions and 'sunbathing' in their underwear, a bond that would ultimately be too strong to fight against. They finally tied the knot after a tempestuous courtship that featured more break-ups, reconciliations, scraps and dramas than anyone cares to remember. It was a July wedding which Dave was adamant about. Over and over he stressed to Linda how July would offer a better chance of good weather which would ultimately contribute to the perfect day – *her* perfect day. She, on the other hand could smell bullshit a mile off and knew fine well that what he really meant was that it was the close season and he wouldn't have to undergo the pain and trauma of missing a pint , some lunch and a Rovers game.

Dave, like myself, was an only child, a late one at that. Unlike me though, he always seemed to have an easy and open relationship with his parents, another thing I was envious of. Fran and Eddie were in their forties when he was born, and when they both died last year, sadly within weeks of one another, we feared the worst for Dave. He, however, found an inner strength from heaven knows where and pulled himself through it all with a quiet resilience that everyone at the time agreed was 'Dave through and through.'

Black and white. That's how Dave tends to see things. And while he has kept all those traits he first showed in the dinner hall he has, over the years, collected a whole bag of new characteristics and idiosyncrasies most of which would make you either smile or wince. The other day I was raking through a pile of old letters and junk when I found some notes I had made for the Best Man's speech I wrote for Dave's wedding. Scrawled on four stuck together yellow Post-it notes, in nervous looking handwriting, was my initial list of observations that that I felt were worth mentioning. They brought a smile to my face again as they still sum him up quite well;

- He brushes his hair before he goes to bed at night
- He has 7 direct debits on his bank account: to the RSPCC, Arthurston Hospice, Playboy TV and 4 credit cards
- He gets stroppy at McDonalds when asked if he would like something else he hasn't specifically ordered, always replying through gritted teeth, 'if I had wanted it I would have asked for it.'
- He despises MPs, councillors and taxi drivers in equal measures and gets particularly

aggravated by women who don't have their money ready when they're in a queue to pay for something in front of him.

- He deliberately drives up close to cars with "Baby on Board" stickers in the back window.
- His favourite band are U2, who he has seen 17 times live. He maintains the first record he ever bought was U2's 'Two Hearts Beat As One'. I know for a fact it was 'Seven Tears' by The Goombay Dance Band. I know 'cos I was there.
- He slings 5p pieces and coppers he finds in his pocket into the bin.
- He has an irrational hatred of faulty technology. He lost his first job as an office clerk for doing irreparable damage to a photocopier by repeatedly kicking it in front of his stunned, open-mouthed workmates.
- He shouts at policemen
- He cries at 'It's a Wonderful Life'

Hard to pin down. That's how I would best describe him. Just when you think you're there something else pops up. He says something or does something that you think, 'Wait a minute, that's new'. Take right now for example. Its midnight, I'm standing at the doorstep in a t-shirt and boxers and I'm staring at Dave who is slouching in the pouring rain sporting his black leather jacket over what looks like a pyjama top with Batman and Robin pictures printed on it.

2.

"She's kicked me out." He mouths in a barely audible whisper.

I stare back at the drowned rat of a man in front of me, my tired mind unable to find any words of valuable response.

"Come in." I eventually conjure up and put an arm round his sodden shoulders pulling him into the warmth of the house.

Sitting in a damp patch on the couch in the living room Dave recounts his evening which makes painful listening.

What started as a minor disagreement over bath towels apparently escalated rapidly into an almighty, marathon barney, torrid even by Dave and Linda's tempestuous standards. Small time sniping quickly gave way to a vicious riot of mutual condemnation - everything from lifestyles and values to personalities and friends were torched into cinders, and before Dave knew what had hit him, he had been handed his jotters and pushed from the premises without as much as getting a chance to pack his bags.

"It was like she was possessed or something." Dave says slowly, still ashen faced." She called me a self-absorbed, unreasonable, arse-hole"

"Don't worry about that, you're not a arse-hole Dave"

"That's exactly what I said" cries Dave in an animated manner. At this he pauses and looks thoughtful. He's about to add something but remains silent and looks at the carpet.

"What happened then?"

"She threw my Rovers mug at me"

"Bloody hell, which one?"

"Last year's, the nice one with the old black and white photos on it. "

"Did she hit you?"

"Nah it went flying over my shoulder and smashed off the kitchen unit." He replies wide eyed, "But it had a dribble of cold tea in it that splashed over my face – some went down my neck" he adds quietly

"I liked that mug," I offer a little unhelpfully.

"Me too. When I bent down to rescue the pieces she went crazy screaming about how I cared more about 'that bloody team' than her!"

I tut, looking momentarily skywards.

"It gets worse," Dave sighs, " Guess what she then finds lying perfectly to hand on the breakfast bar?" he pauses then goes on "My season ticket."

"She didn't?"

"Ripped it into confetti in the blinking of an eye. She was like Edward Fuckin' Scissorhands on smack once she got going. I think …" Dave stops and turns in on himself obviously fighting to remain in control. Its as if every feeling he has ever had is fighting to get out at the one time..... A painfully awkward silence blankets the room.

"Look," I eventually mutter, "It'll be alright." I try to appear firm and confident but I can't help thinking myself how hollow and utterly useless I sound.

"Are you going back tonight?" I venture.

"I thought I'd try but if she won't let me in I reckon it'll be ok to go round to Jonesy's, what do you think?"

"Yeh, why don't you give him a call and I'll make us a cuppa."

I never know what to say for the best in difficult situations and I'm almost relieved to make my escape to the kitchen. 'Lets have a cup of tea!' is my 'go to' line, the answer to all of life's ills. You could be broke, your house burned down, your spouse has ran off with someone else and you've just been told you've not got long to go and I would be absolutely amazed if the prospect of a nice cup of tea wasn't enough to steady the ship.

When I come back armed with two cups of Cure-All Dave has spoken to Jonesy and arranged his alternate accommodation should the need arise.

"So are you going to the game on Saturday?" I ask lifting my cup from the mahogany coffee table, wincing as I notice the nasty ring its left on the wood surface.

"Oh yeh," replies Dave vaguely, "But I'm not optimistic of seeing anything uplifting. The Hibs game was one thing and losing three nil against Celtic at Parkhead was a bit predictable but losing one-nil at home to Falkirk on Saturday was a sore one. If we don't get back on track soon things are going to get difficult."

"Things ARE difficult!" I interject. "We're ninth in the league, only three points off Partick Thistle who are BOTTOM and there's no sign of this new defender Schnabbel keeps talking about."

The conversation heads off in a typically masculine direction with both of us, I think, glad of the diversion, safe territory away from the complexities and sensitivities of life. We chat in low murmurs for another half hour or so until Dave claps his hands on his thighs, stands up and announces that it is 'time to face the fire!'

"Ok, well let me know how you get on." I offer rubbing the back of my neck, guiding Dave gingerly to the door.

He turns round and makes to say something but no words come out.

The rain patters off the path insistently

'Right!" we both say at the same time. Dave smiles thinly and turns to go out the door. I pat him briefly on the back so softly I'm not sure he notices the gesture.

"Hey - about Saturday!" I shout gently as Dave disappears down the pathway and into the darkness. He stops briefly and looks round shielding his head with one bent arm. "Look on the bright side, at least its not a home game – you won't need your season ticket."

Another weary smile and a wave over his shoulder and he's gone into the storm. As I close the door slowly I can't help thinking that for all its drawbacks, I'm glad to be living my own life at the moment.

3.

At 2:13 am my mobile beeps. Giving off a ghostly blue hue that lights up the tip of my nose and up the side of my arm, the text is from Dave and it is stark in its simplicity.

Going 2 stay @ J's for time being. C U Saturday. D

4.

There's a rawness in the wind that suggests that the cold, brittle fingers of winter aren't too far away. Standing in the car park of The Moorings Hotel in Motherwell with nowhere near enough clothes on, it feels like they are here, round my neck and running themselves down my back. Its all a bit bleak and uncomfortable and I feel as grey as the clouds above my head.

Its just gone midday and we have arrived, in deepest, darkest Lanarkshire, much earlier than planned. For once I have managed to unearth the best route to our chosen destination and have negotiated it perfectly without a hitch.

And we've seen the sights along the way. As we skipped along the M74, Jonesy, in animated fashion like a package tour guide, pointed out the landmarks. On our left, Strathclyde Park; home of the Boy Racer and the spindly roller-coasters of 'Scotland's only theme park'- Disneylookverygoodland. On our right the domed roof of Hamilton Mausoleum and that motorway service station you always have to stop at for a pee on the way home from down south. You know the one I mean. It turns up just after that nondescript, roughly tarred stretch of road past Lesmahagow which you can barely see through the driving rain that began at the 'Welcome to Scotland' sign an hour previous. It lures you in with relieved thoughts of an empty bladder, while at the same time provokes unrest from your fellow, travel-weary, passengers the moment you turn on the indicator and mutter ' Ah cannae hang on any longer' in an strained yet apologetic manner.

With the peak of Tinto Hill straight ahead in the misty distance we slipped off the motorway to the left, crossed over the cheeky, adolescent River Clyde, and pushed onwards up the Hamilton Road in search of food, drink and merriment.

Stuck at the traffic lights beside the town-side entrance to Strathclyde Park we were treated to a massive bill-board proclaiming forthcoming attractions at Motherwell Concert Hall and Theatre

Aug 21-22 Jessie Rae –The King of Highland Funk
Aug 28 The Lena Martell Story
Sept 1-5 The Singing Kettle
**Sept 8 Chaka Demus and Pliers – The 'tease me again'
    tour**
Sept 7-8 Joss Swank with the Joss Swank Dancers

Sept 14 Serge Moldovan's Hypno-Bingo Night
Oct 1 - Punk Floyd/ Swiggy Pop

Its almost like being on Broadway. I've made a mental note when I get home, to check my diary to see what I'm doing on the 14th of September.

Through the lights, continuing up the steep hill past the Harvard-like Dalziel High School buildings, we quickly spied the ivy covered frontage of The Moorings on our left. In no mood to trail around we quickly agreed to stop and accept whatever food and drink was on offer.

5.

Avoiding the main, front entrance to the hotel we slump our way up a short flight of steps and through the doors of a conservatory extension- type affair signposted as the Bar Restaurant.

Inside, the tables are almost fully taken up by what is quite obviously a black-attired, low-murmuring funeral party.

"Oh great," I mutter to no-one in particular, "They'll have run out of steak pie then."

"Do you think we should be in here?" whispers Jonesy out the side of his mouth.

"Yeh its fine" I answer back dismissively, "Look , there are menus on that table and I'm sure that couple over there haven't been to a funeral..

We cross the room and sit down at a small table for four set against a red patterned wall crammed full of framed prints and other objects of non-interest. Looking around, the restaurant has all the feel of a slightly better appointed roadside chain restaurant.

A cheery looking waitress decked loudly in TAARRTAAAN!!! comes over to take our order. Jonesy and Dave after some humming and hawing plump for the fish and chips while I stand firm with the Steak, Guinness and Mushroom Casserole (in a crisp pastry case) option – Steak pie to you and I. We complete the order with two pint of lager and a lager 'tops' from the bar which I can just make out tucked away in another section of the restaurant.

In the time it takes our food to come Dave fills me in on his marital developments of the last couple of days. Linda seems to be holding firm as far as the split is concerned maintaining that is been 'on the cards' for a while now. Worryingly she is trotting out tried and tested phrases like she's 'not sure what she wants anymore', 'things have changed' and 'Where is the spare key to the door?' On a more positive note she seems to be giving ground in the big bath-towel debate that kicked off the fight in the first instance. Dave seems very matter-of-fact in his description of things but all the while he's talking I notice he is tapping his fork nervously on the table in front of him. As he sets off on a tirade about Linda's mother who , in Dave's words 'is doing more stirring than Nigella Lawson', my attention is snagged on a gorgeous looking blonde girl in a black trouser suit who is standing at the end of one of the tables in the other corner of the room. She is nodding her head and smiling a dazzling red lipped, white toothed smile at a group of old fogies who are grinning back in an entranced manner. As she throws back her golden hair in natural laughter I swear I hear a symphony orchestra strike up in the background.

"So what about that then?" Dave's voice comes back to me, "You wouldn't believe it would you?"

"Em... no. Absolutely shocking " I suggest taking a gulp of my too- sweet pint.

"You said it mate" adds Dave shaking his head.

At which point the food comes. And pleasantly good it is too. While the boys tuck in to a healthy helping that wouldn't look out of place at Blackpool's finest gourmet establishments, mine reveals itself to be a particularly tasty affair. And it's not quite steak pie either, at least not as we know it. It's more of an open pasty than steak pie but I'm not complaining. Its delicious. The only down side to the serving is the carved chunks of mixed veg

191

which look more like carefully sculptured willies than healthy eating, subjecting us to a volley of bad 'Carry-On film' type puns from Jonesy . He is just about to take things too far when a soft voice breaks into our world.

"Hi.. em.. thanks for coming"

Its her.

The gorgeous blonde.

AT OUR TABLE.

Huh? grunts Dave with a mouthful of chips. Jonesy looks on momentarily with a blank expression.

"Sorry I haven't spoken to you sooner but, you know, you've got to get round everyone. " She smiles apologetically, waving a delicate hand in the general direction behind her.

Dave and Jonesy say nothing

"No problem." I stutter without thinking "These things are always.. em....difficult"

"Aren't they" she says gently. Closer up she is even more attractive than I imagined. 5' 8' or 9, with her shoulder length wavy hair, blue eyes and perfect complexion she looks more Scandinavian than West of Scotland. She is now standing close enough that I can smell the light, sweet smell of her perfume and I am transfixed by her beauty.

"So, how did you know my dad?" she asks

Its now I should have pointed out the mistake. Excused myself from the conversation and went back to talking about phallic vegetables and team selections. And in fact I am all set to do this except when I open my mouth, horror of horrors, out comes:

"We.. eh.. used to work together. Yes … we ..eh… did quite a lot of contract work a while back and I got to know him then."

I can feel Dave and Jonesy's incredulous expressions on me but I am melting into the blue perfection of Heidi's (for I have named her Heidi) eyes and I cannot be saved.

"Poor Dad, maybe if he had stayed away from that office a little more he would be here today. But, hey, you know how hard he worked."

"Oh yeh, "I answer nodding like a dog in the rear window of a car, " a real workaholic!". I'm blushing like a school kid. I know I am. And the same words are running through my head again and again. 'Finish this and escape, finish this and escape'.

"So how's your mum bearing up" I continue. To my side Dave splutters into his glass.

"She's doing ok" replies Heidi turning slightly and glancing across the guests who are now chattering away in a relaxed manner clearly relieved that the worst of the day's formalities are now over. "It's the next bit I'm worried about. You know …. when things quieten back down around the house. Do you know her at all?

FINISH THIS AND ESCAPE!

"I think I met her a couple of times – just in the passing"

"Well you should come over and say hello", says Heidi, "She loves talking about dad and she'll definitely remember you. She never forgets a face."

"Oh eh …maybe later.. that would be nice." I stammer, "I don't want to interrupt her just now , she seems quite …. Em…. taken up" I nod in the general direction that Heidi had looked previously. She glances round and thankfully agrees.

"Oh well, I'd better move on" she sighs and then turns to me, "but promise me you'll come over before you go. Mum would like it …. I would too." She drops her eyes briefly and smiles an innocent yet tantalising smile.

I'm so captivated I can't speak. So I simply nod.

She makes to move away then swirls back. "Sorry," she says apologetically," I don't know your name."

"I'm Craig" I croak

"Its been nice to talk to you Craig" and again she makes to leave.

This time its my turn to look embarrassed "Em …. I don' know your name either."

She stops again and smiles.

"Its Heidi" she says simply then slips back into the throng behind her.

6.

Strapping ourselves into the car Jonesy is twittering on like budgie.

"I think I met your mother a couple of times!" He says in a sing- song voice widening his eyes and twirling an imaginary hair round his ear." You know, one of these days I'll enjoy a relaxing drink without having to make a sharp exit because of something you guys have said or done. I mean , what were you *thinking*?"

"I'm sorry" I sigh, " I don't know what the hell came over me. You know me I wouldn't dream of lying to anyone. I feel bad"

"Don't beat yourself up" says Dave soothingly. "She was lovely and you got carried away. I would have done the same."

"Really?"

"No. I would have gone over and met her mother but that's just me."

"Yeh but I feel bad about missing ….well… a chance. I really think she liked me. Don't you?"

"Hmmm, possibly." grunts Dave signalling for me to take a left turn back on to the main road. "Difficult to tell with women. One minute they're with you, giving all the right signs, making you feel good. Then BANG, they don't want to know. I just don't get women these days. "And with that Dave folds his arms defiantly and stares blindly at the glove compartment in front of him, the conversation apparently over.

The centre of Motherwell is the town planning equivalent of Michael Jackson's face and at first glance divests in you the same instant revulsion as witnessing a dog licking its own nuts. Viewed in the rain it would prompt even the most optimistic of individuals to question the meaning of life and reach for The Samaritans help-line. The main shopping area is a pedestrianized slope about 400 yards long, with 'Woolies' and the obligatory McDonalds perched at its top and an ugly, bruiser of an ASDA supermarket loafing around at its dingy bottom end. In between resides an enthralling collection of cheap chemists, banks and card shops catering presumably for locals who have a headache, want a headache or know someone in hospital with a headache.

All the while this grey chunk of concrete consumerism is surrounded by a looping Scalextric ring road that wends is way around the town centre in a cunning, ill-defined manner. If you are a first time visitor to the town and are unsure of your destination then be prepared for numerous circuits round the block before almost certainly being spat back out in the wrong direction, on the road to nowhere or worse .... Wishaw .

I'm happy with where I'm going and soon find myself on the main drag trundling past the Job Centre and an old school-type building proclaiming 'Dalziel Workspace' on the side. I can remember clearly the route to the ground from here yet somehow I manage to take my eye off the ball and take the wrong turning off one of many mini- roundabouts dotted along the way. We end up mysteriously, without warning in ASDA's car park where we spend a pleasant few minutes driving round the small tightly packed enclosure looking vainly for the exit. On our third time round Dave eventually spots our escape hidden amidst a collection of brick walls and paving and we continue on our way.

Its still only 1.30 and we decide that there's time to get another pint in. Given the limited options in the area we plump for a trip back round the loop for a swift one in The Railway Tavern. We've been here before and know it to be a reasonable boozer. It's a bustling, light and airy pub with a nice square bar sat bang in the middle of proceedings. In fact settling down at a small table and looking round at laughing punters tucking into some standard pub grub, Its difficult to work out why we didn't just come here in the first place.

Over another round of two pints and a softie we have an entertaining conversation about past Motherwell managers. This arose from Jonesy's throw away comment that they had gone through 'some amount of them' over the last few years, eight in under twenty years by his reckoning. We had a go at naming as many as we could.

"Tommy The Hamster' was the one I think of most" started Dave incredibly tearing into a bag of Cheese and Onion crisps by my watch only twenty minutes after finishing his lunch.

"Tommy McLean? Yup " agrees Jonesy, " He was around for a while though. Got them promoted from the first Division and took them to the Scottish Cup final. Not a bad record."

"Wasn't Willie McLean their manager as well" I ask.

"Willie McLean? Bloody hell that's right" splutters Dave, a damp crumb of cheese and onion crisp flying out his mouth hitting Jonesy on the ear. " The third McLean brother. I'd forgotten about him. I wonder if he was as exhilarating a personality as Jim and Tommy. Can you imagine the chat at that dinner table?". We all have a chortle at the thought.

"What about Ally McLeod, he was at Motherwell for a while. " Jonesy settles into his seat. In his element now, able to regurgitate names and facts in an endless stream. Not for the first time I can't help thinking that if he could have been as switched on to work related subjects he would be a very rich man by now.

"Yes he was. God bless Ally McLeod!" We clink our glasses together over the centre of the table.

Jonesy carries on, "There was Bobby Watson, and Billy Davies. He didn't last very long, "

"David Hay," chips in Dave, " and that foreign boy. The guy that was a disaster."

"Harri Kampman! He was from Finland" exclaims Jonesy getting up from his seat and heading off to the bar. Surprisingly he's back almost immediately placing a duplicate round of drinks on the table.

"Kampman lasted only a few months – he wasn't a disaster as such, it was more that his teams were deathly boring." explains Jonesy sitting back down and getting comfortable. "I remember reading in the papers at the time that he sacked 20 players in the one day. Quite an achievement. I think he fell out with their Chairman, John Boyle and didn't last long after that."

"Yeh," chuckles Dave," there was only room for one kampman at the club". Sniggers all round.

"Who else….. Alex McLeish! Big Eck was there before he went to Hibs. And Jock Wallace, that's another one"

Its my turn to get involved. "I've got a good one you've not remembered – Roger Hynd" I sound pleased with myself.

Both Jonesy and Dave look blankly.

"Roger Hynd" I repeat, " He must have been in charge round about the Argentina World Cup. 1978 or so."

"Awwww yes I remember him now "agrees Jonesy, "He looked like one of those slacks-and-pullover-wearing catalogue models that always posed by pointing into the middle distance, didn't he"

"That's the man!" I laugh, relieved that someone knows what I was on about.

And so it flows on. We spend a further half an hour or so discussing other such meaty issues like why none of the gadgets on 70's TV program Tomorrow's World ever caught on, the current whereabouts of Chesney Hawkes, and the outrageous price of razor blades, especially, we agree, those Mach ones with the eight or so extra blades on them (giving eight times closer a shave - and leaving you little in the way of skin presumably) before checking watches, gathering things together and pointing ourselves in the direction of the game.

7.

The designated car parking for away fans is in or around a small industrial estate on Orbiston Street. The ground is fifteen minutes away from here – a five minute walk plus a ten minute wait to cross the busy main road that lies between us and the ground.

Passing the fire-station and having safely negotiated the Road from Hell we saunter past one of many car-showrooms in the vicinity and find ourselves on a peaceful tree-lined street..

"Are those Fir trees then?" asks Jonesy peering skywards.

"Do I look like David Bellamy?" growls Dave who then shrugs innocently when I throw him a stern look.

We pass a disused, dilapidated building amidst the trees to our right that we all agree would make a handy pub for away fans.

"Ah... but what about the rest of the time? How would it make money? " I ask

"Could cater for car salesmen. The place would be packed." suggests Dave not unreasonably.

Turning the corner we find ourselves in a clearing outside the away fans entrance to Fir Park. The large stand towers into the grey sky above and in between structures we are given a sneaky peak at the main stand and the dull green of the pitch at its feet. Joining the queue to pay in, and despite the spitting rain and cold wind invading my hard to get at bits, the adrenalin as always starts to rise. If it didn't I'd be dead.

8.

I have an admission to make. It almost kills me to say it but long, long ago (in a galaxy far away) I nearly became a Motherwell fan.

It was all my Uncle Dick's fault.

He lead me on.

Uncle Dick was actually my dad's cousin and not my real uncle at all. I remember him as a tall, serious man with a heavy black moustache, wispy dark hair and a permanently furrowed brow. He smoked huge Embassy cigars that he pulled endlessly from brown, faux-leather boxes and when he came to visit, which was pretty frequently in those days, he shrouded the front living room with so much smoke that you had to be guided in to the sofa with a light and a fog-horn. He almost always wore a herringbone suit, however as a nod to casualness he would occasionally remove his tie and unbutton his shirt at the neck. Only after nine o-clock mind. At the weekends he retained his collared shirt and suit trousers but audaciously sported either a bright red or a mustard yellow Lyle and Scott pullover. He was the only man I knew that not only bought stuff from Grampa's shop but ran an account with him into the bargain.

Uncle Dick caught me at bad time. I was 9 years old and didn't know my arse from my elbow. I had only seen Arthurston a couple of times so the bond hadn't quite formed and Grampa, the voice of reason and my ticket to Wilmot Park, had a lot on his mind what with the business and all. So I found myself being transported on a semi-regular basis across the roads and the miles to Fir Park, Motherwell with Uncle Dick who had, slyly to my mind, offered to 'keep up my interest in football'.

Uncle Dick was in Motherwell's Vice President's Club at that time. Quite who the President was and what sort of vices were available through being a member of his club were a mystery to me but I went along anyway. The process of entering via this 'club' was always the same - painful. In we would go through the front entrance of the main stand where immediately I felt the burning eyes of the doorman on me. Then it was up a flight of stairs to be met at a nondescript door by a nondescript 'official' who would point out, *every time,* that I was not allowed in here. Uncle Dick would tut and snap "We're only going in to pick up the lad's ticket" whereby I would mop the rapidly forming sweat from my brow. The chap would reluctantly hand me a perforated ticket without explanation and nod for us to pass through the now opened door into what I assume, due to the amount of smoke in the air, was the Ravenscraig Suite, a tribute to the local steel works of the same name. Then I would stand, self consciously, beside a little bar similar in size to the kind people had in their living rooms in the early seventies as Uncle Dick disappeared into the fog to get my ticket. As he paid a man sat at a tiny school desk at the edge of the room, drinkers would bore holes in me with piercing stares and I would teeter on the edge of unconsciousness brought on, in the main, by my complete inability to take a breath. I would remain stalk still until Uncle Dick rejoined me and gently shoved me towards a second door where yet another lurking dullard stripped me of my perforated ticket, ripped it, then gave me half back, again without explanation. A final push and I was through the exit and magically transported onto the middle landing underneath the main stand.

Having skipped up a final flight of steps into the fray, we were now afforded a rather impressive panoramic view of Fir Park in front of and below us. Directly facing us a shallow enclosure with trees seemingly growing out its roof. To our left and right tall floodlights cemented onto the corners of ample terracing behind each goal. Spread luxuriously in the gap in between, The Pitch. Of all the things I remember about the Fir Park of old the thing that lingers most was the flat, billiard green perfection of the pitch. While Arthurston's park had all the finish of a two-bob barber's hack, Fir Park was a stylish London coiffeur, slicked, shaped and trimmed to sophistication. In those days it was probably the best playing surface in Scottish football.

The view taken in, we were then allowed to sit in a boxed off area with burgundy leather seats that were again unquestionably better than anything Wilmot Park had to offer. The people around me always seemed a glum bunch though with no conversation and even less enthusiasm. Uncle Dick would spend the early stages of every game arguing with a steward who looked uncannily like Shaggy from Scooby-Doo and who would (deliberately to my mind) bob around blocking Uncle Dick's line of vision at every opportunity. The whole time it took to get from the front entrance to being comfortable in our seats probably took less than five minutes but it seemed the longest time of my life.

I don't know how often I went to Fir Park in those days but it was enough that I started talking enthusiastically about Joe Wark, Willie Pettigrew and Stewart McLaren rather than the Rovers players my Grampa extolled the virtues of each Sunday night over my mum's Soup'n'Stew Special. So much so that that Grampa eventually wakened up and smelled the coffee.

Uncle Dick may well have got away with his surreptitious effort to convert me to football Lanarkshire style had he not made one fatal error – teaching me to sing 'Oh 'Well, Oh 'Well we are the Champ–ee-ons!'. I never really thought much of it at the time as I genuinely interpreted 'Oh Well' as being some kind of benign exclamation of resignation. Grampa , on the other hand immediately saw it for what it was as I strolled past him at the dinner table serenading myself gently.

"What's that your singing son?" he asked sharply dropping a piece of stew from his fork. When I repeated it he slammed down his cutlery shouting "That's it, enough's enough!" And so ended my habitual treks to Motherwell in favour of Saturday hikes up the Brew with Grampa who would sometimes come in with me or, when he needed to be in the shop, would deposit me at the turnstile and be there waiting for me when the game was over. I still went along to Fir Park with Uncle Dick now and then as I grew older, but he knew he had lost me, consoling himself by puffing on a new brand of even larger cigars and berating the orange-bibbed car park attendant strategically placed on the small stopping area outside the main stand.

9.

After the first game he took me to, Uncle Dick sneakily gave me a book to read. I can't remember what it was called exactly but it told the history of Motherwell Football Club in the usual bone-dry manner of such publications. (Lots of grainy team photos and names no one alive today would recognise nor remember.) I was young though and sponge-like when it came to any new information and quite unbelievably I can, to my shame, remember bits of that book even today.

Motherwell FC, if I remember rightly, was founded in 1886 as an amalgamation of two factory teams Alpha and Glencairn. The former was an engineering works and the other messed around with steam cranes. Some ten years later they were granted a lease by local rich chap, Lord Hamilton, who gave them an area at the north end of the large Fir Park on his Dalzell Estate. After much thought and debate officials of the time creatively opted to name the ground Fir Park and in doing so created decades of confusion amongst mothers, aunties and other non-interested parties who consistently would get mixed up with Fir Park itself, Partick Thistle's 'Firhill' 'Firs Park' the home of East Stirlingshire and Phil Parks the ex QPR goalie with the big 70's porno 'tache.

Motherwell used to wear blue strips until the early nineteen hundreds when they changed to Lord Hamilton's horseracing colours, the now famous claret and amber. That's *claret* and *amber* now, and *not* purple and yellow as most may think. And its vitally important that people understand this as Motherwell folk tend to get quite uptight about the distinction. So much so that there still exists a local bye-law dating back to 1913 condemning anyone caught making this insulting error to a sound whipping to the arse with a Fir branch by the local librarian whilst being forced to look at pictures of Ian St John's granny playing naked volleyball. Not pleasant I am assured.

Speaking of Ian 'The Saint' St John, it was at Motherwell in the late fifties where the glittering career of this famous young forward kicked into life. Under the watchful eye of managerial legend Bobby Ancell, Ian became the golden boy of the celebrated 'Ancell Babes', so influential in the mid to late fifties. Ancell himself has a lot to answer for in terms of moulding the future of British football. Had he buried St John in Motherwell's reserves and maybe let him go on a free transfer to, say, Cowdenbeath a few years later then all of us would surely have been spared the horrors of 'The Saint and Greavesy' on Saturday lunchtime telly.

He didn't though and The Saint shone in that young Motherwell team. So much so that in 1962 he was transferred to Liverpool with Motherwell using the not inconsiderable transfer fee to replace their crappy wee Subbuteo stand with the bigger, three quarter length structure that is the Main Stand today. Questions were asked at the time as to why the stand was not built to run the full way along the park and there were strong, if unfounded allegations made around the town that the club had ran out of money. Rumours were rife that the directors had donated an undisclosed amount of the transfer fee to a training fund for STV cameramen as watching Scotsport at that time was, in the words of the club chairman, ' like playing a game of 'Spot The Ball' in a typhoon'. It was even suggested that a young local entertainer called Christian had been bribed with a 'sizeable chunk' of the cash to 'go away ' and 'never sing another note again.' For the 'Well fans of the time the reality was much more annoying. Had the stand been built all the way along it would have towered over the house and garden behind it. The dwelling's inhabitant at that time, a Mr V. Meldrew, held the club to ransom over the property which the club offered to purchase. A deal could not be struck leaving the board no option but to leave a portion of the new stand unfinished with bare girders left naked and exposed as a constant reminder of where the planned structure should have extended to.

Throughout this debacle the fans of Motherwell Football Club constantly showed great restraint and high moral standing in respecting the householders' stance. Had this happened in nearby Airdrie for example, a covert militia would have been instantly formed, the home in question would , within three days of the disagreement, undoubtedly have been burned down under mysterious circumstances, with the Meldrews, their friends and family, being placed for their own protection, in a safe-house 'somewhere near Twechar'.

10.

As I said, I did go back with Uncle Dick. A number of times. Only next time round Willie Pettigrew, Colin McAdam, Gregor 'Raw Mince' Stevens, Peter Marinello, and the like had all sauntered gracefully into the sunset. Their excellent mid-seventies strip with the diagonal claret stripe down the front had made way for a slick but sterile shiny Adidas number and amongst the new Steelmen numbered a young Brian McClair, an even younger Gary McAllister, 'punk-rock' keeper Hugh Sproat, the hugely skilful Brian McLauchlin, and super-sub John Gahagan.

John Gahagan. My heart went out to this guy. Every game I saw at Fir Park in those days saw him come on as a substitute and show more skill than the rest of the team put together. He would rape his opponents up the wing for fun yet never, obviously, to the satisfaction of any of the managers he played under. I dare say he must have started some games in his eleven years at the club but if he did I certainly wasn't there to see them. Again it serves to highlight the blind-spots managers tend to show in our game. Or is it a sad indictment of Scottish football how skilful players are viewed as bit-part players in a show that favours brawn , physique and a 'Thou shalt not lose' mentality. Maybe I've got it all wrong and just wouldn't know a player if he came over and gave me a tip for the bookies. Whatever the script, players like Gahagan were, and still are, the reason I pay my money to see the beautiful game. I don't go to see big hefty stoppers, nuthin each draws and lone striker formations. I go to see craft, flair and skill on the ball. Thankfully Gahagan and co have given me enough of these things over the years to keep me coming back for more and I just hope that managers continue to remember that the point of the wonderful game of football is to win by scoring more goals than your opponents.

I stopped going to Fir Park entirely with Uncle Dick in the early nineties. He moved down south to work in the marketing department of a well known frozen food company where his job entailed writing the recipe descriptions for the outside of food containers. You know the sort of thing, little phrases like 'Succulent roasted chicken marinaded in an exotic blend of cream, peppers and onion sauce' or 'Thick, savoury minced beef layered under creamy mashed potato – serves 18'.

As his 'creations' hit the shelves he (ridiculously) became the family celebrity and I remember one New Years my dad standing in our living room proudly showing two bemused neighbours an icy cold box of frozen lasagne.

"This is Dick's best one yet" dad said beaming, and I can picture him standing by the fire reading that box to this day. " Traditional Italian pasta, topped with regional cheeses and layered seductively with prime minced beef in a tasty Ragu sauce – Just like mama used to make! " He said the last part like it was a touching personal memory. I don't know how the neighbours reacted to this overwhelming display of human achievement, I was too embarrassed and had to leave the room.

11.

Even the staunchest of Motherwell fans will admit that as a club they have ridden their luck over the years.

Their first stroke of good fortune came in 1975/76 season when they finished tenth in the old first Division. The fine line was drawn under them to form the shiny new, fit and trim, Premier League and while Motherwell breathed a sigh of relief at their good fortune, smugly sidestepped the bouncers and joined the party, Airdrieonians and Kilmarnock, only two points back in 11th and 12th place respectively, were left outside, cursing the damnable, exclusive rules before staggering off into the night, shouting over their shoulders belligerently how they 'didn't want in to the lousy club anyway'.

Then came 1985/86 when Motherwell finished dead last in the league yet avoided relegation when it was decided that the Premier League should be increased to twelve teams. Given the option of relegating Motherwell and promoting three First division clubs the league predictably allowed The Steelmen to stay with only two coming up from the lower league, a protective reasoning fairly typical of the powers at be in Scottish football it has to be said.

In 2002/03 the club again finished bottom. This time they were saved from the drop by Falkirk's inability to satisfy league rules in respect of the state of their stadium. While the Bairns had been promoted fair and square and, in sporting terms at any rate, were good enough for the top league, the aging Brockville was deemed not to be and Falkirk were refused entry.

Its not all been relegation battles and lucky breaks for the men from Lanarkshire though. For every bad season they seem to have bounced back with an equally good one.

Most memorably they won the Scottish cup in 1991 when they concluded an inspirational campaign by pipping Dundee United 4-3 in one of the most exciting finals in living memory. Strong, evocative memories were borne out of these games. Along the way striker Stevie Kirk scored in every round including the winner in the final and John O'Neil's thirty-five yard strike against Celtic in the semi-final replay probably sparked the most enthusiastic reaction from 'neutral' observers since the Aberdeen fan, a few years back, ran on to the park at Ibrox and booted Andy Cameron in the arse.

In 1994, Motherwell finished second in the league, runners up to Rangers, a phenomenal achievement for a provincial club in these days of Old Firm dominance. The resultant European campaign saw them host German giants Borussia Dortmund in what became known throughout Europe as' Der Kampf der Grausamen Fussballhemde' - 'The Duel of the Clatty Strips'. Unfortunately euro success was not on the cards for 'Well'. Hopes had been high of overcoming a shocked and dispirited Dortmund outfit who had got lost on the town centre ring road on the way to game and ended up, quite traumatically at Carfin Grotto. Within minutes of stopping for directions the team bus 'lost' five wheel-trims and had been boarded mysteriously by a group of 'churchy looking men in robes'. Players were sold a selection of Pope John Paul II cigarette lighters, 'Jesus Saves' golf markers' and Paul McStay oven-gloves, while others, according to manager Otmar Hitzfeld , later complained vaguely of being victims of 'some form of mind control trickery'."They came out of the wilderness like Sand-people !" a clearly shaken Matthias Sammer claimed in the post match press conference, ".... and many of my team mates were left with intangible feelings of guilt and the urge to sing Irish Ballads we didn't know the words to."

Despite the Lanarkshire team's disappointing exit from the competition over its two legs, the overall experience was to be an enriching one for Motherwell's travelling faithful. Not only did they get to see their team play at the Westfalenstadion, one of the best grounds in Europe, they got to drink watered down lager at the game, eat long sausages out of short rolls and watch twenty seconds of porn at intermittent intervals on the TV in their hotel rooms - and that's what European football is all about – ask the SFA Executive Management Committee.

Now you would have thought the monitory rewards of two 'bonus' seasons in the Premier, European involvement, a successful cup run *and* the arrival of a multi-millionaire owner would have been sufficient to create some form of lasting financial security for the Lanarkshire club.

Alas not.

In 2003, the flamboyant, megabucks travel agent John Boyle lead the club confidently into corporate administration after demonstrating the age old directorial style of pissing money (his and the club's) against the wall like it didn't really matter. Under such lax financial control the club spiralled helplessly towards insolvency and oblivion. Luckily for Boyle legal jiggery-pokery was applied and costs were cut, players were jettisoned (illegally in the eyes of many) and key players were sold. Fortunately for the fans, the club survived but it amazes me that a man with such criminal disregard for financial discipline was then welcomed back by officials and fans alike into the fold like some kind of twenty-first century prodigal son. The man took the club to the edge of financial ruin, irresponsibly some may say, losing reputedly ten million pounds of his own money in the process. Anyone displaying such dazzling lack of business acumen as this, as well as such scant responsibility to the employees under his charge, should play no part in the running of Scottish Football. Personally I wouldn't allow Boyle and his like within a hundred yards of a football ground - not even to deliver the pies.

So sayeth me.

12.

Sitting in the lower tier of the impressive South (Motorola) Stand its difficult to envisage any team other than the old firm bringing enough fans to fill the thing. Again we have brought five or six hundred fans with us but our numbers don't even touch the sides. The recent run of bad results doesn't seem to have dampened any enthusiasm amongst the faithful and they are in full, optimistic voice.

The teams are on the field and, having finished their pre-match warm ups, have been called by the referee to half way.

"What's going on?" the guy in the chair beside me asks.

"Not sure," I shrug. "Looks like a minute silence for someone or other."

It *is* a minute silence. The Motherwell players now noticeably have black arm bands on and are standing faces lowered, all round the centre circle.

An elongated whistle, a dull scuffle as everyone rises to their feet, and the stadium goes silent..........

...............Phhheeeeeeeeeeeeeeeeeeeep.

Its over and a traditional, rousing cheer rises from the stands. With little fuss two Motherwell players are over the ball on the centre spot and the game, as they say, is aff!

I have a bit of a problem with minute silences. Nothing to do with the legitimacy of them. Just the way they are carried out. Take the one we've just witnessed. Maybe the home support knew who it was for but we were all left in the dark. Was it in memory of an ex-player, a director, the old kettle in the players' lounge? Who knows? Maybe there was some explanation in the programme, I'm not sure, but wouldn't it be nice and respectful if some form of recognition was announced over the public address system. Perhaps a short eulogy could be read telling us a little about the individual in question, paying tribute to their abilities and achievements when they were alive. That would be nice. It's also worth pointing out, while I'm on it, that I don't go to the football to stand in remembrance of natural disaster victims, murdered kids, deceased pontiffs and royals or any other desperate occurrence on a non-football theme. Its not that I'm heartless, far from it, its just that if we encompassed every terrible moment of human struggle into the minute before a footy match starts, we'd be on our feet forever.

The game as it turns out is as subdued as the weather. In fact its safe to say I've seen more exiting episodes of Weir's Way on the telly at four o-clock in the morning. Its so exciting I spend the mid section of the first half reading the match programme without any fear of missing the odd half-chance, or indeed having to look up at all.

Motherwell's match day programme is a small , hand sized publication sporting a Motherwell player on the front cover and the club colour scheme throughout its thirty or so pages .I start with the inside front page where squads of both teams are listed. I'm about to dismiss this page as I usually do, since normally these programme lists are printed at a much earlier date with no hint as to what the actual starting eleven will be. I stop though as I notice below that last week's starting line-ups of both teams are informatively noted underneath. One point to Mr Motherwellprogrammeman!

Ploughing deeply through the subsequent pages I am firstly drawn to an article called 'Supporters Slant'. It's a halfway gesture towards injecting some fan- opinion into the programme and I can't help longing, once again, for a letters page that would draw out the real, more interesting issues of the Scottish game. Next up comes a couple of historic pieces entitled 'Well Remembered' and 'Those were the days'. The former is an extensive reminisce of the last ten years or so of games between 'Well' and The Rovers in which Motherwell seem to have won them all . (Perhaps the article should be re-titled 'Well *Selectively* Remembered). In any case I ponder this page for a good while as I seem to be unable to remember any of the pre-1997 games mentioned. I must have had a stroke in my sleep around then. 'Those were the days' is a neat little piece on what the other teams currently in the Premier league were doing in a certain year, in this case 1969/70. It was interesting to note that Rangers beat Steaua Bucharest in that year's Cup winners Cup , Celtic got to the European Cup final , losing in the end to Feynoord, and Dunfermline beat Anderlecht in the Fairs Cup. Changed days indeed.

The most accomplished article though is the double page description of 'The Visitors'. Its good because it avoids reproducing a painfully dry list of Arthurston's player profiles. It reads, instead, as an interview with an unnamed fan. This is interesting for both home and away fans as the fan explains this season's highlights, aspirations for the future, views on who is playing well at the moment, how the manager is doing and an opinion of how the last match between the clubs went. Good stuff! The rest of the programme is made up of the usual player profiles, stats and the like. All in all a good read during a bad game.

It may not be the biggest programme out there but in terms of original, informative content it's definitely above average. On the down side Motherwell FC (get a catchy name for God's sake) is £2 to buy. *Again* the fan is being fleeced. If those Sunday newspapers can give you a pile of colour supplements, papers and magazines enough to break the paperboy's back, all for under a pound, football clubs should be able to do it too.

13.

"You're awfully quiet" comments Jonesy as we stand up for halftime. "Not sure which team to support?"

"Aye very good" I reply acidly. Sometimes I wish I had been a little less forthcoming with my friends in the past.

"Think we'll score?" he asks

"Yeh, I think we'll steal it one nil."

"On what basis do you say that." Injects Dave

"None whatsoever. Call it blind optimism."

"Blind optimism eh, the football fan's friend. What *would* we do without it?"

"Stay in bed, play golf, or go shopping." I smile.

"Indeed." agrees Dave with a blank expression on his face.

The game finishes nil-nil. Hardly a chance created by either side with the most riveting moment of the second half being a scuffle between Willie Burgoyne and a naïve young Motherwell wingback who foolishly dared to punch 'Cavey' off the ball. Willie then proceeded to shadow the lad round the pitch until his next touch at which point he sent the youngster into orbit with assassin-like accuracy.

"Go on Cavey. Kick him up the council gritter!" screamed the guy next to me, his right fist clenched in defiance. Everyone takes a little something different from their football it would appear.

For five minutes or so after that the crowd was in the game and there was a bit of bite in the tackle. The excitement soon fizzled out though as the game slipped into the mundane again. In the end they were rotten and we were possibly just a bit worse. So much for the optimism. Walking back to the car there is little to talk about in terms of game highlights.

"Who was your man of the match?" asks Jonesy enthusiastically.

"The ref had a pretty good game." suggests Dave sarcastically.

"No, *our* best player" pushes Jonesy seemingly oblivious to Dave's tone.

" Storrie had not a bad game if I had to choose but really they were all piss poor."

Like everyone around us we are scuttling along the pavement at a fair pace anxious to get shelter from the now drizzling rain.

"Well I think Jerry Kidd did well when he came on." Suggests Jonesy catching up after having fallen behind a few steps.

Dave makes a noise like he's hacking something out the back of his throat. "Kidd? He was only on for twenty minutes and he nearly cost us a goal when he got pushed off the ball at the corner flag , remember?"

"He did well considering its his first game back from injury." Says Jonesy defensively.

" Yeh, how is his injured pinkie-nail anyway?" Dave presses, "The man's feckless…….. feckless!"

"What do you think Craig." Jonesy looks over hopefully for backup. Dave's eyes flit sideways in my direction too.

211

"I thought Scott McLean did ok."

Both the guys tut and fall into silence.

"He played a captain's game today … " I continue but stop when I realise no one is listening to me. The rest of the march back to the car is in silence. By the time we get there we have gathered from the slightly sodden grapevine the rest of the day's results. The big news is that Hibs have won one-nil at Parkhead and Hearts have gone top of the league. There's only been seven games played so far but it's the closest there's been to a break in the Old Firm domination for long and weary. For the first time this year though, we are more intent on looking for the results of the teams below us. Partick Thistle have lost at Ibrox, Dundee United have only drawn and Motherwell were below us before today's draw anyway so by our quick reckoning we are still ninth out of twelve.

14.

Ninth out of twelve. Driving home, staring out from the rain battered windscreen I feel like I'm twelfth out of twelve. I'm in a league with eleven other 'average' guys trying hard to find their way in life and I'm dead last. Relegation is staring me in the face.

Heidi, Heidi, Heidi......

I usually play defensively, try and sneak the odd goal against the run of play. Today I threw caution to the wind. Attacked from the whistle. Except I couldn't put the ball in the net could I. Created a gilt edged chance right enough and the crowd appreciated my style but I didn't win the game. The points stayed at home. All I did was get people talking and pick up a couple of injuries for my effort.

The rain is driving down and I have a headache concentrating on the road. Is it normal to feel so guilty and uptight about life and the way I approach it? Bloody hell, is it normal to rationalise life in footballing terms like I just did. I doubt it - I doubt it very much.

There was nothing to that little encounter in the restaurant and yet I feel genuinely knocked off kilter. It never ends up being natural. That whole 'woman thing'. I say the wrong thing or don't say anything at all. I get all concerned about appropriate behaviour then feel too self- conscious to act appropriately in any case. Why can't I be normal?

Through the rain I see her eyes. They linger out there, staring in through the windscreen then fading into the gloom. Hiding for now but I know they'll be back. In the murkiness I see Dave and Linda standing in church, in tartan and white. Smiling. That image fades too giving way to Ray Stark, running to the fans, hands aloft, the ball nestled triumphantly in the net.

Then the wipers are back. In between their smooth rubber swipes, a blurry signpost says Arthurston 15 miles. All things seem too far off at the moment. Well out of reach.

What's the answer?

I just keep driving.

213

Chapter 9 Saints and Sinners

1.

Its been called the Skol Cup, the Coca-Cola Cup, the CIS Cup, and the year the SPL teams tried to improve the sponsorship deal, the Fred Worksop Lawn Mower and Mini-tractor Repairs Cup. But it will always be the League Cup to me.

Compared with the Scottish Cup, The League Cup has always been the worn guttied, half-mast trousered poor relation. Impossible for wee teams to win due to a ridiculously excessive seeding system, poo-pooed and discounted by the bigger teams (until of course they are in with a shout of winning it at which point it miraculously transforms itself into a valuable component of the football diary), the cup staggers on as a spectacle - but only just.

The competition starts early in the football year, usually late September, and unlike the grandiose Scottish Cup 3rd round draw which is live on TV or radio, you tend to only find out who your team has been drawn against via one of the inside sports pages of your favourite tabloid newspaper. One morning a few weeks back, over a bowl of bran flakes, I casually noticed we had been paired with St Mirren away. Not the best of draws. On the one hand the tie offers precious little in the way of financial benefit to The Rovers, on the other, it represents a damned fine chance of being booted out the tournament at its first hurdle.

St Mirren FC are one of those teams you see. Not quite good enough nowadays to feel entirely comfortable in the SPL but infinitely capable of taking the First Division by storm. Over the years they have flitted in and out of both leagues without really ever finding their true level and in doing so have created a well-worn, battle weary fan base experienced in all the highs and lows Scottish Football has to offer.

The days have galloped by since the draw and the game is upon us. The blandness of the Motherwell game is behind us as is a predictable two-nil defeat at home to Rangers where it was exciting to see the ground full for once but, unfortunately, we were never really in the hunt. It's now Tuesday night, the twenty fourth of September, a 7.45 kick off - we think. While the Daily Record and The Sun are in agreement that the game will start at quarter to eight, Ceefax and the Daily Express are controversially suggesting 7.30pm. We could do the sensible thing and call the stadium just to make sure, but that would be, well, too sensible. We will instead aim to arrive in Paisley well in advance, have a beer, and ask someone when we get there. Sounds like a plan.

2.

St Mirren Football Club.
Saint Mirren.
The Old S&M

Rattle it around in your mind. Ponder it. Say the name out loud even. Guaranteed it will start you wondering and eventually have you asking the burning question;

Who the hell was Saint Mirren and how come he got a football team named after him?

And it's easily answered.

Saint Mirren, Mirin, Merryn or even Merinus depending on who you talk to, was like most of your regular saints of the time – religious, devout, and prone to actions of extreme 'niceness'. He was a good friend of St Columba (they played cards together on the last Friday of each month) and was credited with bringing Christianity to the area in the sixth century. He liked the locale of Paisley so much that he decided to settle there explaining in early writings that ' .... its people are most welcoming, God's bounty from the land is plentiful and verily it is handy for the airport.' He founded Paisley Abbey on its present location and since it was his ba', he became its first Abbot spending all his days spreading the teachings of Jesus to the people and doing other 'monk things'. Revered by Catholics and Protestants alike (a rare feat in the Glasgow area for sure), Mirin lived and died in the abbey where he is still buried today. On Inch Murryn, the largest island on Loch Lomond he still has a chapel dedicated to him and in certain quarters is fully recognised as the Patron Saint of One Way Systems. With his name so intrinsically linked with this West of Glasgow town, Saint M is undoubtedly Mr Paisley

3.

St Mirren FC, nicknamed The 'Buddies' possibly due to the people of Paisley's love of 'The King of Beers, were originally formed as a cricket team and once again, like in Kilmarnock, valuable footy-time was wasted before the original players and officials smelled the Deep Heat and swapped their bats and wickets for studs and shin-pads.

The club were founder members of the Scottish League in 1890 along with ten other teams; Abercorn , Cambuslang, Celtic, Cowlairs, Dumbarton , Hearts , Rangers , Renton, Third Lanark and Vale of Leven. Their ground was named St Mirren Park although colloquially it soon became better known as Love Street in reference to the thoroughfare hidden sedately behind the East end of the ground

Throughout their history St Mirren have traditionally worn black and white strips. There are a number of interesting theories why this should be so and although none are conclusive in their assertions, they more than indicate that these colours were not simply chosen randomly from the wholesale sportswear brochure of the time.

There are three trains of thought as to the relevance of black and white to the town of Paisley. Firstly, and quite plausibly, comes the suggestion that the colour scheme was first sported by the Cluniac monks (named after ex player and manager Jim Cluney) who originally resided in the cloisters of Paisley Abbey and wore distinctive black and white robes. No surprise then that the town's representatives would find influence in these monks who historically played such a major role in the cultural development of Paisley.

Another theory refers to an annual charity football match between the sweeps and the bakers of the town. The black of the soot took on the white of the flour so it is told and out of this competition allegedly rose the combination of the two colours to form St Mirren's modern day attire.

Lastly comes the well held 'River Theory'. Paisley has long played host to the River Cart which runs through the town splitting into two as it goes. Once divided, it then continues on its way with one offshoot known as the Black Cart, the other called the White Cart.

A bit like the football version of eighties quiz programme 'Call My Bluff' really. One of the answers is bound to be right but which one? There's probably a little truth in all of them. Whatever the reasoning, the black and white stripes of St Mirren are as familiar and as constant as anything in Scottish Football and asides from one shocking 'bib' designed jersey from a few years back, always make for a classic and instantly recognisable strip design – kind of like Juventus if they'd 'let themselves go' a bit.

The early years saw Love Street as a tough, uncompromising venue to visit. In 1908 the stadium was closed for two weeks after a referee was pelted with ash and stones for disallowing a St Mirren goal for offside. In the same game, St Mirren's Willie Kay was sent off and suspended for a month after entering the crowd and striking a 'supporter' who had been verbally abusing him throughout the match. This scenario was to be repeated some nine years later when winger Higgenbottom (first name unknown but probably Walter, Frank or Arthur) also entered the crowd to chase an abusive fan. Higgenbottom was luckier than Kay in the punishment stakes though. Due to the war there was an extreme shortage of players and with every man being needed on a week to week basis, old Higgsy got off Scott-free. The records unfortunately don't give us any insightful clues as to whether St Mirren's fans were particularly intolerant at that time or if the players were touchier in those days, yet it seems unquestionable that Love Street was a powder-keg of fervour and excitement. Maybe behaviour like this should be tolerated a little more these days. Scottish football probably needs a few more chasings and supporter/player contretemps to pep up its dull moments. More people would show up that's for sure. Ok they would be the sort that slow down to get a better look at car crashes on the way by but their money's as good as anyone else's. (Unless of course they are counterfeiters as well as morbid-voyeurs I suppose.)

4.

Getting there is easy. From the elevated height of the M8 motorway you can comfortably make out the church spires and high rise flats of Paisley itself and taking the appropriately sign-posted turn off you simply head in their general direction and before you know it, St Mirren Park will be yours for the viewing.

Swinging round the slip road from the motorway, you pass on your left the grass public pitches of St James's park which will invariably be playing host to five or six feverish looking amateur games. On the way by you'll be unlucky if you don't witness either a well celebrated goal or a brutal molestation resulting in a full scale pitch battle. A word of warning though, you wont be the only one drawn by the on-field action so watch out for sudden swerves and veers by other motorists travelling in both directions. It's quite dangerous and really they should erect, somewhere in the vicinity, an adaptation of that road sign showing the back of the car with squiggly tyre tracks under the wheels, modified with the warning underneath 'Danger- Distracted football fans'.

Continue on a few hundred yards more and you bend into Greenock Road, a wide thoroughfare that leads you straight to the ground should that be your prime destination. Arrive early and you'll get to park by the pavement at either side of this road. Turn up late and you may need to squeeze yourself into a dusty looking industrial estate that lies off to the right of the main drag.

Because of this easy access to Love Street there is precious little reason to go anywhere near Paisley's town centre at all. No bad thing considering the complexity of the traffic system around that part of town. At first glance the area around the ground may not look like much but scratch its surface and it offers all a travel weary football fan could want and perhaps just a bit more.

5.

"Park there!" shouts Jonesy making both Dave and I jump in unison. We are half way down the Greenock Road and Jonesy has spotted a space on our left hand side. Not a tremendous achievement in fairness since there appears to be about a hundred yards of empty space further up the street anyway. We park up already knowing our game-plan for the next hour or so. This consists of a pint in The Cottage, a wander past the ground to pick up a programme then on to Alamo Bar for a read at said program and a couple more beers before retracing our steps back to the game. We know this will happen because it always happens. It's our Paisley ritual.

The Cottage is just about the closest pub to Love Street itself and isn't hard to find. Hang a left at the semi -derelict looking Golden City Chinese Carry Out, and walk 20 yards down Mossvale Lane and the completely non-cottage-like 'Cottage' appears on your left. It doesn't look terribly inviting from the outside and with a backdrop beyond it that wouldn't look out of place on the streets of Baghdad (post bombing), you could foster the belief that you're on the wrong track. Gird your loins though and push through the door to the lounge bar and you fall into a pleasant, friendly, wood beamed room that will offer you a nice pint, a square meal, and a swatch at Sky TV. There's a good chance you'll be in the company of a few of your own fans to boot.

Jonesy and I sit down on a rust-coloured cushioned bench at a table in the corner. Beside us a juke box that looks like its seen better days entertains the punters with a golden oldie Queen number. Dave is already at a small, hatch-like bar at the other side of room getting the beers in. He turns and shouts over asking if anyone wants crisps. There are three small red lamps mounted on the wall above his head and they are casting a ruby hue off Dave that makes him look faintly demonic. Thumbs up from both of us and the Devil gets on with his job.

Two things strike you when you cast your eye round the room; The number of blackboards on the wall shouting menu suggestions at you, and the vast array of special offers on the go.

One particularly large board with 'The Cottage Kitchen' hand-written boldly in coloured chalk tempts you with soup, a pint, and a sandwich for £4.95. This doesn't seem the best of deals I'm thinking, but without seeing the goods its hard to say. The pensioners deal on the other wall makes better reading. A 'half and a half', soup and a sandwich (with garnish!) - £3.95. It pays to be old if only for the garnish.

"Look," says Jonesy pointing at the wall beside the door, "If you purchase a drink on a Tuesday you get a free Sausage Hot Pot! I could go some of that"

"Are you serious?" I ask, "You only had dinner an hour or so ago."

"Not really, I suppose." Jonesy sounds disappointed. It just sounds quite good"

Dave appears with the drinks and slides the glasses carefully on to the table. "Anyone fancy a Sausage Hot Pot?" he says cheerily.

"Jonesy was just saying. I think I'll pass."

"Do you remember they used to do roast potatoes in here. " Dave continues, ripping open a bag of Prawn Cocktail.

We must have stared dumbly at him.

"Yeh?" he coaxes, "Remember. You used to get a complimentary basket of roast potatoes. In a dish."

"In a dish?" says Jonesy

"In a Pyrex dish." Dave reinforces. "They didn't used to serve proper food then so they gave you some free tatties to snack on."

Jonesy and I look at each other and shrug.

"They did I swear! Tatties in a dish!"

"In a *dish*?" I ask

"In a ...." But he breaks off. "Are you guys taking the piss out of me?"

"I don't remember getting Roast Potatoes Dave," I smile. Jonesy is shaking his head beside me, "but if you say so, I believe you."

"I'm not asking you to believe me. I'm not making this up I tell you. The place must've changed hands or something." He mutters the last part barely audibly and crams a handful of crisps into his mouth crunching them manfully.

"So!" I exclaim turning to Jonesy in an effort to ignite some sensible direction back into the conversation, " Are you prepared to tell us anything about this mysterious job offer yet?"

Jonesy looks at me, then Dave, then back at me again. A flicker of uncertainty passes over his face which then makes way for an excited looking grin.

"OK boys, hang on to your hats ...."

We lean forward in our seats.

"... I'm going to be a window cleaner!"

We lean back in our seats. There's a momentary silence with Jonesy nodding and smiling expectantly while we digest the information.

"What .... like washing windows and stuff?" Dave asks frowning

"No Dave, like giving enemas to small dogs." replies Jonesy sourly." Of course washing windows."

He sits back and takes a drink expectantly, obviously waiting for the barrage of questions.

"So how did this all come about then? I ask tentatively.

"Well you know my Uncle Len?"

"What BIG Uncle Len?" says Dave grabbing his belly and shaking it about.

"Uh huh" Jonesy continues, " He's selling his business and he asked me if I wanted to buy it. It's a right good earner you know. I could make a packet out of this."

"If its so good why is your Uncle Len selling?" asks Dave

"Well, between you and me ,"starts Jonesy smirking, "Uncle Len has gotten too fat to get up the ladder. He went to his doctor who told him he was a heart-attack waiting to happen. Instead of slimming down a bit like he was told to, he's decided to chuck any unnecessary physical exertion. Says he's happy to concentrate on other opportunities."

"Like being a product tester at McDonalds." Dave suggests.

"Don't laugh. Uncle Len could buy a McDonalds branch outright if he wanted. You want to see the big Merc that he drives. Honestly guys, buying his run could be like inheriting a gold mine."

"How much did you pay for it if you don't mind me asking " I inquire.

" Nah, no problem. I'm paying fifteen hundred quid. For that I get his van, two sets of ladders a whole load of buckets, cloths and those window-wiper things." He moves his left hand in an up and down then left to right motion as if to demonstrate his 'squeegee' technique.

"And…." he continues suggesting the best is yet to come, "I get a bank of about a hundred and fifty customers as well. Just as a starter. But I can see that growing, once the locals see what a good job I'm doing."

We talk these revelations over and bounce some ideas around until Jonesy's as high as a kite and the bottom of our glasses tell us that its time to move on. Grabbing our jackets we pull ourselves together, aim for the door and disappear into the dusky evening outside.

6.

Back on the Greenock Road we head in the direction of Love Street itself. We stroll past a three storey house on our left that must be in line for The Munsters Tribute Of The Year Award. All that's missing are silhouetted bats flying out of its top floor window. Next we sneak a glance into The Caledonia Bowling Club hiding from the world like a Secret Garden behind a five foot high, bristling green hedge. I imagine, lying over this leafy divide, is a world apart from its steely grey surroundings. A world of polite exclamations, the soft clunking of bowls on a Jack and the sipping of Pimms in the sunshine, if such a thing is possible in Paisley (the Pimms not the sunshine). Strangely, we only just noticed the bowling green on our last visit here and that was only because Jonesy fell sideways through the obviously invisible gate after a friendly, laddish jostle with Dave. Twenty odd years of tunnel vision prove the point perfectly that sometimes we look but we don't see.

Then, as if trying to give us a fright, St Mirren Park jumps out from behind a petrol station. A little diagonal slip road leads to a set of gates and beyond these guardians rise the old and the new structures of the football ground on Love Street.

We stop to buy a programme from a sullen track-suited youth who finds eye contact impossible and whose only communication is to grunt 'Tooopown' after handing over his ware. Then it's off again continuing on in the same direction. Past a little clutch of shops and a park on our left. Then a hop across the road and we're skirting along the edge of nondescript buildings, housing amongst other predicable establishments 'Bonars Caladonia Bar' and the 'Stanley's Bet' bookies. Onwards and upwards though and a few sprightly steps further on and we are at the door of one of the most interesting pubs in Glasgow – The Alamo Bar .

7.

'Remember the Alamo!' the saying goes. Once you've been in this pub I assure you, you're not likely to ever forget it.

Its like stepping into someone else's dream.

The first thing that hits you (thankfully not literally) is the low ceiling covered with flags. It is an imposing sky of red, white and blue stars, stripes and saltires that yell out rebelliously in remembrance of Civil War, independence and American fighting bravery. Either that or the owner is really into The Dukes of Hazzard.

The next most obvious feature is the prominent sign behind the lager taps above the cash register warning ' Cowboys leave your guns at the bar!'. To accommodate this sentiment a couple of large leather holsters are nailed to the wall awaiting any 'shooters' checked in by patrons 'not wantin' no trouble'.

Dave is grinning his first grin in ages and asks what we're wanting.

I feel like asking for a glass of Sasperilli and some water for my horse but I settle for a pint of lager shandy. Jonesy orders another 'proper pint' as does Dave. The beers are poured by the barman who sets them up on the bar in front of us.

"That'll be four dollars ninety five gents" he requests cheerfully.

"Cheers." says Dave handing over the next best thing – a crinkled fiver, notably British.

We each grab or own pint and mosey over to the corner nearest the door. Taking the weight off our feet we sink into benches around a small shoogly table leaving a singular, out of place, white plastic garden seat unused.

"Is that the Lone Deckchair?" asks Jonesy dissolving into fits of laughter at his own joke. The many eyes of John Wayne bare down on him from various points on the wall and seem to say 'The hell you will make a joke of this saloon' and, as if suddenly aware of his sacrilege, Jonesy quickly quietens down.

While Dave buries his head in the programme I cant help but continue to look around. Towards the back of the pub I can just make out a dart board. I'm ready to make a comment about having a game of arrows but decide against it. As if to mock my thoughts The Alamo offers me a glimpse of an authentic leather quiver of arrows hanging, again, on the busy wall behind the bar. It taunts me with the thought of punters standing at the 'oche' aiming at the board with gritted teeth, straining on the bow. I bet they've tried it.

On the wall beside me is a framed parchment proclaiming 'Heroes of The Alamo 1836'. The document lists some two hundred or so names of men who presumably lost their lives in that famous battle against the Mexicans. For one fleeting moment though, it occurs to me that this may be a list of punters who perished in the *pub* itself. A glance at the small print at the bottom of the list indicates, however, that the information was supplied by The Daughters of The Republic of Texas and unless these women were a splinter faction of The Paisley Parish Women's Guild then its safe to assume that we're talking about the original battle here.

Just when I'm settling in to the whole western feel of the place I notice we are sitting in a little corner shrine. On the walls, above and around us are framed tributes to the father of the Wild West. Custer's right hand man. Cowboy Number One. The one and only......

Robert Burns.

I must have looked noticeably confused because Dave leans over and says "Yeh , I know. Doesn't exactly fit in does it"

Etched on the wall, by way of explanation, is a proclamation that The Alamo Burns Club was established in 1972 with W. Williamson its proud Honorary President. Again strange visions barge into my mind, the most vivid being of a number of upstanding gentlemen grouped round a honkey- tonk piano singing 'Ae Fond Kiss, then toasting The Immortal Memory with a shot of Jack Daniels.

Jonesy has disappeared to the bog and Dave has returned to his program. A large ginger cat appears in the doorway and one of the bar-flies nods his head to the barman muttering "Therrr its therrr." The cat then proceeds to jump onto the bar and walk along its length, weaving in and out of the beer taps and pint glasses in its way. The bar-flies don't bat an eyelid and not a drop of beer is spilled as the cat makes it to the other end dropping out of sight behind the last leaning man who is supping on his pint and gazing into oblivion.

Jonesy sits back down. I decide not to mention the cat.

"Right then Jonesy, " I start enthusiastically, "Give us a couple of interesting facts about St Mirren ."

"What like?"

"No idea. Something unusual that maybe we don't know. You know- *your* type of stuff"

"Emmm. Ok - Did you know that in 1966 St Mirren were the first team in Scotland to use an official substitute?"

"I knew that." says Dave impassively without looking up.

"OK who was it then?" asks Jonesy slightly irked.

"Archie Gemmill." Replies Dave still not taking his eyes of the program in front of him.

"Against who?

"Clyde"

Looking at me Jonesy whispers "Smart-arse." in a barely audible tone then continues on challengingly.

"Well did you know that back in the 1920's St Mirren opened Barcelona's new stadium." There's no answer from Dave and Jonesy looks triumphant.

"What, the Noucamp?" I ask.

"Naw before that. It was called the Estadio Les Cortes – Barcelona played there until the late fifties before moving to the bigger Nou Camp.

" St Mirren in Spain?" I reply speculatively. "How did that come about then?"

"Well, apparently Barcelona were desperate to get St Johnstone over for the grand opening but someone in Admin. fouled up ."

"Really?" I ask.

"Em, no," continues Jonesy smirking. "I just made that bit up. I don't know why they played that game." Looking at me keenly he rattles his empty pint glass on the table suggestively.

"Another beer Jonesy?"

"Oh, don't mind if I do Craig."

"Dave?"

"Yeh go on. I'll come with you. I'm going to the toilet."

I make it back to the now well populated bar and Dave heads off in the direction of the shunky.

The barman is flitting around feverishly pouring pints and squeezing shorts from the optics on the wall. A new feature presents itself. Hanging up there beside the first holster is, quite bizarrely, a pair of blue edible knickers with 'Scotland' written on the waistband. In my mind I'm weaving an explanation for the palatable pants when a voice from beside me attracts my attention.

"Aye its busy in here tonight!" says a slight man wearing a Scotrail uniform and grasping a newspaper under his arm.

"Yup, probably because of the game." I answer politely.

"There's a game on is there?" the man raises an eyebrow," Whose playin'?"

"Arthurson Rovers and St Mirren - League Cup tie" I add.

"Ahh," says the railwayman nodding knowledgeably. "I'm a hoarses man masel'. The Sport of Kings it is. I used to catch the odd game along the road there but its too expensive now. Much better to get a wee bet on at the bookies there and nip back here for a drink and watch the race on the telly." His eyes flit in the direction of the mounted portable beside the door. "Mind you that's if the racin' is on. Half the time he's showin' bloody Cowboys an' Indians films up there."

I laugh. "It's some place isn't it. The owner must be right into America to have collected all this stuff."

My new-found companion cocks his head and looks confused.

"You know I don't think he's ever been."

I just look at him and say nothing.

"I think he's been to Spain though." He adds helpfully.

Just as an uneasy silence envelopes us a young Eastern looking guy sidles up to us and pulls a handful of DVDs from a big black bag at his side.

"New films eh?" he asks in a heavy accent waving some blockbusters I know are still running in the cinemas.

"Naw thanks mate." answers my new friend trying to catch the barman's attention and failing.

"Wait!" exclaims the boy with a furtive look in his eye. "From my Secret Bag!" and he delves down a side compartment returning with a selection of dodgy looking porno DVDs with pictures of what you might call 'supple' looking women on the front.

"No thanks" we both say uncomfortably in unison.

The boy shrugs and moves off to another part of the pub.

"He's from Singapore or Taiwan or something. The Regulars have got him sussed." winks the train man," When he came in at first he was wanting all sorts of prices for those things. They've got him beaten down to three pounds a go now. I've bought a couple maself, for the weans ye know."

"Oh are you not a regular then. I thought by the way you were talking...."

"Naw son I'm probably only in here.... whit .....two or three times a week."

"Oh right." I nod my head in a concerned manner.

I'm just about to ask what constitutes a regular in here when the barman's voice rings in my ear. "Yes sir. What can I get you?"

The round comes to only three dollars eighty-five this time as I am back on the Irn Bru. When I get back to the table Dave has returned and Jonesy s looking pleased with himself.

"Look what I got!" he says excitedly handing over two DVDS in see-through plastic sleeves. "Five pounds each what do you think?"

"An absolute bargain mate. " I agree sipping some of the sugary sweet orange coloured liquid from my glass. Dave grunts takes one final squint at the match program, returns to the land of the living and chucks it over the table and onto my waiting lap.

Its my turn to lose myself for a while. I can hear Dave and Jonesy babbling away in the background as well as the constant drone of the others in the room but my focus is on the black and white covered 'Saints' offishell program. Two pounds again. I don't care what is in it, it's a total rip off. And reading through its glossy pages it does nothing to alter my opinion of this. It ticks all the usual boxes in unspectacular fashion with the only real point of interest being an article called Collectors Corner spotlighting rare match programmes with a Paisley slant whilst encompassing some local nostalgia along the way. There are more adverts in here than a commercial break on Sky TV and I have to mention that the printers have won the record for 'Most Number

Of Different Typing Fonts In The One Publication'. Style, alas, is not a friend of the 'Saints' match programme. Which is a shame really because I remember in my early days of going to the games how good the St Mirren programme always was. While others were weedy, homemade affairs, theirs was a standout. Thick and glossy, chock full of information, topical articles and big colourful action-focussed photos.

Which also gets me thinking. In the middle pages I'm treated to five 'action' photos from the previous game which take up the whole spread. Really what is the point? The only entertainment to be gained from these images is having a chuckle at the silly poses and contorted expressions of the unlucky players featured. The guys in question must cringe when they see themselves photographed with the posture of the elephant man and the facial beauty of Peter Beardsley getting a chest-wax. All in all disappointing stuff. A mere 3 out of ten if I was a teacher with a red pen.

When I come round Dave has established that it is a 7.45 kick off which is just as well since its half past seven now. Collecting our things and taking one more fond look round The Wild Country we dispatch our empty glasses on the bar and head for the game.

8.

Walking up the first flight of stairs slapped onto the side of the away stand you find yourself on a half-landing that gives you an excellent panoramic view of Love Street. Jonesy and Dave have been caught up in the turnstile queue below giving me a quiet moment of recollection.

There are many St Mirren related memories and circumstances that spring to mind. Moments in history that define the club and fuel the faith of it's supporters.

Of course they won the Scottish Cup didn't they. That's the big one for me. In 1987, beating Dundee United one nil. I watched on the telly as Iain Ferguson smashed the ball into the 'Rangers end' goal at Hampden for the only goal that day winning himself an £850,000 transfer to the Ibrox club for his bother. I cheered for them because they were the underdog and it was their turn. A quick glance at the trusty Evening Times 'Wee Red Book' shows they won it twice before in '26 and '59 but lets live in our world shall we.

They signed Thomas Stickroth from Bayer Uerdigan on the back of that Ferguson transfer fee. St Mirren paid £400,000 for the German George Michael look-alike which struck me at the time as being a *huuuuge* amount of money for a team like The Saints to shell out on one player. However with his European style of play (only trying every third game) and his exemplary knowledge of hair products, it was probably money well spent.

Then there were the forays into Europe. As a club you never felt they had the resources to take Europe by storm but in the years between 1980 and 1986 St Mirren became regular standard bearers for Scotland notching up good wins over the likes of Elfsbourg (Situated 10 miles due East of Dwarfsville) and Slavia Prague in the UEFA Cup as well as Tromso in the Cup Winners Cup. Bizarrely the big debate around that time seemed not to be whether St Mirren could win a European trophy but whether the club should be known as *Paisley* St Mirren for the trips over the water - just in case, presumably, any semi-deranged foreign tourists could be duped into holidaying in the rural splendour of this attractive but previously unknown Scottish hamlet.

No disrespect to Rangers and Celtic but I've always found it that little bit more compelling following the fortunes of the smaller Scottish teams in Europe. Although St Mirren's efforts at European supremacy were short-lived, they were romantic and intriguing in a way that the Old Firm could never emulate. The prospect that the Buddies were possibly only one game away from playing a Barcelona or a Manchester United at Love Street was an enthralling one. And if it was enthralling for me goodness knows how dribblingly spellbinding the thought was for St Mirren fans themselves.

Taking things back a bit further I remember St Mirren winning the Anglo Scottish Cup, making them the only Scottish team to do it in its eleven years existence. Previously the Texaco Cup, the 'Anglo' was competed for by the top English and Scottish clubs who had not qualified for Europe (In its Texaco days, Irish clubs also participated) It also gave rival Scottish and English fans an opportunity to batter lumps each other on midweek forays up and down the country. The travelling punters seemed to enjoy the experience and asides from the jovial thuggery, the lure of eating fish and chips at two in the morning in a soulless motorway service station was too good to pass up.

I'm very clear on St Mirren's Anglo-Scottish exploits of 1980. They beat Hibs, Bolton and Sheffield Utd on the way to the final. And the reason I know this is because I'm an all-recollecting oracle to Scottish Football facts and figures. Except of course I'm not. The only reason this sticks in my mind is thanks to three weeks sick in bed, off school with a very bad case of Mumps (surely there must be a more technical term for this disease?). Confined to bed with a raging temperature and a fatter face than Alfred Hitchcock blowing up party balloons, I was going off my head with the boredom of my enforced captivity, matters made all the worse by having to miss TWO Arthurston home games due to my incapacity. The only thing that kept me going was the newspapers. I remember sitting up in bed, drinking endless cups of tea with toast crumbs in my pyjamas, pouring over the back pages of the assorted daily tabloids brought in every day by my dad. St Mirren beat Bristol Rovers 5-1 over two legs to lift the coveted cup which, by the look of it, had all the appearance of a proper trophy that got shrunk in the wash. I distinctly recall reading the score-line whilst eating some soothing ice-cream for my throat and shouting 'HA HA!' out loud, catapulting a dollop of Raspberry Ripple the length of my bedroom in excitement. It was my first real demonstration of anti-English footballing bias (something I still treasure to this day) and it also marked a watershed in my dealings with the Mumps as a life-threatening ailment. My mother heard the furore, popped her head round my door and diagnosed me in a few short acidic words as being "clearly on the mend." The sore throat, the walrus face and the sympathy it had so graciously afforded me was over.

9.

As I continue to gaze over the park with a mild grin on my face I see brief but enduring snapshots of the St Mirren I have grown up with. Flashed images of Frank McGarvey's moaning face, the seemingly ever-present moustache of Tony Fitzpatrick, the slightly unfathomable but nonetheless exciting appearances of Victor Munoz, Spanish World Cup captain in a St Mirren jersey. Frank McAvennie's hair and teeth.

But perhaps my most vivid St Mirren related memory came at an unlikely location. It was early May 1998 and I was sitting in the 'new' Trinity Road Stand behind the goals at Glebe Park, Brechin. Bored rigid with the typical end of season, 'nothing at stake' brand of football being played out in front of me, I was reclining, feet up on the plastic seat in front of me almost willing a steward to challenge me to sit properly. A small hand sized radio was welded to my ear bringing me Radio Scotland's version of the day's footy goings on and the sparse antics of a donkey, which from this angle looked to be tethered to the back of the tiddly 'main' stand to my right, had taken up more of my attention than the drab second half could ever have hoped to.

So what has all this to do with St Mirren then? Well it was like this; St Mirren were at that very moment playing Stirling Albion at Forthbank Stadium. Defeat for the Buddies would have meant relegation to the second division and in view of the financial plight of the club (there's nothing new under the sun is there?) the black clouds of bankruptcy would have drifted in the direction of the sky above Love Street. Numerous reports came in that it was 'still nil- nil at Forthbank' and that it was 'not good enough for St Mirren.' I doubt the implication of that result was lost on anyone that day and I genuinely felt sorry for their plight.

Then it came. "And we'll go to Forthbank where there's been a goal.!" the radio said sensationally. I was excited. - God knows how any absent St Mirren fan must have felt waiting for confirmation of which team had actually scored. The connection flipped from the studio to Stirling and the sounds of ecstatic fans indicated that there had indeed been a goal. The reporter teased it a bit before announcing that St Mirren had dramatically taken the lead 'with only moments to go'. In stark contrast to my surroundings it was drama off the scale.

"St Mirren have scored" I remember relaying to Dave enthusiastically. "Oh yeh?" he replied carelessly, " that's nothing, the donkey over there just had a crap."

One man's wine is another's old crushed grapes evidently.

But it is amazing how clear these memories are to me, even though they shouldn't by rights mean a great deal. I even remember the scorer of the goal that day. A long time ago, all those miles away, under the gaze of Stirling Castle and the Wallace Monument. It was Hugh Murray. The goal was scored by Hugh Murray. The most important single action in St Mirren's long history. Quite possibly. Until of course the next time.

Yup, flashbacks of instances that define a club. Every one a stand out and as I rest against the railing and look out on to the Love Street turf one more iconic image of St Mirren Football Club comes into mind vision. This one though is different. It is more vivid than all that has gone before. It is what we all have come to know and expect of from our visits to this ground.

It is a man in a furry suit.

It is the Paisley Panda!

10.

Let's get things straight. I'm not big on the whole furry animal, jaunty character, mascot thing. At best this pseudo-Americanised razzmatazz is completely un-entertaining and totally inappropriate to our game. At worst its downright embarrassing for the team involved, their red-necked fans who are forced into looking the other way, and the poor bastard in the suit who is only on to a free program and a pie and can probably smell his own feet.

Just as an aside, what makes a grown man want to do something like that anyway? After all, the ability to plod around, waving inanely whilst wearing a big animal parka is scarcely something to be proud of, nor some great yarn to pass on to a keen eyed son.

"Tell me about your football days Dad, you were a player weren't you."

"No son. It was better than that. I was a big bunny called Tumshie and I wore a tammy and a strip that would have been too big for Pavarotti - If I hadn't married your mother I could have been Broxy Bear you know."

The lad's eyes widen and the inevitable question asked by countless generations of young wannabees arises.

"Dad when can I get my first pair of big furry feet?"

And yet Scottish football seems intent on foisting these oversized mugs on us at every opportunity. We've already seen the squirrel at Kilmarnock this year, Dundee United had a rather offensive lion on the go that gave us the fingers when we were at Tannadice last year in the League cup, Hamilton had that big 'It's a Knockout' Tweedle Dum look-a-like called Fergie and Celtic had, for a while, that annoying Jack in The Box character with the pale complexion, balding head and glasses jumping around the touchline, arms waving madly every time Celtic scored. No! - None of these fantasy creatures have any place in our game and should be sent packing ASAP.

Except one; Our friend the Panda.

In the land of furry oversized feet, the black eyed bear is king. Or at least he used to be. Like so many great artists before him the original Paisley Panda, AKA 24 year old sales rep Chris Kelso, was cruelly taken from us before his time, a victim of the oppressive, intolerant powers at be.

The panda did things differently and it was frowned upon. Where the other mascots were happy to insipidly slope around on the park before the match, waving limply at no-one in particular, the panda spent his allotted time more productively, making sure the players and supporters of the opposition were wound up in a magnificently irreverent manner.

Pilloried for mimicking the countryside 'tastes' of Queen of The South fans with the aid of a blow up sheep, vilified for shaking a large Magic Tree air-freshner at whiffy Morton fans, officially censured for using a Morton team sheet as toilet paper in front of the same irate fans, the panda provoked shamefully, or entertained magnificently, depending on how seriously you tended to view life.

Few could remain straight faced though when the panda turned up against Partick Thistle lugging a huge canvass hold-all onto the park. Initially perplexed, the crowd erupted when out from the bag popped a little mini panda who proceeded to accompany its 'dad' in a Ali-G style, booming hi-tempo dance number.

Arthurston keeper Andy Thomson had a torrid time for a while too. The mascot would always meander over during the pre-match warm-up and offer to shake Andy by the hand. Andy, who to be honest isn't the sharpest tool in the box, fell for it every time offering a big goalie- glove back only for the panda to pull away at the last minute. This happened again and again over a number of matches without Thomson ever learning. God bless him. It was slapstick humour the likes of which Harold Lloyd would have been proud of.

However there's a saying that drifts out of Stirlingshire on the wind - 'Never rib a Bairn (cos they cannae take it) .' A fact Chris Kelso would have done well to have observed. When the panda repeated his bottom wiping stunt against Falkirk, this time with a stolen training top, the natives got restless (ken!).Throw into the mix a dig at The Bairn's not having a stadium at that time and it was too much for certain individuals amidst the Falkirk faithful. Complaints were made, to the cops no less (I would have loved to hear that conversation) and once again Scottish football was shown up as being run, watched and policed by small minded, petty people prone to over-reaction. Kelso was threatened with 'Breach of the Peace (the charge made when the cops can't think of anything else to 'do' you for) and was sacked by St Mirren shortly after.

The panda lives on with a more tempered replacement under the fur but its just not the same. We are Elvis fans being forced to listen to Shakin' Stevens, beer drinkers being offered Calibre lager. Match of the Day fans asked to watch Scotsport.

It's not the same, it doesn't wash and he shall be missed.

11.

Love Street has an all-seated capacity of 10,800. The old main South Stand remains the focal point of the stadium striped in black, white and red like a zebra with a heat-rash. Its not a big building and actually takes up only half the length of the touch-line leaving two untidy corners of nothingness at either side. Directly facing the South Stand sits, quite remarkably, the North Stand. This shallow, seated section houses the noisier, more animated of the home fans and if there is any singing to be done, or baiting of the away fans, the people in here have the pedigree to do it.

And so to the West Stand, the designated away end of the ground. While once again the away fans have been fobbed off with a limited, behind-the-goals view of the match, this time there is a whole new issue to contend with – namely the stand's horrifying, vertigo inducing steepness. Except steep is an understatement. If you want a pie you need crampons and a good set of ropes to make the assault to the shop, and I'll swear that it's the only seated area in Scottish football where the stewards have been replaced with sherpas. The poor sods who end up sitting in the front row, or 'Base Camp' as it is known, don't get out of the ground for a good hour after the final whistle and when they do they emerge sweat stained and red faced with ragged fingernails and pulled muscles. They should get a loan of that expensive chair-lift from the ski slope in Aviemore and install it here. Let's face it, it would get more use.

The joker at the council who gave St Mirren planning permission for this 'accident waiting to happen' must surely be locked up by now wearing a vest with no arm holes or alternatively has been handed a well earned transfer to Accounts. It is only a matter of time before someone rolls down those precipitous stairs like a Bovril wielding Easter egg shouting 'if there's blame there's a claim!' as they go. The whole sorry mess will end in tears mark my words.

But it's not just the dizzy, sickly feeling you get looking down from the upper gantry that is the problem. That's only half the story. The view you get from your seat is weird as well. Any depth perception of what is happening on the pitch is instantly lost as soon as you sit down and away fans constantly 'ooh' and 'aah' as their striker hashes a shot nearer to the corner flag than the goal then stare numbly as the next perfectly met shot flies into the net. And what about the action at the other end of the ground? Well you can just forget that. You'd be better off tuning in to Radio Scotland for updates on what's going on up there rather than giving yourself a level of eye strain not experienced since the Christmas Island Nuclear Explosion Tests.

So why if its so awkward and unpleasant do we negotiate the perils of the West Stand at Love Street. I say the same thing time and time again to those who understand and those who don't.

We do it because its there.

12.

For how much longer though? The answer sadly is not long at all. By next year the club will have completed the sale of the old ground and will move on to pastures new, a custom built stadium on Greenhill Road in nearby Ferguslie Park to be exact. St Mirren, like many other clubs in Scotland have shed-loads of debt that past and present custodians have failed to keep in check. Because, like other similar old Scottish grounds, the Love Street property sits on prime land and is worth money, the temptation to sell is great, especially among the less prudent and astute of planners.

Stadium selling is an unhappy trend that has crept into our modern game. It is an option that gives the speculative new director a 'can't lose' scenario when weighing up whether to get involved in a club in the first place. Further, it offers the existing custodian a safety net to drop themselves onto, a 'Get Out Of Jail Free Card' if you will that negates some if not all of the honking financial ineptitudes of the past in, hopefully, one fell swoop.

Property developers and supermarket chains hover like vultures high above stadiums like Love Street knowing that soon, inevitably, there will be one boardroom arse-up too far, one more unaffordable wage approval that tips the scale, one other 'speculate to accumulate' gamble that of course doesn't pay off and then its CHAAACHINGG! the board will take the easy way out and the 'complex' business strategy of selling the family silver will prevail. After all even a football club director is capable of clasping a pen in his sweaty mit and signing on a dotted line.

And on the face of it, all's well that ends well. The houses get built, the supermarket appears (giving us what the Marketeers tell us we strive for– 'Choice') and the club becomes solvent again. Everyone wins.

Except they don't. The loyal supporter loses big time. They have turned up season after season, through thick and thin at grounds like Love Street and Tynecastle, Brockville and Broomfield, Douglas and Muirton, and revelled in doing so. The ground is as much part of the club, THEIR club, as the strips, the players and the name on the badge . It's an old friend, a favourite uncle, a prized possession that they love to see, are proud to be associated with and have fond, long-standing memories of. To deprive the fans of their historic homeland, as it were, for the sake of a better bank balance and a sounder conscience is nothing short of scandalous and if businesspeople involved with the likes of St Mirren, Hearts, Aberdeen and others with a sneaky hankering for a quick 'asset-strip' want to come round to my house, I'll sit them down and wag a finger at them. I can talk tough when I want to.

I am a traditionalist and if I was in charge I would preserve the spiritual home of my club at all costs. I would always turn the lights off, save '20p off your next player purchase' coupons, enter lots of competitions (my statutory rights being unaffected) and place long, stuffed fabric snakes along the bottom of all the doors. Keeps the drafts out *and* the heating bills down so my mother tells me.

It may not be the easy way and some of the time things might not look or feel all that pretty but at least at the end of the day your trusty old home ground will be there for you. You'll always be able to pull up your favourite chair , burn the tip of your tongue on that first sip of Bovril, and enjoy the show. Excuse me but I can't go on , I've gone all tearful.

13.

From the moment we walked on the park we looked worried. Last year we won both league games at Love Street in confident, free-flowing style. Tonight, though, is different. St Mirren have a point to prove and we are six games without a win.

The team looks too familiar as it lines up for the off. Paul Marker and Jerry Kidd are the full backs (much to Dave's disgust). John Storrie and Robert Crush are our central defenders. The former looks older than I remember the latter more ungainly, standing as he is in what looks like his son's shorts they're so tight.

The arm-banded McLean is in midfield, and beside him, Ally Fairful is the one change from our previous game, replacing Mark Bird for no apparent reason. Tony Bunton is there also, sporting an even shorter hair cut than usual, prompting Jonesy to comment that he 'looks like Roy Keane on Death Row'. Hedge on the right, Stark through the middle and an impossibly tanned and shiny Dinsmore hanging left. All set and ready to go.

Rovers are in their all red away strip, St Mirren - the traditional black and white stripes. The game kicks off to an encouraging cheer from both sets of fans and the ball is immediately howfed straight out the park by Ally Fairful. Not a good omen.

The first ten minutes pass uneventfully, both teams shaping up to each other like suspicious prize-fighters watching for any sudden movements. The Rovers then prove not to have been watching too hard as Kidd, under no pressure, loses the ball wide right and suddenly our flesh is exposed. Our whole team seems to have been caught up the park and its three stripes on two reds. A clever ball is slipped between Storrie and Crush, the keeper comes crashing out reaching the penalty spot before diving at the onrushing forward's feet. The ball is deftly chipped into the air and time stops. The angle is confusing and at first it looks like the ball is heading over. In slow motion though it falls to earth catching the inside left of the net and nestling itself in the corner of the goals down below us. Dave holds his head in his hands as the St Mirren players head off to our left to celebrate in front of their delirious fans.

"Kidd again!" Dave shouts with venom turning to Jonesy like it was his fault. Jonesy says nothing and I choose to look away at the other faces around me. Some are shaking their heads, others are mouthing assorted unpleasantries (I never knew I could lip-read until I started going to the football), most though are just staring dispassionately in front of them, seemingly immune to the circumstances surrounding them.

The game kicks off again with a few limp cheers of 'Come on the Rovers!' but in general there's little in the way of enthusiasm around us. McLean gets a bit of space in midfield and sprays the ball out to Dinsmore wide left.

"That's more like it!" cries someone behind me.

Dinsmore traps the ball skilfully and drives into the space in front of him. He's met by the St Mirren right back at the edge of the box and is forced inside. His pace is good however and he finds a yard to get off a low rifled shot across the goal. The ball slips narrowly wide and a unified 'oooooaahhhh' rises from our end of the ground. Applause all round makes way for a rousing chant. The crowd are alive.

St Mirren seem rattled and give the ball away needlessly in the middle of the park. McLean and Bunton combine well with a series of short passes before Bunton himself wriggles free at the edge of the box and sends a looping curler towards the keeper's left hand upright. The keeper dives but is nowhere. We're already on our feet but the ball pings off the bar flies into the air and falls onto the track behind the goals. Feverish applause this time with almost all the away fans singing 'Come on you Rovers!' loudly and fervently.

Its all Arthurston now but St Mirren are hanging on resolutely. Somewhere high above us thunder rumbles ominously and as I look up I'm surprised to see the clear night sky has been hijacked by heavy brown tinged clouds. The game has become compelling. Every pass is finding its man and the Rovers seem to have a couple of extra men on the pitch. Crush wins a biting challenge and carries the ball over half way. He slips the ball through to the rakish Ray Stark who shields the ball with his back to a beast of a defender who looks like he could blow him away without even trying. A swerve of his boney hips though and Stark slips off to his left taking the hulking defender with him. Dinsmore cuts in the opposite direction heading for the far post obviously looking for a reverse ball. But it never comes. Stark is flattened by a clumsy challenge and the referee immediately blows for a foul. Dinsmore looks skyward while Stark looks at the ground, from close quarters. The fans are outraged, upstanding and pointing in a threatening manner.

"This is a chance" says Jonesy . "Five minutes to half-time , a good time to score!"

Like there isn't a good time to score.

Dinsmore and Bunton are over the ball, the wall of players in front of them is being furiously marshalled by an agitated looking keeper.

"Go on Tony have a go" yells Dave so loudly into my ear that he gives me a fright.

Its all set and the whistle blows. A darting dummy run by Dinsmore into the wall is followed by Bunton swooping on the ball. Instead of shooting though, he angles the ball acutely right to Jerry Kidd who is lurking at the right hand edge of the penalty box.

"Aaaarhh" yells Dave beside me like he'd been shot.

Kidd feints then cuts straight into the box blowing past two defenders who are clearly caught by surprise. A third defender has reacted and makes to shut Kidd down but the Rovers wing back is quicker and turns inside slotting the ball through the stopper's open legs. In an instant Kidd is through on the goalie and with a drop of the shoulder curls the ball round his outstretched hand, left footed into the far corner of the goals.

The place goes mad. Jonesy is over grabbing the hood of my jacket. Dave is punching the air. Everyone this side of the ground is on their feet cheering.

"IT WAS LIKE ARCHIE FUCKIN' GEMMILL AGAINST HOLLAND!" shouts Jonesy over the mayhem around me, still clinging on to my hood for all he is worth. "Jerry Kidd!" he finishes with, a smile on his face like he was talking about his son out there.

As we fall back on our seats I look around for any fatalities who have fallen down the stand. Thankfully everyone seems to be safely reinstated in their seats. Amazing really.

What a goal eh?" I say in Dave's direction. Jonesy is looking front and centre.

"Aye not bad." He says with a rye smile on his face, "Who would have thought it?"

The game shuttles around excitedly for a few minutes more before the referee blows for half-time. It is the Arthurston fans that are cheering as the players leave the field and as the last man disappears under the small main stand to our right, another boom of thunder bursts in the sky and the heavens open.

14.

The players look genuinely surprised when they run back out into a deluge. The floodlights are casting bright reflections on

242

the recently formed puddles on the ground as well as the vacated soaked plastic seats in the lower rows of our stand, and on John Storrie's baldy head.

The referee takes a concerned look at the sodden turf in front of the main stand and, satisfied of nothing, continues to the centre circle to start the second half.

Arthurston begin where they have left off. Despite the heavy underfoot conditions and the relentless rain they are moving the ball about well. St Mirren are sticking to their task though and despite the Rovers having the bulk of the possession, it's the men from Paisley who create the better chances with their alarmingly burly midfielder testing out Thomson twice from the edge of the box.

"Come on Rovers, sharpen up at the back there!" I shout as if a) they can hear me and b) they will immediately obey.

"Anyone going for a pie?" Jonesy asks hopefully.

Dave and I look in unison over to the steps then up in the direction of the pie-stand behind us. Deep exhalations are followed by shaking heads. Again in unison.

"Nah , me neither. " concludes Jonesy in a disappointed tone.

Kidd is being effective pushing up the right side and Mickey Hedge is beginning to send in some dangerous crosses as a direct result of his wing back's effort. For the third time in succession Hedge throws over a wicked cross towards the goal in front of us, and while the first two have been clutched at the last moment by the confident St Mirren keeper, this time he comes out flailing, his timing just too late. Just as he reaches the ball, Dinsmore leaps and gets his head on it an instant before they both collide and send each other sprawling in the muck. Russ has done his bit though and the ball slaps down on the mud and squirts into the back of the net, a despairing Saints defender following it in on his backside.

We are up, grasping the air with outstretched arms. The yells are of joy and relief in equal measures and we are congratulating ourselves heartily when Dave puts his finger up. At the same time I notice the referee pointing to the ground near to where the goalie fell and the St Mirren fans are cheering and waving.

"Whaaaat?" I shout. "He can't be disallowing it surely!"

"He is." Confirms Dave simply. "He's saying the goalie got fouled."

The referee does indeed indicate that he felt the keeper was impeded and Arthurston Rovers are the latest to suffer from the perennial fixation of referees to protect the goalkeeper at all cost. Boos ring round the stand but nothing changes. Russ Dinsmore and Ally Fairful both pick up bookings for arguing.

"At least that's Fairful one step closer to a suspension" says Dave uncharitably. No one laughs.

We reach the final minutes and things have turned tense. I still feel we are in control but the conditions have worsened and every break up the park by either team has a lottery feel to it.

"We'll just need to regroup and get a couple of subbies on for the extra-time." says Jonesy not taking his eyes off the park.

"I make that time up" replies Dave looking at his watch then back at the ball which is slopping around harmlessly in mid-field. A stramash has developed inside the centre circle although with the rain sheeting down its difficult to see exactly what is going on. There are about six or seven shadowy figures hacking at the ball which presumably has got stuck in a puddle out there. Suddenly the players look up and the ball appears to have been flicked out left to the waiting St Mirren winger who is in acres of space. Off he heads into the curtain of spray and suddenly everyone is heading desperately towards the faraway goal. The ball is released and I barely make out the chunky St Mirren boy drawing a boot back. The noise from the other end of the park, however, says more than anything I can see.

The ball is in the net. No question. The referee is running back to the centre and St Mirren fans and players are going ballistic.

Somewhere out there.... I think.

"Did you see it? " I ask a stony faced Dave beside me.

"A bit. Their guy met it perfectly and drilled it in the bottom corner. Thomson never even moved."

Thomson never even moved. The words ring out in my head as the referee blows the final whistle. The phrase repeats itself annoyingly as we trudge back to our car in the rain and it's still in there when we trundle down Arthurston Mainstreet some time later. Dave's suggestion of catching last orders at the pub falls on subdued ears. I explain that I need to pop round and see Grampa, Jonesy mutters he wants to have a bath and get an early night. We make our farewells and I am dispatched on the street corner, left with my thoughts. Of course it's still in there , rattling around, like a pea in a pot..........

...... Thomson never even moved.

15.

Grampa is staring at me intently. He hasn't made a sound for a good couple of minutes save for the regular wheeze of his breath and one short stifled cough.

"I've not been feeling so good lately" he eventually says flatly

"I know that." I reply solidly

"I can hardly get about at all."

"I know that too."

The clock on the mantelpiece ticks on and on. He's still looking right at me and I'm looking right back.

There's the barest of softening in his expression. Not much but I catch it anyway and right there I know I've got him.

"We would need to be there a lot earlier than kick off," I throw in lightly, "and wait a bit after the final whistle."

Grampa looks down at floor, between his feet, his brittle fingers scratching on the upholstered arm of his favourite chair. When he looks back up there's an unmistakeable glint in his eye.

"Aye" he says slowly then pauses thoughtfully." The Thistle game you say?"

"A week on Saturday. I thought that would be the best one. There won't be a huge crowd and we might even win!" After a short moment of consideration I add, "Well maybe. We're pretty crap at the moment."

"Son, right now I'd tear the hairs off you to see us lose ten nothing to Albion Rovers in the sleet." He smiles and I break into a grin myself. Shaking my head I start on the cuppa Grampa insisted making before he sat down. It tastes like life itself.

"Dad's not going to buy it you know that don't you."

"Son, your father wouldn't buy a new suit for a wedding. Don't you worry though, I'll deal with him. " He points an unsteady finger at me confidently and with a note of intrigue finishes "Naw , Don't you worry about that, I've got money in the bank where he's concerned."

And that's that. A conversation I had been putting off for days is over and the outcome is more than I dared to hope. The only drawback being that Grampa's newly installed enthusiasm transplant demands that I relive tonight's game blow by painful blow and worse than that, I've finished all my tea.

Chapter 10 One for the road

1.

I've lost count of the number of times my mother has sighed after asking me 'How was the game?' and I have grunted a well worn reply of 'Rubbish'.

"Why do you go if its always rubbish?" is invariably the next question. And she's right to ask it. It is a good and fair question.

The obvious answer is that it isn't always rubbish. Sometimes it's actually quite good. We win, we play quite well and the football sporadically displays a level of art and spectacle that no other sport or entertainment can ever hope to match. Sporadically.

But not that often. The standard of play we watch week in week out unfortunately doesn't offer any consistent, reliable quality, at least not enough to reasonably account for our religious attendance in all weathers at not-inconsiderable expense.

So what is the real, mysterious, underlying reasoning that pokes away at this addiction of ours (for it is an addiction of sorts). I've heard all the theories, intellectual and otherwise, and I tend to agree in part with most of them. The pack mentality, the need to belong, gardening, shopping and DIY avoidance. They are all part of it but I'm sure there's more.

It has become a name synonymous with hangers on who only come to football when the team is winning but deep down when you look at it we are all 'Gloryhunters'. We want, maybe even need in some cases to ...... *succeed* I think. In work, in our leisure, in all walks of life really we strive for, and are attracted to, the idea of being successful or being associated with someone or something that succeeds – that grabs the glory and wins the day. We feel good by our association.

More than that though we want that glory, *our* glory, to be experienced with and witnessed by, our friends our family, and the people we care about. There are others too. People we appreciate, casual acquaintances, people we don't always agree with but certainly people we can identify with. We want them all there. To see us *feel* and to see them feel as well, in the same way. In agreement.

It means nothing without them. Its like watching a funny TV program alone. Seldom do we laugh out loud sitting on our own in these situations and when we do have company the whole experience is richer for it being a shared one. We turn round don't we, at the punch-lines, and smile or laugh along with whoever we're with and when they laugh back they *agree* and life is good for it sort of says we're winning but we're winning together.

As I say it means nothing without them.

2.

There we are. Four guys all in a row. In the practically empty Main Stand at Wilmot Park. It's a quarter past two and asides from the optic lemon clad stewards and a ragged looking character sitting away to our left with his arm wedged in a tube of Pringles, we are the only ones in the ground. With Wilmot Park being reasonably close to the town centre, the crowd tends to pile in right on kick off so our current solitude is not altogether surprising.

It's a perfect day for football. The sun is putting in some October overtime just for us and judging by the expression on Grampa's face the fresh air and the pre-match build-up has been well worth the painfully slow, stop-start journey to get here.

"Are you ok then?" I ask Grampa who in fairness looks a little pale. I can make out little beads of perspiration glinting on the old man's wrinkled forehead.

"Aye, I'm fine. Just a bit shaky after that music Chris put on in the car"

"Yeh, well it makes us shaky too." I reply

I look over to my left. "What was that you had us listening to ?"

"The Legendary Stardust Cowboy." Jonesy replies with a smile on his face.

"It was God-awful whatever it was." injects Dave sharply.

"It should be, it was voted as one of the ten worst albums of all time" Jonesy says still grinning.

"So why the hell are you listening to it then?" cries Dave looking to the heavens, "And more to the point why were *we* being subjected to it as well - Indian whoops and whaling bugles are *not* my idea of music -Why?"

"I don't know. Its just ....different. You have to admit though, it was precious when he did the birdcalls and animal noises, wasn't it?" A silence descends on Jonesy who shrugs and digs his head into the refuge of the match programme.

Dave leans over and whispers confidentially in my ear. I smile widely, nod appreciatively and look my friend squarely in the eye. A feeling of genuine affection for him flows through me and I'm about to whisper a reply back when the calm is broken by a crackle, some electrical feedback and then the unmistakeable, cotton wool muffle of Jimmy Bently.

"Methming Methming, um, ooo, nhreee"

"Some things never change" croaks Grampa dissolving into a fit of half laughter, half coughing. I touch him on the arm but he waves me away producing a huge, iron creased, burgundy hanky from his coat pocket and uses it to gently dab the side of his mouth and chin.

A blunt beat cranks up from the rafters mixing itself awkwardly with a tuneless, tin-can scratching noise and we're treated to some pre-match 'music'. The melody seems vaguely familiar and we collectively narrow it down to either Nutbush City Limits or a 'Dance' version of Ave Maria. Throughout this vague rendition, high above our heads, the bulbous grey speaker vibrates alarmingly against the roof girder it's mounted upon, threatening to shake itself free at any moment.

"I can mind young Jimmy's first time on the PA like it was yesterday" says Grampa and, like a living, breathing advert, unearths a big bag of Werthers Originals from deep within his jacket and passes them along the row.

"*Young* Jimmy?" I ask incredulously taking a sweet and popping it into my mouth, "He must be sixty-five if he's a day!"

"Aye, well he's young to me son. He must have been, what, only nineteen when he started doing the teams and stuff, Young Jimmy's all I've ever called him."

We are all sitting in a row loudly sucking sweeties and staring out on to the strip-mowed pitch where a couple of distinctly unofficial characters are wandering around with rakes vainly looking for holes in the turf to mend.

"Jimmy Bently was an unlucky lad." says Grampa slowly, rattling his dentures with the hard candy in his mouth. "Did you know he was on the Rovers books at one time?" Dave and I shake our heads, Jonesy says nothing but shifts forward on his seat.

"Oh aye, he was a fair player was Jimmy. He played a few times for the reserves and would probably have made it if it wasn't for his accident." Grampa pauses for effect enjoying the attention he's generated.

"Did he get injured then?" Dave asks with genuine interest in his voice..

"You could say that. He was in a car accident with his father." Grampa looks gravely out to the park in front of him." Ploughed into the back of Auld Johnny Reid's butcher van, so they did. The bloody thing had broken down in the rain on the Old Wet Road. Johnny was back in town arranging a tow when the Bently's came along, didnae see the van in the dark, and hit it full on. Some said they must have been going over seventy miles an hour when they battered into the thing. Anyway the old man never even made it to hospital, and the lad suffered terrible injuries - lost his leg from his thigh down eventually. They said he was lucky," Grampa sniffs. "Luck yeh? – Didn'ae sound too full of fortune to me."

"So Jimmy Bently's got a wooden leg?" I ask wide eyed.

"Have you never noticed his limp ?" replies Jonesy quietly.

I had now that it was mentioned it but had never thought much of it.

"Of course," I admit staunchly, "but I just thought it was down to arthritis or something."

"Nah, nah," picks up Grampa again, shaking his head and slapping the thigh of his trousers, "Artificial leg son. To make things worse it came out that Jimmy was going to get the nod for the first team. That same week as the crash. Can you imagine it? Its the sort of story that could finish a man but young Jimmy, to his credit, kept his head up. Once he got himself on the mend he went back up to the games, stood himself right behind me at the same barrier where his old man used to stand, and shouted the boys on."

"Is that when he started on the PA then?"

"Naw, not quite but I think he *did* work for the club round about then, for a while. Got a small job running errands, cleaning the boots and stuff that was until he went to the lawyer's office in the town, and got his qualifications."

Grampa's rolls on, hardly stopping for breath. "He started doing the announcing after Frank Hillhouse got sacked for being drunk on the job. That was a laugh in itself. It was a cup replay against either Dundee or Dundee Utd, one of them, I cannae quite remember. But Frank, who liked a drink or two, must've been having a wee party to himself in the box for halfway through the second half he turned the mike on and started singing, gently mind, 'The roads and the miles to Dundee' over the system. It was a cold night and his deep, slurry voice echoed right over the whole ground. The players stopped playing an' everything - after all Frank was no singer." Grampa catches my eye and smiles. "I'm rambling a bit eh son?"

"Not at all." I reply, "It's good stuff. So Jimmy became the PA man then?"

"Aye he did. Frank was kindly asked to take his singing elsewhere and when they put an advert in the local paper, Jimmy was up knocking on the door the very next morning. And I'll never forget his first game either. It was a brilliant match against Raith Rovers. You know, a classic. One of those ding-dong battles with the ball flyin' from end to end. The game should have finished about ten each but in the end we edged it four-three. Anyway with all this going on, the excitement, and it being his first game and all, Jimmy announced a substitute but forgot to turn the mike off. For about five minutes or so we were all treated to him sitting up in the box willing the team to score. He was up there shouting like he was on the terrace. Stuff aw anxious like 'on ye go!' and 'send it wide man!' and we could hear every word. Luckily we scored the winner not long after that but before he could say somethin' out of turn, ye know." Grampa laughs, "He *did* do a braw bit of commentatin' on the goal mind yellin' 'Hit it man!' then screamin' 'Gooaaaalllll' like that daft Brazilian commentator off the telly when the ba' cracked into the top corner"

"Surely he didn't keep talking after that. Someone must have gone up and told him." Dave asks.

"Naw, he announced the scorer, wee Dickie Ralston it was, there you go…....." Grampa beams at his own memory, " …. then he turns the thing off as normal and its all quiet on the western front for the rest of the match." Grampa rests back in his chair and takes a laboured twisted glance behind him at the window of the PA room.

People are starting to drift in all around the ground and a group of thirty or so fans decked in red, yellow and black appear from the entrance to the opposite stand, shield their eyes from the glaring sun then make their way up the nearest flight of stairs to their choice of seats. The first 'away' bus is in.

"Was that the best Rovers game you've seen Johnnie – the Raith game? " asks Jonesy still somehow sucking away on the sweetie I finished ages ago.

"The best Rovers game?" Grampa looks hard and his wrinkled furrowed brow concertinas itself up even more than usual. "Must be - almost. Mind you the day we put Rangers out the Scottish Cup was super as well."

"1970 wasn't it." says Jonesy with a hint of regret in his voice.

"Aye something like that, it was the Third round I mind that. That was a great game too. Coming back from a goal down to win two-one and playing the kind of football we did was magic. Of course they were good too, a lot of big name players on show but for once we didn't let the occasion get to us. We didnae show them any more respect than they deserved and for the last twenty minutes played them totally off the park. I don't think I've ever seen as many shots at goal, at both ends, as there was in the second half that day. Brilliant !"

"I've heard lots of folk talk about that game" says Jonesy enthusiastically, "Must be the best game you've ever seen live then, what do you think?"

"Well not quite" Grampa replies knowingly." I once saw a better game than that but it wisnae here. Hell, It wasn't even an Arthurston game." He finishes with a trace of guilt in his voice.

"What was that then? Asks Jonesy now leaning at such an angle off his seat that he looks set to fall off.

"It was a European game down at Rugby Park. Autumn of 1964 I think it was. Aye it must have been because your Gran and I had just moved to Collection Street." He looks round at me with an irritated look," Mind yon house with the leaky taps and the crowd next door with the dogs!"

I must have looked confused.

"Naw of course you wouldn't" he says tutting, "Not even born then... Were you?... Naw." Grampa pauses slightly to get breath and collect his thoughts. " So it was like this. I used to work with this guy, Jamesy Mullen up at the Post Office. He was a bit of a slacker but a good laugh all the same. Now his cousin got a game for Kilmarnock in those days . Whatwozisname now? Awww it was emmm….. Naw wait…"

"It doesn't matter " I suggest seeing the old boy getting noticeably agitated." It'll come back to you when you stop thinking about it."

"Aye maybe" says Grampa sourly "more likely he's another one kidnapped away by my auld age, never to be heard of again - JAMIESON!, that was it!" he looks brightly momentarily then slumps his shoulders, "Naw, wait, that was the milkman's boy that played for Stirling Albion., och , I dunno."

"Never mind, go on with the story." I say soothingly.

"Oh aye, well, Jamesy scored a couple of tickets from his cousin to see Killie play Eintracht Frankfurt in the Inter City Fairs Cup, you know, the old UEFA Cup. It was a Tuesday night and me and the bold Jamesy skipped off early from work and drove over to Kilmarnock in his brother's works van, which it turned out he had nicked without permission. Now there's a story for another time. Anyway we had a few bottles of cheap beer for the drive through and by the time we got there we were feeling pretty good. It was a grand night out for us."

Grampa stops and offers round more sweets before carrying on.

"Killie were three – nil down from the first leg and didn'ae really stand a chance. Nobody thought so. But I hadn't seen a European game in the flesh before and was right up for it. Well, we got held up by the crowd didn't we, There was around twenty thousand in Rugby Park that night and could we find a parking space in those hooses round the ground? Jamesy ended up knocking on a wifey's door and asking her if he could park the van in her drive. And she let him as well!"

Grampa laughs and shakes his head.

"He was some man with the ladies, Jamesy. Anyway, by the time we got into the ground the Germans were one up. Only missed the first couple of minutes mind but there it was – Kilmarnock four goals down on aggregate. We'd travelled all that way full of life and the sauce and the game was dead on its feet. Even when Killie snatched a couple back and went in two – one up at half-time I remember thinking it was all over bar the shoutin'."

Dave turns round in his seat and ruffles his hand through his thick black hair. "I've never heard of this game. Was it a good second half then?"

"Good? It was the best son. Killie came out in the second half like a wind out to knock the hooses down. The football was, well, breath-taking, its the only word for it, and when the lad McFadzean pulled another one back the place went wild.

Jamesy and I got quite carried away and I remember us both singing 'Come on Killie'. Not bad for an Arthurston fan and a Celtic sympathiser. The finish was incredible. Kilmarnock scored twice more in the last ten minutes and Rugby Park went berserk. There were fans on the park after both the goals and I remember dancing up and down hugging some big Ayrshire lump who was reekin' of sweat and kept bawlin' 'Ronnie is a God' in my ear. Either he was talkin' about the boy that scored the winner or the lad was in some strange religious sect, I'm no sure. You never know about these Ayrshire folk do you?"

"So they won five – four on aggregate?" asks Dave obviously enthralled by the story.

"Aye they did. Five–one on the night. Frankfurt were no slouches either. It was only a few years previous that they had played in yon European cup final with Real Madrid. It's a far cry from nowadays isn't it? Any Scottish team in this day and age would have given up long before Kilmarnock did. I'm not sure what that's all about." He shakes his head with a furrowed brow

As we sit in the shade of the sinking October sunshine and contemplate Grampa's ponderings none of us seem able to come up with any meaningful reason either. Maybe somewhere in the late 1980's players got lazy, or the confidence went, or maybe their allegiances to their clubs rather than their paycheques just got too tenuous to mean anything. I don't know and by the silence around me not many do for definite. All we can do is sit around, all in a row, and hope that those days come back again. Soon.

3.

The players make their way on to the park to the languid, rhythmic, echoing handclaps of the more enthusiastic fans in the ground. Some jog on full of purpose, others stroll absently, self absorbed, like they are walking in their back garden, as far away from the rest of the world as they could possibly be. Individual stretching and faffing around with one of the many balls on the park soon gives way to more organised limbering up directed by the respective coaching staff of both teams.

As always, Arthurston look resplendent in red and white, the sun only heightening the dazzling freshness of the colours against the green textured backdrop of the pitch around them. Grampa seems mesmerised moving his eyes from one end of the park to the other.

"Well are you...." I start but Grampa holds one finger up at his side not for a second breaking his concentration from the scene in front of him.

"Ssshhhhh...... " is the only sound that leeks out through his lips.

The Rovers players flow across the pitch in two lines of eight or nine, only the goalkeepers in their differently styled grey strips breaking the uniformity of the pattern.

Grampa breaks his gaze and smiles, " I'd forgotten what it was like. I mean you see the snippets on the telly but its not the same as being here. A bit like watching those cooking programmes and not getting to taste what they cook isn't it?" I nod my head but say nothing.

The ground is filling up nicely. In days gone by I used to love being in early and watching the crowd build. Big games were the best. Cup ties, infrequent Rangers or Celtic games, or when one of the other teams could possibly win the championship on the Wilmot Park turf. Whichever, I found it fascinating to witness the old familiar scene slowly change it's appearance over that half an hour or so before kick off. From the rattling, quarter-empty sparseness that was ever the norm, to the cramped, oppressive cauldron of intensity that came with the stands being full to bursting. The process was transfixing and the transformation never ceased to be exhilarating. This fascination for crowd watching would multiply itself tenfold when I would go along to Scotland games at Hampden (the old Hampden at any rate). I would insist upon Grampa or whoever was accompanying me that we *had* to be in our seats a good three-quarters of an hour before the game started 'just to see the crowd come in'. They must have thought I was mad but the spectacle of watching the high banked East terrace fill up and people appear in the precarious seats above the North Enclosure was brilliant.

Today we'll be lucky if there are three and a half thousand at the game so my days of fixation are over (and not just in terms of crowd watching I fear).

4.

At twenty to three 'The Associates' start to arrive - The guys that sit in our immediate vicinity in the stand, not the dodgy 80's 'New Wave' band. We call them 'The Associates' because collectively it's the best name for them. Not friends as such yet somehow more than just nodding acquaintances. I see them more often than some of my family and we've shared so much over the years, despite the fact I don't even know some of their names. It's a strange one. There's even a blurred line as to who qualifies as an Associate and who doesn't. Folk who sit two rows in front are not considered to be part of it yet the guy with the rounded glasses and scar on his left cheek who sits God knows where, is. I meet him at the end of every game at the same spot on the stairs and exchange a pleasant comment or two on the match. A smile or a shake of the head later and we go on our separate ways heading for opposite exits. An Associate.

Being habitual football fans The Associates tend to arrive, for the most part ,in order. First in is Billy. A man in his late sixties with tousy grey hair and a lived in look about his face that would have made Sid James look good enough for the Nivea advert. He has sat in the row behind us since we moved to these seats in our late teens (we used to sit over in the TP Hughes stand behind the goals until we realised how crap the view was and decided to move.) and he spends the majority of his time cursing the referee and furtively trying to light large brown cigars without any of the stewards seeing him. I won't ever forget Billy pressing twenty quid into my hand one Christmas a fair few years back insisting 'take the boys for a wee festive drink on me son." He is a gentleman and despite the fact I don't know what he does or where he lives even, I hold a great deal of affection for the guy. Kind of like a favourite uncle really.

"All right boys" he says jovially as he squashes himself and his camel coat into his seat behind us and produces a cigar from his pocket in a sneaky fashion.

Next up comes Billy's two mates, Alistair and Harry. Alistair is a plump red faced man with a gentle, pacifying nature while Harry is a tall, pale drink of water who wears a pair of 'Two Ronnies' glasses and seems constantly irritated with every player who has ever dared to don the red and white stripes of the Rovers. In the nicest possible way he talks guff all the time and over the years Alistair has saved him from many an altercation with fellow Associates and non-Associates alike. Alistair winks at me as he sits down, Harry flaps an arm self-consciously in our general direction.

A quick look at my watch tells me its ten to three. The players have trotted back off to more substantial and encouraging applause and are no doubt getting final directions from Wilf Schnabbel deep in the belly of the stand as we speak. A second glance shows Grampa sitting quietly. He seems outwardly contented and comfortable looking. Were it not for his left leg jiffling madly and his finger tapping out Morse code on the seat at his side I would have called him relaxed as well.

Parka-Man appears next so called due to his propensity for wearing his furry hooded jacket rain, hail or shine – we don't know his real name. He is closely followed by a dapper, middle-aged chap with a hooked nose and closely razored grey hair, 'down to the wood' as my dad would say. He smiles thinly and slopes into one of three empty chairs if front of us. This is Jeff Singer, a Maths teacher from Arthurston High School who was once a local celebrity of sorts. His flirtation with fame came courtesy of an appearance on Mastermind in the mid-eighties. His specialised subject as he steadfastly announced sitting on the famous black chair was "The history of Arthurston Rovers Football Club , Magnus ." Well of course it was - it should be everyone's, and I cheered when he said it. Thinking back, I'm sure the whole town must have watched him on TV that night. When he blitzed into the lead with his undeniably impressive knowledge of the club I for one was shouting 'Go on Jeff!' at the inanimate telly in the corner. Unfortunately for the man, his wider appreciation of the world around him wasn't quite as thorough. Outside of The Rovers and Pythagoras's Theorem he pretty much knew nothing about nothing, and the additional two questions he got right in the general knowledge round were only good enough to secure him third place. He would have been last had it not been for an Inland Revenue officer called Frank Swilley (a name that must have raised a snigger from schoolboys the length and breadth of the country – "Name? Frank Swilley", Specialised Subject? The insides of Frank's Y-Fronts. Well come on , its why I remember him!). *His* specialised subject had been something to do with politics in post-revolutionary Russia and he clearly didn't know his Stalins from his Kerenskys. If I remember correctly he only got one right.

Had Jeff's fame been limited to his brief appearance on national TV then things would have been all well and good. Had he chosen not to get caught in bed with the heat winner, a blonde 'mutton dressed as lamb' expert on the works of DH Lawrence (the writing was on the wall there I feel) then things would have been fine. Had it not been a slow news weekend and had the Arthurston Gazette not been staying in the hotel room next door then maybe no-one would ever have known. Except it wasn't, he did, it was and they were. The Gazette lead somewhat sensationally for them with 'He was Lady Chatterley's Lover!" whereas the rest of Britain were treated to The News of the World's front page headline of 'Master-Grind!'. Jeff's wife left him of course and he only narrowly avoided getting the sack after a long and protracted inquiry through the Education Department. Still, as far as the Rovers were concerned no one will be able to say he didn't know his stuff. And maybe he learned a bit about DH Lawrence too. Life is, as they say, an education

As if reading my mind Dave whispers in my ear "I wonder how Frank Swilley is getting on" and chortles away to himself happily.

5.

We really need to win this game. I seem to have been saying this for a while but now its getting dicey. We lost again last week against Hearts at Tynecastle and with Motherwell winning at Thistle, we are now second bottom of the league. While we apparently played well in the first half, we lost two bad goals (those bad goals again) in the second and ended up being well beaten. I say apparently because I missed my first game of the season spending the afternoon at home, in bed with the worst of head-colds, the result I'm sure of getting soaked on the way home from the St Mirren game. I'm sensitive that way and I'm utterly convinced that it will be pneumonia that carries me off eventually, when I'm old and wheezy and my immune system has packed up and left town.

"Here they come!" I cry just a little too loudly, grabbing on to the sleeve of Grampa's coat. I'm surprised at my reaction. I'm obviously more excited that usual. I don't know whether it's the fact that Grampa's here or maybe that I missed last week's fix but I'm definitely wired up for this one.

The teams run on to the park and everyone around us barring myself and Grampa stand up and applaud our heroes. When everyone settles back into their seats the pitch comes back into view with the usual home ensemble of Arthurston on our left and the all black away kit of Partick Thistle on our right. To *my* immediate right Grampa is smiling and he is smiling hard.

I like hitting towards The Benches in the first half. We always seem to do better playing the other way in the second, towards our own fans behind the other goal. It must be psychological or something. With no fuss the ball is placed on the centre spot and a quick peep of the whistle pushes us off into another one. Here we go again.

6.

As the game starts I can't help stealing sideways glances at Grampa. After looking pale and drawn as the kick-off approached, there is now a little flush in his cheeks and he looks like an excited kid sitting under the tree on Christmas morning.

"That's not a bad team he's put out there." he says shifting on his seat, " I mean I know I've only seen them on the telly for the last wee while but they look ok. McLean's not the worst in the middle and the English boy, Bunton has bit of dig. Has Frankie Boyle been getting a game?" he asks, a hopeful tone to his question.

"A bit here and a bit there, " I reply, "I'd heard he hadn't turned up at training a couple of times. Not sure if that's true though."

"Aye, that sounds about right – What a waste….."

Grampa is about to continue but stops as Scott McLean picks the ball up at the half way line and drives forward. Thistle's opposite number tries to close him down but only succeeds in sliding through McLean's dark trailing shadow. A couple more paces and a vicious right foot drive is unleashed low to the keeper's left. The Thistle goalie sees it all the way but the ball is skimming the grass so quickly he can only get half a hand to it and palm it on to the post. As the ball deflects out for a corner, the crowd noise rises for the first time in the game. The diminutive Mickey Hedge, who seems to have forgotten the way to the barbers , skips over with his shampoo ad hair to the corner spot far to our right to take the kick.

"Is he wearing one of those tie-back, hair-thingies the Italians wear?" I ask.

Dave seems to know what I'm on about, "Aye, he looks a bit of a throbber doesn't he."

Before I can agree with this less than complimentary assessment, the long-haired one has launched the ball high in the air towards the packed penalty box. Its pace and strength carries it over everyone in the goal-mouth and it falls conveniently to Paul

Marker out left who carefully watches it fall then thunders a volley goalwards without the ball touching the ground. It whistles inches over the bar and the crowd uniformly cry 'oooooohhhhh!'

"Good start eh?" I look to Grampa who nods his head. I turn to the guys and they do likewise. Behind me I hear Harry mutter that "Marker needs to learn to keep the ball down a bit better."

Thistle seem unable to pick up the pace of the game and give away a dangerous free kick at the edge of their box, their centre half mistiming his challenge on the sharp-looking Ray Stark. The crowd grows restless as the referee finds it difficult to get the wall back the required ten yards. Players are shoving and pushing one way then the next. Others are complaining hard. None are currently any more than six or seven yards away from the impatient ball which is lying waiting to be dispatched into the beckoning goal. Hopefully.

"Book one of them!" screams Dave, "that'll get them back!"

The referee chooses not to and another ten seconds or so is wasted with the Partick defensive wall jostling around trying to gain as much advantage as possible. Stark and Dinsmore are over the ball and the expectancy rises as the ref steps away happy now that the thistle players have settled down.

"Hit the dead ball." invites Grampa quietly, shifting in his seat in a laboured manner.

Dinsmore takes two steps back then makes to hit it. As he is about to make contact Stark rolls the ball slightly to the right for Tony Bunton who is shaping up for the shot. The rolling ball has given the wall time to make up some ground though and when Bunton eventually hammers the ball he hits one of three player bearing down on him. The ball rolls out the side harmlessly for a shy.

Grampa is shaking his head. "I've never known whit they do that for. Give 'em the chance to blooter a stationery, well positioned ball from that range, and they instead want to try an' hit an awkward moving one with a gang of maraudin' defenders breathing all over 'em. I dinnae get it."

I have to agree. The quality of shooting in the Scottish game is terrible as it is. Why indeed would the players opt to make things harder for themselves.

We're now some half an hour into the game and as the shadows are lengthening I'm starting to worry that for all our domination we don't have the goal that we need and indeed deserve. As if in reply to my concerns, out of nowhere Marker avoids being caught in possession deep in his own half and humps the ball ferociously towards Thistle territory. The Partick defence is suddenly caught too far up the park and as the ball drops over them, the alert Stark streaks past, takes it on the bounce, carries the ball a few yards into the box and passes the ball low into the corner of the net beyond the outstretched keeper. The stand around us erupts and the Arthurston players swamp Ray Stark finishing as an untidy pile of bodies on the ground beside the near side corner- flag.

The relief around us is palpable.

"Hopefully that will settle us down and we can grab a couple more " cries Jonesy still on his feet applauding the goal, "They've not been in it at all."

We all agree and settle down for more of the same. Except it doesn't transpire. Despite being on top for so long and being clearly the more able team, Rovers immediately fall back deep in their own half and surrender possession and territory to Partick Thistle who suddenly look like a new team. A couple of shots at goal and the Thistle players have an appetite for the game that was previously missing in action.

"Aawwww" groans Dave. "Why does this always happen. There's no need for us to hang back like this. WE NEED TO BE CONFIDENT!" He finishes the outburst in a 'we will fight them on the beaches' sort of way and Parka-man looks round as if to say something but changes his mind and turns back to the game again.

Thistle take a throw-in directly in front of us and the ball finds their lank haired forward who has come wide in search of some action. Without really looking he heaves the ball hopefully into the box where only John Storrie is waiting. The nearest

Thistle man is a good ten yards away and slightly awkwardly, squinting whilst looking into the direct sunlight, Storrie controls it high on his chest and in turn humps the ball up the park. At which point the referee explosively makes a bee-line for the Arthurston box and reaching the area, points directly to the spot. The Arthurston players look incredulous, the Thistle fans, realising they have been awarded a penalty, start to jump up and dance ecstatically. The referee is immediately surrounded by hordes of red and white stripes and at least two yellow cards are flashed in the ensuing bedlam. Storrie himself is ushered away by Scott McLean presumably before he does something he might regret while Thomson, the keeper, remains directly in front of the ref patting his massive gloved right hand continuously on his left shoulder and practically forcing his other hand up one or both of official's nostrils.

The home fans boo and jeer but to no avail. The greasy haired Thistle forward is already taking his run up and with consummate ease strokes the ball high to Thomson's left into the roof of the net.

One all.

Howls of derision ring out as the ball is kicked disconsolately back up to half way and an angry exchange between Storrie and a bulky Thistle midfielder needs to be broken up by the match official who is now getting more than he bargained for from the game.

The match kicks off with the crowd still barracking the referee senselessly. A quick look at my watch shows that there is five minutes to half time. Arthurston are back, reasserting themselves in the game now that they have to and Russ Dinsmore nearly catches the keeper out with a cheeky lob from the corner of penalty box. Unfortunately the ball drops harmlessly over the bar for a bye-kick.

The keeper squirts the resulting clearance out wide to the right, straight to the feet of Mickey Hedge who immediately brings the ball under control and feeds the ball forward. Dinsmore collects it a couple of feet inside the box, tries to turn but is closely marked by the opposition centre half. Dinsmore turns again, this time the other way knocking the ball past the waiting defender. The move is sharp, too sharp for Dinsmore himself and he goes over painfully on his ankle his arms flailing as he falls. In an instant the referee is again sprinting into the box, left arm straight out in front of him, pointing, quite clearly to the spot. Sometimes it can be unclear whether the referee has given a penalty or not. They quite deliberately *don't* point to the spot and instead hare off to a different part of the pitch (possibly to avoid being assaulted) and everyone gets confused. But this is obvious. It is Thistle's turn to feel aggrieved. We have a penalty!

"That was soft." Says Dave clapping his hands feverishly nevertheless.

"It was never a penalty" agrees Grampa, "The referee was just making up for the last one."

And Grampa is probably bang on. Scottish referees have always had the habit of applying the 'two wrongs make a right' policy when it comes to bad decisions they've made. I can't count the number of times a howling decision against us has been equalized shortly afterwards by an equally bad one. Or vice – versa. Better to get it right first time I would have thought, but hey, what do I know?

The Thistle players are quite justifiably, complaining bitterly. One is trying to lift Russ Dinsmore off the ground as the Rovers forward is still lying on his side where he fell. At which point, Eddie Holland, the Rovers' physio arrives on the scene and pushes the Partick boy away from Dinsmore who actually looks genuinely injured. Out of the crowd of players a black arm pushes back and suddenly its like a bar-room brawl. Players are pushing, fists are flying and the poor referee is fighting to get between at least three separate scuffles at the one time.

Every fan in the ground has seemingly risen to their feet straining their necks for a better view of the stramash. Football fans, despite what some may argue, like a good fight. We're like kids spectating at a playground punch-up. As long as it's not us involved we're quite happy to watch and even do the odd bit of egging on.

Credit to the referee and the two captains, order is quickly restored and miraculously no one is booked. Dinsmore is still on the grass being treated and after a good few minutes, the physio signals for stretcher.

Cue the St Andrew's Ambulance duo. Scuttling into the arena with their little legs pumping like pistons holding the stretcher in one hand while gripping tightly onto their red hard-hats[4] with the other. It doesn't look good for Dinsmore who is grimacing in pain as he is carried off the pitch below us. The home support are following tradition by standing applauding the player's willingness to die for the colours although as Dinsmore disappears into the tunnel I'm sure I catch him run his fingers through his hair.

Dinsmore himself usually hits the penalties so it is left to Ray Stark to step up and meet his fate. He confidently places the ball on the spot, looks to the referee who blows his whistle. Two steps back, two forward and he drives the ball up the middle of the goals. The keeper dives to the right and can only watch the ball hit the back of the net.

Two- One.

7.

"Does anyone want a pie" asks Grampa rummaging around in his pockets and eventually pulling out a faded tartan purse cum wallet.

We've reached half time with little further incident and people are standing up or milling around full of enthusiasm, stoked by the prospect of holding a lead and winning the game.

Everyone is up for a pie, and a Bovril too it is decided, but when I refuse Grampa's money and offer to buy them myself I may as well have insulted my Gran's memory. His look is as black as thunder

---

4   Scottish Health & Safety Executive guidelines insist that hard-hats must be worn at all times for protection in the event of flying pies, bits of floodlight or random players falling from above.

and after some pointless to-ing and fro-ing of 'no I'll get them' has been dispensed with, Grampa's stubborn indignation wins through in the end and I am dispatched to the pie-hatch clutching a chunk of Grampa's pension in my right hand.

As I return a good ten minutes later precariously carrying the order in an upturned Mars Bar box lid, Grampa appears to be deep in conversation with Jeff Singer.

"As I say, they're definitely dumbing down the program now" I catch Jeff Singer saying, " It was much harder when I was ….. ahh here's your grandson with the half-time sustenance now!"

I grin mechanically and pass the 'tray' carefully along the row. "The queue was like an execution down there. I think everyone must be having a celebration pie cos we're actually winning."

"I wonder if we sell more pies when we're winning at half time or when we're getting beaten?" injects Jonesy who has been relatively quiet so far.

Confused looks are thrown back in his general direction.

"Well you know" he adds falteringly, " that would be good market research for the pie-stand people to know don't you think. If the Rovers are winning, pile more pies in the oven – bigger profits!"

"Go down and tell them." suggests Dave "No really, this could be a breakthrough in the economic theory of supply and demand in the catering industry. On you go."

Even Jonesy realises he talking nonsense at this point and he smiles and falls silent.

"What's happening with this new job of yours son," enquires Grampa quickly, "I hear you're a bit of a businessman these days.

Jonesy perks up a bit and rubs the knees of his faded, skinny-cut jeans with the palms of his hands energetically "Well I wouldn't say that, Johnny, but , yeah, I guess the run's coming along."

"When did you start?"

"Just on Monday there. That's me just done my first full week."

"Good stuff son," says Grampa cheerily, "How's it been then?"

"OK I suppose." Jonesy crosses his legs awkwardly landing a red baseball shoe and an embroidered 'Clangers' ankle sock perilously close to Dave's groin area. Oblivious to the expression clouding Dave's face Jonesy continues. "The run's not bad but it's a bit scattered around. And the customers aren't the friendliest either. 'Where's the fat man?' they keep asking." Jonesy screws his face up and puts a whiney voice on.

"That's the general public for you, son" injects Grampa, "some of the folk that used to come into my shop were among the rudest folk I ever met."

"Yeah I know what you mean, talk about a grumpy bunch. Never mind, I put out some leaflets around the area so that should hopefully make the run more substantial. I guess they just need to get used to me, Uncle Len's just been a hard act to follow, that's all."

"Seen any naked women yet? Asks Dave keeping one eye carefully on Jonesy's twitching foot.

"Not yet but I've heard that sort of thing happens all the time in this line of work." Jonesy looks knowingly at each of us in turn. "I feel it would be my duty as a gentleman to avert my eyes in such a situation." He covers his eyes melodramatically then peeps through the gaps in his fingers furtively.

"Seriously though, " and after a slight pause he continues," I'm still a bit worried that I've jumped in too quick. This whole thing cost quite a lot of cash and I sometimes wonder if its been a bit of a step back for me."

Dave snorts. " The only thing that I can think of that would qualify as a step back from your last job would be quality controller in a ping-pong ball factory." I snigger slightly but Grampa flashes Dave, then myself a look that's on skewers.

"You should never criticise a man on two things," Grampa says slowly his gaze straight ahead towards the park, "His choice of a woman and his choice of work. You would do well to remember that. Both of you." He then turns round, wincing slightly in the process, and looks at Jonesy.

"Son, There's no such thing as a step back in life. This is all about seein' things from a different angle for a while. That's all. I think its great what your doing, you have to try new things and if this doesn't work out well, you'll just need to think on something else."

Jonesy looks thoughtful and nods his head gently. Dave lowers his eyes and momentarily looks like a chastised schoolboy. Just as the silence is cocooning the immediate area surrounding our four seats, applause rises and shouts 'Come on the Arthurston!" Numbers appear on the backs of shirts, players run onto the pitch and we settle ourselves down for the second half,

8.

The sun has slipped over the roof above us and is walking down the Brew, its job done for the day. Wilmot Park's roof-mounted floodlights, four on each side of the pitch, have picked up the slack and are beaming down on the unnatural lime green grass below, the long singular shadows of dusk giving way to four short blotches of darkness looking to trip the players above them every step of the way.

Arthurston have made one change, Dinsmore has not reappeared and has been replaced by the versatile Mark Bird who looks set to play in midfield pushing Jay McDonald into a more central forward role. As the game kicks off, Grampa hands me half his pie.

"It tastes great but I can't finish it." He declares regretfully. Two hungry bites from me and its gone.

"Could've done with some sauce "I decide licking away the heavy greasy feeling from my lower lip.

The game restarts tepidly with plenty of huffing and puffing and precious little in way of creative play. Arthurston are limited to a couple of long range efforts from Scott McLean and a half chance from McDonald. Unfortunately the one time Jay is allowed a little space in the box, he snatches at the shot and it trundles into the keeper's arms from about ten yards out.

"Och - a kepper!" shouts Grampa slapping his hand on his thigh in a frustrated manner as the Thistle goalie gathers the ball easily.

Just as it looks like the game is waiting for everyone to go home McDonald drops deep and picks up a loose ball centrally about ten yards inside the Partick half. Instead of shutting our slim forward down, the Thistle players in his vicinity are momentarily indecisive and give the lad some room.

"Go On" I hear Grampa breathe through tight lips.

McDonald pushes the ball in front of him and stretches his legs into elegant yet forceful movement and suddenly his momentum is too strong for any of the opposition even if they had wanted to get near him. His movement carries him faintly to the right and he rides one sluggish, tired looking tackle then the next. Breaking into the box, one final touch scrapes him past the final defender and Thistle are exposed. His final contact has pushed him wide right and the keeper has read the situation, scrabbling out from the safety of his goal line like a spider collecting its prey. Just as it looks like the keeper will get to the ball first, McDonald stretches out his left leg tipping the ball past the now diving goalie.

The crowd lean forward necks straining. Some rise to their feet in expectation. The Rovers man impossibly stays on his feet and just as the ball is threatening to slip out for a bye kick McDonald slides and scoops the ball back across the face of the goal. It hangs in the air, spinning and cutting in slow motion. Slower and slower until time stops. From the midst of the statue like defenders, Ray Stark is the only man to react and from ten yards out starts a stumbling run to the far post meeting the ball full on his forehead. From a couple of yards he can't miss and the ball is sent solidly into the back of the net with Stark slipping into the back of the goal coming to rest in a tangled bundle of arms , legs and red and white netting.

9.

Grampa got to his feet. I don't know how he did it but he did. We hugged and smiled. I clapped, my hands high above my head and Grampa's shaking fist seemingly as strong as it ever was. All around us are smiling faces , slapped backs, grabbed arms and in the case of a young couple down at the front, held hands waving in the air.

And then it all faded, slipped away like a smell on the wind And the stadium became quiet again, empty, except for four guys, all in a row.

Dave looks over at me suggestively, I nod and he gets out of his seat, clambers over the numbered wooden chairs and skips down the main exit under the stand.

"Where's he off to?" asks Grampa stretching his right leg awkwardly, letting out a small 'ooaah' as he manoeuvres it into the isle and straightens it fully.

"Oh, the toilet I guess... Dave always goes at the end of the game. Kind of a ... ritual."

Jonesy waits for Grampa to look away then hisses in my ear, "What's going on, Dave never goes to the toilet in here, its vile down there. What is it?"

"Sshhh, just be quiet and wait a minute." I whisper back. Grampa looks round and I smile lightly at him.

The floodlights suddenly sink to half power giving the arena a ghostly Brockville-esque hue. Over in the far right corner, between the benches and the away stand, the overhanging tree lurks in the shadows suspiciously, its darkness stealing the wall and the seats beneath it. The eternal groundsman doing the last shift with his rake looks more like a grave-digger in the spooky half-light. I shiver, noticing the chill in the air for the first time and dig my hands into my pockets "We'll give it five minutes and that should do it. The crowds should be well away by then,"

Just then Dave appears accompanied by a face-slappingly familiar figure, smartly dressed with a ball under one arm. As

Dave slowly climbs the stairs with Ray Stark at his side I hear Jonesy mutter an excited ' Bloody Hell '.

"Ray, this is Johnny Donald" announces Dave with a generous smile on his face. Grampa struggles to his feet with the help of my arm and the hooked wooden stick pulled from under our seats where its been hidden all afternoon. Once steady on his feet he holds out his hand in greeting.

Stark silently wipes his hand on the side of his trousers and offers a limp looking salutation back.

He looks shorter than he does on the park. Standing there in his grey shiny suit and black patent shoes, white shirt unbuttoned at the neck and his red and white diagonally striped club tie loose around his neck, he can't be any more than 5" 9, a good couple of inches shorter than myself. His damp, oily black hair matches his footwear and is swept back behind his ears and down to his back leaving noticeably damp patches on his suit shoulders and collar. Up close the man's hooked nose is outstanding. Together with his sallow skin stretched almost painfully over a sharp chin and protruding cheek bones, and those hooded, shadowed eyes, Stark looks more like an Eastern European hit-man than a Scottish footballer.

After a short silence Dave clears his throat. "Johnny hasn't been for a while and Craig here brought him up for the game as a birthday treat."

Stark sniffs and looks around him. "Oh Aye." he says airily, sniffs again and looks at his watch.

"That was some game you had today." pitches Grampa.

"Aye well, they were shite like," Stark replies dismissively in a thick Edinburgh accent He pauses then, as an after-thought, adds " but tae get the goals was spankin' man."

"When did you last score a hat-trick Ray?" I ask, keen to be part of a memorable chat with one of our heroes.

Stark is looking off to his left where a well-fed character with a red face has appeared sporting a wrinkled version of Stark's suit and the same club tie.

"Marshal McGovern, the director" whispers Jonesy low enough for only me to hear.

Ray Stark holds his right hand up in our direction and then slides away, along the connecting passage to where the club official is now standing. We watch an animated conversation with Stark waving his arms around wildly and intermittently smoothing down the back of his oil-slick hair . All the while McGovern puffs away on a huge cigar which is hanging out the side of his mouth. At one point they both laugh loudly and look over at us. Then, with a pat on Stark's shoulder , the plump director makes for the exit and Ray saunters back over to us with a thin smile on his face.

"Arsehole" says Stark to us all in a confidential tone "So, Jimmy" he says looking directly at Grampa, "This'll be your last one then. Good to go out on a win, like."

Before any of us can even begin to respond to this Stark continues. "So here's a ball, like," and he hands Grampa a slightly dirty, white leather Mitre.

"I've signed it somewhere with a wee message, like." He looks away to his left again   pulling out a cigarette from an inside pocket. He lights it and takes a long draw spewing a stream of smoke out the side of his mouth. "It's not the match ball or anythin', he continues, "My wee laddie will get that, like. He's got five of them already but he likes tae kick them around the garden, like. The wee man's spankin' so he is." We all nod stupidly.

Before the silence can get a grip again, Stark looks at his watch then at us, announces an "OK then" in our general direction, turns and skips down the stairs from whence he came.

"Good luck for the season! "calls out Jonesy tentatively. Not breaking his stride, Stark holds a left hand up in the air in scant recognition as he disappears under the stand.

We stare at each other not quite sure what to say. Dave finally breaks the disquiet. "Look Johnny, I'm ...er.. sorry about that. I...em.."

But Grampa holds up his hand. "David son, that was a lovely thing to organise. Thank you very much for that. Its been a perfect day and now I've got a ball to remind me of it. I can kick it round my living room." He laughs at the thought and I smile thinly.

"And its signed too" Grampa continues spinning the ball round in his hands looking for any signs of the writing.

"Ah here we are"

"What does it say " asks Dave wincing.

Grampa pauses, straining his eyes at a small black scrawl on one of the patches on the ball.

"Jimmy, Hope my goals sent you home smiling". Grampa speaks the words slowly and when he stops he looks up and lifts an eyebrow.

"Well it could have been a lot worse than that I suppose."

"Yeah I thought it was going to say 'Have a Spankin' time' or something." sniggers Dave

We burst out laughing. All of us, including Grampa.

"Do you know what would be nice and would mean a lot more to me than having the whole team on there – If you would all sign it."

After a brief, self conscious moment I take the ball, pluck the ever-present Bic pen from my inside jacket pocket and scribble on the leather. Dave clears his throat and follows me. Jonesy completes the job, pausing slightly for a brief moment of contemplation.

Taking the ball back in his hands he quickly examines our handy work, nods his head and as I gently take his arm he draws a deep breath, and takes a slow, sweeping look from one end of the ground to the other.

"OK?" I whisper

"Ok."

And as the groundsman finally gives up his search for rogue divots and dead bodies, the floodlights dim even further, and the last four men slowly walk to the exit.

10.

Dad was waiting for us when we got in. Grunting something sounding like 'Good game?" as we struggled in the door, he lurked in the hallway, offering no help as I negotiated Grampa into the living-room and settled him down on the couch. He glowered in the corner as Mum listened faithfully to an in depth report on the game with a glazed look on her face (When Grampa eventually stopped talking she asked if that meant Arthurston got to stay in the league. Seemingly every game has to mean something to my mother or she can't reconcile our need to be there at all.) Then, after dinner, things changed and dad became quite ridiculously protective, fussing around Grampa, expressing huge concerns over his well-being. Nipping away at me and asking every five minutes or so if Grampa was worn out and would he like to go bed.

"Pay no attention to him" Grampa whispered confidentially when Dad went out to boil the kettle, "I think he feels a little out of it."

Out of it indeed. If by 'it' you mean the 'Normal & Rational Persons' Club'. Anyway I'm determined not to ruin the day and after making a couple more itchy comments, Dad settles down with Mum to watch the TV, lottery tickets held at the ready. Grampa and I sup instead on tea from flowery china mugs and talked of days gone by.

"Have you still got the Big Sweetie Tin?" I ask licking my sugary fingers clean of Battenburg cake, "I haven't seen that in ages."

"Oh aye, its still about somewhere." Grampa replies.

The Big Sweetie Tin used to be the highlight of my Sunday afternoons. I would pelt up Grandma and Grampa's driveway leaving Mum and Dad trailing, bang the front door open then with a loud 'Hello!' to no-one in particular, fly into the kitchen and reach for The Big Sweeie Tin that was always there, in the corner of the worktop, waiting generously for me to arrive.

The tin was huge, burgundy in colour and had a painted picture of a sleek silver car from a bygone era on its lid. It must have been ancient and its ornate design probably made it quite collectable. All I was interested in though was what was inside. And it was always the same – A packet of sweets, usually Opal Fruits or Poppets, two bags of crisps, Savoury Straws or Cheese and Onion Ringos were the favourites from what I remember, a Cola Qwenchy-Cup and the prize of all prizes, that week's copy of Roy of The Rovers. Latterly, Roy got replaced by 'Shoot' or sometimes 'Match' magazine but they never quite inspired the same level of excitement in me as the captain of Melchester Rovers did.

"Sometimes I wasn't sure if you came to see us or The Tin " laughs Grampa letting out a huge yawn then looking quickly at Dad to see if he has noticed. Dad, however, is too wrapped up in the tumbling, coloured balls on the TV to notice anything for the moment.

"It was The Big Sweetie Tin, no question." I reply cheerfully. " Once I had my goodies and my Roy of the Rovers, I would lie on that rug in front of the fire and lose myself. That was me until the football came on the telly. In another world."

"Aye Sundays were good then." agrees Grampa, " Arthur Montford on Scotsport with those patterned blazers that made the TV picture wonky or Archie McPherson on Sportscene on BBC."

"That's right, they used to swap over each year didn't they. STV got the Saturday night slot one season then swapped to Sundays the next season."

"Aye but either way all they ever showed was Rangers or Celtic games against whoever they were playing that week." Grampa sniffs indignantly showing that old wounds don't necessarily heal well, " The only chance you got to see The Rovers on the box was when it was snowing and all the other games were off."

"That's because people wanted to see proper football", chucks in Dad not taking his eyes off the screen which is now filling up with numbered balls.

"Did I mention that your dad wet the bed until he was twelve years old." Grampa says lightly.

"Whassat ? " grunts dad absently, feverishly looking to and from the pink ticket clutched in his hand.

"Ah nothing." says Grampa.

"That's right " I continue, "Arthurston were pretty good at getting games on in those days weren't they?"

"Aye that was mostly down to old Albert Smith, God rest him. He used to put a power of work into keeping the Wilmot Park pitch in good order. " Grampa is about to launch off into what has all the hallmarks of another old-time Arthurston yarn when the spiel is hijacked by a monumental yawn that leaves Grampa sagging in his chair like . All of a sudden the old man looks pale and watery-eyed.

"You're looking a bit tired now." I suggest keeping my tone conversational.

"Yes, I suppose I am son. Its been a big day all round." Grampa sighs

Dad, satisfied only after about his tenth look at his lottery ticket that it is not a winner has a short, fussy conversation with Grampa about negotiating the stairs to the spare bedroom. After much awkward movement, the two of them manoeuvre themselves out the room and into the hallway. Ten minutes or so of dull non-descript dunting from upstairs then things settle down.

Thinking it might be a better option to make myself scarce I breathe out my excuses to Mum, who is too wrapped up in a TV detective drama to even notice my leaving. As I steal out the living room into the relative cold and dark outside I jump badly as I come face to face with Dad who himself looks ashen and worn out.

Neither of us speak.

I immediately want to say that I'd done the right thing, that life was too damn short to just accept the easy option all the time. That in spite of the strain, Grampa had really enjoyed himself. Except I don't. I don't say anything at all. I hold dad's stare for a few more insolent seconds, mutter something unintelligible to either of us, then skip up the stairs, turn off the upstairs hall light and slide into my room closing the door firmly behind me.

So signalling the end of a tiring day. A day full of sharing, happiness and life.

11.

Oh, and we are back up to ninth in the league again. The Championship dream is alive!

Chapter 11
The Return of Danny Rainbow

1.

The sign says in purple, comic-style lettering 'Dundee - City of Discovery'. Like a homemade birthday card greeting computer literate mums knock up on Microsoft Publisher. Certainly not the proud, historic proclamation that Scotland's fourth largest city deserves.

Nevertheless, it means we are nearly there. Slipping gently downhill on a stretch of dual carriageway that is as familiar a milestone in football travelling as it gets. Polythene crop tents are spread on our left keeping the hills fresh beneath and the BP petrol station slides by on the opposite side promising, no doubt, a stop on the way home for a drink and a packet of crisps to keep us going before tea.

Ahead, high-rise flats have sprouted out of the horizon, their urban dismay at odds with the natural greenery around them. They stand like uneasy guardians not quite sure of their purpose, unclear as to whether they are keeping people in or out of the city. The car slows for the first time in a while as we approach the large roundabout that heralds the last stretch before Tannadice, the spiritual home of Dundee United Football Club.

We've had a great conversation on the way up. After briefly discussing the merits of our win against Thistle followed by the reasonable one each draw at home to Dunfermline last week (A 30 yard wonder-strike by Tony Bunton giving him his first goal of the season), I got to thinking about Grampa, that conversation about 'The Tin' , and the goodies that it would always contain.

"You guys got Roy of the Rovers when you were younger didn't you?" I asked leadingly. The answer was a concise 'Of course.' from both Dave and Jonesy much as if I had just asked if they had been inoculated as babies.

"Can you remember all the stories that were in it?" I continue, and so begins a magical trip back to time when Snickers were still Marathons, cola flavoured Spangles were my favourite sweets and Scottish professional footballers were just beginning to miss their sideburns.

And we did not bad. Bearing in mind that Roy of The Rovers first appeared as a character in the Tiger in 1954 and it was way back in '76 that the character became a comic in its own right, we could be forgiven for a touch of haziness to our memory. For our part though, I'd say we nailed most of them. Eighteen or so iconic blasts from the past that warmed my heart to think of again. In no particular order we came up with;

Roy of the Rovers – The chisel chinned, golden haired man himself, Roy Race. Captain of Melchester Rovers, hero of England and all round good egg. Along with best friend and team mate, Blackie Gray and tasty wife, Penny, Roy majestically strode through his career beating teams like Everpool, Liverton, and Walford for fun. I particularly loved it when Roy yelled 'GET IN THERE!' just as he struck the ball and sent a 'Racey's Rocket' into the back of the net.

Mike's Mini Men – Featuring wimpish Mike Daily and his formidable team of err… Subbuteo players. Lacked realism as not once did Mike play a game on the floor and break his players by accidentally kneeling on them.

The Safest Hands in Soccer – The almost ever-present fortunes of Gordon Stewart, a goalkeeper with rugged good looks and 'hauns like bananas'. He spent the bulk of his career at Tynefield City with influential manager and mentor, Jimmy Rockwell. The strip eventually became 'Goalkeeper' and followed the fortunes of Stewart's son Rick instead.

The Kid from Argentina - The everyday story of young Argentinean, Jorge Porbillas and his efforts to play football the British way. Starring for Manton County, the lad was slight of foot and full of South American flair and trickery. Unfortunately he was never the same after they sank the General Belgrano and ended up on a free to East Fife where he instantly became the best English speaker in the town.

The Hard Man – Allegedly inspired by Neil Cooper in his Aberdeen days, Johnny Dexter knocked over all who stood in his way. Under the certifiably mad gaze of Victor Boskovic an alarmingly fat, bald manager with a penchant for tight fitting tracksuits, Johnny consistently took no prisoners. In the words of Grampa he was 'hard but fair'.

Billy's boots – Young Billy Dane lived with his Gran and played for Groundwood school team in the ancient chewed up boots of his hero Dead-Shot Kean. The boots gave Billy fantastic skills and seemed to relive the events of Dead-Shot's career when he was alive. This was one of my favourites and was undoubtedly the inspiration for the footy movie 'There's only one Jimmy Grimble.'

Hot Shot Hamish – The famous Herculean Highlander, Hamish Balfour, who played for Princes' Park. Despite being in the Scottish League, every game inexplicably seemed to have two hundred thousand fervent fans crammed into huge stadia. At least once every game Hamish would hit a thunderous shot so hard that the 'keeper would end up in the back of the net with the ball. Other memorable characters were Mr McWhacker, Wee Wallie Campbell and McMutton the Sheep.

Mighty Mouse- The detailed career of clinically obese junior doctor, Kevin 'Mighty' Mouse. From his days turning out for St Victors' hospital team, incurring the wrath of Dr Mender and Mad Annie the Matron , to his 'professional' career playing for amongst others, Alftown Hotcakes, Tottenford Rovers and Princes Park alongside Hot Shot Hamish, the strip eventually merged with Hot Shot Hamish to become Hamish and Mouse.

The Wheelchair Wonder- Danny Kidd, tragically mowed down in a car crash at the age of fifteen is nursed back to fitness to resume his budding football career. All week Danny can barely walk, yet on a Saturday he manages to pull on his boots and snatch a couple of goals for Overbridge by way of a crazy, curvy shooting ability , the direct effect of his accident leaving his foot in a 'funny' shape. Based on a true story.

Nipper – Gritty Northern realism prevailed as winger, Nipper Lawrence plied his trade for Blackport Rovers. Other characters included Mike Bateson, Len Duggan. Andy Stewart and Stumpy the dog. Not only did Andy Stewart never once sing ' A Scottish Soldier' in this story, he never even got his kilt on.

Millionaire Villa – David Bradley, rich young playboy bought Selby Villa on the basis that he would give himself a game – despite being utter rubbish. I always figured I would eventually do the same at Arthurston – It'll need to be next year.

Tommy's Troubles – How mullet haired schoolboy Tommy Barnes formed his own football team, Barnes United and, aided by his specky pal, Ginger Collins, thwarted sworn enemies Adam Waller and Cyril Swate. Ginger ultimately moved to Ross County under the Bosman ruling and Tommy eventually lost control of his club when Barnes United were taken over by a mysterious consortium from Raith Rovers.

The footballer who wouldn't stay dead – Bizarre tale of Mel Deakin who continually saw, and conversed with, the ghost of dead Wayside Wanderers star, Andy Steele. A warning shot on the effects of drinking Buckfast in the morning if ever there was one.

Roy Race's School-days – These stories only actually turned up in the Roy of the Rovers Annuals and the big thick Summer Specials. They did exactly what it said on the tin chronicling Roy Race and Blackie Gray's early days as youngsters at school. Highlights included Roy's first wet dream, Blackie getting caught sniffing glue behind the bikesheds and Racey's sister getting pregnant by Mr Sands the careers advisor.

Other honourable if sketchier mentions went to Durrells Palace, The Marks Brothers, Tipped for the Top, You are the Star and The Boy Who Hated Football. Ahhh happy days !

2.

Jonesy's CD of the day, some sort of Peruvian incantation music, lasted precisely three minutes on Dave's car stereo before being popped back out and we are currently half-listening to the build up to today's games on the Radio. While Dave continues to get irked by these growingly diverse' musical' offerings, Jonesy's seems happily intent on pushing the boundaries of decency when it comes to the shining discs he impishly produces from his pocket and slips into the stereo just as soon as he feels we are suitably off guard.

We're well on our journey with the likes of Kinkell Bridge, Tibbermore, Glencarse and Pitroddie (not Pittodrie) now behind us. Familiar names to me after years of trawling up this road to see Arthurston play at Perth, Dundee, Forfar and Brechin and yet sadly these are places I've never been to. We frequently pass so close to these little dots on the map but never go so far as to seeing what they have to offer. A real shame I think.

"Did you see that silly looking sign for Dundee back there" says Dave, " It looks terrible. Surely they could have come up with something better than that?"

"Actually its *meant* to look like comic writing," injects Jonesy, " Its symbolic of the influence journalism has had historically on the city. You know, DC Thomson, the folk that made The Dandy and the Beano comics - They're still Dundee based you know."

"They do the Sunday Post as well don't they." I state, happy to be showing at least a portion of the knowledge Jonesy seems to have constantly at his disposal.

I used to quite like the Sunday Post. With its friendly type-face and competitions that lured the reader in with such extravagant prizes as a pair of tea-towels or a packet of seeds for the garden. OK it rarely offered any level of insightful, hard hitting journalism (Doug Baillie would probably shiver at the thought of such reporting) but in terms of covering Saturdays games, it was good and reliable. You always knew that despite only being First Division upstarts, The Rovers would get their 15 or so lines of coverage no matter who they were playing. Better than some of the other Sunday papers who, if you were lucky, would mention the score or sometimes, for no apparent reason, intermittently omit anything to do with Arthurston altogether – much my disgust of course.

I also got a kick out of reading the reports on the Premier league games. Not so much the actual details on the game , nor for that matter the scores. It was more the 'crime count' that I was drawn to. The Post seemed singularly intent on highlighting how many fouls, bookings and sendings- off each team had incurred during the game in question and then, in a scolding and parental manner, would stamp the incriminating statistics on the report in bold black type at its most eye-catching, prominent juncture. All that was missing was a couple of tuts and a wagging finger from the editor. Such violent behaviour was, after all, *not* what your typical Sunday Post reader expected or should be subjected to. No sir.

Strangely though, it's not the Post's football coverage that holds the most vivid of memories for me – It's the golf.

The 'Sunday Post Putter' to be more exact.

For the uninitiated, this was the much sought after prize awarded by the paper to those who got a hole in one in medal play on their local golf course. Winners would send in a copy of their scorecard highlighting the said hole in one and not only would they see their name in black and white in their favourite, cuddly Sunday publication but could expect to receive, return of post, a golf implement worthy of any seaside public putting green you care to mention.

A friend of my dad's, Ralph Slater was his name (although he couldn't have made a suit from a pack of cards), won the Sunday Post Putter. Now it must have been the summer of '86 because he interrupted us watching the Scotland v Uruguay game in the Mexico World Cup to stand right in front of the TV and tell us the 'wonderful ' news. Ralph, you see, was so far up his own arse that his face scarcely saw sunlight and anything vaguely resembling personal achievement, in Ralph's eyes at any rate, was worthy of an announcement through Reuters, a Papal blessing and the Nobel Prize for.... well... 'Being Ralph Slater'.

Anyway, he turned up that day with this ....*club*, stroking imaginary golf balls down our living room carpet, all the while graciously letting us breathe his air , banging on about *The* Hole In One (the only one ever), The Mmmaaarvelous Sunday Post, and how 'select' it was to have 'one of these beauties.' I of course took great delight in picking it up, taking a practice swing and judging that 'it was a bit on the heavy side and would probably only be of use on heavier greens.' Oh and I deliberately called it a golf 'stick' too because that always annoys golfers.

"It's a golf *club* son," Ralph said lighting a cigar, totally oblivious to the room full of patently agitated folk craning their necks to see the telly behind him.

Not long after that Ralph won another newspaper competition and we had to endure him regaling us on how he kept a ' 6' off his scorecard. 'Consistency's the name of the game' he drawled knowledgably as Mum ducked around irritably trying to see the cliffhanging episode of Dallas that was concluding behind his ample frame . "A good golfer plays the percentages" he concluded tapping the side of his nose mysteriously.

I later found out from a guy at school whose dad checked the cards at the golf course that Ralph did indeed keep a six off his scorecard – what he didn't tell us was that he shot a 90 – all fives! The man's handicap was ten for Christ sake, it was a terrible round!

Oh to have so much confidence and so little self-awareness.

3.

The winter of '62/'63 was a cold one. Ask the sparrows. So cold that for a while there was scarcely a game of football to be seen in Scotland (Except of course at Kilmarnock where, as we know, Jack Frost fears to tread.) Dundee United Football Club fared worse than most in those bitter weeks incredibly managing to play only three times in the three months between December and March.

Of those three matches that *did* get played, one in particular was worthy of mention - a home Scottish Cup tie against Albion Rovers. On the face of it not a remarkable looking fixture. In reality however, it would go down as one of the most significant happenings in the modern history of Dundee United Football Club.

To say that the United directors were keen to get the game played would have been putting things mildly. Yet another Saturday was approaching and the Tannadice pitch was covered in a good few inches of snow and ice. Faced with another inevitable postponement someone at the club desperately suggested renting an industrial tar burner to thaw the pitch out. All and sundry agreed this was a fabulous idea, the machinery was duly hired and on reflection, the idea partially worked. Within minutes they melted all the snow and ice off the pitch with an ease that had all in attendance nodding at one another in a satisfied manner.

They also burned all the grass off the pitch.

Smiles vacated and, faced with a scene from the Battle of the Somme, it was suggested (possibly by the same chap who thought about the tar burner in the first place) that if they covered the mud in sand no one would notice, least of all the referee who by the law of averages would probably be registered blind any way. After further backslapping had subsided they did exactly that, dumping several lorry loads of Broughty Ferrie's finest on the big brown rectangle that, at that point, was the vision of Tannadice Park.

Miraculously or predictably, depending on how much cash was actually slipped into the referee's pocket that Saturday morning, the pitch was declared playable and the game went ahead. United ran out comfortable three-nil winners prompting observers to comment that the Dundee team 'took to the surface like Arabs.'

And so an affinity was made. The fans, never slow to pick up on a vibe, embraced the idea and, for the next few games, rudimentary Arab headgear (towels to you and I) was the preferred attire for the Tannadice faithful. The dressing up then became more widespread in the 70's and 80's, particularly on the bigger occasions, and slowly the fans and by association, the team itself, became known as 'The Arabs'. And although United still hang on to their original nickname of 'The Terrors', it is their other, more mysterious Eastern image that endures as the moniker of choice for the fans and players down Tannadice way.

4.

Of course it all began for Dundee United a long time before those wintry days of 1963. Fifty-four years before to be exact, in 1909. Borne out of the city's Irish settlers, the club started on its way as Dundee Hibernian FC. They wore green and white strips and controversially chose to play their games at Clepington Park, the ground on which the current Tannadice Park stands today. I say controversially because this was already the home of another Dundee team, Dundee Wanderers who were to be unceremoniously booted out by their landlords in favour of the new club who had sneakily offered to 'up' the rent for the privilege of playing at this ready made football ground.

This choice of Clepington Park. however, backfired on the Dundee Hibs committee somewhat when, in a 'get it right up ye!' gesture, The Wanderers completely dismantled their ground right down to the goal posts and took it away with them leaving the dismayed new tenants with nothing more than an open space and the natural contours of the land with which to develop.

Dundee Hibs took over the site with resolve though and keen to stamp their own identity on the place, immediately took to renaming it. The main entrance to the new ground would be on Tannadice Street and after a healthy couple of hours of creative teeth-gnashing and debate the committee could come up with only one option – 'Street Park'. Some felt the name lacked impact but with no other suggestions forthcoming it looked as if the name would surely be adopted. Then in a dramatic eleventh hour turnaround, Club Secretary, Pat Reilly, on returning from a much needed comfort break, controversially threw another name in the ring. As the now historic minutes read;

> *'Secretary Reilly proposed with much gusto for the ground be named Tannadice Park .....This was immediately seconded by Goalpost-Convenor O'Hanlon and after a short but heated discussion .... the motion was approved seven votes to three. .... Secretary Reilly further proposed that more toilet paper be placed in the lavatory.....This too was carried unanimously.'*

In June of 1910 Dundee Hibs entered the Scottish league filling the vacant slot created by the amalgamation of Ayr and Ayr Parkhouse. The two teams had formed Ayr United as the latter's league status had become tenuous after being unable to gain local council planning permission for a new Gents toilet and a pie stand. These early years were not kind to Dundee Hibs who were to quit the league twice over league reconstruction issues. With a growing reputation of being 'a gang of 'grippit' whingers'[5] the club retreated into the wilderness of the Independent Central league where they were to play for seven years, all the while campaigning vociferously for the ICL to be incorporated into the Scottish League itself. Ironically in that seventh year, the ICL *was* adopted as the new Second Division, only for the hapless Tannadice club to finish dead last and find themselves relegated out of the league, once more left on the outside looking in.

In 1923, on the verge of disbanding, the club's luck was to change. Having replaced Celtic Reserves in the 'Scottish Plumbers and White Van Drivers Alliance League (West)' they were re-elected to the Scottish League proper on the understanding that ' any future complaining was to be kept to a minimum'. The club agreed and in an effort to gain wider appeal (i.e. to attract Proddies as well) they decided to drop the 'Hibernian' from their name and opt for something more universally acceptable. The initial proposal was to become Dundee City however arch rivals Dundee F C, being the petty stirrers that they were, complained and the

---

[5]   'Displaying a mean and complaining nature'. Ref - 'Dundonian, a different language' by HR Goldrick

club eventually, after many more hours of barren debate, resorted to Dundee United.

5.

Dundee United 1920's to late 1950's – The 'Pish in a poke' years as they came to be known.

There's no better way of describing them. Sure they got to the final of that War Cup malarky in 1940 but then, in the foggy years of ration books and sketchy memories, didn't everyone. The rest of it though was pure torture for the Arab loyal. As erstwhile fan, Andy Sheever of Provost Road, Dundee enigmatically penned in his letter of February 1957 to the Dundee Courier, 'yonder team are about as United as a pickled egg!'. Andy also went on to compare the manager to a horse-box and the chairman to a wicker likeness of Musollini he had 'hidden down an old Wellington boot in the garden shed'. Andy probably had mad eyes and dribbled a lot.

Then things took a turn for the better. Manager Jerry Kerr came along, steadied the ship and in a groundbreaking move for the times brought in a hoard of Scandinavian imports to inject some European flair to proceedings. Persson, Dossing Seamenn and Wing all pulled on United's black and white strips prompting accusations from many quarters that these were clearly made up names. It was also mooted that they weren't Scandinavian at all and were in fact contracted whalers from Carnoustie who had disguised themselves with blonde wigs in a reckless effort to avoid another vomit inducing North Sea stint aboard a boat the size of an enamel bathtub. These allegations were never proven although a number of opposing players swore that when they shook Finn Dossing's hand they were left with a definite smell of fish on their fingers'. Whatever their story it turned out they were great team players and collectively went a long way to establishing United as a more consistent force in the Scottish game.

The alert amongst you will have noticed the black and white strip reference back there. No, this is not a typo. For the youngsters out there Dundee United *did* used to wear white tops and black shorts. Surprisingly, it was only as recent as 1967 that they changed to the now familiar tangerine numbers and if it hadn't been for the wife of a former director, there's a good chance that black and white would probably still be the order of the day.

That year, '67, United played in an inaugural competition over in the States to publicise the budding North American Soccer League. In a bizarre set of circumstances teams from around the world turned out as the various US cities chosen to host NASL teams. Dundee United represented Dallas. Aberdeen, who had also been invited, played as Washington (none of the really cold cities were left), Hibs were Toronto and an assortment of teams from England, Ireland ,Brazil, Uruguay, Italy and Belgium made up the rest of the representatives. Anyway, back to the director's wife. The Dallas strip worn by Dundee United was a brilliant tangerine in colour and whether it looked particularly flattering in the sunshine or wouldn't be such a bitch to keep clean through the winter months, our soccer spouse liked the design so much that when the team got home she suggested United adopted it as their new, official kit. Feminine persuasiveness being what it is, United were soon sporting the new, funkier ensemble.

Anyone still not completely sold on the conversion, and there are low mutterings of disapproval on Tayside even nowadays, should take consolation in the thought that it could have been worse. During the same trip, the wife took in the celebrated stage show of 'The sound of Music' and was heard to comment afterwards in the theatre bar how she had 'loved those little curtain outfits!' worn by the Von Trappe children. Arabs, think on and be thankful!

The club's development was to take a further turn in 1971 with the arrival of Jim McLean - International Man of Misery. Famous then for nothing more than his dreary mono-tone voice and extensive collection of brown ties, McLean was to embark on an association with the club that would eventually span four decades.

He had a vision. The club would stand on the firm foundations of a sound youth policy and by signing up talented, wide-eyed youngsters on 'standard' thirty-seven year contracts, Jim ensured continuity, fostered loyalty and made sure that at least some of that early crop of kids would die through natural causes in the service of United. As someone worthy once said 'Death comes at the end of life. ' And at United, those young men lived - on bread and water mostly - sometimes not seeing relatives for weeks on end, sometimes wearing leg-irons but always living, breathing and doing ball-work under the domineering shadow of Jim McLean.

He lived the dream at Dundee United

Under McLean's steady guidance United took on Rangers and Celtic and were triumphant. If winning the Premier League in '83 with the financial inequalities of Scottish football stacked heavily against them was nothing short of a miracle, then the subsequent exploits on the European stage were beyond Biblical. They joined Aberdeen as The New (if only temporary) Firm and ruled an era where others like them saw hope, possibility and opportunity. They held internationals in their ranks (as many as five Dundee United players played for Scotland against Israel in '86.) and many of their squad members experienced all the glitz and glamour a successful football life could offer, opening church fairs, hospital annexes and advertising local pine furniture stockists on the radio.

But let's not get carried away. It couldn't last and it didn't. By the early 90s United were back in the clutches of mid-table obscurity; 'also rans' in the new and improved Old-Firm show. From there we barely noticed their steady decline until suddenly at the end of '95, they found themselves at the bottom of the Premier and relegated to the first division at which point even the tangerine decked, out-his-face drunkard in the corner woke up and realised that the party was over.

And what of Jim McLean? Were it not for a spectacular event in Scottish televisual history, Jim would probably still be knocking around in the Tannadice background as we speak. Unfortunately for Jim his willingness to live the dream went one step too far when he took exception to a particular line of questioning taken by BBC reporter, John Barnes (THE John Barnes to his friends and family) during an 'on-camera' post match interview. Times were tough for the club, United had just lost 4-0 to Hearts and the interview had began with McLean being asked about a demonstration outside the ground by United fans followed by a short dig into the appointment of his brother Tommy, that very week, onto the club's coaching staff. Under Barnes' persistent questioning the mood of interview gradually deteriorated culminating in the following unforgettable passage;

Barnes: How long do you give (manager) Alex Smith to get it right on the park?

McLean: You think I'm going to answer a stupid question like that?

Barnes: I'm only asking it

McLean: I told you before I wouldn't be fucking answering it. And make sure that's cut! And I'll tell you something ….. (thump) Don't ever fucking offer me that again!

At which point the picture cut to the studio where a more shell-shocked than usual, Dougie Vipond stuttered " What followed then was a serious assault on our reporter."

Weyhey! A bit more of that please!. Human frailty laid bare, toe-to-toe confrontation, a member of the press being popped. To the morbid voyeurs amongst us – compelling stuff. To everyone else – well … I think I can make out tutting at the back there. Oh yes – definitely the noise of tutting being tossed down from the high ground but come on now, admit it; this is the sort of thing that gets all our blood running isn't it? Possibly even more so than the best of goals or the most sublime of touches of skill. A ten player stramash on the pitch always has us all on our feet snarling like wolves, igniting even the dullest game. A flailing punch, a head-butt even or better, a bit of improvised strangulation is always good to get the primeval juices coursing through the veins. Anyone claiming to be repulsed by such behaviour is either a much, much better man than me or, more likely, a wee lyin' toe-rag.

6.

We've passed the Swallow Hotel and The Gourdie Croft Beefeater to the left of the crushed dual carriageway which bisects an up and coming area of retail parks , modern commercial properties and industrial units. Our decision not to stop-by means that if we are looking for lunch now, we would need to head closer to the centre of Dundee itself and away from the vicinity of the stadium. While there are a few pubs dotted around Tannadice ahead, proper sit-down food with plates, cutlery and other fancy accoutrements isn't really an available option.

Gliding sedately up the said dual-carriageway well within the speed limit (Dave got a fine and 3 points on his licence doing 44mph along this stretch about ten years ago and we're always on our guard now.) we have had our usual argument about which turn-off to take. I want to take the first available slip road signposted Couper Angus but Dave holds firm and continues on half a mile or so to the next one. Both exits rise up on our left hand side, curve over the road above us and generally look very similar but only one takes us directly to the Clepington Road area where we can leave the car, grab some cash from a handy hole-in-the wall, have a pint and be within walking distance of the game.

We manage to take the correct turn-off, which engagingly invites us to the nearby crematorium, leaving me feeling quite sheepish about my heated assertions that Dave was 'definitely going the wrong bloody way!". We seem to have the same argument every time we play the Dundee teams and indeed it is a replica of the verbal joust we also have en-route to Raith Rovers as well. Is it the Kirkaldy East or Kirkaldy West turn-off that's the quickest? (It's Kirkaldy West for the record) The same arguments year on year and yet we never learn. It's like we drive back across that expansive bridge over the River Tay, wind in our ears, Perth nestled down to our right and someone wipes our memories clean. Either that or we're just daft.

We also manage to get parked up on Clepington Road, the main thoroughfare skirting the brow of a steepish hill that slopes down to the football grounds of both Tannadice and Dens Park, the dusty home of local rivals Dundee FC. The tenement streets that cling on to said slope also make for good parking although you frequently have to wedge your car into a small space on a pavement corner or worse, abandon it at an odd angle against a dividing road-island or roundabout . This doesn't pose a huge problem however the irregular facilities do prompt two or three concerned glances over your shoulder at your less-than-plum parking causing you to wonder how you ever passed your driving test in the first place. There's also the lingering concern that this will be the time you'll get your car clamped for excessive 'sticking-outage'. So far so good though, it hasn't happened yet.

Our Clepington Road berth saves us any such concerns though. Clambering out and stretching in unison the three of us stare at each other expectantly. Up this end of the town we have a choice of thirst quenching venues dotted along the Clepington route. Not a vast array of choice but choice nonetheless. Will it be 'The Glens' with its too bright exterior paint job and bemused wall mounted stag's head that can't quite come to terms with not looking out onto the hallway of some stately home or other? Or maybe the split levelled, wood panelled refinement of White's Bar on the corner? The down-at-heel friendliness of The Centenery Bar? Or possibly 'The Clep' with its cheap yellow signage and tight, drinking man's claustrophobia. All, to be fair, are acceptable options for a pre-match swipe at life and football.

"I reckon we should have a pint in The Centenery!" I suggest brightly.

"Why so definitive?" asks Jonesy hands in pockets staring over the car roof at me.

"Well, it's right behind you for starters …."

Jonesy wheels round then looks back slightly suspiciously, as if someone had wheeled the pub in behind him when he wasn't watching.

"Oh yeh." He exclaims absently and without further encouragement announces "Let's go then!". Faced with two doors, he makes his way through the right hand opening and into the 'Bar' area of the tolerantly waiting pub.

7.

I'm standing at corner of the bar like the Invisible Man without his Nicorette patch on, tapping away tersely on the beer drenched surface with a rolled up tenner in my hand. The young barmaid in front of me seems remarkably calm considering the number of blokes , mostly Arthurston fans by their look, clamouring to get served at the one time. There would appear to be a couple more bar-staff through at the other side of the large central-partitioned square bar but one glance says they have their hands full dealing with a flurry of tangerine decked United fans equally as committed to sampling the house specialities as we are in here.

"Three pints of …… " but someone else has caught her eye over at the other side of the bar − Buggerritt!. Resigned, I take a moment out to survey the scene around me. The pub seems to be a little bit shabby and down at heel, made up of two hexagonal shaped rooms, painted an insipid green colour with big telly screens and puggies aplenty. Each room, split obviously today between home and away fans, offers standing room at the bar and a raised seating area divided off from the rest of the pub by a series of carved wooden arches and posts.

Peering round one of these posts Jonesy catches my eye and hangs his tongue out his mouth then, satisfied he has my attention, makes a hand gesture indicating, I think, that he would like a bag of crisps to go with his pint. I shrug my shoulders and turn back to the barmaid who, to my disgust, has just started to pour a healthy round of Guinness pints. A collective groan rises from the surrounding punters.

Ten pound note still in hand, absent-mindedly shaking it in the direction of the beer tap in front of me, I turn to look at a variety of holiday photo's plastered on the wall at my side. Row upon row of glossy, bright red holiday faces that look like they've been dipped in a chip pan. Waving cheerily at the folks in the pub back home smiling smiles that say 'We sincerely hope it's lashing with rain where you are right now.'

Not for the first time I wonder why publicans partake in this strange decorative ritual. What does it say about their clientele other than a) they have never heard of high factor sun-tan lotion, b) they spend their holidays much like they spend their spare time at home - in the pub, or c) they're collectively not a very photogenic bunch and you're not going to pull a 'looker' in this particular establishment on a Saturday night.

Whatever happened to the traditional gantry decoration of the scantily clad young women with packets of 'Big-D' peanuts tantalisingly covering their interesting bits. In those days you were *happy* to linger at the bar for a time. Maybe even have a bag of nuts with your pint – as long as it was that particular bag third down on the right that is. Certainly better than viewing a variety of snaps taken in the Burns Unit of Torremolinos General that's for sure.

Thankfully I catch the girl's eye at just the right moment and spluttering out my order rapidly in a tone several pitches higher than my normal voice, the deal is done. Looking at the resentful eyes boring into me I swell my chest and take a teasing sip from the first golden glass that has just been laid in front of me.

8.

As I steer myself gingerly towards our table, the guys are rounding off a strange argument concerning Jonesy's unauthorised use of Dave's best deodorant as fly spray.

"Well it seems to work, don't you find that worrying?" finishes Jonesy leaning back on his chair, folding his arms as if he has totally vindicated himself.

"Just leave my stuff alone alright!" Dave growls, " I know you're doing me a good turn letting me stay but if you do it again, I swear I'm moving out."

"Bloody hell, all over a can of deodorant!"

" No," says Dave slowly and thoughtfully, "there's those snottery hankies you leave all over the place, soggy or crispy depending how long they've been lying, and those little shits you leave in the toilet pan."

Jonesy looks around in an agitated fashion then leans forward. "That's a dietary condition," he hisses," They honestly refuse to flush awa…"

" AND your skidmarky pants that lie all over the house," Dave persists, "spread on the floor like you just stepped out them and walked on your way. AND there's my washing."

"What about your washing. I don't touch your washing" says Jonesy indignantly.

"Oh yeh so you didn't stick that blue 'Trainee Sex Slave' t-shirt of yours in with my whites making them a mouldy grey colour, and you *haven't* been using my clean work shirts out the basket as pillows when you're lying on the couch watching TV then?"

Jonesy looks uncomfortably at the floor then up at me. I'm still on my feet, mesmerised by the domestic being played out before me.

"Where's the crisps?" cries Jonesy seizing the opportunity to steer the conversation in another direction . I come to and tentatively lay the drinks on the table collapsing into a dark green upholstered bench with a sigh

"Aww man, I forgot." Taking a look back to the bar, the gap I created by leaving has well and truly been swallowed by thirsty punters.

My expression is pathetic enough for Dave to mutter that I didn't need to go back.

"We'll talk later." he then warns Jonesy ominously.

A silence falls over us as we all take simultaneous draws on our pints, Dave and Jonesy each staring blindly into the middle distance. Under pressure to fill the quiet I summon up some courage and casually ask Dave if he's heard from Linda.

Dave exhales slowly through his nose. Deflating like a tyre. Just as I think he isn't going to answer he grumbles under his breath "Nope, not this week – but I have heard from her pal Alice"

"Alice from your New Year's party?" I ask, catching Jonesy's face flush out of the corner of my eye.

"That's the one" he continues grimly, " It seems she's worried about Linda." Pausing as if to pick his words carefully, Dave fixes his stare on the ashtray on the table in front of him. " She thinks that Linda may be seeing a guy from the salon."

"Whaaat!" splutters Jonesy, "You never told me this! A guy from the salon? Don't be ridiculous, they're all as camp as a row of tents in there - apart from that bloke Gerry with the eyebrows and I've heard he's into grannies. Is it…"

"Its not a workmate, it's a customer from the salon" Dave interrupts like he's got a bad taste in his mouth.

I'm stunned. As usual I can't think of anything useful to say. Jonesy seems to be in a similar state. A raucous conversation floats over from another table, a nose wrinkling tale of someone or other's big sister vomiting into a pair of CAT boots. Normally the sort of interlude that would cause us to turn round and grin appreciatively. Right now it slips off us practically unnoticed.

"I'm sure its nothing though. She's got enough on her plate right now to be thinking about without bringing other guys into it."

"How do you mean?" I ask.

"Well she's…" and Dave looks uncomfortable," She's thinking about chucking her job, you know doing something …… different and… she's looking at flats as well…"

"Wait a minute!– she's thinking of *moving*!"cries Jonesy outraged. "What is the woman on?" he continues, "I mean its only been a few weeks, surely she should be coming to her senses and getting things back in order rather than all this .... *new* nonsense."

"Maybe she *is*." replies Dave quietly. "Maybe things *are* being put in order and it doesn't involve me."

Loud braying laughter from the CAT boot people involuntarily steals our attention from the matter in hand. Dave conjures up a diluted smile and suggests gently with a tired expression that we don't waste the day and that we talk about something else.

"What about you" Dave eventually says turning to me. " Any sign of Miss Right heading your way?"

I make a sound of a short, airy fart out my mouth.

"I'll take that as a no then." He responds sharply. " What happened with the girl from the pub the other night."

I look at Dave suspiciously but say nothing.

"Oh yes. Chris here may well have mentioned the goings on once I left O'Jay's last week.

The Girl from O'Jays

Sounds like a hit from the 60's; '...... *Shakin' her hips with her white boots awwnnnnn baby!*'

Last Saturday night. Not my finest hour.

Her name was Diane. She worked in a nursing home. And I sat on her hamster.

It had all started so well. We talked for a bit in that nightclub-shouting-in-each-other's-ear way then did a bit of dancing. We had stuff in common - we were both pissed. So I got an invite back to hers; a cramped flat with a bike in the hall, dim lights, and a Jack Vettriano print hung over the three bar fire. I sat down briefly on the couch then stood up to receive a rather hefty looking vodka. I was about to sit back down when Diane pointed behind me and yelled 'Clliiiingerrrr!" in a tone reserved for patrons of the Wailing Wall. On the cushion behind me, contrasting against the grey upholstery, was the side on view of a golden hamster. 'Like one of those stone-age cave paintings' I remember thinking as I stared without blinking.

Diane shrieked something about reviving Clinger, for Clinger was apparently its name, whereby I made a glib remark about not being well versed in mouth-to-snout resuscitation. Diane called me a bastard at that point then started rushing round the living room and adjacent kitchen muttering 'revive him' repeatedly in a low madness.

She then disappeared into the hall and I swear on my life that what happened next is the Gospel truth.

She reappeared moments later waving in her hand the black mini pump from her bike. "Revive him!" she demanded, thrusting the pump at me viciously.

Cowed by her steely eye and venomous tone, and to my eternal shame, I took the pump and seeing no other option knelt on the floor, tilted Clinger's head to the side and prised open his mouth. With a nauseated grimace on my face I slid the pump nozzle into his mouth. And in time to Diane's counting, I pumped Clinger.

At 2.13 AM Clinger the hamster was officially pronounced dead and at 2.16 AM I was on the pavement digging my hands into my pockets and heading for home. I didn't get her number.

"I'd rather not talk about it." I murmur grimly.

"Ahhh, don't knock being in the action," Dave says with a rye smile, "Better getting a boot in the arse going for the ball than sitting safe on the subs bench, don't you think?"

"Trust me in this case no."

"Well you can tell us in your own time mate." Dave is now smirking. "What about the Chickolita at that funeral? Done anything about that?"

"What? The girl in Motherwell? Are you serious?"

"All I'm saying is that Sherlock Holmes never solved a case by sitting at home fiddling"

Jonesy splutters the last of his beer back into the bottom of his glass and I stare at Dave not quite sure what he's implying. Uncomfortable with the spotlight turned firmly on me I opt for diversionary tactics.

"Another beer?" I suggest hopefully.

"Actually I think we should move on." Dave suggests," By the time one of us gets served I'll have died of thirst and er... need revived."

With a snigger both the guys get up and sharply head for the exit leaving me momentarily sitting contemplating the foamy residue at the bottom of my glass. "Hey wait ! Why did you say th..." I start to yell, but the guys are out of era-shot and a final crash of hilarity from 'the laughing table' derails my train of thought. Sliding off my seat and shaking down my trousers more laughs carry across the room and as I head sharply for the door I can't resist a self-conscious glance backwards. Just to make sure they aren't laughing at me.

9.

A few hundred yards back along the road , White's bar has a more sedate air to it. Its also better appointed. Mr White unlike the owners of the Centenery has a pot of paint and isn't scared to use it. The pub itself is of a strange split level design due in the main to the precarious position it occupies on the steep slope of Provost Road. We are settled on the lower level beside a prominent chimney arrangement and a supporting blackened stove. Hanging Victorian lights illuminate the room necessarily as the day outside has darkened ominously, like a murder is on the way.

We have been talking about Dundee United's European exploits of old. Back in the 80's when we all had more optimism, United of course had two great 'proud to be Scottish' cup runs. The European Cup adventure of '83 where the guns of Malta's Hamrun Spartans , Standard Liege and Rapid Vienna were all silenced before United finally succumbed to the might of AS Roma in the semi-finals. Then the UEFA cup exploits of three years later. It 's at this point that Dave surprisingly digs two folded, slightly dog-eared pieces of photocopied A4 from his pocket and subconsciously flits his eyes back and forth between Jonesy and myself.

"I .... eh, found this in one of my office drawers when I was doing a clearout last week. Its ..... em .... a poem. "

"A whit? "

"Umm ..., a poem. Jake Swinburn gave me it one day years back when I was slagging off his team."

" Jake Swinburn! – there's a name from the past. " I laugh, "You used to give that guy a real hard time. No wonder he left."

"No wonder indeed, the man was soooooo irritating. Singing yon Deacon Blue boy's 'Proud to be an Arab' to himself all day! Can you *begin* to comprehend what that was like to work with?" Dave's tone darkens and he continues, ".... And I'm proud to be an Arab, Proud of my home team, And I'm Proud to be an Arab, Old times and new. LOOK! – I even know the words I heard it that often! *And* it Doesn't even bloody-well rhyme!"

Just as he looks like he's going to burst he pulls himself together and quietly in a resigned manner says "Anyway...."And in an exaggerated, low dramatic tone recites this poem about United's last great run in European competition. A sip of lager, a small clear of the throat and off he goes....

The Terrors of '86

The stories on Tayside run long in the night
'bout a squad full of heroes, willing to fight,
and die for the jersey – the tangerine dream
of the UEFA cup being won by the team

It started in Lens, the dark horses from France
Where United were lead in a bit of a dance
They lost it one-nil but it could have been more
Billy Thomson 's heroics kept down the score

Back in Dundee, the attacking was torrid,
But for 54 minutes the French wall stood solid
Lens had it sewn up, at least so they reckoned
'Til Milne got the first and Coyne bagged the second.

Now Uni. Craiova were next to be shocked
John Clark filled the void with Paul Hegarty crocked.
Big John scored a header and Redford got two,
A three goal advantage would surely get through.

Were the Craiovan players depressed? – by no means,
They each returned home with a caseful of jeans!
And a one-nil reverse sparked Rumanian pride
But the terrors of Dundee were now in their stride

It was on to the third round against Hadjuk Split
With Mclean's brave young lions beginning to knit
as a team that all Europe was starting to see
Were a force to be taken seriously.

Split came to Scotland without some star players
And within half an hour were saying their prayers
Jim McInally had just tapped one in
with Hadjuk's defence looking scared out its skin.

The Slavs went two down just after the break
Clark pouncing on Billy McKinlay's mistake
To drill the ball home like a shot from a cannon
They might have scored more if they hadn't lost Bannon

But two-nil it stayed and a tie nothing each
In the nervy return gave United a peach
of a draw in the quarters against a 'wee' team
From the south coast of Spain, if you know who I mean

Barcelona came forth and give them their dues
Lineker, Zubezaretta, and Hughes
Were true world class, really hard nuts to crack
Could the Arabs waste Venables' plan of attack?

United came out firing, swift, strong and bold
Catching the Catalan superstars cold
From a throw on the right, Sturrock's pass by God's grace
Found young Kevin Gallagher standing in space

Only two minutes gone and the lad's curling lob
Found the back of the Spanish team's net just the job
The sceptics all wondered if Kev really meant it
The 'experts' could tell by the way that he bent it

The world's richest club had been rocked to the core
The twenty-one thousand home fans screamed for more.
They began to believe they were in with a shout
When Lineker fluffed a great chance four yards out.

The ref's final whistle blew – no further score
The worried fans cheered but thought 'Did we need more
than a one-nothing lead to take over to Spain?'
Where Barca could not be as timid again.

The 18th of March , almost twenty years on
From United's first Europen tie which they won,
In the very same ground, 'gainst the very same team
A similar scoreline would be like a dream.

A goal up at halftime, the Spanish had thoughts
That their team would go on now and murder the Scots.
But with four minutes left Clark again was the star,
Pulling them square, heading in off the bar.

The home crowd went silent, the Arabs went mad,
And what happened next made all Scottish fans glad.
From the left Sturrock crossed, as the cup semis beckoned,
Ferguson stooped down and headed the second.

That night full of drama and wonder and awe
Rewarded the club with another tough draw.
Against Monchengladbach, the first leg at 'hame'
A cup final berth would need more of the same.

The Germans looked class in the first forty-five,
But Dundee's resolve kept the fans' hopes alive.
An Ian Redford shot off the post turned the tide,
While a Ferguson goal was chopped off for off-side.

So nil- nil it finished, but what can you say,
'bout the Terrors' who then won it two-nil away.
As fine a performance as in the last round,
In 'Gladbach's real menacing Bokelberg ground.

And so to the final - a two leg affair.
'gainst IFK Gothenburg. Those who were there
Will tell of a heroic fight to the death
Each player donating their very last breath

A poor playing surface would hamper United,
Bumpy and dry – the home fans were delighted
When the ball took a horrible bounce out a hole
Over poor Thomson and into the goal

The Ulevi Stadium erupted in song,
The two thousand Arabs sang back just as strong.
But the Swede stars seemed fresh while United looked jaded
And Dundee failed to score as the bright evening faded.

United to win the home leg? – time would tell,
A capacity crowd saw United start well.
The Swedes, though, took over and it wasn't a shock
When Gothenburg scored, 22" on the clock.

The UEFA trophy was slipping from view
But the weary United lads weren't quite through.
A gutsy revival by Sturrock and Co.
Saw Clark equalise with a half hour to go

A Gallagher blast then a penalty claim
Kept the crowd on their toes 'til the end of the game.
But The ref blew for time, with United's fate sealed
As the gracious support clapped the Swedes off the field.

Proud Jim McLean wept in front of the shed,
As his tired but heroic young players were led,
In before all the faithful to take one more bow,
A vision that staunch Arabs 'mind even now.

The story's been told now and all that's required
Is a toast to United, so skilled and inspired.
To the best Arab team in the last twenty years!
The Terrors of '86 - Here's to you, Cheers!

Dave pauses for dramatic effect, folds the paper up then quickly unfolds it again.

"Oh, and the full squad is listed here too" he adds quickly," want me to read it?"

We both nod enthusiastically and Dave finishes off naming the players again in a low dramatic voice.

"B. Thomson, Main, Malpas, McGuiness, McKinley, Clark, Sulley, Nary, Beaumont, Holt, Hegarty, McLeod, Bowman, Bannon, Kinnaird, Kirkwood, Gallacher, S. Thomson, Coyne, Redford , Milne, Sturrock, Ferguson"

After a short pause for reflection Dave once again folds the poem up and puts it back in his pocket.

"That was ok wasn't it" he states matter-of-factly."I thought it might be a bit cheesy, but it's quite interesting don't you think?" He looks at me challengingly and gives a short sideways glance to Jonesy .

Quite legitimately, we both nod our heads and congratulate Dave, our newly appointed 'Poem Reciter Extraordinaire.' Looking pleased with himself he takes a long drink of his pint and settling back in his chair with just a hint of a smile on his lips sighs "Ahh ... old Jake Swinburn – always liked that guy."

10.

Walking along the hard Dundonian pavement, an unpleasant wind has whipped into our faces all of a sudden, bringing with it a smattering of light rain. Having nipped back to the car for jackets we are heading, along with a steady flow of supporters, down Hindmarsh Avenue, past a small parapet wall commemorating 'The Fleming Trust Housing Scheme', and downwards through dreary stone housing to the football grounds of the City of Dundee.

Eight towering floodlights loom ahead casting wary glances at each other across the dividing thoroughfare of Tannadice Street.

To our right the blue painted stands of Dens Park, home of Dundee Football Club. To our left the corrugated grey metal of Tannadice, home of course to Dundee United.

If one scene could sum up the irrationality, the wonderful stupidity of football I would have to say this would be it. Two teams, two stadia, two sets of fans, four dressing rooms, eight corner flags ... ahh you get the picture ... all separated by the length of a goalie's kick out. It must be enough to make the money men of our game have sweat soaked nightmares and yet from a fans point of view it's a perfectly feasible, thoroughly embraceable arrangement.

Questions beg, yet evade, logical answering in terms of this strangest of situations. There are *whys* aplenty once you get thinking on it? Why on earth would you have two separate teams representing the one relatively small city? (especially in the absence of any current religious or geographic divide). Why wouldn't they merge and become Sporting Club Dynamo Dundee? Why don't they at least share a bloody ground and enjoy a better quality of corrugated iron cladding that they have at the moment?

Why not? Because it would be affront to the fans that's why not. The traditional loyalties would be at best tested, at worst severed. Habits would be broken, identities crushed. These are vital factors of life for football fans, not just in the City of Dundee, that go way beyond the realms of what makes financial or practical sense. Cut the ties and rupture the independencies of each loyal band of fans and the likelihood would be that rather than build a 'Superteam' with increased resources and double the fan base, a Frankenstein's monster of a club would be created that *no one* in the town could summon *any* allegiance to. Few would go to the games and Saturdays in Dundee would be punctuated by packed pubs, full to the gunnels with football fans reminiscing over the 'auld days', the rivalries , the exaggerated glories and the like. Naw, once the damage is done, once the links are forged there's no room for manoeuvre. Two teams in one street in Dundee is where it's at and where it always has to be. Anyone who wants to bring their stupid common sense and practicalities can go and get stuffed.

That said there's an ill divide to the Dundee situation, - certainly in my world at any rate. While I take limited pleasure from 'The Tannadice experience', and apologies to Dundee fans for this, I hold a healthy disregard for all things Dens. Like a farmers wife from 'All Creatures Great and Small', Dens Park could only be described as ugly but functional. Despite the two new stands at either end of the ground the place remains drab and soulless. Like the ugly brick coal-scuttle out in the garden that can neither be demolished or improved upon. Combine these aesthetic shortcomings with Dundee FC's inability to play the welcoming host card terribly well and what we're dealing with is an away fixture that would be top of your 'games to miss if you absolutely had to' list.

Yet Dens Park holds an interesting record for me as an away fan. It is the only ground, to my recollection, where Rovers fans over the years have been allocated space in every side of the stadium. Ok, not *interesting* as such but certainly remarkable. Normally, and quite peculiarly now I think on it, we tend only to see each venue from the same vantage point time and again. And it's a weird almost disconcerting feeling when you're moved and given a new perspective on an old familiar viewpoint.

So its Dens for variety then. The first time I was there we were out in the snow, packed into the tight terraced area in front of the musty, main V-shaped stand. The next, we made it up into the big wooden fire hazard itself on a day, unfortunately, we lost six-nil. Since then we've stood in a sand storm on the old terraced section at the Tannadice end of the ground - the sand in question being blown by Hurricane Bella off the trackside and into our weather-singed faces. We've spent a cold, damp night under a leaky roof behind the other goals, standing on cold concrete. And once, although I'm not sure why, we sat on the little skelf-inducing benches under the shed directly across from the main stand. Nowadays the away fan is sometimes let loose in the new stand behind the goals however generally, if you're a team like Arthurston, things have come full circle and you're situated back in the main stand . Once mugged at the gates by the most expensive pricing in the lower leagues, you'll be herded into the cramped left hand wing which offers limited viewing and painfully little leg room. Here you'll be greeted by the malevolent Tayside police (I'll talk about them another time) and a sour band of stewards who will insist you don't, under pain of death, sit in the front row of seats in case you get either a better view of the game or are tempted to toss yourself over the barrier onto the players tunnel below in a protest over the prices at the pie stand - We're talking 80p for a NORMAL sized Mars bar here and a bank haul for the mince or steak pies which possess flavours and aromas that are disconcertingly unfamiliar to the seasoned pie-eating connoisseur. I haven't bothered looking for a programme in my last few visits to Dens as I assume they'll come in at somewhere round about a tenner.

Such irritations are in the past though. As we scuttle down through the triangular swing park adjacent to Tannadice Street reaching the main drag, we thankfully turn left for the Premier League instead of right for the First Division and head towards our goal - the Jerry Kerr Stand which conveniently is now looming directly in front of us.

11.

'Bitty' would be the best way to describe the inside of Tannadice Park. While the two tiered George Fox Stand (The Foxy George Stand as Jonesy calls it) across from us is splendid in its orangey togetherness, the rest of the ground is an untidy melange of add-ons and stuck-ins. Which I quite like to be honest. Bland symmetrical football grounds have never been my thing and Tannadice's haphazard construction offers an interesting alternative to the grey concrete boxes that are more and more becoming the modern idiom.

We are in the Jerry Kerr Stand (Upper Tier), a welded-on extension to the old L-shaped Main-Stand which has lurked around the South East corner of the ground for as long as I can remember. This strangely shaped structure with its odd location apparently harkens back to the '60s when , in a fit of optimism, United planned to build in a similar manner all the way round the ground. Business planning being as it is in Scottish Football, they got about an eighth of the way there before the money ran out. I suppose it's the thought that counts. The financially bereft directors of the time were admirably best-intentioned and credit must be given to them, I suppose, for designing the first cantilever roof in the Scottish game. For the non-engineers out there that means 'Nae poles', and no doubt the forty-eight people who made up the capacity of the stand really appreciated their clear, unbroken view of the game.

To our left, the West Stand is a shallow seated area populated by home fans. Football supporters are creatures of habit when it comes to which area of the ground they choose to view the game from and if I was a guessing man I would suggest that patrons of the West Stand probably used to stand in that area when it was still terracing. If I'm wrong they can send me a ten pound note in an envelope and tell me why they *do* sit there and I'll agree with them.

In keeping with the general higgledy-piggledy-ness of the ground the seats in the West Stand run out before the end of the rise leaving a couple of hundred square feet of unfilled cemented area in one corner. To my mind there are two possible explanations for this gap. Ever accommodating, the directors left the area bare as a corner of banishment and reflection for 'wallopers' who have overstepped the mark in terms of moaning, shouting or just plain 'talking pish'. Friends or acquaintances in the close proximity to the said 'walloper' can request that they be grabbed by a waiting steward and manhandled in an 'off-putting' manner to 'The Corner' thus offering those around the offender a few minutes of welcome respite to enjoy the game in peace. That's got you all thinking now, eh?

Conversely , I'd like to think that the same directors may have left the space unseated in symbolic protest to the Evil Taylor

Report (ETR). Fans are then secretly encouraged to sneak along every so often and stand defiantly for a brief moment, arms folded and grim faced, before scuttling back to their enthusiasm-sapping plastic 'bucket' seat for the rest of the match. If I'm wrong then the directors can send me a twenty in an envelope with the real explanation and I'll agree with them too. Hell, they can probably afford it.

Arabs of a more excitable disposition will find their way to the two- tiered seating behind the opposite goals in the East Stand. From the boisterous rendition of 'Beautiful Sunday' welcoming the players onto the park to the final whistle, patrons of this area appear to scarcely sit down and you get a real sense of the fervency of the support coming from this section— more so than I've experienced in most away grounds to be honest. I've spoken to others in the past who have claimed that Tannadice lacks atmosphere. All I can say to that is they've obviously never seen the East Stand folk in full tilt. Nor indeed, have they ever been to Recreation Park, Alloa, midweek, in the rain.

12.

"Isn't that Danny Rainbow down there?" says Jonesy leaning forward on his seat and pointing towards the lower tier of seating below us.

Following his direction Dave and I search the small band of Rovers fans scattered there, our eyes coming to rest on a compact character with a startling bush of brown curly hair, heavy birds' nest eye-brows and a ruddy red complexion.

"Yup," agrees Dave," That's him alright. I don't think I've seen him at a game since …."

"Since the Clyde game at Broadwood when his cap blew off in the wind." interrupts Jonesy laughing."

"God , yes!" I agree, "That was like a tornado that day. I mean Broadwood's a wind tunnel at the best of times but that day was awful."

"Yeh , remember Danny jumping the barrier and chasing after his hat down the red ash closely pursued by two stewards and about forty swirling crisp pokes!"

We are all in knots at this and as I catch the eye of the guy in the row behind me, another familiar face with no name, he is smirking too, nodding his head in an 'I saw that too' sort of way.

Danny Rainbow is a man of mystery. Everyone knows him but nobody '*knows* him' if you get my meaning. Over the years there have been all kinds of rumours and behind-the-hand remarks about Danny. Not one has ever been substantiated mind and Danny remains as curious an enigma today as the first day he sauntered into Wilmot Park.

Some say he won the lottery a couple of years back but judging by the moth-eaten 'charity shop' tweed jacket and burst red baseball boots he constantly wears, there's nothing to suggest money about him at all.

No-one knows exactly where he lives but he can frequently be seen cycling to the Rovers home games on a huge non-descript bike, painted by the look of it, with rust coloured emulsion. One day a few years back I bumped into him and his bike outside the main stand and, in between huge gasps for air, (he had just cycled The Brew, after all) he asked me who had won University Challenge that week on the TV. I didn't know and told him so but, curious to glean any snippet of background to this strange guy, I commented politely on his reliance on his bike for transport. Looking sharply both left and right he confidentially informed me that parts of it were made from left-overs from the Forth Railway Bridge. Before I could comment further he lowered his voice to a whisper and explained that he 'had to be off, he was on a secret police mission.' And off he went, this wee man on his huge bike. And there's another part of the mystery – none of us have ever worked out where he stashes the bike during the match. Wilmot Park doesn't have a special bike park or anything like it and he obviously doesn't take it in with him and yet I've never seen it about. I harbour suspicions that he's a weird street-magician with special powers and evil motives and I'd be lying if I said I wasn't a bit scared of his spooky demeanour.

Then there's Danny's party piece.

He hangs on to things.

Not a particularly productive pursuit admittedly but one that has given us a few chuckles over the years.

His favourite is hanging on to the ball. If it goes out of play in is vicinity he scrabbles around for it and if he gets it in his hands he'll put it in a vice like grip and cling on for all he's worth. By my reckoning he's been ejected from grounds on at least three occasions for refusing to give the ball back, each incident degenerating into a bizarre tug of war between Danny and either an unsuspecting official, steward or a member of Her Majesty's Constabulary.

Danny isn't just a one trick pony though. In another memorable incident a couple of winters back at Station Park, Forfar, we were all huddled together in the long, shallow enclosure that runs down the length of the pitch (opposite the stand and the wee Bridie shop). The ball flew out for a shy and, after rattling around the cement steps of the terracing for a bit, it came to rest in the welcoming arms of Danny Rainbow. Everyone in the Arthurston contingent looked on expectantly while a tall skinny Forfar player wandered over arms outstretched looking for the ball back.

Danny skipped down the three or four steps to the barrier and surprisingly and somewhat disappointingly, handed the ball straight back to the waiting player. Just as we were raising our eyebrows wondering if Danny had turned over a new leaf, it happened. Danny stuck out his right hand offering a friendly handshake and, slightly taken aback, the Forfar lad took it, his other hand clutching the match-ball to his chest. After a couple of friendly shakes the player tried to let go but Danny held on.

And held on.......

And...... quite majestically........ held on.

With grim determination Danny held on to that man's hand for a good minute without ever looking like letting go. The player was eventually forced to drop the ball and for one moment it looked like he was going to be pulled over the barrier into the enclosure alongside Danny and the rest of us. A couple of team-mates arrived on the scene and tried to prise him free but Danny held firm. It was only when a rather rotund cop lumbered up the touchline and whacked Danny on the arm with his truncheon that the dazed footballer fell free. The crowd by this time were falling around in hysterics and as Danny was led away to the exit for the fourth time in his career, a rousing round of applause following him. Even the old Forfar farmers with their sticks hooked over the barriers had a wee smile on their ruddy red faces.

It wasn't big, nor was it clever but it sure as hell was quality entertainment.

13.

Unlike the first half hour of the game which hasn't been.

Playing from left to right as we sit, United have just scored a second goal - *Another* header – and lead two-nil. The tangerine faithful packed behind the goal to our right are on their feet completing a rousing rendition of 'I can't help falling in love with you' (YEW-NITE-ED!)

"Well that's that." grumbles Dave, "Another three points down the toilet-pan."

I agree but Jonesy shakes his head and says " No, no there's time yet. "

A noise like a deflating balloon escapes from Dave's lips and he slumps lower in his chair arms folded in front of him.

Down on the pitch Mickey Hedge finally beats his man and sets up a dangerous looking attack. At which point the surge is stopped cruelly by a desperate sliding challenge from the covering defender. Hedge flies into orbit and everyone is on their feet screaming and pointing in unified rage.

Over to our left an argument breaks out as a low-browed, ginger haired steward has speculatively chosen to force an elderly gent on one of the aisle seats to sit down. I'm too concerned with the happenings on the park though where Hedge is on the deck being attended to by the physio and the United man is getting an extended talking to. As the referee continues his lecture The Rovers contingent starts chanting hopefully OFF! OFF! OFF! but as the scene progresses another golden rule of Scottish Football kicks in. Namely, the longer the referee lectures for, the less chance that the appropriate level of punishment will take place. Proving the point perfectly, howls of derision go up as the United defender nods his head , turns round and sprints back into position without as much as a booking.

As the crowd settles down I glance over to where the steward incident has been. All seems resolved now although the steward is now at the top of the stairs silhouetted menacingly against the translucent Perspex wall behind him, his arms folded glowering in a menacing manner at the crowd below him.

"What's your lasting memory of Dundee United?" I ask turning to Dave who is staring enviously at two guys in front of us munching hungrily into pies. "I mean we talked about Europe in the pub but that's an obvious one don't you think?"

"Dick Donnelly." He says immediately, without even thinking.

"Eh?" I reply in reflex.

"Dick Donnelly!" he repeats assuredly. "The radio reporter that always covered the Tayside games, remember?"

And I do.

"Welcome to a dour, dreich, Dondeee Derby at Dens" he would start in a nasel tone that suggested he was close to squeezing the microphone up his nose at any second. He would then go on and regale the listener with details of the howling wind or driving rain that he was being exposed to, then proceed with a hearty description of the desperate lack of action and excitement being played out in front of him.

Despite the deprivation of anything positive around him Dick always managed to sound relatively upbeat." No shots on goal so far but Davie Dodds has just passed the ball back forty yards to his keeper!" he would announce cheerfully. Then " Dondee thrillingly replied by winning a shy two yards inside their own half!" followed by "The sleet is really coming down now swirling in the Northerly gale-force wind!"

Dick Donnelly must have said something horrendous to his boss at a Christmas party to have been lumped with that most constant and demanding of assignments. Worse still, if I'm not mistaken, poor Dick also got sent to Aberdeen periodically, no doubt to witness some *real* rain and hailstones. Whatever Dick's failing , and it must have been something BAD; kitten-molestation perhaps, defiling the Rangers News possibly, asking for a pay-rise. He was a rich and constant character that belonged to our Saturdays at the football and if we ever forget about him and his blocked-nosed brilliance it'll be a sad, dire, rain-soaked, gale-buffeted day.

"Dick Donnelly eh?" I sigh

"Mr Dundee to me." confirms Dave definitively, continuing to stare at the pie eaters ahead, one of whom is grimacing having let grease run down the side of his arm and, almost certainly under the cuff of his jacket.

14.

Out of nowhere Arthurston score. A hump up the park from Storrie, instantly before being flattened by his overzealous marker, has us off our seats once again in black indignation. The game flows on though and as our necks collectively jerk round to follow the play, Scott McLean traps the high awkward ball deftly and from the edge of the penalty area wheels round and drives a poker straight shot low past an unprepared United keeper.

And then, THEN, just before we've quite calmed down, an equalizer of such breathtaking exquisiteness that I see Rovers fans around me looking skywards, arms aloft in gratitude and wonderment.

Frankie Boyle, looking slightly overweight it has to be said, takes the ball on the edge of his right boot and, impossibly, in one motion, flips the ball over an astonished United midfielder, slides past him and on the half-volley sprays a ball wide to Tony

Bunton. Two paces taken, then a driven-in cross just below eye-level finds Ray Stark at full tilt having scorched by two stationery defenders. At full stretch the skinny man toe-pokes the ball past the onrushing keeper who has only spotted the running man at the last second. A vital second that makes him just too late to stop the equalizer.

The players go berserk ending up in a collapsed rugby scrum of celebration at the edge of the United penalty box and from the bench the enigmatic Wilf Schnabbel appears and starts dancing a peculiar jig that looks a cross between a paddy-bah and some ill-defined martial art.

15.

The chatter in the half-time queue is enthusiastic and excitable. Its amazing the difference a few key moments can have on the opinion of the masses. Had Arthurston not hit the net but had otherwise put in an identical performance, the mood would undoubtedly have been one of doom , gloom and unbridled incrimination.

Far from it now though. I myself am basking in a rosy glow of contentment and Dave is beside me eying up the wall mounted price list ahead of us. As if to run a knife through my curtain of joy a dull wave of unpleasant realisation hits me.

"You know about the hamster don't you?"

Dave looks at me , looks at the floor then looks up again , a trace of a smirk on his lips.

"Don't you?" I press.

"Well of course I do ya brammer, she's Jonesy's cousin isn't she."

"Whit?" I splutter.

"Jonesy's cousin, " he repeats with wide eyes, ".... as in Craig I'd like you to meet my cousin Diane."

"He never said that! She wasn't ! I'm sure he never ...." Dave is nodding his head though in an annoyingly knowing manner.

"She was right on the phone bending Jonesy's ear first thing the next morning" he continues. He looks like he's about to say more when the guy in the queue in front of us turns round and pointedly asks;

" What time does the Glasgow train go at from here?"

Neither of us say anything as Danny Rainbow looks at us with a blank expression then puts his finger in his ear and gives it a juddering poke.

"Eh?"

"Emmm don't really know" I eventually offer, "We came up in the car"

Danny says nothing but continues to gaze at us casually.

Uncomfortably I look over his shoulder willing the three guys in front to hurry it along a bit.

"So… emm   haven't seen you at the games for a while Danny."

"Naw," he says pointedly, "I was over in Afghanistan on a job."

"Oh .. right" I reply a little unsure.

"Aye," Danny continues, having another productive houk in his ear,   " Infiltrating Al-Quaida ." he continues as if he had just said he was fitting windows. He pauses for effect though and I raised my eyebrows obligingly.

" Top secret stuff an' all!" He looks nervously left and right then whispers confidentially "We nearly got him, so we did."

"Who?" I ask encouragingly

"Bunn Laiden" he hisses back. "At one point he was in the next room tae me but the wee bastard got away." He looks vaguely at both of us with the same dull, worrying eyes.

"So how come *you* were over there Danny?" asks Dave in a bored monotone voice.

"Ah can talk the lingo" Danny replies simply.

"Ahhh" I say nodding my head slightly. Dave tuts.

"8 pies and six Bovrils!" I hear the boy two ahead request in a loud voice. My shoulders sag and I look back at Danny's pale, expressionless face.

"Aye," he goes on, " Speak fluent Afghan so ah do and ah kin blend in – know what ah mean. " Danny looks briefly mysterious then his blank-canvass expression returns.

"Interesting stuff Danny " injects Dave, a smile suddenly spreading on his face. " Why don't you order us up three pies in Afghan, I'd like to hear what that sounds like."

I dig Dave in the ribs but he shakes his head and looks intently at Danny Rainbow who, to his credit, seems un-phased with the request.

"I cannae" he says austerely.

"Why not Danny." pushes Dave, " thought you could talk Afghan fluently."

"Danny Rainbow looks first at me then at Dave, still with that disconcerting faded look and replies calmly,

"Thur's no word in Afghan for 'pie'."

An uneasy silence descends then just as Dave seems set to say something else, suddenly and quite deliberately, Danny lets out an elongated ' uuummmmmmm' , steps out the queue and sidles off back in the direction of the stairs to the lower tier seat.

Dave and I look at each other but just as we're about to make some kind of sense from the conversation that's just taken place another voice breaks into our midst. This time its more comprehensible, friendly…. Normal. And this time the answer comes a lot more naturally from my lips.

"Ohh…Yes, can I have three pies, two teas and a coffee please?"

16.

The second half is a tight affair. More documentary than soap opera but strangely engaging nonetheless. Both teams are working hard, picking away at each other tentatively and, looking round, everyone's eyes are on the park. Captivated, intrigued and expectant expressions surround me. Pies and crisps are being eaten on autopilot, trips to the shop or the toilet are scrambled, purposeful affairs with no signs of dallying.

Then comes the craziest five minutes of my football-supporting life.

It all starts with the Rovers taking the lead. A neat ball is slipped through by Gerry Kidd and is lashed first time high to the keeper's left by Russ Dinsmore . And the fans duly go wild. However mid-celebration I notice out the side of my eye a scuffle breaking out amidst the cheering upstanding fans. A squint of the eyes shows it to be the same steward and the elderly gentleman from before. The old boy on the face of it looks quite distinguished with his grey beard, a deerstalker on top of snowy white hair, and the tweed coat he's wearing. Without being an expert in lip-reading I gather the old man is being asked to sit down. Clearly annoyed by the old boy's unwillingness to do so mid-celebration, the steward tries to man-handle him back onto his seat whereby the old chap pulls out a broadsheet newspaper (The Glasgow Herald by the look of it) rolls it up and starts battering the steward over the head with it. Within seconds the police are there. The old man's deerstalker falls off as its owner is dragged away in police custody still aiming swipes at the steward who hasn't had the sense to vacate the vicinity.

Meanwhile United equalize.

Not a good goal but one that silences our section of the ground and sends elsewhere into raptures. John Storrie uncharacteristically takes his eye of the ball and instead of clearing his lines, slices the ball behind him. The ball falls to a waiting United forward who jumps on the chance to crash the ball past a helplessly exposed Thomson.

And then the icing on the cake.

A typically mis-timed challenge by 'Cavey' Burgoyne results in the ball squirting out of play below us and the United winger writhing on the ground clutching his ankle. It's the Arabs turn to vent their fury from the stands

As treatment is administered and Cavey takes his booking, Few notice that the ball hasn't been returned back into play. I do though and, as I nudge Dave and then Jonesy, a smile breaks out simultaneously on both their faces.

Down below us sitting in a tensed up hunched position with, what can only be the match ball in his lap, is Danny Rainbow.

Danny is only three rows from the front with no Arthurston fans immediately around him so its only a matter of time before he's rumbled. And it's a young ballboy that spots the situation first. Coyly reaching over the barrier the lad holds out his arms gesturing to Danny Rainbow to chuck the ball to him.

I can only see the back of Danny's head but I can visualise that blank look on his face as he stares at the boy. Motionless but ready for the storm.

The game has resumed again with another ball but no-one this side of the ground is watching it.

All eyes are on the now alerted steward who has approached Danny and has obviously asked for the ball back. A short delay punctuated by inaction and the steward suddenly lunges for the ball. A cheer goes up and after a short wrestle the steward straightens up, brushes himself down then catching the attention of two nearby cops points down at Danny Rainbow who still has the ball and still hasn't moved a muscle.

The cops come over.

They bend down.

Words are spoken.

The cops pounce and start wrestling.

A louder cheer goes up

The vice stays shut.

At one point both cops are pulling and pushing in unison in an effort to retrieve the ball. Danny Rainbow is there, in the middle, swaying back and forward alarmingly but not once does he look like he's going to relinquish possession of the ball.

Another two policemen wander up. The second of which I recognise as the one who was last seen dragging Old Deerstalker off to 'the back of the van'. He looks faintly repulsed at the idea of dealing with another over the edge Rovers fanatic and noticeably keeps the other officer between himself and the bold Danny Rainbow.

A three pronged attack fails, As does a covert assault from behind. Looking increasingly embarrassed at the howls of laughter around them the original two plods employ one last superhuman effort and this time get enough purchase on the ball to lift it four feet in the air – with Danny Rainbow still attached.

The place erupts in hysterics and, clearly unsure of what to do for the best, the two policemen edge their way to the nearest exit, Danny Rainbow in between them in a foetal position with his red boots three feet from the ground. As the strange group get up momentum and head for the exit a round of applause starts as a ripple then spreads across the away support. And if I'm not mistaken, just before they disappear from view, Danny takes his acclaim by shaking his right leg back at his adoring fans.

Wow.

I would have paid double to see half of that. And when the referee blows for full time the Arthurston fans stand tall and applaud the three each draw as if it had just won us the league.

It was a necessary point as it turns out . The radio on the journey home informs us that Kilmarnock, on the same points as us before kick-off, have got a point at Ibrox and Livingstone have moved off the bottom with an away win at Motherwell. All in all though not a bad day's entertainment.

17.

A spectral mist hangs over the hallowed turf as the ball is passed slowly but supremely from player to player. Each time it finds a foot, or is passed along, a dull thud shudders my view. I run on to the field with the panicked thought that someone is chasing me and when I look behind me I see menacing, shadowed figures just beyond the fog. I start to sprint and as my breath puffs out in front of me someone shouts in a deep booming voice "Craig , go wide and I'll buy you a bag of Big-D nuts!" I go wide, keen for nuts, and the ball comes flying towards me at chest height. I know I'm going to control it like I know Christmas is coming but what will I do next?

"Shoot!" Danny Rainbow shouts, casually leaning over the barrier.

I look round and he's only ten yards away from me. Me, out wide and him hanging over the barrier.

"Shoot" he mouths, no sound this time.

A panic rushes through me and as I stop with the ball at my feet I hear scuffling in front of me. Squinting into the fog and darkness I make out a huge hamster, heading straight for me. Its eyes are on the ball not on me and as it lunges I cut inside and beat it on its right.

"Shoot it man!" yells Danny from the side.

But just then I see a red and white shirt over on the penalty spot. I can't see the face but one arm is up waving, wanting the ball.

Without thinking I slip a slide-rule pass into the middle. The waiting figure pounces on the ball and lashes it into the empty goal. As it hits the back of the net the figure turns and runs away from me. The fog clears a little and I see the name on the back of the shirt.

'Heidi'

My stomach lurches involuntarily.

As Heidi disappears into the gloom I hear Danny Rainbow again from out to my right. His voice is echoing like he's moving away from me.

"You could have scored Craig!" he shouts and then once more, softer and further away ,"You could've scored."

Standing in the mist made more ethereal with the light from the floodlights high above me, I'm suddenly left alone. The shadows are gone, the hamster is gone and Danny Rainbow has gone.

'Head up son' I think to myself but my head is down. Down and looking at my boots which miraculously have turned into big, long clown feet covered by shiny red shoes and green laces. Slack shouldered, I start flopping my way back in the direction I imagine the tunnel to be when out of the haze an object loops over my head and falls with a cushioned thump somewhere between me and the now completely obscured goal. I stop and stare, squinting into the cotton wool mist where I can see nothing but swirling fog. I flex my huge red-pepper feet and shuffle peculiarly in no apparent direction. And then I fall completely still and silent. After what seems an age I make to step forward but my legs seem to have disconnected themselves from my brain. They feel cold and not part of me. I strain to push my right foot forward and when nothing happens a wave of panic flows through me and my heart dives to the floor and back. Another extreme effort and my right foot clumps awkwardly forward. "Yesss!" I shout and plant an equally awkward left foot alongside its partner.

And another.

Then another.

And I can see it in front of me. Another few strained, heavy steps and its right in front of me.

The ball. And beyond the ball. Beckoning. The open goal. Surely I can't miss. I don't even think about it. One more flop forward and …

BEEEEEE DEE DEE DEE DEE. ….BEEEEE DEE DEE DEE DEE DEE

My hand flies over in reflex, slamming the clock off and my eyes spring open like a waking vampire. My bed feels sweaty, the duvet and my t-shirt clinging to me uncomfortably. Lying, staring at the ceiling the moments pass and gradually I understand the Sunday morning noises coming from the other side of my bedroom door. The Sunday morning light is straining through the blind and the Sunday morning smell of grilling bacon is pinching away at my nostrils.

Slowly and deliberately I pull the quilt off my chest and swing my legs onto the floor. Bringing myself into an upright sitting position I'm relieved to note that my feet have returned to normal size.

Something is different though.

Its not my bed or my feet or, looking around me, my room.

Left then with no other option, I figure its got to be me.

I know what has to be done.

Better, I feel I'm just the man to do it.

And, as if someone just turned a light on in my mind, if I'm not very much mistaken, I have a plan.

Chapter 12   The Northern Lights

1.

You cant help feeling a sense of foreboding when you witness an East Coast 'Har' drift in off the North Sea. It is a thief of fogs. It steals the horizon effortlessly like an old pro then creeps inwards towards the waiting, nervous mainland, greedily looking for more treasure to claim.

Its coming. Its coming to get us. And by the look of it, it'll be here soon.

Our weather has been slowly getting worse as the journey North has progressed. Splashes of watery November sunshine saw us off from Arthurston about three and a half hours ago. By Perth the heavy dark clouds had mugged the sky and now, having just passed by the sweeping turn-off for Stonehaven, the first drops of rain are spitting from the vague, grey blanket of sea spread below us to our right.

On a clear day this stretch of expansive road offers a stunning panoramic view of fresh blue-green water and rich Angus farmland. You get the feeling that from this high vantage point, if you really look, you can just about make out the tip of Norway on the horizon. Today though, everything is blurred, diluted, starved of life, and although you are still drawn inexorably to the view of the sea, you feel uncomfortable, slightly depressed and anxious to be on your way to a more hospitable place.

The dark graveyards to the summer's yellow gorse flash past at speed as we swallow up the remaining miles to Aberdeen and its not long before a grey stone army of houses, kirks and high rises invade the scene ahead quickly engulfing us as we descend into the Granite city.

2.

It is Saturday the 9th of November and Arthurston Rovers are in the mire. Despite a reasonable point at home last week against Kilmarnock, results elsewhere have hurt us. In particular, Falkirk's two wins and a draw from their last three matches has seen them skipping their way up the table leaving us nestling uncomfortably in eleventh place in the league. Thank heavens for Partick Thistle who can't buy a win and remain five points below us in the damp and dirty basement position.

Wilf Schnabbel has assured us via The Arthurston Gazette that a deal is close to being completed with an 'over- the- sea defender'. Better than signing an over- the- hill one I suppose, however in the same interview he disappointingly made it clear that no more cash would be available to strengthen the team further at this time. In many ways I respect our board's restraint from spending money we can't afford, yet the absence of new blood and plenty of it has us all a little unenthused with proceedings. Fans like new signings. Whether they are affordable or even good enough is, by and large, irrelevant. As long as they are a fresh face, one that gives us five seconds of hope that they might be the 'next big thing' then we'll all be happy … at least until its time to get shot of them to make way for the next potential Pele that is.

Elsewhere in our little world, Dave is energetically deflecting thoughts of Linda by trying to sell his car. Jonesy continues to clean windows and complain about his unfriendly customers, and Sandy still expects me in at nine as assistant, confident and general ear-piece. The bills chase us, the news scares us and women confuse us. Its all pretty much business as usual then.

3.

Movement from the back seat as Jonesy, after an hour or so of fitful slumber, rejoins the land of the living. With a drawn out groaning noise he pokes a pallid face through the head rests and breathes a less than charming, stale beer aroma into the front half of Dave's car.

"I feel awful" he whinges , smacking his lips together in a slow, dry manner.

"I said we should have gone home didn't I. ", I press "It was your idea to go on to O'Jay's."

"It felt good at the time didn't it. " he whimpers back.

Over the King George VI Bridge we slide, skirting round Duthie Park with the languid River Don on our right and we're soon picking our way around roundabouts and through traffic heading towards the docks and onwards to the seafront. Dave stops at a glaring set of traffic lights and we're treated to what I think is one of the most memorable and vivid sights in Scotland. To the left of the street sits a normal, if slightly suffocating, selection of bland office buildings, straggly looking pubs and the like. To the right though, where you feel there should be a bus stop, a car park or a tree or something, is a huge towering boat, peering down at you like its about to fall over itself and join you on the road. Then another one , taller than the first, rising into view blocking off the horizon in a claustrophobic manner. Its just not what you expect to see here and the effect of Aberdeen Harbour is nothing short of awesome.

"Look at the size of those things" says Dave craning his neck to get a better look. Are they fishing boats or cargo carriers or what?" he asks.

The silence that follows suggests that we have no sea-craft experts on board our own little ship of fools. As we crawl round the harbour's edge I count five hefty, tall-hulled boats moored tight to the harbour walls. They are impressive indeed but there is no grace about them. They are bulldogs; stout, hard working vessels more used to rough seas and rough passengers than leisurely cruising with affluent holidaymakers on board.

As they disappear out the back windscreen with Jonesy and I twisting back, still gazing at the scene, Dave declares "There we go, signs for football traffic. We're nearly there."

And indeed up a hill, round a corner, and in stark contrast to the tight, oppressiveness of the harbour, we have in front of us the windswept openness of Aberdeen's seaside 'promenade'.

"What are we going to do then Dave?" Jonesy asks, still with a pathetic tone to his voice. Dave is our accepted Aberdeen 'expert' having spent some time up here with his work a few years back.

"Well its ten-past twelve," Dave replies tipping his wrist on the steering wheel, "and you boys don't look like you are quite ready for a pint.,"

Head shakes and hums of agreement.

" So I think we should have a coffee and a seat in the Café Continental. What do you think?"

"Where is it?" asks Jonesy who over the last minute or so has gone a clammy shade of green.

"See that old fashioned promenade building. Its just beyond that. I'll park just up there, we can walk the last wee bit along the front and you can get a bit of fresh air which, by the look of you, you could use."

Jonesy nods like a man agreeing to a cut-price enema.

4.

And you *could* call it fresh. In the same way as you could call the North Pole 'snowy' or the Atlantic Ocean 'damp'. Looking out onto the deserted, weather-battered beach from outside the Café Continental I can't help thinking of Billy Connolly swimming in this very sea as a youngster with his heavy woollen trunks, blue shivering body and disappearing testicles. On this evidence Aberdeen could indeed be ' Gaelic for hypothermia.'

When Alex Ferguson was the manager here in the eighties, he frequently held training sessions on Aberdeen's beach and as I stand grimacing against the stinging rain I can almost make out shadowy figures booting a ball around on the hard-packed sand underfoot. Echoing voices rise up on the wind and I can just about catch a young Gordon Strachan wailing "Boss my ears are hurtin' wi' the wind", Ferguson replying "betta than havin' sand up the cwack in yewa fuckin' weeewend. Get on with it!" and from elsewhere in the mist, the club doctor pleading "It's no use gaffer Harper's got the frostbite if we don't get him in soon I'll need to amputate!"

For every poison there is an antidote though and as quick as you can say 'bozlikewalnutz' we're through the door of The Café Continental, the jackets are off and we're collapsed onto waiting low slung leather couches and matching arm-chairs with Dave off in search of three 'non-footballesque' Cappuccinos and hopefully some of those wee crunchy Amoretto biscuits you get in these places.

"Feeling a bit better?" I ask looking at Jonesy who has a little more colour in his cheeks.

"Yehhh," Jonesy sighs in a war veteran sort of way, "think I'm over the worst."

"It's not the best of drives with a hangover is it?"

"No." Jonesy states affirmatively. "Although at least I'm going to see a game at the end of it, Eh Craig?" At which he smiles a thin smile.

"Ahhhhh" I say, nodding my head slowly, " I wondered when that would be brought back up again, well I'm glad my unhappy driving experiences are therapeutic to you and your misery."

"As good as some vitamin C and a bottle of freezing Irn Bru, Craigy Boy" he laughs pulling himself upright on the chair that's threatening to eat him whole.

Despite my apparent comfort, a wave of nausea flows over me as the subject of Jonesy's amusement flits gleefully across my mind and I remember what must go down as one of my most painful football Saturdays ever.

It all concerns an away fixture against Inverness three Decembers ago. Jonesy had begged off the trip suffering from a bad cold he claimed to be 'advanced pneumonia' and Dave had his office Christmas 'do' on so if I wanted to go, I was on my own. Snow was in the air and the team were on a particularly poor run of results but I was harbouring a burning sense of martyrdom and was keen to score a few 'commitment points' against the guys. Even so, I dwelled for more than a few minutes on the possibility of spending the afternoon in bed watching 'The Dam Busters' on BBC2 with Worcester Sauce crisps and hot Ribena on ready supply. Such notions, though, were eventually driven out by an irksome 'Call yourself a fan!' argument that snuck into my mind and refused to go away. Thoughts of huddling miserably in Inverness Calay's exposed main stand, staring balefully at the Kessock Bridge against the storm laden skyline ultimately won through in the end. Damn its lacy seduction.

So, at approximately 11.30 AM I grabbed a couple of bags of the Dam Busters crisps, slung my jacket and scarf over my arm and headed out to the waiting car.

WORST – DECISION - EVER.

The coffees arrive and we lean forward and take the first pleasurable sips of piping hot, milky coffee. Jonesy, a creamy moustache on his upper lip smiles.

"Eh Dave? What about Craig's solo trip to Inverness?"

"Daft bastard." smirks Dave with a slight shake of the head and I'm sent packing, back to my oh- too-vivid memories.

5.

I'm off on my own, heading North with a full compliment of soapy scoosher for the windscreen, the crisps, a couple of 'fun size' Mars Bars (what exactly is 'fun' about finishing chocolate in two small bites?) and an assortment of battered looking cassettes beside me on the passenger seat, all containing music I got fed up listening to well over a year ago.

The first leg of the journey joining up with the A9 to Perth was uneventful, the clear blue sky and bright, clean scenery had me in a cheerful frame of mind, so much so that I remember listening to some R&B rap dude on the radio and *not* automatically thinking 'you're a talentless, undeserving, no-cause fashion crisis'. As I say da' sun was shinin', ah woz down wid da ho's an' da bitches, an ah had respec' for da riddims ……. ….emmm……..Mutha'.

Slipping round the Broxden Roundabout and heading off towards Dundee I remember gliding past the left hand exit that takes you down the poker straight dual carriageway to St Johnstone's McDermid Park. Memories of undeserved defeats, frustrations at the lack of a decent pub in the vicinity and the hours wasted trapped in their bloody bottle-necked car park flooded my mind as I gritted my teeth and headed the wrong way to Inverness.

So who would have thought that Inverness wasn't 30 miles or so beyond Aberdeen then? Not me for sure. I worked that one out a good couple of hours later when, as I approached the outskirts of Aberdeen, a signpost flashed by on my left screaming Inverness 112 miles. I did a double take, shook my head and thought I must have misread it. Except two nervy miles later, a second conspiratorial sign claimed that it was now only 110 miles to Inverness. The dawning realisation was sickening. I had to stop by the side of the road in order to pull myself together and, as I sat there with hundreds of vehicles passing me by, they mocked me. Their drivers - all completely sure of where they were going and how to get there-Better drivers than me - they mocked me.

I actually speculated whether it would be quicker going back down the road and somehow cutting cross country, but all my pristine conditioned UK and Ireland roadmap, dug out from the boot of the car, suggested was that no such option was possible and had I perhaps looked at the damn thing before I started, then this might not have happened.

With little option I continued on my way with a new found hope that I could limit the damage and get there, with the aid of a good run through, in time for the second half. Thanks to a fleet of tractors, combine harvesters, HGVs and docile weekend drivers I made it to Inverness for twenty to five. Just in time to hear that the Rovers had won 3-0 putting in, according to some halfwit on Radio Scotland, their best display of the season.

So I filled the car back up (£50 quid in petrol for the round trip) and headed for home. Not, however, before I made one last bad decision. With the crisps and chocolate now just a distant memory I stopped off in a chip shop in Inverness town centre and wolfed down a black pudding supper in the voracious, guzzling style perfected by my Aunt Maria's black Labrador, Toby. A dog who is so fat, greedy and stupid that it regularly gulps down paper, weeds and his own faeces if nothing better is available. I don't even *like* black pudding but my inability to wait five minutes for fresh fish to be fried was to have repercussions beyond anything I could have imagined. For one day only, Toby had a worthy adversary.

6.

Somewhere around Carrbridge my stomach gurgled. A mile further on came the contractions and, by the outskirts of Aviemore, the black-pudding supper was reeking a level of havoc with my innards that had I not experienced since the 'humorously' titled ' Wokked Dog' on Arthurston High Street got shut down by the Environmental Health a year past in September. (My Aunt Jess, the family gossip, swears they found a box full of collars and name tags in a storage cupboard in the staff toilet - items once owned by an assortment of domestic pets now mysteriously missing in action. I however, have it on good authority that the place got closed when the health inspectors somehow discovered that the head chef of 'Wokky's' owned a rather rare, illegal monkey which he kept tied to the microwave oven during working hours. Sitting in close proximity to the 'bagging' area as it did, our simian gourmet was free to 'pick from' and 'add to' the complimentary prawn crackers being cooked and bagged in its immediate vicinity. During a daring lunchtime raid the inspectors swooped and amongst other checks, exact measurement of the rope found around the monkey's neck also brought the sweet and sour sauce pot, the chicken noodle soup and the fried rice container 'into play' as it were. The 'Wokked Dog' is now 'under new management' I am lead to believe)

Anyway, the left hand turn off for Aviemore could not come quick enough and as I eventually skidded, indicated and plunged into the total darkness of the B-road leading into the little ski-town, the ballooning pressure in my nether regions was unbearable. It felt like the creature from Alien was residing in my lower stomach simultaneously blowing up balloons whilst doing The Twist and I knew in my heart of hearts I wouldn't reach the town 'fully laden'.

Then, out of the pitch-black , lit dimly by a small ornate lantern, a lay-by and an entrance-way presented themselves. Making, what was for me, a super-quick decision, I screeched the car to a halt and in a panic stricken manner, haphazardly twisted around and groped desperately in the back seat for any suitable substitute for Andrex I could find. Another monumental growl and my guts sank a foot nearer the floor. I remember moaning and abandoning my search, instead falling out the car door and running headlong up a muddy track away from the glowing light behind me.

Now this last part I have never admitted to the boys and I am confident I never will. Standing breathless but now very much relieved amidst brittle branches and twigs, with cold sweat trickling down from my forehead, I was faced with the inevitable 'clear-up' problem. After a couple of precarious slips and stumbles, my forced down jeans and pants awkwardly constraining any ankle movement, it soon became obvious that leaves were out of season and there was nothing immediately at hand to even partially wipe up the carnage I could not see but could clearly imagine (and could most definitely smell).

So I decided to hop for it. In the total darkness. Maybe I could get back to the car for a more thorough look around the boot or the glove compartment. Crackling branches underfoot, I shuffled my way back onto the track and was about to head downhill in the direction of the car when the undergrowth pleasantly flattened out and I ran awkwardly against a large brick-like object, sending a sharp, shooting pain up my foot. Cursing loudly, I slowly lowered myself down onto my hunkers and groped for the object. Despite being only inches away I could not make out any discernable features through the inky darkness.

Clutching It in my hands it was about a foot in length, heavy yet smooth, and running my fingers across its grooves and contours it felt like a lumpy missile.

Perfect, I thought, I could use the smooth tip to get the worst of the clinging mess off my butt (and upper legs by the feel of it) then continue down to the car to complete the job at my leisure.

Except sometimes life and circumstance moves so quickly and unpredictably that you're powerless to resist. Sometimes its impossible even just to jump out of the way. At the very instant the tip of that nobbly, nondescript hunk of enamel touched skin, an ear-bursting roar broke the silence and the immediate area around me was momentarily lit by a blinding white light. Seconds later everything went black again leaving me in the same slightly bent position, a wave of shock coursing through my body and my eyes bleeding through the strain. The flash-photo image of me standing in the middle of a ring of garden gnomes, trousers at my ankles apparently forcing the leader of the gang into a close-up view of my rectum will no doubt stay with the respectable looking jeep family for some time to come. For my part I can still see the look of surprise, then confusion then disgust on the young mother who held my gaze as the four-by-four tumbled past taking with it its searching, intruding headlamp beams.

I got home at 8 o-clock GMT, a mere nine or so hours after starting out. When my mum met me in the hall and cheerfully asked how I enjoyed the game I couldn't bring myself to speak. When I saw her nose involuntarily twitch in my direction I excused myself sharply and retreated to the bathroom where I remained, head in hands, for some considerable time.

7.

Dave's mobile goes off and after answering with a sharp "Dave here" he slips off the sofa and slinks over to stand in a small vestibule area in the company of a healthy green pot plant and a cigarette machine.

I pick up a copy of the Daily Record we've brought from the car and start flicking through it. Jonesy is quietly dabbing a muddy puddle of spilled coffee from the table around his mug. After seconds rather than minutes, Dave glides back to the table just as I am laying down the paper. Wrinkling my nose at the black inky mess that's now all over my fingers, I grab a paper napkin and ineffectually try wipe my hands clean.

"Well that's that done" says Dave cheerfully.

We look at him vaguely.

"I've sold the car!" he beams.

"Oh, right" I nod

"Got three and a half grand for it. IN CASH. I can go ahead and get the Audi I was telling you about."

We both look blankly"

"Yehhh , I told you last week. The guy at work who's looking for a the quick sale 'cos he's going to live in Dubai." Dave looks expectantly at us smiling enthusiastically. He then fingers his coffee cup and settles his gaze on Jonesy.

"Just one thing," he says tentatively," Could I put the money in your account Jonesy? Just for a little while."

"Em... no problem "says Jonesy shrugging his shoulders, "any particular reason?"

Dave looks a little uncomfortable," Call it an over-reaction but I just don't want to put to put any sizeable cash into our bank account right now."

"What, you think Linda's going to steal your cash? Oh for God's sa..."

"Look will you do it? " snaps Dave, a mixture of frustration and irritation crossing his face.

"Erm, sure." says Jonesy in resignation, shrugging again.

"Ok. Thanks" Dave finishes slowly and deliberately. He sits back down and lets out a sigh that almost empties him of air.

Keen to change the subject but equally intent on steering it well away from the memories of Inverness I opt for safer ground.

"My first ever away game was up here." I volunteer cheerfully. And so begins a pleasant few minutes of childhood recollection, the type of which always leaves me with a warm glow yet also a with strange sense of longing to be back there, in the days with no responsibilities and the bulk of my life in front of me once more. Another chance to do it all again only, maybe, better this time.

8.

Aberdeen, in view of its relative inaccessibility, seems a strange place to experience your first away fixture. The reason being I was on holiday with the folks. A miserable, drizzly week in Stonehaven, and with interesting entertainment at a premium, my dad had slyly suggested to mum that we could break the monotony with a shopping trip to Aberdeen. *And* while we 'waited for her' we could go to Pittodrie to see Arthurston who by happy coincidence (for me at any rate), happened to be playing up there in a pre-season friendly. Yes it was a dull holiday that one. Asides from witnessing an old man having a full blown heart attack after plunging into the 'invigorating' waters of Stonehaven's outdoor swimming pool, the football match remains the only other thing I can remember of that trip.

There are two photographs in the family photo album of that day. One is obviously taken by dad and has me standing in front of the famous grey granite entrance at the corner between the South Stand and the Merkland Stand. Its one of those cringe-worthy homages to the tastelessness of the '70s that makes you wince at the site of yourself and curse your parents for their blatant child cruelty. There I was, captured in front of the thick bricked wall with its raggedly stepped triangular hat and the 'Aberdeen Football Club Ltd' sign stretched above my head, sporting a untamed sandy brown Busby hair-do that, for all the world, looks like I'm hooked up to a Van de Graaf generator. The bright excitement on my face is in stark contrast to my grim surroundings. I'm wearing a plain red cagoule with just the hint of a multicoloured tank- top underneath and a pair of wild, light-blue flared crimplene trousers. A fashion crisis that gives me no comfort in understanding was being echoed the length and breadth of the country at the time.

The other photograph, taken by me clearly, is split diagonally in two with the bottom half made up of a blurry finger, and in the top corner a glimpse of sheepskin jacket and half my dad's younger, slimmer, side-burned face .

The Rovers lost four-nil that day and I recollect quite vividly my dad slumping from blatant condescension to sheer indifference at the eventual outcome.

"Ah well son, never mind" he said patting me on the shoulder as we headed up Merkland Road East in the general direction of Union Street, "your boys were never going to win really. Its not like the 'Gers coming up here, the Rovers just aren't up to it."

And I was livid. "*My* boys?" Nowadays I'd have pointed out that being born and brought up in Arthurston, they were *his* boys as well. I'd have given him ten reasons, quick as a flash, what was wrong with a statement like that and then pointed out vehemently just how such a gulf in standards could be easily bridged to the benefit of everyone concerned with just a small amount of vision and understanding being displayed by 'his' boys.

Being ten years old though, all I knew was that I was wounded and mad. So mad I aimed a kick at a nearby passing lamp-post. My swipe was so swift and forceful that my sandshoe went flying off my right foot, sailed over a tall granite wall and into someone's garden. With no clear entrance to the garden in sight, Dad, after consecutive moments of disbelief, remonstration then dull resignation, had to climb the wall and while he was in the process of retrieving my sand shoe, was firstly accosted by a bad-tempered Scotty dog and then verbally molested by a snarling, dried out old codger who called him a 'Fitba' yob' , threatened to call the police and then bizarrely threw a slice of white bread at him as he scrambled back over the wall to freedom.

We drove back to Stonehaven in silence and when we got there my dad, as a' treat', took me to the outdoor pool where I was forced to go in while my dad sat under a brolly drinking from a hot flask of coffee and reading the paper, safe and sheltered from the incessant, driving rain.

9.

After a pleasant three-quarters of an hour we decide to move on in search of something stronger to let loose on our livers.

Whooooosh! The weather outside grabs us at the door by the ears and drags us breathlessly out and away from the warmth of the café behind us. Heads down we start walking along the front, our black waterproofs giving us the look of three staggering bin-bags exposed to the elements.

Dave makes a pointing gesture and we dive down a flight of cement stairs in seek of a little shelter. The low lying position of the walkway is keeping the worst of the wind at bay and we find it instantly possible to hear each other speak again.

"Quiz question Dave," cries Jonesy as we stride manfully through a little collection of chain - eateries consisting of TGI Fridays (£15 for a burger but you get a refill on your coke – cheers!), Frankie & Benny's square roomed 'Crapola Italiano' joint and Burger King (Whopper in your mouth – salad down your front).

"Oh God," starts Dave, "I never get …."

"You'll get this one, its easy" Jonesy insists, wiping the collecting rain water off his brow. "Name all the teams Aberdeen beat en-route to winning the '83 Cup Winners Cup?"

I stay silent. Of course I remember the final well. When John Hewitt dived to head the winner in injury time on that rainy night in Gothenburg I leapt off my chair and punched the air as if I'd sat at the Beach End of Pittodrie all my days. There it was, the mighty Real Madrid humbled 2-1 by the plucky boys from Aberdeen. It was fairytale stuff however, beyond that its all a bit sketchy for me. I must be getting old. Mind you the Dons had so many good European results around that time , its difficult to sort them all into the correct year. That's my excuse and I'm sticking to it.

By the triumphant look on Dave's face, his memory is less foggy than my own.

"Right then," he begins, "First round they beat Sion of Switzerland, gubbed them in both legs!"

"Ha, not quite!" injects Jonesy pointing an accusing finger at Dave.

"WHAAT! It was so. SION OF SWITZERLAND!"

"Yeah but it was the *preliminary* round" Jonesy says smugly.

"Oh bloody hell, give us a break man!"

"Well you've got to do it right or not at all"

Dave bites his tongue and starts again. Carefully and methodically he goes through them all. Tirana of Albania in the first round proper, a tight one nil aggregate over two legs . Then the Polish outfit, Lech Posnan giving the Dons a wonder draw against the big guns - Bayern Munich, Breitner, Augenthaler, Rumminegge and all. I join in at this point, memories flooding back to me. Aberdeen two-one down with fifteen minutes to go and that bluff free kick when Strachan and McMaster pretended to bump into each other before wee Gordon planked the ball on McLeish's nut for the equaliser. And of course super-sub, Hewitt's winner one minute later - fantastic!

On to the semi final with Warterschei from Belgium. Hat's off to Dave for that, I'd never have remembered that if I'd stayed up all night. A 5-1 victory at Pittodrie paving the way for that wonderful rain-drenched night in the Ullevi Stadium against the Spaniards..

Dave takes all the plaudits for our little quiz which has momentarily taken our minds off the deluge around us but enough is enough. Jonesy makes a comment to the effect that the 'fresh' air has well and truly cured his hangover and it would be nice to get a pint somewhere less windswept than our current location.

10.

There are lots of little bars dotted around the dockside area, some less salubrious looking that others. In order to get a descent , relaxing beer I cant help feeling it may be worth while edging closer to Union Street and the centre of Aberdeen in general. Having jumped back in the car and scooted by a couple of dodgy looking establishments this is my very suggestion but Dave is adamant – The Fittie Bar on Wellington Street will do us proud. So, heading back the way we came in, passing the front entrance to the Queen's Links Leisure Park (named after Her Majesty's favourite sausages) and steering in the direction of the docks yet again, we find ourselves outside the pokey looking Fittie Bar.

"Why is it called the Fittie Bar then?" Jonesy asks Dave standing in front of the emblazoned green sign with a dubious look on his face, "Is it where you go for a pint before goin' tae the *fittie* tae see the Dons." He says the last part in a poor effort of an Aberdonian accent. One which has an unmistakeable Welsh lilt to it and a dash of Indian thrown in for good measure.

"It refers to a place actually" replies Dave pleasantly."

"Oh, " sighs Jonesy obviously disappointed having no doubt harboured a vision of interesting old photos and memorabilia stuck on the wall as far as the eye can see. "Why don't we head towards Union Street , we've got plenty of …….. " But Dave is already through the door leaving us no option but to follow.

Once inside all thoughts of heading up-town are immediately dispelled. The pub is warmth and friendliness personified. As if to ward off the grey dreichness outside, the snug little bar area is cosy, well lit and populated by enough cheery souls to suggest that this is a more than acceptable place to spend an hour before continuing on your way. Faced with the option of moving into a small lounge area to the side of the front door we decide to sit on the polished mahogany bench round a table at the window. While an 'on the mend' Jonesy makes the three step journey over to the small bar running along the left hand wall, Dave and I study the strange set of framed, autographed photos on the wall behind us. There are three of them and the top one is, quite understandably, a picture of Sir Alex Ferguson celebrating yet another Red Nose Day, presumably in this very establishment. The other two make less sense. Both are signed with messages to effect of 'To all at the Fittie Bar' etc etc etc. but quite why Cilla Black and more bizarrely , Joanna Lumley should have found themselves anywhere near here who can rightly say. Dave and I look at each other and shrug simultaneously.

When Jonesy sets down the beers in front of me I'm straining towards the other walls in the vague hope of spotting a photo bearing the message 'Great pint of Tennents Folks !– Meg Ryan' or 'Thanks for the hospitality!– Prince Ranier of Monaco. Alas any evidence of famous yet inappropriate visitations seem to be limited to our little corner and a couple of old boys sat in the other corner are now looking at me strangely.

Ducking their probing gaze, a typically Jonesy conversation ensues where amongst other richly pertinent factoids about the Dons we discover that Jonesy's mum once caught a glimpse of Willie Miller in his pants in a changing room in Marks and Spencer. A sterling piece of footballing trivia for sure. Quite what she was doing in the gents fitting rooms of Marks and Spencer is anyone's guess (assuming it *was* the Gents I suppose) and neither Dave nor I have the appetite to delve any further.

The juke box cranks up and starts shovelling out a hearty rendition of 'Football's coming home'. Much as I hate to admit it, the old England World Cup anthem is a belter of a good song. Scotland's version, 'Football went out ten years ago for fags and a paper and hasn't been seen since - although rumour has it, it went abroad and was seen working in a theme pub in Puerto Banus' never quite had the same impact I felt. I'm just on the verge of taking the risk and commending Skinner and Baddiel's ditty publicly when, in unison, we all sniff the air and look with concern to the bar. The unmistakeable smell of burnt toastie is spreading quickly across the room causing consternation amongst the locals not least one of the old staring boys who looks so put out that I can only assume that its his toastie that's gone down. Despite this cremation, however, inquisitiveness has got the better of us and the three of us are, a mere ten minutes later tucking in to the pub speciality, cheese and ham toasties (mysteriously lacking any ham whatsoever) and Jonesy is cheerfully crunching away whilst regaling us on the why's and wherefores of former Aberdeen manager Ebbe Skovdahl

Skovdahl came to Pittodrie in 1999 on a lucrative £300,000 a year deal, an arrangement that would no doubt have had former chairman and founder member of the Extreme Prudence Society, Dick Donald, turning in his grave in despair. Having worked miracles with Danish club Brondby, a club of similarly modest size and means, he had been brought in to turn The Dons around in the wake of disappointing reigns by Alex Miller and Paul Hegarty. Working on a tight budget- after all he was getting all the money- Skovdahl shrugged off a disastrous initial run of results that left Aberdeen stastically the worst team in Europe, and slowly developed a system and a sound youth policy that would hopefully guarantee the club more successful times in the future. When he finally left Pittodrie in late 2002 the team was undoubtedly in a better state than it had been in on his arrival. Quite whether it was over £800,000 worth of 'better' is debatable and I fear that this is another sad tale of Scottish Football resource slipping out the game and into a slightly undeserving bank balance or pension fund.

"You know what the funniest thing about Ebbe Skovdahl was?" chortles Jonesy, dabbing the side of his mouth then looking forlornly at the few small crumbs remaining on the little plate in front of him, "Ebbe Skovdahl wasn't his real name"

"Really?" asks Dave dryly raising an eyebrow, "What was it - Sven Jorgen Erikkson, c os he got shed loads of money for old rope as well?"

"Not quite," replies Jonesy unmoved, "his real name was Ebbe Hansen. Skovdahl's his middle name." After a pause for thought he adds," It's Danish for 'man with a pine-fitted sauna'

I'm about to seriously question this when I catch a glint in Jonesy's eye.

"Not like you to be humorous." I grunt.

342

"Indeed.... No, seems he played in a football team when he younger and he had a team-mate called Ebbe Johansen. To avoid confusion he got called Skovdahl and the name stuck."

"Jonesy, the utter pish you learn and retain is astounding." ventures Dave finishing off his shandy and throwing a hopeful glance at the bar. "I'm going to start calling you Rainman I think."

"I'm an excellent driver." Jonesy mumbles smiling again, "And there's more, I bet you didn't know Skovdahl was Michael and Brian Laudrup's uncle!"

And so it goes on. Jonesy wittering on in his element, recounting excitedly of how Ebbe Skovdahl's sister married Danish international Finn Laudrup and together gave birth to those two famous footballing brothers. Then onwards to a multitude of facts and figures about old Arthurston v Aberdeen fixtures. Reminiscences and memories of great goals and bad refereeing decisions which, had they gone our way, we'd be Champions League contenders by now.

And as I sit and watch him rabbit on about his trivial 'stuff'. Stuff that most folk would dismiss and think of as dull or pointless and by virtue of that, probably dismiss Jonesy in the same way, a strong wave of affection flows over me and I can't help feeling how he fits in and how necessary he is to Dave and myself. If he wasn't there to fill in the gaps with 'utter pish' then I'm not sure where we'd be. We'd be 'utter pishless' for sure.

11.

Back in the car we're off to the game. As we drive round past the Patio Hotel, a couple of guys walk out adjusting red and white scarves around their necks .

"Do you recognise them?" asks Jonesy

"Nope" I answer then as an after thought, "Of course they're probably not our fans are they?"

I always find it quite strange looking at opposing fans decked in 'our ' colours. I *do* always assume they are supporting

Arthurston especially when they're wearing a traditional, no fuss, 'bar scarf' similar to my own. Honestly, I know I could go to London, walk down the Highbury area of the city just before an Arsenal home game, and double take all the Arthurston fans that had shown up. Obviously I've been strangely conditioned.

Dave brings the car to a halt at the foot of a grassy bank with a red ash pathway climbing its way out of sight above us. While he expertly angles the car into the one conveniently available space at the side of the road, I look across the way at the rain hammering off the shiny roof of a small bowling clubhouse. My gaze then stretches across a wide expanse of grassland outward to the faint, unclear promenade and the shadowy banking which is obscuring the winter sea beyond. An involuntary shiver slips down my back.

"Is it ok to leave the car here?" I ask anxiously. I'm always irrationally worried about leaving the car somewhere that it might get clamped or ticketed.

"Yeh its fine," he replies, "you asked that the last time we were here too if you remember."

I don't remember. Its been a while. "Oh yeh" I agree vacantly.

We pull on various layers of wool and crackling waterproof like we were heading for Everest then jump out into the wind and rain. Coming from the fan-heated cosiness of the car the jolt of cold and wet is, once again, a shock to the system.

Heads down we join a small stream of people forging their way up the pathway no doubt en-route to the football like ourselves. On reaching the crest of the mound, Pittodrie Stadium, the home of Aberdeen Football Club, is there below us in all its rain-soaked glory. If buildings had hearts and souls and voices this one would surely scream "Get me a scarf and a parka – right f**king NOW!"

Edging our way across the gassy summit the wind is shoving and slapping us in all directions. The tiny, staked trees that are scattered along the pathway are clinging to the hillside for dear life. They don't stand a chance you would wager. A large graveyard has spread itself over the undulating land to our left, hundreds of gravestones marking the final resting places of people no doubt glad to be in out of the cold. Down to the right a golf driving range comes into view, its flooded, swamp-like flatlands looking more like a World War One battlefield than a sporting facility.

Front and centre is the towering majesty of what must surely be the grandest stand in Scotland. Sitting like a father at the family table the Richard Donald Stand dominates the rest of the stadium and its protective qualities and close proximity to the sea make it possibly the biggest wind break in the country. Richard Donald, Dick to his banker, was the moody ex-chairman of the club as well as being a Bingo hall mogul in his spare time, and his commitment and sound stewardship was prime to the level of success enjoyed by his club in the eighties. A prudent man, Donald wisely refused to spend money he didn't have and must be congratulated on his common- sense, down to earth approach. Slightly eccentric in his ways he reputedly wore a trilby hat which, depending on the angle it was sitting, reflected what kind of mood he was in. If you found the said hat stuffed half-way down your throat he was having a bad day and it's fair to say he probably didn't like you.

Even from such an elevated view the two-tiered Richard Donald Stand is a hell of an impressive building and with its four striped divisions of red brick separated by contrasting cream panelling, you can't help wondering ....well... Why? Did Aberdeen really need a structure this size? It cost £3.5 million to complete and you cant help speculating that they could have built something smaller yet adequate and spent the rest of the money on more worthwhile projects like golf outings, team monogrammed dressing gowns or investigative' research' trips to the local lap-dancing bars.

A hundred yards or so from the stand entrance sits the handily placed Broadhill Bar. An inhospitable ' home fans only' sign on the outside wall ensures we keep on walking, across the road and along the length of turnstile entrances towards the invitingly warm looking club shop. The crabbiest , most chisel- faced old steward I've ever seen is standing menacingly outside the last entrance to the stand. He has a coupon like a dried walnut and his low, furrowed brow looks like it is ready to collapse over his eyes and large hooked nose any second. As we slink past I feel his eyes boring into me and although he says nothing, I can hear him thinking 'Saft Southern Pansies,'

A quick skip round the spacious shop and ticket collection area rams home how much bigger a concern Aberdeen FC, for all their assertions otherwise, is in comparison to Arthurston. Efficient looking operatives sit poised behind computerised screens waiting to be of assistance, while rail upon rail of swish official merchandise whisper alluringly to the assortment of home fans milling around listlessly. Finding little of actual interest to us we eventually head back to the door, not mind you, before we have all agreed wholeheartedly that we wished our shop was even a little bit like this.

12.

A common theory suggests that Aberdeen Football Club were nicknamed 'The Dons' when, in 1881, a group of footy enthusiasts, drawn mostly from the teaching profession, met, complained about their pay and conditions , then took the first tentative steps towards forming the club we know and sniff at today. This *may* be true although a more generally accepted view holds that the team were first heralded as 'the Aberdonians' which soon became shortened to 'The 'Donians' and in time was clipped into 'The Dons'.

Disappointing accounts to say the least. Having grown up as a thoughtful yet excitable child, I held two equally imaginative notions concerning the Dons. One; that the original team may, quite plausibly, have comprised completely of hairy arsed ginger-beardies *all* called Donald and who marauded round football pitches of the late nineteenth century like a pack of wild-eyed David Bellamys, hacking and slashing at anything in their way.

Even more palatable to my boy's own mind was the vision of the team as a slick, amply- proportioned bunch of olive skinned, Marlon Brando-esque Mafia gang leaders, all jowls and trouser-braces, possibly lured to Aberdeen from the warm shores of Sicily by the promise of good quality beef and ample city- centre parking. The reality, for me, was always going to be somewhat less than compelling.

Having skiddled along for eight years or so, these most academic of football enthusiasts moved the club to the improbably named Police Dung Hill where they immediately issued all squad members with their own personal clothes-peg for nasal purposes then set about renaming the ground Pittodrie Park after the owner of the land, a certain Mr Erskine of Pittodrie (Not Pitroddie).

Aberdeen Football Club Ltd, as we know it today, came into being in 1903 when the original 'Dunghillers' joined with Victoria United and a small club called Orion, so called because of its reliance on their manager's plainly designed Ford automobile which the cash-strapped home team utilised as, amongst other things, changing rooms, club headquarters, and the venue for their popular monthly fundraising tea-dances. Thankfully no underlying 'dung-related' issues nor complaints over the club vehicle's lack of optional extras were to undermine the intention and enthusiasm of the new partners and a firm amalgamation was duly secured.

However success was a long time coming for the new Aberdeen FC. In the early years decked in their original, all white strips they won precisely nothing. When these colours gave way to a typically boggin' gold and black ensemble, temporarily earning themselves the nickname of 'The Wasps, they still won hee- haw. And even when, in the thirties, they changed one more time into the modern, all-red strip that we associate with Aberdeen today, they ploughed through the best part of another decade still with nothing to show for their efforts. Strange circumstance indeed as it wasn't as if they were bereft of talented players. In the twenties there was the legendary goal-scorer Benny Yorston and co-forward Alec Cheyne, the man who, when he scored directly from a corner-kick against England at the national stadium in 1929, is genuinely considered to have inspired the Hampden Roar. The 30's saw the suave, Vaudeville sounding duo of Mills and Anderson plying their considerable talents at Pittodrie, and the forties brought in heroes such as Tommy Pearson with his mysterious double shuffle, Don Emery a stout-hearted fellow with a fearsome shot who once played a game sporting a broken leg, Jackie Hather with his lightening pace and Fred Martin who, peculiarly, was signed for The Dons as an inside forward and ended up as a goalkeeper who would ultimately play between the posts for his country.

13.

Then there was an interesting chap called Donald Coleman. Associated with Aberdeen as player and coach, from 1907 through to the late '30s Coleman was a footballing legend in every sense. Aged 29 and slight of build, the right-back arrived at Pittodrie having been handed a free-transfer by Motherwell. Four years later at the age of 33 Coleman would earn his first cap for Scotland and be widely considered as the best right back in the land, not only proving that the player had ability and tenacity that belied his years but that Motherwell wouldn't have known a player if they fell over one.

Coleman played for the Dons until the ripe old age of 42 then incredibly squeezed out five more years playing with Vale of Leven and Dumbarton. With time catching up with him the defender eventually hung up his boots and focussed his attentions on amongst other things boxing, dancing, singing, football coaching and, naturally enough, inventing.

Donald, you see, had an inquiring mind. Long before the appearance of the super cool 'Puma Dalglish' brand I had as a kid, he investigated the possibility of moulded soled football boots, then in 1931, after Celtic goalkeeper John Thomson tragically died at Ibrox in a collision with Rangers player Sam English, Coleman creatively set about designing protective headgear to ensure such a disaster never happened again. The equipment he designed unfortunately proved to be too unwieldy but his failure was not through want of trying.

Finally however Coleman did succeed in his quest for innovation making Aberdeen the first team to have dug-outs in their ground. Necessity *is* the mother of invention and in an effort to get out of the biting wind one particularly painful Baltic Saturday at Pittodrie (during a friendly against Everton actually), Coleman dug a fifty cubic foot hole in the ground with his bare knuckles lending himself and the gaffer of the time some meagre shelter from the East coast elements. The folks from Merseyside were impressed though and the idea caught on so popularly that soon managerial teams all around the country were happily hurling abuse at their charges from the comforts of their own little subterranean confines – all thanks to Donald.

14.

On the subject of firsts, Aberdeen Football Club hold the somewhat dubious honour of becoming the first in Britain to make their stadium all seated - a bold move that would install Pittodrie as one of the earliest exponents of the morgue-like atmosphere that sitting down at the football often conjures these days. Not too long ago Aberdonian fans were famously criticised for the lack of atmosphere at their home games. It was alleged that you could tell when the home fans were excited as 'the rustling of sweetie papers got louder'. Knowing what we know now, this seems grossly unfair on the Dons faithful and maybe we should not be as quick to judge. Don't forget these poor sods have had to deal with being forced to sit on their backsides at the football longer than anyone else on these shores. No wonder they've lapsed into silence. They're dying to stand up, to jostle, to sway with the crowd and to dance and sing but now they're not allowed, even if they wanted to. For the second time I find myself denying Lord Justice Taylor and his damnable report and I predict that I shall do it one more time before the cock crows. He is *not* the saviour of our game. I don't know him, I've never met him and I don't ever want to meet him. For I would probably smite him down in his tracks - from my plastic bucket seat. So it is written.

And as for our Aberdonian sweetie rustlers? They are to be sympathised with and not maligned in bitter fashion for there but for the grace of God go us all. Soon will come the day, if we're not allowed to stand up at the football again, that we'll all become so glumly inhibited that the ripping of Revels and the molestation of Maltesers will be simply be considered the norm. The partisan and openly intimidating scrunching of crisp pokes will be practiced by the edgier sections of supporters and police intervention will be necessary to quell orchestrated 'humming' by the hooligan element (pre-arranged on an internet message-board undoubtedly.)

One 'first' cruelly stolen from The Dons though was the honour of being the first Scottish team to play in Europe. As we already know, that fell to Hibernian who played in the European Cup of 1955. This was by virtue of the involvement of Hibees chairman, Harry Swan who, admittedly, had been the driving force in making continental football a reality in Scotland at last. However nobody at the time could honestly have predicted that the SFA would overlook Aberdeen, who had notably won their first ever league championship in '54, and instead invite the Easter Road men to be their inaugural representatives in the competition. But alas, eccentricity and sheer buffoonery *did* unfortunately prevail. Swan, typically self-interested like most club representatives (past and present), lacked the common decency to turn down the oh-too-gracious SFA offer and resultantly, Aberdeen would be forced to wait a further twenty-five years before participating in European football's premier competition. 'Boooooooooo!' we shouted in pantomime style.

15.

Built on a foundation of family values, Aberdeen Football Club has historically resisted the lure of the 'Big Team' mentality. Even at the peak of their success in the mid-eighties, with all of Europe at their feet, the small club 'feel' was fostered and encouraged within the walls of Pittodrie. Groups of local pensioner volunteers would come in every day to tidy the ground and look after the players' kit and boots, team training would take place on easily accessible public areas and afterwards, when other teams would disperse to play golf and feed their spiralling gambling habits, Aberdeen's players would remain within the confines of Pittodrie to enjoy innocent social activities such as table tennis, snooker and fondue cookery with their team mates. And its perhaps a lesson to the mega-business orientated clubs of today the way Aberdeen conducted itself, *particularly* in the 1980's at the height of their achievement, in terms of resisting the impersonal, 'corporate way' embraced by other major clubs within the sport. During this highly successful time in Aberdeen, cash incentives for the players were not particularly high, pricey foreign imports were shunned and the development of youth was actively encouraged. And yet the passion for the club sparked, smouldered and was fanned into a burning conflagration of enthusiasm, belief and talent that saw the club rise so far beyond the potential of its constituent parts that envious glances were thrown from Glasgow to Genoa, Dundee to Dortmund.

Alfredo Di Stefano, legendary player and manager of Real Madrid on the night Aberdeen whipped his stars in the European Cup Winners Cup final, summed it up when he asserted "Aberdeen have what money can't buy – a soul; a team spirit built in the family traditions." He also went on to complain about the price of a pint in Gothenburg and how the Swedish meat balls served up in the team hotel 'weren't as good as the ones you get in IKEA', but in his assessment of Aberdeen Football Club he nailed the secret of success squarely on the head and in doing so got as close to describing the holy grail of footballing success as anyone could hope to. He would also, however, have been the first to admit that it is one thing knowing what you're looking for and another thing finding it.

16.

And yet one man in The Aberdeen Story seemed to have the map and compass where team building and spirit lifting was concerned – Sir Alex Ferguson. He may not be everyone's smashed cup of tea but even his staunchest of critics would have to admit his style gets results

Alex, lets drop the noncy English 'Sir' thing shall we, came to Aberdeen from St Mirren in 1978 . He was in the process of challenging the Paisley club for wrongful dismissal, an action he would ultimately lose, and he jumped at the chance to replace Billy McNeil who had been co-opted by Celtic to replace the legendary yet diminishing Jock Stein.

It was a sound move for the Govan born manager as he inherited a team with real potential. In season 76'/'77 Aberdeen had, under Ally 'Tartan Army' McLeod, won the League Cup, and the following year, with McNeil at the helm, had made it to the Scottish Cup final and had narrowly lost the league to Rangers by only two points.

In the time Ferguson held the reigns of the club, Aberdeen well and truly dispelled the modern ethos that if you don't have the facilities you can't be good. Fergie's Dons built on McLeod and McNeil's sound foundations and reached for the sky winning 3 league championships, 4 Scottish cups, a league cup, the European Cup Winners Cup and the European Super cup (competed between the winners of the European Cup and The Cup Winners Cup – Aberdeen beat Hamburg to be crowned 'Kings of Europe') During these times the players built up muscles over the exposed beach dunes and dipped their injuries in the icy North Sea allowing its salty, healing qualities to take effect. They trained in such exclusive locations as the University grounds, the park beside St Machars Cathedral in the town, or at the nearby Gordon Highlander barracks. And in doing so developed and reaped the benefit from honest graft and natural teamwork nurturing their skills light years away from the money fuelled trappings experienced by the bigger teams in the game.

It wasn't all sunshine and roses though. It was alleged by some that Ferguson was a bully who ruled by fear and intimidation. He in turn accused a number of his Aberdeen charges as being self-motivated and disloyal. As interested bystanders we may never know the half of it but his story unquestionably remains a fascinating one. Do yourselves a favour and buy Ferguson's autobiography 'Managing my life' as well as 'The Boss – The many sides of Alex Ferguson' written by Michael Crick. You'll not be disappointed as they're both cracking reads. Take them out to the caravan at St Andrews or the time share in Florida, read them back to back, compare and contrast to your heart's content and form your own opinions. Whatever you come up with though, and however harsh it may seem on the great players that represented the club in that era, one has to concede that Alex Ferguson *was* Aberdeen of the eighties. His style and influence was etched on everything coming out of Pittodrie at that time and his legacy continues through his managerial offspring in the likes of Gordon Strachan, Mark McGee, Eric Black and Alex McLeish.

And Ferguson's influence and achievement doesn't stop there. Asides from these more obvious successes Ferguson has scooped from Scottish football, he has left his mark in so many other, often overlooked ways. For example;

- He has provided material for thousands of irritating office impressionists who were now able to add ' vewwy pwowd of my pwayas' to their repertoire of classics such as 'ooh betty!' ,'now then, now then, guys and gals', and 'Gonnae no dae that!'
- He was the inspiration for the nasally-resplendent, y-fronted patient in classic kids game 'Operation'.
- He was Gum chewers Weekly 'Chew-dude of the Year' three years in succession.
- He has been granted freedom of the city of Aberdeen, an honour which affords him the titles of 'Free Burgess'[6]

---

[6] For the record other famous 'Freemen' include Winston Churchill, Nelson and Winnie Mandela, HMS Scylla the city's adopted warship (eh?), and (of course) Mikail Gorbachev.

and 'Guild Brother'. This, I understand, grants Fergie the privilege of owning one of those big, gold-foiled chocolate keys to the City Gates, thruppence off a library card and allows him to drive his sheep down Union Street without fear of challenge or prosecution. As useful as useful as an Ikea voucher to a Big Issue seller in other words..

- He successfully entered the world of racehorse ownership and in tribute to 'Rock of Gibralter' his most valued equine gift/'business arrangement', Fergie did what all successful steeds do at some point in their career namely had a shit on a public highway and didn't get done for it.
- He called Arsene Wenger 'a ratchet- faced, bad losin' tit-popper on live TV. Actually he didn't but I'm pretty sure he thought it and that's good enough for me
- He managed East Stirlingshire to their glorious 'two in row' victory streak of 1974. A feat that still moistens eyes down Firs Park way to this day.

As we all know, or should I say 'all bar my mother' knows, Alex Ferguson has gone on to secure legendary status in the game through his successful stewardship at Manchester United. Whatever these subsequent achievements with the Lancashire club amount to though, I'm afraid my enduring memory of Alex Ferguson will *not* be of him shouting from the Old Trafford dug-out nor will it be of him pictured with the Champions league trophy, standing with his arm around David Beckham. No, it'll be of an Alex Ferguson dancing across the Easter Road pitch in a camel coat after thumping Hibs 5-0 to win the league for the first time, or possibly of a Fergie falling flat on his face in a puddle before sliding his way on to the rain sodden Ullevi turf in celebration on that historic night in 1983. Alex Ferguson is a Scottish Football icon. And these images, for a dedicated follower of Scottish Football, are the right and proper memories to focus on.

17.

But all this has been the common view- Everyone's Aberdeen. What of *my* Aberdeen. The team that I grew up thinking were so far away, and out of touch with the 'real' world. Way up North, in a greyer, colder world of their own.

My Aberdeen started with plain red strips with floppy white collars and not a badge or insignia to be seen. Wee fat Joe Harper, Stuart Kennedy and Arthur Graham were winning international caps and were about to give way to Willie Miller and Alex McLeish possibly the most recognised and respected central defensive partnership in modern Scottish Football times. Miller's hairy 'tache flapping at referees in dissent at the latest poor decision and McLeish, clearly a close relation of Patsy Palmer once of Eastenders fame, scoring vital goals with his ginger napper and defending the cause bravely. And big Doug Rougvie, hard to beat, hard in the tackle – even his name sounded hard. Rougvie for me epitomised Aberdeen FC down to the ground. The club suited him, it fostered him and I think it made him a better player than he actually was if you get my meaning. He later moved to Chelsea, away from the comfortable environment that he had so obviously thrived upon, and he wasn't half the player he was at Aberdeen. Wonderful proof that some players are just destined to play for one club I'm sure of it.

I loved the story of Rougvie fancying himself as a bit of a Moto-GP racer and turning up to training in full leathers and helmet on a newly purchased motor- bike. Ferguson however, on clapping eyes on Angus's answer to Barry Sheen (more like Mr Sheen), immediately transfer listed the big man until he got rid of the offending mode of transport. An indignant Rougvie consequently gave in, bought himself a bicycle instead and proceeded to get hit by a truck ending up in hospital for his trouble. Lucky Doug they called him (but not to his face).

What else do I think of when I think of Aberdeen? Again, its funny to consider my slant on things. When it comes to Pittodrie, its *not* the sparkling, comfy new stand that springs immediately to mind, it's the old wooden benched, high fronted 'grandstand' that I feel dominates the surroundings. Despite being nearly destroyed in a fire of 1971, which incidentally almost claimed the Scottish Cup as well, and despite being weather beaten over the years, probably more than any other football-related structure in the Scottish game (save for the gents 'brick-wall' toilet off the terrace at Gayfield, Arbroath which gives a new meaning to the phrase 'pissing in the wind') it still stands defiantly as a winner of tradition over 'progress'.

Then what? I think on flocks of seagulls appearing constantly in the background of post match Pittodrie reports and interviews poised, by the look of them, to take over the world in Hitchcock fashion. And also of how dark and mysterious it always looked behind the goals under the low roof of the Merkland Stand – especially on the telly. Who knows what manner of mischievous dealings went on in that inky, shrouded darkness.

Then finally there's that daft club crest. Designed, by the look of it , by Dick Donald's grandson, aged 5 and a quarter . The A in AFC made out to look like a goalpost with a big huge 'baw in it. Its just plain rubbish - FIT WIR YE THINKIN' ABOOT? What The Dons need is a proper crest, something grand and dramatic yet poetically relevant. Something like a big huge seagull, wings spread , standing on the Dunghill in a hooded Gortex jacket with the legend 'King Billy was Gay!' scribed in Latin underneath in proud gold lettering. Simple yet stirring.

18.

A huge replica Aberdeen jersey crawls and billows its way down the Richard Donald Stand, engulfing hundreds of fans simultaneously in red-hued excitement. 'Red Army No 12' is emblazoned boldly on the massive red strip and as a flock of seagulls circle for a closer look, another large elongated banner twitches in the wind and proclaims that 'The Red Ultras' are here and they mean business. The teams emerge to a rousing if damp welcome from the North East corner of the ground between the

Main Stand and the 'Big Dick' Stand which I have to say looks even grander and more imposing from inside the ground than out.

We are huddled together tightly in the right hand corner of the South Stand, a little corner of football-spectating wretchedness that offers no more than an average angle to the pitch but a much more favourable view of the wild and rugged coastline outside. Our seats are particularly well positioned to be snagged by the piercing wind and driving rain that is shooting in off the grumbling North Sea and is, like thousands of little guided missiles, assaulting my right ear-hole and prying its way beyond my hood's defences and down the side of my neck.

By half time I'm more miserable than Elvis in a health food shop. The right half of my face is red but numb. Staring up at the glass fronted corporate boxes that divide the two tiers of the Big Dick Stand, I can just make out white shirts and ties peering out, no doubt enjoying a beer or a warm cup of tea and a miniature pork pie. I'm not big on the whole corporate football experience as a rule. The muffled sound of the crowd outside and the inability or unwillingness to shout what's on your mind is too limiting for my liking. However today the two words 'Lucky bastards' are at the forefront of my mind as I imagine legions of egg-mayo sandwiches and cups of piping coffee being enthusiastically consumed inside those little rooms of centrally heated heaven.

Arthurston are a goal down and I have consumed two pies. A steak one and a mince one. The steak pie was roasting and good. Having smeared some of the warm beefy gravy on my cold face and neck for bodily warmth, I devoured the rest hungrily. The Scotch pie was boggin' though. Death Valley dry and practically tasteless. After spending a good five minutes trying to fashion the offending pastry product into a hat I give up, let it slip to the ground beneath me and squeeze myself as low into my seat as is humanly possible.

No conversation is coming from the boys. Each is facing grimly forward seemingly intent on blocking the reality of the icy shower curtain which is hanging over each of our faces in a mask of pain. As if to compound the torture an up-tempo version of 'Whatsa-matter-you' by Joe Dolce inexplicably enters my head and starts looping incessantly with no sign of abatement. What form of hell is this I beg you!

19.

The second half then? Hmmmmm. No shots at goal for us, Aberdeen deservedly score a couple more and, in view of the localised numbness I'm feeling from my head to my hip, I develop the nagging thought that I've had a stroke down my right side (much like the Arthurston team I have to say). Conceivably, I will be the proud owner of a dragging, lopsided walking action like The Mummy from the Tomb when its my turn to descend the stairs to the exit. The locked feeling in my knees adds to the probability.

Were it not for the thought of the walk back to the car, I'd feel that I'd been pushed as far as I humanly could be. I vow there and then that next Saturday I'm going to lie in bed until two in the afternoon, have a bath, then sit for the rest of the day, on a towel, beside the open oven, pre-heated to gas mark 4 – whatever that means.

20.

It's a long haul to Aberdeen. It's a longer haul in the cold and the wet. And its just plain bloody misery when your team just got beaten three-nil and you have to turn tail and head back, the roads and the miles to whence you came. To be huddled in your car wearing damp jeans with the windows steamed up *without* there being the cover of darkness and an unfussy female involved only adds to the despair.

You don't get much post-match analysis on a day like this. Fifteen minutes of us collectively reiterating the same-old theories and explanations, only in higher pitched voices this time, kills the football talk dead for the rest of the journey. The remainder of our travels I'm pleased to report is painless.

"Great company you were. Did you boys enjoy your sleep?" Dave mutters sarcastically as he brings the car to a standstill outside my parents house. My neck is aching and my left hand is tingling furiously having slept for goodness knows how long in an awkward, Elephant-man-type posture. The driving rain has followed us down the road and the gloom outside has me wondering if I could just huddle in the warm, safety of the car until the sun comes out again.

The lure of a big, roasting cup of tea washed down with some Jaffa Cakes, possibly the whole box in a 'wunner', wins through though and after the briefest of goodbyes I gird my loins and dive from the car towards the driveway, then the door, then the wonderful, wonderful central heating system.

21.

Flicking through the rough cut pages of the small local newspaper my pulse involuntarily quickens. After an initial clumsy and excited sift, my heart rate calms down again. Nothing.

I start again from the front page.This time turning the pages slowly.

Three quarters through the 11th of September's Motherwell Times I find them. The births, marriages and deaths.

'Couldn't see them for lookin' at them' I mutter under my breath.

Running my finger down the obituary column, I try to remain focussed but I can't help lingering on some of the messages. You know the sort - where stoic Central Scottish sentiment uncomfortably meets shallow American evangelism. By the first column I've noted no fewer than six 'taken too soon's , three 'dearly departed's and four demised souls who are, I was reliably informed, now performing a variety of their recognised earthly duties 'in the sky'. John is now golfing *in the sky*, while Francie is tending the garden and Wee Rab is 'pullin' burds up there '*in the sky*. Ouch.

And for the more poetic we have, 'Granda Marsh – where you are now there is no wind or rain. Only joy and happiness." Granda Marsh isn't actually dead – he's just gone to Centre Parks (probably to get away from his overly dramatic family). And finally there's the clutch of lucky sods who died 'peacefully in their asleep', a statement that clearly represents a final two-fingered salute to the poor sods who went 'violently while awake'. Who'd have thought it? All this theatre in half a page of small town journalism.

Pay attention I tell myself.

And with attention comes the result. Taggart could surely never have had it this easy.

Half way down the second column of obituaries is the entry I was hoping for.

'Jack Ellis. Suddenly at home. Leaves wife Jean and daughters Rachel and Heidi. 10.30 Crosshill Parish Church, 11.30 Holytown Crematorium.

Ha!

Then on to stage two.

Not so lucky.

Not one J. Ellis in the phone book.

Never mind. Stage two – Plan B

"Hello, is that The Moorings Hotel in Motherwell? ...... Yes I wonder if you can, I'm phoning on behalf of Mrs Jean Ellis. We held a funeral in your hotel a few weeks back and we arranged for you to send us out a couple of brochures, there weren't any available when we asked so the girl said she'd send something out..... uhuh...... well we haven't received anything as yet and I wondered if you could arrange to have a pack or something sent out..... it was the 14th of September .... Sure, no problem ....
....
...hello, yes.................uhuh, great! Em can you confirm the address you have just in case the last stuff went AWOL ....

uhuh … 4 Erskine Avenue , Bothwell… yup that's right….ok brilliant, so we can expect something in post this week…… ok thanks for your help , bye now.

Like taking sweeties from a baby really.

22.

A couple of wins will see us leap up the table I'm thinking. Supping away at a damn fine cuppa and munching on a slice of buttery toast I'm back staring at the tables in the Sunday paper.

Scottish Premier League

	Pld	W	L	D	GF	GA	PTS
Hearts	14	8	2	4	21	14	28
Celtic	14	7	2	5	23	8	26
Rangers	14	7	2	5	18	7	26
Aberdeen	14	6	3	5	20	10	23
Hibernian	14	5	4	5	18	16	20
Dunfermline	14	5	6	3	17	18	18
Dundee Utd	14	4	5	5	24	24	17
Kilmarnock	14	3	4	7	10	15	16
Falkirk	14	3	6	5	14	21	14
Motherwell	14	2	5	7	13	17	13
Arthurston R.	14	3	7	4	13	28	13
Patrick Th.	14	1	8	5	9	22	8

However our next two games are both at home against Hibs and Celtic respectively and even with my blinkered enthusiasm, I can't see us taking six points from those games.

Dad wanders into the kitchen and starts rummaging noisily in a drawer muttering to himself about green twine. I'm about to comment on the excessive clanging going on when I'm drawn to the top right of the 'Shorts' column of sports news. I smile and a little of that old child-like excitement flickers somewhere deep down inside.

Arthurston Sign Slovenian

Arthurston last night secured the signature of 31 year old Slovenian defender Ivan Pecnik. The former Lyon, Slavia Prague and Wolves man has signed a one year deal and will go straight into the squad or next week's home match against Hibernian. Manager Wilf Schnabbel was delighted to finally get his man and although he was unwilling to disclose the fee involved, did joke that Pecnik was 'reassuringly expensive'.

Looking up from the paper, dad is still clanking around in the kitchen drawer.

"We've signed a boy from Slovenia – a defender." I announce expectantly.

"Eh?" mutters dad dropping what looks like a pencil sharpener realistically shaped like a Bourbon Cream. A vague recollection of buying the novelty toy one rainy childhood holiday momentarily yanks my memory.

"I said we've signed a …. Oh never mind. What are you doing?"

"I'm looking for something for the garden."

"Isn't your gardening year about done." I ask feigning an interested tone.

"I suppose," he replies, turning round looking at me earnestly, "but there's still lots to do. I need to cut back a lot of the bigger plants and compost one more time before the really cold weather hits us."

"Oh right," I say nodding my head , slightly sorry I asked. A pregnant pause settles as I rack my brains for something else to say. A light goes on in my head an almost excitedly I ask, "How's that new tree doing that you planted ?"

A flicker of something that looked like, well, gratitude and dad wanders over to the kitchen table where I'm sat. "Ahh not so good son. It hasn't taken so well. I mean its still alive but I can't get the damn thing to grow at all. If I don't get something from it soon, I can't see it lasting the winter."

As he shakes his head my father seems genuinely saddened by his little tree's failure to sprout. "I see your team bought a new defender" he says turning his back on me and edging his way to the back door, "Slovakian or something?"

"Slovenian," I correct him, smiling, "but close enough."

"Uhuh" he responds and stops in his tracks, looking as if he's going to say something else. He doesn't though and instead grabs a pair of threadbare looking gardening gloves from the window sill, mutters another confirming "Uhuh" and slips out into his garden.

Chapter 13 A Tale O' The Hun

1.

On December 4th 2007, a clear, crisp winter-cold Wednesday, my Grampa died.

When it happened I didn't cry, I didn't feel sad or angry or lost. I felt nothing.

The doctor informed us in a monotone voice it was an 'osis or an 'ism of some sorts but to be honest I wasn't really listening – the details didn't matter much. He was gone and that was it.

He hadn't felt well that morning, so much so that he had called mum on the phone asking her to come over and sit with him. By lunch-time he'd had an ill defined 'seizure' of some sort and was duly being 'monitored' in a private room in Arthurston General. And at 3:52 on this bright and brisk winter's afternoon, with the sun sinking in a smouldering, burned-out sky, he shut his eyes and he stopped living.

We were there. My dad, hands deep in his pockets, staring out of the window seeking refuge in the world outside. Mum, sitting straight as a poker on an orange plastic bucket seat at the side of the bed. And me, perched on the edge of the bed itself. Anxious and unable to sit still, slipping to my feet every few minutes, pacing the room, inspecting its corners then returning to my place on the bed.

I had rushed over from Sandy's as soon as I had heard the news and when I burst into the room and saw Grampa, drawn and frail, hooked up to all those drips, pumps and monitors, it felt like someone, a large, muscle-bound someone, had hit me square in the chest with a big heavy mallet. I moved to the window, my back to everyone, and cried a few silent tears of shock before hastily wiping my eyes and turning back to face the music.

"He's going to be ok?" I nodded at my parents quietly as Grampa lay, eyes closed, an oxygen mask covering his face, making short and shallow breathing compressions with the help of the hard working machine hooked up beside him.

The dark looks said not.

He came to for a while, as we sat and waited. Watery eyes looking to each of us for comfort. Or possibly to offer comfort, I'm not sure. At one point, one of the pieces of bedside equipment had suddenly beeped loudly and aggressively. Stark fear flooded into those same eyes, full and wide and scared.

"Its ok." I said quietly, clasping Grampa's bony hand and the fear subsided more gently than it had arrived.

At 3:27 on the expressionless white clock on the wall, Grampa struggled awkwardly to peel the oxygen mask slightly to the side of his face then beckoned me close.

'Y'alrighh son?"

"I'm ok Grampa" I croak, my throat dry and dusty.

"Think...ah....just lost......." he whispered, then paused, concentrating every part of himself on getting his breath back. His mouth moved again,"... a bad....goal." The smallest glint of a smile pulled the corner of his cracked lips and I tightened my grip around his fingers.

"Since when did we ever lose a good goal." I reply slowly, falling into a broad smile of my own. A little raise of the eyebrows from Grampa in agreement.

At 3:41 he tried to sit up. Mum told him not to move too much and Dad came as close to the bed as he had dared all day. Grampa was adamant though and with a little help from Mum, myself, and three industrial strength support pillows, he got himself into a slightly more upright position. Hands quivering, he slipped the mask from his face then awkwardly but in determined fashion, swept the sticky monitor pads off his chest.

Mum started to say something, Grampa shook his head and Dad barely audibly said ' No love, let him be.'

And at 3:52 it was over. The deep wrinkles of age and worry, etched for all those years on Grampa's forehead slid away in an instant and he was gone. I stood quietly, forever, as I waited for Grampa's eyes to open up and for him to say he was 'feeling better thanks' but as the minutes went by nothing happened. I think a nurse came and quietly explained what we should do next but I'm not sure. Finally, after sitting, standing and mulling around in the fog for a while we were eventually told we could go home.

2.

As we walked back to the car, through the floodlit hospital car park, people around us got on with their lives. They started their shifts, ran for a bus or bustled towards the supermarket. We drove home in silence as cars flew past in the opposite direction. At the top of Arthurston Main Street two women stood staring at their respective vehicles, perplexed at the bump which had just occurred. An illuminated queue stood in 'The Last Supper' chip shop waiting to feed their deep fried laziness and a group of pale youths hung on the corner outside Semi-Chem jostling each other in mock battle. The world was getting on with it whilst mine had stopped.

In true Donald family tradition we all looked our own way. Words of support went unsaid and personal thoughts and feelings remained just that – personal.

The funeral was on the Friday morning and by the time the last of the steak-pie had been polished off in the dining-room of the Arthurston House Hotel, friends had reminisced, and close and not so close family had reacquainted in varying degrees of awkwardness. All had agreed 'what a shock it was' and how 'badly Grampa would be missed'. All had left to resume whatever it was they did with their lives.

I was still numb.

3.

"I really don't think I should be going to this" I mutter sullenly for about the tenth time in the half hour we've been in the car.

Dave looks at me carefully. "What the hell else would you have been doing today? Helping your dad in the garden?"

"No ... but"

"No but nothing!" Dave continues, his tone with a steel tip to it. "What would Johnnie have wanted you to do? I know that sounds like a corny cliché but ... well.... would he have had you sittin' home feelin' sorry? – I DON'T THINK SO."

Before I can answer Dave rounds off gently, "He'd have been damned adamant that you got on with it and he'd have been especially determined that you went see the Rovers. You know he would."

And I know he would but I can help feeling guilty and inappropriate by skipping off to see Rangers v Arthurston Rovers, a mere three days after my favourite person in the world has died.

Asides from the moral dilemmas camped in my head I'm of mixed feelings about heading to Ibrox Stadium anyway. On the one hand, watching the Rovers play on one of the biggest stages in British football has me enthralled at the prospect. On the other, it can be an aggravating trip for the small town fan. Some of the more *extreme* attitudes, shall we say, that prevail with many of the Rangers faithful can be difficult to come to terms with and I tend to get unduly worked up by it all. And there's a lot of them. AND we could get a hiding. So, on reflection this may not be the best of grounds to visit for a relaxing afternoon of sport and camaraderie in the current circumstances.

We're being clever. Instead of crawling painfully along the 'Devil's own' M8 and then forcing our way through Govan's gridded streets, like the rest of the numpties, we have cheekily skootched our way along the Clyde-side Expressway and taken the slip road leading to the Crowne Plaza (The old Moathouse Hotel). Three pounds to safely park in their car-park, a couple of over-priced beers and a sandwich, then a short but pleasant walk across the bridge to Glasgow's Science Centre will leave us a stone's throw from Ibrox Stadium without any of the ensuing hassle traditionally experienced when visiting the Gers.

Ingenious.

4.

Lunch is duly had in the hotel lounge, an airy, open-planned area that sprawls itself around a centrally placed, marquee covered bar. Jonesy and I plump for sandwiches while Dave has a Panini of some sort. At £6.95 and £7.95 respectively I fully expect of a drop of sex thrown in as well. Unfortunately a couple of sprigs of rocket (man!) and a carrot stick are my lot. Amidst the indoor trees and dark wood furniture, Dave and Jonesy chatter away with chintzy cheeriness. I, on the other hand, find my gaze lost over in the direction of the huge 'history of the Clyde' mural on the far wall and its only when Jonesy shakes my shoulder and tells me its time we were making a move, that I drag my full attention back to reality.

A sharp icy wind scratches at us as we cross over the Clyde on the exposed 'Millennium' footbridge. The sky is as blue as on a Spanish postcard. My cracking lips and involuntary muscular spasms, however chase off any lingering thoughts that we are anywhere other than Glasgow on a raw winter's day.

The metal gray Science Centre looms in front of us, with the adjoining IMAX Cinema sitting like a big shiny, robotic maggot in the sunshine. Looking over, It's pal - the Glasgow Tower, hangs around guiltily whistling in the wind. Over four hundred feet high and costing ten million pounds to build, the structure has all the appearance of a caterpillar gripping on grimly to a garden cane.

The tower is Glasgow's foolhardy equivalent to the Millennium Dome. Promising spectacular views of the Glasgow skyline it craftily lured tourists and locals alike to it's grand opening in 2001, only for the expectant visitors to be informed that the lifts were too heavy to operate safely and no one would be allowed to make the ascent that day or indeed, for the foreseeable future. Then the rotating structure which, according to its designers, would 'usefully' inform the people of Glasgow which way the wind was blowing (towards frivolous misspending of public funds I would suggest), unfortunately 'slipped out of alignment', whatever that meant - before finally sinking alarmingly into its own foundations. Early indications suggested the attraction would be closed for two months while waiting for replacement parts to arrive. Those parts must have really got lost in the post as, some five years later, the tower still appears to be in a state of closure. What a dreadful state of affairs – a shocking waste of money on a goofy, not-particularly-pleasing-to-the-eye, piece of kit that doesn't work anyway. Not only that, the good folk of Glasgow have been left for years now, wandering around aimlessly, clearly unsure of prevailing wind direction. Its just not good enough.

We stroll through the gap between the Science Centre and the new boxy, glacial BBC offices where Jonesy only narrowly avoids stepping into the shallow moat of water around the IMAX building. Behind us, up on the hill in the distance, the spire of Glasgow University surveys the Glasgow scene below in a slightly superior manner. To our right, the more grounded Govan Town Hall welcomes us to its territory. We are now very much in Rangers country.

5.

Onwards to Ibrox, on Copeland Road now, and the trail of football fans has built up substantially out of nowhere. Street corners are suddenly adorned with Union Jacks, red, white and blue scarves, fanzines and the like, all being sold by a selection of menacing individuals who have clearly been temporarily separated from their Waltzers, Dodgems and Shire horses if only for the afternoon.

As if by magic – a pub appears. The Stadium Bar no less. A single levelled, windowless cube that looks about as inviting as female oxter hair. Dave looks at it carefully, visibly slowing his pace. However, just as it appears something momentous may be about to occur he looks the other way and picks up the pace again.

"Not fancy it?" I ask puffing my way level with Dave who seems lost in his own world.

"Eh?.... Nah, I'm trying to cut down a bit." He pats his belly gently. " Lose a few pounds maybe."

"Yeh, well it doesn't look very nice anyway." I venture.

"Actually its fine inside, "Dave replies airily, "Never judge a book by its cover."

Jonesy , who had been lagging even further behind than me, catches us up waving a match program in his hand. "Ivan Pecnik is named in the squad and the boy back there says he's definitely going to play!" he cries excitedly, his laboured breath clearly visible in the air in front of him.

Unfortunately due to a freak 'training injury' Pecnik hasn't kicked a ball for the club yet – 'ankle ligament damage' so the Arthurston Gazette reported. Frustratingly, in his five weeks at the club, the closest he's got to the pitch is waving bravely to the crowd from the touchline at the home game against Hibs (a tousy game we contrived to lose 2-1 despite the Edinburgh side having two men sent off and losing their keeper in an incident involving his head and 'Cavey' Burgoigne's elbow.)

We could really have done with him too. Two further defeats against Celtic at home and Falkirk away took us to within one point of bottom team, Partick Thistle and the situation was looking desperate. Out of nowhere, however, came last week's rousing 4-1 victory at home to Motherwell. The lads were majestic with Ray Stark and Jay McDonald each grabbing two goals. Psychologically it was even more important than just the result. With the Steelmen themselves picking up only one point from their last five games, we joyfully leap-frogged them into tenth place in the league . One worrying footnote to the whole Pecnik saga was the unsettling rumour that the Slovenian's injury was not quite as it seemed. A reliable source of Dave's confided to him in the pub on Friday night that Pecnik came with a 'bit of a Playboy reputation' and that the twisted ankle was actually the result of him falling off the revolving floor in a pole dancing club during a 'welcome to the club' night out with a few of the other players. Hmmm. Hopefully not.

Passed the peeling, white terraced houses that have seen better days and the constant brown tenements, then down Harrison Drive where the bustling crowd multiplies tenfold almost instantly. Program sellers punt their wares from little stalls, people are meeting and greeting each other while others plough on to their goal. Ahead of us looming large and imposing is our goal too. Its big. And its fearsome....

Its Castle Greyskull.

6.

Rangers FC were formed in 1872 from the origins of a local cricket team...........

Aye right! Can you seriously imagine a cricket match in Govan?

"Howzat!"

"HOWZIT- NO, ya dobber man?

A barney ensues.

No. Cricket may have been at the root of several of the other Scottish teams but not Rangers. In reality It was down to four young men; Peter Campbell, William McBeath, Moses and Peter McNeil who founded this club which would eventually go on to become one of the dominating monsters of the Scottish game. Ironic considering that these young men stood on Fleshers Haugh on Glasgow Green and plotted the birth of their football club without money, kit or even a football. The latter threw up an obvious problem to say the least.

In the absence of the proper accessories to boot about, the first few training sessions were interesting affairs with the lads being forced to make do with whatever was at hand. Resourceful souls to the core, they experimented, kicking around, amongst other things, strapped up cardboard boxes, dead crows, left over body parts from the nearby gallows on Glasgow Green and outsized Scotch Eggs nabbed from the back door of the nearby butcher. In the face of this rich array of kickable options, they opted perhaps controversially, for none of the above. Instead, and most unanimously, they chose to use William's wee sister's hedgehog, Billy.

'Once Billy wiz rolled in cotton wool he made a gem wee ba' commented McBeath in issue 2 of The Rangers News. The fluffed up rodent became so synonymous with the lads and their early dealings that they became well known locally as 'The Billy Boys'[7]. When the team ran out from their changing bushes kitted out and ready for action, many of the old worthies on the Green were even heard to comment expectantly ' Hello - hello, here come the Billy Boys' . And so Glasgow's relationship with this most interesting of clubs began.

The team was called 'Argyle' however they lost their first game to Callander FC, a team made up predominantly of fudge-makers, outdoor-wear retailers and woollen-mill owners, prompting Moses, an uncompromising player more inclined to parting plums than parting oceans, to rename themselves 'Rangers', a name he had read of in a rugby publication of the time. Inspirationally, the team beat Clyde in the next game 11-0, disappointing Peter Campbell intensely as he was intent, in the event of a second defeat, on calling the club Dukla Softy-Peewanker United.

The club went from strength to strength and in 1899 they moved to the current location of Ibrox Stadium where they immediately made history by winning the league without dropping a single point - a record that still stands today. In the years approaching the first World War, Rangers were, along with firmly established rivals Celtic, the dominant force in the Scottish game. Together they were well and truly , The' Old Firm' – a faintly accusing term stretching back to the early nineteen hundreds inferring that both Rangers and Celtic, despite their intense rivalry, were a single commercial entity, guilty of colluding

---

[7]   many refute this assertion claiming the terminology is actually in reference to the famous horse-riding homosexual, William of Orange who
died of acute chaffing in 1702.

in their own self-interest. Even their own fans in the early days, were suspicious that matches were rigged to maximise revenues for both clubs!

The 'War To End All Wars' was imminent and it was during this time of instability that religious intolerance arrived in Glasgow and infected many of the Rangers following to a level that certainly had never been experienced before. In actuality, prior to 1912, there had been very little in the way of serious trouble between the Old Firm supporters beyond that of natural local rivalry. So where did this wind of change blow in from? Why were large sections of the predominantly Protestant Rangers' faithful suddenly injected with anti-Catholic feeling? As in most historical arguments, reason and blame could be draped over any one of a number of factors.

The historical tensions borne out of the hoards of Irish Catholic immigrants fleeing their country's potato famine for a new life on the Clyde-side were still simmering in the lower reaches of Glasgow life for starters. 'Protestant' jobs were being taken by a Catholic workforce eager to work longer and harder and for less pay. The home-grown resentment for this was palpable.

Add into the mix the influx of Irish Dockworkers to the war-galvanised Glasgow shipyards, together with the arrival of Belfast shipbuilders Harland and Wolff, bringing with them their notoriously sectarian employment policy to an area in such close proximity to Ibrox Stadium, trouble was obviously brewing.

Finally, throw into the fray an individual the likes of newly elected Rangers chairman John Ure Primose, an outspoken anti-catholic, and its clear to see how all these ingredients stirred up a bitter mixture that became as awkward to throw away as it was unpalatable to the taste. Primrose was not only a man of prejudice, he was also a calculating man who quite possibly realised from a very early juncture that a fuelled rivalry between Rangers and Celtic in the prevailing climate could bring with it substantial financial returns. Sharpening this rivalry with religious 'moral justification' only made the sell that little bit easier to the strained populous around the Govan area of Glasgow. And so it began.

The rise of sectarianism in Glasgow and its ultimate attachment to Rangers Football Club is a complicated issue. Too complicated in all honesty for a wee book on football to reflect on wisely. The dark roots of today's problems are clearly borne out of all the factors mentioned above and Rangers FC purists, for their part, must feel justifiably unfortunate to have become embroiled in the whole thing in the first place. They are after all just a football club. They are *not* a political movement nor are they the prime guardians of social equity who must bear sole responsibility for many of Glasgow's misguided failings. Yes the club profit from age old bitterness , Yes, they could be more intolerant at times with sections of their support where it is within their powers to do so, and because of this the spotlight of suspicion will always hover over Ibrox, but all in all Sectarianism is an unwanted legacy that must hurt the genuine fans and benefactors of what has always been a proud and disciplined club.

7.

Unfortunately Rangers Football Club, over the years, haven't been without their tragedies. Two infamous incidents have shaken the club to its foundations and although Rangers have soldiered on with heart and character, the marks of sorrow have been left indelibly on the fabric of Glasgow football for ever.

In April 1902 Ibrox Stadium witnessed its first disaster when a section of its old fashioned timber terracing collapsed during a Scotland v England international fixture. Twenty six people died and over five hundred were injured on the East Terracing (now the Copeland Road Stand) when the weight and motion of the packed crowd caused the structure to give way below them. The disaster struck only ten minutes into the game and the players were quickly led from the field as rescue teams struggled to restore order amidst the mangled structure. Incredibly, in a bid to avert additional panic or rioting, the teams eventually returned to the pitch and, amidst the rescue operation being carried out around them, finished the game. As a club, Rangers were so distraught by the events that they put all of their 22 professional players up for sale in a bid to finance any necessary work to improve the overall ground safety at the Ibrox Stadium.

If this was enough to cast a shadow over Rangers FC then the events of the 2nd of January 1971 shrouded the club in near darkness.

The final old firm derby of the season was virtually over with Rangers trailing one-nil by a late strike from Celtic winger Jimmy Johnstone. To make matters worse for the Ibrox faithful, Celtic were out of sight in the chase for the league and en-route to a sixth successive championship victory. When Colin Stein scored a dramatic last gasp equaliser the previously subdued Rangers fans exploded. It was only when the excitement began to abate that there was a dawning realisation that something was far wrong. Over on Stairway thirteen leading from the ill-fated East terracing, the steel barriers had buckled under the pressure of the jubilant crowd using the exits. The resulting pile up quickly developed into mass panic and before the hour was out 66 people had lost their lives in the suffocating carnage. Grim.

Because the Ibrox disaster happened before I started watching football the events seem like ancient history to me. Except it wasn't really all that long ago. This terrible accident happened in my lifetime - in 'modern day Scotland' so to speak. This wasn't some sepia-toned, grainy-filmed catastrophe borne out of an older, less developed world. People who died on those wintry stairs would easily still be alive today had fate not taken a cruel and unfair hand that January afternoon. It could have been a dad, or an uncle. It could have been me or it could have been you - just out for a day at the football for a bit of fun, or some banter with your mates.

Sixty- six sheet-covered bodies lay on Ibrox turf that evening, stretching from the corner flag to the goalpost as a reminder that life is fragile. Fragile for even the toughest and bravest of us. More often than not we finish the day safe and unscathed, in much the same state as we started it. Sometimes, however, something happens in those intervening hours that alters the status quo so badly that we may never be the same again. I guess its how we deal with these slings and arrows that makes us who we are as people, as groups, or as clubs, businesses and organisations. 'What doesn't kill us makes us stronger' is a well used slice of maternal advice but it remains one of the truest maxims I've ever heard. The experience of these two horrendous events could have brought Rangers FC to its knees. The fans could have given up. Fear, blame and disillusionment could have set in, leaving the club as an empty husk. But it didn't, Rangers were not killed and the human resolve shown by everyone associated with the club and touched by its disasters is an example to us all. As for being stronger, the club has gone on to accumulate 51 league titles, 31 Scottish Cup wins, 24 League Cup wins and a Cup Winners Cup triumph to date with little sign of decay. With this in mind it would fair to say they are more than just a stronger outfit. They are in every sense an immovable force.

8.

One thing Rangers are good at is holding on to their managers. While other teams (look away Dundee United) change their bosses quicker than they change their under-pants, Rangers have always remained incredibly loyal to their man in the hot-seat.

In the century and a bit that the Ibrox club has been in existence they have had only twelve different managers at the helm. William Wilton, who was tragically killed in a boating accident near Gourock, held the honour of being the first manager of the club. Bill Struth, voted third 'Greatest Ever Manager' behind Jock Stein and Alex Ferguson in the Sunday Herald's poll in 2003, remains the longest serving steward whilst Jock ' get up them fuckin' sand-dunes' Wallace and Walter Smith take the honour of being the only men to have held the position twice. The full list is;

William Wilton	1899 – 1920
Bill Struth	1920 – 1954
Scot Symon	1954 – 1967
David White	1967 – 1969
William Waddell	1969 – 1972
Jock Wallace	1972 –78 and 1983 - 1986
John Greig	1978 – 1983
Graeme Souness	1986 – 1991
Walter Smith	1991 -98 and 2007 - date
Dick Advocaat	1998 – 2002
Alex McLeish	2002 - 2006
Paul Leguen	2006 – 2007
Walter Smith	2007 - date

That Rangers have only had these twelve souls in charge over such a long period is a little surprising considering their relative lack of European success. This is a club with serious aspirations in that area and it can only be testament to fan and boardroom acceptance of domestic domination that more managerial sackings and appointments haven't been forthcoming. In an effort to obtain the right blend to ensure success in Scotland, while at the same time realising Rangers' potential as one of the major forces in Europe, one would have expected less tolerance . The conclusion has to be, therefore, that despite overtures to the contrary, everyone out Ibrox way *is* really quite contented at being that proverbial outsized, aquatic creature - the big fish in the small pond.

And then there's the playing style adopted by these bosses. I can't speak for the earlier teams since I never saw them, but I have always held the notion that the Rangers managers of my era built their teams on solid, physical attribute and honest hard work above and beyond the need to play attractive 'silky' football. Contrast this with rivals Celtic who, I feel, have traditionally placed that bit more focus on flair and creativity and consequently have been the more fluid team to watch. (God, I can hear the arguments starting already)

There I've said it! Or at least inferred it. In pure footballing terms, I have always preferred watching Celtic than Rangers. While Rangers, in my opinion, have consistently been more workman-like, better organised and, in a positive sense, defensive minded, Celtic have always been that bit more pleasing to my neutral eye. Not that achieving aesthetic superiority has necessarily been the best and most successful approach mind you. After all, Walter Smith, throughout the nineties, consistently dismantled attractive, attack-minded Celtic teams along the way to his nine-in-a- row championships, and he did it with the emphasis on excellent tactical awareness allied with keenly motivated, quality players that fitted neatly into the system. *Not* by teaching his players to dribble round six men five times each before engaging in ten minutes of ball juggling.

And here's the rub. When the final whistle was blown and the points were counted, who would you rather have supported during that era? Celtic with their pretty patterns, dainty touches and runners-up medals or the highly efficient, unbeatable Rangers machine with nine unanswered championships behind them? Not a difficult answer irrespective of your persuasion.

9.

But hold on – Why drag Celtic into this at all? Why contaminate this blue, blue sea of prose with anything to do with the Bhoys from the East side. I'll tell you why. For the neutral supporter, and I always think this is an unfortunate cross that the Old Firm fan has to bare, I'm afraid that its got to the point the two clubs *are* bound together - they are well and truly viewed as being The Old Firm. Who's gong to win the league? Rangers /Celtic. Who is eyeing up pastures new or pushing for a bigger piece of the pie? Rangers/Celtic. Who is on the back page of the paper? Ranger/Celtic. They are so often as one that when it comes to many of the opinions and talking points of the day, they cannot now be untangled.

And the thing is , through the excessive press exposure 'enjoyed' by the Old firm, we as fans of the other clubs can't help but know so much more about Rangers and Celtic than their fans could ever know about *us*. In many ways Rangers and Celtic have become public property of the masses. There is so much written about the Glasgow teams on a day to day basis that I find myself infinitely more equipped to argue the whys and wherefores of the latest issues at Parkhead and Ibrox than I could ever be discussing the intricate goings on at, say, Falkirk Stadium or East End Park. The idea that everyone's an expert must be a real pain in the crotch for old firm fans. As far as *their* team goes, we *all* know who's doing well. Who's arsed things up. Where the money's going, what the supporters have been up to and worse, because of the antagonistic wedge between Old Firm fans and Non-Old Firm fans that nowadays tends to exist, I think we as the 'non' variety are more inclined to put the boot in where we can. For this I sympathise, I really do. I know I hate 'outsiders' criticising my team. Unfortunately for the Old Firm fan, not only does such scrutiny come with the turf, the turf gets re-laid several times a week and often by folk who aren't even gardeners.

Anyway, to get back to my point – Rangers have had some great defences on which they have built championship winning teams. The best of which would indisputably be the 'Iron Curtain' defence of the late '40s. Brown, Young, Shaw, McCoy, Woodburn and Cox made up the backbone of a defensive line which struck terror into the hearts of forwards the length and breadth of the country. As a gauge of their worth, even Hibs' celebrated 'Famous Five' got tangled up in the folds of this fearsome unit as Rangers squeezed out the talented men from Easter Road to win the 1948/49 championship. Such was their strength, passion and organisation.

10.

If history shows anything though, it shows that Rangers fans like nothing better than a good riot. Over the years, their 'squad' has done more for the ancient art of 'bringing a game to its knees' than perhaps any other team in the country. And small, localised skirmishes just aren't their style. Clearly if a job is worth doing, its worth doing well and if you can get a few thousand on the pitch rather than a few then all the better. Here are a few of my personal favourites;

The West of Scotland Cricket Ground riot of 1877 – The Bears first really successful effort at mass rioting occurred in this Scottish Cup Final replay against Vale of Leven. With the game delicately poised at 1-1, Rangers looked to have scored an extra-time winner were it not for the fact that the ball , after crossing the line, struck a fan then rebounded safely back into the keeper's arms. Referee Kerr[8] chose not to give the goal provoking the seething masses into a pitch invasion that eventually lead to the game being abandoned. The resultant replay became the first ever final to be played at Hampden which Rangers incidentally lost. The change of venue arose from complaints that the original ground wasn't big enough, it offered poor crowd control, and that the players kept running into the wooden stumps in the middle of the pitch.'

The 1909 Cup Final Replay Riot – An historic event in which Rangers and Celtic fans uniquely joined forces to rampage around Hampden Park in a state of drink-fuelled hysteria. It didn't take much to spark spectator fury in those days and when it became apparent that with the game finishing in another draw, extra time would not be played and *another* replay was necessary, the 60,000 crowd went ballistic suspecting that both clubs were milking the opportunity of further revenue. When the players disappeared down the tunnel, fans invaded the pitch whereby they tore down the goalposts, dug up the turf and then set

---

[8]   Referee Kerr, despite standing at height of 6" 3" weighed in at only 10stone 5lbs. It was this physical appearance which prompted Rangers fans to sing, for the first time, en-masse 'Who's the Lean-yin in the black? A chant which is still sung by their fans today in the wake of poor refereeing decisions.

fire to the Main Stand and turnstiles using what little left-over whiskey they had as fuel. After the dust had settled both clubs were ordered to pay Queens Park compensation for the damage and the SFA sought further punishment by withholding the cup and the players medals.

The St James Park Riot in '69 – Mayhem ensued as Rangers tumbled out of the Fairs Cup in the semi final away-leg against Newcastle United. Hundreds of Rangers fans, armed with bottles and beer cans (all empty), poured onto the park from the Gallowgate End of the ground in a futile attempt to have the match abandoned and, meeting little in the way of resistance from rival United fans, were forced into an improvised scuffle with the local constabulary. Finding this too tame for their tastes, they then proceeded to battle amongst themselves for a good twenty minutes over what many claim was a heated disagreement over the names of the firemen in classic kids' TV programme Trumpton.

The '72 Cup Winners Cup riot – Some blame police heavy handedness others point to the unfavourable cycle of the moon. The long and the short of it was that fans spilled on to the hallowed turf of Barcelona FC in celebration at having hung on to beat Russian cracks, Dynamo Moscow 3-2, at last giving the Gers their first taste of European success. It was third time lucky for Rangers who had previously lost in Cup Winners Cup finals having been edged out by Bayern Munich in '67 and Fiorentina in the inaugural competition of '61. As more and more fans piled onto the playing field things turned ugly as itchy Spanish police clashed with bevvied Scottish dafties. As Andy Belmont poignantly wrote in his 1984 book 'Och Aye the Nou-Camp', '… *sheer excitement got the better of me and by the time I made my way down from my seat in the back row of the top tier of the stand….. the floodlights were off, the place was in darkness and everyone had gone home.*'

In the wake of the goings on outside in the arena, a makeshift presentation ceremony took place in a little stuffy room under the main stand and when John Greig finally took the Cup Winners Cup in his hands, only a few officials and UEFA representatives were there to see it.

Kind of sad really.

The Scottish Cup Final Riot of 1980 – Held in great affection by both sides of the Old Firm, television brought this visual feast to armchairs the length and breadth of the open-mouthed nation. It was genuine end to end stuff with literally thousands of blokes, who didn't look like they'd seen a bar of soap in a decade, knocking the crap out of each other in what the Guinness Book of Records officially recognised as the World's largest bar-room brawl. Dedication's what they needed and both sets of fans had it in spades that day. In the aftermath, police officials called for all old firm games to be played behind closed doors. By way of compromise the SFA promised to ensure that at future Old Firm clashes, Lena Martell, Sydney Devine and Ally Bain records would be played before kick off and also at half- time to 'give the fans more to worry about than the opposition'. The police agreed. Celtic won one nil after extra time that day but that was honestly 'by the by'.

The Burger-Bun Riot of 2003 - A home midweek CIS cup tie v Falkirk turned to near disaster as thousands of livid Rangers fans rampaged when , ten minutes before half time, it became apparent that there were no more burger buns left at *any* of the eatery stations throughout the stadium. The news spread like wildfire and by the time referee Hugh Dallas blew for the break, wild gangs of red, white and blue maniacs were lumbering and wheezing their way through the long Ibrox concourses bursting Quenchy-cups open, prodding snack-bar assistants with little white plastic stirring spatulas and gang-raiding the ovens for signs of anything resembling bakery products.

Injury on a grand scale was only averted when, in a last gasp of desperation, former director, Donald Findlay announced over the public address system that if everyone returned to their seats he would send out for pizza.

The gesture worked quickly if only temporarily. Placated by the promise of an al fresco Italian 'tightener', the crowd settled to watching Rangers record a comfortable two-nil victory. Fighting, however resumed and continued long into the night when the pizzas failed to materialise and it became common knowledge that the delivery boy from Dominos had taken the 18,000 'Mighty Meaties' and 6,000 Texas Bar-B-Qs to a 12" by 8" lock up in Anniesland by mistake.

11.

It is always worth taking a walk round to the front of Ibrox's main stand. Just for a wee look. The red brick frontage and tall arched windows are a sight to behold, they reek tradition and you are instantly transported back to the days of flat caps, rations, and heavy industry on the Clyde. Squint and you can almost see the legendary Bill Struth wandering to work from his nearby tenement home, readying himself for another athletic training session.

Physical fitness was paramount in those days and Ibrox's running track was well used. Athletics, in fact, played a big part in the development of Ibrox as a stadium. Like most of the Scottish league clubs of the time, Rangers encouraged their ground to be used as a venue for running and cycling events through the summer months. 'The Ibrox Sports', which remained popular well into the 1950's, were the biggest and most celebrated of these meetings. Olympic champions such as Englishman, Sydney Wooderson, 'The Flying Finn' Paavo Nurmi, and Chariots of Fire stars Eric Liddell and Harold Abrahams all ran on the blaze track surrounding the Ibrox turf, while all the major Scottish football teams clamoured to play in the 5-a-side competition that became integral to 'The Sports'.

At the Copland Road end of the old main stand frontage, the bronze statue of John Greig stands unflinching, ball in hand, in commemoration of the two Ibrox disasters. The figure is the epitome of defiance as thousands pass by, at every match, remembering its relevance as they go. Dave, Jonesy and I linger in front of Greig's imposing form, each of us lost for a moment in the sentiment.

Nowadays Ibrox Stadium is an altogether safer proposition and holds the coveted UEFA 5 star classification. There are twenty-nine stadia in Europe that meet the governing body's requirements for such a prestigious award in terms of ground capacity (minimum 50,000) , pitch size, security and TV surveillance systems, the *absence* of protective fencing, and adequate floodlighting and changing facilities etc. Currently in the UK only Hampden, Old Trafford, the new Wembley Stadium in London, The Millennium Stadium in Cardiff, and Ibrox itself satisfy the various criteria although it is expected that once Peterhead put a latch on the corner portacabin where they sell their strips and programmes from, Balmoor Stadium will soon follow suit.

"I still always think about Rab Kyle when I come here." says Jonesy fondly as we turn away from the statue and head back round the stadium towards the visitor's turnstiles.

Dave and I join Jonesy in a smirk for surely Rab was a character and a half. One of Jonesy's dad's drinkin' buddies of old, we had all experienced Rab at one time or another, grinning from the Milne's living room couch, invariably sporting a multitude of fresh shaving scars on his plump ruddy face and a can of Skol welded into his hand. To my knowledge he still stays in Arthurston although I haven't seen him around in years. His story, however, is an interesting one.

12.

Rab Kyle was a Rangers fan. In his own mind he was THE Rangers fan. No one cared as much as him, no one suffered for the cause as much as him and, most certainly, no one had the right to criticise *his* team in the way he was allowed to.

Cos he'd 'paid his dues' as he was forever telling anyone who was prepared to listen. Season ticket holder, owner of every XXL home and away top designed over the last twenty years or so (even the bizarre Muslim version without the drinks sponsor logo on front – just for completeness), and proud collector of the largest range of Rangers tat this side of Derry's Walls. The John Greig testimonial dish- towel was his. As were the commemorative, 50th League Championship, pack of 3 Boxer Shorts (worn only once since being bought in 2003 - in the bad month when the washing machine packed in). And, of course, his prize 'Nine-In-A-Row', red, white and blue, four- slice toaster.

And Rab had seen it all. He was on the pitch in the Noucamp in 1972 when Rangers beat Dynamo Moscow to win the European Cup Winners Cup. Despite being photographed as one of the first over the barriers, Rab still strenuously denies being part of the invasion which would ultimately earn his team a one year ban from European competition. Rab, instead, has remained adamant that it wisnae him, that he was ' in the shunky with the diarinkies at the time, fightin' aff some dodgy paella'. Adamant indeed but if you look sharply, you'll catch a flicker of guilt in those grey puffy eyes that says it all. In '89 he burned his season ticket on national TV when Rangers signed Maurice Johnston, the first dodgy track-suit dealer to sign for the team in almost 70 years. A staunch man of principle, Rab phoned up the club two days later and pleaded for a new ticket claiming his dog had eaten the old one. Being a lucky man as well as a principled one, Rangers obliged. And In 2003 he was arrested for standing bollock naked, *very much* ' the worse for wear' outside manager, Dick Advocaat's house, singing 'Have you seen the Glasgow Rangers ?' whilst intermittently screaming 'AWAY HAME TAE DUTCHLAND SHORT-ARSE AND WASTE YER ANE MONEY!' at the top of his voice. This would have been all well and good had Advocaat not left the club in 2002.

As a loyal Rangers man though, a real 'Berr', Rab had one aching want in his life. Something that would make him complete. It wasn't winning the Champions League, nor was it urinating in Peter Grant's temporarily unattended pint. It was more than that;

For Rab, above all else in his small, war-torn, Glasgow life, wanted to meet the Queen.

There had been a couple of close shaves. Three feet away from a handshake at the Opening of Arthurston General's new Psychiatric wing, and straining to be next in line to say 'A pleasure maaaam' , Rab, in his doggish excitement, put excessive weight on his right ankle and at the key moment collapsed back into the waiting crowd who duly swallowed him up like a killer-whale on a seal. The conveniently nearby A& E unit diagnosed ligament damage quickly and professionally but Rab's moment was lost. More frustrating was his near miss at the Royal Garden Party at Hollyroodhouse Palace in Edinburgh. Procuring an invite through Violet Hilderbrand, a friend of Rab's sister and District Organiser of the Womens' Royal Voluntary Service (all of her members were too old to stand outdoors for more than three minutes at a time without falling over or needing to pee, and thus uptake on her invites was minimal) our man Rab waltzed into the fray fully expectant of a gratis Barcardi Breezer , a mushroom vol-au-vent , and a brisk yet informal tete-a-tete with the Walking Handbag herself . Alas it was not to be. With the monarch once more a mere stone's throw away and Rab's pulse sky-rocketing to over 120 a minute, a rogue cloud on an otherwise fair and sunny day conspiratorially blew over and emptied itself indulgently over the attending masses. The near-biblical deluge sent everyone scuttling for nearest shelter, not least the Queen herself who was skilfully whisked back indoors, leaving a stunned and forlorn Rab Kyle standing on his own. On the grass. Looking skywards. Dripping.

The Queen, predictably, did not return and the damp guests were only semi- appeased with the provision of newly prepared mini-quiches, glasses of Appeltiser and small silver plates of ridged Pringles.

Which is round about when desperation set in. Rab *had* to meet the Queen and nothing was going to stop him. Spurred on by the constant taunting from his mates, all of whom amazingly *had* met her Royal Highness themselves in some shape or form over the years. Understandably Rab was pushed to the brink.

After a night of particularly aggravating So- Rab-you-met-the-Queen yet?- type comments, Rab decided that desperate times called for desperate measures. It may not have been big or clever but Rab's feelings were of a 'what the hell' nature. The decade was coming to an end, he wasn't getting any younger and as he assured himself in the longer, darker nights, John Greig would have done exactly the same in such adversity.

That's how in the Autumn of '79, Rab *happened* to take a long weekend break in Windsor. It also *happened* that Liz was in residence at Windsor Castle at the very same time, home, no doubt, from one of her energy-sapping tours of the unspoilt beaches of her rapidly declining empire. Ambition at bubbling point, Rab laid a plan. It wasn't a good plan. It wasn't even an average plan, but then again Rab didn't have 'World Planning Federation's Planner of the Year' branded on his ass. Nor would he ever.

He had journeyed down south by virtue of his brother's borrowed white Transit van, a choice of vehicle which fitted nicely into his guise as Robert Kyle and Sons, Plumbers by Royal Appointment. Not a complex thinker, Rab had reasoned that even the Queen had to periodically take a dump (although he refused, out of regal respect, to form any mental pictures of the act) and where there was dumping going on there was, generally at any rate, toilet pans in the vicinity. Toilet pans that every once in a while needed mending.

So it was that Rab drove boldly up to the main entrance to Windsor Castle and calmly announced himself as being there to fix a couple of faulty cisterns in the private quarters. Security being somewhat slacker in the late seventies than at present, Rab was miraculously shown in by a slightly harassed House Manager who gushed that he was aware of the 'faulty units' in question but added absently that he couldn't remember sending for the plumber though.

Within minutes Rab and his tool-bag containing a hammer, two rawlplugs, a toothbrush and a Bounty, were being marched up wide, thickly carpeted stairs, along stretching wood-panelled corridors until finally reaching a marble convenience the likes of which had not been seen since Xanadu returned to the dust it had been built upon.

It was about now that Rab, I imagine, wished he had chosen a job he could actually do. As an electrician to trade, he didn't know a stop-cock from a pump-valve which, as an aside, makes it all the stranger why he didn't choose electrics as a cover in the first place. Anyway, luckily for him, he was left on his own to do the necessary. Unluckily for him he decided, before downing his 'tools' and embarking on a swift scout around to find the Queen, to have a quick rinse in the nearby royal basin. After a precursory splash on the face, however, he reached out, eyes closed, for the hand wash only to mistakenly grab an inconveniently placed plastic bottle of detergent instead. Within seconds of liberally applying the cleaning fluid over his mug , an allergic reaction had burst onto the scene and was in full, angry red swing. Luckily for Rab only one of his eyes had been exposed, however in the shock of his error, the offensive liquid snuck into his open mouth causing his tongue and inner cheek area to instantaneously swell up like a big, pink soufflé. Disorientated and groping around for a towel in considerable discomfort, Rab fell out the toilet door and blundered his way semi-blindly down the hallway, all the while moaning incoherently and dribbling down the front of his royal blue overalls.

With the pain inside his mouth growing in line with the size of his inflatable tongue, Rab chose what he thought was the doorway to the main stairway area and staggered through - only to find himself in a small peaceful study room and, spectacularly, face to face with Elizabeth II, the Monarch of our Realm.

For an instant they both simply stared at one another.

No doubt trained in how to react to such matters the Queen fixedly inquired, "And who sir are you?"

Rab, whose face now resembled a half pound of corned beef and was twitching involuntarily with his streaming right eye said nothing.

"Again Sir , who are you and why are you in these quarters?" Insisted the Queen deliberately.

Slowly coming to terms with the situation Rab cleared his throat painfully and embarked on the highly emotive, from-the-heart speech he had ran through his head in his quieter moments a thousand times before.

"Phllaankkkks lafflablaaa mfffffflabllmmm" began Rab sincerely bowing his head and only slightly dribbling on the carpet beneath.

 Within minutes Rab was in police custody.

Were it not for the confusion surrounding Rab's demeanour he would, undoubtedly, have been in serious trouble. However, bemused security officers were at a loss as to what to make of the sweating, crimson faced specimen who was now holding his head at constant forty-five degree angle, who had given up trying to respond to any form of questioning and who instead was now reduced to murmering what sounded like "shawwwuurrkweeeen" and "Shiinnndervvvictorrrus" repeatedly with wide , pain stricken eyes.

"The man's clearly deranged." muttered the 'in charge' cop almost confidentially to a concerned looking subordinate and after much debate and low- murmered discussion, Rab was hoisted to his feet and gently escorted from the premises.

Despite being what would nowadays be considered as a serious compromise in security and a field-day for the press, wider exposure of the event was limited to a small, unspecific inside article of The Reading Standard claiming;

'Stroke victim in Castle breech!'

No names were mentioned although the paper alluded to the suspicion that 'The Intruder' was 'possibly a war-veteran from the

Korean conflict' and went on to disclose a helpline number for those suffering from Post Traumatic Stress Disorder.

After the application of various steroid creams and an industrial strength course of anti-histamines, Rab returned home the conquering hero.

"Twice she called me Sir" he boasted to the pub-ensemble, to the butcher, his barber, the postman, the common man in the street, and pretty much anyone who happened to cross his path." Makes me practically a Knight of the Realm" he would conclude with that grin of his etched onto his 'well-slapped' looking face.

So Rab got to live the dream. And the Queen got to meet Sir Rab Kyle of Arthurston, Scotland. No doubt a memorable experience for both of them. The last time I saw Rab was in Jonesy's parents house the week before Jonesy's dad left home. He was in his usual place on the middle of the couch, straining its cushions into a v-shape with his sizeable, ever expanding ass. A can of Shlitz lager in hand, he was watching a live European tie on the TV. Rangers lost the game one nil if I remember but Rab was unabashed and having told us one more time about the time he went to Windsor, he proudly pulled out his 'new wee treasure' from his jacket pocket. It was a plastic oval topped paperweight.

Inside the paperweight was a mini-model of Ibrox's main stand and when he shook it, snow fell gently and hypnotically on its roof and the grey ground of the adjacent Edmiston Drive . All the while the snow was settling Rab grinned and picked at one of the many scabs on his neck. Once it was done, Rab took a slug from his can, smiled, sat back, and shook it again.

13.

Rangers have had so many great players on their books over their long and successful history that it would be impossible to single out even a hundred of them such has their lure been to the greats our country and further afield has produced. If pushed, though, I reckon I can pick a team of not necessarily the best but certainly the most noteworthy or 'memorable' players that, in my eyes at any rate, have graced the Ibrox turf. This team of mine, my vestibule of fame if you will, would be as follows - naturally starting with the goalie;

1. Peter McCloy – The big tall keeper who, if you mention his name in company, will motivate at least one person into spouting 'Ahh, The Girvan Lighthouse' like they were the King of Football trivia. Signed from Motherwell in 1970, many will remember with relish his huge kick out to Willie Johnstone for the winning goal in the '72 Cup Winners Cup Final. A keen golfer, McCloy was last seen sporting an industrial strength windcheater, meeting and greeting rich folk and corporate spongers alike onto the first tee at Turnberry's Ailsa Course.

2. 'Wicked' Willie Woodburn - Nominated for his channelled use of temper in a sporting arena. Willie launched his reign of terror in 1948 with a 'violent exchange' involving himself and Motherwell centre forward Dave Mathie. As a first offence, Willie was only banned for fourteen days, precisely five days before Mathie himself finally got full feeling back in his various extremities. For so long a model of repentance, and under extreme provocation I like to think, he eventually cracked five years later when he aimed a sweeping haymaker punch at an unsuspecting Clyde player. Granted he missed but he got sent off anyway and the SFA, who clearly had his card marked, gave him a twenty-one day ban. The following season it all went badly wrong for poor 'Wicked' when, after an admittedly bad challenge by young Stirling Albion forward Alec Paterson, he retaliated with a well executed head-butt leaving Alec with a constant high pitched ringing in his ears and the distinct impression that he was, in fact, a soprano in the in the Moscow State Opera named Wilma Vitt. Woodburn, with no credit left in the bank, was banned *sine die*, for life and didn't kick a ball professionally in Scotland again.

3. John Greig- Voted the 'Greatest Ranger Ever' by fans in a 1999 pole ,the legendary right-half captained the club, won international honours and managed Rangers from '78 to '83. Graduate of the club's 'Find An Old Boy A Job' Program, John now holds the position of Director and I have strong recollections of him spending most of the late '90s being photographed collecting Sebastian Rosental from the airport after the striker's latest trip home to Chile for 'expert medical attention'. John also remains memorable as being a dead-ringer for our local window-cleaner, Frank.

4. Daniel Prodan – Product of the Gers' shrewd signing policy of the time that unfortunately didn't involve an examination incorporating any 21st Century medical techniques whatsoever. Daniel hung around Ibrox for two years and did not as much as start one game due to the alarming knee injury he had when he signed. Rangers persevered patiently with the defender only to mysteriously send him packing after he made a surprise but adept comeback with the Romanian national team in the 3rd year of his Rangers contract. Daniel now owns a gogosi (a huge doughnut) shop in a small town near Bucharest and still talks fondly of BUPA's West of Scotland facilities.

5. Colin Jackson – Well thought of centre half whose Rangers career spanned the early '60s through to the 1980's. Sticks in my mind as being possibly the oldest looking player I ever saw playing professional football. The clear result of 'bad digs' *and* an 'uphill paper round' I suggest.

6. Graeme Souness – Lured from Sampdoria to become player manager, Souness brought about the 'English Invasion' with signings such as Mark 'Fashion Crisis' Hately, Terry 'Bloody' Butcher , Ray 'Uncle Fester' Wilkins, Graham 'The Conductor' Roberts, and Trevor ' No nickname' Francis. His signing policy would change the face of Scottish football forever prompting the other clubs, in a vain effort at keeping up with the Joneses, to ditch their home-grown talent in favour of expensive second rate foreign imports. Advancement in the style of nuclear power really– efficient but dangerous.

7. Alex McDonald – For his brammin' sideburns.

8. Paul Gascoigne – Stole a bus, crashed another one, booked a ref, ran over a fan, rifted into a press microphone, paid £20 for a Mars Bar, set his mate up with a transvestite, spoke to the President of the Danish FA doing an impression of the Swedish Chef from the Muppets, faked his own suicide and brought a dead snake to training. All in a days work for the bold Paul. My favourite though had to be the incident when he took the BBC documentary crew to a scenic little cottage which he inferred he had just bought. Explaining he had forgotten his key, he knocked on the door and when an old dear appeared he announced he was doing 'The Doorstep Challenge' and could he ask her what her favourite washing powder was. Comic genius.

9. Davie Cooper – Remembered for his monumental skill. A silky left-winger bought for a bargain £100,000 from Clydebank in 1977. He played twelve seasons with Rangers and I can well remember lying on my belly on the furry rug in front of the telly watching the footy programmes on Saturday nights and Sunday afternoons, marvelling at way the ball seemed to be glued to Davie's foot. Cooper, who was only 39 when he sadly died of a brain haemorrhage a few years back, scored what many Rangers fans consider to be the best goal ever seen in the 1979 Drybrough Cup Final versus the 'Tic. Those lucky enough to be there that day witnessed him dribble round about sixteen Celtic players TWICE before slotting the ball home to the ecstatic delight of every Rangers supporter present . For the rest of us the penalty against Wales won't be forgotten either.

10. Brian Laudrup – The Danish dynamo who, week in week out, ran past his opponents like they weren't there. Laudrup was exceptional but you couldn't help feeling he was put on this earth to show just how poor the rest of the players in the Scottish league had gotten. I also seem to remember he'd too much hair for the one man and that his obviously frequent visits to 'The Rainbow Room' must have cost a bloody fortune.

11. 'Slim' Jim Baxter – The fife-born , ex-miner who signed from Raith Rovers in 1960 and spent two spells at the club spanning over 250 appearances in the blue jersey. Sunderland

and Nottingham Forest took up his attention in the intervening period but Ibrox was where Jim really showed his elegant midfield mastery. Well renowned as a gregarious *bon viveur*, Jim was once asked whether the vast amounts of cash paid in today's game would have made a difference to his lifestyle compared to when he was a player. In typical Baxter style he answered "Definitely. I'd have spent £50,000 a week at the bookies instead of £100 !" Jim retired from the game in 1970 at the surprisingly early age of 31, an act that many felt represented a personal demonstration against the fast approaching Decimalisation in the UK. Others took the more pragmatic line that all the necessary playing and training was keeping him out the pub…. And then there was the Wembley keepie-uppies wasn't there.

Sub : Peter Huistra - The Dutch left-winger who sneaks into this team of worthies by virtue of having more pronunciations of his name that any other player in Scottish Football History . Journalists and commentators vying with one another to scoop the 'real' way of saying it, confidently suggested Peter 'Howstra', 'Histra', 'Hooostra', 'Hweestra' and 'Hoystra' before eventually unanimously plumping for 'The nippy number 7'. Rangers fans themselves elegantly avoided the weekly confusion by calling him 'Wee Man', 'Fannybaws' and 'ya fuckin' sand-dancer'.

14.

Arthurston shouldn't be playing here. Its all too much. Sitting in my blue plastic seat in the tight corner section between the Govan Road and the Broomloan Stands, I gaze around the best stadium in Scotland in some kind of mesmerised wonder. It's the crowd again and I have a laugh to myself. If I had been a few years younger I'd have truly relished watching these 50,411 seats gradually fill up around me.

Arthurston's travelling support, despite being hugely outnumbered are making the bulk of the noise. While the red and white contingent are suffering from a kind of infectious, rabid hysteria, the Rangers fans are a subdued bunch, hanging over their knees or lounging back in their seats, an tangible air of expectancy dulling their senses.

A booming orchestral medley featuring Rule Britannia and the theme's from The Dambusters and The Great Escape' comes to an end in 'Last Night of the Proms' fashion. It should all have sounded so dramatic. Instead it comes off as being a faintly inflammatory, 'get it right up ye' gesture, demonstrating no more than the club's continued willingness to pander to their questionable 'Billy Britain' image.

Next up we're treated to 'Granny's Favourite' and popular pantomime dame, Andy Cameron, who scuttles into the centre circle in his suit and slip-ons , microphone in hand, and proceeds to rally the home crowd with a bit of Glasgow banter. The Bears in the stand are suitably impressed whilst, predictably, howls of derision rise up from our vicinity. I remember seeing Cameron give a moving performance as Buttons in Cinderella at the Kings Theatre back in '79 and consequently I find it hard to join in the lambasting of such a consummate pro. I can't however, resist a hearty shout of 'BEHIND YOU!' which gets a laugh from the punters around me and temporarily elevates me to the position of 'Stand Up King of the Moment'. The honour is immediately revoked with my follow up ' Who's the Rangers captain today, Widow Twankie?' comment. A tumbleweed skips down the stairs beside me as I clear my throat self consciously and stare blindly at my feet.

Disappearing as quickly as he arrived, Cameron's departure heralds the arrival of the teams and as the Rovers men run on to the pitch I'm surprised at suddenly having a big lump in my throat. Everyone is upstanding around me, hands clapping well above head height and I find myself fighting back the rising panic that I'm about to burst into tears. Thankfully nobody notices and the feeling abates as I focus manfully on the team in front of me. Scanning the players it doesn't take me long to find the new guy. Ivan Pecnik is clearly the tall, slim, swarthy looking guy with the Ming the Merciless beard, who is presently pumping his fist like a maniac towards the our general direction. It's well known that my eyesight isn't the best but even I can make out the mad Rasputin eyes that are staring out from his under lank dark hair.

The kick-off sneaks up on us. I'm so busy looking around me, taking it all in, that I barley notice the game is in full flow. After an initially flurry of exuberance from both sides the game settles down to a scrappy midfield joust. The Rangers contingent remain mostly subdued despite the valiant efforts of the small brass band up to our right who are 'oompaahh –ing' an endless stream of Rangers standards enthusiastically. Slowly but surely, though, its dawning on the Arthurston lot that Rangers are not infallible and the singing and shouts of encouragement are getting more confident and heart-felt . With twenty minutes gone we all expected to be five down by now. Its just the way it is when you play the Old Firm. Even when they're off form, you feel that a pasting never comes as a bolt from the blue.

Outside the first five minutes, though, Rangers haven't created a clear cut chance and their fans seem to have completely switched off. All the noise that is echoing round the big stadium is coming from the thousand or so Rovers fans and a taunting "Sssshhhhhhhhhhhhhhhhhhhhhh!" rises from our midst as we all hold our index fingers to our lips to emphasise the quiet.

As if to mock us, Rangers work the ball free of the midfield quagmire and flow up the park dangerously. As the ball falls wide the noise rises like someone twiddled the volume knob sharply. A rapier like out-swinging cross flies over, picking out the darting Rangers front-man, who gets a solid head on the ball and fires it inches past the left hand goal with our keeper nowhere.

"OOOOOOOAAAAAHHHHHHHHH" washes over us loudly and the true sound of Ibrox is unleashed upon us. Wakened from slumber the big crowd senses something in the air and sure enough, another sweet move unfolds with Pecnik's desperate defensive header saving another vicious cross from finding the unmarked man at the back post.

Again the crowd rise to the moment and you feel that they could shout our poor lads into submission at any point. Scott

McLean, slaps Pecnik on the back as Rovers funnel back to defend the resulting corner.

The new boy is doing ok. The Rovers fans have been enthusiastically applauding even the most basic of touches he has made, convincing themselves that he's a player. A couple of clumsy, misplaced passes are explained away by his team-mates not 'reading the situation' or the ball taking a' bobble'. By and large it is encouraging, well meaning applause that follows everything he does.

The corner floats over to the penalty spot where the big Slovenian heads it easily clear. Jonesy digs me in the ribs.

"He's not bad is he? Eh? Eh?"

I nod my head. I'm trying in vain to enjoy the individual steak 'n Gravy pie Jonesy has recently presented to me. He looks at me carefully " You better eat that, I've just been shafted £1.70 for it!". I smile thinly and chew on. More dough than in Ronnie Biggs' mattress I'm thinking to myself.

Dave glances over and murmurs, "I'm not sure about Pecnik's distribution but he's certainly getting his head to the ball."

Again I nod my head. I'm not really with them though. Once more I'm taken in by the size of the stadium. Its almost hypnotic the way it encourages me to stare at it and not the game itself. The three tiered Main Stand looms massive, sitting as it does between two internal staircases enclosed by small panelled windows and the same traditional red brick that features outside. My view pans around the ground and I'm warmed by the two electronic scoreboards situated in the middle separation of the tiered stands behind the goals. Each comfortingly reports Rangers 0 Arthurston Rovers 0.

I turn to Jonesy. "How much must David Murray have ploughed into Rangers over the years to end up with a place like this? "

Jonesy whistles silently. " Well I know for sure that when Murray bought the club and became the Chairman he paid, whatsisname?........" "Lawrence Marlborough." Dave injects with his mouth full, staring distastefully at the pie in his hand.

"Marlborough yeh, he reportedly paid just under £7 million for the club itself. Then, in the ten years after that Murray sunk £52 million into the stadium and £90 million on players. I'm not sure about after that but add to that the Murray Park training facility over in Milngavie which cost him £14 million, we're not talking small beer here."

"That's for sure." I agree, "Don't you sometimes wonder what Ayr United fans must think about that level of investment bearing in mind Murray was originally going to buy them, wasn't he?"

"Yeh he was, but hey, they got their own rich-man chairman on board didn't they. And surely they can take comfort in how far Bill Barr, took Ayr United in the time he was at the helm." Jonesy replies grandly. We both look at each other then burst out laughing.

The half time whistle goes. It's still goalless with everything to play for but whilst everyone around me stands to applaud our heroes off the pitch, the Rangers players walk off to boos ringing in their ears. Ah, the ill divides of this game of ours.

15.

Our half time chat consists mostly of our most vivid Rangers associations. Jonesy kicks off, quite unimaginatively I feel, pointing out the number and frequency of new strip designs they seem to have. ("Right up there with Man Utd" he ventures) He's right though. Parents of young Gers fans must despair, year in year out, at the blatant commercialism of it all. At forty quid a pop they must speculate if, perhaps, the club hadn't bought Tore Andre Flo then they could have *given* everyone, not just the kids, one top a year for at least three years, and not been out of pocket any the worse! Ah, if only.

Dave, more uncharitably, feels moved to complain about how Rangers fans always manage to turn up in season ticket areas of every other team in the league in their own ground. "How do they do it?" he cries, arms flailing in the air, "Especially on a big game day, like a cup tie or a day they can win the league!" he concludes, sitting back down red faced and harassed.

My own personal association is altogether more ..... exterior. I opt for mentioning the wee boys outside the ground that ambush you when you get out your car and shout "50p tae watch yer motor mister? I like this and have never had any problem with the concept of giving the wee guy a bit of cash to feed his weans (they grow up so fast these days don't they?). A lesson though, when one of these young Prince's of Extortion approaches you, the correct response is "Certainly young man, congratulations on your entrepreneurship, I'll give you the money when I get back ." And when you return to your vehicle you keep your promise and do precisely that – if the lad's about at any rate, which he more often than not isn't. You do NOT, as Dave did, reply tersely "Yeh, you can watch it if you want but it won't do anything", feign a sarcastic smile, and then stalk off to the game . Because what transpires when you do that is that you come back to your car a couple of hours later to find the window smashed in with a sizeable piece of masonry lying waiting for you on the drivers seat.

'Yeh, you can shout and swear at that brick if you want but it won't do anything!'

As we cleared out the front of Dave's car I nearly said that out loud but luckily managed to stifle my death-wish inclination at the very last moment.

Life is, after all, a learning curve.

16.

The second half is much brighter affair. Rangers come out guns blazing and create three clear-cut chances in the first few minutes. Then, just as it looks like we're going to succumb to the pressure we get a break.

A nice move involving Mickey Hedge and Ally Fairful (Yes Ally Fairful! On the very same turf as Henderson, Baxter, Brand and co. once played– Its like Keannu Reeves playing Hamlet at The Globe) results in a brilliant saving tackle from the Gers left back and we have a corner. Hedge himself swings the ball over with a bit of pace. So much pace in fact that the ball whips through a ruck of players untouched and is last seen heading for a throw-in on the far side.

Enter the referee who blows his whistle and points groundwards having obviously noticed an infringement. 'Cavey' Burgoyne immediately commences a volley of abuse, clearly claiming that despite being nearest to the ball's flight he didn't touch his marker. He stops mid rant however when it becomes apparent that the ref is actually pointing to the spot.

After a surreal number of dead, silent seconds, realisation hits everyone setting off a cacophony of sound. Our lot go mental while their fans go ...well ... MENTAL. The Rangers players surround the official in a state of apoplexy while I actually see Cavey walking towards Scot McLean and shrugging in a mystified manner.

After much mulling around Ray Stark steps coolly up to the spot, places the ball, takes his run.... AND MISSES.

Two feet over the bar if he's lucky.

The ground erupts as the keeper casually retrieves the ball and prepares to hit the bye-kick. All around me I can see heads in hands and disappointed expressions. Our support rallies though and a chant of 'BREWERS-BREWERS-BREWERS' rises from our little corner of the stadium.

I'm gutted but I can't help thinking that poetic justice was served by Stark gouging the ball over the bar. In fact I can't help pondering on how often that scenario plays out in football with the undeserved penalty failing to be converted. God moves in mysterious ways, especially on a football pitch.

17.

There's no time to go. We're going to get a draw. The safety announcement, warning us all to be careful when leaving, is long over and our crowd are whistling in impatience. An angry and half-hearted sort of encouragement is being vented from the Rangers faithful who have waited to the end, but like the rest of the game their players don't seem to be listening.

We are all up on our feet singing 'We love you Rovers (We do!) Everyone is up. Everyone is so happy, so elated. Life is good again.

By the time the chorus is finished the ball is in our net.

The blue shirted Rangers players are chasing the goalscorer to the corner flag and Rovers, to a man, are staring at the grass.

I don't know what happened, I was looking at our fans, the jumping fans, the singing fans, the smiling fans. The same fans who are now slumped back in their seats wincing at the wall of noise around them.

It doesn't matter to the home crowd that they've only just beaten the lowly Arthurston Rovers. A last minute goal in a tight game is like winning the cup and their fans are rightly going loopy.

We have just enough time to re-spot the ball and knock it forward before the ref blows for full time.

A jubilant roar goes up and we, in a slightly bemused fashion, make for the exits.

Another one has got away.

18.

Looking out of the car window its dark, cold and forbidding. As the industrial shadows of Glasgow slip past suspiciously, Dave and Jonesy talk in low strains that I can't quite make out over the sound of the radio. The drab, bored-sounding drawl of Jim Traynor is bumming up his imminent presentation of 'Your Call' - the accommodating phone-in for irritated Old Firm fans to debate their tedium of the day. Despite the wintry, murkiness outside, I feel warm and slightly woozy. The heater is churning out a soothing waft that has me sinking lower and lower into the comfortable contours of the back seat.

As Trainer finishes his effervescent pitch with a depressed sigh, anchorman Richard Gordon's cheery voice takes over making an announcement that jerks me out of the funk I'm slowly descending into.

"As promised, It's now time to go over to SFA headquarters for the live draw for the third round of the Scottish Cup!" he cries in rapturous fashion.

I drag myself back upright in the seat and force my head through the gap in the headrests. A tingling sensation flutters gently into the pit of my stomach.

Dave reaches over and cranks the volume up , Jonesy stares at the radio in wide eyed anticipation .

Anticipation - for this is a major event in the Scottish football fan's year. The preliminary and first two rounds of the cup are over with the remaining bloodied and battle-hardened teams from the Highland league , amateur and junior leagues , and Scottish Second and Third divisions now staggering forward with resolve towards their sunshine-dream of playing at Hampden Park in May. This round of the cup however , is where the dream frequently dies. Where the 'big teams' enter the fray bringing with them their superior fitness, organisation and dubiously unfair refereeing decisions designed to boot any cheeky upstarts out in conspiratorial fashion.

Strangely, for the ardent fan, this long awaited draw stimulates more trepidation and anxiety than the any of the other subsequent ones. Once your team gets through this tie, I suppose you thank your lucky stars and are happy to take what is thrown at your heroes. Fear, however, of an embarrassing exit on the first rung of the ladder, against a tricky wee team on their patch is probably the main root of our worries. Almost as bad, however, is going out to a team of similar size and stature in a match that fails to attract any of the romance of the cup whatsoever, or indeed without making a bit of money from the day. The psyche behind a successful cup draw in a deep and complicated one.

"I hope we get Rangers or Celtic at home" chatters Jonesy excitedly. "That way we get a good lump of cash and have an outside chance of winning."

"Nah," injects Dave, " A nice and easy away game at a second division team. It gives us a day out, we'll stroll through with little worry then get a bigger game in the next round. I'd take Alloa or Brechin I think - one of those."

A quick poll also indicates that we definitely *don't* want to play Ross County or Inverness away – the travelling is a bitch. Nor do we fancy going to St Mirren again, Dundee or indeed Hamilton because of their rotten 'skill killing' plastic pitch. We also decide, in view of their unfathomable 'trickiness', that we'd rather not get involved with Airdrie at all.

"Shhhhhhhh" cries Jonesey suddenly , flapping his right hand and diving to turn up the volume on the radio even further. "Its starting!"

We fall silent . Jonesy and I stare intently at the radio while Dave who normally fixes his eyes on the road ahead religiously, flits his eyes in the direction of glowing red '94.3 RADIO SCOTLAND' display on the dashboard.

"Good evening and welcome to the draw for the third round of the Scottish Cup" says an officious, nasally voice. We then get a brief introduction of the two lumps no doubt standing at either side of Sinex-man, poised to draw the home and away team balls from some form of velvet bag or other.

A clearing of a throat and a couple of nearby coughs and with the noise of balls clicking together as they are mixed up, the draw begins;

"Number 4…"

"THAT'S US!" yells Jonesy giving me a fright.

"….. Motherwell." The nasal voice announces. Jonesy looks at me perplexed.

"I don't think they do it that way now." I suggest.

The teams were always numbered in alphabetical order before. That meant, providing Alloa were still in the competition at this point, that we would be number four in the draw behind them,

Aberdeen and Airdrie. Simple. Except the numbers seem to be all random now and inexplicably, some of the excitement of it all is lost somehow.

Click, click, click

"Versus number 20 …….. Clyde"

Click, click, click, click.

"Number 12….. Partick Thistle"

click, click

"Versus number 17 ……..Rangers!"

A barely audible ripple of exclamation with a dash of laughter breaks the silence of SFA headquarters and then silence again. Onwards.

"Number 6 …….Ross County"

"Noooo..no…no….no" breathes Jonesy anxiously

"Versus number 19 ……………………. Dundee United!"

Phhheeeewwwwwwwwww . We all breathe.

"Number 11 ………Airdrie United"

Wide eyes, no breathing again. "Please no" I mouth silently. Click, click, click.

"Versus number 25 ……….. Arthurston Rovers

"Aaaawwww" wails Jonesy.

"Occhhhhhhh no" I moan.

Dave tuts and returns his eyes, thankfully, to the road ahead.

The draw rambles on but we're not listening anymore. A few animated minutes of debate and we decide that although it could have been a lot better (Airdrie have a brilliant cup tradition for a First Division club), we *are* playing a team from a lower league and all things being equal we *should* be able to get a result at Excelsior Stadium.

On the radio, the nasal voice is bringing proceedings to a close.

"All matches" he concludes with an air smugness, "will be played on Saturday the 25th and Sunday the 26th of January. Thank you." And with that its back to the studio for some swift opinion on the talking points of the draw.

The excitement is over. The draw hasn't been kind. But once again, the heat of the car creeps over me. The guys chat of today's game and cup ties of old fade off in the distance as I feel my eyes getting heavy. The car engine purrs comfortingly and the last thing I think of before I nod off is that we're heading for home and that's a good thing.

19.

Grampa's house is cold. Not just cool or drafty but COLD like the frozen food isle in the supermarket on a hot summer's day. I shiver involuntarily as I pull another box from under the bed and haul it over to the glare of the bedside lamp.

This one has, amongst other things, some Second World War adventure novels, no fewer than four electric alarm clocks (none working), and a small dusty collection of old LP records consisting of an Al Jolson compilation, some brass band 'classics' and the cream of the crop - 'Glen Daly live at the Pittenweem Fisherman's Club'. I can't resist a closer look at the last one. On the front is a balding man with side-burns grinning inanely from inside a huge yellow collared shirt. The reverse side proclaims, presumably to those small but lucky band of Pitteneweem residents with more than a passing interest in fish, that 'Mr Glasgow' is back in town singing the old favourites such as 'The Wee House 'mang the heather', 'Wild Colonial Boy' ,'I belong to Glasgow, and 'Mary, dae the dishes in yer pants again!'. Mr Glasgow indeed – a strange moniker considering the back sleeve further informs us that old Glen was born and bred in Ireland.

I sigh and push the box over into the corner beside the growing collection of bits and bobs destined for the next church jumble sale. Straightening up and wincing as a sharp pain shoots through my spine, I decide a cup of tea is in order and slouch my way over to the door , out into the dark hall and on to the kitchen.

Whacking the kettle on, I reach into the wooden jar with 'tea' carved on the side. The kettle slowly starts to whisper as I drop a tea-bag into a handy mug then slope over to the big kitchen cupboard in search of anything resembling a chocolate biscuit.

The door creaks open and I'm met by a comforting wall of warmth contrary to the hanging chill elsewhere in the house. Up by my left ear is the old fashioned, stumpy black switch which I yank on automatically. It drops thickly and the three shelves on each side of the cupboard are illuminated dimly by a single, bare half- a- watt bulb hanging from the ceiling On the shelf to the left, three large piles of newspapers reach up almost to the ceiling. Grampa had a thing about not tossing out papers that either had articles of interest to him, or else had an unfinished crossword in it. I clutch at an old tartan patterned, short-bread tin on the shelf opposite and am mindlessly rummaging around the small but varied selection of Kit-Kats, Blue Ribands, yo-yos and Twix fingers when my attention is drawn to the gloomy rear of the cupboard.

On the shelf, at the back, almost disappearing into the shadows are two objects. Despite the general clutter of the cupboard, space seems to have been cleared neatly around them, exposing them like prize exhibits in a museum.

I awkwardly stretch over the assorted debris on the floor and clasp the scuffed Mitre football in my hand. I read the first message.

'Jimmy, Hope my goals sent you home smiling' is scrawled in sloping black handwriting, followed by a barely legible squiggle that I just make out as Ray Stark. Underneath, easily identifiable in small, deliberate script is 'Dave Beaumont' followed by the looping stringy signature of Chris Milne with my twitchy handiwork completing the job at the bottom.

Running my hands round the ball's contours, feeling its contrasting ridged and ragged grooves and smooth panels, I give it one final firmness- testing press then return it gently to the shelf beside the only other object in the vicinity.

I stare at the big rectangular tin. In the half light I can just make out the words luxury mint selection etched in classy swirly writing on its burgundy body. Memories flood back of me sprinting into kitchen, rudely ignoring my grandparents hello's from the hall, falling over the boxes on the cupboard floor and knocking a couple of the newspapers off the shelf at my side. All this haste and panic culminating in me stretching anxiously up to the tin, high above my head, precariously lifting it towards me with only my finger tips then removing the lid to reveal the goodies inside. It was always with relief that I scooped up the contents as time after time I held the worry that that there wouldn't be anything in there for me. Of course there always was.

A soft smile wanders on to my face and I reach over and firmly grab the tin. Bringing it to me, I hold it in my hands for what seems like an age. The smile doesn't move but my heartbeat quickens as I stroke the smooth edge of the lid and admire the sleek classic lines of the painted silver sports car. Slowly I lift it off and place it on the nearby shelf.

I needn't have worried. I gently pick out the new FourFourTwo magazine and the packet of cheese and onion crisps that are waiting for me and replace the bowl gently in its place.

A draft flits through the hairs on the back of my neck and I turn round involuntarily. The clock on the kitchen wall ticks at me and out in the kitchen the blowing kettle clicks and fades into silence.

I sigh and, clutching my magazine, my crisps and the Blue Riband I have chosen (only 5% fat I believe), I edge back into the kitchen.

And with my free left hand I reluctantly turn out the light behind me.

Chapter 14 The Kingdom of Fife

1.

The view from the bus window is like a Christmas card scene. A light powdering of snow covers the rolling hills like dandruff on a suit and the clear, cloudless, blue sky is big, wide and brilliant.

My trousers are tight round the waist from excessive quantities of turkey , wine, nuts and After Eight mints. What can you do though? It's Boxing Day and it would be rude not to have indulged just a little over the holiday period.

The St Andrews bus is chugging its way through the Fife countryside at a workmanlike rate. Although it's final destination will be the little East coast town famous for its golf and English University students, we will be jumping off considerably sooner than that, at Dunfermline bus station to be exact. We're meeting 'Mad' Mike McKechnie at 12.30 prompt in The East Port Bar for beers 'n' banter and its important we get there on time – Left to his own devices for anything over ten minutes, Mad Mike could bring down a government.

The bus is populated by an odd assortment of individuals. Front and right we have an excitable trio of fifty-somethings who, by their high volume conversation, collectively have enough ailments and maladies to bring the NHS to its knees, are one step away from murdering their respective husbands, and are heading to Dunfermline for the shopping trip to end all shopping trips. Two seats back from them, a thin scholarly gentleman in glasses and a tweed jacket is buried in a weighty tome entitled 'Garden Shed's of our age '. Every time a burst of raucous laughter escapes from the women ahead, he looks up from his book, shakes his head and scowls disapprovingly before rubbing his elbow patches absently and returning to his reading. A middle-aged couple are seated directly in front of me and by the various 'einfahrts', 'umfens' and 'geflaggens' rising over the headrests they are, to some extent, German. For some ten minutes now they have been wolfing their way through what smells like a toxic mixture of chicken tikka sandwiches and raw garlic cloves, washed down with onion water and Tabasco gravy. The fumes emanating from their little two-seated world are deathly but apparently localised. I have two seats to myself with Dave and Jonesy behind me muttering in low, barely audible tones, neither of whom seem in any way conscious of the culinary atrocities unfolding in front of me. A particularly foul and spicy waft hits me full on pushing my face sideways in revulsion and I'm afforded a somewhat enforced view of the countryside slipping by.

We are ploughing our way through the neighbouring towns of Oakley and Carnock. The former, a bleak collection of grey council houses, a ghostly white bowling green and a dreary junior football ground, casts envious eyes up the gradual incline to Carnock, a confident optimistic order of modern new-build homes, extensions and conservatories. You can't help feeling that the walk up the connecting main road here is more than just a physical exercise.

The bus rumbles on. Through the one street towns of Gowkhall and Milesmark, onwards to Dunfermline. It'll be good to see 'Mad' Mike again. Its been well over a year and a half since he got us kicked out the pub in Edinburgh. An incident involving the changing of channels on the TV just as Scotland were about to win the Calcutta Cup. What motivated him to grab the handily positioned remote and flip to live coverage of an FA cup tie, deftly pocket the controller batteries and then sprint out the nearest exit is anyone's guess. He said it 'represented a fitting protest against middle-class oppression of the working man'. I think he was probably just being an arse.

But he's a likeable arse all the same. I can clearly picture that deranged grin leering out from under an explosion of crazy, Highland ginger hair. Hair that seems constantly intent on escaping as far from Mad Mike's head as is humanly possible. Discerning hair you'd have to say.

It'll be interesting to see what Mike is doing with himself these days. His job choices are legendary. Over the years he's held down, albeit temporarily, positions home and abroad that make our own lives dull and pitiful in contrast. He's been a cage-assistant at Edinburgh Zoo where he got sacked for smuggling a ring-tailed lemur home for the night as 'a wee bit of company', a tram driver in Zagreb, Croatia where he memorably crashed his tram into the Prime minister's limo (seriously) whilst confidentially trying to beat his 'circuit record' round the city centre. He's taken rich tourists shark fishing in the waters off Miami Beach, given golf tuition at an all-inclusive holiday resort in Bulgaria (despite never having played golf in his puff) and memorably, held down the position, for a whole summer season, of Entertainments Co-ordinator at Wonder-West World in Ayr.

During that extraordinary season, campers were treated to such legendary acts as Leo and his Singing Fishes, The Amazing Stretching Viking and 'Rula and her Nooks and Crannies'. Mad Mike was eventually asked to leave in the aftermath of an eventful performance by a bee circus called Honey-Belle and the Swarm. Honey-Belle was a rampant alcoholic and 'The Swarm' proved to be less controllable that a ten year old ASDA Trolley. The result - eighteen holidaymakers requiring emergency first-aid treatment for multiple bee-stings and Honey-Belle spending a night in Ayr police-station after assaulting the improbably named, yet singularly 'mouthy' resident pianist, Arnie Schitt. The incident made page five of The Sun if I remember correctly and Mad Mike was suitably thrilled.

We first met Mad Mike a number of years ago in the 'Grande Place' in Brussels. Embracing the age-old ritual of watching Scotland fumble their way around Europe in the only manner we knew how ie by getting rat-arsed in pleasant surroundings, Mike introduced himself into our company, and regaled us with hilarious tales of mental nuns, stolen cows, uncontrollable flatulence and inappropriate uses of Ski Yoghurt. We all got on like a house on fire and became firm friends from that point forward. Mad Mike may be a Dunfermline fan for his sins but in all other aspects he's as sound as a pound (Well 94p at any rate, if I was to be absolutely pushed on it.)

2.

"Do vee get auf heer for Saint Androos?" inquires the slightly concerned looking German female from the seat in front as we slide into the Eastern- Block concrete greyness of the bus station.

"No, no," I reply soothingly, "This is Dunfermline, you've got a while to go yet."

As an afterthought I also add self-consciously "And don't worry it's a lot nicer than here – there's … err…. more grass."

With that we edge our way awkwardly down the narrow central passage and hop confidently off onto Fife soil. One great leap for mankind and all that.

"There's more *grass*?" questions Jonesy jumping off the bus wincing slightly as he goes over on his ankle " Aiyah!" he mutters before quickly recovering, " Your patter with women is getting worse I swear it. "

Negotiating ourselves out of Vilnius Central Station we find ourselves but a short stagger to Dunfermline town centre where The East Port Bar makes itself known to us almost immediately.

Dunfermline's hub is a bustling place laced with cobble-stoned history. The thing is that unless you have, like us, a reason to be in its vicinity, there's a good chance that if you're bound for East End Park you would miss it – every time . Most football fans from out of town probably swoop round the Sinclair Gardens roundabout in their bus or car, park on or around Halbeath Road, sink a swifty in the nearby Elizabethan pub or make their way straight into the stadium itself. In doing so they deprive themselves of a number of good pubs to sample and enjoy, a stroll past The Mercat Cross, or possibly a quick meander down to Dunfermline Abbey which is only a stone's throw away.

Crossing the busy main thoroughfare of the 'East Port' with the shops beckoning to our right, we aim for the bar's grey-stoned doorway and slip self-consciously past two meaty doormen clad in long black cardboard coats who are hanging in the shadows clearly not quite sure why they are there. 'Orrright lads' they growl menacingly almost imploding into their low foreheads.

"Nnnrrrghhh" we all grunt simultaneously with traditional resentment avoiding any semblance of eye contact. Dave lingers slightly and looks like he may be cooking up a Smart Alec comment but I'm right behind him and I shove him sharply into the warmth of the pub.

3.

The untidy crowd hanging immediately in front of the bar mysteriously part revealing a pale couple wearing complimentary black T-shirt and jeans ensembles. Both are nursing half pint glasses of dark brown liquid and are staring blankly in opposite directions somewhere over their respective horizons.

The man is tall, possibly 6"2" or 6"3"with slouched shoulders and a vacant, jowly expression draped under his fiercely razored skull. Rusty red stubble traces a faintly receding hairline and as he hangs at the side of the bar, he nibbles the side of his lip absently. The woman is small, thin and bloodless with lank, mousey brown hair, thin tight-drawn lips and fierce bushy eyebrows, correction, eye*brow* – the gap in between is negligible, giving her the look of a woman with a constant frown on her face. Dave takes a couple of unsure steps forward. "Mike?"

The big chap slides out of his trance and a flicker of recognition ignites in his sunken grey eyes. A small smile curls on the corner of his mouth momentarily then disappears as quick as it came.

"Oh hi Dave," he drawls in a low Highland brogue and, holding out a limp looking mit, gives Dave, then Jonesy, then myself a wet salmon handshake that slips through my hands like lottery winnings.

"Chris...... Craig." He nods with all the enthusiasm of a rotting banana then turns to Frau Uni-Brau and murmers "Emm...this is Ingrid Ruffin.... my ..emm …. wife. A watery and slightly nervous smile conquers Mike's face

Ingrid flits sharp, almost accusatory glances at all three of us then in a disconcertingly deep, almost baritone husk, nods and says "So you're the pals". She says the word 'pals' but it sounds more like 'serial paedophiles with wife-beating tendencies'

"Yeah," I reply too cheerily "Not his only ones though, ha ha". Ingrid raises the eyebrow speculatively then brings it back to rest in dark, brooding menace.

We move away from the bar area choosing a spot beside a tall round table to rest our drinks on. A moment of silence hangs in the air before Dave pulls himself together and opts for "Sooooo, you're eh... married then. When did this all happen?"

"Eight months and three weeks ago." Mike answers mechanically and then unprompted, embarks on the meaty yet uninspired explanation of how their two hearts become one.

They met at a nudism demo, of course. Mike had wangled a job as a junior reporter for some local rag somewhere down Dorset or Cornwall way. Ingrid was part of a pressure group calling themselves 'Perfect Skin' proclaiming the right to 'git nekkid' whenever and wherever they jolly well pleased. Mike was on hand to interview members of The ' Skins' who had collectively chained themselves to a prominent bandstand amidst a stirring rendition of Elgar's Enigma Variation's attended by, in principal, a large group of Scottish OAPs on an Urquart Tour of the South Coast of England. Mike had scooped an eye-to-eye interview with Ingrid in her glory, Ingrid had, in minutes, succumbed to Mike's probing style, while the Urquart tour had seen some unforgettable sights that were clearly not part of the itinerary.

"We didn't just chain ourselves to bandstands. We ran an orchestrated series of appropriately strategic manoeuvres." Ingrid chipped in malevolently yet informatively.

'Appropriately strategic manoeuvres' apparently included a naked parachute jump into a county flower-show, a raid on the local Oxfam clothes shop where The PS savagely cut all crotch and breast areas away from the clothes in stock, and the coup de grace, the mass kidnapping of a number of 'high profile' show dogs from the Falmouth Canine Club who were then duly shaved and returned to their distraught owners sans-fur and tres-embarrassed.

"And it was Love at first sight then?" I pitch in smiling.

The eyebrow sank a couple of inches. "We don't believe in love." Ingrid boomed in a style uncannily like Gordon Brown delivering the budget. "Love is a media-propagated weakness that limits and undermines ourselves both collectively and, more importantly, as individuals. Michael and I have a higher-plane mutual understanding based on the self-need within us. We are two but we can co-exist together as The One." She held her two index fingers up, pointing at the roof then intertwined them in a hook-like configuration. This would have looked better if she hadn't, in doing so, poured the remains of her half pint on the floor.

"Emm, more drinks guys?"

Slightly shell-shocked nods and Mike heads off through the rapidly increasing throng with Ingrid in hot pursuit. Three sets of eyes follow them until they are out of sight then turn and look at each other wide eyed in wonder

"Can you imagine her naked?" whispers Jonesy, "I bet she's got legs like Frodo Baggins."

"And oxter hair you could back-comb." agrees Dave quietly.

"Do you think he's happy?" Jonesy ventures, " Mad Mike doesn't seem very …. well … MAD anymore does he? Hardly full of the joys."

"I'm sure he's fine," I reply less than definitively, "After all this 'higher-plane mutual understanding based on the self-need within us' *is* a many splendored thing eh?"

We all laugh but nobody looks sold.

4.

Its like Mad-Mike had kissed this …. Woman-thing and she'd sucked all the life from him beyond that which is the necessary minimum required to stand straight, sigh and offer wane, half-smiles.

They spent their honeymoon in Findhorn Bay but had to leave after three days because Ingrid objected to the blatant lack of 'earthly values' shown by their fellow visitors.

A warning to us all - You've gotta respect the hemp! (man)

When they moved in together, into Mike's flat on James Street, the first thing to go was the TV. Mike looked on in a drug-like trance as Ingrid described the BBC as a 'manipulative lie factory' and the folks at Channel 5 'lewd and impure fornicators'.

'So you haven't seen Scotsport recently' injected Jonesy at that point.

The wind whistled audibly round the pub and in the faint distance I swear I heard a bell tolling in torment.

Then comes the revelation that The McKechnie/Ruffin co-existence have recently 'rescued' a stray dog from the local pound. For no apparent reason they called it 'Monk' and almost immediately our hearts go out to Monk. Ingrid and Mike, it would seem are 'Strato-Vegans', and as such are only allowed to eat towelling, biscuits which have fallen to the floor of their own accord, and certain varieties of tree-bark, so the chances of Monk seeing a steak again are up there with Lou Macari's prodigal return to Parkhead.

"Monk is a very sensitive animal and he agrees with our principals." sniffs Ingrid. "He would just die if we fed him dog food. Wouldn't he Michael?"

Mike nods balefully.

Monk has bitten Ingrid three times yet has failed to draw blood we discover. I swear I saw a glint in Mike's eye when he described in unnecessary detail Monk attacking Ingrid's ankles and then how he had gone on to destroy her best grey tweed shawl.

After a third half- pint Mike seems visibly more relaxed. Nothing to the Mad Mike of olde but definitely a portion less disconcerting than half an hour ago.

"This pub used to be owned by John Watson and Norrie McCathie ye know", Mike says casting an appraising eye round the place.

"Bonny Langford owned this pub!" exclaims Dave laughing into his pint. Mike looks at the three of us strangely which prompts us all to snigger in a schoolboy manner.

Former Dunfermline forward Watson was, and will forever be, known to us as Bonnie Langford. This was by virtue of his long curly ginger hair that flowed impressively at one time over his bulky shoulders. A matching bushy red moustache further added to the likeness. Despite the moniker though, John was certainly no girlie on the football pitch. He put himself about big style and was a constant thorn in our side with his strong runs and aerial prowess. A strange cross between Obelix from the Aterix the Gaul cartoons and Spanish golfer , Miguel-Angel Jiminez , Watson was a fearsome sight bearing down on defences.

His business partner and former club captain, McCathie is sadly remembered as having died of carbon monoxide poisoning in a domestic accident a few years back. Again though, another tough customer who typified the strength and physical nature of the Dunfermline Athletic of our youth. Dave explains the reference and Mike smiles.

"Mind you," he says "The pub's no' as good now. Its more open plan than before an' there's nowhere near as many footy fans come in afore the game." His wandering eyes come to rest on the ledge on the top of the bar. "There were boys sittin' on top of that ledge the night we got promoted back to 'the Premier. Man it was heavin' that night. I mind ah was sick down the back of…" But Mike gets caught in the Glare of Ingrid Ruffin® and unfortunately we never find out who or what Mike was sick down the back of.

5.

At the surprising, and somewhat brave insistence of Mike we head off to pastures new for a further pint. Ingrid flashes that look we have already come to know and love but this time Mike's gaze has conveniently settled elsewhere.

Outside a light, almost invisible feathering of snow is in the air. Its biting cold and thankfully our scuttle is but a short one. Heading from the City Chambers in the direction of the abbey, we totter down the sloping 'Kirkgate' a tranquil route off the main thoroughfare. Encouraging us to the right hand side of the street, Mike hastily ushers us into the cramped entrance of the blue frontaged 'Old Inn'.

Inside a tight little hallway we push through a double, stained glass doorway on the right-hand wall and find ourselves in a long thin room immediately facing a busy well stocked bar.

Its like we're in a church, ready to worship the Great Omnipotent Lager Lord and The God of Shorts and Chasers. Large imposing stained glass mirrors religiously proclaim sacraments such as ' McEwans - 'The Old Inn' cask ales' and 'Gilbert Rae Aerated Water Manufacturer, Dunfermline'. Old Dunfermline Athletic memorabilia hangs framed on the walls, and particularly eye-catching is a match program hanging near the corner of the bar from the Scottish Cup Final against Celtic dated 24th April 1965 . Dunfermline didn't even win this game but its treasured presence shows how important cup final appearances are to provincial teams like The Pars. From another frame, goalkeeper James Herriot, stares down at you. Involuntarily you look at the name, look at his arms and ponder if one of those limbs had recently frequented a cow's back passage. You get the impression that not much has changed in the Old Inn in the last century or so. Which is good. The pub is warm and snug, full of character – a sanctuary from the bitter elements outside.

'Well gents,' announces Mike dramatically with the first real sparks of life flickering in his eyes, " this is where it all happened." I hold my breath awaiting another gut-wrenching tale about Mike and Ingrid's road to happiness. 'Please God don't let this be where they first *did it*', is the thought that immediately flashes into my head.

'Don't yiz know about The Old Inn then?'

Three slightly disconcerted faces say not.

'Ah well, this is where Dunfermline Athletic FC was founded, it was in here that aw the plans were made and the organisin' was done. Mike pauses for effect, waves to the conveniently on-hand barman for five pints and begins a short but fervent explanation of how his beloved club came into being.

6.

It would never have occurred to you but Dunfermline Athletic actually were once part of a cricket team. Formed as 'The Dunfermline Club' in 1874 its sole purpose was, just like Killie and St Mirren, to maintain the fitness of its members over the winter months. A good, healthy dose of energetic free-flowing football was considered just the thing to prepare the chaps for a lengthy summer of hanging around 'silly mid-off' watching the seagulls, rubbing that red wooden ball against their privates in a disturbing fashion, stopping for tea and embarking on frightfully exhausting sessions of backslapping, wicket thumping and moustache twiddling.

In 1885, reputedly due to an argument over half a cheese sandwich, the two factions went their separate ways. Dunfermline Athletic Football Club was formed and immediately moved its headquarters to East End Park . The cricket club , in defiance, started a replacement weekly backgammon club and hastily organised a hypnotist night which the Dunfermline Press and all eight remaining members present agreed was ' a vulgar and deeply inappropriate experience.'

The club spent much of its early years jousting with a rival local team who were now playing from Athletic's old home at Ladysmill. What began as playful nips, towel flacking, and Chinese burns escalated alarmingly into inter-club hostility punctuated by equipment theft, kidnapping and unsubstantiated torture sessions incorporating sharp, rusty scissors, pop music hits played on pan-pipes and female stand-up comedians. The rivalry became so fierce that in the wake of a sketchy incident involving both club managers, a man dressed as a female nurse, and a rubber glove filled with lard, Athletic were suspended from the Fife Football Association forcing them into eight years of exile as a junior club in the Pittenweem & Anstruther Industrial - North League (The PAIN League as it was known colloquially and otherwise).

Yet as Dunfermline Athletic flirted with non league football, East End Park developed into the best sporting arena in the area. At the outset however the stadium's original location was problematic. The playing field was surrounded by the gaol, the cemetery, the poorhouse, the hospital *and* the railway-line. Not only did the fans find visiting East-End Park deep-down depressing, it became impossible to get any of the players to retrieve the ball if it went out for a shy. Over the years two players were hit by trains, three were eaten and twelve were fondled inappropriately as they bent to pick the ball up by a sixteen stone 'Lifer' known affectionately as 'Marigold Martin'. Something had to give.

So in 1920 the club eventually moved slightly East to the safer, cheerier three-acre site which remains the home of East End Park today. Back then the playing surface was surrounded by a cinder track and natural embankments that could accommodate and afford an incredible 64,000 people a view of the pitch.

With the team jumping from the Central League back to Division 2 the public were now being treated to regular, quality football however the Fifers traditional appreciation for racing of any sort had them clamouring for a more varied spectacle at East End Park. Cowdenbeath, after all had the stock-car racing, Burntisland (not in fact an island) had their highly entertaining Over 60's , Downhill Wheelchair Slaloms , so naturally the good folk from the 'Old Grey Toun' wanted theirs.

1932, therefore, saw the introduction of greyhound racing at East End Park. The meetings were an immediate hit , so much so that some fifteen months later, in an extravagant bid to keep the dogs on the track, a rabbit was installed. 1933 saw 'Defensive Jim' win the first fully completed race from the inside trap at 3-1 and the fans were ecstatic.

East End Park was under constant development and in 1934 the ground was upgraded in unusual circumstances. Using timber from Cunard's famous luxury 'Super-liner' the Mauritania, which had been recently scrapped at Rosyth, the east terrace was rebuilt and strengthened thus affording supporters a clearer, safer view of the games. A strange end indeed for such an historic ship. Sister to the ill-fated Lusitania, the Mauritania had transported royalty and aristocracy across the Atlantic Ocean, negotiated troops to dangerous foreign locations and jousted with enemy u-boats during the First World War. Now it had finally been laid to rest under the feet of football mad, pie-eating Fifers. An arguably inauspicious end for such an important piece of maritime history.

The improvement of the ground continued apace with roofing, new floodlighting and crash barriers all being introduced. 1962 saw the construction of the sizeable new main stand and notably in 1990 the TV gantry was moved from the back of the main stand over to a specially built suspension above the North Terracing. Not only did this give the armchair fan an annoyingly less panoramic view of the game, it afforded the more excitable Dunfermline fans , directly below the new gantry , the opportunity to throw stuff at the cameramen in a playful yet intimidating manner.

The final piece of the jigsaw was the refurbishment of the Main Stand in 2002 incorporating new bar and conference facilities as well as cleaner, fresher smelling toilets. The old ones, for the sake of public safety were burned to destruction and the remains hermetically sealed before being buried in a secure waste disposal location 'somewhere in Uruguay'. Some season ticket holders swear they can still smell something when the wind blows in a certain direction but club doctors assert that any continued reaction is purely psychosomatic.

By the time the last nail had been hit and the last screw tightened, East End Park, in its many guises, had seen it all. It had enjoyed promotions and anguished at relegations, experienced European competition, had visited the bowels of the second division, the lowest league in Scotland at that time, and welcomed two glorious cup wins (against Celtic in '61 and Hearts in '68). Supporting Dunfermline Athletic throughout this was never going to an easy or predictable ride. And realistically the future doesn't map out anything different for the Pars and their fans. But it is this unpredictability that adds to the pleasure of supporting a team like Dunfermline. The downs are painful and all seems lost but if you hang around and show a bit of character the 'ups' return and are in every sense exhilarating - a religious experience akin to a good fish supper or getting the temperature of your bath water *exactly* right.

Fans of teams like Dunfermline are proud of who they are. They know their roots, they revel in their glory *and* misfortune and they understand their place in the pecking order of Scottish football. That's not to say that they don't have expectations – for thy do - often delightfully unrealistic ones at that. Its just that these expectations are tempered with humour and a resignation that despite having gubbed the Old Firm the week before, a hiding from Clyde is right around the corner.

7.

"Where's the toilet mate? " Dave asks Mike as he drains the last dregs of his pint.

"Out the door there," Mike replies, "but I'll show you, I'm just goin' myself."

The two of them down their glasses and disappear into the corridor leaving Jonesy and myself with the glowering Ingrid who is sipping on her beer like it was boiling tea. However, as if to destroy this image she then takes a huge draw on the drink and drains the glass, not once taking her eyes off either of us as she does so.

Jonesy circles a puddle of beer on the bar nervously and I clear my throat awkwardly.

Ingrid fixes us with narrowing scrutiny.

Racking my brains for something to say, a light suddenly goes on in my mind "Sooo ehhh how….."

"Do you masturbate?" she barks pointedly.

"Eh?

"DO YOU MASTERBATE?" she repeats slower and more insistently.

I look at Jonesy who is staring back at me wide eyed and clearly petrified.

"I… ehhh ….. ffffffwwwwwww" I venture meaningfully looking at the ceiling and expelling all the air I have in reserve.

She turns to Jonesy. "DO YOU?"

Jonesy visibly jumps but remains wide eyed and unblinking. I can see beads of sweat forming on his brow.

"Do you?" she persists.

"Possibly …. only on the odd weeken…"

"I BET YOU DO! I BET YOU BOTH DO!" Ingrid interrupts venomously. "Think of the lives you're killing. MILLIONS OF THEM!"

The barman glances over and Ingrid continues in a lower smouldering voice. "Millions of potential living beings, cruelly …. spent….. murdered by you, by all of you, for the sake of …"

And she almost whispered the last part, painfully slowly, her pale face shaking in fury,

"….. ssselllfff grrratiffficationnnnnn."

Neither Jonesy or I are even breathing now. Out of the corner of my eye I see the barman, who had seemed poised to offer us more drinks, sidle off to the other end of the bar with an anxious look on his face.

The pub seems strangely silent. A forest with a predator in its undergrowth looking to strike.

I'm about to pass out when - OH GOD, AMEN HALLELUYAH – Dave comes through the door closely followed by Mike.

The strain must surely be etched on our faces.

Everything ok folks? Dave ask s lightly, catching the attention of the now reticent barman and holding up five fingers in a 'same again' appeal.

"Oh yeh… eh… fine," I reply shakily, "Ingrid was just asking us about our … emm… hobbies." Jonesy is nodding his head like a string puppet.

"Good stuff" Dave concludes somewhat warily, scooping out a clutch of five pound notes from a slick black designer wallet and laying them on the bar.

He looks carefully at Jonesy. "Is it too warm in here, you're sweating there mate." Without waiting for an answer he leans over and starts distributing the drinks which have been efficiently organised by the now patently skittish barman.

"So boys," Mike exclaims, " How do yiz like the birthplace of The Pars then?"

We agree unanimously that the Old Inn is a quality boozer and Mike beams like he'd built it himself.

"Can I ask you something though, just when you say that" says Jonesy gulping at his pint like it was the elixir of life, " How come your team are nicknamed the Pars anyway. I mean I could never work that one out."

"Ahhh, young man, a good question," replies Mike dramatically, clearly relishing the opportunity to be centre stage again, "There are a nu…"

"Ishn't it time we werr walking to the shoccer?" Ingrid slurs in a slightly irritated tone.

"In a minute dear," dismisses Mike and continues, seemingly oblivious to the Death Ray that has just been fired from Ingrid's eyes in his very direction. " Aye, there are loads of theories as to The Pars bein' our nickname, because we weren't always known as that. In the beginning we were 'The Dumps', kinda' short for Dumfermline ye see." He stops and takes a considered sip of his pint then continues.

"Some think that the newer name wiz to do with the parallel stripes down the shirts. Others link it in to when we got into the league for the first time and were now on a PAR with the best teams in the land."

"Those don't sound particularly good reasons to be honest." says Jonesy shaking his head.

"Nah, I agree. There's an argument goes round that it may go back to an old court case in 1912 involving Cowdenbeath of all teams. A solicitor, in order to establish the 'Beath's current standing in the game, asked the club's representative in court 'Were they on a *PAR* with Dunfermline?' I'm no sure on that one either. Oh, and someone came up with the idea that we were called after the name for a young salmon – a parr. They're black and white apparently."

"Is that what you think then?"

"Oh no," Mike says, shaking his head and taking a slug of heavy, "I think its one of two reasons. *Either* it goes back to the 50's when the team was so bad that the players were accused of playin' like they were *para*letically drunk - again the shortened version was the name that stuck. *or* its to do with the English workers at Rosyth."

"How do you mean?" I pitch in, enjoying the flow of the conversation.

"Well, its said that a while back, a number of English workers stationed at Rosyth Dockyard and at the armaments depot at Crombie, bein' big footy fans started coming along to see Dunfermline. The majority of them, it turns out, were Plymouth Argyle fans but they got so taken with the club that they called themselves the Plymouth Argyle Rosyth supporters club. They took it so seriously that made a big flag with P.A.R.S written on it and brought it to the games."

"And somehow Pars got adopted as the nickname!" Jonesy finishes, laughing

"AYE!" exclaims Mike like he'd just proven the Theory of Relativity.

We all agree we like the last one best and reluctantly also agree with Ingrid that it is now time to leave the pub and head for the game.

Outside in the cold we resist the curious urge to stop in on the intriguingly named 'Creepy Wee Pub' which sits next door to The Old Inn. Instead, though, we dip our heads and aim back up the hill towards High Street, East Port and the way to East End Park.

Mike and Ingrid lead the way setting a bullet pace and, after a rally of vicious whispering, I overhear Mike evidently ending the debate by firmly stating "And for God's sake Ingrid, what have I told you - its not soccer its football luv, FOOTBALL!"

8.

Its absolutely Baltic and we don't make it to the ground without stopping for one more refreshment. In truth we only make it five minutes round the corner to a busy little place called 'Somewhere-Else' where we find a small band of Arthurston boys getting so wrapped up in the bevvy that it has clearly got to that debateable stage whether they will go on to the game at all. The pub itself seems a little unsure whether it wants to be a sit down café or a bar however today, at any rate, its certainly doing a better trade in alcoholic beverages than crepes and pasta.

"It used to be better in there" Mike says as we once more hit the biting cold winter wind and strike out in the direction of the ground, "I don't think they encourage the football crowd so much now."

"It seemed ok to me, a wee bit cramped maybe but good on a day like this." I answer taking my hand reluctantly out my pocket and braving a look at my watch. The cold slips down my sleeve and I make a mental note to get a pair of gloves for the next game.

My watch tells me its just after two o'clock.

"So how is your team playing lads?" asks Mike as he fumbles around in his heavy donkey-jacket pockets and digs out two black and white scarves and hands one to Ingrid. Initially Ingrid looks at it disdainfully but as a fresh whisk of powdery snow bites her in the face, she has a change of heart , grabs the scarf and ties it round her neck.

A bit tough down the bottom of the league there?" he continues laughing slightly.

"Aye its not easy. I thought we were dead unlucky to lose at Ibrox and it was a TRAVESTY of a penalty that cost us at home to Hearts. "Two weeks on and I'm still fizzing about

"Funny they got a jammy one against us too – the boy took a blatant dive and it got given. Always the same against the bigger teams eh?"

"Aye." I agree in a resigned tone. "Losing one nil to Hearts stuck us bottom of the league, but last week was the worst, eh guys?"

"Awwwhhh" comes the pain-filled reply.

"How we lost two-one to Partick Thistle , AT WILMOT PARK TOO! – it was a joke!" Jonesey' s frustration is there for all to hear and to compound his misery, he absently stubs his foot on the pavement kerb in his way. An exclamation sounding like "Ahhhyafffffuuuyaaa" escapes quietly. Like Jackie Chan in a library.

"Honestly Mike, they were up the park twice and scored both times." I grumble, trying to ignore Jonesey who is now hacking his way along the pavement doing an impression of Douglas Bader on ice.

"Yeh I believe you" consoles Mike, "I saw them on telly a couple of week …." A streak of panic spreads on Mike's face but too late, it's out there.

"When did you shee the television?" demands Ingrid vaguely from inside her scarf which she has now tied in a bonnet type of arrangement round her head and under her chin.

"I … ehhh….. ochhhh … when I was away on that course remember. There happened to be a TV in the room and I ehhh…. Turned it on by mistake!"

"By mishtake?" she retorts then hiccups violently.

"....Aye .... ehhhh.... I thought it was the air conditioning remote I had and here it was the telly!" Before Ingrid can counter attack Mike's feeble defences we hit the main road.

It seems funny negotiating the big Sinclair Gardens roundabout on foot. Its one of those 'familiar away-day features' we have driven round so often on our way to our games with Dunfermline. Along Appin Crescent, to the bottom (or is it the top) of Halbeath Road where the stands and floodlights of East End Park spring into view. Then usually on to park the car where we can. Either round between the North Stand and the graveyard in the designated car-park or if we're feeling more risqué, abandoning the whole of the car up on the wide pavement of Halbeath Road itself. I wait expectantly for the day to come when I return to find my vehicle stripped, burned and towed away with an old codger, who looks like Adolf Hitler in a beige cardigan, standing in his bay window arms folded with a satisfied grin on his face. Its never happened yet though and I tip my hat to the relaxed perspective of old Adolf, his tolerant neighbours and his local law enforcement representatives.

We're early but there's already a steady flow of black and white decked families and friends heading along this short distance to the stadium. It always strikes me as a funny place to have a football ground. The situation has a Wizard of Oz type of feel to it, like the whole stadium blew in on the wind and dropped slap, bang in the middle of the affluent, Yorkshire grey bungalows that are a feature of this residential area. A protruding pair of legs sporting ruby slippers is all that's missing from under the main stand which looms large over the raised front gardens of those lucky enough to live so near to their home-town team.

As we skip past the palm tree-guarded porch entrance and onwards beyond the door to 'The Gallery Restaurant', I can't help feeling things have moved on from the East End Park of my formative years. The visit to Dunfermline was always a nerve-tingling affair. All of us tightly packed under the corrugated asbestos roof of the North Terracing as it was then. It was probably one of the worst views in Scottish football, what with the low slung TV gantry and enough twisted segregating wire to keep the Mongol hoards at bay, but that didn't matter. The atmosphere was electric and the singing that reverberated around that tight semi-enclosed area gave you the feeling you were part of a ten thousand strong army.

It was even better under floodlights. Tousy cup ties and hard-fought rearranged league matches always seemed to have even more of an edge in the evening with the dark shadows nipping at the players feet, and I reckon I must have seen more men sent off here than any other ground on my travels. Because you had to fight to get anything at East End Park, it was always the same. Especially when we were both in the First Division. Dunfermline were always one of the big guns of that league and you knew that if you beat them you would be well on your road to promotion or a good cup run. It was good, old fashioned down an' dirty football you got here , every time, and as we come to the end of the main stand I agree with my own slightly intangible feeling that the stadium now looks a bit too neat and polished to play host to those grimy, wonderful games of old.

9.

And it wasn't just the action on the pitch that got the blood boiling. East End Park was where I was introduced, for the first time by my recollection, to the concept of the 'controlled container'.

Because, for a while at least, the Fife Constabulary were mightily obsessed with 'controlled containers'. I can remember it to this day.

"Stop right there son! – you can't go in with that, its a controlled container!"

I was rummaging through a rich assortment of pockets at the gate to the North Terrace, slowly but surely coming up with enough pound notes to see me into the game when the copper grabbed me and shouted again.

"I said get rid of the controlled container!"

I was lost. I'm looking down at my feet, patting my trouser legs to prove , quite bizarrely, that I didn't have an Kalashnakov, tins of tear-gas or a matching set of steak knives concealed anywhere around my person.

"THAT !" spat the cop pointing to my hand.

And it dawns on me what all the fuss is about. For I have in my hand one of the most feared weapons in twentieth century warfare. The Scourge of Beirut , the Korean Widow-Maker, the Assassin's Comrade ...... A Robertson's Orange Quenchy Cup.

"You can't take that in with you"

"Why not?"

"It's a controlled container"

"How do you mean?"

"It could do damage to a player."

" Yeh but only if he took a drink and was allergic to additives" I respond quick as a flash.

The cop looks confused.

"What if I took off my shoe and threw it?" I press.

"Eh?"

"Well my shoe's more of a weapon than this drink." To reinforce my point I hold up the orange plastic cup and squeeze it then look down suggestively at my feet.

"A shoe isn't a controlled container."

"Are you saying my shoes are uncontrollable then?"

"What?"

I was then about to reign the conversation back in by asking what actually DOES constitute a controlled container when I spied my final argument.

"Look!" I cried in horror, "That old man's taking in a brolly he could harpoon the wingers with that! "

The policeman and I both looked at each other and it was at that point that I knew what was coming. The age old copper's comment when there is no logic or justification to what he's saying or doing;

"Do you want lifted?"

Now this all sounds quite amusing but honestly I was getting really hacked off by now. The only blessing was that Dave was already through the turnstile and unable to stick in his tuppenceworth as well.

Deciding the civil liberties issues surrounding a small fruit drink (no actual fruit contained) were unworthy of an extreme political standpoint, I plied the damned drink open, defiantly downed it in a wunner , crumpled it up in manly fashion, and tossed the plastic ball into the handy wall mounted dustbin.

I would have stared at the cop in militant fashion and then brushed off coolly into the game were it not for the coughing fit and the severe 'catching' in the back of my throat that had rendered me helpless. It took all my guile and energy to point myself in the direction of the turnstile and fall through the entrance, paying, if I'm not mistaken a pound too much to get in. Maybe if I'd bought the cola flavour instead none of this would have happened.

According to the 'Police Information- Scottish Legislation Section' a 'controlled container' is ' a container of any description which is, or was;

- **capable of holding liquid and;**

- **is made of a material which, if the container were to be thrown or propelled at a person could cause injury to that person.'**

There you go, just as I thought. My shoe *was* a controlled container therefore all shoes, especially those filled with liquid, should be confiscated on the way in to games. I demand it on the grounds of consistency.

10.

"Controlled containers" I mutter out loud as we approach what is the self same turnstile as all those years ago. I stare suspiciously at the pleasant looking policeman standing at its side. He smiles back with a tired expression on his face and I guiltily smile back.

"Bloody hell Craig, there are elephants more forgetful than you "says Jonesy reaching for his wallet.

"And you as well obviously" I reply laughing.

Standing, waiting in the queue I turn and look over the car park at the graveyard on the hill behind the dividing wall. I always find myself doing this when I'm here, its like it draws me to its clean, grey headstones and dark gnarled trees that look like withered , wiry old men watching us head to the game. I always think graveyards look a bit bleak, desolate and depressing but this one always seems calm, serene and inviting. I think I might request to be buried here when I die – that way I can lie there and listen to all the nearby sendings off and 'controlled container' arguments in peace .

Our hosts are honouring us by sitting in the North Stand along with the rest of the Arthurston contingent. Mike seems altogether brighter whilst Ingrid, who I caught staggering down the stand stairs, has collapsed on her seat and is thankfully keeping her own countenance. We're seated in that same tight area where we used to stand and bark at the moon on those cold, thrilling nights. The place strangely still has the same feel to it only the view is a little better. Someone has obviously been up there, on the roof above section 'M' with the wire cutters and I can just about catch the far end of the pitch, talk about advancement.

Over to our left, the big and boxy East Stand resides where the old 'terrace with no fans' used to be . In all my years of coming here I never, ever saw a single spectator standing on that expansive stretch of terracing behind the goals – even pre Taylor Report. I've no idea why. It wasn't like it looked in disrepair or anything. I can't even remember seeing it full on the TV when the Old Firm came to call. That doesn't mean it didn't happen I suppose.

One thing to be thankful for is that the pitch is back to being grass again. For in 2005 the turf at East End Park was of the artificial variety and boy did that cause a rumpus. In that very year, UEFA had commissioned a study into the use of artificial playing surfaces at the 'highest level of the game. Before they did that, however, they gave Dunfermline a £125,000 grant to play on a plastic , all weather pitch and study the results. The Pars laid first one pitch and then another after the initial one was deemed to have been of poor quality. The surface at East End Park was known as XL Turf which in the fullness of time turned out to be the supermarket's slightly inferior 'yellow pack' version of Field Turf, the cutting-edge, real deal in artificial sports surfaces. An almighty stramash ensued with the SPL looking to ban the pitch and Dunfermline stubbornly holding on to their vision of renting out the pitch to balding overweight white-van drivers and electricians on Monday and Thursday nights for £7 a head. Amid concerns for player safety however, the pitch was eventually re-laid with natural grass and the experiment was declared a failure.

Which was good because plastic pitches are the Devil's work. Currently only two clubs in Scotland still plays on an artificial surface – Alloa and Hamilton Accies. And their pitches stink. I can honestly say I have never seen even a semi-decent game at New Douglas Park and I have seen a fair few First Division tussles there. And it has nothing to do with the quality of players on show either. The ball bounces so high and skids so sharply off the surface that for the players, trying control a pass is like trying to trap a squirrel. Unforced errors are more frequent than a rise in prescription charges and the ball spends as much time rolling out of play as in it. Unless each pass is perfectly weighted then odds on the move will break down with the ball ending up lost in that 'attractive' health and safety hazard wasteland that runs the length of the Douglas Park pitch opposite the main stand.

I feel so sorry for the Accies fans who are subjected to these random pinball matches week in week out. They don't get value for money and in view of how few of them ever make it to an away game, they've probably forgotten what a real game of football looks like altogether.

Football should be played on grass, and possibly sand and maybe the carpet in your mum's front room. But nothing else. If

God had meant us to play football on fake grass he would have invented fake lawn-mowers.

And he didn't.

Enough said.

11.

The players are on the park and already things have failed to live up to the revered days of old. One of the brilliantly unique features of East End Park was the way the players made their way on to the pitch. They made a real gladiatorial entrance as they walked along a balcony half way up the main stand, dramatically descended a flight of stairs then sprinted on to the pitch at the half-way line. By the time your guys were on the park you were whipped into frenzy of excitement and anticipation not felt since they gave out the free butter from Arthurston Town Hall as part of the EEC surplus allocation.

By way of contrast, the players today now slip on to the pitch from the South West corner between the Main and Norrie McCathie Stands to the tune of The Skids 'Into the Valley'. Its functional but its not theatre.

With the game kicked off I pluck up the courage and turn to Ingrid , who is sitting directly to my right. My conversational olive branch, I have decided, will be 'So what exactly is Humus anyway?'

Incredibly though, with all the shouting and hullabaloo going on around her, Ingrid has fallen asleep. Her eyes are closed, her head is tilted slightly to the left and a little bit of dribble had formed in the corner of her mouth. I nudge Dave at my other side and nod my head in her direction.

"I know." he whispers back, " She's been like that for five minutes now. Scottish Football has definitely lost some of its excitement factor don't you think?"

The game is lively enough and the crowd oohhhh and ahhhhh appreciatively as early chances fall to both teams. Already it would appear we are not going to get the rub of the green from today's referee as a couple of wrongful decisions go against us igniting the fury in the fans around us.

East End Park still retains a level of the old ground's character and atmosphere due in the main to the presence of the original main stand. The big, dusty old construction remains the centre-point of the stadium preventing East End Park from falling into that boring 'generic new stadium' category which I have come to despise. Two tiers of seating and private boxes clearly designed by the same folk who did the sheds and glasshouses down in the Clyde Valley nurseries make up the stand which pleasantly proclaims 'Welcome to East End Park in big letters on the dividing wall.

Looking around I'd say there are about three and a half thousand folk at the game today. At its capacity, the ground can hold 12,500 so the fact that there's a real atmosphere today is again testament to East End Park's appeal. To our left, the sizable East Stand is desolate. Had Arthurston had a better away support today, we would have been undoubtedly been housed over there. I personally think we've won a watch and are better where we are. The behind the goal vantage, as I have already opined, is not a good one and once again I dwell on and question those who actually choose to sit there given the option. Like the folks in the Norrie McCathie Stand to our right. Even with the main stand's annoying poles, and the low , shallowness of the North West Stand, the view must surely be better than up there behind the goals. Mind you the world would be a dull, dull place if we all thought the same I suppose.

12.

Maybe its through a combination of the drink and my bad eyesight but after half an hour of play I've just noticed that Robert Crush is back in defence with Ivan Pecnik nowhere in sight. When I ask the guys why he's not playing I get the same shrug from both of them.

As if to hammer a 'YES ITS ME!" signpost into the proceedings, Crush chases a hopeful Dunfermline punt back into his own half and, under only nominal pressure from their forward ,plays a woefully short back pass to our keeper . Thomson, who can't keep the startled look off his face, starts scrambling forward but the Dunfermline forward hurtles past Crush, easily beats the keeper to the ball and swerves round him before crashing the ball into the empty net.

"Awww mannn!" yells Jonesy. Dave is shaking his head. Mike somehow manages to look sympathetic, amused and delighted all simultaneously.

Incredibly, despite the huge roar from the home fans, Ingrid remains dead to the world. In fact she actually gives a small snore just after the announcer has given the scorer.

The cold is beginning to seep into my very being and I'm delighted when Jonesy presents me with a Bovril and a steak-bridie thingy. Unfortunately the Bovril is on the cold side but the food is great. Well worth the purchase.

As half-time approaches we are struggling to grab a foothold in the game. We haven't had a chance in the last ten minutes or so and our problems are being compounded by the referee's unwillingness to give any decision our way. As if to reinforce his standing, the ref watches Scott McLean being blatantly pushed off the ball then waves play on in a stupidly exaggerated hand-ushering manner.

"AWAY YA GO YA HOMER!" I scream, my patience at its limit.

"Craig!" comes a shout in my left ear.

"Yyyaaaahhhh" I yell, visibly jumping.

For the Cracken wakes

"I really don't think its clever to be casting aspersions on the that man's sexuality. I thought you of all people would be more ..... tolerant shall we say."

I look at Ingrid carefully. " I called him a HOMER. " I insist

"Uhuh?" The eyebrow rises majestically.

"It's a sort of *footballing* word- It means that the referee appears to be biased towards the home team. He's a *homer*."

"Oh I see."says Ingrid in a matter of fact manner.

"Anyway. What do you mean *me of all people*?"

"Well, what do you think? Michael tells me you haven't had a girlfriend for ages."

"What .... Do you think I'm GAY!" I cry indignantly then look around frantically as at least three people turn and stare at me. I quickly lower my voice to a hiss. "Cos I'm certainly not!" I hold up my hand in a halting manner, " Not that that there's anything wrong with being gay mind you, but I'm just not ok?"

"Whatever" she shrugs, then half closes her eyes and exaggeratedly whispers the word "Denial"

"DENIAL?" I shriek. More folk twitch and steal a glance. "I AM NOT ..... Oh for the love of God!" I stop, shake my head and turn back to the game just I time to see the referee give a blatant Rovers throw- in to Dunfermline. A homer indeed.

Beside me I can feel the shaking of Dave's laughter all the way from my shoulder down to my knee.

13.

Footballing terminology *can* be confusing and unintelligible to the uninitiated though. The more poetic, colloquial or obscure terms and phrases are often lost on the 'newbe' fan and I feel moved at this point to present a helpful pocket guide to anyone looking to advance their footballing word-power towards that of a more experienced supporter. I would suggest novices attempt integrating the following into related conversation. Successful usage will undoubtedly project the image of a football veteran and as they say, practice *does* make perfect. Here are a few to be getting on with;

Handbags at dawn *(phrase)*– A low-level, insignificant contretemps between two opposing players, usually punished by the referee in a manner disproportionate to the seriousness of the flare-up in question . Sometimes referred to as 'Handbags at 10 paces' or simply shortened to just 'handbags'.

The channels (*noun pl.*)– A strange, mysterious non-specific area of the pitch where 'knowledgeable' managers insist the ball should be 'fed'.

Man on! (*phrase*) - Standard alert to a player nano-seconds before being rear-ended by an opponent in a semi-sexual manner.

Early doors (*phrase*) – The initial stages of the game defined specifically in 1995 by an SFA Investigative Committee chaired by Ernie Walker as 'the first seventeen and a half minutes of open play'. *Usage* – 'He was pure mingin' early doors but the lad has come on tae a right good game!'

A game of two halves (*phrase*) – Inexplicable scenario whereby your team are notable world-beaters in one half, scoring at least two goals in the process, then clumpy half-wits in the other, losing at least two goals.

A six-pointer (*phrase*) – A vital 'must win' game between two teams in close proximity to one another in the league table which, determinant on the final score, could result in a six point swing relative to each teams position, the gain or loss in the season's momentum, and a shed-load of fighting outside the ground.

Fan-dancer (*noun*)– A seldom effective player who, although prone to moments of skill 'flatters to deceive'. Usually prefixed by irate fans with 'Ya' and the 'F' word. Not to be confused with a 'Sand-Dancer who although possessing many similar attributes, has less mobility and slightly thicker ankles.

Flatters to deceive (*phrase*) – Well-loved phraseology, especially amongst older football supporters, inferring that a player's overall impact on proceedings may not be as influential as his 'flowery' possession suggests.

Flowery (adj)– Like a flower.

Kepper (*noun*) – A non-threatening shot of minimal height and velocity which is easily collected by the goalkeeper. Often hit by a 'Fan-dancer'.

Bunshin' (*verb*) - The incidence whereby too many players of the one team inhabit the same, small, localised area of the pitch. Frequently compared unfavourably to the player positioning 'in a kiddies game' or 'after five minutes in every Subbuteo match ever played'

The carpet (*noun*)– Slang terminology for the surface of the grass. In the eyes of every fan of every team, 'on the carpet' is their measured opinion of where the ball should be, giving their boys optimal opportunity to win the game. By stark contrast, 'their boys' on the park will frequently, in situations demanding that the ball be played 'on the carpet', resort to howfin' the ball as long, hard and high as they can up the park. An act that persistently results in diminutive forwards being gang raped by tall, sturdy defenders and is certainly of little benefit to the objective of winning the game. Supporter frustration ensues.

Arsewinder (*noun*)- A potent strike of the ball with power and accuracy that if attempted too numerously in a game presumably affects the feeling in one's anal region. *Usage* – ' Send fur the ambulance, he's been melted in the bawz by an arsewinder!'

Hot potato (*noun*) – Descriptive reference to the ball whilst held in possession of a team with limited confidence in their own ability to do something useful with it, individuals preferring to hand responsibility to other team-mates in a rash and nervous manner.

The Red Mist (*phrase*) – Mythical shroud of anger that is said to have 'come doon' over temperamental players who usually have an ongoing reputation for such behaviour. All self control is lost with the affected player invariably punching, pushing, head-butting, gobbing on, or drawing the boot off, the subject of his annoyance. A red card will invariably follow.

Sitter (*noun*) – A chance in front of goal that is easier to score than miss. Notably more frequently used in terms of 'missing a sitter' than 'scoring a sitter'. Understanding this fine distinction in usage is vital if the novice is to maintain an experienced and knowledgeable air.

To appear even more of a football aficionado one could also try other, less popular terms that have, unfortunately, very nearly fallen out of popular usage completely. Try using the following;

Fatulism – The feeling of absolute certainty that one's team is about to buckle under extreme mounting pressure and concede a last minute goal (particularly against Celtic)

Fectal – The mixed smell of sweat, Deep-heat and Right Guard Original that emanates from all football dressing rooms. *Usage-* 'yon air was fectal'

Scoober –A pie in which, on close inspection, the mince content has become separated from its surroundings in one solid 'burger-like' block.

Gebbled   - The act of getting yellow 'safety' paint from the stand-stairs on one's shoes and the back of one's trousers. *Usage-* ' Aww man ah've gebbled ma good trakkies!

Jimmie-shooker – An extended bout of involuntary knee shaking, muscular spasm and chest tightening experienced by seated spectators after 22 minutes of watching play on a bitingly cold winter's day.

Broadwood Jimmie-shooker – As above after three minutes

Ragmush – A season ticket book that has been through the wash in the back pocket of a pair of jeans.

Shovney – A small pre-arranged pile of pound coins, held by the turnstile operator, representing the exact change of a £20 note paid over as entrance money.

A Clinget of Shovneys – Rows and columns of pre-arranged pound coins representing the exact change of £20 entrance money. *Usage-* "Hurry up man ahm missin the match!", - "Ahm doin' ma best but ma clinget of shovneys has fallen intae a big pile an' ahve lost ma coont"

Johnson – A match official whose upper-body is disproportionate in size to the length and build of his legs.

Flitter – A collection of seven or more empty crisp pokes, paper cups and assorted debris blown on the park by the wind which then spends most if not all of the match being buffeted and spiralled collectively in a strange and hypnotic manner.

Strinkle – The half centimetre of urine absorbed by your shoe from the damp floor of the gent's toilet.

Scunty – The non-committal angle the linesman points his flag indicating he has no idea which way to award a throw-in whilst awaiting the referee to make his decision for him .

Glour – The welcoming glow of a football stadium's floodlights over the dark night sky as seen from a distance away. *Usage* "We must be near Brockville by now but I still cannae' see the glour anywhere."

Ramshamble – A supporter's highly audible, irate and critical shout that fades off to nothing as the individual embarrassingly stutters and loses track of what he or she was trying to say in the first place.

Brogan – The act, particular to football players, of clearing one's nostril passage of phlegm by blocking the other nostril with one's index finger and blowing hard.

Moving-Brogan – A more accomplished version of above completed whilst running.

Cacky–Brogan – As above occurring when the offending phlegm does not disengage from the nose fully and attaches itself to the side of one's face and down the inside of one's arm.

14

The game finished two nil. To be honest though, by the end of it no-one cared. It was so cold we were just glad to be back indoors. After a short scurry round the extremity of East End Park we are sitting warm and comfy, beers in hand, watching the scores come in via SKY Sports News on the high mounted screens of 'Legends' – the bar under the main stand of the stadium.

The bar is so named because it is indeed a place of legends. It is said that that in this very room foreign donkey, Vettle Anderson, pulled NINE women in a half hour stretch. Others tell that a barmaid once threw a cloth at goalkeeping coach, Scott Thomson in order to quickly mop up a spilled pint ….and he caught it. Some say the room just has mystical powers that make Fifers, of all ages and from all walks of life, feel compelled to buy a round of drinks.

It is a long, thin room with an elongated bar along the inside wall. We are neatly ensconced by the window which affords us easy access to the bar as well as a nice view of the illuminated deepfreeze that is the Halbeath Road outside.

With Ingrid nicely subdued by the early vestiges of a hangover, Mike's eyes have the old twinkle back as he reminisces, prompted by Jonesy, over his earliest memories of his beloved club.

"The first thing I can remember?" he ponders

"It's a bit of a funny one but it would have to be the programs." He eventually says. "When I first started coming here they were these long thin things. All black and white with Dunfermline Athletic stamped up the left edge and the hand-drawn picture of diving goalkeeper, Hugh White, catching the ball in front of a set of flying goalposts. They were right distinctive and we must have kept the same design for about …oohh….five years or so. "

"I've still got about a hundred of them up in the loft at home" he whispers confidentially, and looking in Ingrid's direction who is engrossed in peeling the label of a bottle of Budweiser bottle, adds with a drunken snigger, "They're in a big box I marked as crockery when she moved in." He laughs a wheezy, conspiratorial laugh which fades away too quickly to a sigh.

Legends is a far cry from the old brand of corporate hospitality formerly on offer by Dunfermline. I remember in a previous life doing the 'corporate thing' at East End Park and being ushered at half time into a wee musty room deep under the stand that had all the lure and many of the features of the lower reaches of a slave galley. The hospitality in question amounted to a mound of egg sandwiches on a big plate set on a pool table, a cup of dirt infused tea and a Jammy Dodger all in close proximity of a leather clad, nazi-esque Iain Ferguson regaling assembled club officials with tips on how to buy a good second hand car. Ah the simple days.

So we're in this slickest, most Americanised, split level chrome 'n' foam 'sports bar I have been in this side of the water. All that's missing is a dodgy foreign policy and an unhealthy dose of fear. A black spiral staircase leads upwards to a mezzanine floor and as Mike skips over to the bar to get some crisps in, my first thought is 'God I wish I'd won the contract to fit the laminate flooring in here.'

My attention is newly taken up by the four telly screens fitted above the bar. As always, I can't decide which one to watch and my eyes move from one to the other in a shifty fashion. Anyone watching me would swear I had something to hide. I can never work out why bars fit so many screens in such close proximity. They must be desperate to get their money's worth out of the licence fee or something. The choice is giving me a headache so instead I level my gaze on the sloping ceiling above my head which presumably mirrors the gradient of the main stand

"You know I'm surprised we scored a couple today " Mike says staggering precariously to the table with yet another round of drinks, " Goals have been pretty hard to come by recently, we don't have a real natural goalscorer at the club right now.

"Nah your right" Jonesy agrees, "It'll sound like a blast from the past but you could use a George O'Boyle character out there."

"Or an Andy Smith." Injects Dave. "He wasn't the worst."

"When he was with Dunfermline Andy Smith should have played for Scotland ! I exclaim somewhat dramatically, dunting my pint glass on the table and sloshing the foamy head of my lager everywhere.

"Oh come on, he wasn't that good" argues Jonesy, "Not international class at any rate."

"Well I don't know. What's the criteria for getting picked for Scotland then ? Being the best player in your position at the time I'd have thought. And Big Andy was the top scorer in Scotland for a while *and* we didn't have a single recognised goalscorer as a justifiable alternative."

"He would have played for Scotland if he had been with an Old Firm team." growls Mike before taking a huge gulp of heavy then licking his lips defiantly.

I nod my head in agreement glad someone has backed me up.

"And sometimes its better to be lucky than good." Mike continues. "Our record scorer at Dunfermline was a guy called Charlie Dickson. My old man used to watch him in the late fifties , early sixties and he always said that Charlie wasn't *that* great a player. Enthusiastic and hard working yes, but not naturally gifted or anything. And yet the guy scored over 200 goals for the club!" Its Mike's turn to get overly excited and he inadvertently spills some of his beer into his lap.

"What are we arguing about again?" he drawls as he finishes mopping his crotch unselfconsciously.

"Goalshkorers." mutters Ingrid without taking her eyes of the now naked Budweiser bottle In her hands.

"Goalshkorers indeed!" repeats Mike spilling more beer and fixing his stare on each of us in turn. "Did you know?" he pronounces deliberately. "Did… you …. know …. " he repeats, his eyes starting to dance in his head, " … that Alex Ferguson scored ninety goals in three seasons at Dunfermline ?"

"I did not know that." I reply trying to sound casual and indeed sober. My own deliberateness betrays me.

"Oh yes," Mike says definitively, "And then he fucked off to St Johnstone!"

"MICHAEL!" swipes Ingrid.

"Shorry luv" he mumbles huffily , "But he did …. Fucked … Right…. Off !" He lifts his glass and waves it around dangerously, "To Shirr Alex Fergushon - Ninety goals then he Fucked Right Off!

Before Ingrid can become outraged again we all lift our glasses and repeat the toast together;

"TO SHIRR ALEX FERGUSHON – NINETY GOALS THEN HE FUCKED RIGHT OFF!" We down our beers then burst out laughing.

15.

Nature calls and I get up and make that drunken floaty meander to the door. The one that simultaneously announces inside your head 'I'm ok' but screams to any nearby voyeurs ' He's not ok , he's wrecked'.

Its quiet in the toilet. Mainly because its not the toilet I'm in. I've found my way to a dining room.

"Can I help you sir? asks a slick gent with a shirt and tie on.

I was looking for the toilet, where is this?

"This is the Gallery Restaurant, sir"

I look around at the chic glass tables and their ornate place settings, pause for thought and then spectacularly ask. "So, you can get a meal in here then?"

"Yes sir," the shirt and tie replies in a tone that says 'well anyone else can but you can't.'

"Really?" I sniff, raising an impressed eyebrow. "Well I'll be off to the toilet then."

"Its out the door beside the stairs sir."

"I thank you" I reply over politely.

Somehow I find myself in the dark. I shouldn't have come down stairs at all and now I'm in the dark. Standing beside a door saying 'The Jock Stein Suite' to be exact.

'That's not a toilet' I reason.

"That's a suite", I actually say out loud. "Jock Stein's Suite!" I again exclaim out loud, this time giving myself a fright at the sound of my own voice. I look around subconsciously, suddenly worried I am somewhere akin to the restricted area in a top secret government facility and someone is about to appear suddenly and take me away for intense questioning and an anal probe. I try the door which accommodatingly falls gently open. Peering into the dark, empty room I'm somewhat disappointed to view a small but tidy conference room with chairs neatly laid out and plasma TV mounted into the wall.

After a moment of indecision, I shrug and close the door behind me. Quickly retracing my steps I soon find myself back in the land of the living.

"Where were you?" Dave asks

"Toilet." I reply then add, "No wait, I wasn't . Never got there. Went to the dining room and then the Jock Stein Suite."

"Jock Stein has a suite?" Dave slabbers eyebrows raised, eyes glazed.

"Oh yes" I reply, "but its very dark and it doesn't have a toilet."

"Ah never mind" says Dave grabbing his glass, "To Jock Stein and the Jock Stein Suite. May it be forever in darkness!"

"To Jock Stein" we chant in unison.

I'd join in the new conversation about legendary Dunfermline managers but right now it seems I need the toilet.

16.

With due respect to the other managers who have wedged themselves into the hot seat at East End Park over the years, two men have stood out as real movers and shakers of the Fife club.

It almost goes without saying that the first is Jock Stein. The legendary status Stein attained at Celtic often leads us to forget how important and accomplished a role he played at Dunfermline.

When Stein came to the club in March 1960, he was a relatively inexperienced manager having, at that point, only coached Celtic's youth and reserve teams. The Pars were drastically languishing at the foot of the old First Division and with six games left, Dunfermline realistically had to win all of them to have any chance of staying up. Stein, who had turned out for Albion Rovers in his younger days once spoke to a Tory voter down Coatbridge Main Street one lunchtime , so was no stranger to miracles. He claimed to have 'no magic wand' when he first set foot in

East End Park however some form of mysticism must have been brought to bear as they indeed won all six games in the run in and avoided the dreaded relegation by a hair.

Galvanised by this Houdini-like escape Stein strengthened his squad in somewhat confusing fashion ensuring that Tommy Callaghan, Willie Callaghan and Eddie Connaghan would all play in the same starting eleven. Importantly, but much to the dismay of the board of directors, he also journeyed to Italy where he studied Helenio Herrera's training methods at Inter Milan. The club chairman, in an impetuous rush of enthusiasm, had encouraged the young Stein to take on any training he saw fit as the club 'had a budget for that sort of thing'. He did later admit however that he was thinking more along the lines of a First Aid Module at nearby Lauder College or maybe getting someone in to teach the ECDL. However, the promise was honoured and the trip was money well spent. Stein came back with a tan, eleven 'I♥Milano' t-shirts for all the first team players, and a new found training ethos that focussed on ball-work rather than the traditional Scottish emphasis of a hard slog towards physical fitness.

The change paid off in spectacular style. The very next year, 1961, the Pars shocked the nation by beating Celtic in the Scottish Cup Final. One of the greatest goalkeeping performances of all time by Eddie Connaghan, saw Dunfermline see off the 'Tic two-nil in a midweek replay bringing the cup to East End Park for the first time whilst at last elevating Dunfermline above Raith Rovers as the premier team in Fife.

The scene was set then for the Pars to enter the European stage, notably before the likes of Celtic or Liverpool had ever tasted such an experience. They played in the cup winners cup and then, memorably, in the 62/63 Inter-cities Fairs Cup where they disposed of a shell-shocked Everton team who had insultingly called the Pars 'Country Hicks' in the press prior to the ties. This victory, however, paved the way for one of the most memorable European nights in Scottish football history.

Drawn against Spanish giants Valencia, Dunfermline found them an altogether different proposition from the overconfident Scousers. They lost four- nil in Spain effectively killing off any hopes of advancement in the competition. Or so everyone thought. In what must have been the most incredible forty-five minutes of football East End Park has ever witnessed, Dunfermline went in at half-time sensationally *five-one* up.

AGAINST VALENCIA!

Not only that but they held their nerve and finished the game six-two victors. They would ultimately lose the following play-off in neutral Lisbon but Dunfermline and more pertinently, their able manager Jock Stein had made a clear statement of intent as to what the future held for the Fife club.

Of course Stein's achievements in the game are well documented. He would eventually spend four years at East End Park before departing for Hibernian, en-route to Celtic. But it is the legacy he left at Dunfermline that may be one of the underestimated achievements in our game. They would win the cup again in 1968 and between 1961 and 1970 go on to play forty-two European ties in a total, the pinnacle being reaching the Cup Winners Cup Semi-final in '69 where they unfortunately lost to Slovan Bratislava .

As with most provincial clubs, success was hard if not impossible, to maintain in the longer term though . Slowly but surely mediocrity seeped back into the pores of East End Park and by 1983 Dunfermline were rock bottom of the second division, the lowest of the low with memories of the glorious sixties now just that - memories.

Enter our second saviour.

A man called Jim Leishman

17.

Jim Leishman, imaginatively nick-named 'Leish' , was only 29 when he was given the task of scraping the Pars off the arse of Scottish football. Looking back, it was probably destiny that such a man would be the one to lead the club out of the wilderness and succeed where the likes of Tom Forsyth and Pat Stanton had failed miserably before.

For he was a Dunfermline man through and through. As a lad, he admirably rebelled against his Rangers supporting father and walked the not inconsiderable distance from his home in Lochgelly to Dunfermline to see the Pars in action. A promising left-back , he also realised his dream of playing for the club, turning out eighty times in the black and white stripes between 1971 and 1974. Unfortunately for Jim, his budding career was severed in a clash with current Kilmarnock boss and then Hearts player ' Jim Jeffries.

"My leg broke in sheer boredom." recalled Leishman in recently discovered, unpublished memoirs. "Yon monotone voice was enough tae send ye mad like. After standin' beside the dour bampot for twenty minutes the leg-brake was a Godsend - Ah was glad to be goin' aff like!"

Once again, Dunfermline's meteoric rise was one for the history books to whistle and shake one's head at in mild disbelief. Leishman, with his strong motivational personality and Grecian 2000 treated moustache, steadied the ship and within two years, his team had romped up the table and won the second division title. The very next year they became one of only three teams to gain promotion in consecutive seasons gaining entry to the premier league on the shirt tails of First Division champions Morton (Gretna and Partick Thistle were the only other clubs to equal such a feet however the latter were shortly afterwards to become the first and only club to be *relegated* two divisions from the Premier in consecutive seasons)

It was around this time that the bold Jim went a shade off the rails. You see he started spouting very bad poetry at strange, inappropriate moments. It was almost like he had a rare creative strain of Tourettes Syndrome. Whether it was during post match comments or TV interviews, Leish just couldn't stop bursting into McGonnigalesque verse that must have made even the staunchest of Pars fans wince in pain. The subject matter of these creations were so inconsequential that the jists of them have faded into the mists of time.

Until recently that is.

During the final stages of the Main Stand development, an old tatty jotter was unearthed with 'The Dunfermline Edition' scrawled in a rough hand across the front. The parchments, through the carbon dating process, have been pinpointed as being from the mid eighties to the early nineties. Although Jim himself denies their authenticity, experts are firm in their assertions that in view of the said carbon testing and Jim's prevailing red neck, the works were indeed 'early Leishman'. The Dunfermline Edition held thirty-seven poems in various states of completion and legibility. Classics such as

'The Ballad of Dick Campbell's bunnet'
'We're goin' all out tae win it ! (wi' ten men behind the ball)
Ross Jack can fair heid a ball, but watch him tryin' tae lay slabs.
and '**Ode to a mad red and pink Hummel away top.**'

all appear for the first time in their entirety while previously undiscovered works such as;

' **Oh   Istvan Kozma ,you looked like Tommy Steel (you scored a goal from the half-way line - at your feet I kneel)**'
' **Bert Paton talks like my Grampa.**'
'**The strange arousing qualities of Widow Twankie's tights.**'
'**Irritation, thou ist The Eastenders theme tune.**'
and ' **Milos Drizic – shall I compare thee to a pun 'o tatties?**'

all render the find invaluable in terms of the man's celebrated work.

Eventually Leishman realised that the poetry was threatening his credibility as a serious manager and was at his most poignant when, during a historic press conference he eventually conceded "The verses are gone, the were makin' folk yawn, am aff now tae ASDA in ma blue hatchback Mazda."

Henceforth Leish concentrated on the fitba-managing and gave the verse a bye. In his up and down world he flitted from the manager's chair to the boardroom and back, serving Dunfermline Athletic wherever and whenever he could. After a recent spell of managing the club he has once more retired to the shadows as the Director of Football at the club. You get the feeling though that it is only a matter of time before the club once more get on the Bat-Phone, ring his number and Jim will appear like a grey-haired super-hero to run into the dug-out, cape swirling , to save the day.

And we'll all welcome him too – as long as he doesn't do any of that bloody poetry.

18.

We said our goodbyes amidst the cement of the Dunfermline Bus Station. Mike insisted on walking us to the stance while Ingrid sought refuse from the cold in the starkly lit waiting room.

"Well, thanks for coming over," he offered as he shook each of our hands in turn. There seemed to be just a hint of regret in his tone as he did so and as he headed off in the direction of the waiting area, he stopped and turned round.

"You'll need to come back over soon and the five of us can go out for a meal or something" he said enthusiastically "I was just speaking to Ingrid and she said she really likes you guys."

The surreal silence hangs momentarily before Dave shakes himself and says "Well yeh, of course – we'll be in touch."

Satisfied that sufficient closure has been made we wave awkwardly and jump onto the chuntering bus that has conveniently just pulled up. Within seconds the door has closed behind us, we're seated and the bus is straining its way out of the station.

As we pass by the last grey concrete pillar a couple are huddled together at its side gazing in our direction. The tall man with a vague, distant expression and a shaven head waves tentatively . The much shorter woman stands rigidly, a black and white striped scarf tied tightly around her head. She momentarily looks as though she too may wave at the bus however at the last instant she digs her hands into her coat pockets instead. And as the bus heads slowly for the station exit it may or may not be a trick of the light but I'm sure I make out a small smile from beneath the scarf just before one big black eyebrow lowers itself deeper and deeper then deeper still into the woman's pasty white forehead.

I wave, expel a small chuckle and settle down for the journey home.

19.

The headline screams off the front page of the Sunday paper causing me to spill my bran flakes on my lap.

Scots footballer has (S)ex - Factor!

Popular X-Factor girl group '3 Piece Sweet' were last night at the centre of saucy 'four- In- a- bed' sex allegations involving a professional footballer currently playing in the Scottish Premier League.

Slovenian football star, Ivan Pecnik (31) , who recently signed for SPL strugglers Arthurston Rovers, last night admitted to being involved in a 'disturbance' sometime during the early hours of Christmas eve in an executive suite of Glasgow's Hilton Hotel.

Hotel staff notified the authorities when residents complained of loud repetitive banging , the sound of 'breaking glass' and noises 'not unlike a donkey braying'.

One eyewitness claimed 'when the door was forced open, I recognised the girls immediately. They were all naked along with a drunk looking man who was on the back of one of the girls,riding her like a horse whilst singing what sounded like 'Rawhide' in a heavy foreign accent. They seemed to be enjoying themselves'.

Superintendent Russell Maitland of Strathclyde Police confirmed that 'a drug and alcohol related incident had occurred at around 3.45 am on Christmas eve in the Glasgow Hilton '. He went on to suggest that '4 members of the public were involved and that the hotel owners would be pressing charges"

Earlier today X-Factor judge and creator, Simon Cowell confirmed that 3 Piece Sweet's continued involvement in the TV competition would now be under review. Group members, Leanne (23) , Ashley (21) and Demi-Lee (20), all from Glasgow, were said to staying with close family over the next few days and were unavailable for comment.

For more see pages 5,6 and 7.

Beside the article are two pictures. One is of three short-skirted, almost pretty girls, singing into microphones on the, now familiar, X-Factor set. The other is of our man Ivan, decked in his striped Rovers kit with a couple of faded Rangers players in the background. Under his photo is the small bold narrative 'Ivan the terrible?'

I'm about to skip dutifully to page five, then presumably on faithfully to pages six and seven for the sake of completeness when the phone rings. I let it go as it is never for me. However just to prove me wrong my mum answers it , murmurs a few low words, then shouts "Craig – Its David for you!"

I jump neatly out my chair and hop into hall, collapsing lazily onto the little three legged stool beside the telephone table.

"Alright?" I say bringing my knees up to my chest, resting the soles of my feet on the wall on the other side of the thin hallway, "I bet I know why you're on…."

And for a good thirty seconds confusion reigns in my mind.

"Uhuh, I know" I say

"Its in the paper"

"Honestly, its in the paper"

452

"What?"

"No , that's not what you said – We *are* talking about Pecnik here?"

"Pecnik and those girls from the X-Factor?" I say falteringly.

Dave's voice rambles on insistently and by the time he's finished his news is starting to sink in.

"I'll be right there." I finish and hang up the phone. Biting my lip I try to comprehend what Dave has just told me but it just doesn't fit. I'm on the phone there, listening to Dave telling me all about Pecnik being arrested for taking drugs and yet that's not what he was saying at all.

My mum interrupts my whirling thoughts by shaking me on the shoulder.

"Is everything alright?" she asks

"Emmm no its not" I reply, "Listen, I'm going to have to go out for a while."

"Is it important son because you were going to help me move those boxes, remember?"

"Yeh it is a bit," I say slowly as I fumble the wall mounted rack of keys for those belonging to my car

My words hang in the air like death.

"Jonesy's been arrested mum."

She looks at me.

I look back,

Shrug,

Then walk out the door.

Chapter 15
The winter (jail) break

1.

Arthurston Police Station smells like the unpleasant alliance of a hospital ward and a chicken and mushroom pot-noodle. The public area is deserted. As I nervously edge my way to the reception desk then stare hypnotically at the 'press here for attention' button (a light switch crudely stuck to the desk with freezer tape) I can't help feeling indefinably guilty over something I didn't do. Plucking up some courage, I'm about to ring for attention when the door behind me flies open. In bursts a consternated Dave who slumps on to a chair and runs his hand through his hair. He slowly looks up at me.

"Sorry mate, had to go to the toilet. Jesus what a day!" He leans back, crosses his legs and smiles wanly at me.

"Well?" I ask.

"Well what?"

"Well - What the hell is going on?"

"He's been arrested for … get this … drug dealing!"

"Eh?"

"I know. Chris Milne…*Our Jonesy* …" he states deliberately in clear disbelief, "… is currently being detained at her majesty's convenience as a drug dealer!"

"Where did they get that from? It *must* be a case of mistaken identity surely."

"The police think not. They've been questioning him for over an hour now."

"To what end though? There's no way Jonesy will be able to answer questions about drugs." I can hear my voice rising in pitch.

"Yeh, well of course he won't but in the meantime we'll just need to wait and see."

I don't feel much in the mood for 'wait and see' but in view of the fact that there is nothing else we can do, I slump into the plastic seat beside Dave and systematically start to bite my fingernails.

2.

Jonesy has never been the luckiest or most together person you could meet. In fact since his old man left you could say that his life has been a series of mishaps and accidents that belong more to some bitter-sweet slapstick movie than to anything resembling real life.

In the time I've known him stretching back to our irresponsible schooldays, I've lost count of the number of illnesses, personal injuries, mishaps and downright bizarre incidents that have wrapped themselves around Chris Milne. Over the years he has fallen off gymnasium treadmills, been assaulted by grannies with shopping trolleys, ravaged by cats and peed on by babies. A catalogue of Basil Fawlty mahem that makes him who he is and the rest of us shake our heads in chronic disbelief.

Surely it can't be that bad? – well let me give you a few examples;

The stray dog incident.

Jonesy was in his late teens and during the holidays he had happily volunteered to mend a broken chest of drawers for his mum. I was also in my late teens and had volunteered to watch him do it. It was summer, the weather was particularly warm and sunny so in order to keep the house free from the smell of the super-fast, super-strong adhesive he was using, he took his project al fresco, to the driveway at the side of the house to be exact. As

Jonesy explains it, events unfolded so quickly that thinking wasn't really an option. I'm not sure.

Midway through this intricate furniture reconstruction he paused for deep breath, sat back on the monoblok ground and lent the palm of his hand fully onto the lid of the glue tin which he had been using as a sort of mini- dispensing tray. As such, it was full of adhesive. Almost simultaneously a small, sandy haired mongrel dog appeared from nowhere, scuttled up the driveway from the street, sniffed my knees economically then in a relatively friendly fashion launched itself onto Jonesy who was still sitting hand in lid. In reflex, he grabbed the dog, scrambled to his feet then stood grimacing as the over excited little mutt tried to climb his chest and lick his face. Of course the real drama only started when Jonesy tried to put his new little friend down.

The dog bit him five times before we could subdue it enough to cut it free from Jonesy's left hand and was last seen scurrying back into the street with a bare buttock and a ravaged expression. Jonesy, for his part, had to get a tetanus injection in *his* bare buttock and had to sport a hairy hand for a good fortnight afterwards.

The one night stand incident

Jonesy met Angie in O'Jays the night the last episode of Friends was shown on the telly. Jonesy was canned and after disappearing for half an hour came back to our corner with a girl he introduced as Angie who worked for a construction company and who looked, according to Jonesy just like Jennifer Aniston. To say she looked more like the woman who ate Jennifer Aniston would be closer to it however our lad seemed happy enough and the two duly headed off in the back of a taxi together just before chucking out time.

Jonesy, keen not to subject the girl to the toxic horrors of his own flat was happy to accept an offer to go back to her's which as it happened turned out to be a swanky 'designer' pad in the brand new estate out in the neighbouring town of Lingford.

Formalities were dispensed with and an alcohol enhanced sexual encounter duly took place which Jonesy in his own words 'was surprised didn't register on the Richter Scale'.

Our man then slept the sleep of a man with ten pints of lager and six shots of Apple Sours in his system and only awakened in the morning by a gentle shake of his shoulder. Opening his eyes he came face to face with a middle-aged couple, their young Gameboy playing son and a bemused, smartly dressed young woman holding a clipboard who immediately demanded to know why Jonesy was lying naked in the master-bedroom of her 'show house'. Angie, if that was her real name, was nowhere to be seen. After overcoming a near fatal attack of shame and heartburn and a painful, fruitless search for his left sock, Jonesy made his red-faced getaway. Dave, after laughing for what must have been an hour solid, urged him to call the builders and track 'Angie' down, Jonesy felt more inclined to let it go and stalked off to buy a box of Rennies and a single ticket to Guatemala.

The hospital incident.

The week after his twenty- first birthday Jonesy was stricken with a bad case of tonsillitis. For reasons best known to his GP , he was referred to the renal unit of Arthurston General where in quick succession he was given a barium meal, a dose of Picolax and an enema. Jonesy being Jonesy said nothing until the violation was complete. Sitting gingerly on the edge of thin bed behind the screens, still in his paper smock, he eventually plucked up the courage to ask in a weak voice, when would they be examining his throat.

The apologies came quickly and seemed genuine. A new paperwork system and an equally new admin. assistant were seemingly to blame for the mistaken identity. Jonesy, for his part accepted the situation in fair grace although for a good week he complained to us in private of the strange white poos he was 'experiencing'. Dave and I reacted as any solid, considerate friends would do in similar circumstance – We gifted him a piles cushion and nicknamed him 'Chalky' which to his irritation, stuck for the best part of a month.

3.

"Mr Gorman could we have a word?" A thin, pasty faced young policeman with short red hair and the remnants of bad acne asks, popping his head round a door in the far wall I hadn't even noticed.

Dave shrugs his shoulders at me then disappears off through the door and into the bowels of crime and punishment. Twenty minutes later he's back sitting beside me regaling me with as much as he has gathered from a less than pleasant interview with a couple of cops sensationally called Detective Inspector Decker and Detective Constable Black.

"Black and Decker!" I exclaim grinning, "No way. Did you laugh?"

Dave apparently didn't laugh but did smirk enough for DC Black to open with "There's nothing funny about this situation sir." in that superior yet irritatingly un-confrontational tone they all must learn at basic training.

From what Dave can make out it would seem that although he's not, as yet been charged, Jonesy is strongly suspected of using his window cleaning run as a cover for selling a rich array of illegal drugs to the Arthurston public. And why would the police think that? Because that's exactly what his Uncle Len – alias 'The Fat Man' was doing before skipping the country and handing over the 'family business' to Jonesy.

"No way!" I cry again, "Uncle Len eh?"

"Think about it though," Dave reasons, "Those flash cars he always had and the big house. I always thought that was pretty good going for a window-cleaner. I get the feeling the cops had been staking out Len for ages and just when they were about to bust him, he got wind of it and bailed."

"And remember what Jonesy said" I exclaim, " When he first started he was always complaining that the run was all over the place and that the customers were unhappy about him doing the windows – they weren't wanting their windows done at all were they?"

Dave shakes his head."*And*, of course, they were always asking him about 'The Fat Man'." he concludes.

We both look at each other.

After a lengthy silence I reason "Clearly they've nothing on Jonesy though."

"Well that's the thing," replies Dave frowning, "I think they've got his bank statements."

"So what?" I shrug, " He hasn't done anything wrong. His bank statements aren't gong to show anything unusual are they?"

Dave's frown degenerates into a pained expression."Well it depends on what you mean by unusual. He paid a huge chunk of cash to Len for the round didn't he, and he emm ......" Dave looks at the floor and mutters a few more low unintelligible words.

"Whassat?" I demand scrunching up my forehead .

"..... AND HE HAS MY THREE AND A HALF GRAND!" he repeats audibly.

"Three and a half grand, "I reply stupidly, "What for?"

"The cash from my car sale remember."

The blank expression remains on my face.

"Jonesy agreed to let me pay the cash for the sale of the Golf into his account. " Dave continues, clearly irritated at my flaky memory, "I also drew out my wages in cash and paid them into Jonesy's account."

"Why the hell did you do that?"

"Look, I'm just not sure about Linda right!" he cries defensively. "I was just being careful."

"You think she's honestly going to take your money?"

"Well she can't take what she doesn't know about that's for sure."

"How often did you transfer cash then?"

"Twice." Dave replies. "Then took it back out in chunks of £200 at a time ... you know... for spending money. I also took some out for the deposit on the Audi." He sighs then gets up and paces round the stark grey room, pausing under a Drug information line poster. 'Together we can beat the dealers!' it says optimistically in big bold lettering. Dave snorts then trudges back to his seat.

Another sigh as he crosses his legs and stares at the wall.

This time I reply with a sigh of my own.

4

The clock on the wall says midday. We've been seated in the waiting room for another hour. No more information has been forthcoming.

"Its just typical of these bastards to be so heavy handed." Dave mutters scuffing the side of his shoe on the grey laminate floor. "Eight o-clock this morning they turned up at the door. Like a dawn fuckin' raid!

"They're just doing their job" I reply wearily.

"Oh you've changed yer tune!" he replies confrontationally, "When did you suddenly become Defender of Police Activity for the area. You never have a good word to say about them."

"That's different. "I counter, " I just don't like the way they deal with football fans sometimes. That's all."

And that's an understatement. I know policing is a difficult job and I certainly wouldn't want to do it, but sometimes, just sometimes when it comes to overseeing football matches they get it so badly wrong that you wonder just what the motivations to their actions really are. You travel long distances, around the country, optimistically intent on an enjoyable day out, hopefully watching your favourite team win against the odds, and yet somewhere in the mix are the local police division. Waiting for you, intent on wasting your day by causing as much self-generated friction as is humanly possible within the bounds of 'acceptable' force and intervention. I can feel the blood-pressure rising already.

Football fans like it or not, still seem to have this stigma attached to them that says 'We are trouble-seeking maniacs on the edge of violent conduct at any given moment ' It doesn't matter who we are , what we look like or what we're doing, the boys in blue look at us like we're on the ex-offenders summer picnic or something and need watching at all times, just in case.

Granted not all cops are the same and it would be grossly unfair to insinuate that police heavy handedness is a global problem. It certainly isn't. One bunch of characters however, that cannot escape specific criticism and are a group that ardent away fans will know well.

They are twisted, they are mean. They have no humour and their disdain for football fans of all ages, sex and standing knows no bounds.

They are, my friends, The Tayside Police.

Now clearly there is a policy at work here. Granted it may not be one advocated by the organisation as a whole but nonetheless we are talking about a policy adhered to by certain individuals which has long since abandoned the principles of zero tolerance and is now reaching well into the negatives. For we experience some form of excessive reaction or intimidation *every* time we venture North-West to play Dundee, Dundee United or St Johnstone. I have read comments on the internet forums of many other Scottish teams that echo my concerns about law and order Tayside Style to the extent that I'm confident that this is not some form of tailored anti-Arthurston initiative.

The problem, in my opinion, is as clear as day

Individuals, I suspect, within the Tayside Police *want* trouble.

You can see it in their eyes.

They don't want a quiet, hassle-free uneventful couple of hours. They crave the confrontation. They take perverse pleasure in annoying and intimidating normal, respectable people and, with a bit of luck, they'll succeed in so far as someone will react and give reason to be ejected, or arrested or better still ignite an angry little scuffle offering the opportunity to deal out a little tough love.

Last season we played Dundee midweek in a cup tie and the chain of events typified the treatment football fans get in that neck of the woods.

It starts with us cheerfully and enthusiastically assembling in our designated area of the ground. While friendly greetings are made amongst the familiar groups and the younger lads gathered enthusiastically at the edge of our crowd, the police presence looks on offering suspicious , glowering looks to all and sundry . Inwardly the surveillance unit in attendance has just switched to DEFCON 1.

DEFCON 2 quickly follows as a group of Rovers fans starts that provocative and patently hazardous activity …..singing. We all look on with interest as the three cops at the foot of the stand suddenly multiply into seven or eight officers, all of whom are staring malevolently at the crowd above. A couple looked like they were already on the radio requesting back-up in case, presumably the singing dangerously fell further out of tune.

The game has now started offering our itchy officers the opportunity to hit DEFCON 3. The crime for this escalation – standing up. Wooahh ! Do not, I repeat, DO NOT attempt to stand up at a football match under the auspices of the Tayside Police because it is a one way ticket to the cells my friends. Its ok to do it at half time, its ok presumably if you raise your hand and are given permission to go to the toilet, but stand up midway through the match with no good reason other than your reaction to what's happening on the field of play, then you're toast.

They are now amongst the crowd and choosing three or four unfortunate victims they stand either directly behind them breathing on their necks or right beside them, admiring their ear-wax. Willing them to say or do something wrong.

And it 's at this point that they cast their net wider. A group of respectable looking middle aged gents rise to their feet in excitement as the Rovers come close, and quick as a flash two cops are over demanding that they sit down.

At last one of the younger group cracks and says something to the cop who's inside his jacket with him. As the young boy (fifteen years old if he's a day) is huckled, arm up his back by two burly officers down the length of the stand, fans start to shout their displeasure at the unnecessary interference going on. Slowly the collection of boos and heckles grows. Another middle aged man who is on his feet straining to see what the commotion is, is pinpointed and asked to sit down. He says something in retort and his arm is up his back and he's being manhandled down the stairs as well.

The boos ring out louder and more agitated. The lads start singing in greater, more restless defiance and the Tayside Police get on their walkie- talkies with relish. And as another squad of goons enter the fray we have now reached DEFCON 4. Another youngster is lifted and now everyone is more concerned with the events unfolding in the stand rather than anything in the game itself. The tension is palpable as an argument breaks out between another cop and an elderly gent down to our right. He's a familiar face to us all. A man in his late sixties who drinks in our pub and who is a real, nice and pleasant guy. It becomes apparent that one of the younger guys just lifted is his friend's son. The old guy, although persistent, is neither threatening nor abusive. After a good couple minutes of what looks like controlled , reasoned conversation however, he shrugs his shoulders, shakes his head and accompanies the fiery looking cop down the stairs – yep you guessed it – with his arm forced up his back.

The Tayside police, in all their glory, have lifted a pensioner.

Now, out of nothing, we have a real situation. We are in a segregated area almost two hundred yards away from the nearest rival fan. The propensity for crowd trouble is practically non existent. And yet here we are – people who have paid (through the nose) for an enjoyable evening's entertainment being subjected to a hostile atmosphere that has rendered any form of enjoyment impossible – with no justification.

Its back to my question of motivation. Had the three original police officers just stood at the bottom of the stand and observed, not one incident worthy of intervention would have occurred. A quiet shift for the boys in blue. And yet they chose the alternative. Why exactly? The answer of course is deeply worrying.

And of course this was not a one off incident. We have been subjected to this sort of treatment, in varying degrees, on two or three other occasions in the last couple of seasons. The same police force virtually ruined a recent family oriented Challenge cup final with a similar antagonistic approach to proceedings. Havoc again being created in an environment more reflective of a Sunday-school outing than a security threat.

Its insulting, inflammatory and does nothing for police public relations. The matter needs to be highlighted and addressed. A similar incident happened to us down at Stranraer a few years back but we put it down to an isolated incident arising from the high profile that football related violence had at that time. Despite matches being altogether more orderly affairs these days, however, the 'football fans are scum' mentality still seems to raise its ugly head now and again – particularly as we have seen on Tayside. This view is not acceptable, it is degrading and I for one am anxious of the repercussions. I certainly don't want to be around on the day when those officers reach DEFCON 5.

5.

Jonesy was held overnight as the police sought to verify Dave's assertions on the cash transfers. By the middle of the next morning after much scrutinising of vehicle registration documents and bank confirmations, a pale, shell-shocked Jonesy staggered through the door to freedom, tired looking and disoriented.

Sandy gave me an hour off the shop to collect Jonesy and take him home. He hugged me tightly as we met in the waiting room of the station, and as we quietly headed for my car his eyes glistened in the bright January sunshine.

By the time we got home he was perkier. I made him a cup of tea, of course, and once that was done we watched a bit of Jonesy's highlights tape, a compilation of all the 'too brief' appearances the Rovers have made on Scotsport this year.

As I sat on the sofa he scribbled some details on a scrap piece of paper, purposefully extracted a number from the phone book and made a phone call.

Three days later I sat at the kitchen table reading The Arthurston Gazette. Turning to the classified section, second down on the extreme right hand column under 'Miscellaneous' was a small ad.

> **For sale : Window cleaning round.**
> **Includes van, 2 sets of ladders,**
> **assorted equipment and cleaning**
> **materials. Price on application –**
> **Thick skin a necessity.**

Dwelling on the entry only momentarily, I took an extra big spoonful of pro-biotic yogurt, shook my head and folded the paper away.

6.

Arthurston Rovers 2 Dundee United 3
Kilmarnock 2 Arthurston Rovers 1

Jonesy may well be off the hook in the lead up to the winter break but the same, unfortunately, cannot be said of the Rovers. Two further defeats leave us completely marooned at the bottom of the table and many of the fans have resigned themselves to the fact that we're going down. Comments like 'We should just enjoy it while we can.' And 'Its time to rebuild for next year' are already doing the rounds. But people talk a lot of tosh sometimes don't they. I mean look at the table;

Scottish Premier League

	Pld	W	L	D	GF	GA	PTS
Celtic	24	16	2	6	49	10	54
Rangers	24	12	5	7	32	16	43
Hearts	25	10	6	9	29	27	39
Dundee Utd.	24	10	7	7	37	30	37
Aberdeen	24	9	6	9	31	18	36
Hibernian	24	8	7	9	30	28	33
Dunfermline	24	9	10	5	27	28	32
Kilmarnock	24	6	8	10	19	24	28
Falkirk	25	6	10	9	21	35	27
Motherwell	24	5	10	9	27	39	24
Patrick Th.	24	4	12	8	18	40	20
Arthurston R.	24	4	16	4	22	47	16

Three wins and we're back up to tenth place! Assuming no one else plays a game that is. But I have a good feeling about things – its not like me. Unlike those 'glass is half empty' pessimists I can see us turning things around. We led in both of the last two games and only our keeper getting sent off against United and a late, dubious penalty at Rugby Park cost us the points. No, all things being equal, I reckon we're on the verge of greater things.

Elsewhere in the league, with injuries and suspensions kicking in, the Hearts challenge has finally stuttered - being forced to play Scotsmen has clearly reeked havoc with their game-plan. Dundee United have gone all season without sacking their manager (applause please) and indeed recently presented their boss with a carriage clock for his seven months loyal and, quite frankly, inspired service.

Partick Thistle remain our best hope for avoiding the drop although their plodding 'point here and a point there' style has admittedly given them a small breathing space over us in recent weeks.

Thankfully the winter break has been reinstated. Playing with such a small squad as we are, the time will be well used resting tired limbs and healing niggling injuries. Some clubs will utilise the opportunity to travel to far flung locations to develop their branding, others will elect to trounce third rate Scandinavian outfits and pretend they're winning the Champions League. Most, however will head to Marbella, play a game against the hotel waiters (which they will lose) and spend the rest of the holiday, I mean tour, drinking 'two for the price of one' Tequila Slammers, wearing towels tied into togas, and singing 'Hey baby will you be ma girl' at girls with pink sun-burn around their bra-strap areas called Chantelle, Michelle or possibly Ashleeeen.

The winter break is one of those modern day features of our game that the powers at be cannot decide is a good thing or a bad thing. Whether it is necessary or indeed useful is a matter of debate. Two weeks off to avoid the worst of the weather hardly makes much sense since the propensity for snow in April seems as likely as in January these days. Resting players seems a smoke screen also. As we've already noted, playing extra games abroad together with all those exhausting visits to the STD clinic when they get home are clearly counterproductive to the benefits of a slackened workload. Not to mention the stress of the pending paternity suits over little Juan and Juanita or Kylie and Jordan depending on the cultural preferences of the player concerned.

Nah, there's really little justification for the winter break and the clubs would be better admitting its just a good excuse to massage the club overdraft, for fisticuffs on a chartered aircraft, and for saucy misunderstandings in striped beach tents like in 'Are you being served – the movie'(When the staff went abroad and Captain Peacock rented a deckchair and he ' .... couldn't get it up'. Fnnarr, fnnarr.)

For the rest of us its worse. Faced with no games to go to we have to make alternative arrangements, think of other activities. It might involve doing some exercise, shopping with the wife or partner, visiting relatives.

Things may even be more desperate than that.

7.

My heart has been beating quick-fire since my arse touched the seat of the car. By the time I've hit the A74 I have whipped myself into a panic, calmed myself down, cranked up the fear and dread again then pulled myself together ... oohhh something like twenty times so far.

Cos I'm rock solid me. Sound as a pound in all manner of difficult situations. 'Why am I doing this?' keeps flashing into my head.

And every time the question is asked, the chorus of Eagles' Desperado slides into my mind.

'Desperado, why don't you come to your senses.' What d'ya know I have an inner psyche with a sense of humour. And even it's mocking me.

I decide to concentrate on my computer printout instructions and making sure I turn off at the sign for Coatbridge , Bellshill and East Kilbride which has just appeared, I slip back under the motorway , negotiate a couple of well signposted roundabouts and in no time at all I'm in the tight, affluent looking main drag of Bothwell, South Lanarkshire.

8.

I bring the car to a halt across the road from a pair of white gateposts each with a black ornate number 4 attached three quarters up. The house is a sizable mock Tudor detached with a pristine front lawn and a BMW and a red and white Mini Cooper parked in the cobblestone driveway. The BMW is black and rich, the squat, chunky mini looks shiny new and is sporting the private registration number HEI D16. Directly outside the low hedged whitewashed wall, parked in the street is an army green Freelander jeep and metallic gold Porsche Carrera again with a private registration which I can just make out on the angle as being JED 1.

'Oh man they're loaded' I think involuntarily as I pull the keys out the ignition and the engine is killed. "What the hell does that matter?" I say out loud, my own voice sounding weak and out of body. I look in the rear view mirror and set my jaw in a manner that eradicates any traces of a double chin that may or may not be there.

"Nothing!" I answer myself definitively. "Nothing at all". I run my fingers through my hair and then look appraisingly at the palm of my hand which is awash with tiny droplets of moisture. A deep but wavery breath is taken.

"Right lets do this!" I announce to the air and with steely purpose I shift my buttocks, grab the door handle and ....

.... Let it go again, turning back round to my original position.

"Fuuuuck!" I wail, laying my hand on the gear stick in search of a steadying influence.

'Why am I doing this ?" drifts once again to mind.'

'Because feint heart never won fair maiden, that's why.' my internal database of wise-ass old-fashioned sayings announces.

Feint heart indeed. There's nothing remotely feint about the bongo drums in my chest announcing that a human sacrifice is about to begin.

'Don't think about it – Do it!' is the last thing I think before I find myself out of the car, crossing the road and floating up the driveway.

The doorbell rings cringingly loudly. Beating down all urges to leg it back down the driveway I stand my ground. Through the frosted glass door I see movement and my heart tilts as I know that escape is now no longer an option.

I've played the scenario thousand times in my mind already. Heidi comes to the door. I smile and say hi. She smiles back and says hi. I coolly say I was just passing and thought I'd look her up. She smiles again warmly, invites me in for a coffee and we casually talk small talk alone at the kitchen table, laughing and getting to know one another. I have just enough time to fit in one more comfortable vision of this before the door opens in front of me.

I stare at the dragon in the doorway.

"Yes?" she barks, managing to look me up and down five or six times in the time it's taken her to say her opening monosyllabic greeting.

"Yes .. emmm…. Is Heidel in?" I slurp.

The woman who looks uncannily like that vampire that's married to Tony Blair furrows her brow, tilts her head and says in an overly dramatic manner "Heidel?"

"Emmm… Heidi ……. Sorry … Heidi ….. yes!" I'm nodding and trying to hold my brow line steady.

"Who are you?" she demands like a prosecuting lawyer.

"I'm … emmmmm ….. Craig …. an … errrr …old friend of Heidi's."

"M. Craig." She replies officiously, "Can I ask what the M stands for?"

"Eh?" I reply momentarily lost. "Oh… ehhh …. sorry … ha …. Yes… no… that was just me …. stuttering… ehhh my name is Craig. Just Craig." I can feel sweat forming along my hairline.

The woman stands for what seems an age appraising me.

"Well you'd better come in I suppose."

With that she turns with a swirl of pink pleated skirt and stalks back into the house. I hastily follow her through a hallway that seems to be one big mirror, passed a few closed doors and find myself in an airy, modern kitchen.

"Why are you following me young man?" the woman squawks, "I'm in here for another gin." She flaps her hand back at the door we've just come through and suddenly screeches at the top of her voice "HIYDEEEE, IT'S A FRIEND OF YORRRS !"

Notwithstanding the fright I've just had, I remain resolute if wide eyed and rooted to the spot. The woman slips out of sight behind a shiny white worktop and reappears clutching a bottle of Bombay Sapphire. She looks over at me again in an irritated fashion.

"Out the door, first left then first right dear!" she waves before pouncing on half a lemon she has spied on a nearby saucer.

Left with no other option I turn in slow motion and do as she says. Out the door, first left, then first right.

9.

I'm in the whitest room I've ever seen. This room is so white if it was a person it would be a saint. Facing me like a group photograph of a royal family is a collection of people perched uncomfortably on a big white leather couch, and two equally sprawling white leather chairs. A white frosted glass table and a white squashed looking pouffe make up the rest of the whiteness. To a person they are looking at me.

"Emmmmm ... Hi." I venture raising my right hand slightly then flapping it back against the seam of my trousers.

Silence hangs as the assembled group look like they are in the midst of a close encounter. Except, that is, for a glowing smile in the middle. I meet Heidi eye to eye and feel myself blush a deep warm rush of red.

She starts to speak "Hi ehh ......"

"Craig" I finish sharply, "Craig Donald."

"Hi Craig" she quickly says, "Mum, you remember Craig from the funeral don't you." Heidi looks over to the chair nearest the broad, blanched wood mantelpiece.

A sharp rush of relief flushes through me. At least I'm in context.

"Oh yes" says her mum in a tone that says ," I have no idea what you're talking about."

"Listen I was just passing by," I start, valiantly trying to hold it together, "but you're obviously busy, I'll maybe come back anoth….."

"Sit down Craig and have a beer" Heidi smiles. She is more beautiful than I remember. Her golden blond hair is held up in a pony tail giving her a casual look that shows off the delicate curve of her neck. Her eyes are so perfectly feminine that I can't bear to look into them. I drop my gaze and look to sit down. With all the seats and sofa space taken, I'm left with no option but to take the pouffe. It collapses under me leaving me sprawled, semi-upright, inches from the floor with everyone looking down on me.

""Sorry Craig, where are my manners," Heidi says , "let me introduce everyone. This is my sister Clara." An older, more severe version of Heidi sitting on the couch nods with the merest glimmer of a smile. "My Aunt Fiona." Vampira has just returned from the kitchen and slipped on to the edge of the settee . She tilts a crystal glass in my direction. "And in between them, my boyfriend , Jed."

The words suck the life out of me and I feel the room surge ten feet towards me and then back into place . Four months of fantasy squashed instantly.

"Hey." says the boyfriend in a bored manner. He's a ridiculously handsome so-and-so. Sandy haired with a tan leather jacket to match his tanned leather face. Brad Pitt meets Captain Testosterone meets Gnarly Ski-Dude meets.... Ahh you get the picture.

"Hi," I reply "That'll be your car outside then, the Porsche.... Either that or there's a Star Wars geek next door." I add lamely. A white tumbleweed blows across the carpet.

"Yeh it is." he eventually replies.

"Nice. " I venture stating the somewhat obvious.

"What do you drive yourself bud?"

"Emm, a Fiesta." I reply , suddenly ashamed, "Gets me from A to B." I add unnecessarily.

"And what do you do for a living Bud?"

"I'm errr.... in hardware" I smile weakly. Jed has his mouth open to inquire further when Heidi interrupts.

"And finally Craig, over in the corner there is Grampa Brewster. " Heidi motions to a pile of bones, cardigan and loose skin in the other single chair in the room. "Grampa Brewster furrows his brow and sighs a little.

"Grampa is going into hospital tomorrow for a hip replacement operation." Explains Heidi moving behind the old man and lightly laying a hand on his shoulder " And he's a bit worried, aren't you Grampa?"

"Eh?" he squeaks

"A LITTLE BIT WORRIED !"

"Ohhh no. I don't like hospitals." he replies, the blood draining from his face visibly.

"MY GRAMPA HAD A HIP REPLACEMENT" I shout over to Heidi's Grampa

"Huhhh... Is he alright now?" Grampa Brewster asks in a quivering voice .

"HE DIED !" I cry.

"Ohhhhhhhh," exclaims Grampa Brewster like he's just fallen out of a moving train.

Gasps and tuts escape from the couch.

"Oh no, sorry - I mean , he died recently. Not from the hip. replacement." I'm stuttering." HIS REPLACEMENT WAS A SUCCESS!" I shout over but I don't think Grampa Brewster is listening as he is looking at Heidi gripping her sleeve. I put my head in my hands. "Oh God." I mutter.

"Can I get you a cup of tea or something?" asks Heidi in a benevolent manner, clearly satisfied that Grampa Brewster isn't going to have a panic attack.

I nod gratefully and absently run my hand across my damp brow. "That would be lovely thanks."

"What do you take?"

"Milk and one sugar thanks."

And with a quick nod she's off leaving me on my own, reclining awkwardly two inches off the floor, surrounded by a pack of wild carnivores.

Thankfully the conversation steers off in the direction of Jed's college degree which they had obviously been discussing before my grand entrance. From what I can gather Jed graduated an unspecified number of years ago from Bell College in Hamilton with a turbo honours, HNSVNQ featuring a peculiar combination of architecture, Industrial Portuguese and Wine-tasting. I'm trying hard to pay attention but introspective flashes of panic and terror keep taking over urging me to find an excuse to leave.

"......yeh , I mean Bell College was great," he is drawling," the courses then were almost as good as University ones and to be honest I didn't really want to travel to Glasgow or Edinburgh so it worked out well." He blows on about the student life, the complexity of his 'degree' and the multitudes of friends he made 'on campus' as he kept referring. Campus indeed. I may be wrong but if my memory serves me Bell College's 'campus' consists of fifty square feet of mono-blok, a bench and a bus-stop. Anyway I'm barely listening to his embellished tale of academic achievement, instead seeking refuge in the trees outside in the front garden which I can see through the huge window that takes up most of the wall on my left.

Heidi comes back with a white Denby mug of tea just as Jed is finishing off an indulgent reminisce about his first drink in the Student Union. As she walks by, Jed grabs her around the waist and holds on. As he does so he turns to me and gently caressing her waist asks, "So Colin, you got any qualifications worth mentioning?"

"Emm yeh," I start," bit of a time ago but I did similar to you actually."

"Jed looks sceptical,. "What, you get yourself a diploma or something before getting into hardware?" he laughs slightly.

"No actually I have an honours degree in Architecture" I reply flatly.

The smile fades from Jed's face.

"Where did you do that?" asks Clara proving she is still alive on the corner of the couch.

"Edinburgh University." I reply nodding and giving her a small smile.

Aunt Fiona turns to Jed and with a sly expression says ," Looks like you've got a bit of competition there, eh Jed."

Heidi flashes her a look , breaks free from Jed's grasp and picks up another white mug and takes a drink, staring into the bottom of the cup when she's finished.

Jed looks at me contemptuously. I cannot hold his gaze as I shift my buttocks uncomfortably on the pouffe while racking my brains to come up with a benign subject to talk about.

"So can you tell us a bit about your job Bud?" Jed asks deliberately. I look back at him and I swear I see a twinkle in his eye. Somewhere not far off I swear I can hear David Attenborough whisper ' And the threatened Alpha male vigorously defends his territory.'

"As I said, I'm in hardware at the moment." I reply in the most matter-of-fact tone I can muster.

"Own business?"

"Emmm ....no"

"Management?"

"Something like that."

The hyena can smell blood.

"So what's your role?"

I sit up a little straighter. " I'm an assistant in a small store over in Arthurston. I used to have my own picture framing business but it didn't work out and I basically had to take what I could get." The details roll out a little too easily.

"I thought you used to work with my husband." Injected Heidi's mum sounding confused.

Clang !

"oohh erm ... yeh I did Mrs Ellis. ..... a bit ..... through a previous employer, " I squirm and I hate myself for lying. " I was seconded to your husband's business for a while a few years back."

Jed looks about to pounce when

clink – splash – yelp

Aunt Dracula knocks over her gin and tonic. It falls off the arm of the couch where she had evidently placed it for easy access and into her lap. The ensuing kafuffle undoubtedly saves my bacon and as Fiona skuttles to the kitchen in search of a cloth and a refill, I take a huge gulp to finish my tea and decide to make a bid for freedom.

Agonisingly there isn't a suitable break in the conversation with a now animated Clara explaining how to get a variety of household stains out without using upholstery cleaner. Five minutes go by and my lack of assertiveness is starting to irritate me. Clara stops briefly and silence prevails.

"I…" I start.

"Why….." Mrs Ellis begins at the same time.

"No , on you go." I say politely. Mrs Ellis smiles and then starts a unfeasibly long inquisition into the choice of a white lounge as the main room in your house. I want to scream and only take comfort in the sneaky glances I'm snatching at Heidi. Once she caught me, smiled and yet again I felt myself flush.

At last a pause in the chatter presents itself.

"Well," I exclaim loudly, slapping myself on the knees and hoisting myself off the pouffe, "I'd better be going then."

A friendly round of "Oh Craig do stay a while longer' is not forthcoming.

Heidi gets up as does her mother who walks over and takes my hand. She begins to explain how her husband would have been touched that I had come in today. I start to nod but my attention is distracted by movement in the garden outside.

"Jack was always so busy at work…." She continues but my vision is now fully taken up by the two dogs humping like jack-rabbits on the front lawn. The corners of my mouth curl slightly and I force myself to look at Heidi's mum's face.

"…….. his illness was hard on us all ……." I hear and nod. Over her shoulder though, a large brown non-descript mongrel is on the back of a much smaller King Charles Spaniel and is going at it like a fiddler's elbow. The relative size of each dog is making life difficult for the mongrel but to his credit, he has adopted an uncomfortable looking 'bent leg' technique and is making do.

" ….. so many kind friends……."

Nerves are taking over and I let out a slight giggle which I manage to just about stifle with a short fit of coughing. I try with all my nerve and control to fix my eyes on Mrs Ellis and to beat down the irrational need to laugh.

".......a nice touch and something that was fitting to his memory." She continues. My eyes slide sideways just in time to see the mongrel pushing his special lady round the lawn in a tight circular pattern all the while staggering with that lowered hind leg position being held and maintaining the 'rhythm of luurve' in his private parts . They begin their third rapid revolution when I burst out laughing.

Heidi's mum stops talking in astonishment. Heidi who is standing with her back to the window, looks on wide eyed and confused.

I'm hysterical with laughter and the more I try to stop the more my face contorts painfully.

"Are you alright dear?" Mrs Ellis asks.

My face is bright red, I'm shaking uncontrollably and tears are now streaming down my face.

"Oh my , I'm so sorry." she cries suddenly, "You're poor Grandfather has just passed away and I've upset you with all this talk of dying haven't I?"

In a grande-finale I catch the dogs skite straight across the lawn like a gardener running with a wheel-barrow and I wail in pain, the aching down my sides and in my kidneys almost unbearable.

"No...its ok...." I just about manage before exploding into a further bout of convulsions.

A glass of water is sent for and eventually I manage to control myself with a strange painful grimace the cover for my exquisite need to smile and start laughing again. Once my breathing has returned, Heidi offers to see me out with a distraught Mrs Ellis fussing around in the background. I'm about to accompany her out into the hall when I ask for 'a minute' and skip over to the room past the patently uncomfortable grandstand to Grampa

Brewster. A few quiet words, a nod of the head and I skip out the door self-consciously.

"I'm sorry about all that, " I say breathing the fresh air at the open door like I had been on the verge of suffocation. " I don't think I should have come."

"Don't be silly. " Heidi smiles. "It was nice of you to do so."

"Well, I said I'd look you up."

"Did you?"

"Errr… I'm not sure I did actually" I reply and we both laugh gently. "But the football wasn't on," I continue valiantly, " *and* I was in the area sooo ….."

"Ahh, Football. What team do you support ?"

"Arthurston Rovers." I reply nodding like one of those novelty dogs you see on car dashboards.

"Uh huh." Heidi nods back, "Bit of a nut eh?"

"Yehhhhh ……. Hardly miss a game. They're not so great but I guess being a fan is … well…. character building."

A nervous silence descends and brief panic spreads in my mind as I think I might say something. Something possibly inappropriate.

The urge subsides though and instead I give her an apologetic smile and a quick "Well, see ya" and I'm off down the path as quickly as politeness dictates. As I get to the end of the driveway I allow myself one final glance. I turn round to casually wave but when I do the door is closed and Heidi is gone.

A small laugh cum breath escapes my mouth and I head for my car. I'm not a doctor but suddenly my heart seems in every way normal again.

It must have been something in the tea.

10.

The sign on the door reads 'Beware of the guard-dog'. An excessive measure for a third floor flat possibly. Sometimes though, Jonesy's sense of humour kicks out into odd directions and the only thing to do is shrug your shoulders and acquiesce.

Dave answers after I knock for the third time.

"He is one *lazy* bastard!" he snaps pointing behind him into the flat, " I swear a couple of weeks in the jail would have done him some good."

I follow into the dark hallway with Dave muttering the likes of "never thinks to answer the door or pick up the phone!" and "fuckin' pants lyin' everywhere!"

"Hey." I say to Jonesy who is stretched on the living room couch nibbling on a Tunnocks tea-cake only partially liberated from its red and silver foil wrapper.

"Alright?" he replies looking up from the book he's reading, a dog-eared paperback of 'The Man in The Iron Mask.'

"Yeh," I sigh.

"What's up with you?" he asks folding over a corner of his page to mark his spot then laying the book down, "Hard day?"

"Hard life more like." I reply removing an empty yogurt pot and two copies of NME from the corner of the couch and flopping down carelessly.

"That doesn't sound good, fancy a beer?"

"Nah," I shrug don't really feel like one."

"Cuppa then?"

"Emm… aye, I'll take a cup of tea." I say brightening

"Good man, I'll have one when you're making it." I look for a sign that he's kidding but the fact that Jonesy's picked up his book again and is fingering his way back to his marked page suggests not. Dave brushes into the room with a pile of shirts in his arm.

"Lazy Bastard" he affirms continuing out into the hall.

I figure if I want something to drink then I'd better make it myself. Struggling to my feet, I slump my way into the narrow, rust coloured kitchen and slap on the kettle. The faint hope that there may be a chocolate biscuit on the premises fills my head and I set about investigating the cupboards at hand.

They say you can tell a lot about a person by what they have in their kitchen cupboards. Currently on Jonesy's main food shelves he has two pot noodles (one 'Toxic Spice' flavour , the other 'Savoury Plastic'), a bottle of soy sauce, a giant container of

Saxo salt, a half empty pack of Doritos and a bottle of Head & Shoulders shampoo.

Jonesy's cupboard tells me he's a lazy bastard.

"Where's the tea-bags then?" I shout. "WAIT - I've got them!" Having opened the fridge in search of milk, I've found a small box of PG Tips on the ledge beside three bottles of Peroni and a can of Magners.

Jonesy wanders into the kitchen pulling at the neck of his 'Muppets-Velcro Dawn!' t-shirt. Casting a regretful look in the open cupboard he pulls the neck out further."I ..errr.. need to do a bit of food shopping ."

"I'll say." I reply sharply, What's the shampoo for, dip for the Doritos?"

"Shampoo? Aww cool, I wondered where that had had gone." He grabs the little white bottle and looks at it like it might grant him three wishes.

Somehow I manage to clear Jonesy out the kitchen area, where he clearly feels uncomfortable anyway, and by the time I've brewed up three teas Dave has joined us in the living room and is reclining on the sofa, hands behind his neck and is glaring at Jonesy who is doing his level best to avoid any kind of eye contact.

Relations are clearly strained. A good ten minutes of bickering takes place before the conversation unpredictably turns to me and I'm forced to explain my trip to Bothwell.

Jonesy looks horrified while Dave nods in approval.

"At least you did it eh?" Dave says encouragingly, " I mean, it sounds rough an' all but how much would it have eaten away at you if you had done nothing. I bet you felt better once it was over."

"After I'd stopped shaking." I reply with a rueful smile. "No , but I know what you mean."

"I couldn't have done that for the world." says Jonesy shaking his head with a look that is two parts admiration to one part abject terror.

"Nah, you'd have phoned her from that chair ya lazy b…"

"Dave!" I interject "give it a rest will you. We get the message – *Don't we* Jonesy?"

Jonesy grumbles in barely audible agreement.

Rain suddenly patters off the window outside and Jonesy slips off to turn the heating on. The conversation skips around from my work, to our up and coming cup tie with Airdrie. Dave , who has clearly been reading the paper informs us that Ivan Pecnik has had the charges against him dropped after offering to pay for all damages. And according to Jonesy after their threat of expulsion, 'Three Piece Sweet' got booted off the X-Factor anyway after a shocking rendition of 'The Eye of the Tiger' during the 'Songs From the Movies' night.

"Cowell said it sounded a bit karaoke." Jonesy cried," A BIT KARAOKE? When did anyone NOT sound karaoke on that programme?"

Then, bang in the middle of all our idle chit-chat Dave butts in awkwardly almost whispering "I met with Linda this morning."

A nervous silence hangs in the air with neither Jonesy or I seemingly brave enough to ask the outcome. Dave however takes the lead and explains how they had talked for a good hour or so and things seemed better until that is, he asked her about the other guy.

"It was the way she said his name that set me off." Dave says slowly "Gary isn't the issue she said. But there was an intimacy there, I heard it. In that name - Gary. FUCKIN' GARY!" Dave flushes and looks at the floor.

"And then I started shouting didn't I. All the good stuff went out the window. She said she didn't want to see me until I *matured* and was ready to talk properly. And all I did was shout some more. Why can't I learn to just shut the hell up? All I wanted to say was I'm so sorry and all I want is to have her back and what do I do? ..... I ...shout...... and...."

And Dave is suddenly crying. Stripped of any anger or shame or self-awareness his head is bowed and he is crying. Barely a sound comes out but unrelenting pain is etched on his face and a huge tear rolls down his face and drops onto the knee of his jeans.

Another cup of tea just isn't going to cover this and, judging by Jonesey's shell-shocked expression, he's not about to do a Claire Rayner and take control.

I shuffle over and put my arm round Dave's shoulders.

"I know this is all fucked up for you just now but it'll sort itself out. Honestly it will." He continues to look at the floor.

"I'm sure things will be alright but you have to come to terms with the fact she *might* not come back and I know that's difficult thought. If that happens , well, you'll just have to move on. But that's ages away isn't it? We'll cross that bridge if we come to it, and look at the positives here…" Dave looks up and wipes his puffed up face with the back of his hand

"…. she wanted to talk didn't she. So that's something. And your outburst, well I kinda get that. That's understandable. She's your wife after all. The next time, you won't lose the rag and you'll tell her how you feel. After all that's all you can do really isn't it." I stop and look into Dave's eyes trying to muster all the sincerity I can.

"Do us one favour will you?" I add gently.

Dave nods.

"Next time you organise to see her, let us know."

Dave nods again.

"That way I can be less of a lazy bastard." injects Jonesy quietly, "I'm sorry mate I've been a right pain this last few weeks…"

And so we move onwards and upwards. The rest of the evening is spend pleasantly, the pressure having been released. Jonesy's highlights tape, the apparent cure for all ills, gets another airing and if anyone was to wander into that living room and found us, three guys, yelling at the TV screen, arguing over tactics, complaining about refereeing decisions, you would have thought 'There's a bunch of boys happy with their lot.'

And who knows, deep down, away from the horrible realities of the real world, maybe they'd be right.

Chapter 16
A diamond in the rough

1.

Driving round the John Smith Swimming Pool on Airdrie's town centre bypass you can be forgiven for thinking Motherwell isn't so bad after all. On one side of the road the elevated railway line is partially obscured by an unkempt straggle of trees, nondescript foliage and assorted indigenous litter. While on the other, oddly angled whitewashed flats and a compact brick-walled bowling club sniff disgustedly at two deceased supermarket carcasses lying grotesquely in a barren, empty car park behind blue and grey flaking railings. Having just driven up through the green rimmed, landscaping exuberance that is Coatbridge, the unkempt, untidiness here is stark in contrast.

Unlike Motherwell's grim town-centre though, you can see glimmers of potential in the Airdrie locale. Negotiating the gently sloping roundabout that links the town's ring-road to the nearby railway station, a glance left allows you a brief look up Broomknoll Street towards the bustling throng that is Airdrie Cross. And despite the frayed edged surroundings, it makes for an almost appealing scene. Complete with its imposing clock spire and the regal sandstone building of Henderson the Jeweller, you can imagine a neater, more prosperous Airdrie of old. Indeed it leaves you speculating just how much better the place would look if Coatbridge did the decent thing and sent up a few of their rampantly enthusiastic gardeners with a couple of Fisons Growbags, the leftover pansies, and some quick growing conifers.

Cultured foliage aside, we've been to The Tudor Hotel for some of the best steak pie this side of heaven and washed it down with a quick pint in the welcoming arms of the nearby West End Bar — an excellent boozer with good beer, a nice big telly screen and classical music playing in the toilet. We have three quarters of an hour to kill before the excitement of Scottish Cup football hits our veins like a pint of Red Bull topped with sugar-icing, and we find ourselves cruising slowly up the wide expanse of Graham Street, the town's main thoroughfare, as usual looking for somewhere to stop for one more pint.

2.

I bring the car gently to a halt in front of 'The Double A' bar. With its cheap neon signage and a tiled, indented entrance, it exudes all the allure of Archie Knox, naked in a rusty tin bath. This was an old haunt though back in the days when Airdrieonians played at Broomfield Park, directly across the road, and we know it to be pleasant and bustling with a good mixture of home and away supporters. Not today though. The pub, for all its promise of a thirst quenching pint and some banter with a local or two, is closed and no amount of peering through the gap in the grey door shutter is going to open it.

As we climb back into the car, I stop and look over the road, half expecting to see the low, roof mounted floodlights of Broomfield, Airdrie's old ground. Instead, however, the yellow and black branding of a Morrison's Supermarket peeks out of the dip in the landscape - not a hint of floodlight in sight. I sigh and click the car ignition back into life.

Slotting into the steady stream of traffic, I take an immediate left turn up a short hill then another sharp left, retracing our steps down a back road towards Airdrie town centre. Jonesy fumbles around in his jacket pocket and with a triumphant grunt brandishes a blank tape which he slaps into my cassette player and starts rewinding.

"Wit tull ooz eer riss!" he glows then winces in pain as he touches his slightly swollen left cheek.

"How's it now?" Dave asks with little real concern in his voice.

"Weeely fore" he replies in an indignant tone.

Jonesy, it would seem, lost a big grey, lump of coal filling to a slice of Thin 'n' Too Crispy Dominoes pizza last night. His threshold for pain is minimal and now, almost seventeen hours since the 'accident' and an emergency trip to the dentist under his belt, he is still in a state of mild shock.

"Re toof faiwy iz a bahshtad wif rat dwill!" he grumbles sullenly.

"You need to stop calling him the Tooth Fairy," I suggest pointedly, "Gay folk could take umbrage at that don't you think?"

"Aw eez naw gay, eez jissst ur but efffewimmet." Jonesy forces out spraying more dribble about the place before mopping the side of his mouth gingerly with a sodden paper hanky. "Oo wan ta shee iz wife. Shiz wuvwy. Awazin woh a Porshh an a viwwa in Schpain dush foh a mam!" he grunts.

"Eh?" both Dave and I say at the one time.

Jonesy looks irritated and makes no effort to repeat himself.

The rewinding tape snaps to a finish and Jonesy gives us a lopsided grin whilst dribbling again slightly out the left side of his mouth. Instead of mopping up with his hanky he makes a huge slurping noise which sounds like dirty bathwater dregs disappearing down the plug.

"Oh for God's sa...." starts Dave in disgust but is stopped in his tracks by an another obscene yet strangely familiar noise that suddenly blasts from the stereo. At first it blares in distorted protest but as Jonesy leans over and reduces the volume slightly it becomes clear what we are listening to.

Most people would think that having a tape of ice-cream van music was well beyond the bounds of normality. I would have to agree and the tortured bing-bongs of glockenspiel as recorded on, by the sounds of it, a wood panelled deck and mike set from the 70's, is a step too far for even Jonesy's 'eclectic musical taste. I make to pop the offending tape back out but incredibly, Dave reaches out and blocks my arm.

"No no no," he shouts above the din in a tone laced with intrigue, "Let it go a bit."

"You're kidding."

"Nope, it has a certain …. something." And with a little smile and a shake of the head, he looks out of the window. I drive on making a mental note to invest in a CD player and new friends.

3.

We seem to be back where we came from at a mini roundabout at the top of Airdrie town centre's pedestrian precinct, beside two more derelict looking supermarkets and a structure proclaiming itself officiously as Airdrie Sheriff Court.

"Eh Jonesy? Eh?" beckons Dave towards the grey, blocky building, "Want to go in and see yer mates?"

Jonesy glowers over the back headrest. Dave smiles innocently and shrugs. The statute of limitations on *not* ridiculing Jonesy's temporary incarceration is evidently up.

"Nyahh fwaag gunnya " Jonesy grunts enigmatically and falls back on the car seat.

Dave and I look at each other again and shrug simultaneously.

"Right ,"cries Dave tapping along to the booming strains of 'The Teddy Bears Picnic', "Stuff this driving around aimlessly, lets stop and ask someone where the nearest decent pub is."

I agree and Jonesy also nods his head once to give his seal of approval.

We slide to the side of the road outside 'The Bon Bon 'cake-shop and stop beside a rotund, middle aged gent standing dreaming at the edge of the payment. The man is in a world of his own leaning all his weight on a chunky looking but slightly small bike at his side. Dave winds down the window and shouts 'excuse me!' crisply and clearly in the cyclist's direction. In the background a tinnitus inducing rendition of 'The Halls of Montezuma' cranks up majestically.

"EXCUSE ME!" Dave repeats and the chap jolts out of the self- induced coma like someone wired him up to the mains.

He seems an interesting sort. Flat tweed cap on head, he is sporting a beige, ill-fitting fleece that says Bailey's Irish Cream on the breast, sagging and heavily-pilled, navy blue jogging bottoms tucked into grey and purple argyle patterned socks, and heavy, black formal brogues. The term 'Baw-face' was evidently inspired by this man as his blotchy red cheeks are inflated to the extent that he appears to be storing nuts for the winter.

"Wwhaaa!" he rasps, focussing first on Dave then on Jonesy's lopsided features peering out of the back window before finally glancing in a disconcerted manner at me as the loop of 'Montezuma' trundles on unabashed in the background.

"Can you tell us where the nearest pub to the football stadium is?"

"Whit?" he barks and reaches for a half empty bottle of Irn Bru that is hanging precariously out of his fleece pocket and takes a huge draw on it.

"Where's the nearest pub mate?" Dave repeats.

Baw-face stops, thinks, and absently tries to put his half- empty Irn Bru bottle back into his pocket. It refuses to fit and after three or four unsuccessful attempts his body slips into a contorted spinning motion much like a dog chasing its own tale. After a couple of revolutions he gives up trying to wedge the bottle where it obviously doesn't want to go and stands puffing, looking in mystified fashion at the bottle in his hand.

He then remembers us and looks up at Dave. In doing so he looses grip on the bottle which falls and smashes to the pavement with a crash and a fizz.

"Naawwwwwwww!" he yells with a look like he dropped his cone in the sand. A uncomfortable moment passes with Baw-Face staring forlornly at the toxic puddle at his feet.

"Where urr yeez fuckin' fae?" he eventually asks in a guttural, low- pitched voice, eyeing Dave suspiciously and stroking the crossbar of his ill-fitting bike on which I can just make out the faded, semi-peeled letters G R I F T E R.

"Arthurston." He replies sounding outrageously polite in comparison to Baw-face beside him.

"Fuckin' Arburston!" he looks thoughtful" Fuckinnn... Aye... Fuck......... Where the fuck is Arburston? An' fuckinnn….." he looks like he's about to say more but again the nauseating sound of the electro-glockenspiel wafts out of the car and Baw-face looks past Dave again, knocked off his train of thought.

Dave sighs and, more in hope than anything else, says "Nearest pub?"

"Ahm no fuckin' telling yiz!.... Fuckinnnnn...aye.... Bastardin' forrinners'"

"You're not telling us?" Dave drawls in an exaggeratedly tolerant tone, "Foreigners! Oh for fff... "

Dave turns to me wide eyed and shaking his head . "Craig lets go!" he yells over the stereo then makes to wind up the window.

"WAIT!" Baw-face shouts anxiously, rummaging around his trouser pockets in a disgusting manner.

His panic stops us momentarily in our tracks.

Brandishing a couple of pound notes and some coppers he drawls "Giz a '99', a Black Man, a bottle o' Bru an' a fuckinnn Toffee Crisp!"

Dave looks skyward for Devine guidance, hesitates only briefly and with a 'wagon ho! 'tilt of his pointing finger we are off up the road leaving Baw-face standing in battle stance, waving a handful of ragged notes in the air.

"Stop here!" cries Dave a hundred yards or so farther up the wide expansive main road. I stop the car again to find us once more in front of the Double A entrance. Dave sharply winds the window down again.

"Hi, can you tell us where the nearest pub to the football stadium?" he asks not without an air of trepidation.

The guy, who has wandered over to our car, smiles. Thin, silver rimmed glasses, an Africa–Corps type cap and the suggestion of shaved blond hair give him the air of a sensitive nazi. The sort who appears in war-movies, mid- interrogation and apologises for the behaviour of the attending psychotic SS officer before delivering the standard line 'I am sorry, veee are not all barbarians like him."

"Sure," the chap says in a friendly manner, "You lookin' for a pint before the game then?"

"That's it." says Dave enthusiastically, "Any suggestions?"

Colonel Clink looks at his watch. "Well I would have gone to the West End Bar back down the road there – its probably the best pub in the town - but now that you're this far up you could try 'The Albert'. Its just up a bit and on your right there." The guy looks momentarily thoughtful "Although nowadays it's like a morgue in there, mostly old guys watching the horse-racing. To be honest you'd be better biting the bullet and heading up to the stadium itself. There's a small bar open under the main stand. Its not much cop but at least you're there, close at hand for the game starting."

"You heading up yourself" Dave asks passing the time of day.

"Absolutely," comes the savouring reply, "Wouldn't miss Scottish Cup 3rd Round Saturday for the world - a big crowd and a bit of niggle - can't be beaten!"

"Well listen, we're going up right now, can we give you a lift?"

Clink looks left and right then glances at his watch. A smile once again breaks out on his face.

"That would be great guys, I'm running a bit late to get my mates as it happens. You'd bale me out, thanks. "

Dave gets out and springs the front seat forward. Just as the guy is about to duck into the car a red-faced man on a bike that looks just too wee for him powers past with legs pumping at a ridiculous rate of knots. Baw-face is blowing hard and makes no effort to slow down. As he draws level with the car, he shakily points his left arm straight out at us and through his puff he yells, scarlet and trembling with visible fury, "TELL 'EM FUCKIN' NUTHINNN!" and with that, he sails off into the distance. We all follow his path then look at each other in bewildered fashion. The silence is only broken when Colonel Clink sighs "If only that sort of thing was unusual round here…"

He's about to go on and make some sort of sage social comment when a confused expression spreads on his face, he sits a little closer to the edge of the back seat, briefly hums a few bars along to 'The Theme from The Third Man' then says slowly and very deliberately.

"You've not got a Mr Whippy machine in here have you?"

4.

'Diamonds are forever' sang Welsh wriggly-mouthed crooner, Shirley Bassey. It was a song she was moved to perform, aged twelve, whilst presenting the 1924 Scottish Cup to Airdrieonians captain , George McQueen after their surprise Ibrox victory against a shell-shocked Hibs eleven. Wearing a spangley red dress and white FMs she congratulated each Airdrie player individually before entertaining them with a second tune, a sultry jazz number entitled 'Boot the crap out of 'em boys', a song which sentimentally would later be adopted as the club anthem.

But forever is a long time. Ask anyone who's watched a whole edition of 'Machair'. And on the 1st of May 2002, one hundred and twenty four years after the club's inception, 'forever' no longer became an option to Airdrieonians Football and Athletic Company Ltd when they sensationally became the first club since Third Lanark to go out of business and lose their position as a member club of the Scottish League. For Airdrie's small band of faithful fans, dismal times indeed and we'll come back to that later. For the moment though lets step back those hundred and twenty four years to a happier age when life was simpler, the offside rule was understandable, and few if any in the realms of football, had even heard of administrations, insolvency practitioners, creditors meetings and the like.

Formed in 1878 as Excelsior, this team from the quaint weavers' town of Airdrie (latin for 'Dry wind of the Anus') took little time in making their mark. Indeed early records show the club's first decade as being a notably eventful one. First up their home ground of Mavisbank Park interestingly bore witness to the world's first penalty kick, taken and clinically converted by a Royal Albert player exotically known as 'The lad McLuggage'.

Following on from this momentous event the team name was then changed to Airdrieonians (*not* Airdrieonions as I once amusingly noticed on the scarf of a young Diamonds fan visiting Wilmot Park), and with this new elongated moniker came an impressive number of early victories, non possibly more so than a 10-2 gubbing of Rangers one snow- bound Saturday which remains the Gers record defeat to this day. Finally came the club's first honour via the prestigious Lanarkshire Cup, a crushing defeat of Cambuslang by five goals to one. As the Coatbridge Express reported it '.... *the young Airdrie fellows, fresh from their annual team holiday taking the waters of the local spa at Drumpellier Loch .... defeated their Glasgow opponents in fine and proud fashion . Were the 'Onians' to have shown full vigilance throughout the game and refrained from stopping to enjoy the view of the nearby Orange Walk parade, a clean sheet would surely have been secured.* '

In 1892 the club moved from the damp, unkempt squalor of Mavisbank Park to Broomfield Park, a venue that the club chairman of the time insisted enthusiastically was ' a bit less inviting." Little did he realise that in completing the move he was establishing an unnerving home that almost one hundred years later, would be cited by ninety-five percent of Scottish League players profiled in the Daily Record as being their 'Least favourite away ground'.

And why was it so bad? Well there was the pitch for a start. It was so narrow a ten year old could score from a corner, and its course, patchy surface hid a series of dips and trenches that you could comfortably repel a German invasion from. Then there was the stand. With its high frontage and wooden benched seating, it was like a mini version of Pittodrie's old main stand only with older, grumpier, more psychotic supporters housed in its centre section. Managers and substitutes sitting on the bench level just below the scalping line got it the worst but the abuse could carry. Sometimes as far as the terracing on the other side of the pitch where it would be absorbed, considered, then spat back with interest, decapitating any poor unsuspecting player who wasn't paying attention or didn't have the common sense to duck.

The rest of the ground was little better. The terracing was so close to the pitch that mental old Jakeys smelling of Buckfast tonic wine whispered in your ear when you took a shy. A narrow blaze track ran round the pitch ensuring that when you were dumped unceremoniously out of play, fairly or otherwise, you would spend three weeks picking red ash out your hair, toes, ass and the big sceptic gashes on both your knees. As if things weren't bad enough, the changing- rooms were housed in a small Pavilion Stand sitting in the North-West corner of the ground. Assuming the players and officials safely negotiated the low cemented stairs leading to the pitch without breaking an ankle, the first volley of abuse from the 'posh' seats perched high above them in the Pavilion's rickety wooden body, would be enough to send a distasteful shiver down the most muscular of backs.

History tells that in the last competitive match played at Broomfield a talented and accomplished Dunfermline side missed out on promotion as they fell to a mediocre Airdrie team with little to play for in competitive terms, and this pretty much sums Broomfield up. A man-trap for skill and ambition, a trip wire for the cocky swagger. Broomfield was a horror story for away teams and worth a goal of a start to Airdrie, and when it was finally bulldozed in the summer of 1994 you could almost hear cheers in the wind from past players, managers, club and match officials, journalists, and away fans all of whom were no doubt ecstatic at the thought of never having to play there again.

It will come as no surprise then that I quite liked it.

5.

Due to their relative size and provinciality, the modern Airdrieonans were a club who pretty much acquiesced to their role as hearty also-rans of the Scottish game. But it wasn't always like this. The 1920's saw The Diamonds emerge as a real powerhouse in Scottish football. Without ever managing to break the predictable Old Firm stranglehold, they came runners up in the league to both Rangers and Celtic no fewer than four years in a row from 1922 to 1926. Their cup win in '24 offered some consolation however few would disagree that the record books don't properly reflect the greatness of the Lanarkshire team at that time.

Under the managerial reigns of Willie Orr, that Airdrie team of the 20's boasted a formidable array of promising youth and seasoned professionals. Although they were a team in the truest sense, without question one name stood out on those old team sheets well above the rest of the rank and file.

That name was Hughie Gallacher .

Hughie was the 'Gazza' of his era, with a similarly controversial lifestyle and demeanour, but arguably in possession of a more prodigious talent. Working down the pits when he was fifteen, married at 17, separated aged 19; by the time the diminutive 5"5 Gallacher moved to Airdrie he had already seen more of life than most. John Chapman, the Diamonds manager of the time, who would soon make the notable leap down south to manage Manchester United, had seen Gallacher in action for Queen of the South and had been so impressed with the tenacious forward that he signed him almost immediately. The typically fickle Airdrie fans took to the young Bellshill lad like he was family and when inevitably bigger clubs came sniffing for his signature they threatened to burn the stand down if he was sold (Some tried the night he eventually moved to Newcastle for £6,500 but even with a rented blowtorch, 3 gallons of four star, and a batch of Hydrogen Peroxide, they couldn't get the old, damp structure to light.) Their fervour was warranted though for his marksmanship was keen. Despite taking extreme punishment from the defenders of the day he scored 101 goals in his four seasons at Airdrie and 24 goals in 20 games for Scotland. A member of the great Wembley Wizards of 1928, Gallacher also went on to play for Chelsea, Derby, Notts County and Grimsby.

After the death of his second wife , Hughie sadly lost his way and became deeply depressed. In a series of overblown events that culminated in him being accused of assaulting his youngest son, Gallacher heart-breakingly took his own life by stepping in front of a train near his Gateshead home. One of the greatest, most volatile, tragic and yet compulsive players in British Football history, Airdrie supporters are quite right to proudly claim him as their own.

6.

Airdrieonians FC to me, were always a bit of a mystery. Especially in my early years of going to the football. Here was a team hailing from a wee town at the edge of the M8 with a micro catchment area, not many fans and a crappy ground. They were part time when most of the big boys had full time squads and on Saturdays more blokes got on buses from Airdrie to travel along the motorway to see Celtic and (more particularly) Rangers than from probably anywhere East of Glasgow. And yet they competed. They were always there or there abouts, challenging for promotion, signing the cream of the crop from the competition around them, and scaring the crap out of bigger teams in the cups.

HOW THE HELL DID THEY DO IT?

Part of the answer became at least semi-transparent when sponsors started appearing on shirts. To those living outwith the boundaries of Lanarkshire, Dalziel the Baker probably didn't mean much, however local coconut sponge-man, Jake Dalziel, was a wealthy old codger and a fervent Airdrie fan to boot Through his support from the shadows, players came to Broomfield over the years of a quality that today's First Division outfits could only dream of. Owen Coyle, John Watson, Alan Lawrence, Kenny Black, Jimmy Sandison were all among the modern influx but throughout the 80s a steady stream of players with reputations as the best in the lower leagues ensured that The Diamonds remained one of the teams to beat if you had any aspirations of playing top flight Scottish football.

Ahhh, those tops with the Dalziel logo emblazoned on the front. What a sad day sponsorship was for this shirt design, blighting, as it did, the ultra distinctive diamond that gave the team their nickname . It pains me to say it but the coolest design of strip in Scotland, nay Britain, *isn't* the red and white stripes of Arthurston Rovers. The colours may be right but the look doesn't quite project the panache of Airdrie's traditional white top with the red diamond. On a clear, crisp day nothing looks quite as striking or distinctive as the lads from Lanarkshire lining up to get stuck right into you.

And some fair players have pulled on that diamond jersey over the years. Hughie Gallacher, as I've mentioned , perhaps tops them all but others have followed that are also worthy of mention. Forward, Bobby Flavell, veteran of nine years at Broomfield, became the first British player in modern times to move abroad for serious money when he signed in 1950 for Colombian cracks Millionarios, a made up 'Roy of the Rovers' type name if I ever heard one. For 'El Flavio' however, the thrill of playing alongside a certain Alfredo Di Stefano could never hope to compare to the feeling of lifting the Lanarkshire cup or scoring a pre-season winner for the Diamonds in the heaving rain at Stenhousemuir. And while the frequent flyer air-miles he clocked up between Bogota and Glasgow were all well and good, Flavell's record of 'Scottish footballer to experience most rectal cavity searches by UK Customs'[9] eventually led the wayward Diamond back to the safety and comfort of his beloved Scotland.

And there were others. The great Stanley Matthews incredibly wore the Diamond once in 1940 when he guested for the club in the Scottish War Cup and a young Bob McPhail started out with Airdrie before going on to an illustrious career at Rangers.

Now here's a quality sports quiz question – 'Which Prime Minister also went onto become the President?'. Hang those anoraks up folks, Ian McMillan, the 'Wee Prime Minister', also holds a special place in the hearts of the Airdrie faithful. As a Diamond in the 50's he represented his country five times and established his reputation as one of *the* gentlemen of the game - He would   complete his 20 year career encompassing spells at Airdrie and Rangers without receiving a single booking,

---

[9]   Source - Peeworthy's Sporting Facts& Records (4th Edition)

something you couldn't hope to achieve for over twenty minutes these days. In his time at Airdrie McMillan has been a ball-boy, a player, reserve team coach, manager (twice) and shareholder. These days he has added the positions of director and Honorary Club President to the various other roles he has fulfilled at the club thus answering the earlier question and staking himself as one of, if not *the* greatest servant to the club in its long, and latterly turbulent history.

Final honourable mentions must surely go to Drew Jarvie with his Bobby Charlton wrap around hair-do, chisel-chinned legendary captain courageous, Derek Whiteford and Jimmy Crapnell who may indeed be the club's most capped player but who ultimately can't escape the fact that his surname sounds like a slang word for the toilet. Schooldays must have been hard for The Crapmeister no matter how you look at it - Kids, after all, can be so cruel.

These men, and many others like them have been wearing the diamond through thick and thin since 1912. The design has been a constant in the ever changing face of Scottish football, recognisable by everyone with even a passing interest in our game. It's a funny one but every time I catch the horseracing on TV and see a 'silk' with the popular diamond design I involuntarily think of Airdrie. I wonder how many hopeless nags have had money stuck on them over the years at telephone-number odds by sentimental Airdrie fans just so they can shout for the diamond down the final furlong. Lots I'll bet, especially round Grand National day.

Asides from those few early pre-1912 years when the team uncharacteristically experimented with both vertical and horizontal stripes, the club admirably haven't deviated from the diamond design in any way. With the exception of one season; In the year 2000, the start of the new millennium and notably also the year the club first hit the skids financially, Airdrie turned out in a manky 'Avec' red and black tram-lined fiasco which must be a fair shout as a Jersey Hall of Shame entrant . Quite a step for the incumbent board at that time you'd have thought - spend all the money *and* get rid of the diamond. They must have been well popular down Airdrie way. An ominous lesson is there to be learned for anyone with the temptation to mess with Old Man History though;

Tinker at your peril.

7.

Filed under Memory B, and I'm going back a bit here, were the Lanarkshire club's old programmes. On my first trip to Broomfield my Grampa bought me this red, white and black tent cover which, on closer inspection, turned out to be the man-sized Broomfield Bulletin. The thing only had about 6 pages but it took you all game to read it and, holding it straight out in front of you, not only made you feel the size of a hobbit, it rendered you frighteningly susceptible to random gusts of wind catching you and blowing you over the wall back into the street outside. As a shrewd sales ploy, you had to buy the said 'Bulletin' in order to get the half time scores from the rest of that day's games. Instead of announcing them over the PA, a wee man would plod round at the break and hang the scores onto a board mounted on the advertising hoardings behind the away end goals. Each game was allocated a letter, usually A to L or M , which would correspond with the fixtures of the day as printed in the programme. How the club ever went out of business with ingenious money making schemes like that on the go I'll never know.

Perhaps predictably, 'we' of the First Division waved good-bye to The Diamonds in season 79/80 when the part-timers secured promotion to the Premier League for the first time in their history. With enthusiastic ex -Ranger Bobby Watson at the helm and a youthful local lad called Sandy Clark banging in goals aplenty, their team of teachers, miners, engineers, plasterers, salesmen and civil servants miraculously retained their top tier status first time around and only succumbed to the vice-like grip of relegation the following year when a peculiar glut of PTA meetings, tax enquiries and Aimes-taping contracts completely scuppered the

Diamonds usually rigid and cohesive post Coronation Street training sessions.

It was to be season '91/'92 before the Premier league would see Airdrie again and although manager Jimmy Bone led the club to the First Division runners up position behind Jim 'Anaesthetic' Jeffries' Falkirk, it was another ex- Rangers stalwart, Alex McDonald who would pick up the Premier baton and ultimately lead the Broomfield revolution successfully into the nineties.

Under the increased glare of the press spotlights, The Diamonds proceeded to make life iron-tough for anyone who dared to enter the same field of play as them. So much so that that headlines such as 'Rough Diamonds' and 'Beastie Boys' became regular fixtures atop the team's match reports in the Sunday sports pages, reflecting their *alleged* excessively physical approach. I say alleged as the hatchet-men reputation never quite held true for me. I saw that team on numerous occasions before they were promoted *and* subsequently on TV. To be honest they didn't seem that bad to me, in fact if anything they were a bit lightweight. With diminutive fullbacks and players like the skilful Alan Lawrence and Davy Kirkwood, the elegant sweeper Jimmy Sandison, and stick- man Owen Coyle, most of them couldn't tackle a ninety year old blind man with weak ankles, heavy shoes and a sign round his neck saying 'Tackle me, I'm not as strong as I look'. That said Walter Kidd and Kenny Black clearly needed a licence and a muzzle at times so maybe the team was better 'balanced' than I remember.

However the press love an angle and its fair to say that with the Diamonds they widened it as far as they could. Not that the image necessarily hurt Airdrie at the start. They formed a circle and created that inspirational Alex Ferguson-type siege mentality and as our impressionable whistlers got tetchier, the Diamonds got more committed to the cause. Except the wedge being forced between the club and the establishment would eventually grow and grow until it became obvious that a point of reckoning was approaching, and when that point came, the club would truly suffer.

And I think I can picture that very moment of reckoning to this day. Its like the JFK assassination for conspiracy-sympathetic fans of underdog teams the world over. On the 24th September 1991, during the league cup semi-final between Airdrieonians and Dunfermline played at Tynecastle Park, Edinburgh, referee David Syme drew blood when he became party to the most blatantly suspicious refereeing decision seen since Willie Young's final set of annual sprint test results. With The Diamonds cruising to an historic one-nil victory which would take them into their first ever League Cup final, a loose and hopeful punt was unleashed by Dunfermline high and handsome into the glare of the Tyncastle floodlights. When it came down to earth there wasn't a Pars player within thirty yards of the ball. Such tactics were meat and drink to the reliable Jimmy Sandison who controlled the ball and returned it with interest. That was when Syme blew for the penalty. Despite the fact Sandison had taken the ball on his *chest*, a yard or so *outside* the box, the ref gave a penalty. A bemused Dunfermline outfit blessed their luck, converted the kick and went on to final, settling the tie after extra-time and penalty kicks.

I know this happened. I saw it on Sportscene. And I watched it over and over as a head-shaking Dougie Donnelly and the normally non-committal studio pundits failed to rationalise the decision in their post match summaries. Its in situations like this that you question the overall, consistent impartiality of some refs in our game. Syme *had* to have had an agenda to award that kick. In fact you see ref's do it quite frequently. A ruck of jostling players at a corner, the ball swings over and the guy blows for a penalty having seen the slightest of infringements somewhere 'midst the ensuing bedlam. To see these things means you're *looking* for them to happen and to be looking in such a peculiarly fastidious manner clearly displays a bias against one team – it must.

The motivation? One can only speculate. Past conflict between a player and the referee may be at the root of things, the 'reputation' of certain players may have whistlers reacting out of preconceived notions. Perhaps the club or the manager previously 'disrespected' the ref in some way or maybe a supporter likened the man in black to the illegitimate son of a traffic cop, who knows. I just think once in a while something flips with these guys and if you're lucky, whatever slanted judgement he meats out on your team doesn't do too much damage. And if you're unlucky, you're Airdrie – and its no final for you my lads.

8.

The success of Peter Kay's mind-numbingly cakky cover of 'Amarillo' was to be a slur on Airdrie fans like none before. Every cheekily smiled line was an insult, every 'sha-la-la-la-la-la-la-la' a mocking two-fingered salute to the club's proud history. For Kay's version was by no means the definitive cover of the Tony Christie 'classic' indeed many would argue the toss that 'Airdrie for the Texaco Cup!' was actually penned well before Christie himself recorded his jaunty bilge. Whatever the odds, The Diamonds' exploits in that peculiar competition became legendary the length and breadth of Stirling Street and indeed some of the windy little back roads as well. Not that they ever won it mind, but they did come damned close.

The Lanarkshire part-timers featured in two of the early Texaco competitions. In the inaugural event of 1970 they caused a major stir by knocking out Nottingham Forest, a typical professional top-flight English side containing of no fewer than four internationalists, a soon-to-be-internationalist, three gang-rapists, two alcoholics and a crack addict. Both legs finished two apiece and the Broomfield climax became notable in that it was the first ever cup-tie in world football to be settled by a penalty shoot-out[10].

It was to be the '71/'72 competition that set the blood pumping for The Diamonds though. They started in style by dispatching Manchester City in the first round. The Maine Road team, managed at the time by Joe Mercer and the 'flamboyant'

---

[10]   Games of this calibre were previously settled by tense 'best of three' bouts of Ker-plunk! until complaints were increasingly made over the length of time it took to fix the straws and load the marbles.

Malcolm Allison, were serious challengers in England's Division 1 and it was red necks all round for the cocky English chancers when the Diamonds stole a two-two draw in Manchester then duly dispatched the light blues two-nil at Broomfield in the return leg.

Airdrie marched proudly on to the next round while the might of Manchester returned home in disgrace. Allison, a Graduate of the Big Ron College of Jingly Bling, and an all round big-mouth to boot, reportedly took the defeat particularly badly. So badly that he flounced from the Broomfield Pavilion en-route to the team bus sporting his signature garb - a sheepskin jacket , a Fedora hat and huge cigar - and stalked past a small crowd of straggling fans of both teams audibly criticising the ground and its facilities. One young lad, munching casually on a gratis left-over pie, took umbrage to Allison's disrespect for the home of his heroes' and loudly questioned the manager's ménage-running abilities. The livid fop wheeled round and insinuated that the lad was diminutive in stature and prone to engaging in sexual activities of a solo nature, at which point Allison was hit squarely on the head by the partially eaten pie with, as was reported in the Airdrie & Coatbridge Advertiser, '... much of the grease and pastry sliding down his face but the majority of the mince lodging itself in the brim of his hat.'

Amidst that small crowd of onlookers was thought to have been a young and impressionable Noel Gallagher attending his very first away match, en-route to visiting a Scottish based female cousin (he had 'bout a dozen) who reputedly had a 'one in the oven'. The incident struck a chord with Gallagher who would be moved to pen, that very night in the back of his dad's car, the lyrics to 'Don't look back in anger'[11], a song that many years later would resemble most of his other songs, would patently sound like Beatles, yet earn him shed loads of money which he would successfully use to fuel his growing obsession with cosmetic

---

[11]   Source – 'Oasis, the truth and the lies' by Ken Sigley (Tenuous Publications 2003)

surgery in an effort to look like his childhood hero, Parker the retarded 'chauffeur' from Thunderbirds.

Airdrie went on to skelp Huddersfield and Ballymena before meeting Brian Clough's formidable Derby County in the final. A nothing each first leg in Scotland paved the way for a thrilling return at County's Baseball Ground where a packed crowd saw Derby win the match 2-1 and lift the trophy. An accomplished outfit, The Rams would also go on to win the English League Championship that year. By all accounts though, the Diamonds fought bravely and may have drawn more success from the match had the referee for the day not been English, international ranking mug, Jack Taylor who, on blowing the final whistle, hugged Derby forward Kevin Hector, pulled down his own shorts to reveal Cross of St George boxers, sang two verses of God Save the Queen (which a number of the Airdrie contingent stopped complaining and joined in with) before accepting a brown paper package from Clough and disappearing happily down the tunnel.

You can't keep a good team down though and Airdrieonians would soon ultimately scoop the Lanarkshire Cup again in front of 67 fervent fans at Albion Rovers' Cliftonhill (many were still on holiday in Skegness while the rest were understandably put off by a particularly icy Glasgow Fair deluge.) They also went on to reach the 1975 Scottish Cup Final where overly adventurous tactics cost them a 3-1 defeat at the hands of Celtic and then of course there was that successful Premier league season in 1981 where the Diamonds held their own and finished a creditable seventh in a tight league of ten.

But there's resources and there's resources and a team like Airdrie, who were and are essentially a First Division team, couldn't hope to maintain such heady living indefinitely. In these situations, gravity has a nasty habit of kicking in, and the Diamonds returned from whence they came the richer for their Premier League experiences but in their heart of hearts, understanding their role as plucky over-achievers.

9.

But plucky over achievers or not, on Wednesday the 5th of May 2002 , through a combination of mismanagement, an overly adventurous bid to conform with the Taylor Report, an extended period of ground-sharing with Clyde at Broadwood (in which 20% of their season ticket holders died of hypothermia) and some questionable liquidation shenanigans, Airdrieonians Football and Athletic Company Limited as a business entity finally bit the dust. Newspaper reports of the time were sketchy, with few journalists grasping, or indeed caring about, the complex issues that would ultimately conspire against the club and frustrate its loyal supporters seemingly at every turn.

Unlike Motherwell, Dundee and Livingston who had also flirted with the dark spectre of insolvency, Airdrieonians' administration process was dogged with problems. These problems were related in no small way to the involvement of opportunist businessman Bill Barr, owner of Barr Construction, the company who had built Airdrie's new 10,000 seater stadium a few years earlier. Those loyal to Airdrie felt that Barr, who was then the chairman of Ayr United, had protracted the process to his own ends and had been, at best, 'difficult' for potential investors to deal with. The hourglass eventually ran dry on the Lanarkshire club and with no credible takeover bids on the table that could satisfy the demands of the liquidators or Mr Barr and his fellow creditors, the doors of Excelsior Stadium were locked. Meanwhile in typical Diamonds spirit, the team soldiered on under the creative stewardship of Ian McCall and, under the darkest of circumstances, incredibly ran Partick Thistle a close second in the race for promotion to the Premier League.

With the league decided and slim hopes of survival extinguished, one more game was left to play on the 27th April '02. Players contracts would run out after the match and then The Diamonds would be done. Irony of Ironies. That final game - It was away to Ayr United and their ever-popular chairman …. Bill Barr.

10.

Airdrie broke the bar but the Barr broke them.

The club's last game in senior football lasted precisely 21 minutes before being abandoned on police advice. With Ayr winning one-nil, and the away fans in a state of wild, mad-eyed hysteria, a faction of Airdrie supporters stormed the pitch, reached Somerset's Railway End goals and in protest of Barr's involvement and the liquidator's handling of the whole affair, they brought down the crossbar . The game could not continue and Airdrieonians bowed out of senior football in circumstances which some would call 'shameful' and others would claim to be 'justified through provocation.'

Looking incredulously at the pictures of those ruined goalposts in the paper the next day I was instantly reminded of a similar incident from my childhood. It all happened up at Jubilee Park in Arthurston during the summer holidays following my first year at the High School. We had been playing a nineteen-a-side bounce game with kids from the other side of town all afternoon and, in testament to the importance of the match, instead of using jackets and tops as goalposts we had erected 'proper' goals fashioned from six rusty oil drums with a line of thick string stretching across the divide as the crossbar . The sun was shining, the heat was intense and the niggling that frequently punctuated such encounters amongst young boys had grown and grown over the long, hot afternoon. Being bigger than us to a man, all the dodgy decisions were going the other team's way. There was much backhanded moaning about this but little audible complaint from us and when we had the gall, at around half past four, to take the lead for the first time in the game, the big boys started cheating like blazes. Its worth mentioning now that self-proclaimed hard-man 'Big Jeff' aka 'The Cleaver' had joined our ranks for the day. He didn't hang around with us much and was the sort of acquaintance who you welcomed uneasily, remained uncomfortable with while he was around and breathed a sigh of relief when he went on his way again. So far his input to proceedings had been negligible since, like most of his type, he was a rotten football player who had no balance, less coordination and kicked the ball like a player from the old kids' football game 'Striker'- not that anyone ever had the guts to point this out mind. However he was here, he was on our side and tellingly, he was getting frustrated like the rest of us.

So, after our hefty opponents had disallowed two further perfectly good goals and hammered wee 'Rash' Buchan into the air just as he was about to score a brilliant solo effort, Jeff seemingly had had enough and took a total 'maddy', sprinting ungainly towards our goals yelling indiscriminately as he went . Once there he launched himself at the string crossbar and yanked it to the ground tipping over two of drums and knocking Jamesy Johnson's 'Grand Nationals' clean off his face.

Shouting 'I am The Cleaver and the Cleaver says NO!" he pointed savagely at a tall, bug-eyed lad in the other team who had obviously annoyed him more than the others, then ran off in his inelegant manner into a clump of nearby bushes. In reality it transpired 'The Cleaver' had been called in for tea by his mum and was back half an hour later with red spaghetti hoops stains on the corners of his mouth and more down his front. It may have been infantile, it may have been daft but the political message was loud and clear – Unfairness will not go unchecked, especially around meal times.

11.

So Airdrieonians died. Possibly in a web of deceit worthy of a Shakespearian play, possibly not. But they died nevertheless. Even in death though, the controversy surrounding the club rumbled on.

The one-team-short Scottish League, never fond of the obvious route, chose to reject a bid from local businessman Jim Ballantyne to reinstate a new Airdrie-based club into the league - a move that would effectively have allowed his team to start again in the lowly third division. Borders club Gretna, it was decided, was to be elected in their stead despite having no fans, a paper thin business plan and an inferior infrastructure at that time. But the League Management committee was intent on making a point of sorts. In desperation, with his hand forced, Ballantyne bought over the failing Clydebank FC who had for some time been hanging on to solvency with the aid of a life support machine. Once successful, he renamed the club Airdrie United and opportunistically picked up where 'The Bankies' had left off in the second division. The loss of the Glasgow club in the circumstances was a black day for Scottish football and Airdrie United's unpalatable act of club-cannibalism could surely have been avoided. On a plus point, the League would welcome new club Gretna into the fold safe in the knowledge that they had admitted an organisation with sound financial foundations and the potential to contribute to Scottish football in a positive sense for many long years to come.[12]

The new Airdrie United club crest features a striking, blue, two- headed bird. That the creature looks uncannily like a phoenix rising from the ashes is perhaps coincidental but nonetheless poignantly symbolic of the club's circumstances. Airdrie are a team who ambitiously looked to meet the ever changing demands of SPL stadium requirements and the frankly ludicrous Taylor report. Granted they didn't do it very well but, unlike others who sat back and did nothing or slowly, persistently worked around a policy of complaint and avoidance, they at least tried to be a part of what the powers-at-be deemed to be a developing and ambitious set-up. That their ultimate reward was financial ruin and then, ironically, exclusion from the league was yet one more exposed frailty in the moral code of the Scottish League set up. That a club such as Clydebank paid the ultimate price in the whole sorry saga is just downright sad.

Never mind. That a club still hails from Airdrie is heartening – it gives everyone a chance to learn. A chance to understand that the books must be balanced, that two perpetually empty stands in a stadium isn't necessarily advancement even if they

---

[12]   In the spring of 2008 Gretna lost their Division 1 status due to insurmountable debt and cashflow issues. Shortly afterwards they went out of business.

are all seated, and that League representatives have to take a more practical viewpoint in creating rules that are prudent as well as fair and equitable to all of its members, making sure such difficult days don't ever come around again. If these values prevail then I for one hold the hope that the next phoenix visiting the Scottish football scene is new and full of real potential and is spotted circling over the skies above the shipyards in the far west of Glasgow.

12.

Colonel Clink , real name Rik Porter, is justifiably excited by the prospect of a Scottish Cup run. In the few minutes he's been in the car he's proudly regaled us of his club's admittedly phenomenal cup record over the last decade or so. Its only when you digest the Diamonds achievements back to back do you understand the true scale of what went on through the nineties and into the new millennium. Outside of the Old Firm, the Edinburgh clubs and possibly Aberdeen, it would be fair to say that every other team in Scotland holds reaching a final or even a semi-final as a kind of exalted dream, something to be cherished due to its understandable infrequency. From 1991 to 2001 though, Airdrie reached no fewer than four league cup semi-finals, two Scottish cup finals and three Challenge Cup finals. By virtue of Rangers having already qualified for Europe as 91/92 league winners, Airdrie also found themselves as Scotland's representatives in the now defunct Cup Winners Cup. To see the UEFA flag flying high above the Pavilion the night that Sparta Prague came visiting must have made even the most optimistic of Diamonds supporters rub their eyes in disbelief (then swell their chest in pride). In typical fashion Pavel Nedved and co were made to fight all the way and only scraped narrow wins in both legs to stop Airdrie's European dream in it tracks. Airdrie's cup exploits in list form ram's home the magnitude of this small club's achievement and the details must surely bring back pleasurable memories to the Diamonds faithful.

Season 91/92 League Cup Semi Final (Lost on penalties to Dunfermline)
Season 91/92 Scottish Cup Final (Lost to Rangers)
Season 94/95 Challenge Cup final (Beat Dundee)
Season 94/95 League Cup Semi Final (Lost on penalties to Raith Rovers)
Season 94/95 Scottish Cup Final (Lost to Celtic)
Season 95/96 League Cup Semi-final (Lost to Dundee)
Season 98/99 League Cup Semi-final (Lost to Rangers)
Season 00/01 Challenge Cup Final (Beat Livingston)
Season 01/02 Challenge Cup Final (Beat Alloa)

Of course it's not the same now" Rik laments with more than a hint of regret in his voice. "We've slipped back in with the also-rans a bit. Don't get me wrong we still always manage to raise our game when we have to, but year on year we have fewer decent players in the squad. Its not like we even get a lot of credit for bringin' on new talent. The transfer rules being as the are, the bigger teams just wait 'til our best prospects are out of contract and pick 'em up for nothing. After us risking their signature in the first place, developing and training them, giving them a chance – it doesn't seem fair really."

The three of us nod in agreement. Last year we lost a young right-sided midfielder to Aberdeen. A guy who looked a real hot ticket. First sign of a bigger club being interested he was off like old meat. You can't blame the lad for it but it would have been nice, like days gone by, if a transfer fee had been involved, allowing us to get a replacement in, duck and dive a bit in the transfer market, and remain at a competitive level. There seemed to be more ... well... *sport* to it that way. Nowadays money talks and if you've got it (although there are no guarantees) you are at least in with a shout. If you haven't, you've got nae chance.

"Take a right turn just here" says Rik. We slip off the main drag, down a dip then over the brow of a hill past a dour, militaristic collection of buildings. The sign on the gate says

Tollbrae Primary School. You can almost see kiddies in football strips and netball uniforms being marched around 'the drill yard' in Hitler youth fashion. I shiver in reflex. Then, from our high vantage point amidst some nicely appointed detached villas, the tall floodlight pylons come into view.

"You'd be better parking around here," suggests Rik, "It's a short walk but it means a quick getaway after the game avoiding the car park queues."

I take him up on his suggestion and bring my car to a halt at a convenient spot down the rise and just off the road junction, outside a small grocers shop. The engine dies and the contrasting silence, free from Jonesy's 'music' is soothing to my system. We quickly pull ourselves together, grabbing coats and scarves and mobile phones. A quick wallet check and we're off joining the straggle of red and white decked adventurers who have started to make their way to the game.

13.

In front of us, acting as a backdrop to the busy Carlisle Road, is Excelsior Stadium. The first thing that strikes you is that it looks like a grey and red version of St Johnstone's McDermid Park, or is it Livingston's all-seater, flat-pack stadium before they filled in the corners, or even Broadwood with an extra end. Its safe to say the architects involved in this one didn't stay up too late being innovative, that's for sure.

As we cross the road at a set of pedestrian lights, the guys and our newly found friend Rik are debating why Alex MacDonald didn't get another job in football after he left Airdrie. After all the guy's record was phenomenal. At Hearts he was brilliant, almost breaking the Old Firm's league domination as he did, and in his days as the Diamonds manager, well that cup record speaks for itself.

"Maybe he just didn't want to do it any more." Suggests Jonesy

"Maybe when you've been the manager at Airdrie its better to go out at the top." injects Rik. We all look at him before all of us, including Rik himself, burst out laughing.

Excelsior stadium, sits slightly elevated on the brow of a small rise ahead of us. To our left a couple of football matches involving either kiddies or midgets (or both), are taking place on the wide grassy expanse of Craigneuk Park . Surrounding the park and the stadium, a grim, grey collection of council houses hang around resentfully having long given up the hope of being featured in TV's 'A place in the sun – Home and away'.

As we march purposefully up to the main stand, the tinny strain of 'Can't help falling in love with you' hangs in the air. Elvis, it would appear has left the building and we are instead being treated to a tin-flute version recorded by some Irish Wino or other. We reach the large glass frontage of the Stadium where Rik thanks us for the lift, wishes us luck and disappears into the little door he informs us is the club shop. Before doing so he points further along to the far end of the stand indicating the exact location of the supporters bar where we have been promised a convenient but under-whelming drinking experience.

And under-whelming it is. Airdrie United's Stadium Bar offers all the ambience of a Tupperware container ….. with the lid off. We are in an 'L' shaped room (the 'L' quite possibly standing for 'Lets stay for one then GTF') with canteen tables and waiting room chairs dotted around randomly. Near to the door a freestanding TV set is showing horseracing on Grandstand. How they have managed to even approach the feeling of a tacky 70's working mens' club in such modern surroundings is a 'tribute' to the interior planners sense of style. The room for all its 'lacking' is well on the road to being full and it takes me a good while to squeeze myself through to the light-wooded bar area where a small band of bar-staff, self consciously wearing red, white and black tartan tunics, are beavering away like animated picnic rugs desperately dipping in and out of a refrigerated cabinet on the wall behind them. Eventually I am served only to find that there is no draft lager on and that the fridge unit has been a smoke screen with the bottled beer in fact being the temperature of vending machine soup.

Nothing can dampen the growing expectancy of the game though and soon our warm lager's are slipping down like … emm…vending machine soup and the chat has turned nicely to our chances of actually winning a game. I'll spare the details of our in depth, balanced pre-match analysis, suffice to say that we are quietly confident.

Resisting the prospect of a second beer that holds the allure of being possibly ten minutes colder than the last one, we decide that at twenty five to three we can get away with heading round to the away section of the stadium. With an economic gathering of bottles which Jonesy dispatches on the nearest table we wander to the door and, taking a cursory glance at the Asian guys grilling each other at table-tennis on the telly, stride out into the bright, sunny daylight.

14.

Excelsior stadium for all its newness is all that's bad about today's facilities. It's boxy conformity and atmosphere sapping countenance leave you cold in its midst. The need for all-seater stadia is debatable enough. What isn't up for debate is my need to not be sitting in grounds where I have to check on the front of the match program to remind myself where I actually am and who we're playing. I'm worried that soon, most, if not all grounds will look and feel exactly the same with the only variation possibly being the views sneaking in from the unblocked corners or the variety of overpriced chocolate bars at the pie shop.

The Taylor report which instigated so many of these 'improvements' was a knee jerk reaction capable of firing a cold Mitre 5 into orbit. Let's use old Broomfield as example. Who in the their right mind could come to the conclusion that a Hillsborough type of accident could ever happen at that ground. There are forty-two senior grounds in Scotland. Surely Taylor , or one or two of his buddies, in view of the major implications his findings would have on our national sport, could have taken the time to assess each venue separately and made specific allowances and recommendations? Rather than the broad-brush approach they took of course which has put so many clubs pointlessly under financial strain in order to comply.

Financial implications aside, The Taylor Report did nothing to satisfy my thirst for character and individualism. And in my admittedly romantic 'all-things- football-related' book this is a big, big issue. There used to be so much more variety in ground styles when you travelled the country and I much preferred it that way. Some grounds have still retained their unusual features while others have either 'cleared them out or the 'stadiums' themselves have been replaced by more sterile, modern efforts. As I sit in my Airdrie plastic bucket seat which feels an altogether similar experience to being on a Raith or Partick or Clyde plastic bucket seat, my mind slips off to happier times and pastures old. In a pleasant five minutes I manage to conjure up images of some wonderfully unique features from the Scottish football landscape. Features that give (or gave) away trips a feeling of place and of spectacle. The ten wonders of the Scottish football world , if you will:

1. The Hedge at Brechin – Running the full length of Glebe Park's rather sloping touchline, the spectacular big green hedge gives away fixtures at Brechin City FC the feel of a kick around in the back garden. Punting the ball high over this horticultural divide was always a good time waster although disappointingly, in these modern days of multiple replacement balls on hand, the offending 'punter' is no longer required, as a ground rule, to jump the hedge, knock on the neighbour's door and ask politely, "Can we have our ball back please?". Shame.

2. The Wall at Cliftonhill – Based on a number of loose assumptions, Albion Rovers have, in their long and sometimes painful history, missed out on £112,324.80 of gate receipts through sponging fans and cheapskate local residents viewing their games from outside the ground on a walled vantage point, high above the corner of the away terracing. This ever-present group of voyeuristic freeloaders are of predictable constitution, seldom being less than five in number and typically consisting of one man in a snorkel parka, and old bloke with a dog on a rope, a snotty lad wearing a 'Sellic tap' and a wee boy on a bike that's far too big for him.

3. The Stranraer Bandstand – Not content with providing breathtaking views of Ailsa Craig from the cliffside route to Stranraer, the trip to Stair Park offers the opportunity to stand in, sit on, walk through or simply look at, the multicoloured Victorian bandstand which sits cheerfully amidst the kiddies swings just outside the home of Stranraer FC. Not strictly part of the ground, this quaint little structure was built to commemorate the coronation of King George V in 1911. Relocated from another part of town where apparently it was obstructing traffic, it plays host during the summer months to a variety of musical renditions. Its red roof and blue and yellow supports once played host to me singing 'Nessun Dorma' supported by a choir of lunchtime beers, to commemorate a fine Fourth Round cup win. 'Nessun' and 'Dorma' were of course the only actual Italian words that made it into my 'modernised' version, nonetheless a fair few of Arthurston's more discerning supporters did comment favourably on the performance.

4. Kilbowie Park's Big Social Club Windows - Situated in the corner of the ground farthest from the nearby railway line, Clydebank's Social Club sported two rows of large windows that looked directly on to the hallowed Kilbowie turf. These heavily curtained windows would, from time to time, allow the odd sneaky drunk a brief gander at the game taking place outside of his world of booze and horseracing. This was before being unceremoniously hooked backwards into the smoke and beer by a random club official and issued with an invoice, signed by Chairman Jack Steedman, for at least half the entrance money. Our main hope, as avid away fans, was that someone would hit and smash the windows with the ball. Alas I never saw it happen.

5. Annfield House, Stirling - This was a big grey stone mansion house which figured prominently in Stirling Albion's old Annfield ground and which was used originally as changing rooms and club offices. With its slate tiled roofs, turreted brickwork, multitudes of chimneys and the Ochil Hills in the background, the building had all the characteristics of a countrified venue for an Agatha Christie murder. Unlike the pitch which regularly witnessed murder of a plainer more Scottish Football related variety.

6. The Broomfield Pavilion – Build in the days when small houses at the corner flag were all the rage (Fulham had one similar at Craven Cottage if I remember rightly), The Dunsmore Pavilion, named after local spirit merchants of the time, reeked of class and individualism. It was a tiled-roof affair sporting red and white latticed paintwork and a big white flag-pole adorned with a swirling Union Flag. The players ran out from two separate doorways at either side of the building with the away stars risking molestation by arriving home fans standing at a little red fence between the pavilion and the main stand. A couple of hundred or so seats accessed via an external flight of stairs made up its viewing capacity, and sometime before its eventual demise, these seats were enclosed by a large pain of glass, installed one would assume, to stop home fans pouring burning oil on anyone causing offence below – the away team or otherwise.

7. The Cowdenbeath Tyres – Littered around Central Park, Cowdenbeath are huge, chunky-gripped rubber tyres, presumably linked to the banger racing that goes on at the stadium when the 'Boys from the Blue Brazil' go home for their tea. I'm not sure there are as many tyres now as there used to be or if the ones left are quite as enormous, but they make an interesting feature to the ground which won ' Stadium most resembling a small, decaying communist sporting facility ' trophy at the PFA Awards five years in succession. Personally, and I'm just tossing it in there as an idea, I always thought it would be exciting to have the football *and* the stock car racing on at the same time. How cool would that be? It would certainly make throw ins a more interesting facet to the game.

8. The Kircaldy Windows – Its a chilling indictment on the design of Raith Rovers' Starks Park that the best seats in the house aren't actually in the ground at all. They do, in fact, belong in the distinctly *un*-private, upstairs bedroom windows of a small row of houses adjacent to the Main Stand side of the pitch. Owners, favourite uncles and treasured friends can sit on deck chairs in the dormer windows with homemade soup and adequate toilet facilities close at hand, peering over the Stark's Park wall at the somewhat inconsistent action below. Great if your in the mood to watch some football. Not so good if you're 'on the bone's' with the wife or girlfriend …. one would speculate.

9. Tannadice's Big Banked Corners – It's the simple little things that count in life. I used to love the old terracing design at Tannadice where the low advertising hoardings ran the length of the touchline until they reached the ends then banked thirty feet or so, in whitewashed splendour, around the corner flag. It gave the ground a strange, distinctive European look and afforded Dundee Utd supporters the opportunity to gob on the heads of corner-kick takers. Value for money indeed.

10. The Arthurston tree – Standing regally in the corner of Wilmot Park, hanging over 'The Benches' section, tickling the roof of the away stand, is 'Madelaine's Tree'. Planted in 1878 by club founder James Wilmot , the domineering mature Maple represents a rare spark of sentiment by the old man, dedicated as it was to the memory of his second wife Madelaine who had died ten years previously. As a sapling it stood in the middle of a small open garden in the corner of the original Arthurston Brewery. When the business moved however and the new stadium was built on the small hilltop site, James's son Renton insisted that despite the awkwardness of its location, the tree could not be disturbed. And so with no room for manoeuvre, the ground was forcibly designed around it leaving no option but to retain Madelaine's tree some three feet inside the West wall's perimeter.

Wonderful uniqueness and a sense of character; it used to be everywhere. And its so important to the football experience. I know its my fuddy-duddy traditionalism kicking in again but I would genuinely prefer to stand up at every game, possibly in the shadow of hedges and trees or maybe underneath leaky cow shed roofs, certainly being afforded a good panoramic view of odd shaped stands, strange little huts and assorted stadium accessories (clocks, scoreboards, floodlights pie-stands and the like). If there are any designers out there pay heed. When St Mirren's new ground goes up, or if Falkirk and Clyde's are ever actually finished I demand to see variety. Water features, big chimneys, missile launch sites, baked potato mountains who cares. Just give me something that isn't boxed Meccano – that's all I ask.

15.

And so to the game. Our pre-match predictions were right on the money. It *was* much edgier, tackles flew in sharper and harder than usual and the crowd was there every step of the way, except more so. With temperatures running high we managed to have a short altercation with a nearby 'fan' who stepped over the line in terms of player abuse. Robert Crush who admittedly has been having a poor season and indeed was not having a great game today either, was the target for the said abuse, however being called a 'clumpy c**t' and having his play likened to that of 'a big fat f**k with a f**king peg-leg' was not going to help matters and Dave rightly told the boy with the big mouth exactly that. After a bit of verbal argy-bargy where we, and a good number of folk around us, backed Dave to the hilt, the boy quietened down and let us, and presumably Robert Crush, enjoy the game a bit more.

When the halftime whistle blew we were a goal up through a Scott McLean penalty. When the final whistle blew the score-line was the same, Andy Thomson the hero saving a nail biting last minute spot kick from a nervy looking Airdrie forward who never looked up to the task. When the players left the field we stood and applauded and all was well again in our little world.

Perhaps the best moment of the game came just before half-time however, when the guy in the next seat whispered to me in an admiring tone how great I was with my retarded brother. At first bemused, I then smiled and made no effort to explain Jonesy's oral predicament, letting Chris happily chatter away and shout stuff in his unintelligible style of the day. Imagine then, the look on Jonesy's face when he had finished bawling "Mell munn Wovas!" at the top of his voice as the game finished only to catch the moist eye of the beaming bloke beside me. The guy then proceeded to ask Jonesy who his favourite player was, did he enjoy his pie at half time and were Arthurston his favourite team then? Jonesey suspiciously answered 'Hott McWain', 'yef' and 'yef' before the guy cheerfully ruffled Jonesy's hair , winked at me and disappeared off to the exit blowing his nose heftily into a big white hanky.

"Wov ee oh-kay?" asked Jonesy , his still swollen face etched with concern.

"Oh I think he's fine" I replied trying not to laugh. "I think he's just glad we're into the next round of the cup."

16.

Saturday night sitting in the glow of my computer monitor – its a rock'n roll lifestyle for sure – I'm pouring over the Arthurston Rovers unofficial web-site message-board which is 'as usual' punctuated by comments on today's game. 'On the Brew' dot-com has long been the site of choice for Rovers fans and tends to be a better source of news and views than the club run www.arthurstonrovers.co.uk site. It can however be a lot more annoying.

Our 'fans forum' message-board can often be a worthy and entertaining platform for debate amongst a cross section of the Rovers support however more typically it tends to be populated 24/7 by the same five or six characters who clearly have no jobs to go to, operate a zero tolerance approach to any opinion that isn't their own and who clearly have better IT skills than me considering the little moving-picture personal icons attached to their postings.

I don't post entries that often however tonight I have been moved to start a thread on the subject of player abuse in view of the verbal ear-bashing Robert Crush was subjected to today. Making the cogent point (I felt) that such abuse is unacceptable and is indeed counterproductive to the team's performance I went on to point out that never have I seen a player improve his game through barracking on a personal level from the stands.

The response quickly flew back from one of those ever-presents 'Wrecker07', who aggressively pitched the well worn argument 'You pay yer money, yer entitled to say what you like.'

My reply, suggesting that since I'd paid by broadband subscription, could I call him a rude intolerant half-wit without him getting unduly uptight somewhat proved my point when a volley of abuse hurtled back across the information highway concluding that I was a 'namby-pamby f**king fan-boy just on to wind him up' and that I was 'hiding behind a name he didn't recognise anyway so get tae fuck!' Ahh the power of structured rational debate.

My final posting before I shut down went pretty much as follows;

'Sorry, Wrecker07, that you think any level of personal abuse is acceptable for the price of the entrance ticket. In truth I bet you're one of those low self-esteem guys who winds players up to disgraceful levels then acts outraged and offended and howls for police action when they have the temerity to react back.

For your info, £17 does not give you carte-blanche to insult a player's appearance, disrespect his wife or question his sexual preferences. If the player is playing badly or isn't good enough for the team, its not his fault, its the manager's fault for having him out there.

And as for hiding behind an anonymous log-in name Mr Wrecker (are you of the Somerset Wreckers?), my details are at the bottom of this post . Sorry for not being as frequent a contributer to this forum as your good self which would have clearly lent my views more credence, however I have friends, other interests, and I enjoy the fresh air far too much.'

Chris Donald
24 Westview Crescent
Arthurston

At which point I got up in a state of anger, irritation and agitation and headed purposefully for the cupboard to hide - just in case Wrecker07 was on his way round to my door to get me.

Chapter 17 Strangers in Paradise

1.

All I can say is I'm glad I've got my parka on. Two T-shirts, a wooly-pooly and a tracky top are also present and correct and yet the cold is still seeping through and I'm very much of the opinion that the added layer of a vest wouldn't go amiss.

Not that I'd wear a vest mind you. Even if no one could see it I'd know it was there and it would….. well, make me feel … 'soft'. It's a legacy of my schooldays. Thinking back, there was always a certain guy in class who would attract the unwelcome attention of the hard-nuts more than anyone else, who would take more stick and get more kickings. And it wasn't because he was necessarily smaller than the others, nor did he talk more politely or even that he did homework, read books and knew stuff. No it wasn't that at all.

It was his vest.

That tell-tale shade-change above the shoulder and under the arm-pit of his shirt that acted as a call to arms to all the classroom bullies of the day. Kind of like an ultrasonic dog-whistle for neds. The unfortunate undergarment would predictably reveal itself, usually in the changing rooms before PE, as being of either white cotton variety or the strangely popular 'brown with a cream border' number. Both would typically be accompanied with thin muscle-free, milk-bottle arms dangling at the side limply. The brown and cream variety seemed to incense the thugs particularly, coming as it frequently did in a matching set format with equally lame, brown with cream bordered, nappy Ys. The poor victim seen sporting this hapless ensemble was in all honesty lucky to reach puberty. Our next door neighbour, Mr Desmond wears a vest all year round and he breeds canaries. I'll say no more.

This morning though, its cold enough for a vest. One of those biting, pinkish starts where the light is pale and wispy and the colours are all faded like they've seen too many spin cycles. The grass is crunching under my feet as I take Sparkie on her Saturday morning drag across the wintry expanse of Jubilee Park. We aim as always towards the echoing, high-pitched shouts and intermittent whistles ahead, climbing the gradual rise away from the park's main entrance. I soon make it, with a reluctant dog in tow to the edge of the first of 'Jubilee's' two ash pitches where the game is in full flow.

Time has been a great healer in respect of my views on the 'wee boys' football I used to play when I was younger. Back when I was eleven years old the pulling on of the yellow, scratchy, Admiral branded top of 3rd Arthurston Boys Brigade's football team held, at best, mixed appeal. It was all well and good during the Summer Cup at the start of the calendar and the league run-in around March but winter duties were an altogether different bag of walnuts.

The Saturday morning alarm going off at eight o clock to the accompaniment of wind and rain battering off the window sank my heart. As did the freezing last-minute ritual of squatting at the back door scraping last week's clods of mud and turf from the studded soles of my girder-soft football boots. The shivering, tired coldness continuing as we stood, as a team, on the steps of the church hall waiting for the straggling late-comers to show up so we could jump in our entourage of vehicles and head for the park. There we would be, a bunch of small boys in tracksuits and cagouls forlornly holding canvass Rucanor satchels, faux-leather Adidas shoulder bags or grasping on to dangling boots by the their long black laces.

The team was a mixed bunch made up of essentially three types of player. Wee boys that were quite good, wee boys that were no' very good, and wee boys who were mingin' but had a dad with a car.

"Where the hell's Danny?" Jim Henderson the BB captain would agonise as we hung on impatiently on the steps, now only ten minutes away from kick-off time.

One of Danny's sidekicks would waken up from his stupor to inform us that Danny 'wisnae cummin' as he was 'away tae his grans for the weekend". Jim would then loudly and angrily question why no one had mentioned this 'on Wednesday night when the team was read out' or indeed a quarter of an hour ago saving us 'hangin' around like a bunch of nuggets'. No one would be listening to him though as, by that time, we were all running to the cars , the quickest off the mark securing the prime seats in 'Big' Brian's souped up Fiat where a captive and inquisitive audience would be regaled by the eighteen year old junior officer's tales of drinking beer and touching girls in places below the neckline. Envious eyes would follow these four lucky individuals as Brian's Fiat wheel-spun out of the gravel car park and headed for Jubilee Park where we played our games. It was the same story every Saturday morning.

In the liniment smelling dressing rooms (which was strange since there was never a tube of Deep-Heat to be seen) Jim would have his weekly 'eppy' as he produced only seven of the total thirteen strips from his big, black bag before embarking on his ' How many times have I said bring the strips back washed and ironed before opening service on Wednesday nights.' lecture. The other six would then miraculously appear in various states of cleanliness, some like props from the end of an Ariel advert, others sporting suspicious brown or rust coloured stains and omitting repulsive damp-garage odours.

The games themselves remain a blur to me beyond vague recollections of icy patches, muddy puddles, tissue thin shorts that were too big and Mitre 'Mouldmaster' footballs that were to be avoided mid-flight at all cost for fear of life-long maiming. Being hit on the thigh by a dimpled Mitre Mouldmaster was every boy's fear. It happened to me once and it not only felt like my thigh had been ravaged by a shoal of pissed-off, ravenous piranha-fish, I was left with a pink and grey spherical stain on my leg, no bigger than a tennis ball, which I still had over a fortnight later.

Cut then to lying in a steaming bath around mid-day like a battle-weary gladiator. The leg that has all the hallmarks of being attacked by a dwarf with a cheese-grater due to an ill advised sliding tackle is still nipping like hell in the hot water. Fortunately it seems that all the red ash has been removed from the nasty weeping laceration that earlier Jim Henderson wiped roughly with a dirty grey window-cleaning cloth, patted encouragingly, and described cheerfully as a 'wee scratch'. Time could then be devoted to mulling over my performance of the day as well as looking forward to a pie for lunch (with HP Sauce) and pondering the prospect of witnessing yet another easy Arthurston Rovers home win - The hypothermia inducing coldness of the morning thankfully forgotten for another week.

2.

Sparkie sits patiently as I take ten minutes to watch the kids doing their stuff. The 'Near' pitch, the higher lying of the two with its line of fir trees running along the far side touchline, was always the best one to play on. The other one down the hill diagonally to my right was typically covered in puddles even in the summer. This was due presumably to its close proximity to 'Arthur's Stream' which trundled its way merrily by, into the Jubilee Woods and away. Valuable minutes could always be wasted kicking the ball into the stream and I'll never forget one classic encounter when an opponent's irate father took undue exception to the fact that we were 5-4 up and had kicked the ball into the stream for the fifth time in succession. "UNGENTLEMANLY CONDUCT!" he kept yelling red-faced and livid, every time the ball splashed into the grey running water. On the sixth time leather touched water the father could contain himself no longer and sprinted down to the water to retrieve the ball himself. We all looked on as Hyper-Dad fought to quickly prise away the ball which had wedged itself under a fallen tree trunk. We laughed as he predictably lost his footing and staggered into the shin-deep flowing water . And we stared open mouthed as he finally extricated the ball from its wooden–armed captor then instead of sending the ball back to the field of play, turned and booted the ball high into the nearby trees, screaming 'Howz that for time-wasting then!'. I guess he'd had a bad week or something.

The icing on the cake for me however wasn't the guy's outburst or his falling in the water even. It was the referee's reaction that did it. He sent the guy to his car. Seriously. Sent him to sit in his car and wait for his (totally mortified) son to finish the game. And the guy actually went! Like a sullen schoolboy he went - Priceless! Can you imagine that guy going home to his wife and being asked how the game went.

"Disappointing dear, we lost five-four but I did my bit by shouting like a madman, falling into a burn, going in a huff and getting sent to my car .... Now take off that pinny Marjory and treat me like a man!"

Ahh yes , proof if it were ever needed, that football does something to a man. It thieves his self-control and strips him of his very senses.

3.

The ball looks way too heavy as the twenty or so tiny pretend smokers chase around puffing their breath in front of them, at least half with expressions like they'd rather be gutting old fish than playing deep-freeze football at this precise moment. The ball scuffs off the crusty red surface and trundles along taking a variety of unpredictable skids and bounces.

"THINK ABOUT IT GUYS, YIZ ARE BUNSHIN!" yells a chap on the sideline who , in his long padded Nike jacket, is just a bit too seriously involved in the on-pitch activity and, in view of his animated motions, body language and too frequent verbal infractions is clearly living his football managerial dream vicariously through these kids.

"FRANNY, WEE-MAN! FEED THE CHANNELS!" he shouts in agitated fashion at a stocky lad who returns a mystified look before chasing after the ball, head down and arms pumping.

"COME ON GUYS – BUNSHIN!" he repeats, waving his arms and pacing up the line like he was in charge of the Scotland World Cup effort.

And of course they *are* bunshin'. Its what wee kids do in the Arthurston Battalion Junior Section Winter League. They follow the ball and they 'bunch'. All of them. Like a swarm of bees. Every player barring the goalies, is ignoring the position they are meant to be playing, instead homing in on the ball and flying after it in the vague hope of 'getting a touch' and scudding it ever closer to the opposing keeper who stands , at best, a third of the height of the MASSIVE looking goals behind him.

The 'manager's' team, decked out in all black Nike strips score two goals in my few minutes of spectating. The manager clenches his fist each time and hisses a 'yessss' quietly to himself.

"What's the score?" I ask casually as he brushes past me purposefully on the side-line.

"Eleven nil to the blacks," he replies without taking his eyes off the pitch." Should be twelve but that arsehole ref disallowed a perfectly good goal in the first five" he adds informatively.

"How long to go?" I raise my voice as Arthurston's own Jose Mourinho heads off up the line.

"Just about half-ti...DANNY MAN-ON!!! " he shouts, shaking his head, still not looking away from the action for even a second. In confirmation the whistle blows and the teams scuttle off to their respective sides of the pitch for hot orange and a gee-up by their respective 'benches'.

I look into the beautiful pink skyline and head off, with my dog on its lead, towards the alien sun. A red sky in the morning's a shepherds warning as they say. Not a good omen as we travel this afternoon to Celtic Park playing catch-up to the league and facing a towering Celtic team with only two defeats to their name this season.

To make matters worse we have now gone eight league games without a win and in that time only a solitary point, from our one-all draw at home to Aberdeen a fortnight ago, has been forthcoming. Adding insult to injury or injury to insult I should say, Ray Stark pulled ligaments in last week's 3-1 mauling at Hibs and it would appear he will be out for at least a month. Who's going to not score the goals we're not scoring now then?

As I leave the young lads enjoying the game behind me I take one more , almost rueful glance over my shoulder and not for the first time I wish I was back there. No responsibilities or pressures, with my whole life in front of me again.

I feel anxious. I'm not sure why but there's a growing, unsettling panic in me that has me worrying or over-complicating things at the drop of a hat. I was sure that once I had knocked the Heidi 'thing' on the head I would feel better, and for a while I suppose it did. But I'm noticing an almost constant angst creeping in to my day to day thoughts and actions. Just little things really, but lots of them. In the supermarket I've started getting paranoid that they don't take into account my 2 for 1 offers I've picked up. In the petrol station I can't put a drop of petrol in the car without first checking (sometimes twice) that I have my card on me to pay for it. I haven't bought a CD or a DVD in months that I didn't agonise over in case it was rubbish and it would be construed as a waste of money.

And then there's the stuff I'm putting off doing. Paying bills, renewing insurances, going to the dentist, getting my eyes tested. Not that my actions actually seem to matter anyway. Even if I do attempt to sort things out I remain surrounded by confusion. I'm living in a world of banks that lose my information, Indian call-centres that don't understand what I want, cars in constant breakdown mode and wallets that get lost under spooky , inexplicable circumstances. I'd book myself into rehab if I could honestly come up with something damaging that I needed to give up. Maybe its the football – maybe its eating my brain.

4.

1888 was a hell of a year. Jack the Ripper spent much of it introducing himself personally to a number of young ladies' innards, Van Gogh cut off his own left ear, John Gregg first published Gregg's Shorthand (surprising many down Ibrox way who weren't aware he could even write) and, purely coincidentally I must stress, the first deodorant was invented by the Mumm company .

For it was also the year in which Celtic FC officially played their first match beating Rangers 5-2 in a 'friendly encounter', a match that the BBC impartially reported as being 'a travesty of the Queen's justice and a scurrilous victory for pure, concentrated evil over God's chosen messengers.'

It had all started one year earlier when a devout and religious fellow called Andrew Cairns felt moved to do something to alleviate the poverty and squalid living conditions suffered by the immigrant population of Glasgow's East end. Brother Walfred, to give him his Sunday 'Marist' title, founded the club specifically for this purpose and in doing so also created 'The Poor Children's Dinner Table' charity, which raised money to provide platters of spaghetti hoops, Iceland fish-fingers, spam and strawberry pop-tarts for many Glasgow households of the time.

Inspired by the success of Hibernian over in Edinburgh, Walfred sought to create a team in Glasgow which could compete against the slick capital outfit as well as existing for the betterment of the Irish workers of the Clydeside. The former was achieved relatively quickly. As we've already noted, Hibs rapidly found their first team squad plundered by Celtic's already superior cash resources and on that momentous first day victory had no fewer than eight 'guesting' Hibernian players in the ranks. The 'guests' ultimately chose not to leave and while the Edinburgh team lost the core to their success overnight, Celtic looked well prepared for domination straight from the offing.

And dominate they have done. In the years since 1888, they have to date won the Scottish League title on over forty occasions, the Scottish Cup 33 times and the League Cup 13 times. Together with arch rivals Rangers they have, over the years, dampened the enthusiasm and sporting resolve of more managers, players and supporters of opposing teams than any weekend dose of the common cold could ever have done. And the Old Firm fans love it. For them, this is how it should be.

5.

And this is how it is. As we dig our way through the first decade of the twenty-first century both teams' superior resources now dictate that they really shouldn't ever be beaten over the course of a season. *Of course* they shouldn't and they seldom are. This sense of inevitability doesn't dampen the elation of winning for the big two's fans however. Their elation at, what is, in essence, the beating of each other knows no bounds and winning is in every way expected which is fair enough I suppose.

Except it becomes difficult for all the rest of us to put up with the moaning and angst when they don't win. Because when they don't, all hell breaks loose. The 'Devine Right' kicks in. The Devine right to win everything, always and forever. The Devine right to stamp collective feet like spoiled children during the momentary blips rather than sit back and patiently accept how lucky they are that another cup or championship is, in reality, just round the corner.

Celtic fans were better for a while. Wait, I'll qualify that. The 16,000 or so *loyal* fans who turned up in the 'darkest' days of '94 were better. Amidst Rangers '9-in-a- row' dominance of the nineties there was an air of humility about Parkhead and their support became much like the rest of us. Unhappy and disappointed but steadily more understanding of defeat. Unsure, hopeful of future success, but more accepting in their uncertainty ..... for a while.

But things inevitably got better. As they do for a club like Celtic. Managers Wim 'the perm' Jansen and Dr Josef Venglos (surely the name of a Nazi war criminal with a penchant for static electricity) stopped the rot and expectations slowly started to rise. By the time Martin O'Neil had woven his magic the 'Devine Right' was again prevalent with the slightest hint of a poor domestic result or performance once more sparking intolerant insurrection in the masses.

And the press stir the pot. If either Old Firm club lose three in a row or God forbid, fall momentarily below third in the table, the troops are whipped up with 'Club in Crisis!' headlines and radio phone ins inviting, stimulating and accommodating fan outrage by simply offering a forum for the more extreme views going around at that time . They know that the Devine Right is always there with some folk. Smouldering away in all its unjustifiable glory. They just need to press the right buttons.

'Celtic in 15-minutes-without-a-shot-at-goal-at-Inverness fiasco. CLUB IN CRISIS!'

Get real.

Complaints of Old Firm 'trials and tribulations' in a playing sense are a slap in the face insult to fans who, week in week out, really do face the thin end of the wedge. Griping about disastrous Old Firm form is like running through the Cancer ward complaining of a runny nose. Hibs have faced amalgamation with their bitterest of rivals. Dundee, Motherwell, Airdrie, Thistle and Livingston have all stood *properly* at the brink of extinction. East Stirlingshire have lived with almost constant failure for years now. A gaggle of clubs will never know anything other than the lower leagues and face relegation and financial uncertainty *every* season they step onto the August grass. *These* are clubs in crisis. These are fans with real issues.

And yet its all part of the play isn't it? Another facet to the storyline, another character in the cast. They'd cut their hands off rather than admit it but most Celtic and Rangers fans view their teams in a broadly similar manner. They have evolved into similar beasts with similar expectations, with the same intolerances and the same motivations.

Similar except for possibly one differentiating feature....

Celtic's paranoia.

..... Celtic's deeply contagious, constantly smouldering, wonderfully entertaining paranoia.

Yes entertaining. It's a cheap shot but I'm allowed. Its all I've got really. I'm never going to be able to 'lord it' because my team is better on the pitch than Celtic, and Celtic are never going to implode on themselves to the extent that I sympathise and feel no longer able to have a little snicker at their inconsequential little frailties, so for now I can talk about the paranoia with an easy mind. In fact I can feel the corners of my mouth twitching already.

Its unfaltering you see. Year on year managers, directors , players and smatterings of the general public remonstrate about Celtic's treatment by all and sundry in a particular manner that, in their opinion, more than implies that everyone is out to get them. To certain individuals, the SFA will always be looking to disadvantage their club. Certain referees will always be against them , fixtures will be organised to disadvantage Celtic FC as much as possible and leagues will be 'fixed' to ensure that Celtic lose on the last day through the suspect performance of other teams and certainly through no fault of their own.

And this psychosis seems to affect everyone who goes near the club way beyond any concerns prevalent in any of the other Scottish clubs. Normal, balanced individuals seemingly take a breath of Parkhead air, disappear behind the couch, then reappear as mad-eyed, slavering cynics with enough chips on each shoulder to pave the M8, the A9 and still have some left over for a small feature at the bottom of the garden.

In 2001 rumours were rife of a shocking, no-holds-barred press release which would voice the club's displeasure at their general treatment once and for all. For a number of reasons 'The Paranoia Statement' as it was known, never saw the light of day. An unnamed source deep with MI5 however recently leaked its contents amongst other politically sensitive documents such as The Princess Diana car crash file, missing drafts of The Hutton Report and the manuscripts of the eighth JK Rowling masterpiece 'Harry Potter meets the Wife-swappers'. This is the first time the public have viewed the contents of this sensitive and provocative statement and one can only suggest that care must be taken in its interpretation. It is reproduced below in its entirety for reference only and no responsibility as to its accuracy or validity rests with this author or those associated with the document whether alive, dead or in a state of pleasant inebriation.

Celtic Football Club Ltd
Press Statement : PS274FM
Date : 15/02/01

'In response to a plethora of perceived attacks and undermining criticisms on and of Celtic Football Club, we as representatives of Celtic Football Club, feel the time is right to make known certain of our own observances. For make no mistake, we are aware of, and are sensitive to the aforementioned æattacks and criticisms'. These are not loud, obvious attacks and criticisms but quiet whispers we can definitely just about make out when we turn the TV right down. It must be stressed that we, as individuals and as an organisation, are not paranoid. We do not like this word. We do not necessarily feel the whole world is against us as we concede there are many predominantly water based areas non-supportive of human life, however we would take this opportunity to cite a number of concerning incidents which we feel may or may not be linked to a wider conspiracy to undermine Celtic Football Club in a surreptitious fashion or otherwise;

1. We have recently been expected to kick off a number of our matches at 3pm on Saturday afternoons. In view of our ongoing contractual obligations with Satellite and cable television

companies, such rogue arrangements are intolerable and are clearly designed to undermine the digestive systems of our players who are now unsure at what time to have their pub-lunch, when to administer the Rennies, and when to go for a dump and get a good read at the Saturday morning newspapers.

2. People are digging tunnels under Celtic Park. Late at night we can definitely hear digging noises. We don't know what they are doing but can assure these diggers right now that we're on to them, they won't find anything, and any hopes of getting in to the stadium without paying at least for a guided tour are completely futile.

3. Last Wednesday morning someone looked over the chairman's shoulder at a cash point on Argyle Street and could possibly have noted his pin number.

4. Our table at the PFA dinner for the third consecutive year was placed nearest to the toilet door. Last time we could barely taste our Beef Wellington for the smell of stale urine and liquid soap.

5. Celtic player registrations are continuing to be held up. We are not unreasonable but our recent clearance dated December 1999 finally allowing us to play Dino Zoff has come intolerably late for us to utilise what was a promising young goalkeeper in our first team plans.

6. The main stadium entrance off London Road is periodically being watched, we are convinced, by a bearded man in a red, Ford Escort van with the words 'Royal Mail' written on its side. He appears mostly in the mornings when the players are arriving for training but is sometimes spotted later in the

day as well.
7. Our electricity bills appear to be getting bigger. We have strong suspicions that the envelopes are being intercepted, possibly by the aforementioned bearded man, possibly by Jim Farry, steamed open and the amounts are being altered to the detriment of this club.
8. On telephoning the SPL, pressing option 2 for 'player registrations' and being placed on hold, callers experience Dean Martin singing 'That's Amore'. Play this backwards at half-speed and midway through the second verse the line 'The Celts are goat-eaters' can clearly be distinguished.
9. People are continually distracting us and putting us off what we're doing.

In respect of these circumstances and others of a similar nature too numerous to mention, Celtic Football Club are hereby formally giving notice of our displeasure and demand a formal inquiry immediately.
I would finally draw everyone's attention to the collection bucket now in circulation and ask everyone present to give generously. We are endeavouring to install a satellite surveillance system or possibly to erect a big curtain to pull round Celtic Park, whichever is cheapest. Without your help this worthwhile project may not come to fruition.

Thank you for your time and consideration.
(Pause for applause)

According to a club source who is unwilling to be named, this release was ultimately withheld on the belief that a) the club would be misquoted in another room when all its representatives had gone home, b) the club would be asked further, possibly related questions and c) No one could be trusted to read it out accurately and with the 'right intonation'.

In much the same way as Roman Catholics suffered in West of Scotland society over the last century, Celtic FC *will* historically have been disadvantaged in Scottish football through religiously motivated prejudice. Of that there is no doubt. Whether Celtic's rough treatment stretches well into the new millennium in the sinister form that some allege is another matter. Sure football's governing bodies can be petty, they are inefficient, illogical and even incompetent in their dealings but I'm thinking that at any one time there will be a whole clutch of clubs grinding their teeth and complaining that rules and situations are unfair and detrimental to their club in particular . Its not just Celtic suffering here.

I have a theory. The more fervent the allegiance a fan holds, the more passionate and sensitive their reaction is to outside treatment, criticism and opinions of that allegiance. This holds true in all walks of life and Its fair to say that everyone associated with Celtic FC are of a fervent disposition when it comes to their team. Commendably so. Isn't it fair then to suppose that through this zealous commitment to the cause, there is a heightened sensitivity to all that relates to their beloved Celtic and that it might just be blind devotion getting in the way of more objective viewing? I'm going to stick my neck out and suggest this is what its all about. There's a back handed compliment in there somewhere too - I'm sure of it.

6.

By the early 1900s Brother Walfred's firm foundations had impressively been built upon. 1905 to 1910 saw Celtic scoop five titles in a row. And over the First World War years, they chalked up another four-in-a row series of league wins. The club had already become an institution of attacking, free-flowing football, an image which would hold fast throughout the club's long history.

Naturally, huge crowds flocked to see the Glasgow giants play their attractive brand of football and in 1937 a remarkable 147,365 people crammed into Hampden Park to witness Celtic beating Aberdeen in the Scottish Cup final, a record attendance for a European club match which understandably stands today. The statistic remains even more impressive when you consider that the entire Aberdeen contingent travelled to the game in a convoy of three unicycles, a single-decker bus, a trailer drawn by an early design Massey Ferguson tractor and only numbered twenty-four in total.

Lean times would descend on Celtic Park however and while the Forties roared the Celts unfortunately squeaked. Under the guidance of former player, Jimmy McGrory, they stuttered their way through his twenty five year tenure with the highlight questionably being their winning of the '53 Coronation Cup celebrating the crowning of Queen Elizabeth II. They beat Hibs in the final of a tournament which involved the cream of both the Scottish and the English game.

Board members of Rangers were appalled by such an outcome to the extent that a formal complaint was submitted immediately after the final. Fortunately 'Its no' fair she's more our Queen than theirs' wasn't considered ample grounds to reverse the outcome and Celtic retained the trophy which still resides in the Celtic Park trophy room to this day. For their part, the men from Ibrox were left licking their wounds and with all the defiance they could muster, swore to clinch the Pope's Ordainment Shield should one ever be introduced into the Scottish football arena.

By 1965 it was clear that a managerial change was needed and so McGrory stepped down to allow a new era to begin in earnest. Fresh from his astounding successes with Dunfermline, Jock Stein was given the job of heaving Celtic out of the doldrums. The new appointment paid dividends almost instantly with Celtic winning their first Scottish Cup in eleven years. The next year would be even better with the league title coming to Parkhead as well as a Semi-final appearance in the Cup Winners Cup where they narrowly lost two-one on aggregate to a Liverpool side who would go on to lose the final to Borussia Dortmund at Hampden Park.

Onwards they strode into 1967, the year which would prove without doubt to be the greatest the club and its supporters have ever known. Recovering from the suicide inducing disappointment of England winning the World Cup the previous summer, Celtic girded their loins and by May of that year found they had won the league, the Scottish Cup, The League Cup, The Glasgow Cup and had they put a team in for the Synchronised Arse-scratching World Championship, they would have probably won that as well.

Then, with the lighter evenings, the warmer air and domestic duties done, attention moved to the club's thus far successful European exploits. The European Cup had never been won by a non-latin club , let alone a British one but there was an excitement brewing in Glasgow that wasn't totally due to Sandy Shaw winning the Eurovision Song Contest with 'Puppet on a string'.

Celtic had reached the final of Europe's premier knock-out competition and all eyes now fell on Lisbon's Estadio Nacional where now only Internationale Milan stood between them and the record books.

7.

They were Christened the Lisbon Lions by a man of unknown origins who possessed a fondness for dangerous safari animals and lethal alliteration. And they were Scottish to a man. Each and every one of them was born within thirty miles of the ground they call Paradise, indeed eight of them, due to an unscrupulous landlord called Mark Skid, 'Skid-Mark' to many wry acquaintances, actually stayed in the same house at the same time without ever realising it.

And they were a team in the truest sense of the word like none before or after. Eleven names with only one goal - to bring that big daft looking, shiny silver cup back to Parkhead. Those players were;

Ronnie Simpson (Goalkeeper)
Jim Craig (Right Back)
Tommy Gemmell (Left wing back)
Billy McNeill (Capt. Centre half)
John Clark (Left half)
Jimmy Johnstone (Outside Right)
Bertie Auld (Inside left)
Bobby Murdoch (Right Half)
Bobby Lennox (Outside Left)
Willie Wallace (Inside Right)
Stevie Chalmers (Centre Forward)

Few in the game thought that Celtic had it in them to dismantle the dour, well drilled 'Catenaccio '[13] Milan defence. Inter Boss , Helenio Herrera, an honours graduate of The Craig Brown Academy of Hingin' On , was confident his stout defence would not be breached by a bunch of hoop-adorned Johnny-Come-Latelys from Glasgow, and the cup would be winging its way to Milano before the night was out. And after seven minutes of play he looked to be Celtic's prophet of doom as his team took the lead from the penalty spot.

True to their reputation, Inter packed their defence; Herrera drawing on every nuance of the hundreds of old Meadowbank Thistle videos he had watched and memorised over the years. For an eternity it seemed like it wouldn't be Celtic's night. They pounded the Italian defence hitting the bar twice and bringing save after save out of 'Greasy' Giuliano Sarti in the Inter goal.

The West of Scotland boys didn't give up though and just after the hour mark Tommy Gemmell drove the ball home for the equalizer. The 7,000 Celtic fans in the stadium went ballistic and willed their team on to glory with added fervour. With the Italians hanging on to the ropes bruised and bloodied, the winner was struck. Gemmell again was involved, laying the ball off to

---

[13]   A system featuring no fewer than seven central defenders, a consultant doing a Powerpoint presentation on Health and Safety in the work-place, and a stereo playing 'Mull of Kintyre' on a constant loop in the background.

Bobby Murdoch who rasped a long range effort at goal . Fortune this time favoured the Celts and the ball was deflected by Steve Chalmers past the helpless Sarti. Herrera threw his arms up in the air and yelled in anguish his now legendary vow, "Curse you Signor Christie and your defensive Meadowbank tomfoolery, I shall from now on take risks like a man walking the streets of Garthamlock after dark!"

The final whistle went and hoards of Celtic fans flooded onto the pitch to engulf their heroes, nick the turf and perform a synchronised victory dance choreographed by a young Michael Flatley to music by Bono, Rod Stewart and the bloke with no teeth from the Pogues.

Twenty four hours earlier Kilmarnock had lost out in the UEFA cup semi-final to Leeds and, six days later , Rangers would narrowly lose out to Bayern Munich in the Cup Winners Cup final. For one week only, Scotland were well and truly the driving force of European football and all bowed before us . For longer than that though the Celtic team of '67 were recognised for what they were - Glorious pioneers of the British game who would never be surmounted in terms of what they achieved under the circumstances.

8.

Whenever I think of the Lisbon Lions, which is fairly frequently considering the number of anniversaries and commemorations they go through, I think of Jonesy's old next door neighbour Danny Grant.

'Not one of *the* Grants.' He would always smile and stress when first introducing himself, as if that should mean something to whoever his new acquaintance may be. Danny was a tremendously likeable man who stayed with his sister Bernadette on Delivery Crescent, Arthurston, in the small semi through the wall from the Milnes when they were still a family. Always quick with a line as he jumped out his green Austin Allegro and met us playing football out in the streets, he would tease us about our 'training to play for The 'Tic'.

'NEVER,' we would shout appalled at the thought, 'We'll play for The Rovers!'

'Good for you!' Danny would laugh before producing mint imperials from his pocket, passing them round then skipping up his driveway with a heavy looking cardboard box from Fine-Fare containing what he always explained were 'Our Bernadette's messages'.

Danny was Celtic through and through . From the day he saw his first match, Celtic beating Everton in The Empire Exhibition Cup at Hampden in 1939, he was hooked. And the day, some nineteen years later, when they beat Rangers 7-1 in the League Cup Final, well, as he tells it he was "as happy as a dog with a stick.'

So when Dukla Prague were soundly dumped in the European Cup semi-final, amidst all the euphoria *that* caused, Danny knew that plans had to be made. Money was tight though and not only could Danny ill-afford to get to the final himself, there was Liam, his 22 year old son to think of. In student digs and training to be a doctor, Liam couldn't buy a round let alone get himself to Portugal. But he would have to be there too. Danny knew it.

So Danny sold his car. His trusty, slate grey Morris Minor. Bernadette shook her head as he set off that first morning to walk the two miles or so to work and swore under her breathe that he was 'mad as a brush'. Danny made it to the Arthurston Public library for a quarter to nine where he duly commenced his assistant- librarian duties claiming to everyone that day that he 'really felt the benefit of the fresh air' and moreover 'should have got rid of the car ages ago!'.

On Monday the 22nd of May 1967, three days before the game, father and son, Danny and Liam, set forth for Lisbon. On what was to be a protracted trip of shaky bus, rolling ferry and trembling train, Danny, unused to foreign travel, was sick on three occasions. Twice in the foul smelling toilets of the claustrophobic, cross channel ferry and once over a small chatty man called

Ardel from Leopardstown who refilled vending machines for a living , kept a worm farm in his garage and was also en-route to the final. For Danny had only been abroad once in his life - a trip to Lourdes with his wife some seven years before, but that was business not pleasure. Lisbon was different. His nausea was probably two parts excitement to one part travel-sickness and in spite of his wrenching gut, Danny was captivated by all that was going on around him. All roads to Portugal it seamed, were a flow of green and white. The banter was precious, anticipation was high, and by the time the first foreign beer was consumed, in a little café bar called 'O Papagaio' , Liam had a hero in his father and Danny saw a man in his boy. Together, like thousands more of the Celtic faithful, they had been drawn to the show like hypnotised children , pushed and buffeted on a wind of hope and expectation. And in a matter of hours they knew that the world would be theirs and that they would be witnesses to its presentation

When Liam lost his ticket outside the stadium that world, *their* world stopped. Around them things seemed to speed up, crowds flashed by, snatches of singing skipped over them, but for the two statues from Arthurston, decked in rosettes and green and white scarves, the world just shuddered to a halt. Pockets were searched. Then the same pockets were searched again. Steps were retraced some way back along the five mile walk from centre of town, but amidst the grid-locked traffic chaos the hunt soon proved hopeless. Other Celtic boys were asked. No joy.

Pockets were searched again. Sympathetic smiles came from those recognising their fix, those with purpose, those heading excited and carefree for the turnstiles. One old boy with a ginger beard and matted hair that looked like the comb had just point-blank *refused*, offered to vouch for them at the gate. He didn't have a ticket himself he admitted casually but he was 'ok with that', wasn't this, after all, 'a great way to spend yer 70th Birthday?'So he said in a very serious tone .

A few painful goose-chases for imaginary spare tickets ensued and as it turned out, the bearded fellow held no sway on the turnstile. As kick off approached the dawning realisation was one of hopelessness. Five minutes before kick-off Danny shook his head and smiled at Liam. There were no recriminations to speak of as Danny sauntered over to old Beardy and gave his ticket away. Gave it away mind, no charge. Old Beardy looked set to cry as he and Danny gripped each others' right hand and looked into each other's eyes. As the old man headed for the gate he looked round every few steps fully expecting for the joke to be played but he finally disappeared into the stadium with a final wave, out of sight. Danny and Liam sat down on the concrete ground and waited.

They found out the game was on the TV in a café just down the way but they decided to sit on the pavement where they could be closer. Where they could hear the cheers. And when the final whistle blew they knew Celtic had won. It was everywhere, it was the biggest thing, too big to grasp.

When Danny told us all this, Jonesy had laughed a wee boy's laugh and said something like 'All that way to sit on the street'. Danny though didn't chortle his usual cheery response and I felt bad for him.

'That's terrible' I quickly said clearing my throat self-consciously.

'Oh no son, not at all." He said gently, 'Just being there was the thing.' Danny's gaze drifted off beyond the horizon.

'To think we were so close that night...' he went on," ... closer , probably, where we were sat, to the goalposts the boys scored into than some of the folks in the ground if you think on it. We breathed the same air as the players, and we saw the same sky. That was enough….. '

'And it wasn't about us anyway, Liam and I. We were just one sentence of one page in a big book, it was ….*more*…. much more, it was for all of us. A true success story for everyone down through the times, that we did all by ourselves and …. " he stopped and thought for a second or two and looked confused,

' But maybe it *was* all about us, you know. People still comment how awful it must have been for us but it wasn't. It was the best. Like payback for the bad times.'

'The truth is, sitting there, looking up at all those trees around the ground against the clear foreign sky, I never felt more at peace than I did that night. Aye...' he said thoughtfully, '...payback."

And with that Danny picked up the box at his feet and slowly straightened up. We thought he was going to say something about getting old, or the nuisance contents of his big box but instead he slightly narrowed his eyes and started speaking in a low, measured lilt;

Where were you when the Lions walked out
Onto warm, dark Portuguese soil
Where were you sat when the Lord paid us back
For our honest and hard working toil.

Where were you when we fell a goal down
And the candle-light flickered in fear
From Lisbon to Glasgow and roads in between
As we pulled for the things we held dear.

Did you let yer chin drop when we twice hit the bar
Thinkin fate was forever our foe,
Did yer heart hit the clouds when Tommy's shot flew
Past the keeper so hard and so low

Where did you dance when the winner went in
With the men from Milan on the rack.
Who did you hug as the ball hit the net
Defence being slayed by attack

So where were you Friend when Big Jock held the cup
With more pride than a grown man could bare
In the pub, on a shift, Whether home or away
The truth is that we were all there

Does the distance between take away from the love
Do your eyes need to witness to see
Is it yours to behold when its not there to touch
Can we grasp it or must it fly free ....

Danny opened his mouth to continue then stopped and looked at us both equally. And then he smiled and awkwardly negotiated the ever-present paper bag of mint imperials out his pocket. We took one each and said thank you politely as we always did.

"Damn Bernadette's messages!" Danny said as he wrestled his box to a more comfortable place in his arms. As he walked sedately up his driveway I remember Danny still with that contented smile on his face although I'm not sure how I know this as we were already haring back to our positions shouting 'You be Sarti and I'll be Gemmell!' as Jonesy aimed and lamped the ball past me into the gatepost goals.

9.

There was a song sung loudly and fervently that suggested 'Rangers were watching the Bill while the Celts took Seville!'. Uncharitable but probably true. For the legions of Gers fans sitting at home on the 21st May 2003 it was a potentially painful night. Collapsed on their Rangers tartan couch covers, seeing off the last of the weans' Easter eggs while flipping the channels furiously, they probably were faced with a form of TV hell. On one hand they could indeed have sampled the taught characterisation and tight woven plottery of Springhill's hard pressed constabulary. It was either that or watching their arch-rivals, the unmentionable ones, take on Porto in the UEFA Cup Final. With every other channel taken up with a variety of cooking, dodgy singing and 'clever' programmes presented by Carol Vorderman, its also probable that the resulting level of gardening and car washing that went on around Govan, Larkhall and Airdrie from eight o-clock onwards would have been enough to cause a month long hosepipe ban throughout the West of Scotland.

For it was Lisbon for a new generation. A chance for so many Celtic fans to experience what their uncles, fathers and grandfathers had done thirty-six years before. Almost 80,000 hooped pilgrims descended into the baking heat of Seville, the largest travelling support ever for a football match, in the hope of witnessing a repeat performance of that glorious victory in Portugal.

The cobbled Andalusian streets were heaving with green sombreros, grand ornamental fountains played host to sunburned backs and pink bellies and the decaying buildings and crumbling sandstone city walls watched over the biggest party the old city had ever seen. There were packed Irish bars, men in kilts, hooped-taps and trainers, marching fire-brigade bands, sweet senioritas in colourful national dress, the prerequisite big TV screens by the town hall, sunbathers on the beach and in the parks, and of course legions of fans gubbed on the beer, Guinness and Sangria. Most had no chance of a ticket and even the clever forgeries, those ones with the slightly lighter green 'footy-stickmen' logos on, were hard to come by.

A nation was captivated- Scotland almost as much as Ireland. Even Tony Blair sent a fax of hope. 'Good luck' it said warmly,' the good wishes of our country are with you ' it went on supportively 'and if you see any weapons of mass destruction lying around, for heavens sake let me know' it concluded with just a hint of panic.

But it wasn't to be . A three-two defeat with the winning goal painfully being scored by the Brazilian, Derlei in extra-time gave the blue and white striped 'simulators' (cheats) from Porto the trophy. Celtic's army of followers took the defeat on the chin though after all the sun was still shining and there was still drink to be had in Seville's bounteous taverns. Collectively, the fans won the FIFA Fair Play Award. As the governing body put it ' The supporters of Celtic FC were a shining illustration of the meaning of fairplay during their stay in Seville – Jubilant in celebration, stalwart in support and although beaten in the score-line, utterly undefeated in spirit.' Which sort of brings home what its all about. For those thinking that winning is everything , think again. Where the real appreciation lies is in community, enjoyment and getting stuck in a foreign country having missed your plane home . Fans now had their Lisbon and the memory in so many ways overwhelmed the result of the day – the score as any would admit afterwards 'wasn't that important.'

Thus the squad of 2003 slipped into dark shadow of the Lisbon Lions in much the same way as the ill-fated European Cup Final team of 1970. How often is it forgotten, in favour of reminiscing about the Lions, that Celtic won through to their second Euro final in three years meeting Feyenoord at the San Siro? They didn't have a cool nickname (The Milan Marmosets was toyed with but it just didn't sound right), and they had been defeated despite being odds-on favourites to win. Seven of the Lions team were in the team that lost 2-1 after extra time in a match that would have given Britain a clean sweep of European competition (Manchester City had already won the UEFA Cup and Arsenal had taken the Fairs Cup) but a combination of complacency, underestimation of the opposition and the promise by Daniel O'Donnell to bring out a victory record to mark the occasion undoubtedly cost the Glasgow men a trophy that should really have been theirs. If proof were ever needed that no-one remembers the loser then surely this must be it.

10.

Celtic Football Club remains an influential cultural icon in West of Scotland society. And as such they clearly take their role very seriously. With historic and ongoing projects such as Bhoys Against Bigotry, Youth Against Bigotry, the 'Celtic in the Community' coaching programme, and the 'Celtic Against Drugs', the club have responsibly tackled difficult social issues with sensitivity and concern. They are however more than capable of seeing the lighter side of life. Less well published initiatives such as the Deedlee-Dee Music Awareness Project and the Petrov Community Acting & Drama Group have also carried out sterling work in the east end of Glasgow.

While the club have always purported to be 'of' the community, 'for' the community there were many who argued that by the early nineties, the incumbent board of directors paid only lip-service to these ideals and were interested in nothing more than feathering their own nests. The Whites, Grants and Kellys were family dynasties synonymous with the ownership of Celtic FC stretching as far back as the earliest of days of the company and yet all the while they grasped tightly with white bony knuckles to the reigns of the club it became clear that, aspirationally and financially, the club would remain at best restricted and at worst compromised by their presence.

Through such inflexible ownership the board became known for its 'biscuit tin' approach to running the club. The biscuit tin itself, for a while at least, became the most talked about asset to be found within the confines of Celtic Park . Yet despite its obvious significance to the fate of Celtic FC, little is actually known about the tin itself.

Sports Historians have always argued as to what the tin actually looked like and leading on from that, quite naturally, the types of biscuit that were originally in the tin. One train of thought suggests that it was tartan in design, filled with butter shortbread and had 'A present from Oban ' etched on the lid. Another maintains it was filled with the uneaten Bourbon Creams from years of Crawfords 'Rover' Assortments that had passed through the club's offices. Gerry McNee in 1983 'exclusively revealed' on Radio Clyde that it was full of Kit-Kats however nobody believed him and he subsequently went off in a huff.

Some time in the late 80's a scroll was found in Santiago De Compostela dating back to the early first century. Written in 'conversational' Latin , the document was loosely translated as claiming ' he who is in charge of the biscuit tin will have it in him to dominate all of Scottish football'. Mysterious fireside tales are told of an ultra-secret priory of Catholic monks who carried an old and unmarked tin from its place of origin in Ireland to the east end of Glasgow before secreting it in a dark and impenetrable vault deep below Celtic Park where reputedly it lies to this very day.

Others controversially suggest that it may not be a tin at all. It may, in fact, be a person; A Devine being who would act as a talisman to the ongoing fortunes of the club. Some suggested Billy Connolly was the One, others insisted a link could be made to Gerard Kelly off City Lights who once allegedly had the Dalai Lama round for tea and a Lees Snowball but never told anyone. It was Tiger-Tim Stevens though who was favoured by many 'disciples' as being the legitimate 'biscuit-tin' until the fateful night he misused the Celtic Park PA system for the sake of an amusing dig at their Old Firm rivals. In calling for a half-time minute's silence in memory of Rangers who had just been knocked out the European Cup by Levski Sofia, he certainly got plenty of laughs but in doing so failed in many learned eyes to be in possession of the necessary integrity and wisdom to be truly considered as the chosen one. He was duly sacked and asked in no uncertain terms to hand back his unused '30p off match entry 'coupons as well as his limited edition club key-ring which doubled as a pound coin deposit for unhooking shopping trolleys.

Whatever the myth, ownership of the biscuit tin eventually became too heavy a burden to bare for the directors who, by the mid-nineties had become so despised by the club's supporters that they were as welcome as a tea-time 'We're in your area' marketing call for fitted-kitchens and doors. Threatened with receivership, a step the bank may or may not have been prepared to take, the Kelly's, Grants and Whites, took one last lingering look at the proverbial 'tin', stroked it fondly and rode off into the sunset on poor quality horses they supposedly got for a bargain after haggling for a fair number of hours at Bridgeton Cross.

11.

Enter Fergus McCann. A man with a bunnet, big specs, shed loads of cash and a daft accent that sounded like a phonetics experiment gone wrong. Although he looked and often spoke like a 'right warmer' he was, financially, nobody's fool and after five years at the club managed with aplomb to build a 60,000 plus all seated stadium, win the league title averting Rangers' record breaking yet tedious 'ten in a row' bid, convert the club into a profit making business *and* place the ownership of the club in the hands of those supporters who had a spare £700 to blow on the minimum investment as dictated by the Great Share Issue of '99.

Yet despite achieving so much, and quite possibly being the modern day saviour of Celtic FC, McCann was not held universally in esteem by all who squeezed through the Parkhead turnstiles. He put bucket seats in the Jungle for a kick-off. A crime punishable by death in the minds of many of the faithful. He also allegedly ordered Cardinal Winning out of his office, a sacrilegious act that sent shock-waves across Sunday morning masses the length and breadth of the country. But worse, much worse than that, McCann had the temerity to … get this…. take a *profit* from his buying and selling of the club. Dick Turpin you have a sidekick!

This blatant profiteering went totally against the grain for some of the more die-hard, politically principled fans as did many of McCann's abrasive and ruthless actions. For those with the view that Celtic's role was above all, one of a social and community based organisation, the idea of McCann walking away £31 million richer on the deal was a distasteful one and to be truthful , I can see a bit of this and admire the pure socialism of the viewpoint. That said, when sections of the crowd booed McCann as he unfurled the Scottish League championship flag in August 1998 , it was difficult not to view the perpetrators as being somewhat ungrateful and to sympathise with 'The Bunnet'. Not only had he achieved all the major goals of his 'five year plan' but he had completed his exit strategy without calling on outside institutional investors, a philanthropic act that surely held true to Celtic's traditional notion of mutual self-help and quite probably fostered a significant element of community pride in all those individuals who invested in the future of their club.

When any fair-minded Celtic supporter looks back on the outcome of the roller-coaster events of 1994- 1999 they will hopefully conclude that Fergus McCann's purposeful tenure was the saving of the club. Looking at the alternatives how could any other conclusion be forthcoming? For those hung up by the thirty-one million pounds residing in Fergus's bank account console yourselves with the thought that he did offer an interest-free payment plan to assist individuals in buying the shares, he also donated £1.5 million of his profits to the funding of Celtic's youth academy and lets be honest, thirty - one million pounds doesn't buy you nearly as much as it used to do.

So, what of Fergus McCann nowadays? The Bunnit returned to America (Club Class of course) Where by all accounts he started a travel company which is doing reasonably well. He resides in New England with Mrs Bunnit and the two little bunnits and recently realised a personal ambition by starring on Broadway as Professor Hubert Farnsworth in the stage production of 'Futurama'. A life fulfilled by the sounds of it.

12.

As a nipper I used to get quite skittish when Celtic came to town. There was always trouble, or so it seemed to an impressionable, nervous ten year old. About town there were cars squeezed in everywhere. Double parked on the narrow residential streets below 'The Brew'. Abandoned in big lines along the main street.

My old-man used to go mental. Total outrage exploded from him as cars cheekily parked outside our house and out jumped guys brushing themselves down and adjusting green and white scarves around their necks.

"Christ on a conveyor-belt, I'LL NEVER GET MY CAR OUT BECAUSE OF ...THEM!" he'd shout despite the fact that there was room enough to manoeuvre an HGV and he wasn't going out anyway. The police station number would then be located from the phone directory but the call of complaint would never be made.

Not that all this happened too often. A couple of times in the old first division at the outside edge of my childhood memories, and the odd cup tie but still, they were memorable events for a small town like Arthurston.

And it was amazing to see Wilmot Park full to bursting. In those days, before clubs started hiking the prices for the 'big' games, the Old Firm would bring a heaving away support, an almost guaranteed capacity crowd. The old ground was vibrant. Ok there was always a certain unfounded resentment that 'your place' had been taken over for the day by a rival fan but it was still better than hearing the players voices echoing around the pitch like in dull, nothing-at-stake league encounters with Hamilton Accies and the like.

What I loved more than anything was watching players you knew from the telly, the supposed big name, quality players being utter mince on your pitch. Alan 'Rambo' McInally – there's a good example. He may have scored goals in the Bundesleague but at Wilmot Park, as Grampa used to say when he'd had a few, he couldn't trap custard. No I don't know what it meant either. Paul McStay – there's another one. I never thought his shooting was particularly clever for a player of his undoubted ability but at Wilmot Park he served up such a rich array of keppers, sclaffs and howks into Row Z that the Rovers keeper of the day, a five foot five, pot bellied alcoholic called Gordie Blake actually sat down on the grass as one of McStay's rapier-like goal attempts squibbed towards the corner flag. It doesn't pay to get too cocky though, especially if you're a five foot four keeper. Celtic had the last laugh that day when Frank MacAvennie scored the only goal of the game managing to 'chip' Blake when he was on his goal line. The Bhoys behind the goals loved that one and as clear as day I can remember them joyously singing the Oooompa lumpa song from the beloved but disconcerting kiddies film 'Charlie and the Chocolate Factory'.

Oompa Lumpa
Bobbidy Beed
We've chipped the ba' right over yer heid!

We had to laugh. Gordie deserved it.

As a footnote, Gordie Blake went on to land himself five minutes of fame by very publicly falling off a third floor balcony on a club 18-30 holiday in Salou. Despite falling over a hundred feet, through a plastic canopy and onto ornamental paving he got up, in front of around fifty witnesses attending the ever popular 'Stuff A Balloon Up An Orifice Night' and walked away totally unscathed. Incredibly this feet of 'imbalance' made all the red top scandal sheets with The News of the Screws uncharitably running the story under the headline 'Going Down' (but not what you had in mind mate!)

For our part we couldn't work out what was more inexplicable, the fact that he didn't hurt himself or that he was allowed on the holiday in the first place. He was thirty-two when he'd played with us and that was four years previously – Dirty old bastard.

13.

Anyway, back to Fergus McCann and the biscuit tin one last time. A guy that comes in to the hardware store sometimes told me this and it's worth repeating because it must be true. No, I know what you're thinking but this is a good source. His wife's brother is mates with a guy who is a painter and decorator and who painted Brian Dempsey's kitchen (Cool Azure Blue , I believe) and he's as sound as a pound. Well now, he overheard Dempsey and Wayne Biggins talking about this 'find' of McCann's over an afternoon latte and a mint Viscount and he swears its on the level.

The rumour was that McCann, after spending in the region of a hundred grand in exploration costs had eventually dug up the original biscuit tin. In the fabled tin wasn't money as expected or even how to go about obtaining said money. Instead inside was a single piece of ragged worn parchment with what appeared to be a coded message. Expert code-breakers and symbologists were drafted in and after weeks of painstaking scrutiny and research it was discovered that it was written in Comic Sans Bold Italics.

Down deep in one of the old Celtic Park basements , by the light of an oil lantern (Fergus had turned off the leccy again to save a few bob) the letters were identified one by one to reveal what soon appeared to be a prophecy. It simply stated;

A Swede with golden locks and boots of magic will come amongst us and alight Glasgow in the East.

Scholars immediately debated the prophecy's meaning and many have remain convinced to this day that it refers to Agnetha from Abba playing the Apollo with the band in 1977. Others, with the benefit of hindsight are willing to swear on their professional reputation that it may, in fact, relate to Henrik Larsson.

Henrik Edward Larsson MBE, came to Celtic in the summer of 1997. Hard on the heels of a frustrating spell at Feynoord in the Dutch Eredivisie, the Swedish international could not in his wildest dreams have predicted the impact he would make in the green and white hooped jersey. Signed by Wim Janson for what would prove to be a charity shop bargain of £650,000, Larsson would eventually become Celtic's third top scorer of all time behind the legendary names of Jimmy McGrory and Bobby Lennox, impressive when you consider a double-leg break suffered against Lyon in the UEFA cup kept him out the game for almost a year.

Celtic fans were scarcely enamoured by early glimpses of the young Swede though. With his hanging blonde dreadlocks and half-cast complexion (his father was originally from the Cape Verde Islands) Larsson, in truth looked more like a young Egyptian Pharaoh than a footballer of the SPL. Indeed initial outings suggested he had all the ability of an Egyptian Pharaoh – one who, in Pharaoh School, was regularly the last to be picked for the playground kick-abouts at that. A misplaced pass against Hibs on his debut cost Celtic the match as perennial whinger

Chic Charnley pounced on the stray ball to rifle in the winner. An own goal in his first European appearance did little more to endear himself to the Celtic faithful either. By the time Larsson bid Celtic Park farewell some seven years later however, he had lost the dreds but attained God-like status amongst the Parkhead legions. In 2000/01 he won the Golden Boot award as Europe's top scorer, and throughout his Celtic career he picked up numerous player of the year awards voted for by fans, his fellow professionals and the media alike. Perhaps his proudest moment came in 2005 when he was awarded an honorary degree from the University of Strathclyde. Larsson took his qualification seriously and in a tip of the hat gesture to the educational fraternity he subscribed to the Socialist Worker, lay in bed for thirty-two afternoons on the trot watching 'Tricia' and applied for a student loan which he subsequently spent completely on beer , fags and Pot Noodles.

Surprisingly Larsson didn't turn pro until he was the ripe old age of 21 when he signed for his home town team of Helsingborgs IF. He had originally been on trial with rivals Helsingborgs WHEN but ultimately put pen to paper with the former as, in his own words, he 'enjoyed living with the uncertainty'.

A private family man, Larsson proved it was indeed possible to play for the old firm without getting into scuffles with pikey scumbags every second Saturday night in a Glasgow nightclub. Living a sedate lifestyle in sleepy Lanarkshire hamlet of Bothwell, Larsson spent quality time with his wife , Magdalene his son Jordan (named after Joe Jordon when he was born with a powerful looking forehead and no teeth) and a daughter Janelle (named after a woman with white stilettos, gold dangling earrings and a magnificent cleavage Henrik once saw on the popular MTV show 'Pimp My Ride' .) Shunning the fast-lane celebrity lifestyle, the Larsson family much preferred the simpler life of nipping out to Equi's for an ice cream, feeding the killer-swans in Strathclyde Park and visiting the garden centres of the Clyde Valley on Sundays where they would regularly partake in some of the most overpriced tea and caramel shortcake in Europe.

As Henrik Larsson packed his bags and waved goodbye to 'Paradise' talk was rife of his imminent retirement from the game. Now my dad's idea of retirement consists of pottering around the garden, watching 'Murder She Wrote' or Columbo while wiring into a multi-pack of cheesy Wotsits, and trimming his nose hairs with a set of safety scissors. Larsson though, chose to scale down his career by playing for his country in the World Cup finals, signing for Barcelona, appearing in a Champions league final then moving to Manchester Utd on loan. Its good to finally get the time to pander to your hobbies a bit isn't it.

Henrik Larsson will not be quickly forgotten down Celtic Park way. He played an exceptional game in the most sportsmanlike manner and showed genuine commitment to the club in an era where the top players in the game have often appeared mercenary in their approach. Ok when he first turned up his hair was a mile out but once it had all fallen out after the first Glasgow cold snap he settled down, started banging the goals in and proved himself as one of the few genuine world-class players to have graced the Scottish Premier League. The 'tic, you feel, will do very well to sign his likes again.

14.

The Friday night, in the pub, 'brilliant-at-the-time-but-now-a-bit-dubious-in-the-cold-light-of-day idea' was to get off the train in Glasgow's town Centre and walk to the game. Credit where credit is due though, after a few 'Do you really want tos ?' and a good number of 'You sures?' we've done just that.

It started sedately enough with a 'gird-yer-loins' pint in McChuill's on High Street around mid-day. From there we picked up our slackening hangovers and headed along The Gallogate towards the locale of Bairds Bar and the Glasgow Barrowland, a historic patch of Glasgow if you're into music or hooky electrical gear. The strip of small shops and take-aways has impressively resisted the overall facelift Glasgow has had over the last twenty or so years and retains all the atmosphere of a 'downtown' scene from Starsky and Hutch.

Bairds is a legendary Celtic pub cramming bags of (predominantly Irish) atmosphere into its tight, memorabilia laden confines. In it I was soon accosted by Joey McGlinn, a small elderly gent with a well-tanned bald head, few real teeth to speak of and who smelled vaguely of the moss on our back garden wall. Joey took no time in telling me he only had one lung and that he was personal friends with all the Celtic greats. "Oh aye, I know them all!" he proclaimed grandly. When pushed, it turned out that he once met Billy McNeil in a pub in Largs, used to work at the Council with one of the groundsman and he lived two doors down from the guy who fell off the top tier of the Celtic Park stand at the Old Firm league decider in '99. Somehow managing to extricate myself from Joey's verbal vice I managed to get the round in and, sitting at a small round table in the corner, we succumbed to a respectful pint of Guinness and a good discussion about Celtic's grotesque away tops over the years. While we are in sound agreement that the green and white hooped top, white shorts and white socks combo is, with the exception of Airdrie's Diamond, the most outstanding strip in Scotland, their second strips however have always left a lot to be desired. Generally more subdued in appearance, they have consistently sported cheap looking collars, dirty spray effects and random splashes of shade giving them either an untidy inside-out appearance or the feeling that they've been made from leftover off-cuts from the factory floor.

Yet despite this general mankiness in design the fans have continued to buy and buy, and buy. Merchandising and branding offers huge potential revenue to a club like Celtic and like Manchester United, Barcelona and the like they haven't been slow to recognise the global possibilities of this. The Asian market in particular has clearly been identified as an un-reaped harvest and the signing of Shunsuke Nakamura was a bold move which, if one was being cynical made as much marketing sense as it did footballing. Compared to the poorly attended 'An evening with

Tommy Nakajima at Uddingston Driving Range' though, it was a slick piece of business.

Fuelled with the life-giving qualities of Dublin's fine stout we stepped out from under the fluttering Brazil flag hanging over Bairds' doorway and continue on our way. Past the unlit neon facade of The Barrowland where U2 once played to over two hundred thousand folk (if the numbers claiming to have been present that night are to believed) and onwards along the Gallowgate towards Parkhead. Past the 'Hielen Jessie' and 'The Drober'. Beyond The Bellgrove Hotel which almost certainly *doesn't* do room service, nor complimentary mints on your pillow, nor possibly carpeted flooring. As the Forge Retail Park appears ahead and the last of our shoe leather wears gossamer thin, the monstrous, imposing structure of Celtic Park rises out of the horizon like the product of a massive Emerald earthquake.

15.

Celtic Park is huge and intimidating. With a seating capacity of 60,832 it dwarfs both Ibrox and Hampden Park easily. Behind its shiny façade though you can't help noticing there's a 'fur coat, no knickers' feel to the stadium. While these other two grounds have sweeping, well appointed concourses and stairways, Celtic Park has a more Spartan underbelly. It looks more like ….well, a football ground with its cramped staircases, stone tunnelled walkways and boggin toilets. Its almost like it was deliberately designed with this no frills approach in mind.

Like Ibrox though we've spent a lot of money to get in but have, *again* , been given the worst seats in the house, squashed away in the corner section of the lower Lisbon Lions Stand. Not that the towering stadium around us isn't still a breath-taking scene. Three quarters is a constant two-teared flow of seats, hugging the pitch and the sky like the edge of a massive bowl. The pattern is broken down the south side by the old main stand which despite being a fair size itself shrinks pitifully under the stern gaze of the rest of the ground.

The Rovers are in all red today and as Dunsmore and Jay McDonald stand over the ball ready for the off, the spine tingling finale of 'You'll never walk alone' is being completed by the Celtic fans in attendance. The background music has been turned off and only human voices, around forty thousand or so of them today, are echoing the famous song round every nook and cranny of the stadium. Scarves are held aloft . No defiant counter singing is coming from our usually boisterous away support. It would be almost disrespectful. In actuality most of the supporters around me, including Dave and Jonesy, are caught up in the moment with glazed expressions and far away looks their common feature.

Irrelevantly, the game has started and it takes a strong will to focus on the action rather than getting lost in the hypnotic curtain of green and white that is shimmering from the stands. The anthem draws to a close and indeed 'with hope in our hearts' we settle down as faithful Arthurston Rovers fans, ready to push our team on towards the near-impossible – a win at Celtic Park.

Our crowd have found their voice. No longer cowed into silence by the unified Green Machine, they are upstanding, belting out the old standard 'We'll walk a million miles for one of your goals ohhh Ro-oh-oh-verrs!' . Howls of derision come from small sections of the home support but really they're going through the motions. You can feel that they aren't threatened by us on or off the park. We sing on defiantly nonetheless.

With four minutes on my watch (I'm clock watching already) Tony Bunton finds a bit of space in the midfield and tentatively, almost suspiciously edges his grey, razored head forward. Frankie Boyle, at the corner edge of the box drops off his marker and as Bunton threads it through to him, he lays it off deftly, first time behind the Celtic defensive line . Russ Dinsmore is the first to react and slipping into the penalty area takes one touch and rifles the ball towards the Celtic goal. The keeper doesn't move as the ball hits the top right corner of the net.

I think I'm going to have a stroke of some sort. I'm screaming in ecstasy but no noise is coming out. Around me is bedlam. Jonesy and Dave are hugging and dancing simultaneously and the guy next to them has almost fallen over into the row in front of him. Only the firm grasp of the bloke to his right is preventing him from falling forward. I've just found my voice when a loud jeer rises from the home support and we notice the referee's assistant away on the far right.

His flag is up and I get a sinking feeling in my gut.

"OFFSIDE?" yells Jonesy maliciously, "He couldn't be, Russ ran from behind the man!"

"Might have been Jay," starts Dave, "he made a run beyond the last man too."

The referee, evidently unsure himself, jogs over to the assistant who, as if to reinforce the point, still has his flag pointed out in front of him intently. After a brief exchange, the ref skips over to the penalty box, points in the direction of where McDonald had been lurking then sprints up the park followed by at least three livid looking Rovers players.

"AAWWWWW NO WAY" I yell.

"HE WAS NEVER INTERFERING WITH PLAY!" screams Dave, his sentiment echoed ferociously by Jonesy despite not having seen the offending run in the first place.

Outrage ensues as once again the overly complicated off-side rule causes controversy

"You never get anything here. EVER!" vents Jonesy loudly with evil in his eyes, "Away an' learn the rules!" He shouts pointlessly before slumping to his seat in what has all the hallmarks of a toddler's huff.

The off-side decision indeed stands and I can't help wondering if that was our only chance blown. As play rages on though, the boys in red seem to think not. They've clearly not read the script for this one and are, in fact dictating the flow of the game. Storrie and Pecnik are confidently nipping any early threats in the bud and are creating a number of attacks by playing simple short passes into Bunton and McLean in midfield who are surprisingly being given acres of room to continue the move forward. Boyle is drifting around the right-wing showing some sublime touches while Hedge and Dinsmore are linking well down on the left.

"I don't think the Celtic boy wants to go near Mickey Hedge's hair" says Jonesy wrinkling his nose in disgust, "Look at it, its like a flock of birds that died in an oil slick. You could power a generator for hours with those locks". Dave and I both look at him questioningly.

" ....assuming you could refine it" he then adds somewhat unnecessarily. We both turn back to the game without comment.

The first half draws to a conclusion quite joyously with no score. A couple of fitful moments are all we've had to endure so far and asides from the grave injustices of the first five minutes, a draw is just about fair.

16.

Our half time conversation revolves around the 'R' word. Relegation isn't something we've discussed as yet. Our heady optimism and our 'live for the moment' enjoyment of our Premier adventure has prevented it. But failure's hand is clawing at our ankles ready to drag us kicking and screaming back to Division 1 and its getting hard to ignore.

Its Dave that brings it up first. "I'm thinking we better enjoy all this while we can." He affords himself a panoramic look around the stadium and sighs.

"Yeh, things aren't looking good. It just feels like everything and everyone is against us just now. " mutters Jonesy disconsolately. " Its like they want us to get relegated."

"Who exactly are 'they'?" Dave asks half-amused.

"THEM" he replies in an agitated fashion looking around him at nothing in particular. "The Powers At Be. The League, the SFA, The bigger clubs. Lets face it , we don't make them much money do we, we're just a nuisance."

I'm about to open this debate further when a rousing cheer goes up and the Rovers take the field lead by the three sprinting officials clad in their nasty optic lemon shirts and matching socks. These 'shoutfits' as we have christened them (for they *are* louder than bombs) are a damn disgrace. We do not pay good money to see rotund referees squeezed into skin tight tops . Its like watching whole frozen chicken's packed in radio-active cling-film. The lemon one is the retina burning worst but there now seems to be a wide range of multi-coloured figure hugging 'creations' in various unflattering colours. What may have looked *Euro-chic* on the six-packed, chisel-chinned design models on the cat-walk of 'Le Collection d' Officials' though does not hang well on Fats McLardygut, Scottish grade one referee and erstwhile pie-crammer. Man-breasts are not cool; Trapped, squashed man-breasts suffocating in such a public manner are just plain wrong. If I was forced into a definition of the image generated I think I would opt for ' The opposite of sex'. Its that bad.

Referees should wear all black and that's that. Good old black cotton jerseys with a good couple of centimetres of give to shroud any unsightly movement in the 'love handle department. Maybe, *maybe* we can let them off with wearing a red top once in a while , like in the old days, but only if the fourth official has inspected the situation, consulted with both teams, and has agreed that this doesn't appear to drain the ref's facial colour in any kind of an undead, child-frightening manner. Once more tradition should be observed – its there for a purpose.

17.

The game restarts and again, encouragingly, we are sprightly and willing to attack. As it stands Celtic are twelve points ahead at the top of the league while the Rovers are two points adrift at the bottom. Football.... as Jimmy 'Greavsie' Greaves got paid wads to say on the telly when he couldn't think of anything more pertinent, '.... is a funny old game (Saint)' and indeed form can be an unpredictable bedfellow as there is nothing between the teams today.

Arthurston have plugged away manfully and a Pecnik header from a corner and a thirty yard drive by McLean tipped expertly over the bar by the Celtic keeper has had us on the edges of our seats in 'wee boy' excitement. With ten minutes to go though the game has take a predictable turn. The Rovers, on the verge of an excellent Old Firm result have turned edgy and Celtic have found another gear. Suddenly we are giving the ball away more frequently and the hooped jerseys are finding more space, further up the pitch. A swift three man attack has Andy Thomson stretching down to his left to steer the ball round the post for a corner.

'Oooooaaaaaahhhhh' expel the crowd awakening from the deep slumber they've been in. A wall of encouraging noise builds as Celtics big men lumber forward in anticipation of the cross coming over.

It swings in with a vicious curve and is met full on by one of the aforementioned lumberers. He's unmarked and thunders his header goalwards. Thomson , in reaction only raises his arm but does enough to deflect the ball off the bar. It flies high in the air then drops into a melee of players. Flashes of white amidst a forest of legs, the ball bounces around interminably before the red sock of John Storrie meets it and slots it out of play for another corner.

The Celtic volcano rumbles threateningly. "Don't panic!" yells Jonesy shrilly.

We are too nervous to laugh with Dave leaning forward, elbows on his knees, and me with my left hand rubbing the back of my neck scratching an imaginary rash. Another vicious curler torpedoes its way towards the penalty spot and again its met by a Celtic man. This time the header is driven groundward the ball bouncing high and awkward towards the top corner of the net. It looks in for certain and the home support start to rise to their feet..... until Thomson's yellow jersey flashes through the crowded box and two huge hands impossibly pluck the ball from mid air.

'Oh maaaaaannnnnn', moans Jonesy.

"WHAT A SAVE!' I scream,

"'MON THE ROVVERRS!" yells Dave battering his hands together in frenzied applause.

But back charge Celtic and suddenly its seems like we're playing against a hurricane. Wide left Frankie Boyle is panicked into easily giving up possession and Celtic whip forward again. The ball skims low across the lush grass finding their winger in acres of space in the shadow of the main stand. As he roams forward dangerously, three team-mates are all making raking runs into the Rovers box. He sees them and chips a delicate ball into the feet of the nearest. The forward takes one touch then deftly turns on a sixpence and knocks the ball past Mark Bird in the left back position. Bird Is caught all ends up and makes a mad lunge for the ball. Missing his target by miles he instead thumps into the Celtic man's legs (both of them) sending the unfortunate player into orbit.

"Noooooooooooooo!" wails everyone simultaneously around us.

The referee (of course) rushes into the box pointing dramatically at the spot. The Celtic contingent cheer in a relieved manner as Bird hangs his head guiltily with no complaint.

Without fuss the same forward who has just been knee-capped brushes himself down and places the ball on the spot.

I look at my watch. 4.43. We were two minutes away by my reckoning.

Thomson stands on his line motionless with legs slightly bent at the knees, his gloved hands waving slightly back and forward at his sides.

The penalty taker takes three steps back. Stops. Slides forward gracefully, and almost in slow motion, chips the ball languidly down the middle of the goals.

Silence.

Time stands still.

The place erupts.

It was one of those audacious penalties. The keeper chooses one side or the other, drops to the ground on his side and agonises as the ball flies into the space he used to be in and drops into the net.

Except Thomson hasn't moved a muscle. He's stood his ground, resisted the urge to dive in any direction and miraculously watched and waited as the ball flopped into his arms without the need for as much as a stumble in either direction.

Thomson looks slightly bewildered as team-mates pat him on the back and rub his hair. The penalty taker is still standing rooted on the penalty spot and even from our skewed position off to the side, I can easily make out the right belter of a red-neck that's rising up to the guy's ears.

The storm has blown itself out and Celtic play out the last couple of minutes to little effect. Scarcely believing their luck, the Rovers do likewise. The final whistle blows and we stand arms aloft, applauding and cheering as though we had won the league. The players raise their arms similarly, McLean and Bird falling to their knees in exhaustion and possibly relief. News circulates quickly that Partick Thistle have lost to Dundee Utd. A point has been gained on the Jags pulling the Rovers back to within two points. The day has been, to all intent and purpose, a success.

18.

Walking out the ground into the chilly February darkness Jonesy is chattering excitedly.

"I always wanted to see that done," he says shaking his head, "I mean sometimes you just will the keeper to take that chance and not move but its such a gamble isn't it."

"Doesn't half make the penalty taker look daft eh?" I add nodding.

Singing echoes around the high, overbearing outside walls of Celtic Park as a small band of happy fans make their way back to their cars and buses. The mood is optimistic and upbeat and the talk is all about how maybe our luck is changing. It's a good feeling and one that seems to have been absent for so long. It feels *so* good that the walk back to town I had secretly been dreading is as pleasurable as summer stroll in the warm fragrant countryside. As we hit the Trongate, the cold has barely registered and every one of our players has been elevated to a status seldom reached by mere mortals.

And as we wearily stagger towards Central Station and I absently poke my finger into the seldom visited, little tight 'sub-pocket' inside the right hand pocket of my jeans , I scoop out a tiny folded piece of paper which after some clumsy , numb-fingered fumbling,   spreads out delightfully into a haggard looking but resilient twenty pound note.

Yup, its fair to say our luck is definitely changing.

Chapter 18 Up for the cup?

1.

There aren't too many ways of positively describing a 4-1 away defeat in anyone's book. That it happened in the fourth round of the Scottish Cup is doubly painful. Against a team from a lower league than you, well its like eating nail sandwiches really.

No sir, not many positive words spring to mind. I thought about 'sobering'. And I toyed with 'character-building' but that's really two words. The best I myself could muster was 'enlightening'. I now feel its been 'enlightening' as to how bad Ally Fairful really is.

Schnabbel shook his head as Ally trudged off the field after his sending off, own goal and fifty-two minutes of general misdemeanour . "ITS NOT HIS FAULT YA MUPPET, ITS YOURS!" I screamed at our impervious manager, "AFTER TWO YEARS WATCHING HIM WHAT PART OF THAT WOEFULLY INEPT PERFORMANCE CAME AS A SURPRISE TO YOU?" I finish collapsing onto my chair in nervous, shaky, exhaustion.

People round about were looking at me strangely like I was a shade loopy. Clearly I'm not, but they are entitled to their opinion. So we're out the cup and the thought of it resonates like a bucket falling down a deep well.

But then one interesting little thing did come from our ill-fated trip to Dumfries. Jonesy, doing his usual nosey around the internet for interesting tit-bits for conversation purposes, found this little gem on the Queen of the South 'unofficial' web-site message-board under the thread 'Disastrous away games' .... Well, read on.

`Nae luck Danbo72, I can beat that though. A good few years back we went up to Arthurston for a mid-`

week game. It was ice-pole cold and we were all wrapped up like guards in a Russian gulag. Seemed like most of us had wangled a half day and we had enjoyed a good session in the pub before heading for the game. Anyway it was just the usual on the bus with most of us mortal by Lesmahagow and folks screaming for pee stops every ten minutes or so all the way up the A74. We reached the outskirts of Arthurston around five and we're on the main route into town when a boy called Stoory McLenechan, a big lad with funny wee feet if I remember, fell off the bus. Right off. God knows how he did it but he opened the door and fell right out that bus when it was still going at least forty miles an hour. Slap onto the road he went. When we stopped and ran back to get him there he was spread-eagled on his back with his Tennents still vertical in his hand, his head turned at an angle and his gaze anchored lovingly at Shona on the back of the can. I don't think he spilled a drop.

It soon became pretty obvious Stoory had broken his leg and, after a heap of wailing and painful teeth-gritting, mainly by the boys who were itching to get on to the pub, we manoeuvred him back on the bus where we debated what to do with the big donkey. Either we gave him another few beers which would hopefully send him off to sleep and we could deal with him after the match, or else in view of the powerful moaning he was coming out with, we could take him to the hospital. Fortunately, only a few yards up the road, was a signpost telling us Arthurston General Hospital was only a mile and a half up the road. On a show of hands it was (reluctantly) decided to take him to Accident and Emergency where hopefully there would be medical folks there that could quickly bind him up and let us get on our way.

As Tam the bus-driver edged his way into the ambulance bay like the chancer that he was, we got a surprisingly swift and accommodating welcome by a gang of green-clad docs who appeared out from behind a big rubber flap doorway and proceeded to usher us off the bus.

Fat Sam was first off (Who remembers Sam White that ran the supporters bus, the wee bloke with the biggest beer gut you've ever seen. Always wore a faded blue t-shirt with 'Pop a Pomagne!' on the front and had a big tattoo on his arm that said 'HMS Ulysissees'. A guy on the bus once asked about the spelling and Sam broke his nose.) Together with Tam he struggled Stoory over to the door where the big chap was dispatched unceremoniously onto a waiting gurney before being pushed through the entrance and beyond.

Of course we were all blitzed by then and when they cleared every one of us off the bus to a man then whisked us all in after Stoory, not one of us complained. Once inside we were dispatched into cubicles where we were asked to remove our jackets, shirts and tops (which they collected in a big bin thing and immediately wheeled away). Then, one by one, we had our blood-pressure checked and our chests sounded. Again there was no complaints made, indeed most of the boys were glowing and enjoying the seat while one boy, sitting in beside me, actually dosed off as the docs did their stuff.

They asked me how my breathing was. I admitted it wasn't great, well I mean twenty years on the Silk Cut doesn't make you King of the Mountains does it. And then they asked if I was cold, which I definitely was as there was an awful draft firing in from outside. Someone mentioned getting me an oxygen mask then they brought us all tea. I remember thinking that 'The Dumfries & Galloway Royal Infirmary' could learn a lot from these boys.

I'm not sure when the real confusion started but we were all sat, dotted around the A&E unit, supping tea and sobering up when the docs started muttering to themselves. A couple ran in then some ran out and not long after that one of them came over to Sam who was sitting scratching his big space-hopper belly and said, 'Can I ask Where have you all come from?" To which Sam replied proudly ' Dumfries mostly but a couple of us are from Lockerbie – up fur the Qweeenohthesoooth game." He added helpfully.

The Doc looked uncomfortable, like he'd just been asked to make a house-call, 'So you're not from the power plant then?' he asked chewing on his stethoscope.

"Eh?" replied Sam. At which point a dishevelled bunch of about fifteen sorry looking lads with blackened faces and ragged clothes were ushered past us into another section of the unit. As they passed us by they looked at us funny and I must say, we looked at them funny too. Not a word passed between us.

568

So we got booted out at that point. The place, it seemed, was in turmoil due to an explosion at some nearby power facility. There were fears of radiation leaks and contamination and everything. 'You'll have to leave now!' a stern old battle-axe of a nurse ordered us and tried to herd us all out the door as quickly as possible. When we asked for our tops back we were caustically told that they had been burned in the interests of safety. Burned in the interests of safety? — Boy, Fat Sam was hacked off at losing his Pomagne t-shirt I'll tell you, kept yelling that it had 'fuckin' sentimental value'. No alternative clothing was offered however and we found ourselves, mere minutes later, driving into Arthurston , thirty or so blokes, on a bus , tits oot.

It was bitter out. By this time we were sobering up and with our drinking time cruelly taken from us, along with our tops, we dived into a gents outfitters that was surprisingly still open, hoping to buy at least something to keep the wind out at the game. Fat Sam, who was still raging by the way, organised it all and we all trooped through this old boy's shop and picked up a golf shirt or a monogrammed polo-neck or one of a range of many monstrous diamond patterned garments laid out on the display cabinet. Man that gear was hideous! I got a brown short-sleeved shirt with green buttons and a green strip down just one of the sleeves. I felt like a right knob. I don't think the old boy that owned the place could believe his luck. He couldn't have hoped to clear that stuff short of a gaggle of blind golfers breezing through, or possibly some American tourists nipping in looking to purchase some country-wear and possibly a firearm or two.

So we paid for our gear and went on to the game. We were still cold (coldest I've ever been at a match for sure), we missed the first ten minutes for a start, during which we scored the only goal of what was a miserable game. Then the Rovers fans started ripping the pish out of us. They kept shouting 'Fore' and 'Get in the hole!'. The fact that we won the game gave us little in the way of consolation. I was off my work for three days afterwards with a chest infection and my mate Franny ended up in hospital for a week with pneumonia (complicated by mild alcohol poisoning). I never saw Stoory again after that night and Sam White is a face you never see around any more either. Perhaps we can set up a new thread entitled 'Daft Bastards who have fallen out of moving transport' or 'Bad tattoos of our time'.

A guy at my work has one that says 'Meat Loave'. There you go, there's a starter for ten ....

2.

Wilf Schnabbel met the press head on as usual after our four goal thumping. What started on fairly predictable ground with "You cannot take anything away from Queens Of South, you come here and they do exactly what they say on the tin." soon made way for the emotional black-mail of "I ask the boys to be all they can be and feel disembowelled if they do not reach this." This tact quickly steered towards the more understated pragmatism of a shrug, a tepid smile and "Hey though fellas, we must see this as merely a game eh…. and I mean……"and at this point he gave another smile and shrug," … what's the worst that could happen? Thanks fellas!" And that was him. Back to the studio with the permanently bemused drummer Dougie Vipond sitting beside the Scottish Cup, which by that time was clearly stealing the show.

And of course somewhere in that last comment Wilf's on the right track. But when you've just driven for five hours, spent a wad of cash , listened to some terrifying thrash metal music and *not* stopped for chips on the way home, it doesn't feel like he's right at all. It feels like he's being flippant and isn't quite grasping how important this all is. Or at least how important it all *seems* in the hours spent driving home in the car and through the subsequent early Saturday evening, at least until X-Factor is finished and you've cracked open a beer.

I've decided the next time Ally Fairful plays I'm going to write to my MP. Someone has to listen to me. Maybe if I can stimulate a debate on a more serious forum Schnabbel will sit up and take notice. Failing that I suppose I could at least look forward in speculation to the sort of measured response I could expect from our local representative. I mean, they *have* to write back to you don't they. What a system - 'Dear Sir , I am unfamiliar with the Alistair Fairful to whom you are referring but naturally I am concerned by your assertion that he is having a detrimental effect on the community .....'

Baby steps to a better world I think. Maybe one man *can* make a difference.

3.

With Spring in the air Jonesy has seemingly shrugged off his yellow-chamois blues and has committed himself to circulating his CV in the hope of getting some job interviews, preferably in the financial sector. Inexplicably he has also adopted a strange fixation with 'ample barmaid' Charlotte Church and keeps sloping off to the 'Easy listening' section in WH Smiths for an ogle at her CDs and a flip through her , now slightly dog-eared, promotional calendar. Phrases like 'sturdy ankles', ' generous bosom' and ' fine, child-bearing hips' are tripping off his tongue just as soon as his third pint is down. Its all a bit disconcerting and we're hoping its just a phase.

Dave, by comparison is holding his cards close to his chest. We've weedled out of him that Linda has suggested meeting for a coffee and a talk, Sunday the 16th of March officiously being the arrangement. He's playing things down greatly but I think I can see flashes of anticipation in his eyes that I hope are in some way justified. There's a part of me that has a sinking feeling about the whole affair and am readying myself for the worst. Jonesy , although equally supportive, is faced with the added strain of living with Dave and their enforced proximity is starting to take its toll. Confidentially, I think he's on the verge of making an impassioned plea to Linda himself to take him back. I know for a fact he's also quizzed my mother on her views on lodgers and has taken to leaving Remax portfolios dotted around his flat.

If Dave has noticed, he hasn't said a thing.

4.

Soon the clocks will be put forward. The evenings will stretch into soft summer light and Albion Rovers fans will be able to see some home-field action beyond quarter-past four. For now though things are still dark, murky and unsure. A week of respite in the form of a Scotland international presents itself and brings with it its own frustrations. The one sure thing, asides from death and taxes, is Arthurston's failing form.

Sat. February 15th - Arthurston 0 Falkirk 2
Sat. March 1st - Motherwell 0 Arthurston 1
Sat. Mar 6th - Arthurston 1 Rangers 2

God bless Motherwell! They've now given us a third of our total points tally for the season. Its strange how often this happens. How frequently there is one team in the league who can't buy a win against you no matter either team's current circumstances. They may be a technically better team than yours, possibly even riding much higher in the league than yours, and yet something in their formation, their team selection or tactics plays right into your hands and time after time its like taking sweeties from a wean. For us this year, Motherwell *are* that team. Without them (and their lacklustre play) we would have been in the grubber by now. Things still don't look pretty but with nine games to go, a string of wins could see us clawing our way back into the fray. Falkirk find themselves nine points adrift from the team directly above them but with only one relegation place gaping, they will no doubt feel confident that all three teams below them will never be able to overhaul them. For Motherwell, Thistle and our good-selves though, the fear is real;

	Pld	W	L	D	GF	GA	PTS
Falkirk	30	7	13	10	24	42	31
Motherwell	30	6	14	10	30	47	28
Patrick Th.	30	6	16	8	24	55	26
Arthurston R.	30	5	19	6	26	54	21

At least The 'Well have the security of knowing that the league will be reconstructed should they finish in the bottom spot leaving them somehow still in the top flight. Rovers and Thistle hold no such fancy.

We'll just need to win. Fair and square.

Anyway, anyhow.

Ray Stark is set to return on Saturday against Hearts at Tynecastle and the rest of the team are fit. There are good times coming, I can feel them. A new day is dawning . Things are about to go my way in a manner that is both surprising and welcoming. A number of financial burdens will soon be lifted and I should pay particular attention to the advice of a man in a moustache. How do I know all this? I read my stars in a woman's magazine in the Dentist's yesterday.

I await my fate with optimism.

Chapter 19   The talk of the Toun

1.

The score on the vidi-printer stands at Chasings by Hearts fans 4 , Chasings by Hibs fans 7 (seven). In view of this chilling historical statistic, I'm moved to announce that I have the maroon clad Jam Tarts well ahead of the Hibees in the Most Popular Team in Edinburgh stakes. Before Hearts fans pump their fists in jubilation though, bear in mind that had Meadowbank Thistle not been spirited away suspiciously to the New Town sobriety of Livingston, then they would have probably scooped the silverware themselves.

Actually that's not true at all. I'm not sure why I said it. It *should* be the case admittedly, what with my 'wee team leanings' and all, but strangely its not. I have to come clean here and admit that I do have a warm spot for Heart of Midlothian Football Club. And its not just because they charitably have cultivated a shockingly bad record against Arthurston over the years either.

No, there's something about the Hearts that I can't quite put my finger on that stirs this seldom admitted affection within me . Maybe it's the Edinburgh backdrop that does it - that ancient capital tradition, the cobbledy-streeted, Black-death character that Glasgow can never match. But then Hibs share this as well so that can't be it. Maybe Tynecastle Park is at the root of it all. A favoured away ground, crammed impossibly as it is amidst the grey Gorgy shops and tenements with so little room to spare, its tight claustrophobic stands giving every match the opportunity to feel like its trapped inside a pressure cooker with the heat full on. Or maybe its a softer notion than that. Maybe its because I feel Hearts have deserved, over the years, a little bit more from their toils than they've really achieved.

For Hearts have become glorious losers. (A trait I am strangely and inexplicably drawn to) Nearly men who almost better the

Scotland national team in terms of the sympathetic looks and 'never mind' claps on the back they've attracted after their latest bid for greatness has come up a couple of bob short. League titles have been lost when they should have been won, legitimate cup winning chances have been squandered, financial opportunities have not been exploited, and dynasties have teetered when they should have solidified and pressed forward with hope and influence.

Being a Hearts fan over the last twenty years or so has probably been a bit of a struggle and there, I suspect, is where my real attraction lies. When their players trudged off the Dens Park turf on the last day of the 85/86 season it summed things up for the Edinburgh side. With three games to go and five points clear of Celtic (who had a game in hand) they seemed destined, under Alex MacDonald's beetroot faced leadership, to break the mould of Scottish football and lift the Premier League championship. History of course tells that they drew with Aberdeen, scraped a one-nil win over Clydebank and with seven minutes left against Dundee , succumbed to two Albert Kidd goals leaving Celtic, heart-breakingly[14], to win the league on goal difference.

Mind you has it ever really been straight forward for the boys in maroon? I'm not so sure. From the very outset, the club struggled to be an attractive proposition in the nation's capital. For starters they were forced to compete against city rivals Hibernian who were joyfully capitalising on a religious 'draw' that Hearts simply couldn't hope to match. Add to this the relative indifference of many Edinburghers towards the game of football itself in those days then you begin to understand the sheer achievement in the club's ability to endure and indeed flourish beyond those most difficult of times. And it is perhaps testament to the resolve of both players and supporters of the rather quaintly nicknamed 'Jam Tarts' that they ultimately established themselves within the cream of the Scottish game while almost, but not quite, stripping

---

[14]   pun reproduced without the express permission of The Sun Knobby Headline Dept ©

away their fair share of cups and titles from the rest of the 'big boys' in Scottish football .

2.

It wasn't easy starting a football team in Edinburgh in the late 1800s. Rugby was all the rage and it proved devilishly difficult finding a ball to play with that wasn't of the awkward, oval shaped variety. Hoards of young gentlemen of a certain standing seemed entirely prepossessed with hurling these egg-shaped objects around the old cobbled streets of the capital, hand to hand, with questionable purpose, whilst at the same time singing bawdy songs of sex with farmyard animals and playing practical jokes involving the ramming of random objects hilariously up each others' back passages. However while all this seemed top class fun and japery for that certain breed of 'sportsman', the more demanding kids who possessed a degree of speed, craft and co-ordination yearned for something more. Thankfully it wasn't long before a collection of young men of enterprising disposition acquired a more spherical chunk of patched leather, dropped it to the ground and started knocking it around with their feet in an enjoyable and altogether more wholesome manner.

Conflicting theories circulate as to how this pioneering gang of spotty youths came together to 'get a game aff' in the first instance. Some talk of an informal scuff-around that regularly took place on the site of the old tollbooth jail on High Street. The famous stone 'Heart of Midlothian' set into the hard grey cobbles outside St Giles Cathedral allegedly bore witness to early versions of 'Tippy-wanny', 'Long- shootie', 'Off-and-on' and the connoisseur's favourite - 'Rushy-in'. However it wasn't long before these sporting youngsters were despatched by concerned locals, to the nearby 'Meadows' thereby graciously sparing them from the gruesome executions that were still commonplace on the High Street at that time. It was on that large area of grassland that Hearts would first play organised matches.

Hang fire though! Others hold the firm belief that it was to be the energetic bunch of young men who frequented the Heart of Midlothian Dance Hall in Hollyrood Square who would collectively set Edinburgh's footballing wheels in motion. On the controversial suggestion of the local constabulary that 'football was 'better than dancing', the yoofs (around 40 of them) after a particularly bemusing and unwarranted passage of grief from their womenfolk, decided that there might be something in what the cops were saying. One brave soul, a young lad called Andy Grogger from Westfield Road was duly allocated the critical charge of buying the ball. Telling his girlfriend he was 'just nipping out to buy some nit-spray' he scuttled off, early one Saturday morning, to Percival King's on Lothian Street. When he got there Andy, not renowned for his attention span, handed over the collected 'club' funds in return for a 'quarter' of rats' nostrils and a wheel of cheese. The bold lad was duly sent back to the shop just before lunchtime where he successfully, though reluctantly, exchanged the cheese for a fine leather football (The nostrils had been devoured in their entirety by Andy on the short walk home and were consequently non-returnable. Somewhat poetically, however, they proved to be 'of a bad batch', and left the hapless lad with a bad case of 'Black-stool' over which none of his friends offered any sympathy whatsoever.)

3.

In 1874 Heart of Midlothian Football Club were formed under the low roof of their chosen headquarters within Mother Anderson's Tavern on West Cross Causeway (in the third toilet cubicle from the left for historical accuracy). From the outset they used the tavern predominantly as changing facilities en-route to the East Meadows pitch, and it was in homage to the rich aroma of the piles of underpants that were perpetually left drying on the pub's window sills, that Mother Anderson named her now immortal home-brewed ale, 'Dead Man's Crotch'.

The team started off in all white strips most probably in deference to an early Edinburgh club 'White Star' who may or may not have been Heart of Midlothian's immediate forerunners. In 1875 they joined the Edinburgh FA who at that time consisted of a tight-knit group of pale men with stale oxters, long, wavy beards, and who were prone to extended hours of introspective frowning and the whistling of 'Over the sea to Skye' annoyingly under their breath.

The white strips soon made way for blue ones which were in turn replaced by red ones. Then after a freak accident in the washroom involving the luckless Andy Grogger, a 'cumly' wench invitingly called Laura Love and a jar of pickled eggs, the jerseys got mixed up, the colours ran together and when Hearts resurrected themselves from a short period of disbandment, they did so playing under the name of St Andrews with somewhere in the region of thirty woollen maroon coloured tops at their disposal. There were many grumblings from stalwart Edinburghers concerned that the club was unnecessarily aligning itself with another, much smaller town, however once it became known that as a concession, players and supporters would be allowed to visit The Bottle Dungeon at St Andrews Castle for half price on weekends and public holidays, the dissenting voices soon abated. For his part, Andy Groggar was booted out the football club and his final reference in the annuls of Edinburgh history comes surprisingly by way of an excerpt from The Scotsman's review of the Edinburgh Fringe.' Sensational, side-splittingly hilarious, Andy Groggar's bombastic brand of humour will have you in hysterics right from the off.' It announced . Surprisingly indeed since every paying customer who saw Andy's stand up act thought it was a lot of bollocks, didn't laugh once and felt strongly compelled at various stages of the performance to demand their money back .

Hearts first taste of silverware came in 1878 when they gratifyingly beat Hibs 3-2 in the fourth replay of the Edinburgh FA Cup Final. The Jam Tarts at that time were finding it much harder than their local rivals to recruit quality players. Hibs, because of their religious ties, had a seemingly unending line-up of young catholic men longing to pull on the famous green shirt. Hearts simply couldn't match this strong pull and so, when captain , Tom Purdie lifted the FA trophy, it was considered by all and sundry to be a major achievement. All except for the small group of Hibs fans that is who felt it was a major inconvenience and insisted on giving the jubilant Purdie a 'right good doin' in the street on his way home from the match.

The East Meadows was becoming an increasingly difficult place to play as it was regularly overcrowded with spectators milling around and generally interfering with the matches trying to take place there. For a while Hearts solved the problem by playing their bigger games at the EFA's ground at Powburn. This not only offered the club a more organised , self contained venue, but it attractively gave the club the opportunity to charge fans to get in. It was only a short term solution however and 1881 saw a permanent venue change for Hearts as they collected their things and headed for a field on Wardlaw Street. Now based in the Gorgy area of the town, the club laid down its roots in what would become known as Old Tynecastle Park. It was while they were there that the club suffered the dubious honour of being the first club to be investigated by the game's governing body for 'illegal practices'. While the official transcripts accuse the club of illegally paying two players wages to turn out for the then amateur outfit, rumour held that the club were in fact guilty of the much more serious crime of illegally renting 'much valued' horse-drawn carriage parking spaces in the city centre to desperate businessmen and office workers.

The early years of the Scottish League showed a clear bias against the East coast with only Hearts and St Bernards hailing from that side of the country. Hibs, for their sins were considered to be 'Irish', as in the phrase 'as radioactively pollutant as the Irish', and despite being a well established club and always available at short notice for a kick-around, they were forcibly excluded from Scottish football's early dealings. After some six years at Old Tynecastle, Hearts jumped across the road to the current site where they unusually started to build the stadium around two pitches. After two years of painful indecision as to which park to play on, it was eventually decided to dispense with one set of lines and goalposts and go with the traditional single pitch approach.

The first league matches took place on the 16th of March 1890 and on a day that 10,000 saw Celtic beaten by Renton, a crowd of around 4,000 watched Hearts succumb easily to Rangers at Old Ibrox (Start as you mean to go on I say). The Gorgy side did little to set the pulses racing as far as early league performances were concerned. They did however establish themselves as an excellent cup side and lifted the '90/'91 Scottish Cup beating Dumbarton in the final. Again the centre of controversy, Hearts prompted outrage when in an earlier tie against East Stirlingshire, the maroon shirted outfield player Jimmy Adams punched away an almost certain goal yet he suffered little in the way of punishment. This, together with a clutch of similar incidents, forced the league into adopting the concept of the penalty kick into the rule-book[15]. Making up the rules as they went along was a notable feature of those early encounters and it's a concept that many of our more traditional whistlers still happily adhere to today.

We probably can't leave the early days of Hearts without mentioning the great Bobby Walker. Nicknamed 'Bobby' he joined the Jambos just after the famous Scottish Cup final of 1896 - Hearts had run out 3-1 victors over Hibs in a fixture that was to be the only Scottish Cup final ever to be played outside Glasgow. Walker was Hearts first bona fide superstar. Slight but tenacious, had you met him on the street you would have looked at his thick neck and short dark hair and probably have taken him for a featherweight boxer rather than a football forward. But a skilful football player he certainly was and in those early days where players liked, primarily, to show off their dribbling prowess , Walker was better known for his expertise in passing the ball

---

[15]   It has been mooted that in 2011 the rule will be extended to away teams playing at Ibrox or Celtic Park however nothing official has been confirmed at this stage.

and bringing his fellow team-mates into the game. He became known as 'The Father of Altruistic football' and his rare (at that time) brand of football earned him twenty-nine caps for Scotland. Bearing in mind the national team played a lot fewer games back then, usually confined to contests with England , Wales and Northern Ireland, this was a fair haul and impressively his international career spanned some 13 years. In the 1934 Football Encyclopaedia, Editor Frank Johnson referred to Walker as ' The greatest natural footballer who ever played. Hearts captain of the time, Charlie Thomson, also dubbed him 'The best player in Europe'. Thomson, however, was later quoted in a match-day programme profile as saying that his favourite comedian was ' the immortal Andy Grogger' so we must treat the player's claims with relative suspicion.

There was no doubting the validity of King Haakan of Norway's opinion though. In Hearts first overseas tour of 1912 , a trip which took them somewhat adventurously to Scandinavia, the football loving regent had expressly wished to see the Scottish forward play. After the game Hakaan was asked what he thought of Walker's performance. Painfully nervous amidst such international media attention, and with a remarkably poor command of English he replied ' Take my hirsute wife and brand her like a prize ox! '. Shortly afterwards he was violently sick into the champagne flute of a prominent SFA official who happened to be in attendance. The gentleman in question, who was apparently on an official 'fact -finding' review of soap dispensers in European stadia toilets, took great offence to this action and an international incident was only narrowly avoided when Hakaan promised to supply George Square with a Christmas tree for the next hundred years and send sub-standard entries to the Eurovision song contest in perpetuity.

4.

It's a beautiful Spring afternoon. The kind of day that sneaks up like an early party guest and has you habitually kitting yourself out in a shirt, a jumper *and* a jacket before you become dully aware that your pants are uncomfy and there's a moisture to your underarms reminiscent of your first job interview.

The trip through has been a pleasant affair with Jonesy's music being of greater mass appeal than normal (a tuneful band called The Desperados who had our toes tapping with a wonderfully poppy number called 'Grease stain on my brand new tie') The car windows have been tentatively edged down a couple of inches to allow some pleasant fresh air to circulate and we seem to be, for the first time in a long while, collectively at peace with the world.

It's a simple route into Tynecastle these days providing you can clear up in your own mind whether you are aiming for City Centre Bypass North or South. Having correctly chosen South *and* having quick-wittedly taken the slip road that leads up the hill to the roundabout at the People's Ford garage, and *not* having plundered cheerfully onwards to the likes of Musselburgh , Berwick upon Tweed and Marrakesh, then it's a direct line into Gorgy Road from then on.

A predictable palate of conversation then strikes up. Predictable because the same subjects arise every time we hit the main route into Tynecastle from this side of the city. Firstly it consists of me anxiously asking ' Is it okay to be driving up this bus lane then?', nearly crashing the car as I crane my neck to read the road signs flashing by. Then Jonesy comments on the inappropriately named 'Corn Exchange' music venue which we're now in the vicinity of , and how its '…. like listening to a band in yer school assembly hall' apparently. Finally Dave glances contemplatively out the window as Saughton Prison slips past and speculates to the air more than anything, 'I wonder how James is doing these days' . Silence typically follows with slight shrugs or barely discernable shakes of the head our only response to the question.

James Ingram was a university buddy of Dave's. For a while, in those new, post high-school years of adjustment and enlightenment, they were pretty tight. Of course Dave still saw us but James was a new friend with university life and university people in common. He came originally from up North somewhere, a small place near Bara with one vowel and four g's in its name, and had come down to the big city of Edinburgh to be educated on the back of a hefty collection of 'A' graded Highers gained admirably against the backdrop of having recently lost his mother to cancer. His lilting accent, ruddy complexion and a shockingly full head of wavy, sewn-on caramel hair were typically Hebridean and it wouldn't have seemed unreasonable for him to whip an Arran Knit sweater over his head and break off into a verse of Flower of Scotland at any given moment. During the odd weekends I spent in his company I always found him to be pleasant enough if a touch intense depending on the subject of conversation. He was severely socialist in his viewpoint and had that wearing ability to bring a political stance to almost any conversation. It didn't matter whether we were talking about football, women, or the best variety of peanuts, James could manage to quote Karl Marx or wangle the word 'proletariat' into any given sentence. Impressive in a peculiar sort of way.

Yes, intense would describe him best. That said he was generous to a fault both with his attention and his behaviour. Unlike most hyper-opinionated and vociferous people, James never commandeered the conversation nor resorted to verbal bullying. He, instead, gave everyone their place and always made his point in an annoyingly lucid and winning manner despite having given you a clear runway to land your much stronger argument. So much so that he could almost criminally strip down your mind and have you nodding in consternated agreement that the government *should* nationalise your socks (both of them) and it would be sound political and economic policy if generations of asylum seekers were allowed to live in your bath, under your bed and in your underwear drawer – all rent free.

James wasn't the sort you would have said had a temper as such. But the day he killed that man in the car park of the Ikea near Penicuik, something must have snapped. It was Jonesy that saw the report in the paper and after consultation with Dave and a quick confirming phone call, it appeared the reported

James Ingram was indeed our James Ingram of the islands with the hair and the leftie politics. Apparently he had got involved in an altercation with the driver of a four-by-four who had, in the middle of the busy superstore car-park, deliberately, and quite selfishly we all agreed, taken up two rare and precious parking spaces with his oversized vehicle. James hadn't mean to kill him of course but the stress of the ensuing argument and the climactic punch to the jaw, was unfortunate enough to trigger a cardiac arrest in Mr Four-by-four. Before the evening was out the bad driver was in the morgue and James was in custody on a manslaughter charge. With a gaggle of witnesses on hand at the time wielding bags full of clever yet surprisingly inexpensive 'home solutions', there was no question that he would go down, it was just a matter of for how long.

So Dave's opinionated pal from the university is now three years into a ten year stretch at Her Majesty's Prison Saughton. No longer does he get to rant at smug Tory sympathisers on Question Time, nor does he nip out for a pint of milk when he feels like it. Instead he learns car-mechanics, carves little figures out of rock and has Morgan Freeman audibly narrate his life in a well-paced monotone drawl. Well he does in my mind at least.

"A cautionary tale" Dave says thoughtfully this time as we drove past the prison.

"What, for four-by-four drivers or university graduates with short fuses?" I reply, my eyebrows arched suggestively. I catch a dark look and clear my throat self-consciously. "Sooo ... ehhhh, does its bother you that he's in there, you know ... in jail?"

"Hmmmmnn?.... Nah not really, we weren't that close" Dave adds dismissively, turning away to cast a glazed look at the warm, inviting world outside. At which point The Desperados cut the mood uneasily , picking up another summery anthem with a chorus that was insistent in asking us in repetitive fashion ' Where have all the 2 for 1 deodorant offers gone?' By the third refrain though, all three of us are singing along in full voice; a car-full of consumers with grave concerns over cosmetics availability, heading ever closer to Tynecastle Park.

5.

The first time I ever went to Tyncastle I ended up in the main stand with my dad on one side of me and Dave on the other, crying my eyes out. I didn't look but I assumed they were crying too. I was a young sensitive foal with emotion coming out of my ears and it was a Wednesday evening (when Wednesdays were the standard midweek football night and all the better for it) cup quarter-final replay. I had never seen the Rovers go so far in the Scottish Cup and , much like the rest of the town, I was buzzing. Lee Renicks, a red haired freckly boy in my class had worn a rosette attached lopsidedly to his grey school pullover all that day and Mr Watson our teacher, hadn't make him take it off, such was the fervour of the moment. Dad, in a rare show of graciousness where the Rovers were concerned, had made a last minute commitment to taking us to Tynecastle, and with our teeth chattering with the vibration, had hammered the road, foot to the floor of his Triumph Dolomite, all the way to Edinburgh to get there just in time for kick-off.

The first game had been a dour, goalless encounter but Hearts had come out for the replay in an altogether different frame of mind. They pounded our goal from the start and we could do nothing it seemed to stem the almost incessant onslaught. All around us in the shadowy wooden main stand the Hearts fans got louder and more voluble. On the pitch two men were reeking havoc on our withering defence. A tall imposing centre half called Frank Liddell, who may have been neither tall nor imposing but in my memory he stands eight foot two and worthy of a Scotland call up. And a pale, rakish forward, Willie Gibson, who's control was mesmerising and his danger constant and predatory. Gibson hit the post twice and the bar once, each time the ferocious home support were on their feet willing the ball into the net. Each time they fell back to their seats, shook their heads and licked their lips.

We hung on valiantly until five minutes to go and when Liddell rose in slow motion and bulleted his header high into the net and the universe erupted. My ear drums threatened to burst as the night caved in on me. A wee boy overwhelmed by all the towering, clamouring figures around me.

Then it started. Scattered and hopeful at first but within seconds a defiant, unified tribal incantation. This was the first time I heard the best song in Scottish football and with all those giants around me stamping their feet rhythmically on the old wooden flooring, the stand shook in terrifying fashion and it was all too much.

H-E-A-R-T-S
**If you cannae spell it then here's what it says
Hearts glorious Hearts
Its down at Tynecastle they bide
The talk of the toun are the boys in maroon
And Auld Reekie supports them with pride ....**

That's when I lost it and started bubbling. My team were beat, I was gutted to the point of vomiting myself inside out, and the world was shaking to a steady, incessant , rumbling beat. My dad put his hand on my shoulder but for a minute or so I was inconsolable. Only when I heard the strains of 'We'll support you ever more' rising from the tightly packed band of Rovers fans standing down to our left did I look up with bleary eyes and realise that life had not ended, that everything was going to be alright.

We didn't equalize. There was no miracle turnaround in the final few minutes of the game. I don't think we even got a kick of the ball as the Hearts players , their job done, passed the ball around with the calmness and ease that only relief in its most extreme form lets you do. I had to endure one final ear-drum bursting cheer as the final whistle went but by then I was a harder man.

6.

The next time I visited the tight old ground was a freezing December night in the mid eighties. I know it was round about that era because 'Johnny Banger' one of the mental guys in the Rovers 'squad' had one of those Flock of Seagulls hairdos and, despite it being sub-zero , Dave had the sleeves of his Polar Gear jacket rolled up to his elbows. Fannies.

What stayed with me most about that evening strangely wasn't the game itself but the walk to the ground. I can picture like it happened yesterday. Us being dropped off by the supporters bus up at Russell Road beside Roseburn Street then creeping through the tight, foggy streets towards Tynecastle, shivering with more than just the cold. Round past the Royal Mail sorting office we weaved, under the railway, through the high double arches of the road bridge eventually finding our way into McLeod Street. The icy mist hanging on the ground around the pale white street lamps, killer-trees stretching their bony wooden arms over the fence straining for our throats. And me, squinting in the shadows for a glimpse of Sherlock Holmes or Jack the Ripper abroad on dangerous business - I had an active imagination in those days. Even the normally friendly Tynecastle High School with its arched windows and long row of chimneys along its roof, looked more like a haunted shadowy morgue echoing of ice-cold death and despair. The relief I felt when we eventually rounded the final corner and came upon the frosted glow of the floodlights fighting through the strangling fog was palpable.

Hearts at that time were emerging from an unsettling period in their history. The late 70's had seen them relegated out of the top league for the first time ever and their loyal fans had been forced to experience the highs and lows of seeing their team yo-yo between leagues on an almost yearly basis. This uncertainty would continue painfully until 1983 when, along with St Johnstone they were promoted to the Premier League and they have managed to remain there ever since. On that bitterly cold, mysterious night though, Hearts seemed to have put all their inconsistencies behind them and the three-nil defeat we suffered kept the chill in our souls long after we had jumped on the bus and headed back West from the capital.

7.

Today's chill is of a slightly different variety. Five points adrift at the bottom of the league and with Partick at home to fellow relegation battlers Motherwell, a bad result today could snuff out any hopes of us climbing the table and dare I say it , escaping relegation.

For now we remain upbeat and our chief concern revolves around which pub to drink in. I've been in most of the establishments surrounding Tynecastle over the years and they all hold their own appeal. From the staunchly partisan surroundings of Robertsons where I suggest you practice your best east-coast accent to ensure a hassle free pint, to the light and friendly Athletic Arms (or The Diggers as it is more colloquially known) at the top of Henderson Terrace. Historically a favoured haunt by the area's grave-diggers, hence the name, it is also Jonesy's favourite what with its distinctive coffin clock hanging behind the bar, framed photos of Hearts players, landlords and possibly grave-diggers on the walls, as well as the promise of a game of darts in the back room. Jonesy immediately suggests a visit as we jump out the car into the soft warm air. Dave and I have other ideas however. Our preferred pub in this neck of the woods is The Roseburn Bar. Given its Victorian high ceilinged splendour, its rich array of sweaty ales and the fact that it is a hundred yards from where we have parked the car, it is the natural choice. Together with a mealy mouthed Jonesy, we scoot by the Lounge door at the side of the building, slope our way through the pub's main street-corner entrance, over the circular floor-tiled insignia which pronounces the pub's allegiance to both football *and* rugby, and into the body of the kirk as it were. The bar is Edinburgh through and through and blends its old traditional feel happily enough with the modern air that comes with the presence of plasma TV screens and plenty of them . A quick 'shufty' at the state of play in the lounge tells us that the small side-room is intimate to the point of bursting and we consequently decide to stay in the main bar area. Despite there being a good number of Hearts and Arthurston fans in, the bar feels comfortably roomy. Catching sight of the long, well stocked gantry Dave nominates himself for drinks duty leaving Jonesy and I to find a space to call our own which we do quickly and efficiently, tucking ourselves in behind one of the pub's many varnished wooden divides.

8.

Half way down our first drink Jamie Dott slips momentarily into our company, a half-filled pint of Deuchars in one hand and a blue and white William Hill coupon in the other. Jamie is a pink faced, smiley lad we've been acquainted with since high school. He was never the brightest and my lasting association with Jamie is of a classroom argument in third year where he took on the whole class vociferously, his firm belief being that the teams on University challenge sat one above the other in the studio ('with the team in the upper row having to climb up a flight of stairs to reach their seats', I remember him explaining quite authoritatively). Now a town planner with the local council, Jamie has two party-pieces. One is downing a full pint of Strongbow Cider in a wunner then rifting, in its entirety, the Kylie Minogue hit 'I should be so lucky'. The other is quoting you into submission with a selection from his extensive collection of 'Colmanballs' until you can't take it any longer. Everyone has their thing I suppose and recounting bumbling yet gently humorous football quotes from players, managers, commentators and the like are clearly his.

And he can recite them verbatim on request like he was reading them straight from a book. A skill which has always impressed me and concerned me in equal measures. Yes, Jamie's recollective capacity is remarkable, however after every conversation with him, I am invariably left with the nagging feeling that because I can't do the same, even remotely, I must clearly be several steps further down the path to Camp Alzheimers than most 'normal' people would admit to. For I am incapable of remembering even one.

Jamie shoves his coupon in his pocket and scratches his head through thick Worzel Gummidge straw hair smiling contagiously.

"Heard a good one the other day boys", he starts . Our enthusiastic grins give full encouragement to him to continue.

"Was listening to Radio 5 Live the other night and I swear to God one of the pundits said 'Its now 1-1, an exact reversal of the score-line on Saturday- absolute quality don't you think?

As I said its gentle humour and we smirk accordingly. I, myself, let out a slightly forced guffaw just to be polite causing Dave to throw me a 'it wasn't *that* funny' look and likewise causing me to respond with a nervous shrug.

"My favourite is an Alex Ferguson one' Dave then injects surprisingly. "Fergie once sagely pointed out to an on hand reporter that 'Its a conflict of parallels'. I don't remember what 'it' was exactly but it was funny nevertheless....."

"Ohhh!' butts in Jonesy excitedly, "Remember when they announced on Radio 5 Live that 'Emile Zola has scored again for Chelsea." That was brilliant.

"What's the best ones you've ever heard Jamie?", I ask sipping at a dark, cloudy pint that's as 'reekie' as Edinburgh itself and judging by the aftertaste possible a little bit 'aulder'.

"A top ten of quotes boys?" says Jamie licking his lips, still smiling his disarming smile. "Hmmnnn I don't think I've ever thought about it like that." he continues in a definitive manner that suggests in actual fact he had given it quite a bit of thought. After a short pause for effect he clears his throat.

"Weeeeelll .... I'd probably start with ...." and off he goes with all the confidence of a stand up comic who's been round the block too many times to count and knows his stuff gets the laughs. Jamie's top ten, aided and abetted by the hilarious manner that he spouted them were these belters;

First up at number ten was

'I never predict anything and I never will' - Paul Gascoigne.

Next came David Beckham's legendary comment

'I definitely want Brooklyn Christened but I don't know into what religion yet'

The middle order was packed with some real quality , namely;

'Celtic manager David Hay still has a fresh pair of legs up his sleeve!' *- John Greig*

' My parents have been there for me ever since I was about 7' - again, *David Beckham*

'More football later but first lets see the goals from the Scottish Cup Final' Des Lynam

'So the United States are through to the next qualifying round of this world cup and will play the winner of Trinidad against Tobago' – *Unknown German Presenter.*

'What I don't understand is how a Frenchman can be playing for Manchester United. He's not even from England – *Lord Denning QC (on the legendary Cantona kung-fu incident)*

A bit of a worry we all agree, that last one. The Big Three according to Jamie pick themselves. At number three deservedly came ;

'Borussia Munchengladbach 5 Borussia Dortmund 1, so Munchengladbach win the Borussia Derby' *- Gary Newbon*

and at number two and narrowly missing the top spot was the absolute belter;

'I think this could be our best victory over Germany since the war' – John Motson .

We collectively hold our breathes as Jamie changed over the weight on his feet and paused as if waiting for drum roll. " I defy you to say this isn't the best football quote ever!" he says looking each of us in the eye. Slowly and dramatically he rhymes off his all-time favourite, Jonathon Pierce's much loved intro;

' Welcome to Bologna on Capital Gold for England versus San Marino with Tennents Pilsner, brewed with Czechoslovakian yeast for that extra pilsner taste and England are a goal down. '

He does it in an accent that sounds uncannily like Pierce - the 'More-English- than-the-Chelsea-Pensioners' commentator, and we dissolve into fits of raucous laughter causing most of the folk in our nearby vicinity to turn round and see where the commotion is coming from. Jamie takes the plaudits for his entertainment graciously then laughing and shaking his head, slips back to his group who are hanging round one of the high roof pillars nearer to the old traditional bar.

9.

Whilst Hibs had their Famous Five to revere and hold up in adulation, Hearts had their own 'team within a team' heroes. The aptly named 'Terrible Trio'.

In the 50's and early 60's it was commonplace for fans and press alike to Christen defensive, midfield and attacking units with memorable, flamboyant tags. Hibs of course had their Famous Five. St Johnstone had their 'Thingmabob Three' a highly successful frontline from the mid-sixties who no-one could immediately remember the names of. And of course who could forget Dundee's celebrated 'Fairy-cake Four' of the early 50's, a rakish band of strikers who would cleverly distract the most unforgiving of defences with tempting, homemade icing-covered buns they carried around in white Tupperware containers. The Four scored countless vital goals as the opposition guiltily searched for change in order to 'buy a cake for charity'. And then there was Albion Rovers' 'Effluent Eleven' a collection of much-loved 'tryers' whose desperate persistence spanned decades at the Coatbridge club .

Heart's Terrible Trio were special though. Alfie Conn[16] on the left, Jimmy Wardhaugh on the right and Willie Bauld through the middle. In this formation they scored over 850 goals for Hearts between them. The key was in their 'blend'. Conn standing 5"7" wasn't tall but his stocky frame, tenacious and dynamic style, and his powerful shooting made him harder to stop than an exploding beer can. Bauld by contrast was a more thoughtful player. Prone to stopping mid- attack to perform breeze-velocity calculations with the aid of a wind sock and a compass secreted carefully under his maroon jersey, he terrorised defences with his phenomenal aerial power and intermittent flatulence. Wardhaugh was a dribbler, but not in an old-person eating soup type of way, and his non-stop running and ability to slip past the opposition like a Bryl-Creamed ninja perfectly complimented his team-mates' style.

Yet this collective presence of greatness wasn't enough to spare Hearts once again from the tag of 'Glorious Losers'. Even amidst the relatively successful 50's and 60's, the Jam Tarts were to feel the eye-watering pinch of 'nearliness' on more than one occasion. Despite holding a seven point lead in early March of 1957 they contrived to lose the league that year to a trailing but persistent Rangers outfit. A few years later, in 1965, Hearts excruciatingly lost the league title on the final day of the season. Needing a draw or even a single goal defeat in the last game at home to Kilmarnock, they managed to lose two-nil and finished second with a goal average of 0.042 worse than Kilmarnock, the grateful champions of the day.

---

16   Father of 'Ohhh Alfie, Alfie. Alfie, Alfie, Alfie, Alfie, Alfie Conn', the first player post- war to play for both Rangers and Celtic.

Which brings us neatly if uncomfortably back to Hearts' most modern and possibly most painful of failures – The Disaster at Dens , The Dundee Debacle , The Parade of the Pooh-Packed Pants. Having survived yet another final day disappointment some four years earlier under McDonald's budding tenure when they failed in their bid for promotion back to the Premier (this time at home to Motherwell), it seemed inconceivable that Hearts could fall on their faces again.

But fall they did.

It was big flat noses all round.

And yet it still remains easier to be sympathetic with, rather than critical of, the Hearts effort of 1986 despite the nasty stench of predictability that filled Dens Park that day. Alex MacDonald and his trusty assistant Sandy Jardine worked nothing short of miracles in their efforts to turn a Dads' Army bunch of aging journeymen into a committed and driven squad capable make a serious, concerted, season-long challenge for the league title. Eventually, with a team of familiar, if not superstar names MacDonald steered a ship of hope through a mountain range of challenges and in doing so wove himself a reputation as an ideal subject for mixed metaphors as well as one of the most able (yet cruelly unrecognised) managers ever to grace the Scottish game. It would not be far-fetched to suggest that had Rangers or Celtic overachieved under a stewardship similar to MacDonald's at Hearts (and then Airdrieonians) then Glasgow would probably boast at least one Champions League Finalist by now.

Unfortunately for Alex and Hearts, taking that one little step forward and actually winning something was just too much of a demand for the wee man's somewhat limited inside leg measurement. This was merely highlighted one week after the Dundee defeat when Hearts, presented with a quick opportunity for salvation, lost an oft-forgotten Scottish Cup final to Aberdeen by a resounding three goals to nil. Again, after so much promise, the newly dusted down Tynecastle trophy room was locked back up its grasping shelves remaining empty with nothing to show. Maybe its just the Hearts way.

10.

1986 was to be pivotal for Hearts and Scottish Football in general. Not everyone was happy and encouraged by the Hearts challenge that year and with Rangers finishing some fifteen points off the pace in the championship race, a sleeping giant started to stir.

Some called it a revolution, others, an infection. Whatever the prevailing opinions though, it was clear that Graham Souness's arrival at Rangers and the simultaneous 'Grand Opening' of David Murray's bank book was going to impact the game like nothing had before. First came the English players, most of them aging but still quite useful, then an influx of European talent, highly paid and of a quality the likes of which Hearts couldn't hope to match. The Jam Tarts quickly faded with the curtains and Alex MacDonald was eventually sacked by chairman Wallace Mercer for not keeping up with the pace.

It all seemed hopeless. How could anyone hope to compete against the resources behind the might of Glasgow Rangers? Even Celtic had been taken by surprise, their 'biscuit tin' approach now under more scrutiny than ever before. There were only two options for the other clubs – Focus on good management and nurture young Scottish talent through the ranks in the hope that in the longer term they *could* compete. Or spend like there's no tomorrow and bring in foreign talent to meet Rangers head on and play them at their own game.

Much to the consternation of bank managers throughout the land the bulk of the Premier League teams chose the latter. Except while Rangers paraded their 'real deal' football celebrities, the other clubs touted a bunch of 'Stars in Your Eyes' second string wannabees. 'Tonight Matthew I want to be Brian Laudrup ... or Paul Gascoigne ... or ....' And the Chairmen all paid through the nose for the privilege. Hearts were no different and valiantly they tried to introduce their own brand of Foreign imports. While they found limited success in the likes of Stephane Adam, (Joe) Pasquali Bruno and Christian Salvatori, others were less impressive. Yugoslav Husref Musemic, whose English clearly didn't stretch to understanding ' Move yer arse ya lazy bastard!' and Hans Eskilsson who looked like some unholy merger of 80's Argentina star Alberto Tarrantini and the big daft leader of the Hair Bear Bunch offered two instances where clearly 'European' doesn't necessarily mean 'good'. Big Hans was particularly 'limited' and who around Tynecastle will forget his wonderful public excuse that he missed a virtually open goal because 'the crowd put him off.' (Oooh, oooh Mr Peevely- Someone opened a bag of crisps just as I was shooting!)

Mind you it can't be easy coming to a foreign country, settling in, learning new ways, communicating effectively, whilst at the same time getting rained upon incessantly, and all the while staying focussed and maintaining a quality in one's work.

It begs the question 'How do these Portuguese, Spanish, Slovenian, or whatever characters cope with the demands of the English language as spoken in the indomitable style of your everyday Scotsman. Are they contractually bound to go on courses to recognise words like 'swedger', 'bawheid' and 'Irn Bru' before they sign up? Are they given a welcome to the SPL video that shows them how to deal with doctors' surgery receptionists or unhelpful bank clerks? I doubt it. As Scots we pride ourselves on our friendly and welcoming demeanour but in reality I have the suspicion that we rarely go out of our way to roll out the tartan carpet and offer help where help is needed.

And so for any foreign imports reading, I'm going to rectify this unfortunate lack of support and consideration here and now by turning this section into a condensed yet useful reference manual offering handy phrases to suit almost every eventuality. Hopefully this will help the bemused foreign player through his first few months in Scotland and encourage him to learn more complex vocabulary in due course. For ease of use I have split each statement into suitable categories.

Section 1 : With the press.

These phrases can easily be integrated into post match

interviews with reporters win, lose or draw.

1. "I am over the moon with my goal/with my performance/ to be here and at the end of the day we'll take things one game a time."
2. "........ is the only team I have ever wanted to play for in Scotland. When I was younger I used to listen for the .... result on the town radio every week." (insert team you have signed for)
3. "No , I have no ambition to ever play for my country again."
4. "Didn't you used to play with the Old Firm?"

Section 2: Day to day affairs

Deal comfortably with everyday situations away from the stadium. The following should cover every eventuality;

1. "Ahhh sorry, I have just installed double glazing AND a new kitchen – Do not call again."
2. "Can you speak a little slower please my English is too good for this"
3. "Here is my settlement of your account Mr Tradesman , please feel free to tell all your friends in the pub about my signing talks with Celtic and also of my sexual encounter with the Dyson Vacuum cleaner."
4. "Please explain to me again all these different coloured bins outside my house as they are confusing me."
5. "I'm sorry I don't understand, I'm from Wishaw."

Section 3 : Out and about

Hitting the bright lights of Glasgow or Edinburgh or finding yourself out in Hamilton after a near fatal concoction of Champagne, Carling extra-colds and Aftershocks? Try using these;

1. "I have not been drinking officer, my erratic driving is due to an overdose of Benylin I've taken for a bad cold"
2. "Your skin is an attractive shade of orange sexy Scottish lady, is that a natural tan?"

3. "Yes I can wait ten minutes for a special fish supper"
4. "Do you know who I am?"
5. "How much for the Lesbian show?"
6. "I'm sorry I don't understand, I'm from Wishaw."

Section 4 : At training

Get through the rigours of those long, dedicated, hard-working days between the big games;
1. "The dispenser has ran out, can I have another betting slip please?"
2. "I cannot attend training today as I have flown home to consult with my personal physician"
3. My niggling thigh strain appears to have flared up and I will be unavailable for the mid-week cup tie at Peterhead"
4. "Hurry up, Its your break!"

Section 5 : Miscellaneous

And for everything else;

1. "When is the creditors meeting, I would like my wages please!"
2. "Please take this Kleeneze Catalogue away, I have no recurring need for tight lidded plastic receptacles?"
3. "Excuse me can you explain the difference between biological and non-biological washing powder please?
4. "Take me to Glasgow Airport taxi-man but I will not be paying your foul boundary charge thievery"
5. I'm sorry I don't understand, I'm from Wishaw.

11.

Sitting behind the goals in the Roseburn Stand I can't help noticing a lot of empty maroon seats in the ground. It surely can't be that the lure of the mighty Rovers has failed to attract the Jambos in their excited droves therefore I'm only left to assume that the Tynecastle entrance prices must be as steep as the gradient of it's three 'new' stands. Despite the visit of Arthurston being what Hearts would classify a 'Category B' match ('B' standing for Bollocks opposition), prices for the premium areas of the ground are still in the vicinity of twenty eight quid. Paying ten pounds more for the big 'Category A' games and rightly you'd be miffed that the ticket doesn't include a three course meal, a back rub and a deluxe car-valet with complimentary 'Magic Tree' air-freshener. Hardly a pricing policy to encourage new or casual fans to make their visit more regular I'd venture.

A shiver runs down my spine as I look left towards the old three-tiered main stand. Lower slung than its newer surroundings, it's very presence immediately takes me back to that fearsome and disappointing night I came here as a youngster, the night it held me in its skelf inducing clutches and ran its fingers through my soul. In the gloom, behind eight white, view-sapping support poles, fans are walking up or scooting down stairs, standing conversing with neighbours or sitting in their seats patiently waiting for kick-off which is now less than ten minutes away. High on the red tiled roofing sits the well known fake owl, surveying all below, placed at such a vantage point to scare the birds away now that Stevie Fulton and Davy Bowman are no longer at the club.

Unlike most grounds sporting the new style boxy stands, Tynecastle feels nicely enclosed due in the main to the neatly designed floodlights being crammed into the corner gaps. Adverts and large screen prints of famous Hearts players link the lighting's scaffolding legs and further protect the stadium from prying eyes beyond . Resultantly, what atmosphere is generated in the ground remains in the ground and doesn't escape through the gaps and down the street outside. Away from the bread and butter of league tussles, I've seen Scotland play here and with a sell-out crowd crammed into its confines, Tynecastle makes for a wonderfully fearsome and, intimidating venue.

Casting a critical eye of comparison over the modern sections of the stadium, the Gorgie and Wheatfield Stands and indeed the stand we're in are not quite as steep as Love Street's but they are getting on that way. A Thora Hird stair-lift would probably suffice rather than a funicular railway for transportation to your seat but I still wouldn't risk carrying any more than one Bovril at a time whist scaling any of its faces.

Yes, from the outside Tynecastle constantly looks like it needs a good stretch of its legs. Whether entering from the cramped wee street beside Gorgy Parish Church (as away fans did in the old days) or from the Ticket Centre side of the ground, its tightly wedged demeanour prevails. From the inside however, its 18,000 odd seats are comfortably accommodated in a Doctor Who TARDIS kind of way and as our own maroon plastic chairs are momentarily vacated to give our team an upstanding welcome our cause seems as clear and wide open as the Tynecastle grass in front of us.

12.

Despite needing the win, we lose the game two one. An opening ten minutes of feverish, pressing football soon evaporated into a nervy ineffectual display and it was frankly no surprise when Hearts took the lead on the half-hour. A terrible sliced clearance by Robert Crush, reinstated to the side as cover for an injured Ivan Pecnik, only made it as far as a loitering Hearts forward at the edge of our box. His resultant shot at goal, a half-hit trundler, cruelly deflected off one hairy leg in a crowd and rolled into the net with the keeper wrong-footed in the other direction.

The second , two minutes into the second half, was the nail in our coffin. Again Crush was at fault. Slow to react to a quickly taken free kick , he allowed his man to skip into the penalty box unopposed then, in a desperate bid to make up lost ground, launched into a rash sliding-tackle which the Hearts man saw coming a mile off. A maroon sock was left trailing and Crush could do nothing but slide on through, upending his opponent in high flying style. You'd have thought the Hearts guy was auditioning for 'House of The Flying Daggers' but it was still a foul nonetheless. Thomson got a hand to the penalty but it was a well struck ball and unfortunately it found its way in via the side of the net.

Two disappointing events which subsequently prompted a slightly unsavoury incident between Crush and one of our supporters sitting down near the front of the stand. It happened some five minutes after the penalty as Crush himself retrieved the ball from just behind the goals after an errant Hearts effort had skimmed past the post. I didn't hear the full volley of abuse but I did hear it end with the line "Haw Schabbel, get that waster Bobby Crush aff!"

Now one thing to be mentioned right here is that Robert does not like getting called Bobby. Years of smart arse comments in reference to the *other* Bobby Crush, a velvet suited piano player with a bowl-cut and a salesman's smile from the 70s talent show 'Opportunity Knocks' have undoubtedly left him 'on a short fuse ' shall we say.

'Where's yer piano Crush?',' Yer nuthin but a pianist Bobby!'. Yes I'm sure he's heard them all. The last time I recall a flare up like this was after the final whistle at Stenhousemuir about four years ago when a guy hanging over the barrier yelled in an erudite manner 'Away and tinkle the ivories ya Bobby Crush fudd-ye!'. At which point the nearby defender, who had just scored the only goal of the game .... into his own net and was clearly in poor humour, calmly bent down, unlaced both his boots, slowly took them off, straightened up ..... and threw them, one at time, like black and white guided missiles, hitting the bloke squarely on the head with an accuracy and velocity that Babe Ruth would have been proud of. Robert then sprinted over to the sideline to presumably finish the job by which time the antagonist was legging it, a hand over one eye, to the exit for fear of his life.

Despite today's abuse having fewer instrumental references it would appear to have still struck a chord (thank you very much – I'm here all week) , and rather than walk away the bigger man, Crush picked up the ball and in Joe Montana style threw it ten yards or so into the stand smacking the guilty party on the nose and lower forehead with consummate ease yet remarkable force. Miraculously the referee and his assistants caught none of this and wearing a Les Mottram-esque expression that said 'I know something happened there but I'm not sure what.' the whistler waved for the clearly agitated Crush to hurry up and get the ball into play. The Rovers fans for their part did little to react to the outburst, indeed a bout of laughter followed by a ripple of sympathetic applause followed Robert back onto the pitch.

We scored a consolation goal with about five minutes to go and the crowd got briefly excited but truthfully a comeback was never on the cards. When the referee's final whistle blew, a half-hearted round of applause was observed but seemed scarcely appropriate and as I took one last look at the players trudging of the pitch before I disappeared into the belly of the stand, it suddenly crossed my mind that it might be a while before we're back at Tynecastle again.

13.

I was fortunate enough to witness first hand the ecstasy that May evening in 2006 when Hearts saw off a stodgy Aberdeen side to finish second place in the SPL and therefore secure Champions League (qualifier) football at Tyncastle for the following season. Again, and without wishing to sound like a broken record, It could have resulted in so much more for the Jam Tarts that year. Yet when Paul Hartley struck home the deciding penalty and the Hearts players stood on the pitch and took in the post match adulation of their adoring fans, I still couldn't help applaud along with them and speculate that a new power was on the rise.

It had all started with an explosion of intent so momentous and far-reaching that mums, wives and IT support technicians alike knew that Hearts were under new Lithuanian management and had raced to the top of the Premier League. Talk of their challenge being the most viable since Jim McLean and Alex Ferguson were fresh faced young grump-mongers was rife in supermarket queues, vacuum cleaner repair shops and dog-grooming parlours the length and breadth of the land. So much so that Jonesy's cousin Roy Sutter, a Prestonpans based market-trader with an eye for a fast buck was moved to have four hundred t-shirts hastily printed up in sizes S, M, L and XL proclaiming in bold maroon lettering 'Welcome Lithuananians!' As a result of Roy's substandard education all but five of these are still available on Ebay at a fixed offer price of 99p under the headline 'novelty leisurewear'.

So Lithuanian Oligar[17] Vladimir Romanov had taken over as Hearts Uber-chairman and had appointed softly spoken ex-Ipswich and Derby manager George Burley to run the team. The early batch of results had been nothing short of miraculous and the confident attacking style of play Hearts had adopted had experts and Graham Speirs alike talking of a realistic challenge to Rangers and Celtic's dominance. Then, just when Old Firm eyes were starting to twitch nervously as they looked over to the Capital city, Burley was sacked amidst rumours ranging from rampant alcoholism to slave trafficking on his part. And with that, a chain of events was set in motion that had every newsman worth his salt rubbing his hands in glee and thanking 'Jerrimacknee' the Great Sun God of Scandal and Hearsay for sending the most bountiful boon since Bill Clinton buzzed out on the intercom and said 'Come in and take a letter Ms Lewinski'.

Burley was swiftly replaced by Graham Rix who everyone vaguelyremembered as 'yon Arsenal boy with the bad curly perm'. Rix however was soon exposed in the press as having underage sex with a girl in one of those 'honest m'lud she looked 18' incidents

---

[17]   A mystical Baltic creature; half human, half banker strangely prone to forgetting to zip up his fly first thing in the morning.

that all men of a certain age shudder over and, if we're being honest, hold a certain degree of sympathy with. Unfortunately not only was Rix unsure what a 16 year old girl looked like, he had little idea of what resembled a good football player either and the Hearts legs began to stagger in an embarrassing 'drunk man in the street' fashion (although the e-mail joke about Rix wanting to give Stephen Pressley a free transfer because he didn't like hairy fannies went some way to making the whole debacle worthwhile, even for Hearts fans)

Suddenly Tyncastle's playing staff was awash with supporting characters from Dr Zhivago with so many different Omanovs and Owskisses turning up on the team sheet that Hearts fans themselves couldn't keep track. To confuse matters further, Romanov's own behaviour became more and more erratic. Soon after being spotted in Prince's Street with the X-factor Christmas album *and* a copy of Bertie Auld's autobiography 'Madness – One Step Beyond' under his arm, Romanov took the decision to sack Rix. With the club failing to maintain the season's early promise and the manager making it known to anyone who was asking that it was the owner himself who was picking the team, it was hardly the surprise of the century that the manager got his P45. After fleetingly stepping into the managerial hot-seat Assistant Jim Duffy was then also dismissed having only been with the club for a month, a particularly galling turn of events for the baldy ex-Dundee man as he had just bought his own mug for the club canteen.

Then, spectacularly, the Lithuanian accused the Old Firm of bribing match officials into making dodgy decisions in their favour, a quite ludicrous suggestion since everyone knows they do it free of charge. Romonov's son , humorously named Roman, was subsequently appointed as Chairman and Chief Executive. The lad was clearly in need of a hobby that got him out his room and away from his Dungeons and Dragons and well-fingered Kays catalogue and, having recently won the SPL on Championship Manager playing as Ayr United, his father saw him eminently qualified to steady the Hearts ship.

Rix's replacement was to be, surprise-surprise, some Lithuanian guy who soon went off on the sick to be replaced by another Lithuanian guy who couldn't speak English and took The Jam Tarts on their worst run of results in forty years. He then made way for the original Lithuanian guy who now felt better (or at least felt it was safe to return to Edinburgh as he probably couldn't do any worse than the second Lithuanian Guy). And so with the inner turmoil bubbling away nicely and the club once more embracing mid-table mediocrity, the fans bemoaned their latest near-miss with heaven and the Romanov Dynasty, Edinburgh style, staggered on regardless .

14.

But then all this got me to thinking 'Who is this Vladimir Romanov? Where has he come from and can he knock a tune out of the recorder? The answers perhaps predictably were ' I don't know, I don't know, and most probably, which inevitably prompted the following research. Not being noted as a completer/ finisher in historical terms I hope that the following portrays the essence of the man's life to date if not its fullness. Maybe as a snapshot it will act as a catalyst for others to complete, correct and enhance the account as I have presented it. I hope so.

The Hearts supremo then. A life in brief;

1947 - Vladimir Romanov is born to parents Zinaida and Nikolai in the Tver province North West of Moscow. These early days are punctuated by poverty, hardship and meals containing mostly cabbage.

1952- 1955 Whilst his mother works in a radio factory and father endeavours in the army as a career officer, young Vladimir attends the Alexander Solzenitzen Memorial Playgroup near Moscow where he learns potato printing, wears shoes chosen by his mother which he silently despises, and frequently complains of having cold fingers.

1956 – The family move to a Russian army base in Kaunas, Lithuania where Vladimir attends school at Vilijampole. Despite being a harsh and uncompromising institution, he quickly makes friends with the aid of his collection of oriental battle sabres and a winning smile.

1963 – Father Nikolai dies leaving Vladimir as the man of the house, aged 16. Needing money to support the family, Vladimir readily becomes a taxi driver and has his first brush with fame when he is featured in an early BBC Omnibus documentary entitled 'Young Vlad - The Real Life Latka'.

1964 – Romanov makes his first profit selling black market western music from the back of his cab. He falls instantly for the heady, hip-shaking rock n roll of Elvis Presley and begins writing his own poetry. He is encouraged when his first poem entitled 'Why is my garden cement?' wins third prize in the Vilnius Annual 'Proper Poetry That Rhymes' Competition.

1966 - An 18 year old Romanov is drafted into the Russian army where he is commissioned to serve on the nuclear submarine fleet . He is immediately posted to Murmansk where he meets his wife Svetlana. Despite spending 6 years in the city he never visits the library and doesn't manage to find a good plumber.

1971 - As the Soviet Union begins to relax restrictions on private enterprise, Romanov returns to Kaunas and forms his first company selling 'two pairs for the price of one' Farah slacks to schizophrenics at the local psychiatric hospital. Skinny fit T-shirts with 'Rock-a-hula!' printed across the chest in glitter-ink also prove popular.

1972 – 84 Business really takes off as a more worldly-wise Vladimir progresses a clutch of companies, buying raw materials in Russia and turning them into finished goods in Lithuania. During this time he writes the poem 'Conflicting Fundamental Marxist Indoctrination.' which is adapted into the '82 Russian Eurovision Song Contest entry 'Yeh, Banga - Banga Baby ! '

1985 - Vladimir publicly renounces Elvis in favour of Shakin' Stevens then changes his mind again on the release of 'Lipstick, powder and paint'.

1991 – 'The Velvet Revolution' takes place throughout the Baltic states and Romanov acquires a number of previously state run businesses cheaply at public auction. While his textile based operations flourish, his 'Pot-Cabbage' snacks unfortunately prove to be less successful.

1992 – Joins a consortium to form the Ukio, Lithuania's first private bank. Romanov proves his flair for marketing by successfully luring thousands of students into opening current accounts with the incentive of ten soup vouchers and a free canister of Red Diesel.

1994 – 2006 Romanov consolidates his involvement in football by purchasing significant stakes in Lithuania's FBK Kaunas and MTZ Ripo in Belarus. He then looks to Scotland and has bids for Dundee, Dundee Utd, and Dunfermline rejected before buying an initial 30% share in Hearts. Romanov chooses to spend further 'daft' cash by purchasing the famous K19 submarine (instead of U571 which he agrees 'wasn't as good a movie') and commits to turning it into a museum. Local's and critics alike are beside themselves at the prospect of the first glow in the dark paintings to be exhibited in the Baltic region since The Chernoble Vermeers Exposition of 1983.

15.

Romanov's involvement and influence is a difficult one for the Hearts fans to rationalise and come to terms with. For despite the ensuing mayhem that has become part and parcel of life down Tynecastle way, his intervention *did* single handily scupper previous CEO, Chris Robinson's alarming plans of selling the hallowed Tynecastle to property developers. He also pledged to settle almost £4.5 million pounds worth of debt owed to Scottish Media Group (Its amazing how all those telephone votes for X-Factor add up isn't it) And on analysis even the hardest to please Scottish football critics would have to admit that quite a few of those 'furriners' that he insisted on bringing in weren't half bad.

And yet its all gone pear shaped. For Hearts fans the advent of Vladimir Romanov has been a bit like quickly turning the TV channel and saving yourself from a particularly odious episode of Neighbours only to find yourself watching a documentary on open-rectum surgery instead. Hearts' public persona has frequently been, quite frankly, cringe-worthy and for hardened fans to sit back and watch quality, well respected players forced to leave the club at odds with the current regime, see a shed-load of potential never realised, and eventually witness the club gravitate to a similar 'also-ran' role in the Scottish set up as before, its all a bit frustrating to say the least . Under normal circumstances chants of 'The Board must seriously review their priorities !' would have been prevalent and not unreasonable however its still hard for the loyal Jambos to appear so ungrateful . Maybe time (and couple more straws placed on the camel's back) will make it easier for the fans to vent their true frustrations. Until then Roy Sutter's new batch of 'Goodbye , Lithuananians!' T-shirts will need to sit in his back bedroom until the time is right to unleash them on a disgruntled Gorgy public.

16.

Our day trip to Edinburgh finishes with a visit to the Station Tavern where amongst other things we admire Rhona Martin's wall mounted curling jersey and jock-strap as well as having a brief but pointless debate on whether Hibs fans object to all the buses in Edinburgh being maroon.

Its half past six before we get back to the car and head for home. Despite it having been such a beautiful day, the closing darkness and chilling breeze is a reminder that we haven't shown winter a clean pair of heels quite yet. The rush of football traffic has of course cleared away some time ago and as the remnants of an orange sky hugs the horizon we hit the city bypass and head for home.

Jim Traynor in his radio Scotland Phone-in slot 'Your Call' is babbling away however with the show featuring the usual parade of confused bam-pots and easily provoked Old Firm punters, we are barely listening. Until that is we instantly snap to attention as Traynor announces 'We have Arthurston manager Wilf Schnabbel on the line now."

Our discussion on whether it is indicative of a person's psyche whether they sit in the front or back seat of a taxi stops instantly as Dave beats me to the volume button.

"Am I honoured to be talking with the real Mr Schnabbel then?" Traynor asks in a suspicious tone, his voice now loudly and clearly filling the car.

"Will the real Slim Schnabbel please stand up?" answers a familiar accented voice with a laugh. It is immediately clear that this is definitely our Wilf and further, his recent televisual viewing has evidently encompassed MTV.

"Not the best result for you today Wilf, I have to admit I thought you would maybe get something today"

"Ahh well, you know what the thought did don't you? The thought went to the market, sold the cow and bought magic beans – that's what the thought did!"

"Right.... ehhhh ....." stutters Traynor , for once a shade unbalanced. To his credit however he recovers quickly. "So what can we do for you tonight

"Yeh , this a good and funny programme, you know, and I often hear the questions after games on the Saturday....."

"Uhuh." Says Traynor.

"Well yeh, I'm lovin'it, you know. But I'm driving home in my car again tonight..."

"You're not in the bus then?" Traynor interrupts.

"What? No I have a Rovers car with Manager Schnabbel written on the doors, I don't have a use of public transport.

"No, the team bus I mean. You are not on the bus with the other players?" Traynor involuntarily is annunciating each word like he is on holiday trying to explain to a bewildered Turkish waiter what a haggis is.

"Ahhh , noooooo, noooooo not tonight!" exclaims the Rovers boss, " Tonight I need home early as some friends as couples are coming for beef and the swapping."

".... Beef?"

"Not just Beef, Jean. Succulent Aberdeen Angus beef with a rich cream and brandy sauce, luxuriously glazed traditional farmhouse vegetables and soft aromatically spiced, pan-fried potatoes."

"And the ... ehh... swapping?"

"Yeh there's me and my wife, Roger and Sue, and Peter and Madelaine. I begin with mine but swap with Peter. Then Roger has mine and I have Roger's. A mix of the German, Australian and then some French is good for spicing the night up eh?."

"And after we finish, ha!", Scnabbel laughs "My wife is always red face with blotches down her chest and then we talk about who's was best."

I glance at Dave and then at Jonesy in the back seat. Both are wide eyed with traces of a smile on their lips.

"And ehh, who's is usually the best," Traynor troops on.

"Not usually me "Schnabbel laughs again, "German wine is not always the best a man can get, Jean. It can have too much of the sweetness for peoples' taste so ...."

"So you're on the way home for a night of good food and wine tasting then Wilf?" chortles Traynor with the slightest hint of relief in his voice.

"Oh yes. " Schnabbel admits, " And then we have all the sex with each other's wives."

Jonesy yells "HAAA!" and Dave misses our turn off on the roundabout we are driving round.

"Wilf ... I'm ... ehh ..."

"Haaa haa , I'm just pulling on the leg Jean" Schnabbel cries, clearly appreciating his own humour. "I know what I say, haaa. No , no, no , why I am on Jean is ...." and there is a slight hesitation.

"Ahh yes Wilf, why indeed are you on?" says Traynor who sounds like he's given up.

"Well, for two or four days now I have been in the car listening to my music CDs. Normally everything good, my stereo is a Blaupunkt you see, but not now. One minute I am listening to my Rolf Schrenkenbaum sings the Bob Dylans CD and then BAAABING!, news and roads reports. All radio – no Rolf Shrenkenbaum!"

Traynor sounds like he is choking.

"And it keeps doing it!" Schnabbel continues in consternated fashion, "And I don't tell it to!" he yells with no small amount of indignation."

"And how can I help you with this Wilf?"asks Traynor.

"You are the Radio Man I'm thinking. I'm driving along and I thinking who will know this thing and it is the Radio Man. *You* Jean."

"Wilf?"

"Yessy?"

"I think you should get your instructions for your stereo and read them."

"Awww can you not tell me then, I do not find instructions easily?"

"I don't know the answer Wilf. Try asking one of your players. They'll probably know what's wrong.

"Ha, my boys wouldn't know .... So you can't help me?

"I don't think so "replies Traynor and scratching around for something of journalistic merit to take from proceedings finishes with "So, do you think you can stay up then?"

"I think we will stay up " is the defiant answer "And hey, if not, what's the worst that can happen?" And with that the line goes dead and Jim Traynor is once again left alone.

"Wilf Schnabbel, Arthurston Rovers manager - Bit of a character." He eventually ventures.

We scarcely hear this as we are laughing way too loudly.

17.

After the near miss way back on the roundabout we are on track and heading along the never-ending stretch of the M8 near Harthill services. Anyone that drives this road will be familiar with the strange phenomenon that makes the East to West journey seem a good ten miles longer than travelling in the opposite direction. 'Your Call' has just finished and the Radio Scotland News has given way to the weather forecast. The conversation has ebbed to a silence and I'm just wanting to be off this boring, boring road and closer to home when it happens. A sobering moment, nae a frightening moment, enough to send a chill down the back of the hardest man. That moment in the broadcasting week when tens of thousands of car-bound football fans simultaneously cry 'Awww Jesus' and dive for either the OFF, CD, or TUNING dial on their radio.

"And now..." a clipped voice announces, "Robbie Shepherd's 'Take The Floor'! Within five bars of an accordion striking up Dave has deftly moved the station to Radio 5 where the splendidly belligerent Alan Green is berating some goalie or other for not stopping a shot that according to him, his grandmother could have caught.

For those of you unfamiliar with 'Take the Floor', well done, sterling work! This is a Scottish country dance spot so long running that Paul mentions it in his letter to the Corinthians. Now I'm as patriotically Scottish as the next man but three minutes of listening to this would force you to scurry down past Carlisle, stopping briefly to rebuild Hadrian's Wall behind you before continuing onwards to a safe distance possibly around Antwerp or Nice .

Grampa always liked Take The Floor. Sitting in his chair with a drop of malt in the bottom of a glass, tapping his feet to the likes of Jimmy Shand , Archie Yeeuch And The Fiddlers Elbows and the like. And he wouldn't hear a word against it either. Anytime I came in when it was on and made a disparaging remark he would say 'Away ye go, this is the music o' kings'. It was round about then we started double-checking his medicine.

Twenty minutes of Radio 5 commentary though and we slip gladly along the Old Wet Road. Five minutes after that and I'm hauling myself out of the passenger seat outside my parents' house. Stooping in the car-doorway I ask what the guys are doing tonight. Dave dutifully informs me that he will be catching up on some long overdue paperwork for the office while Jonesy mutters something about looking for some music on the Net.

I'm about to shut the door when I lean in and look at Jonesy one more time.

"That music your looking for?"

"Uhuh?" replies Jonesy uncomfortably.

"Its Rolf Schrenkenbaum isn't it?"

The look he gives me tells me all I need to know and I shake my head, slam the door and trudge up the path towards a Saturday night of Chicken Kievs, gardening programs and conversations about underwear offers at Matalan. Shoot me now.

Chapter 20 Falkirk Ken

1.

Saturday mornings have always been my favourite part of the week. Thoughts of work have disappeared into the wool spun by a good night's sleep and the weekend is stretched out in front of me. In days of old I would have been guilty of sleeping until noon or maybe one o clock before staggering down the stairs, bleary eyed in time to have tea, toast and marmalade in my pyjama bottoms, on the couch in front of BBC's Football Focus. Nowadays, hangovers permitting, I feel a duty not to waste the cannot-be-topped feel-good factor that Saturday morning offers. I like to be up and about by nine in time to complete what has become a regimented process. Stage one, the dog gets walked come hail or shine. Stage 2, I saunter up the main street and have a swift wander around WH Smiths and Woolworths, the only two 'chains' in Arthurston and coincidentally, the only shops with stuff you would even toy with the idea of buying. Stage 3, I stop for some fresh morning rolls (does anywhere sell evening rolls I wonder?) and a Daily Record from the paper shop and then finally, I stand in a queue so long you'd think there was free booze at the end of it, on the shiny black and white floor tiles of McCallum's the butchers, to buy proper[18] square sausages for a late breakfast or early lunch however you wish to view it.

Then, with my bulging full, super-crinkly, white poly-bag in hand, I head home for food, Football Focus and a cup of tea that feeds the soul.

---

[18]   Thick, big enough to take on the morning roll around it & slightly spicy in taste with beefy vestiges of cow contained *unlike* the pink mushy crap 'Lorne'* variety one sees in supermarkets, shrink wrapped to death in wee white trays with tartan stickers plastered over . * Old Gailic word meaning 'lips, hoofs and arseholes'

2.

The sausages are, in a nod to healthy eating, sizzling away to themselves in the George Foreman Grill. Mum is still in her bed reading her Scottish equivalent of 'Hello!' magazine called 'Awright Misseez!'. Dad has just slunk in from the garden and is sitting across from me at the table winding oatmeal coloured string into a ball tutting every so often and giving off a generally consternated vibe.

The mood is catching as I finish the newspaper's preview of this afternoon's match with Falkirk. 'Arthurston Rovers,' it gleefully reports, 'travel to Falkirk stadium six points adrift at the bottom of the league. At this stage in the campaign nothing short of a win will do for the Brewers.....'

"No shit." I say out loud causing my dad to look up.

"What's that?" he said in an aggravated tone he usually reserves for toddlers and dogs.

"We need to beat Falkirk today." I murmur sullenly, slowly bringing my gaze up to meet Dad's, almost challenging him to trivialise my concern. He looks like he's about to oblige then suddenly his eyes soften and he looks own at the string in his hands . Looking back up he seems on the verge of something then elects to let out nothing more than a self-conscious sigh-cum-exclamation.

"There's time yet" he eventually feels burdened to offer.

"Not really Dad," I reply feeling the familiar currents of irritation rising, " It's the first week in May, there's only three games left and that bloody stupid league split is on the go, TIME'S RUNNING OUT!."

Dad gets up and moves over to the kitchen worktop. "These sausages are ready, do you want them out?"

I grunt an affirmative and glower at the black inky smudges that have detached from the newspaper pages and onto my hands.

"I had a trial for Falkirk once." says Dad laying a plate in front of me.

"Eh?" I reply like he had just claimed to having fathered Madonna's lovechild. Dad has wandered over to the window and is staring outside, his back turned to me.

"That poor tree is dying on me" he says sadly

"When?"

"I don't think it'll last the month."

"Noooo, When did you have a trial for Falkirk? I didn't even know you *played* football!"

"You never asked" he says turning round to face me.

"Oh yeh, that's the sort of question that would come up randomly in casual conversation – So Dad, a bit parky outside today isn't it, by any chance did you ever try out for The Bairns when you were younger...."

Dad winces a little and I immediately feel rotten.

"Were you any good?" I ask in a softer tone.

"Wasn't bad." He smiles almost ruefully, "Was probably the best player at the High School when I got called for the trial"

"What position did you play? How did it go?"

Dad starts to make himself a cuppa. After an inordinate amount of faffing with a soggy tea bag and wild clicking of a faulty Sweetex dispenser he continues " Midfield ... I was a right half ."

"And what happened, how did you play?"

"Never got a look in son, the game passed right by me."

"Was it at Brockville, the game?"

"Oh aye, not that it was ever much of a ground as you know but for me to be playing there, where proper footballers played, it was a real big thing. Playing at Hampden couldn't have felt better ."

"So you didn't get asked back then?"

"No I didn't" he replies, another rueful look passing over his face. " Was lucky they let me out for the second half truth be told- I just wasn't anywhere near up to it. I told myself at the time I didn't want it enough, that if it had been the Rangers I'd have tried harder. But I knew deep down. "

Another wave of irritation. 'Don't say anything' I think to myself. ' JUST DON'T SAY A WORD' I repeat.

"... I mean I just don't get it."

"What's that? Dad asks now rummaging around the 'Sweet Drawer' clearly struggling to decide from a international-class selection of chocolate biscuits that would have brought Vanessa Felts out in a sweat.

"The Rangers .... thing

"What do you mean the Rangers *thing*? They're my team." Dad turns around, his look hardened.

"BUT THEY'RE NOT YOUR TEAM ARE THEY?"

My old man looks dumfounded

"You were born and bred in Arthurston -You don't come from Glasgow and you haven't been to a game since Arthur Montford went off the telly! Don't you get it, YOU'RE SUPPORTING SOMEONE ELSE'S TEAM !. You'd be as well saying you were a big Real Madrid man or a died-in-the-wool Boca-Bloody-Juniors fan, for all the connection there is. Face it, *The Rovers* are your team ..... whether you choose to accept it or not" I stop to breathe not to think ".... but , hey, its ok , I'll support them for you."

Dad's nostrils are flaring "Where do you get off telling people who to like and what to choose in life eh... tell me?"

"I can't but you've got to see how your view hurts teams like the Rovers and how it makes you look."

"Makes me look? What the hell are you talking about?"

"Well you either like them 'cause they win or you're aligning with what they stand for. So..... you're either insecure or a bigot, which is it dad?"

Dad's eyes bulge. Mine in turn fly to the worktop at his side in panic that there may be some sort of sharp kitchen utencil handily positioned. Before I lower my view to my half eaten roll and sausage on my plate I catch his left eye twitching rapidly.

I keep my head down waiting for the storm. It doesn't come. Silence.

Eventually dad speaks in a soft voice.

"Why does it matter so much..... who I support, and what my justifications are?" He pauses briefly, considering his words carefully. " Maybe I *did* start to like the wrong team years back

…. *Maybe.* Maybe I should have shown more character and gone against my friends or the guys at my work, but I didn't. And what's done is done. I mean, I've heard you talking about habit and allegiance and getting attached to your team -are you saying I'm not attached to mine?" I look to interrupt but he holds the palm of his hand up, " And since I am , should I just stop wanting them to win just like that, just because my motives were slightly questionable forty-odd years ago?"

I don't answer immediately. "I suppose not" I mumble.

"There's a lot of terrible stuff going on in the world out there, son. Me having a passing interest in what's going on at Ibrox doesn't quite measure up does it?"

" Yeh … but… doesn't all the 'nonsense' make you think twice though?"

"Of course it does, I can't condone any of that sort of stuff but I'm not like that am I? Look at some of those young lads that fight at the Rovers games …"

"There's not that many of them now…"

"No, but they *are* there and do you agree with what they do?"

"Of course not, they're an embarrassment to the club"

"And when their behaviour was at its worst a few years back did it ever diminish your love for the club?"

"No … but…" And my train of thought has been crudely stopped by a points failure somewhere near Moral High-Ground Central. Despite feeling entirely justified in everything I've said , the argument has strangely ebbed away from me. A fresh swell of annoyance hits me but this time I say nothing.

Dad potters around and I chew away on my roll and sausage feverishly like the dog eating a fruit gum. I can hear him clanking and scuffing around. Go knows what he's doing but I can't bring myself to look up and see.

I'm just starting to wallow in thoughts of Arthurston hitting their seventh goal against Rangers in front of twenty thousand fervent Rovers fans, bating the Berrs with a catchy chant of ' How's yer wee team doin' now?' when I become aware of heavy loitering at the kitchen door. I brave myself to look up. Dad immediately looks down and jangles what sounds like fifty pounds worth of loose change in his pocket.

Eventually after what seems like an eternity he looks up and this time we hold each other's gaze.

"Son," he says quietly, "I know you don't like living here – I .... I just wish I could help you more." I'm about to shake my head, screw up my face, protest.... something, when dad offers up a quick watery smile, sighs and slips out of the door and out of my grasp.

"That's ok..." I murmur looking at the close door where my father had stood seconds earlier. I stare back at my lunch in my hand, finger it absently then put in back on my plate. Suddenly I don't feel hungry any more.

3.

Alex Totten once enigmatically pointed out in a TV interview, 'What's Falkirk without Falkirk?' An excellent point succinctly put and the response would probably be 'nothing' if we had, in fact, any idea of what the ex-Bairns manager was going on about. Except, hands up in surrender, we do *kind of* understand what he was so Spartanly trying to convey. Its that idea of wider exposure for the small town again. The thought that the football club represents the most meaningful mass focus that a community has going for it.

Think of towns down south and our sum total knowledge of them. Places like Grimsby, Hartlepool and Wycombe. For a large percentage of the sports-aware population of the UK it's their football teams that pretty much define them . Subconsciously we complete them as Grimsby ... *Town*, Hartlepool ... *United,* Wycombe .... *Wanderers*. And the same thing must happen reciprocally with our Scottish teams . On a recent trip to the borders (as 'down south' as I'm prepared to venture for the sake of sounding well travelled) I investigated this very theory. Taking a group of average punters on Selkirk Main Street (Eyes a bit too close together, unpleasant looking skin complaints, sporting long, heavy knitwear and a faraway look) they pleasingly linked without prompting Hamilton with *Academical* , Ross with *County,* Inverness with *Clachnacudden* (*ha! Caledonian Thistle* ; just stirring the old Highland hornet nest there) and of course Falkirk with .. emm .... *Wheel.*

Yup, it seems to be an unfortunate fact that the most famous feature of today's Falkirk according to the outside world is a big grey cement wheel that looks a bit like a giant tin-opener. Fair enough if they'd mentioned Callendar Park or the wee par three golf course close by, I'd have given them that but the Falkirk ..... *Wheel?* Now I'm not one to decry the obvious attractions of rotating boat lifts however you have to think that Falkirk FC *should* hold slightly more allure . That said I have never actually been in, on, or around the 'Falkirk Wheel' so perhaps I'm being a trifle harsh. I *am* led to believe one can spend a splendid afternoon partaking in the 'Falkirk Wheel Experience' (£8 adults, £4.25 kids, £6 concessions) which includes a boat trip, a quick 'birl' on the wheel itself, and the right to purchase a slightly stale crispy cake in the café and/or a brightly coloured pencil with a rubber on the end from the visitor centre shop. Not that the revolving, wheel-related excitement stops there mind you. If you are really lucky your visit could coincide with the odd falconry display, floating art gallery, craft fair or clog dance. Personally, if I happened to be in the locale I would prefer to visit the shining new Falkirk stadium no matter what the weather and who was playing. Personally I would also prefer a night in with a urinary infection and a wasp stuck in my ear but that's just me.

Luckily the only option on the horizon *is* a trip to the shining new Falkirk stadium - there will be no burning sensations in my lower reaches today. Because the league has 'split' we will, from now until the end of the season, only be playing teams in the bottom six of the Premier League. Eh? I hear those of you unfamiliar with the more modern nuances of our game cry. And it would be a valid exclamation. The May splicing of the twelve team league into two sections of six is the latest in a long line of structural tinkerings with the league and there's a fair chance that it has to be the most hair-brained and pointless one yet.

Modelled on that powerhouse of European leagues, the Austrian Bundesliga, the split supposedly reduced the number of games and adds interest and excitement to the end of season proceedings. But for what necessity and at what cock-eyed price?

Anomalies abound. For starters one team could, over the course of a season, conceivably play a rival three times at home and only once away. Or vice versa. High impact stuff in terms of where the title heads or who gets relegated don't you think! Oh and here's a belter, the seventh or even the eighth team in the league could quite ridiculously finish with more points than the sixth place team because of the relatively contrasting quality of the opposition each now face. Its all just plain wrong!

But its all been wrong for ages. And everyone but everyone who understands and cares anything about Scottish Football knows it. They also know that the solution is simple. Straight and to the point, the top league should have at least sixteen teams in it. Even those with their big greedy financial specks on must also have their suspicions that this is the way forward. Greater variety in opposition , more breathing space to play youngsters , higher motivation for teams in the lower leagues to aspire to top flight status, and a fairer distribution of wealth are all strong reasons to build on the number of clubs playing in the Premier League. What hasn't been helpful is the half-assed chopping and changing of formats for well over a decade now. Modifications that, in reality, have done more to portray the League as a motivationally transparent laughing stock than a well meaning healer of any problems in our game. Lets look at a brief history of league reconstruction in recent years;

1975/76   The old 16 team First division gives way to the Premier League (pronounced 'Preemier' by old men over the age of sixty-five) consisting of only 10 teams. 2 teams are promoted while 2 are relegated.

1986/87	With complaints that teams are playing each other too often the Premier league is expanded to 12 teams. 2 teams are promoted while 2 teams are relegated.
1988/89	Worrying that undesirable factions are sneaking into the fray the Premier League reverts to 10 teams with only one team relegated.
1991/92	Thinking that things weren't really so bad in 1986/87, the league goes back to 12 teams with 2 up and 2 down.
1994/95	Back to 10 teams , one up, one down.
1995/96	Still 10 teams, one up, one down but with the inclusion of a playoff between the second bottom of the Premier and the second top of Division 1.
1997/98	*Still* 10 teams (well done, take a sweetie from the tin gents), playoffs scrapped though, back to only one up and one down.
1999/00	10 teams start with a view to moving to 12 next season. No automatic relegation. First division champions promoted . Bottom of the Premier (Aberdeen) play 2nd and 3rd place from the first Division (Dunfermline and Falkirk) in a round robin with two from the three securing top flight football for the following season. To complete this fiasco, Brockville was considered unsuitable to host Premier league football and with Falkirk eliminated , the playoffs didn't take place at all.
2000/01	The league reverts to 12 teams and incorporates the radical If bewildering 'split' into two with 5 games remaining.

Not bad, eight changes in the space of fourteen years. Can you imagine the meeting to organise the SPL Management Committee Christmas night out?

"Should we invite partners? "

"Dunno what do you think? "

"Well we didn't two years ago but nobody here pulled, no one even got asked to dance – it wasn't very good."

" So invite partners then! "

"Well, we did that last year and it was quite good but the kitty didn't last as long did it. "

"Hmmm good point, I reckon we could pull this year without the partners"

"We couldn't before"

"Yes but this time it will be different"

"I agree........... how?"

"New aftershave"

"Brilliant!"

What gets on my goat is that while all this silly tampering is going on the genuine issues are left unaddressed. The biggest one, and I'm going to whisper this because it sounds a bit soft , has to be 'How do we give other teams a chance of winning? ' How do we inject a modicum of interest at the *top* of the Premier table for a change. For lets be honest, the Scottish Premier league is boring, or at least it's inevitable outcomes are. The same two teams win year on year. Over a hundred years of domination left completely unaddressed. Look at the excitement that is generated when any one of the other teams starts the season well and pushes their way towards the top of the league. Dougie Donnelly and co get in a right lather about it all. Richard Gordon on Radio Scotland has to think of his granny in a thong to keep calm. Just imagine what it would be like if year in year out five or six teams had a genuine chance of winning and the league conclusion was pushed to wire, without it necessarily being the two Glasgow teams at the forefront. I personally think it would be heart-attack inducing.

But how do we achieve this parity? Its a difficult conundrum I realise but to a football visionary like myself, the solutions are many and obvious ;

1. Make the Old Firm players play in Wellington boots. Possibly filled with custard . Excellent comedy value – gets the kids involved.
2. Make the Old Firm players play in past designs of Celtic away tops, the sheer weight of embarrassment would take at least two yards of pace off each player.
3. Issue each non Old Firm centre-half with an old fashioned, wooden handled duelling pistol, a small packet of gunpowder and a licence to kill.
4. Strategically place an assortment of wild animals and drunken Jakeys on the pitch. - Irritated monkeys and indignant hobos are always 'a great leveller'.
5. Let Berti Vogts manage Rangers and Celtic on alternate weeks.
5. Call in the A-Team (if no one else can help *and* you can find them.... of course)

A constant battle is seemingly being fought between what is best for the game and what is best for each individual club's bank balance. The day the directors in Scotland's bigger clubs take an altruistic view of policy in the game unfortunately will be same day that all the cones and temporary traffic lights mysteriously vanish from our roads, the BBC provide live coverage of an SPL relegation 'six-pointer', and Nessie pops her head out of the water and sings 'Sunshine on Leith'- Unfortunate but true.

4.

So we're in Falkirk – In the pub known as 'Behind the Wall' on Melville Street to be exact. Its known as that because that is in fact, its name. In the days when Brockville was still alive it was brilliantly close at hand for both the football ground *and* the railway station, however nowadays its a good twenty minute walk from the new stadium. But old habits die hard and since it's still the best pub in the town that's why we're there.

The mood isn't good however. Dave is on a major downer because, according to him, the world is against him. Firstly a parking space wasn't made immediately available to him in royal fashion. Cue a furrowed brow and some below-the-breath swear words. Then we couldn't find a Motor-Mart for him to buy. Now ordinarily I quite like strolling along Falkirk's main pedestrian-only thoroughfare. With its scattering of turreted sandstone buildings, cobbled walkways and twin-globed, hanging street lamps there's a nice sense of age about it. And of course under the prominent clock tower lies the brilliant Tolbooth Street which at fifty eight feet long its the self-proclaimed shortest street in Britain. I always go out of my way to take twenty seconds or so to stroll its length and wonder when they're going to get around to sticking a mini-roundabout on it. The centre has also got a healthy scattering of 'big' shops like Waterstones, Next, M&S and in spite of the fact that people from Falkirk don't look like they approve of or partake in sex ...... ever, Ann Summers. At the same time, though, quaintly named places like 'Joukiedaidles', Granny's Sookers sweetie shop, Lorraine's Sewing Box and er ... Heaven and Hell Piercings give the place a friendly small town feel.

Today though, there was nothing pleasurable about scuttling along, ten paces behind a grim faced Dave searching randomly for anywhere selling what must be the equivalent of a porno magazine for petrol-heads. It never ceases to amaze me how long and repeatedly Dave can pour over pages and pages of cars all washed and tarted up to get their photo's taken. Each to their own I suppose. Anyway eventually we find one in The High Street Newsagent. Rather than accepting this luck in the same manner as me (a fast, economic punch to the air and a nearly silent 'yessss' forced through gritted teeth) Jonesy grumbled 'about bloody time' in a tone that Dave didn't care for at which point a small set to occurred, much to the embarrassment of myself and the shopkeeper who may or may not have been *the* High Street Newsagent himself.

But we eventually made it to the pub and after a cold pint and a short but distressing conversation about the modern phenomenon of 'The Cankle' (When you can't tell when a woman's fat ankle ends and her fat calf begins), the frost if not completely disappeared, has at least thawed.

I really like BTW. I doesn't try too hard and yet its nicely toning interior of wooden furniture and warm brickwork create a comfortable but fashionable image. A large peculiar painting on the back wall depicting ethnic figures offering themselves to the God of Bright Turquoise and Orange could hang nowhere else but where it is and the blackened fireplace near the front entrance makes for a homely corner if that's what you're after. We are standing in our traditional spot. Superstition dictates that we hang beside the maroon pillar in front of the bar for at least one pint. This dates back to our first ever pre-match drink in here, a good number of years back now. We stood almost hugging the pillar as we drank to our luck in the cup, and when we were stoked up with alcohol and bravado , we went out into an icy cold afternoon and watched the Rovers score four goals and march purposefully into the fourth round. And every time since that we have repeated the pillar visit, we have not lost. Twice by my recollection we ignored the Gods and went straight to the match. Twice, I have to say, we lost miserably. Quite clearly Behind The Wall is a very spiritual place.

Having paid our dues to the Great and Holy Pillar Deity, we are now free to stick Arthurston on the coupon for an away win and move into the adjoining conservatory-type eating area for something of a belly-filling hot food nature. God bless pub grub.

5.

Dave mops up his leftover sauce with his last nacho (BTW does a bewildering selection of nachos on their lunch menu) and in a tone that one might normally reserve for announcements such as 'I'm going out to fill the car with petrol' or ' I'm off to the clog dance at the Falkirk Wheel.' He leans back in his chair and announces "I'm going to ask Linda for a divorce."

"Whaaat?" Jonesy and I both say wide eyed, in unison.

"Yeh," he continues too casually, "I can't go on like this, dangling on a string waiting for the hammer to fall. For her to come in and say David I've met someone else or David I've decided to make a clean break'

"So what are you saying?" I splutter, "Make a pre-emptive strike and that will make things alright?"

"At least I'll have my dignity"

I didn't think now was the time to point out that dignity had marched out the door the second he charged into Linda's salon last month accusing her of seeing half of her male clientele in a manner, he screamed, was 'nefarious and unbefitting of a married women.' Those were his actual words!

'Nefarious and unbefitting of a married woman.'

What motivated Dave to suddenly become a character in a Jane Austin novel and come out with this, only he knows but he surely did. As surely as a disagreement then developed between Mr Gorman and the young, fair Mrs Gorman; absent of wit or delicacy, charm or wisdom, and most certainly beyond the realms of acceptable public behaviour. As surely as Linda then hit him with a set of curling tongs.

Dave seems initially to be unwavering in his view that verbal attack is the best means of defence where Linda is concerned. However after a good fifteen minutes consulting with the two most qualified agony uncles in the nation, he now seems to be leaning more towards some kind of measured physical violence
.

"I can't go on like this !' Dave repeats , mad eyes glinting in the light , remnants of his last mouthful of shandy dribbling out the side of his mouth. Momentarily Jack Nicholson in the Shining springs to mind.

"I know I've lost the plot with her over this at times, but I've been good too. I've listened to what she's said and I take some of it on board"

"What bits ?" asks Jonesy. I look for signs of sarcasm but for once I can't see anything.

Dave sighs. "I know I can be selfish sometimes. *Really* selfish. I guess I've gotten out of the way of putting her first too... I suppose. But I am NOT self-absorbed and I DO NOT fly off the handle at the slightest thing !"

Neither of us answer. Jonesy coughs and rubs the back of his neck

"Do I ?" he repeats insistently.

"Weeeeell....." I start, grimacing slightly.

"OH THANK YOU *VERY* MUCH GUYS!' . Dave looks to Jonesy who averts his eyes towards the bar area. Silence descends.

"So what are you going to do then?" I eventually venture.

Dave shrugs. "Appointment at the lawyers on Monday, Widderidge, Lapel and Gunk up the Main Street." He pauses and takes a drink, "Couldn't find ones with any normal names..... organised it yesterday. I guess I'll do that and see how it goes from there." I rack my brains for something to say to change his mind. Don't rush anything, give yourself every opportunity to keep things together, think of ways of winning her back because you don't appreciate what you've got there....

"Hmmmmmnn." I say meaningfully before sighing loudly and shifting in my seat uncomfortably. Go on my son, tell it like it is!

Our meal on the whole was enjoyable if a trifle strained. While Dave takes our contributions to pay at the bar and Jonesy heads off up the prominent staircase in the centre of the bar to the toilet I pick my way through the now crowded main area, make a slight detour to surreptitiously touch the pillar once more for good measure , then head through the door coming to a slightly unsure halt outside on the pavement.

Fair weather has come early and It's a beautiful shirt-sleeved day. People in freshly creased summer gear are bustling by the entrance to 'Behind The Wall' with purpose. In front of me, beyond a little square pay and display car park, I mindlessly watch a train roof draw into Grahamston Station before casting my gaze up to the clear blue sky where a small white plane is cruising lazily amongst the scattering of small, wispy clouds .

I'm dragged out of my dwam by the sweet, light aroma   of expensive perfume. A shapely girl in her early twenty's glides by in a low cut blouse and a short, light blue denim skirt. Having a natural appreciation of superior fabrics I watch her disappear up towards the town centre. I'm just admiring the quality of the stitching on her back pockets when I feel a stinging slap on the side of my face. I wheel round and come face to face with a feverish looking woman.

"You didn't stare at me when I walked by!" she yells, my hair blowing back wildly in the gust of her voice. Then with an anguished look, and without waiting for an answer she stalks off also in the direction of the shops. Dave and Jonesy suddenly appear at my side. "What did you say to *that* one?" Dave asks .

" I ... emmmm ... nuthin .... Eh?" I come back.

"Oh yeh, nothing? Well smooth stuff anyway Romeo"

I make to say something by way of explanation but frankly haven't got the energy so instead I shrug , stick my hands in my pockets and suggest "Let's go back to the car and get ourselves to the ground"

6.

An old Falkirk Burgh motto goes *'Better meddle wi' the devil than the bairns o' Falkirk!'* Sounds like a form of ancient warning to tie your wheel-trims on tight when you park in the vicinity doesn't it? Why though, have Falkirk's kids historically earned this less than complimentary image? Were the town's parents too soft on their offspring? Was there something disquieting in the water? Did young snottery-nosed urchins travel in packs along the medieval cobbled streets haranguing OAPs and annoying everyone else by skieting around public places on their fashionable 'bread-board-on-wheels' contraptions? Who knows? Whatever was going on though doesn't seem to have limited itself any as an olden day warning.

Back to that most wondrous of engineering feats the Falkirk Wheel, as featured earlier; Its grand opening was delayed for a full *month* due to a gang of mealy- mouthed local waifs storming the facility, forcing open the wheel gates and flooding the place. 'The Bairns o' Falkirk' indeed.

Strange because when I think of the word 'bairn' I conjure up a thoroughly wholesome image of a small, innocent young child , possibly in woolly tartan PJs, smiling warmly on the rug by the fireside . There would however seem to be a darker implication at work here. Better meddling wi' the Devil indeed.

Of course it doesn't then take a genius to work out that Falkirk FC's famous nickname 'The Bairns' was clearly borne from this ancient cautionary remark . What isn't particularly clear is whether Falkirk's nineteenth century footballing rivals felt the fear or indeed got the reference at all. What is strikingly obvious is that visiting Brockville in the early years was very much like going into the big dark cupboard as a child – you never quite knew what was waiting for you.

7.

Top quality entertainment in the town of Falkirk was at a premium in the late 1870s. Those in search of sporting gratification were forced to choose from a peachy smorgasbord of activities that included rugby, cricket, hunting and that visceral sport of kings – quoiting. Faced with such a sorry selection of pursuits the locals, like many rural Scots townsfolk of the time, had contented themselves with more passive exploits such as getting manky on the local ales, 'experimenting' with locally grown herbal 'extracts' and punching their spouses for not getting the dinner on .

Which probably explains why no one can remember exactly when Falkirk F.C. came into being in the first place. Falkirk, the football club, blossomed onto the scene in 1876 or possibly 1877, no-one seems to know exactly. Indeed the Silver Jubilee Dinner in 1902[19] (Held in Falkirk Town Hall and jovially described as 'An evening of songs, poetry, comedy and juggling) nearly didn't take place at all due to complaints from many ardent Bairns followers who claimed it was 'wicked and disrespectful' to be sitting down to a celebratory meal of lentil soup, chicken or beef, and apple pie some twenty- *six* years after the true beginnings of their club.

Whatever the arguments concerning *when* the first tan leather ball was booted by a Bairn in blue and white, it is worth noting that the '*where*'was in no such question. It was kicked, quite significantly, on the original site of Brockville Park, a hedge-bounded stretch of turf rented from local farmer George Morrison, a comfortable site which would in time establish itself as the spiritual home of the club. Certainly, the team would play four of its first seven years on two other pitches at the quaintly sounding Randyford and Blinkbonny but they soon returned to the original Brockville site lured home by its ' gentle slope' and 'enviable proximity to the town's pay and display parking facilities.

Details of those early years are sketchy although it is known that the club lost its first competitive match seven-nil to a lively outfit called Bonnybridge Grasshoppers and that in 1878 the Central club joined the SFA. Despite the relative infancy of Scottish football, quality players were being produced and developed in numbers yet frustratingly it was proving difficult for clubs like Falkirk to remain attractive against the lure of the bigger clubs down south. English scouts often had to turn up at games in disguise for fear of being attacked, indeed as the Falkirk Herald reported in May of 1879, '*Well kent, evil London*

---

[19]   In a notably rousing 50 minute speech, Club President Murdoch McIntyre recounted with gusto highlights from the club's historical achievements so far. For the other 49 minutes he hummed excerpts from 'The Pirates of Penzance and told a joke about a pig with a hair-lip.

Spyer , Willoughby Smyth-Hackett was spotted again at Brockville Saturday, this time dressed as a threshing machine, and was chased by a feverish throng from the limits forthwith'.

By the late 1880's Falkirk had consolidated themselves as one of the best teams in Falkirk however they were still lagging badly behind the likes of Queens Park , Rangers and Celtic in a wider sense. Failing to gain entry into the first Scottish League of ten teams (Rumours were rife at the time that the ropes round the Brockville pitch were not of suitable quality for the top flight.), Falkirk contented themselves by regularly winning the Stirlingshire Cup, The Falkirk Cottage Hospital Charity Shield, The Infirmary Shield and the highly esteemed ' Renal Unit, Ward 4 , Third Bed From The Left (the one with the stained mattress and slightly shoogly wheels) Charity Quaich. Prestigious trophies indeed .

1892 saw The Bairns produce their first internationalist in Jock Drummond, a surly looking fellow with a jowly demeanour who made a low-pitched growling noise when he ate crisps and nuts in the pub and enjoyed arranging his 'family jewels', hand in pocket, every thirty seconds or so no matter the company or circumstance. Professionalism had come to the Scottish League and one year after Drummond's call up, the Scottish Second Division came into being. Brief hopes of inclusion flickered and died as Falkirk again found themselves rejected and it took until 1897 for the club to pluck up the courage to once more reapply to join the League. The silence was deafening in the members room of the Scottish League as Falkirk waited desperately for someone to second their application, and it was almost inevitable when Hamilton Academicals, by virtue of their 'amusing name', were welcomed into the fold instead. A feeling of 'Everyone hates Falkirk' was brewing and when they applied three years later only for local rivals, East Stirlingshire, to be admitted instead violence hit the streets of Falkirk in a manner which was held as being 'brutal and alarming' for the time. Again we look to the Falkirk Herald who described the scenes of carnage;

'.... crowds of youth and worthy alike jostled outside the Toun Hall in a heady manner ...... so much so that a number present had their hats knocked off. Mr Riddoch of Meeks Road ...... found himself warned by Constable 'Pudgey' Brocus against stamping on peoples' toes ...... and a Wellington boot was thrown into a tree.....'

The lynch mob had spoken in the vilest and most shocking of terms. The people of Falkirk wanted a league team and they would not be denied.

8.

And eventually they weren't. In 1902 the First Division was expanded to twelve teams and resultantly Falkirk slipped into the space create at the bottom of the second. The club's luck was changing and at the end of season 1904/05 having narrowly avoided the repugnant prospect of amalgamating with East Stirlingshire, The Bairns found themselves promoted in somewhat controversial circumstances. Sporting fairness *not* being the operative ethos, Falkirk found themselves as runners up in the Second division, yet were approved for promotion by virtue of having larger crowds and presumably fewer dog turds along the touchline than the actual champions of that year, Clyde.

It was to herald a golden decade for the club culminating in Falkirk winning the Scottish Cup in 1913. Raith Rovers succumbed to a classy Falkirk side two nil at Celtic Park and the Bairns finally got a meaningful piece of silver to stick in their trophy cabinet. Luck however was again to desert the club as the war came along and disrupted a team that many considered was destined for bigger and better things.

Then, from out of the post war mediocrity that had unfortunately settled on Brockville Park came a player called Syd Puddefoot. Sounding more like a flat capped , cobbled-street-climbing character from a Hovis ad, this football legend signed in 1922 from West Ham for what was at the time a *world* record fee of £5,000. The England International had impressed greatly when he appeared as a guest for The Bairns in a number of makeshift fixtures during the war years and, as the story goes, Falkirk supporters who are always quick to dip into their pockets for the sake of their club, had a whip round and the London club were asked to name their price. Thinking Falkirk could never raise what was considered such an outrageous amount, the Hammers demanded the Rockerfellian sum of five thousand pounds only to collectively fall off their comfy leather director's box seats when the Scottish club, without batting an eyelid, paid up. The transaction was made all the more annoying for the Londoners as most of the fee was paid in loose change and further, it became publically known that Falkirk would have, if pushed, happily gone to six grand plus ten jars of the Chairman's homemade monkey-nut chutney. The extra cash was one thing but the reputed sexual performance-enhancing properties of the chutney were legendary in the area and for the well to do gentleman of London society, worth its weight in gold.[20]

Puddefoot was hailed as a hero and paraded from Falkirk Grahamston Station around the town in an open top carriage. Men , women and children of all ages flooded the town centre and the scene would have been perfect had Syd not been forced to stand on his own with his cases at his side for over an hour before the ten thousand strong crowd realised he wasn't getting off at Falkirk High. Puddefoot was an out and out success, however like many Englishmen of international class who followed in his wake, he wouldn't even smell another cap for his country whilst plying his trade in Scotland. He scored forty-one goals in his three years at Brockville and in a rare interview for the match programme in April 1923 cagily admitted that he was married to Cheryl and his favourite meal was lasagne.

---

[20] Purportedly a secret stash of the chutney is still kept under lock and key at the club accessible only to the Chairman and selected officials. This, however, is refuted by midfield star Russell Latapy who claims to have eaten all that was left on toast with a 'nice bit of chedder' one Saturday evening before heading out for a night on the town . 'Man, I luurve dat chutney!' he disclosed in a recent interview in the Sunday Sport.

It was Fakirk's unpredictability as a team that was to punctuate the club's journey towards the modern era. One week they would be more than capable of routing the old firm home or away, the next they were being given a showing up by Slammanan Rust Scourers And Slurry Pumpers Second XI. Great players like the diminutive Patsy Gallagher, the powerful Kenny Dawson, Bob Shankly and goal-machine Jimmy Bartram came and went. A Scottish Cup was proudly won in 1957 when The Bairns saw off Kilmarnock in the final and a fair few memorable performances graced the Brockville turf in the years that followed, however asides from winning the modern day Challenge Cup in '97 and the competition's forerunner The B&Q Cup in 1993 (A questionable trophy which came as a flat- pack with slightly misleading assembly instructions) , silverware has been sadly absent from the modern day trophy cabinet.

Of course glory fluttered ever so close to the Falkirk light in 1997 when the Bairns lost one-nil to Kilmarnock in the Scottish cup final but as we'll all bare witness to, being close is no substitute for winning the day. Yet isn't it strange how the cards of circumstance sometimes play themselves. For Falkirk to reach their first final in forty years and find themselves pitted against the same 'unfashionable' club they met and defeated all those years previously seems a peculiar twist of fate . This time round a sclaffed goal for Killie and a disallowed, marginally offside effort at the other end was all that separated the team from immortality in the Ibrox sunshine.

Its not just the slim margin of defeat that Bairns fans have had to come to terms with though (especially as they were probably the better team on the day). Its the frustration of finally reaching a major cup final and *not* having to meet one of the old firm that must really rankle. Opportunity like this just doesn't come round that often in Scottish football and I bet I'd be a very rich man if I'd been given a pound for every pub conversation down Falkirk way that ended in a shaken head and regretful sigh lamenting "That was our chance, man. That was our chance!"

The Falkirk FC of today gives off an air of vibrant optimism and prosperity though. For a provincial club they have done well to rebound from the scare of 2001/02 where, but for the demise of Airdrieonians, they would have been relegated to the life-sucking wilderness of the Second Division . For the time being they have shaken off the shackles of being perennial First Division Challengers and are instead considered as a genuine Premier League fixture. They generally play an uninhibited style of attacking football that attracts compliments if not trophies and there is an underlying feeling that real success may only be a couple of good signings away.

And yet despite all this, Falkirk's position in reality remains precarious. The spectre of the First Division always looms , as it does for the majority of the other teams in the Premier, lurking below like a sea-faring predator. Waiting for the slightest 'bad start' or poor run of results before grabbing at flailing heals, then dragging them kicking and screaming downwards into the deep. For such a club geared up for the Premier League with nice facilities needing maintained and good players to be paid, it can soon feel the pinch of less illustrious surroundings. Then the better players leave following the cash, the punters don't come as regularly, the quality predictably drops and only sound stewardship and a canny choice of management prevent the impending gravitational pull back to the role of First Division battlers or possibly worse. When put like this, its perhaps easier to understand why directors become cold and calculating, jam packed with that trade-mark SPL selfishness when it comes to preserving their own team's top Premier league status . Its still not right but its understandable.

9.

The new Falkirk Stadium stands uncomfortably alone like it has no pals and is waiting for a bus that isn't going to come. Around it a flat expansive area of grass and cemented parking contributes to the stadium's stark and isolated look. From the main road two stands are instantly visible. The most prominent is the main West Stand, a 4,200 capacity beauty that holds the bulk of the home supporters. Opened in 2004 as the first phase of the development it is impressive in its cantilever design. Two grey pill-box type protuberances jut out at either side of the slightly underwhelming main entrance. Three levels of windows stretch across the length of its frontage while Grey triangulated girders peak over the edge of the roof. All in all a nifty piece of architecture.

When we first came here back when Falkirk were still trying to escape the First Division, the West stand was pretty much *it* as the new stadium design went. Away fans at that time were housed behind the south goals in what could only be describe as a seated marquee 'half-inched' from the Royal Highland Show. Offering possibly the worst view ever experienced in Scottish Football, away fans didn't know whether to shout for their team or start the bidding at a hundred guineas for a prize bull as yet unseen. Falkirk FC for their part conceded nothing in their pricing and charged us through the nose for the privilege of cramming into this canvass and plastic nightmare. Resentment abounded and I remember missing my only away game of the season in protest at the exorbitant prices for such poor facilities. Directors take heed - Football fans are like elephants, they never forget (and sometimes smell just as bad).

Now we are living in happier times and the North stand has been built to house away fans. Straight out the 'off the shelf' stadium catalogue it looks a lot like every other end-wedge of seating you could see at any one of ten grounds in Scotland today. A big yawn for the architects then. Our old friend the marquee hasn't quite left us either. Having impressively doubled itself in length, its red low-slung roof stretches the length of the pitch opposite the main stand and now plays host to a scattering of home fans as well as pockets of increasingly impatient farmers desperate to see the Massey Ferguson Synchronised Tractor Fleet, famed from Lanark to Peebles for its 'big-wheeled madness' and 'hilarious tight-turning antics'. Flags representing the nationalities of the playing squad currently at the club fly the length of the stand/tent heading towards the southerly end of the ground which although currently awash with enough billboard advertising to fund at least a couple of DVD purchases *and* coffees and cakes for two at Borders Books, it is devoid of seating or people.

And that's Falkirk stadium. In conclusion- Its out there waiting for us and It'll be nice when its finished. If that day ever comes. Unfortunately for the club, arguments rage on over the safety of the stadium in view of its close proximity to the petrochemical facility at nearby Grangemouth. A three kilometre blast zone as defined by the Health & Safety Executive would appear by sheer bad luck to extend somewhere near to the touchline on the east side of the pitch. This unfortunate fact prohibits the club from erecting a seated area holding more than one thousand people .... just in case. From this we must conclude that in the event of 'The Big Kaabooom' the Executive see one thousand barbecued Falkirk fans as an acceptable loss, but any more than that and people might talk. And so the completion process remains tied in knots with little immediate hope of resolution. Those in the temporary East Stand breath a sigh of relief every time the final whistle blows whilst the rest of the Falkirk support slope off disgruntled at *again* being deprived of a firework show that the Edinburgh Tattoo could never hope to match as well as being faced, for another week at least, with the unimpressive, part finished look of their pride and joy stadium. Hardly ideal.

What *is* impressive about the ground though is its in-situ drinking facilities. The Amarillo Bistro and bar area , named after either Tony Christie's cheesy 1971 hit, my Auntie Madge's semi-bald yellow budgie or the catering company owning the stadium franchise (you choose), sits at the top of the stairs accessed from the main stand entrance and positively throws its arms around you in welcome to its beer taps, comfortable couches , numerous plasma TV screens and generous view, through a big window on the back wall, of the pitch down below. It even has a little bookies desk at the door for that last minute wasted fiver on the fixed odds.

Which is where we find ourselves. Sitting, pints of Carling Extra- Cold frost-bonded onto our hands, making stilted small talk whilst keeping half an eye on the live lunchtime match on Sky. Downing his lager allowance for the day, rashly to my mind, in only three efforts, Dave places the glass on the table and heads off to the toilet.

"What would you define as your perfect moment?" Jonesy asks unexpectedly, taking a considered sip at his pint then casting a concerned look at his blue, frozen looking fingers.

"How do you mean?"

"Well, you know, what would just *do it* for you. Make you think 'God, you can take me now – it can't get any better than this"

"Having the best sex ever with the women I love while 'Do you realize?' by The Flaming Lips is playing away in the background." I say without even thinking.

Jonesy seems slightly taken aback at the swiftness and directness of my answer.

"What, on a loop, or can you get done what needs to be done in the duration of one rendition?" he says recovering quickly.

"Don't even think about cheapening this."

"No sorry, you're right. And in fairness I did ask you."

"You did and I was honest " I reply, strangely comfortable in my forthrightness. "What about you then? At what point do you cash in your chips and say I'll quit when I'm winning?"

Jonesy suddenly looks uneasy and his eyes shift away from our gaze."I was thinking about this last night and ......" he pauses and takes another sip of his pint, his eyes clearly wrinkle in abject concern now. "I *think* it would be if we won the Scottish Cup and we were all there to see it." And then lifts his eyes back to mine.

"Bloody hell Jonesy, you had me going there a bit. I thought you were going to say something mental like Climbing the Scott Monument in womens clothes or humping the Pope in your garden shed or something.

"Its not good is it though?

"What isn't?"

"Being thirty- six years old and having a life where your football team winning a poxy competition is your gut reaction of what perfection is all about!"

"Everyone has their thing Jonesy, its nothing to be ashamed of." I offer soothingly.

"Yeh but I'm getting on aren't I? I'm starting to have doubts. I mean look at me. My Saturdays are lost without the football, I listen to music that only teenagers with identity issues listen to and all my clothes are crap!" A brief pause for breath. "To tell you the truth I'm not even sure winning the cup *is* the be all and end all anymore. And without that then what?"

I find my eyebrows raised. "Its funny to hear you talk like that. I always have you down as this guy who is pretty contented in himself. I've always envied your .... well .... *contentedness* , I think is the best word."

"Yeh well, sometimes it doesn't always do what it says on the tin......"

"What you talking about? Dave asks as he reappears and collapses into his little couch.

"Just the usual," I laugh, "Women and football"

"Both leave you feeling it's an awful price for happiness." he replies pulling out his Motor Mart and flicking through it randomly.

"I'm off to the bar " I smile struggling to my feet , "What'll I get you Dave , a pint of *bitter*?"

"Better make it gin and lemon "he replies with no trace of humour.

10.

When I arrive back at the table Jonesy is, in animated style, bemoaning the waste of a good couple of hours the previous evening watching the movie, 'Mike Basset - England Manager' on the telly when he could have been by his own admission 'doing a million things more useful or entertaining. When pushed a little further he quantifies something more 'entertaining' as getting up at the crack of dawn on a bank holiday, Sellotaping his underarm hair to his nearest nipple, before heading off to IKEA with damp pants on. It would be wrong of me, therefore, to allude that Jonesy holds any love for the movie that is 'Mike Bassett - England Manager'.

"Total guff if you ask me." he mutters pulling at a loose thread on the sleeve of his jumper and succeeding in filling his hand with a fuzzy ball of frayed polyester and giving the inside arm a deformed , snagged look to it. " Why do they always make a hash of movies to do with football?" he continues thoughtfully now trying valiantly to feed the hairy strand back into the cuff and up the side of his elbow.

Football movies *are* on the whole pretty guff though. Its a kind of unwritten rule. Any effort at portraying our beautiful game in dramatic celluloid form sadly seems destined to drown in cringe worthy cliché or die a horribly mutilated death at the hands of a luvvy film-director who has clearly been about as close to a football ground as Neil Armstrong has been to the moon (For a short yet informative perspective of my thoughts on this, send for my highly anticipated yet unpublished scientific research paper entitled 'Moonlandings – My Arse').

For these misguided movie-mutts, football films *must*, it would appear, under pain of expulsion from the Film-makers Scone Club or wherever these daft bastards meet to discuss their next molestation of reality, to have to include a number of set factors or they are just not deemed worthy of releasing onto the hopeful masses. First and foremost the tale must centre around an underdog of some sort. The hero(ine) will be preferably poor, maybe with some form of physical or mental defect and possibly fallen from grace due to some faith-in-life threatening event of the past. A bit of gritty Northern realism doesn't go amiss and the appearance of Ray Winston acting with that just-too- convincing 'wee man syndrome' edge is a given. Whatever the slant or nuance of the film however, it is the ending which must conform more than anything else to the strict guidelines of the Sports-film Bible. By that I mean there has to be a last minute, match winning goal (almost definitely score by our hero), and the said goal *must* be depicted in tension sapping slooowwww mowwwshhhuuunnnn depicting an event so long drawn out that booking a seat at the cinema using the 'convenient' voice recognition system seems positively rapier in comparison.

Which of course sets us off on a heated debate as to the best football movies ever made. The early exchanges centre around the consideration of 'Gregory's Girl' as a football film. Since clearly we are in agreement that it wipes the floor with, well, most films in *any* category, its fair to say it would easily top our chart if allowed. We do however reluctantly agree that despite unanimously thinking Claire Grogan looked a 'dirty wee minx' in it (in the nicest possible terms of course) and Cumbernauld fully deserves its accolade as 'Most Boggin' Place to stay in the Universe Award', the overall footballing theme was just too tenuous for inclusion.

Once that was out the way however we slowly but surely came up with a list that once whittled down with all the skill of a Native Indian .. er... whittler, wasn't quite as sickening as was first suggested. In reverse order for dramatic effect we had....

10. A Shot at Glory (Robert Duvall, Ally McCoist)

A Shot at Glory is the sort of film that will appeal to those people who drive slowly by car crashes so they can have a right good gander at the ensuing carnage. Included in our top ten by virtue that it is so spectacularly bad it's a 'must see', the story of small- time Kilnockie *FC's* trip to the Scottish Cup final attracts and stirs us much in the same way as a two month old bottle of milk does. In fairness McCoist is actually quite good is his role as Jackie McQuillan the playboy striker however Duval's performance as the embittered club manager verges on the laughable. Presenting us with the worst Scottish accent since Brigadoon, Duval eventually degenerates into emitting wheezy 'ironic' laughter, muttering the word

'Aye' repetitively and compulsively shaking his head as if he too can't believe how bloody awful the movie is.

For those in search of authenticity, Andy Gray sensationally turns up as live commentary anchorman for the media extravaganzas that are Kilnockie versus Dumbarton, Queen of the South and Kilmarnock , John Martin gets to a cup final and *isn't* photographed in a tutu or wearing huge goalie gloves, and amidst Rangers' pool of crack international superstars surfaces penalty hero EDDIE MAY to score a vital kick. Oh dear.

9. Bend it like Beckham (Parminder Nagra, Keira Knightley)

Not a manual of cutlery vandalising techniques to rival Uri Geller (Although just about the only thing the ex-England captain hasn't put his name to if truth be told), BILB is in fact a charming tale of deception, forbidden love, sexual inequality and cultural conflict with a sprinkling of racism, homosexuality and teenage angst thrown in for good measure . It's Match of the Day meets Monsoon Wedding as young Asian football mistress Jess spends the majority of the movie sneaking around against her family's wishes banging in goals for the local girls team who are managed in slightly bullying fashion by a sexually repressed, Irishman who can't play football himself anymore due to a gammy knee and a crippling hang-dog expression.

Jess, to my mind must be the most alluring character ever to grace the silver screen. Not only does she brush up pretty well and look good in heels, she'll play you at long shootie in the back garden *and* rustle you up a rip-snorter of a Karahi Bhoona afterwards. In truth though the film probably only sneaks into the top ten by virtue of Keira Knightley's extended presence in silky football shorts and the frequent but faintly arousing conversations about sports bras.

8. Shaolin Soccer (Stephen Chow, Vicky Zhao)

Kung fu *can* be applied to football! Martial arts mayhem ensues as bin-man 'Mighty Iron Leg' Sing and former football legend 'Golden Leg' Fung set out with their team of geeks and lardy-ass ex-kung fu masters to defeat Team Evil (no, really, I'm not making this up) and win the China Supercup Competition.

A Thriller-esque dance routine, a mesmerising ditty called 'Shaolin Kung Fu's Great' to the tune of California Dreamin' , and a plethora of bone crushing martial artistry all contribute to what amounts to a totally mental, yet strangely enjoyable experience that will leave you wondering why David Weir doesn't employ the Shaolin Barricade Shield more often when he's playing for Scotland.

*Winner of Auchinleck Talbot FC's Golden Hatchet for 'Most Realistic Sports Film of the Year' Award 2005.

7. Escape to Victory (Michael Cane, Sylvester Stallone, Max Von Sydow)

The unlikely tale of a group of international footballers all imprisoned in a nazi POW camp that looks spookily like Ochilview Park , Stenhousemuir, and their plan to escape during a challenge match against the German national squad. Presented with a sure-fire plan to disappear from the dressing room at half-time, the boys predictably opt instead to return for the second half to give Johnny Foreigner a sound thrashing that he wont forget in a hurry. Hurrah!

Never in cinematic history has a group of individuals looked as uncomfortable as cameos Bobby Moore , Pele, John Wark, Osvaldo Ardiles, Mike Sumerbee and company do here. Pele in particular looks frighteningly bemused as he delivers a performance only marginally less embarrassing than that male impotency advert of some years later. Not quite as good as you remember it but jaunty entertainment nonetheless.

6. Greenstreet (Elijah Wood, Charlie Hunnam, Marc Warran)

Disgraced American journalism student Matt Buckner (Wood) escapes to London where he quickly gets sucked into the violent lifestyle of a group of West Ham fans (as Harvard under-graduates tend to do when visiting the capital).

Despite being as soft as the Andrex puppy, Buckner joins The Green Street Elite, London's toughest football firm and takes enough punches to the face to make staunch Lord of The Rings haters smirk with satisfaction. The scene when the Millwall fans petrol bomb the pub then jump in through the windows is a cracker. Needless to say they are all now barred.

5. The Football Factory (Danny Dyer, Frank Harper)

Set in 1978, this is the moving tale of Senga Brannigan who loses her job on the Cumbernauld based production line of Adidas Tangos for repeatedly drying her underwear on the company radiators. A mass strike is called on her behalf and ...... ok no, its not about that at all. Its another movie about English football hooliganism .

This time its Chelsea, and a gritty world of tower blocks, drugs , lager and Saturday kickings that makes Greenstreet look like Sesame Street . Quick-fire humour and engaging characters make this a compelling movie even if breaking teeth and Stanley Knife plastic surgery isn't your thing. My favourite scene has jaunty psychopath Billy Bright punishing two younger members of the firm for robbing his house by letting his kids use them as a practice dart board. A soundtrack featuring Primal Scream, The Streets , Buzzcocks and the Jam add to the salty taste of blood in your mouth making The Football Factory a must see in anyone's terms.

4. The Miracle of Berne (Peter Lohmeyer, Sascha Gopel)

From the nation who brought us such filmic classics as 'A Day at the Electricity Pylons', 'Me & my Plank' , and 'Die Alten Dicken nackten Leute, die sonnenbaden gehen' – 'The Old Fat Nude Sunbathers' comes this nice little Deutcher film set in post war Germany during the 1954 World Cup.

It tells the story of 11 year old Matthias who lives in a small mining village and becomes the lucky mascot for local football hero Helmut Rahn. Rahn makes it into the German National squad for the upcoming World Cup in Switzerland while young Matthias has to contend with the return of his 'damaged' father fresh from 12 years in a Soviet POW camp. The trials and tribulations of the father's relationship with his son are gently mirrored by Germany's blossoming fortunes in the finals and throughout, the film offers a thought provoking yet scarcely seen insight into a nation coping with the defeat of war.

Pat Nevin reviews the film on the front cover as 'The Best Football Film Ever.' This , presumably, as he was the only member of the Scottish sports press they could find who was capable of watching the film *and* keeping up with the subtitles at the same time.

3. Goal (Kuno Becker, Stephen Dillane, Anna Friel)

United States border-hopper Santiago Munez swaps the drugs and street-crime of LA for the ... uh ... drugs and street-crime of Newcastle where he lives his boyhood dream of playing for the Magpies and going out for a drink in the December sleet without wearing a jacket.

Great right up until the end when yes, you've guessed it, Santiago scores a last minute goal – in slow motion

– in a finale that offers up about as much tension as the preliminary qualifying round of the Dingwall and Black Isle Over-seventies Hedge-clipping Round-Robin.

Goal 2, the sequel, sees Munez move to Real Madrid while Goal 3 (still in production) captures the heart-ache as a sixteen-stone Munez signs for St Mirren, gets a suspended sentence for nicking two boxes of Hugo Boss from The Perfume Shop and finishes up as trainee Senior Sales Executive at The Carphone Warehouse at The Parkhead Forge Shopping Centre.

2. There's only one Jimmy Grimble (Robert Carlyle, Gina McKee, Ray Winston)

Young Jimmy Grimble hasn't got much going for him. He's a Man City fan amidst a school full of Man Utd supporting bullies, his mum's going out with a psychopathic, judo-wielding biker and he finds talking to women about as easy as forcing a cat down a toilet pan.

Except he's good at football of course. As his school team progresses through the area cup Jimmy shows increasingly gifted form due , in *his* mind at any rate, to an old pair of boots given to him by a mysterious old woman who he met up a dark alleyway (Charlie says ' stay away from strangers unless they're offering grubby, unfashionable sportswear). In a predictable climax Billy eventually gets the girl , some badly needed self-belief and the offer of Ray Winston's sheepskin jacket anytime he wants it, as long as it's not a Friday night when Ray goes 'daaahhn the dogs' and then on to the 'rub-a-dub-dub'. In one brilliant passage, Billy's team come up against a the hatchet men of Wreckingam where, to the backing of 'Two-tribes', the teams take part in a mud-splashed scene of carnage and mutilation not seen since the battle of the Somme. Despite losing a controversial equaliser to a bullet header by the referee (How biased *were* the teachers that officiated schools matches in our glory days?), Billy's team eventually win the day and battle through to ultimate glory with Man City's old Maine Road ground providing the setting for the final scenes. Undoubtedly based on the old Roy of the Rovers strip ' Billy's Boots' and none the worst for it.

1. Fever Pitch (Colin Firth, Ruth Gemmell)

Adaptation of Nick Hornby's book of the same name set against the backdrop of Arsenal's '88/'89 league championship win. Eventually coming to the conclusion that football isn't everything, Fever Pitch ably portrays a London Schoolteacher's life-consuming obsession with The Gunners. Despite straying alarmingly into romantic comedy territory the film rolls over and shows enough underbelly of real football sentiment to bring wry smiles out of the most hardened football fans. The number of 'Oh God, I do that' moments are disconcertingly high.

I remember sitting in the local cinema with the guys and being the only ones guffawing at Firth's meticulous efforts to teach the school kids Arsenal's renowned offside trap (taking two steps out, raising the right arm, then applauding the referee for making the correct decision). Amongst this audience of casual film-goers we felt part of a terrific 'private joke'.

Firth sports his Arsenal boxer shorts in an eminently believable manner throughout while Ms Gemmell courts sympathy as the long suffering girlfriend and gives us hope that if someone as phenomenally unbalanced as Firth can pull a good looking bird then we all can. Having seen Fever Pitch a fair few times now I still manage to get a lump in my throat as the Arsenal fans spill onto the Highbury streets at the end and dance joyfully along to Van Morrison's 'Bright-side of the road'. Brilliant.

11.

Going to see your team play Falkirk and not going to see your team play Falkirk at Brockville is just plain wrong. New shiny stadiums with comfy seats may be all well and good but when they come at the expense of losing traditional, stirring, 'dirt under your fingers' grounds like Brockville, then things simply aren't going in the right direction. It was somewhat ironic that in 2003 Falkirk FC sold their land back to another Morrison - this time of the supermarket and not the farming variety. It was yet another 'new lamps for old' transaction Scottish football style and Falkirk became the latest club to yield to temptation, happy for the moment with their shiny new acquisition but forgetting that their old one was, in fact magic.

So, park the car, head over the 'weak' bridge on the way down to Meeks Road and instead of seeing a dingy but lovable shit-heap of a stadium, a sign on a perfectly built, modern looking wall says 'Welcome to Morrisons , Brockville Park' . The 'not quite as good as Safeway was' grocers have to their credit preserved a little of the old ground in the main shopping area. Images of old Falkirk teams and Brockville scenes are etched on the windows, a photo gallery of eminent Bairns players hang on the wall behind the checkouts, and Aisle 5 sells the AAA batteries they used to power the old floodlights with. On the face of it the windows are a nice touch by the supermarket giants but in reality act as a torturous reminder to the stauncher Falkirk fans of the good old days as they are caught in another stagnant express lane, vainly trying to pay for '2 for 1' toothpaste and peppered beefsteaks for the dinner.

Brockville always got a bad press. The self-same journalistic namby-pambys who sniffed at Douglas Park, Hamilton and turned their noses up at Airdrie's Broomfield looked down on Brockville as if it were a cockroach on the bathroom floor of their five star hotel lives. It was raw, uncomfortable and absolutely *not* what the scribes, commentators and pundits were used to or should have to put up with. So the ground and the club got it in the neck. Brockville, as was the will of the Scottish football press, became a widespread laughing stock and it wasn't long before the criticism extended well beyond the sports pages and radio shows with opposition fans gleefully jumping on the bandwagon, holding up the old ground in cruel amusement like bullies teasing the poor kid in the class about his trainers.

And true, for visiting fans a trip to Brockville could be right royal pain in the butt. A frustrating crawl through Falkirk's bemusing one way system, a hopeful scout round the Municipal Buildings' car park for a mythical space that did not exist , onward round more roundabouts (twice) before ditching the vehicle in a random spot nearer to Buenos Aires than the ground itself. *Trying* to say the very least.

Once inside it got no better. The view was chronic-no matter where you stood. On summer days when the drizzle was pleasantly warm, one would stand behind the goals on the war-torn, uncovered terrace, an experience yielding all the atmosphere of a pavement mime artist on dope. Even amidst a sizable crowd of fellow supporters boisterous and valiant singing would escape harmlessly into the sky above long before it reached the pitch ahead. On all other occasions you would huddle together under the low roof of the shed and view the game from what felt was an almost subterranean view point, casting your eyes through a wire-meshed no-mans land to the far left corner of the pitch where invariably ninety percent of the match would conspire to take place.

And yet now that it isn't there anymore I badly miss it. In the same way as one possibly might miss an itchy bum mind you but there is a sense of loss nonetheless. I miss standing so close to the sideline that you could lean over, tap the linesman on the shoulder and say 'Excuse me my fine fellow but that's the fifth attack in a row of a non-offside nature my team has completed only for you to wave your flag and rule to the contrary-Kindly resist from doing so again.' I miss the partisan outrage that emanated from the main stand more than anywhere else in the league any time the ref gave a decision against the home team, whether justified or not. I miss the black band of scary darkness that ran up the middle of the pitch during evening kick-offs thanks to the woefully inadequate 'candles in jam jars' floodlighting. And I really miss the tense cloying atmosphere that you experienced under that wee shed-like enclosure. Similar to the tension and excitement generated at Dunfermline, fans would pack themselves in shoulder to shoulder, shouts echoing around the metallic rafters and singing that threatened to blow the corrugated roofing into Watson Street behind.

The Brockville atmosphere was always laced with a spicy blend of antagonism and irritation, in equal measures. Which was a good thing I have to say. Falkirk were part of the Bad-Guy Gang in our eyes. A select group of rivals which also included Partick Thistle, Airdrie, and Dunfermline, teams who you just had to beat . The 'Brockville Buzz' was due, in the main, to Falkirk's persistent and infuriating parading of wind-up merchants in their team. In fact for awhile it seemed they only signed the like. From my earliest memories a guy called Gerry McCoy was the chief instigator of all things 'cheaty'. Always willing to deal out the late challenge, a snidey ankle clip, or sneaky Chinese burns, McCoy seemed almost deployed specifically to crank our gears as easily stirred opposition fans. Then, just as our blood pressure was returning to normal levels came ginger haired Sammy McGivern. Never scared to slice a man from tip to toe with the point of his elbow or take eighteen minutes to retrieve a ball resting two feet away, McGivern would send us all into the gibbering stages of apoplexy before popping up, as sure as Christmas, to bullet a header past our hopeless keeper and kill off a couple of our older fans with fatal rage and indignation. And finally there was Paul McGrillen. A man who could be standing up to his neck in snow and still fall over. I once witnessed an Arthrston man's eye-balls pop out his head in fury as McGrillen fell foul of a stiff north-westerly breeze , tipped over and was immediately awarded a penalty. The thing is though these were all good players, good players that 'did us' on a regular basis. Football fans never develop any kind of loathing for second rate rivals. If Roddie Grant, Davie Bowman, Chic Charnley, Andy Millen, Kenny Black and co hadn't been quality players with impact and threat in abundance no one would have batted an eyelid. But they were and we did and burst blood vessels were a small price to pay for the perverse entertainment we extracted from watching them and their like over the years.

For every demon there was an angel though. I got sick fed up wishing we would sign the small but tricky Kevin McAllister. Even when, in the twilight of his career, he came to work using his pensioners free bus-pass and was getting daily treatment by the club doctor for liver spots, McAllister was worth the entrance money alone. Then there was uncompromising defender and habitual streaker John Hughes, nicknamed Yogi after the Lisbon Lion of the same name, and Crawford Baptie, famous for that absurdity of a handle as well as being lamped on national TV by Mick McCarthy. And indeed Russell 'I boozed and got high with Big Eck McLeish' Latapy, the mercurial Trinidad and Tobago internationalist who not only played for both these fine and sunny countries but became a national hero winning their 'Tropical Golden Boot 'Award[21] an unprecedented eighteen times. Who could forget the bold Russell who nearly blew it all by getting nicked for chasing round Edinburgh in a VW Beetle, utterly bladdered, together with his slightly more famous friend Dwight Yorke and two 'up for it' female 'representatives' of the Royal Bank of Scotland. Luckily he only blew some of it as he is (still) quite a player and a pleasure to watch.

12.

The ref and his hear no evil/see no evil assistants are wearing their fetching (rhymes with retching) all turquoise strips today. As the man in the middle blows to kick the game off, a rousing call to arms goes up amongst the red and white contingent in our stand behind the goals.

---

[21]   Award for scoring the most number of penalties wearing a big coral bead necklace and a pair of flowery 'baggies' *after* tanning a basin of Pena Colada and draining a spliff the size of a rolled up sports sock..

For the first time in ages we appear to have our strongest team out. Only the spectre of Ally Fairful stretching at the side of the pitch with the rest of the subs suggests any form of weakness. Boisterous singing surrounds us and there seems to be such an air of underlying confidence that I can only assume everyone here must have visited the pub and touched the pillar too.

As the first bout of singing reaches a crescendo we go one down. The ball resting defiantly in the goals in front of us. Our end goes silent in disbelief while the Falkirk folks stand and applaud with gusto. From five yards inside the Falkirk half, Scott McLean stood on the ball and fell over it. The alert Falkirk midfielder whipped a long looping ball over the heads of both Pecnik and Storrie picking out the lone sprinting forward who took one touch then crashed the ball low past Andy Thomson's outstretched left hand.

We're Blue , we're white
We're fuckin' dynamite
Falkirk Bairns, Falkirk Bairns !

The Falkirk fans bellow out an old family favourite forcing a jeer and some coffee-bean shaking hand actions from sections of our support.

"That's it." announces Jonesy." We're down. May as well accept it; Relegation here we come ." No one reaches out immediately to disagree.

"COME ON ROVERS FOR FUCK'S SAKE!" Dave rattles at the top of his voice then puts his face in his hands. A guy in the row in front of us sitting with a small child swamped in a red and white scarf and hat combo, turns round and glowers at Dave."

"WHAT?" Dave snaps peering through his fingers.

The chap limits his obvious concerns to a shake of the head. Dave takes his hands away from his face and looks ready for a verbal onslaught however Jonesy touches him on the arm and shakes his head. Miraculously Dave shrugs and turns his attention back to the game. Thankfully our heads haven't dropped and the brilliant red and white stripes are darting around the sun-drenched pitch below us clearly eager to make amends.

Mickey Hedge , whose hair and newly grown wispy beard make him look uncannily like Tom *'You weren't there man!'* Cruise in Born on the Fourth of July, wins the ball wide right in front of the main stand and carries the ball away from us towards the far end of the pitch. A deft pass slipped to the side finds Ray Stark who is lying deep. Stark slips past his marker and from fully thirty yards unleashes a rising drive that seems goal-bound from the second it leaves his foot. With the keeper rooted the spot the ball rises a little too far and slams off the bar. Everyone is on their feet, arms aloft and then in unison collapse back to their seat in anguish as the ball rebounds to a Falkirk defender who thankfully batters it out the side for a throw in.

"SEE!" Jonesy wails, "Its just not going to happen!"

The play trundles on with Arthurston stoically chipping away at a frail looking Falkirk rear-guard. Despite looking shaky at the back though, Falkirk are menacing coming forward and the flowing end to end play has us on the edge of our seats. As the referee blows for half time everyone in the stadium stands and applauds their team off the park. Nods and exclamations abound to the tune of 'no' a bad game eh?' and a general optimism prevails.

Jonesy is prattling on in the background about nothing in particular as I stare over the low red roof to my left . Over to where the clear blue sky meets the horizon and industrial hangers bleed into grey council housing. The roof mounted flags flutter excitedly having been wakened from their slumber by a perky young breeze that has blown up from nowhere.

Sometimes half-time seems to drag on for ever however this one is over in the blinking of an eye. Without having passed a single word with the guys, a ripple of noise brings me to, and immediately builds into a healthy encouraging cheer from around the three stands.

"Awww Bollocks!" cries Jonesy, "He's only gone and stuck Fairful on." True enough the Golden Boy himself is jogging on to the field wind-milling his arms around in a frantic stretching motion.

"Who's off?" Dave inevitably asks. A quick check reveals that Tony Bunton won't kick another ball in this game.

Dave looks pensive while Jonesy is hunched uncomfortably with a sagging jowly look on his face. An air of apprehension flits around with the breeze which is now blowing into our faces insistently as the players get into position. The Rovers kick off and immediately push towards us.

A full ten minutes go by and Falkirk hardly touch the ball. Four corners in quick succession get the Arthurston feet stamping but all we have for our domination is thick header by Pecnick which flies well over the bar. Slowly we stake more and more territory until our back four are virtually camped on the half way line, all the play going on well in front of them. Another lively move involving McLean, Bunton and Dinsmore ends with a fierce drive hit too directly at the Bairns keeper. The Falkirk stopper wastes no time in directing the ball away out to our left where a pacey, blond mopped left winger gathers the ball gratefully. Within three steps the lad is motoring and shows Jerry Kidd a clean pair of heels on the outside.

"WATCH THE NUMBER ELEVEN IN THE MIDDLE!" I scream

"THE NUMBER ELEVENNNN!" Dave echoes seeing the same as me. Unlike Jim Storrie in the middle, the winger too has spotted his striker's surging run and lofts a high ball towards the penalty spot. Thomson has seen the danger and is haring out his goals. Storrie though, has clearly lost the track of the ball and his momentum actually carries him by the onrushing keeper. In a flash disaster hits. The number eleven gets to the ball first before Thomson and heads a looping effort goalwards. Storrie, now back peddling two feet off the line, and seeing the ball dropping over his head makes an acrobatic dive and punches the ball over the bar. Within seconds the defender is walking to the stand without even waiting for the referee to catch up and brandish the red card.

Heads fall into hands, some eyes shut. Others look to the heavens. The Falkirk masses bay jubilantly as the ball is placed on the penalty spot. Dave looks at me grim face, Jonesy bites his fist. I just shake my head.

A tall, lean blue-shirt moves the ball slightly on its spot, straightens up and looks at Thomson. He takes only three steps back then scoops a well placed kick to the keeper's top left corner. Its accurate but lacking in pace and Thomson manages to get fingers to and deflects it onto the bar. Pecnick is the first man back and manages to cooly chip the ball wide to Micky Hedge who is standing on the touchline about midway inside the Rovers half of the pitch. Our support are going ballistic waving arms and punching the air. Suddenly though, the cheers for the penalty miss change to screams of encouragement as Arthurston pour forward. Four red and white striped shirts are powering forward and now we have them outnumbered. Hedge looks like he's running on air as he eats up the grass in front of the main stand. As the nearest defender pulls towards him, Micky lowers his head over the ball and skulls it low into the penalty box. Stark the leader in the Arthurston foot-race looks to be reaching it first. Just as he gets there he keeps running and lets it go by.

"Aaaaarrrgggghhhh.... " starts Jonesy but doesn't finish as in behind Stark rakes Ally Fairful who takes the ball in his stride and powerfully side foots the ball past the exposed Falkirk keeper.

"Waaaahhhhhhhhhhhh !" he continues but is immediately drowned out by everyone around us as the celebrations begin. By the time we're settle back in our seats Falkirk are ready to kick off . The score – one all.

"COME ON THE TEN MEN!" yells Dave then looks at his watch anxiously .

"How long have we got ?" i ask.

" I make it half an hour" he replies , "plenty of time."

Plenty of time for eleven men but for the Rovers it quickly becomes difficult. We keep the pressure on for a good seven or eight minutes after the goal and then almost by the flick of a switch we look tired and heavy legged and suddenly Falkirk are striking the ball around confidently and we can't get near it.

"How long now?" asks Jonesy for the fifth time in about a minute.

"About two minutes to go Jonesy." mutters Dave clearly irritated.

"I'd take a draw now wouldn't you." He looks at Dave. Dave doesn't answer. "I'd take a draw now eh?" he repeats turning to me nervously. "

"Not really" I answer absently, not taking my eyes of the pitch where Falkirk currently have a corner but are waiting for one of their players to be substituted. "We *need* the three points here. "

The Falkirk man takes an age to drag himself off the pitch clapping the home support as he eventually reaches his replacement at the side of the pitch. The new man immediately runs to the corner flag, looks resolutely at the ball then chips it straight out the pitch before it gets to the goal. The Rovers fans cheer is relief as much as ridicule. To save his blushes the player opts for the age old ploy of staring at the turf then stamping down the imaginary rut that caused the 'bobble'.

Thomson takes a quick goal kick and sweeps the ball up into midfield where Fairful traps the ball then loses it to the Falkirk man he hasn't seen on his blind side.

"Noooooooooo!" I yell then glance sharply at my watch. We are now, by my reckoning into injury time, Dave's watch would appear to be a couple of minutes slow. To confirm my suspicions the assistant holds up the digital board showing two minutes extra to be played. Falkirk still have the ball in the centre circle and are about to launch it forward when Scott McLean hits the man in possession with a crunching sliding challenge sending the ball spiralling into the Bairns' half. The home fans yell in derision as their man rolls around on the ground in obvious pain but the referee waves play on. Which we were doing anyway. Dinsmore , standing with his back to the last defender collects the ball and with his second touch sprays it out wide to the waiting Hedge.

Mickey has time. He looks up then invites his marker onto him. Showing just enough of the ball to entice the tackle, he skips beyond it as soon as it comes. Three or four more paces then, without even looking, he sends a vicious out-swinging cross into the melee of players desperately trying to find position at the front post. The cross has more pace than that however and as the crowded box watch the ball fly harmlessly overhead we all take to our feet in slow motion as one man in red and white stands waiting at the back post. Alone.

Ally Fairful watches the ball in the air as if he were studying a physics experiment. It drops sharply onto his head and his subtle prod towards goal gives it all it needs to fly into the net at the post with the keeper nowhere.

The place goes mental. Jonesy beside me is doing some horrific zombie Riverdance whilst rubbing my hair in a frantic manner, Dave is standing amidst the bedlam pumping his fist like he has invisible maracas, while the carnage around me that is the rest of the Arthurston support are facing the grave difficulties of remaining coherent and standing upright without falling over the seats, both at the same time. And as the final whistle blows and a triumphant 'Yeeeeesssssssssss!' rises from our ranks I feel a cool, almost liquid relief spreading across my neck, onto my shoulders and down my back and chest. I look to the sky, briefly scratch my ear and that's when I realise this feeling has nothing to with the win, the final whistle or indeed my relaxed breathing techniques. The bloke behind me has in fact spilled his cup of coke all over me in excitement, has buggered off quickly presumably in a state of guilt, and I'm now thinking my jacket is probably ruined.

13.

Ahh the Sunday papers. 'Rovers Return!' announces the News of the Screws. 'Arthurston at the Double!" notes the Scotland on Sunday, 'Come on Rangers!' pleads The Sunday Mail. I read every word avidly searching as always for any compliments that are going our way. All in all pretty good reviews all round . Only the Sunday Herald are slightly luke-warm to our achievement but since they also manage to get three of our players' names wrong (out of either disinterest or incompetence) I dismiss them as one would dismiss Prince Philip critiquing classic episodes of Sponge-Bob Squarepants.

"Goodness!" exclaims my mum as she walks into the kitchen, "How many papers have you got there Craig?"

"I'm just reading the reports on the Rovers game."

"Why would you want to read reviews of a game you were at?" mum seems genuinely mystified. "Don't you know what happened?"

"Yes mum," I reply in a weary voice, "its just good to read about a win for a change."

"Well win or not, see and clear up all those magazines when your finished," She's about to say more but instead picks up one of the supplements and walks off staring in a captivated manner at the back page. Before she disappears out the door I catch the words ' Desirable Special Offer! And make out a decorative plate with the picture of a West Highland Terrier painted on it. Lovely, I think turning back to the paper.

A quick flip over the page and the league table springs off the page.

	Pld	W	L	D	GF	GA	PTS
Celtic	36	25	3	8	67	12	83
Rangers	36	20	7	9	53	24	69
Dundee Utd.	36	16	8	12	49	34	60
Aberdeen	36	13	11	12	46	28	51
Dunfermline	36	14	16	6	37	42	48
Hibernian	36	12	14	10	39	41	46
Hearts	36	14	11	11	41	37	53
Kilmarnock	36	13	12	11	32	38	50
Falkirk	36	8	16	11	29	55	35
Motherwell	36	7	17	12	34	53	33
Patrick Th.	36	7	19	10	27	63	31
Arthurston R.	36	7	22	7	32	59	28

Only two games to go with one of them away to Partick Thistle in seven days time. Assuming we win that then, we could yet save ourselves. Win them both and it could conceivably be Motherwell heading for the First Division. The baw's on the slates now and despite the fact I can't really work out what that means, I'm feeling pretty juiced. In the words of both Doris Day and the Tartan army ' What will be will be'. As I see it (yet choose to ignore when it comes to my own life), a more pertinent axiom would be ' What will be will be - if you make it so'.

I, for one, think we're staying up.

Chapter 21
The Firhill Wind Thrill

1.

There's an air of discomfort in The Barrel and its not just to do with the smell of the cheese. I for one am finding it hard to swallow my steak pie properly and Jonesy seems to be running to the toilet after every other gulp of the lager in front of him. My affliction centres firmly around yet another nasty hangover, one that even a full Scottish breakfast (a pint of water, three paracetamol and a mug of ice-cold Irn Bru) has been unable to blitz. Jonesy on the other hand is, according to him, suffering from a combination of pre-match nerves and the after-effects of a 'Chairman Mao[22]' from the night before.

Jonesy isn't the only one harbouring concerns for the Rovers though. The pub is rammed with agitated, nervy looking Brewers fans grasping onto their pint glasses too tightly and straining towards the plasma TV in the corner every time the SPL league table comes round on the Sky News loop. Also, the periodic waft of sulphur and death that used to be conveniently shrouded by fag fumes suggests that if the Rovers boys aren't shitting themselves over today's game, then they're not far off it. Our own cock sure confidence after last week's result at Falkirk seems long gone and its a hotch-potch mixture of mild hope, measured realism and downright pessimism that is ebbing and flowing its way over our pre-match conversation. Jonesy, when he's not excusing himself in an agitated manner, is repeatedly bemoaning the fact that we will face Partick this afternoon without Russ Dinsmore and Micky Hedge who both picked up knocks in last week's game as well as Scott Mclean, whose dad died unexpectedly a couple of days ago.

---

[22] A bad Chinese

"Of all games to have three of our best players missing for!" Jonesy wails dramatically, slumping over his dirty lunch plate.

"I'm thinking Old Man McLean didn't pop off ahead of an important game on purpose." Dave mutters not lifting his eyes from the fixed odds coupon he's been staring at intently for the last ten minutes.

"I'm not saying he did but its just bloody typical isn't it. Three points today puts us above Thistle on goal difference and with us at home for the last game and them away at Motherwell, well, its there for the taking isn't it?

"Assuming we do something against Hearts" I add absently, also knee deep in my coupon.

"Well, if we get the result today we might not need to win next week....." And Jonesy sets off on a verbal trip of endless result permutations that an autistic mathematician would find hard to follow. His anxious chatter fades to the background as my focus falls on whether Nottingham Forest have it within them to beat Carlisle Utd (11/10) or indeed whether I have it within me not to be sick over the table (Evens).

"So what are you thinking for today lads?" a smooth deep voice pitches in from high above us. A long drink of water of a man has sidled up to us and his sunken, intense eyes are boring down on us fiercely, like an industrial laser.

"Emmm , hey Roddy." says Dave in slightly disconcerted fashion

"Heyyy" Jonesy and I echo limply, our voices ringing with all the feigned enthusiasm we can muster. A brief, uncomfortable silence engulfs us before Dave takes a deep breath and offers the man all the measured insight we've been talking about over lunch.

Roddy Hawk is a strange and scary fellow. Standing there as the tallest man in the room with his bald head, hooked nose and skull face, he's like a (close) relation of Lurch from the Addams Family (if Lurch was prone to wearing a big manky grey duffle coat, skin tight faded black jeans and doc martin lace -ups). Its not only his looks that throw you off-kilter though, its his whole demeanour. Roddy and his strange crew of mates have been lurking around Rovers games off and on ever since I can remember. Not what I would call dyed in the wool men, their attendance is at best sporadic and unpredictable. They'll invariable show for the three or four most important games of the season and then, as if to fudge any hint of a pattern, turn up inexplicably at a miserable nonentity of a midweek match at Forfar in the wind, the sleet and the near fatal monotony.

No one I know has actually witnessed Roddy and his mates fight but there are stories. Stories of brutal molestations, ritualistic beatings, and stories of 'The Burnings'. They may be true, they may not, but the common rumours hinting at how Roddy and his mates' could be co-authors of the hoodlums' handbook; '101 Humorous Yet Sickeningly Violent Uses Of A Naked Flame' are nothing if not blindingly terrifying . If captured by any of these guys you *apparently* could quite happily say cheerio to your eye-brows, ear-lobes, finger nails or any other dangling, burnable appendages that may find their way into the fresh air. It is rumoured that they once caught a St Johnstone fan, tied him to the railings outside St Judes, stripped him topless then singed his nipples with a cigarette lighter, burning off his chest hairs to leave the pattern of the Macdonald Arches etched on the boy's chest. They were also set to do the Dominoes Pizza sign on his back, so it goes, but the lighter ran out of fuel.

"Got your coupons done?" says Roddy his voice sounding as if he's speaking from deep within a bat-infested cavern.

"Ahh, yehh .... well ... almost " I stutter.

Roddy then looks at Dave. "And you?"

Dave shrugs and tosses his coupon onto the table with a dejected look in his eyes. "I guess so but you know what these things are like. I don't think I've had a line up for about a year now - I mean what's the point really?"

Big Lurch looks vaguely thoughtful, wrinkles the size of tractor troughs appearing on his hairless forehead. "Things have not been good with you recently have they?"

"Uhh?" gurgles Dave mid sup at his beer.

"Your wife, she's still away isn't she." It is a statement not a question.

"I don't think that .... ehh..." Dave starts, dark furrows bursting onto his own brow. Roddy holds his hand up menacingly and Dave stops in his tracks.

"It is not a good thing to have too much pain." The big man says in an almost soothing voice. "Come over here with me." And with a beckoning motion he moves away from our table towards the other side of the pub. The three of us look at each other, no one moving a muscle.

"Come!" insists Roddy sounding irritated and one by one we scrape our chair legs, get up and edge towards where he is now standing in a clear spot in the middle of the pub.

"Emmm, where are we going?" I ask barely keeping the raw fear out of my voice.

"Not far." Is all Roddy admits.

We edge through a crowd of Rovers shirts to the far end of the pub. Roddy stops ahead of us to make sure we're still with him. A quick surreptitious look round the bar then he sharply gestures with his head and slides to the end of a short carpet-tiled corridor, past the fruit machine and toilet doors. He tugs on a small handle sticking out of the wall that I've never noticed before and opens up another doorway. Moving into its frame he beckons us through and as we squeeze past him we find ourselves in a dull, musty , perfectly square room featureless asides from another doorway in front of us. Roddy clicks the door behind us and we are all instantly engulfed in complete darkness. Not a word is spoken and the sound of four men breathing in close confines only adds to the claustrophobia of the situation. The smell of beer-breath floats up my nostrils making me instantly want to gag.

"You're going to meet Gordy." The big man's voice booms thickly in my left ear and I involuntarily jump out my skin.

"Uhhuh" I reply, my heart squishing rhythmically in my ears. The name Gordy means nothing to me and without the benefit of seeing the guys I can only imagine similarly vacant looks.

"Three things though - When you meet Gordy....." Roddy's voice says darkly, "Only speak to Gordy if he speaks directly to you first. Okay?

Three mumbled confused sounding okays.

"Do NOT look Gordy straight in the eyes," the voice continues full of menace, " he doesn't like it. And finally, do not even think about sneezing in Gordy's presence. If you think you're going to, excuse yourself quietly and come back out here. Capeeesh?"

"Mmmmm." we again murmer in agreement.

"Right." says Roddy's voice and I feel him brush past me. Four soft but deliberate knocks, an elongated creak and a dull red glow crawls round the frame of the second door.

"Come through." Roddy hisses in barely audible whisper at which the red haze grows tenfold and the three of us shuffle past our morose doorman towards the light, out from the darkness.

The room beyond is dull and smoky, the eerie Venusian glow is emanating from a ruby-shaded standard lamp lurking to our right. Low electric guitar music a la Carlos Santana is playing somewhere in the background as a small wooden table emerges in front of us bearing an intricate piped metal arrangement holding what looks like a row of test tubes half filled with red liquid. Behind the table five murky figures are reclined in the gloom, the most prominent of whom is slouched on the extreme right, seated nearest to the lamp. A busby of fly-away hair, a pair of round-lensed sunglasses and the suggestion of a gaunt, milky white face are just about discernable through the fog. The others remain faceless.

"Gentlemen, This is Gordy. Gordy, these are the guys we were talking about"

The shape with the shades and the Ken Dodd hair nods in our general direction and I immediately feel my nose twitch, a sneeze cranking itself up.

Dave nods his head back appreciatively. "I like what you've done with the place. Early-Seventies Parisian Bordello if I'm not mistaken."

The room falls into silence "It does for us." counters Roddy humourlessly. Ignoring the speculative look on Dave's face he continues pointing his monotonous drone in Gordy's direction "The boys need a coupon up, what do you think?" Some non-descript murmurs emanate from the gang in the darkness and after another short period of silence another nod from Gordy.

My nose feels like someone is tickling it with a daffodil as I try to catch a better view of Gordy who remains silent and anonymous behind his dark round glasses.

"Who were you going for?" challenges Roddy. "Five games!" He quickly barks aggressively.

"Emmm ... well.. Liverpool to beat Spurs.... I think."

"JUST THE FIXTURE!' booms Roddy, "Gordy, AND ONLY GORDY will give the outcome."

Dave looks bemused and Roddy, this time in a more passive manner, suggests "Again."

"Emm .... Liverpool v Spurs?"

Gordy suddenly throws his head back and in a strange, pre-pubescent high-pitched voice gives a strangled yell that sounds something like 'chicken-in-a basket'. Bringing his head slowly forward he looks, what I assume' is in our direction and in the same child like tone squeaks "Home Win"

Dave looks wide eyed at myself, then at Gordy then barely discernibly shakes his head.

"Next one." Roddy prompts

"Burnley against Wolves!" Dave pronounces clearly.

"Chickenninnehbaskkah!"squawks Gordy, his head once again thrown back violently. "Draw." he trills having resumed his upright position.

"Accrington v Barnet"

"Chickenninnehbaskkah! .... Home win"

"Chesterfield v Darlington"

"Chickenninnehbaskkah! .... Away win"

"Eh? "cries Dave, " You sure, Darlington are bottom and Chesterfield are going for the playoffs this y....."

"DO NOT QUESTION GORDY!" booms Roddy. Dave looks suitably chastised and a trifle knocked off his stride.

"Emmm ...... "

" FOREST AGAINST CARLISLE!" I shout involuntarily and then let out a massive sneeze "YAAAHISSSSHHHOOOOOOOO"

"Oh God, I'm sorry!" I wibble. "Really sorry, won't do it again. That's it out now .... haaa ...... gone. " Dave is looking at me, again wide eyed. Roddy is looking at me too. Gordy may or may not be looking at me, I can't tell as I'm frantically avoiding anything that may be construed as eye contact to compound my misdemeanour. An inordinate amount of time passes before Dave clears his throat and says hopefully "Forest v Carlisle?"

Another small pause then Gordy thankfully throws back his head in one final flourish and announces that the Nottingham Forest , Carlisle game will, allegedly, end in a draw.

"Five games" announces Roddy stepping forward. Gordy reaches over and delicately frees one of the test tubes from its holder and downs the red liquid in a single whiplash motion. Four arms reach out from the darkness and do likewise. "You may put a maximum of £30 on your line." Roddy continues, " This will be your only ever chance to do this. Gordy does not help with coupons twice. You cannot mention this to anyone – if you do, we will know. You will not try to find this room again nor will you spend your winnings on food, petrol or dental treatment. If you disobey any of these rules – we will know...... and there will be .... a reckoning."

"Aahhemmm .. well thank you .... and Gordy ... much obliged" stammers Dave "How do you think the Rov..."

"You will leave the presence of Gordy now." Interrupts Roddy firmly and beckons us back in the direction of the door. Needing no second invitation we make for the exit.

"Wait" says Roddy and slides across the room to where Gordy is seated. He lowers his ear to Gordy's mouth and gives a few economic nods before looking up and making his way back to where we are loitering.

"Not you." He says pointing at me. "The others may go but you stay here." Before I can say a thing, Roddy has ushered the other two out the door closing it carefully behind him. In the time it takes me to lift my gaze to the Devil's own Committee Roddy has slipped back into the room no doubt having dispatched Jonesy and Dave back into the pub. The thin bald man looks at me appraisingly and my heart is thumping in my chest. Behind the table a cigarette lighter sparks into a long flame and I possibly whimper.

"Gordy likes you and wishes to give you a message" Roddy whispers as the flame in the shadows reveals a set of lips and nostrils and turns the end of a cigarette molten.

"Ohhhh ehhhh ..... that's ... good" Roddy doesn't reply and instead turns towards Gordy. I do the same.

Without any of the prior neck-whipping or incantation howling Gordy stares in my direction and takes a small sip from the remainder of his laboratory test beverage.

"Do not worry, " he begins in a slow high frequency screech "the daffodils are coming." Low murmers of agreement emanate from the darkness and Roddy beside me nods gently.

"Emmmm..... thank you for that .... ummm ... Gordy ..." and before I can say anymore, Roddy, with a benevolent expression on his face like I have just been sold my salvation, gestures to me that it is time to leave.

To be truthful I don't need a second bidding.

2.

Back outside the guys are standing in the middle of the pub, Dave looking irritated , Jonesy pale and blank.

"That wasn't good was it?" is all I can muster.

"That's for sure," agrees Dave nodding behind him, "someone's taken our table!"

Which they have. And without as much as a dribble at the bottom of an occupying pint glass to our name to prove that the seats are ours, we are forced to order up and drink our next round *a pied* as they say at St Etienne matches. Of course the conversation chiefly surrounds our strange experience with the enigmatic Gordy and his crew. All of us agree we can picture the group of weirdoes from the Rovers games but no-one can remember ever seeing Gordy in their midst.

"Maybe he wears a tammy." suggested Jonesy before being nailed to wall by two 'don't be feckin' ridiculous' looks. Dave of course is off on a rant about them being 'woolly bam-pots' whatever that may mean, ' out their heads on drugs and other mumbo-jumbo". He dismisses their spooky familiarity with us as being 'stuff you could get from anyone round here", and rounds off his assessment by suggesting that Gordy and his band are "nothing that electric shock therapy wouldn't cure". As for myself, I feel unsettled.

"What did they want with you? " asks Jonesy fearfully, almost in a whisper. As I explain, Jonesy listens first with wide eyes and then obvious confusion.

"Daffodils?"

I shrug.

"Well what does that mean?"

"It means Gordy, Roddy, Bobby and Noddy are nutty as squirrel turds." raps Dave squarely. A silence descends as no one is about to disagree. Each of us takes a casual drag on our pints whilst looking to opposite corners of the pub.

"I'm meeting Linda on Wednesday night." Dave eventually cracks, looking at his toes as he says it.

""Oh yes?" I respond, not sure whether this is a good or a bad thing.

"Yeah , we spoke on the phone a bit last night and .... well ......"

"Well what?" I press.

"I don't know !" he spills in exasperation. "I just don't know what to do."

"How did you get on at the lawyers?" I divert the conversation in a casual tone that belies my concern. I've been plucking up the courage to ask this all week but seemed incapable of finding the right moment.

"Didn't go."

"What , you cancelled?"

"Nah, just didn't go." Dave shrugs his shoulders and offers a watery smile. "You don't need to be good at dealing with everything all the time do you?" I shake my head silently.

Discomfort hangs in the air and I nearly ask what he's planning on doing. I catch Dave's eye and I'm sure he's about to tell me but nothing happens and the moment is lost.

"Right, time we were hitting the road to Maryhill" Dave suddenly insists downing the last of his pint.

"Its a bit early."

"Yeh, but we'll need time to get to the bookies."

I give Dave an incredulous look. "After all your mumping and moaning, you're going to put that line on aren't you?"

"Can't hurt to put a couple of quid on it" he replies falteringly and avoiding eye-contact. And with that he shrugs, jingles his keys and heads out into the daylight.

3.

On the 19th of February 1876 'The Thistle of Partick' played their first ever match against an improbably named local junior outfit called Valencia. The location of this match was *not* as many have claimed on the site of Kelvingrove Gallery but at the nearby and somewhat generic sounding Overnewtown Park, the outcome being a narrow victory for Thistle. The North British Daily Mail was present and of this historic Partick Thistle v Valencia fixture, printed a stimulating, seventeen word account stating 'Played on the ground of the former and resulted in their favour by one goal to nothing.' So taken were they with this first encounter that when the two teams met again one month later The Mail chose not to attend, preferring instead to use the much needed column inches reporting on sightings of a large slug on Byers Road and detailing how to treat 'Yeastie Foote' a common yet virulent affliction grimly proclaimed as the 'scourge of the Bakers' Apprentice' and indeed 'not very nice'.

There were a number of amateur teams vying for supremacy in the Partick area of Glasgow at that time. Partick Academy, Partickhill, Partick Ramblers, Partick Violet and Partick Partick were all also toddling around in their infancy however it was to be 'Thistle' with their organised committee, team thermos and unfeasibly large canvass hold-all to keep the strips in who quickly forged ahead and established themselves as the team to beat in the town's vibrant and slightly snobby 'West-End'.

1877 saw Thistle complete their first full season and their newly appointed five man committee (the first body in Scottish football history to include a Theatrical Make-Up Convenor) spent a happy year organising 'friendly' fixtures, poncing around in their club blazers and vying for the attentions of tea lady Mrs Grogan, a woman of a certain age whom The Glaswegian captured the essence of when describing her in an early club profile as 'an accommodating, well proportioned Madame with a familiar derriere and lips like a industrial plunger.' That memorable and exciting inaugural year came to a close with a glamorous social gathering at The Templars' Rooms in Partick where players and officials celebrated a successful season in which the record books show that Thistle played 29 games, won 18, lost 7, and drew 3 (with one match being abandoned due, according to the referee's match report, to 'an awwfy smell of shite' [23])

The new season saw Thistle reach the West of Scotland Cup Final. The match was played at Hampden Park, which in those days was a communal back-garden in Strathbungo, their opponents being fellow junior side Marchton. Thistle scored the only goal of the game, a cruel deflection off a clothes pole, to lift their first ever piece of silverware and their fans rightly rejoiced.

Further success was hard to come by for Partick Thistle however and the early years were to be punctuated by three recurring events. An innate inability to beat the trailblazers of the

---

[23]   An inexplicable climatic phenomena which exists in certain areas of Glasgow's West End near Victoria Park to this day.

day, Queen's Park, a running feud with Third Lanark over such issues as player eligibility, kick-off times and the correct spelling of 'rhythm', and finally there was the club's propensity to move grounds almost as often as the grass needed cutting.

As we already know the club started off at Overnewtown Park however when the pitch fell into disrepair the site was moved to a lower lying patch of land in the vicinity of Clayslaps Road. Moves were made to call the new ground New-Overnewtownpark-underoldovernewtownpark - Park however it was decide by a narrow committee vote to retain the old, original name. 1880 saw Thistle move to Jordanhill Park in the picturesque area of Whiteinch. The ground, which sat just off Dumbarton Road on Edzell Street was considered by 'The Scottish Sport' newspaper and indeed all and sundry to be 'so uneasy on the eye .... that it still made the rest of Whiteinch look like a public convenience .... but one that at least had recently been cleaned '. Three years later came the move to the old strawberry field at Muir Park which lay in close proximity to the West of Scotland Cricket Club , and Partick Bowling Club on Hamilton Crescent however poor drainage and a seemingly ever-present mob of unbearable BBC producers talking in loud affected voices soon forced the club on to pastures new.

Muir Park soon gave way to Inchview Park where they were to play for twelve years. The park was situated beside the present North entrance to the Clyde tunnel and today if you care to look carefully, just before you wrap your car around the central reservation, you'll see a set of goal posts painted on the building wall. Proof, if proof were needed that Glasgow street art isn't up to much.

Thistle's journeys still weren't at an end though and in 1897 they moved for the fifth time to altogether more impressive quarters at Meadowside Park. Adjacent to the Meadowside Ferry, at the mouth of the River Kelvin, the ground afforded a spectacular view of the Fairfield docks and the Glasgow steamers slowly passing by. On a clear day you could easily see the boats on the Clyde as well. The move to Meadowside coincided with

Partick Thistle's first appearance in the old first division. Locals swarmed to the new ground to gain their first taste of top-flight football and while thousands bathed in the summer sunshine, coiffed pies and compared Jesus sandals, the Knightswood Brass Band played a rousing rendition of 'I like to move it, move it' a traditional Glasgow tune of the time which would be revived some 97 years later by piss-poor popsters Reel to Real (feat. The Mad Stuntman). Thistle were to spend twelve happy years at Meadowside and it was only when their current lease was not renewed under faintly suspicious circumstances that the Jags made their final relocation to fresh fields.

4.

It was 1909 when The Clyde Navigation Trust dropped the bombshell that they wouldn't be renewing the Meadowside lease. It was a bitter blow to Thistle who had just spent a shilling overhauling Old Joe Bunton's rowing boat, a barely seaworthy vessel used for fishing errant balls out of the nearby Clyde (a regular occurrence apparently). The Trust maintained that the land could be let more profitably for 'maritime purposes' however a contrary story was circulating that, in a period of dwindling crowds, Rangers were becoming increasingly unsettled by the potential gates being lost to the prominently positioned Partick Thistle FC. Tellingly, at least one Rangers director sat on the board of The Clyde Navigation Trust and was in a prime position to halt Thistle's inconvenient popularity. Even more suspicious was the Ibrox club's 'enthusiasm' in finding a new location for the now homeless Jags. After allowing them to play the odd game at Ibrox itself, a site owned by The Caledonian Railway Company in way-off Maryhill was suggested. A lease would be no problem as one of the Railway Company directors also happened to be ...... ta da! ... another director of Rangers Football Club and it could all be agreed with the minimum of fuss. Thistle's concern over this site would be that many of their customers drawn from the Clyde-side, accustomed to rolling out of the pub and heading for the nearby Meadowside ground, would not now be inclined to hike it all the way to Maryhill to watch a game of football – instead they would probably settle for a short stroll to the much closer Ibrox Park.

Desperate to find a suitable site and find one quickly, Thistle were in a poor position to quibble and so the move was made to Firhill Stadium in Maryhill heralding a new era that would ultimately see The Jags nurtured or shackled, depending on your point of view, into what was generally accepted as being the 'third team in Glasgow'.

Might things have been different if they had remained beside the river? Were they hustled out of a prime location by a bigger, wilier competitor - Who knows? As a footnote to this tale however it's maybe worth mentioning what happened to that valuable Meadowside land – the space, if you remember that was so desperately needed for more profitable uses. The answer ….. ABSOLUTELY NOTHING. After Thistle's unceremonious ejection, the land lay spare and unused for almost five years before the Meadowside Granary (that well known maritime operation) was built giving rise to the question of why Thistle were pushed into moving in the first place. Why indeed?

5.

It was during this spell that the mysterious nickname 'The Harry Wraggs' sprang up. At first glance the name is thoughtlessly dismissed as simple rhyming slang for Jags (and indeed fags) however this alternative, and rather classy moniker can in truth be traced to one of two iconic gentlemen of the era. Harry Wragg Number One, as every cuddy pundit approaching the age of 110 knows, was a successful jockey in the early part of the Twentieth Century. His connection to the Maryhill Club is sketchy at best however it is claimed that one of his lesser known mounts 'Oh So Listless' played centre forward for the Jags for the first half of season 1912/13 and therein lies the somewhat dubious connection.

Harry Wragg Number Two was a bawdy, much-loved music hall entertainer who toured the Glasgow venues of the day with his riotous song, dance and 'Powers of Persuasion' act. Famed for his signature ditties 'Mother McCreadie's Winkle' and 'Pull 'em up Dearie (The minister's cummin)', Wragg enthralled all and sundry with his fascinating ability to lure onto the stage local traffic wardens and get them to rescind tickets even though, by their own insistence, they had 'started writing them'. Common sense tells us that it was Wragg the entertainer and not Wragg the short-legged animal-whipper who found himself immortalised poetically in the fabric of Scottish football. Had he been about today, no doubt he would be found at Firhill on Saturdays trying to persuade everyone that Thistle were a right good team and that the entrance money was well and truly justified. A case that even he might have been stretched to win.

6.

Jonesy has a new job. He broke the news, red faced and stuttering, just after Dave had finished screwing his car into a tight space outside the old school building on Doncaster Street (now the Springbank Centre use by Social Work Services) a few blocks away from Firhill Stadium. Amidst a flurry of handshaking and shoulder slapping we were interrupted briefly by a young lad wearing a red t-shirt with 'You're My Bitch!' emblazoned on it. He wanted 50p for watching the car (Firhill is the only place beyond Ibrox and Parkhead where this still happens) and since we were, collectively, his bitches, then there was no use arguing. Walking away from the car, Jonesy economically embroidered on his revelation informing us that the job was back in banking, one of the banks in Stirling to be exact, his new boss looked like a walrus and the money was "alright but nothing brilliant".

Glancing at him crossing the busy Garscube Street, heading towards the ground there's a sense of purpose and a mild air of confidence that wasn't there before. Nothing too obvious but something a close friend can just about pick out.

We're on Firhill Street just past the aptly named 'Loony Tunes' paper shop on the corner. Clearly you would have to be such to remain open for business in this area with 'things' and 'stuff' and 'money' all 'available' under the one roof for the price of a balaclava and a bread knife. Tall red tenement flats hang over our right shoulders while a row of small, low roofed modern houses make up the other side of the road. These houses didn't use to be here. When I first started coming to Firhill it was the stadium car park that occupied the two hundred or so square yards of land directly in front of the main stand. When I say car park, I use the term loosely - It was more of an off-road mountain-biking circuit than a designated motoring facility. And frequently it was used as a makeshift battleground by hordes of excitable, testosterone fuelled youths who were partial to a post-match ruckus. Those were the heady days of the football 'casual' and the dirty, pot-holed expanse offered an excellent supply of stones, boulders and the odd stripped off car-part for rival gangs of pink polo-shirted, white training-shoed weekend warriors to throw at each other in contrived fury.

It was quite a scene. Watching groups of young hoodlum golfers skipping through parked cars, brandishing muddy bricks and charging at their rivals, retreating madly as the inevitable counter attack was mounted, then scattering like rats as the blue flashing light and ear-bursting siren descended on the scene, as always just a minute too late.

Which was a strange set of affairs in view of the popular reputation held that Partick Thistle fans were a delicate band of pseudo-intellectual art-house fopps. I always wondered where that association came from. Did these violence-loving young whippymylads quote scenes from La Dolce Vita whilst hitting you over the head with a hunk of wooden fencing? Did they fret histrionically at missing out on La Boheme at the Theatre Royal owing to the fact they were incarcerated in the cells until Monday morning? Who knows. What was clear though, was that the number of incidents of bad-feeling towards away fans around the Maryhill area was more in keeping with a John Woo tale of revenge (flocks of doves aplenty) than a French subtitled period romance.

In front of us the corner of the main stand comes into view. Its cream painted top section looks clean and tidy against the blue sky and the large black minimalist modern thistle logo on the side wall is striking against the big yellow and red board its mounted on. Crossing the street we quickly find ourselves on Firhill Road itself skirting the main stand, fighting against the seemingly unending flow of red, yellow and black scarved Thistle fans heading purposefully in the opposite direction towards the home supporters entrance. Past the steps to the main door we jostle, under the two big white globe bulbs mounted on the wall and on up the gentle incline to the nearby away turnstile; Which is convenient in so many ways. Not only does it save us a trek round to the other side of the ground as in days gone by, but it keeps my comrades away from the pond. Ahh yes Firhill's pond- sounds charming and scenic ... you'd think? Alas not. Despite playing host to the odd hardy duck or two and being set amidst indigenous reeds and grassland, it holds all the charm of an old pish-stained mattress, and the point at which it seeps into the passing Forth and Clyde canal patently will *never* be the scene that finds its way into the 'Tranquil Boating in Scotland' brochure. It *does* hold a special place in my heart though as memorably both Dave and Jonesy once slipped into its watery expanse, up to their knees. The story in all honesty is an unremarkable one fuelled by two young lads' quest for the truth coupled with enough Jack Daniels to preserve a dead goat.

Someone in the pub, Wintersgills on Great Western Road for those interested, told them that the original Glasgow Cup was at the bottom of that pond. Thrown there, allegedly, by a former Thistle Chairman in protest at the Old Firm's monopoly on the old trophy. I can still see that red, scratchy faced old man peering over his half of lager recounting his tale *"...... and when the watter's at a certain level you can stand at its edge and catch a glimpse of yon cup stuck in the mud, way doon at the bottom ."* Sobriety is a wonderful thing – you can tell bullshit the minute you hear it. The boys - my friends - had no such protection. Swallowing the story like a python snacking on a small domestic pet, they carried the notion all the way to the game. As soon as we hit the path heading round to the Jackie Husband Stand the two of them tilted their heads over to the water and ran off giggling like a mad combination of Indiana Jones and St Trinians Schoolgirls. I was way too cold and drunk to join them in their quest and kept walking but I was lucky enough to look back and catch Dave standing too close to the edge and instantly dropping a foot in height as he collapsed down into the water. Not before he grabbed Jonesy's sleeve though and brought him unceremoniously in with him.

Our intrepid adventurers then had to spend the entire match sitting with mud caked hands and dark stained trousers from the knee down, Dave only wearing one training shoe, the other having been suctioned into the pond-bed as he hauled himself out. Jonesy for his part admitted two weeks later to losing his little red hand-held radio to Davy Jones Locker and went on about the reception on its inferior replacement for months afterwards.

There's a legend goes that if you stand at the edge of the Firhill pond, *and* if the watter is at the right level, you may catch sight of a Converse tracky and a wee red Binotone radio. And I for one believe it.

7.

Firhill has changed quite a bit over the years. In the olden days , well, olden for me at any rate, we used to enter at a turnstile over in the southwest corner at the right hand side of the old main stand. From there we had to hike all the way round the exposed South Terracing, past the big white, chunky square goal-posts and head towards our designated standing area, high up to the right of the halfway line. Given the option of skirting the front wall or wading through the congregated home fans we always chose the former before climbing the steep incline and hopefully finding a free barrier to lean comfortably upon and enjoy the match. Some ten minutes after kick off the Rovers 'Beastie Bus' would get in. Cue fifty or so well oiled, iron-clad, mentalists snaking their way provocatively into the ground in a long, posturing line following the same semi-circular path we had just done except of course they took the high road when we took the low one.

We would all watch and wait. Closer and closer they got until a shout went up, a scuffle broke out and the previously sedate terracing was instantly turned into a scene of manic bedlam with innocent bystanders fleeing, cops ploughing into the crowd truncheons at the ready and hordes of the usual suspects jostling, flailing wildly, falling down steps and generally making a nuisance of themselves . We didn't mind all this going on within a stone's throw of us in fact on the rare occasions that it didn't happen, we all secretly felt short changed at being deprived of the spectacle. Show me someone who doesn't appreciate seeing inebriated grown men in Doc-Martens and braces tumbling down cement stairs like punk Easter eggs and I'll show you someone who collects buttons and tapes missed episodes of Emmerdale.

Things are a bit different now though. Where the fights used to kick off sits the expansive Jackie Husband Stand. It carries itself the length of the touchline and holds the home fans comfortably in its 6,200 or so seats. In the not so distant past away fans use to grace its right hand corner which gave a pretty good view of proceedings, however on the completion of the North Stand (and the creamy, plastic looking Beersbridge student flats directly behind it) we have been relocated and now tend to be afforded my favourite, wonderfully limited view from behind the goals. And all for the same price of course.

The old South Terrace is still there though. Stark and unpopulated, with its police hut perched on its summit and the distant high rise flats of Cowcaddens poking upwards from the horizon like the legs of an upturned three pin plug. As is the old Main Stand, a peculiar pole-ridden structure that has always reminded me of a dusty railway building due to the strange enclosed section in its most Southerly corner. This houses the changing rooms and for now at least, a number of hospitality areas. In my youthful ignorance though I always I figured there were a couple freight carriages and a spare set of signals in there. Actually nowadays, it doesn't appear so bad. It looks suspiciously like the council, when they were upgrading the facades of all the beleaguered flats in the surrounding city, gave Thistle some of the left over panelling which the club gratefully stuck over the old grey corrugated sheet metal leaving the players' tunnel a little more Glasgow Club than Glasgow Central.

I was fixated with that old stand I think. Probably because of all those games standing, staring at it in despair as the Rovers huffed and puffed and struggled to get any kind of result here. For years two things always caught my attention asides from the Hornby section of the main stand. One was an advertising hoarding slightly right of halfway that proclaimed 'Reids of Pertick' - I never found out what Reids did or why they felt the need to be so colloquial in their advertising but it never stopped me wondering – every time. The other was a big green bulb on one of the floodlight stantions that used to be mounted on the main stand roof. It was only the fascination and logic of a child that could have imagined the scene with the groundsman having opened his B&Q poly-bag, (which they outrageously made him pay for) and finding he's bought the wrong colour bulb, then refusing huffily to take the bulb back - after all its fine, its a bayonet not a screw in so it'll still fit and probably no-one will notice .

Except me.

A part of me also fancied that Thistle had sneakily stuck it in there to make grass look greener. Maybe there was a barren spot down there in the corner that they could do nothing with. Or stray cats were getting in at night and peeing there. I don't know. Either way a Fison's Growbag would probably have served them better. Too much thought already? Maybe I should move on to more weighty matters.

8.

Its funny how peoples' frames of reference can be so different. With football, it's usually down to age. My Partick Thistle is one of gritty, rough around the edges, nearly-men with a reputation that barely allows them the standing of contenders. My Dad, who I had a surprisingly stimulating breakfast conversation with on this very subject before heading for The Barrel, still sees Thistle as the team that won the '71 League cup final. Unpredictable pretenders to the Weegie Throne, the filling in the Glasgow sandwich with a serious part to play in the taste of West of Scotland football. To him they are 'Players'.

Because that's how influential key moments in history can be, however fleeting. We still talk of Celtic's achievement in Lisbon and it perpetuates a European pedigree for the Hoops that they struggle to merit in modern days. Uruguay winning the early world cups still , somehow, makes them a worthy scalp on the world stage, Benfica, Ajax and Athletico Madrid conjure up images of the European greats despite being relative lightweights in today's Champions League gladiatorial parade. And yet they have all had snapshots taken of them that define them as 'Players'. And that picture is the one that prevails, however curled up it becomes at the edges or however much the colour fades.

Make no bones about it, the 1971 League cup final was a defining moment in Scottish Football lore. *The* point in the modern era that fans of the smaller clubs still look to and think 'That's what the *Crystal Moment* looks like – that's what we're striving for." And it must still rank, without fear of contradiction, as the most instantly memorable forty-five minutes seen in Scottish football since Dundee striker Humphrey Lutkin played the second half of a war-time Tayside Derby dressed as Vera Lynn in a gas-mask. Partick Thistle, most will remember, saw three o-clock then took the mighty Celtic apart on that Autumnal Hampden turf, and when they walked back down the tunnel at half-time with their sideburns, dreams of buying a Humber, and one day having a corner-bar in their living room (with bar stools, optics and everything), they did so with a sensational four goal lead (it might have been more if they'd been kicking *with* the wind and not against it). This was a team who only a year before, were languishing in the second division, a team up against Hay, Gemmell, Dalglish, Macari, and Jimmy Johnstone, a team with Alan Rough in goals. Well it was nothing short of miraculous. My old man cheerfully admitted to physically falling off his seat and kissing my Aunt Jean (a woman he always cited as having a face like bad joiner's thumb) when Jimmy Bone score the fourth one, mind you such reckless action may well be down to his own blue-tinged leanings rather that any great appreciation of fine attacking football, empathy with the challenger or the urge to get jiggy with 'Hairy Jean' as they use to call her down at the bowling club. Old people can be so unkind.

9.

Why do they do it? I'm intrigued. What makes a Glasgow football fan a Partick Thistle fan? Because its worth remembering that that these people have also been offered the opportunity to legitimately support Rangers and Celtic, to wallow in the almost ever-present, lavender smelling ease of success. And yet they choose not to. They choose instead the hard, uphill road of frequent disappointment, frustration and consternation. 'Why?'

Maybe the '71 factor bubbles hopefully under the surface in all of them or rather the hope that it repeats itself. Maybe they are just being contrary and rebellious to the point of perversity. Granted there's probably a whole host of plausible explanations for the global magnetism to Firhill - the attraction of the underdog, the distaste of sectarianism , the family hand-me-down loyalty, the need for stimulating sporting action on a Saturday since ITV stopped showing the wrestling. But dig deeper and I'm sure there must be more to it than all these things.

I have my suspicions that really its a lot to do with a congenital evil streak that runs through your average Thistle fan - Possibly something that only shows up on an ultrasound. What needs to be understood is that neither Celtic nor Rangers could *ever* hope to match the snidey, cheatiness of Thistle's finest representatives over the years and it is the yearning to see the likes of Jerry Britton or Chic Charnley torment opponents by both fair but often foul means that I think stirs the Devil's own juices in the folks from Maryhill.

Because getting back to the idea of 'my' Partick Thistle, that's what makes playing Thistle so memorable. Their constant propensity to annoy you. That whole can of 'Bad Boys' has been opened back up again and if we're talking 'memorable' then perversely we are also talking 'intensely aggravating'. And whereas Falkirk had isolated pockets of these characters as I've already mentioned, Thistle had the full patterned coat. Britton and Charnley were just the tip of the ice-berg. George Shaw, Gerry McCoy (again), Roddy Grant, Gerry Collins, Sammy Johnson and Steve Maskrey were all lurking just beneath the surface ready to crank up our blood pressure at a moment's notice. And although I wouldn't have admitted it at the time , their 'mischievous' impact was the thing that tickled our fancy, it was what we paid our money for, the battle, the niggle, the outrage. And the Thistle fans must have lapped that up too. Come on , they *must* have, it was always there in spades.

Yet sadly 'wee twisters' like those mentioned above are a dying breed nowadays. We seem to be heading for a sterile sportsmanlike world that has teams kicking the ball back to each other after breaks in the play or helping each other up after inadvertently colliding. Where's the sneaky rabbit punches, or the flailing elbows when the ref's back is turned? This is what we want, this what we need. A dim and distant advertising hoarding used to proclaim 'Firhill for Thrills!' What it should have said was 'Firhill for joyful antagonism'. Its not quite the same anymore – maybe its time they brought John Lambie back.

10.

Its half time and the news is great. We're one nil up through a Ray Stark poke-in from a couple of yards out and delightfully Partick Thistle simply aren't at the races. We've pretty much held on to the ball for most of the half with Andy Thomson not having a single save to make. Needless to say our section of the stadium behind the North Goals is buzzing. While Dave and Jonesy are chattering away about Frankie Boyle's brilliant first half performance and the two elderly gentlemen behind me are engaged in, from what I can gather, an unlikely conversation about Christine Aguilera's midriff, I am watching a gaggle of young kids hitting penalties. My eyes are glazed however and not for the first time I just wish half time could be over and that the teams were back on the pitch ready for the off.

Its high time the whole concept of half time entertainment was looked at more closely. For, to be honest, wee boys (and now wee girls too) taking trundling penalties at each other no longer cuts the mustard as ripping half-time fayre - unless of course you're a parent of one of the participants or are on some form of register that doesn't look good on a CV. Worse still is the newish, alternative, 'beat the goalie' game where the same small baggy-shirted nippers are expected to dribble the ball from somewhere near the half way line and then finish off by planting a pin-point drive past an onrushing keeper. On paper this seems to be a slightly more enthralling prospect than the penalties. However in reality we are treated to a beleaguered yet heart-wrenchingly intrepid child, tripping over the ball continuously before, some ten minutes later, they reach the edge of the penalty box, out of puff and sweating uncontrollably, only to shoot the ball harmlessly against the keeper's legs micro-seconds before collapsing in a heap of nervous and physical exhaustion. Not the best.

And yet not the worst.

At some point, in the last few years, when no one was greatly paying attention, a number of clubs (who for their own dignity here shall remain nameless) figured that their crowds *were* in need of better quality half-time entertainment and dutifully they went to it to present what they *knew* would excite, nae *enthral* every dyed-in-the-wool football enthusiast looking for stimulation in that fifteen minute lull between the action.

The answer was obvious. It was inspired.

It was cheerleaders.

Not the cheerleaders you see at the LA Lakers basketball or the Dallas Cowboys American Football though. Not the smooth-skinned, long legged California Girls the Beach-Boys use to sing of. No, we're talking cheerleaders Scottish football style and can I say right off the bat that watching fifteen or so pre-pubescent young girls with tartan legs, Muffin-tops and lycra VPLs, slapping around in the mud *almost* to the beat of 'I got the Power!' isn't ... and I'll repeat this, ISN'T entertainment. Its murder that's what it is. Pure .... Unadulterated ... Murder. I'll tell you what song they should dancing to - An old favourite of my great Grandmother's entitled "Come on, get aff the pitch (Thurrs some can see yer pants.)

I don't know what bright spark thought that a Scottish football match, in the sleet, in front of thousands of indifferent football supporters was a suitable stage for under-age *thang*-shaking, but I have a suspicion that it is the same person who wrote 'Schindlers List – The Musical' and introduced the slosh to the world of interpretive dance. I know what you're thinking - I didn't know that Hamilton Accies' Chairman was involved in the arts. Well there you are ...... knowledge is power.

But what's the alternative? I'll tell you right now because I've thought about it long and hard, and quite clearly I'm an exceptional 'ideas' man. In fact I have a fair few that would put those pie-stand highwaymen out of business and have crowds scared to blink even once between 3.45 and 4pm lest they missed a single moment of crystalline pleasure.

The first is Dizzy Penalties. Simple in concept , high in fun-factor, yet remaining true to the traditional roots of half-time entertainment. First the child, for it will be a child, (although midgets dressed like superheroes could be substituted for additional, totally un-PC giggles) stands at the edge of the penalty box and twirls madly on the spot for approximately sixty seconds. On the count of three they will then be let loose on the beckoning penalty. Wildly slapstick staggers and swipes will be the order of day before the process is then hilariously repeated by other little members of the team. Mayhem will presumably ensue .

Next up is a short game of fives which I like to call Foe-Fighters. Here we pit teams of bitter rivals against one another in a no-holds barred opportunity for bitter revenge involving neck-biting, garrotting and rampaging gangs of hot gypsies. The competing teams would be along the lines of long-term convicts (with little to lose) vs warders, wives vs exposed mistresses, law abiders vs people who have more than 9 items in their shopping basket yet stand in the express lane, and minor car crash victims vs the guilty parties who admit liability at the scene then phoned up and deny it when they get home. Players would be given four pre-match pints of Stella Artois and advised that anything except elongated pinging with rubber bands will be tolerate by the referee. Also, the ball must not go over head height.

Finally a game called St Andrew's Cross Ball. The two groups of substitutes stand at either edge of the pitch and attempt to chip the ball into the stretcher held by four St Andrew's Ambulance buddies. The St Andrew's Ambulance buddies, for their part, move around and attempt to catch as many balls for the subs as possible without having a heart-attack, dropping the stretcher or letting their red hard-hats fall off. Winners are the team of subs who get the most balls in their stretcher, with additional bonus points for players who refrain the longest from stopping for a gab about the bird in the club shop who they would 'totally do'.

Back to reality for a moment, I once saw Bayern Munich play at the old Olympiastadion and at half-time they dragged ex-German internationalists onto the pitch and had them competing against each other in events such as speed log- sawing, barrel lifting and 'who can hold two full steins of lager with a straight arm out in front of them the longest . Those Germans eh? They sure know how to live.

11.

A dry, warm wind gusts into Firhill and strokes my right cheek. Having sneaked over the big exit gates which are standing manfully down the slope towards Firhill Road outside, it whispers to me first gently then quickly more insistently . With the penalty kick competition (I say competition but in these days of non-competitive molly-coddling no-one seems to be taking the score) invoking all the tension of a Tupperware full of plain buns, we resort to making our own entertainment. Whilst digging around in my jeans pocket I have found an interesting looking, crumpled up bit of paper covered in my unmistakable, blue-penned scrawl. Before I've fully unravelled the ball I've remembered what it is.

"Awww brilliant!" I exclaim excitedly, "I thought I'd lost this"

"Lost what?"asks Jonesy peering at the battered, dog-eared paper in my hands.

"The list I made of my favourite funny footballers' names." I reply happily.

I had been working a late Thursday evening at the hardware-store a couple of weeks back, usually a pleasantly hectic shift but with the rain assaulting the pavement outside, customers and the distractions they brought with them, were few and far between. So I was on the internet. A two minute perusal of a trade web-site had quickly given way to a more committed scout over the message-board on the Barrel-Boyz. Right at the top 'Lando08' a man clearly with not too much on his mind had recently started a thread with '*What ever happened to Danny Shittu? What a great name for a footballer*'. Being another man with not too much on my mind it set me off thinking about all the great names over the years. Within five minutes my memory had given me four or five beauties. Another entertaining quarter of an hour on t'internet had me picking my starting eleven of memorable names. Some were cool, others bizarre, most would have been main characters in Carry On Football, had such a film ever been made (cue a scratchy Sid James laugh, whaaa haaa haaa)

"Ohh , ohh dont' tell me ...... "cries Jonesy enthusiastically, "Dean Windass! Emmmmm...... Rafael Schiiiite ...... "

"Noooo, way better than those " I laugh. Jonesy looks seriously thoughtful and within an instant we have a bet that between them, Dave and Jonesy can't get four or more names off my list.

"Bear in mind its *my* favourite names " I remind them. And off they go throwing suggestions at me left right and centre. In my hand, the definitive if worn and crinkled list looks something like this;

1. **Norman Conquest** – Brilliantly named Australian goalkeeper who played against England in the early 1920s, a game which English commentators of the time would surely have claimed was 'the biggest game of his life'.

2. **Hector Chumpitaz** – So cool a name drawn from my Panini Argentina '78 sticker album that I called a pet goldfish after him. He was Peruvian if I remember rightly and had big white teeth – the player that is, not the goldfish.

3. **Wolfgang Wolf** – I'd plump for this guy being German. A fair player in his own right 'Wolfi' fabulously went on to manage Wolfsberg in the Bundesliga thereby stimulating the memorable chant of 'Wolfgang Wolf's Wolfsberg Army!'

4. **Frank Awanka** –Based in Luxembourg, a player with the reputation as a hard-man but having great individual skill on the ball. (boom-tscsshhh)

5. **Argelico Fucks** – Brazilian centre half about whom Eurosport sensationally reported his transfer to Portuguese football under the poetic headline plastered across the TV screen, 'Fucks off to Benfica !'.

6. **Bongo Christ** – Hailing from DC Congo. Another classic name with hints of African Despot about it.

7. **Ralf Minge** – East German Midfielder of the '80s. Which is lucky for him. He wouldn't have lasted a minute at our school with a name like that.

8. **Johnny Moustache** – If I were to change my name by deed pole it would be to this. Sounding like a gangster from the movie 'Dick Tracy' the lad is currently an up and coming prospect in Seychelles football. Talent seemingly runs in the family as brothers Droopay and Pornoe are apparently showing great potential too.

9. **Emmanuel Panther** – York City midfielder famous for inspiring the song 'He's tall, he's quick, his name's a porno flick, Emmanuel! Emmanuel!'

10. **Daniel Killer** – Another Panini Argentina '78 album memory (along with brother Mario), Daniel Killer became Hector Chumpitaz's replacement after the poor thing was found in its bowl floating on top the water, undoubtedly a victim of my Mengele-esque experiment investigating whether goldfish liked Ribena and Kit-Kats.

11. **Ars Bandeet**- No seriously! A member of 70's Algerian national team and distant cousin of the famous African sprinter Sheert Leefter.

Dave and Jonesy got four in total but only because Dave remembered the goldfish incident. "Sick Bastard!" he added shaking his head in disgust. Ars Bandeet predictably got the biggest, most incredulous hoot although Jonesy's insistence that a Czech chap called Milan Fukal nearly ended up playing for Leeds and Man City. I laughed but the name meant nothing to me.

So caught up are we in our world that we scarcely notice that the players have snuck onto the pitch and are ready for the off. The Rovers fans around us start to applaud encouragingly as Ray Stark and Frankie Boyle, wind buffering their hair, stand over the ball on the centre spot. The Thistle fans in the big Jackie Husband stand to our left shield their anxious eyes from the sun. A small pocket of directors and hangers on lurk in the darkness of the main stand opposite. The whistle blows and the season edges on.

12.

Its an ill wind that is now buffeting the players every which way as they try valiantly to put some form of control into proceedings. Small wisps of net-curtain clouds slide speedily across the perfect blue Glasgow sky not getting the chance to catch more than a couple of minutes of the frantic match going on below.

Partick, in their black-sleeved, red and yellow hooped shirts and black shorts are making more of a fist of the second half and are currently trying to take a free kick into the goals directly in front of us. I say 'trying' as comically every time the Thistle striker spots the ball and lines up to take the kick, the ball starts rolling towards our goals impatiently. At the fourth time of asking the player manages to hastily hack at the ball having heeled a small quarry into the grass and settled the anxious ball into its contours. We screw our eyes to the brightness as the long awaited effort fires low and inaccurately through our defending wall of players and hits the adverting hoardings to the left of our goal with all the force of an earthbound comet.

We are then subjected to fifteen minutes or so of frenetic ball chasing with neither team quite up to the task of taming the round white terror that is currently spending more time out of play down the sides of the pitch than on it.

Dave is the first one to look at his watch.

"Twenty to go ." he says tersely as he catches my eye.

You can feel the tension rising from the Rovers faithful packed tightly into the away North Stand, a bubbling mass of red and white radioactivity.

Thistle have a throw in just inside our half in front of the shadowy old main stand. The ball is returned into play sharply before being controlled and played into the path of the sprinting winger who for the first time today manages the catch it before it skips out the side again. The squat, ginger topped player (whose hair and pallid complexion are clashing with his strip in particularly poor fashion) drops a shoulder and cuts expertly inside of Paul Marker. Looking up once he clearly catches sight of the one Thistle player making a forward positive run for the penalty spot. The ball floats over dangerously. Almost instantaneously the attacking forward realises he's not getting the ball. Ivan Pecnic too realises that the wind has taken control as he slackens his running and watches the ball pick up pace and elevation. Only Andy Thomson looks worried and, as he starts to scramble backwards to his far post, we all see the conclusion seconds before it happens.

The keeper takes two more backward steps before watching helplessly as the ball drifts into the top left corner of the goals then drops to the grass below bouncing cheerfully a couple of times before coming to rest. The Jackie Husband Stand explodes. Dave beside me swears loudly and venomously.

I look at the grey cement floor beneath me then in a surge of frustration kick the unoccupied bucket seat in front of me. A nasty rending crack sounds and both Dave and Jonesy look at me immediately.

"Oh Christ not again!" cries Dave over the stadium announcer who is completing an elongated confirmation of the goal-scorer with excessive gusto (I feel). I almost can't bare to look at the damage I've done and the memories come flooding back before I can stop them.

For I have 'previous' as far as volatile chair kicking is concerned. The seat in question was a particularly offensive yellow one and was attached, albeit temporarily, to Almondvale Stadium in Livingstone. When Micky Hedge unfortunately missed his vital penalty in our doomed run for the title two years ago, emotion I'm ashamed to say, overcame me and I toe-ended the offending plastic arse-mould with all the frustration of a eunuch at a Girls Aloud gig.

Despite not kicking it 'that hard', to my horror the yellow seat snapped with a loud crack and went sailing into the air. That its forward momentum was stopped when it hit Big Jammy McKnight in the second row from the front, squarely on the back of the head was of little salvation. Two lemon-clad, multi-skilled stewarding operatives stepped forward from their leaning session on the advertising hoardings, picked up the errant piece of plastic from the ground, stared at it blankly, then looked up into our section of the stand presumably for an empty space.

Next up came a couple of police. They took the seat, looked at it like it was a piece of Roswell debris then similarly scanned the length of the Arthurston contingent. My heart bounced off my feet and back and at that point I instantly became convinced I was going to jail.

How I remained undetected I can't fathom. Firstly they could have simply collared the man with the biggest beamer in the vicinity (me) and they would have caught the guilty culprit. Secondly, and this is all the more perplexing, they could surely have read the number on the back of the seat and marched up the column in the stand with the same number until they found one was missing then collared the gibbering, sweating man behind it (me). Luckily neither the security company or police representatives below us were in the hunt for Employee of The Month and beyond another five interminable minutes of scouring , analyzing and consulting with one another, they seemed capable of nothing more than some continued, low eye-browed 'looking' and some casual, through the side of the mouth, yammering into their little lapel walkie-talkies. And so the Phantom Toe-basher remained at large. I still suffered though. The last fifteen minutes were torturous. In my mind, I imagined squads of cops and yellow-vesties waiting at the exit, ready to grab my arm having carefully examined CCTV evidence and cross-linked it with some sort of non-specific DNA (an errant toe-nail or something) that came from my shoe and got stuck on the plastic. It wasn't to be though and as I drifted conspicuously out the stadium like a first-time shoplifter and headed to our car, the mortal fear quickly changed to showy bravado and the battle was won. I felt a little guilty for a while after all poor Livvie, doing their best with their spooky Stepford fans and their flat pack stadium , well, they didn't deserve any part of my wanton destruction did they? Then, last season, they tried to charge me FOUR pounds to use their car park and I thought 'Dirty Robbin' Scumbags' and immediately wished I'd kicked two of their seats. And my guilt was purged.

Unscrewing my eyes slowly, my shoulders lurch and I breathe a sigh of relief when I see that the Partick Thistle seat is still intact, directly in front of me.

"Lucky man." Is all Dave remarks in a low tone before looking back at the match and bellowing "COME ON ARTHURSTON!" at the top of his voice.

The elements are against us though. By the time the ref finally blows the final whistle, the gale is so strong that the corner flags are straining at forty-five degrees and the old boy behind me has lost complete control of a grey, sweeping, comb-over which has been flapping devilishly for most of the second half. The wispy appendages which have revealed themselves to be, in their full glory, at least a foot long are now hypnotically waving like a sea-anemone on a strong tidal current. The old guy, for his part he has given up his fruitless palm-licking and hair-flattening and, taking one rueful look at the now deserted pitch, him and his lively shed head for the exit. I marvel at the spectacle and for a few choice minutes my disappointments of the game are tempered. Oh for a pair of scissors I think, not for the first time.

13.

We're sitting in the car, listening to the football results read out by James Alexander Gordon. This is because James Alexander Gordon of the English BBC is our results-caster of choice. James Alexander Gordon is not like the cheeky, wayward young upstarts of today's world of football result-announcement. He has well practiced predictability to his style and delivery and this is what we like. When James Alexander Gordon reads out the first part of the result , like "Arthurston Rovers - one," you can immediately tell by his plummy English tone and enunciation whether the opposition goal tally will amount to a win a draw or a loss, before he's even said it. A rare talent indeed. To illustrate – "Arthurston Rovers one (finishing on a high , suggestive inflexion) is completed by "Dundee" (said low and regretfully) .... nil. Or Celtic one (matter of fact), Arthurston Rovers (excited and laced with anticipation) SIX ! (finishing high, loud and proud) Its a scant saviour from today's ruthless, unfeeling world but endlessly comforting nonetheless.

So far we've been through the English Premiership, the Coca-cola Championship and League One results. Dave is insisting on shouting 'Chicken-in-a-basket! at the top of his voice after each correct result and excitingly we have three results up. Exciting for me at any rate because its usually my first result to be read out that messes up the line leaving all other results redundant and completely inconsequential , my coupon scrumpled in a wee ball in between my feet on the rubber car mat. Resultantly anything beyond that first result represents a rollercoaster ride of lusty fervour on my part.

So Liverpool have beaten Spurs, Burnley and Wolves was a one all draw and Forest v Carlisle ended up scoreless. All we're waiting for is the Accrington score and the dubious Darlington away win at Chesterfield.

"Coca cola League 2" exclaims James Alexander Gordon regally, on the verge of ordering up Fois-gras on fingers of toast and a glass of Port to wash it down.

"Accrington one (slightly upwards inflexion), Barnet (low monotone, slightly bored – no sweat, its in the bag) nil.

"CHICKEN-IN-A-BASKET!" we all shout deliriously. Dave dunts his hand rhythmically on the centre of the car wheel a deranged smile on his face.

And without giving us time to think, or get nervous, keeping the high octane fervour pumping along comes ;

"Chesterfield (confident and to the point) ...... versus Darlington .... late result ."

The car becomes a vacuum.

Eventually Dave breathes.

Then Jonesy.

Always the sheep, I do to.

"LATE RESULT!" yells Dave through gritted teeth. He hits the steering wheel and the car veers alarmingly to the left then back as he quickly gains control briefly glancing apologetically at me. Only briefly though before dissolving into a volley of swear words that segue into one slithering continuous profanity.

"Settle down it'll be around soon, once the Scottish stuff is done " I soothe

"Isthmian League Division one" announces James Alexander Gordon playfully.

"Aaaaaaaarrrgghhhhhh!" we yell in wide-mouthed , Charlie Brown unison.

"Abbingford Napkin one (suggestively), Nuneaton Borough (expectantly) 2

"Chingly and Bingly nil, Ketchup Town nil"

"Aaaaaaaaaaaaaarrghhhhhh"

And on he trots, on and on ....

"Wait!" whispers Jonesy after James Alexander Gordon pauses having waded through a screed more English town names that have never made it anywhere near a motorway signpost . "This is it, this is the Scottish ones coming up!"

We hush in anticipation

"Marmite Central Premier Division"

"Aaaaaaaaaaaaaaarrrrgghh!"

"Hoolipool Magnet 3, Scubby 2"

"Scubby! SCUBBY!" screams Dave red faced "THERE'S NO SUCH FUCKIN'PLACE!"

"Didn't that used to be the Dr Marten's League ?" muses Jonesy

"WHO GIVES A SHIT JONESY! I DON'T CARE IF IT WAS FORMERLY THE HUSHPUPPY PATENT WINKLEPICKER LEAGUE- NORTH! I JUST WANT HIM TO STOP!........"

"........ I just want him to stop" Dave repeats pathetically almost whispering. Breathless. Childlike. Spent.

"Remind me, what are we waiting for here?" Jonesy asks through the headrests.

"Away win" replies Dave with tight lipped economy.

"Clydesdale Bank Scottish Premier League " James Alexander Gordon announces and we're on the final leg. We look at each other in apprehension as the Rovers result flows by. Down into the first division. Then the second. Then slowly and inexorably through the third. Stranraer finally beat Albion Rovers two nil and that's it- no more results left.

Just as a big black pause threatens to engulf the radio and all those around it , a feint rustle of papers floats over the airwaves and the elegant James clears his throat,

"Late result just in" he begins, calmly readjusting his monocle and gesturing to his butler to put another log on the fireplace. "Chesterfield two,"

"AWWWWW...." starts Jonesy

"Darlington three!"

"Yeeeeeeeeaaaaaaaaahhhhhhhhh!" we yell in unison.

"CHICKEN-IN-A-FECKIN-BASKET !!!" screams Dave once again thudding on the black dimpled steering wheel.

"Aww man" he gasps, "I knew it when he said *Darlington* in that tone. Didn't you?" He looks at me blowing air slowly out his mouth. I nod.

"Old Darlington eh, who'd have thought it."

"So how much do you reckon you've won then? Two draws and a reeker of an away win, it'll be good odds I'd have thought"

"'Bout thirty to one."

"Jeez, Can you imagine if we'd stuck on the thirty quid Roddy said we were allowed." Jonesy pipes in his head still peeping through the black leather divide. Dave smiles enigmatically and quietly says "Imagine."

"You didn't?"

"Did you?" I press

"YOU DID!" I finish as Dave's smile spreads all over his face.

"Put a tenner on for each of us," he smirks, "I mean, how often are we in the presence of one the likes of the Great Gordy."

"You called him a dippy bastard when Craig was still in the back room with them." says Jonesy blankly.

"Awww dippy, schmippy Chris, the guy's obviously a genius of sorts. Okay, maybe not a genius, but a .... lucky talisman, shall we say. Aye, he focussed our luck for us ... Or .. emmmm .... something." Dave seems unwilling to be drawn any further on Gordy's influence on our windfall and gives his steering wheel a couple more enthusiastic bangs for good measure.

The untidy, gristly sprawl of Glasgow is far behind us and as the sun softens in the sky, comfortable landmarks start to slip by. The big white house on the hill with the four huge fir trees cutting into the sky, The sign saying 'Arthurston 4 miles' and behind it the smaller one pointing down the narrow pot-holed 'B' road to Lingford, 'The Meat Wagon' burger van sat in the lay-by before the Old Wet Road (always accompanied by someone waiting to be served come rain, hail or shine) Things that say, for good or worse, 'welcome home'. Tonight must be for the better though. As I clamber out Dave's car and make my goodbyes I feel a rush of wellbeing flowing over me. Despite the day's obvious disappointment The Rovers will be in it right until the final whistle of the season is blown, Jonesy will once again soon be in full employment and by my reckoning I've got a good three hundred quid coming my way. I might splash out and buy myself a carry-out and some razorblades.

As they say in the best parts of town ; Chicken-in-a-basket !

14.

I have to use my key to get in the door. 'Its like Fort Bloody Knox trying to get into this house' I think, not for the first time. The dull murmur of voices wafts under the living room door and I recognise my mum's shrill laughter amidst the vague muffled drone. No doubt the Church Folk are in which means tea will be well behind schedule. 'Never mind' I decide graciously, in view of my new found wealth I may just treat myself to a Chinese take-away.

Hanging my jacket up in the big cupboard under the stairs, I'm just about to head for the kitchen to dig out the 'Wokked Dog' menu from the drawer when my mum's voice rings out.

"Is that you Craig?"she trills in her pleasant 'Reserved for Visitors' voice.

"No its Ted Moult, back from the dead, just in to check if you've got Everest double-glazing." I shout back. Before I can take another step towards my beef chow-mein though, mum's face is round the living room door beckoning to me like she's got a tick in her eye.

"An old friend from school is here to see you." She says in an exaggerated, too loud manner.

My stomach twists and I involuntarily think 'Don't let it be George Dowie from my Second Year registration class out on probation. '

"Who?" I mouth silently but my mum gives me a 'just get in here' look, beckons with her hand, then disappears back out of sight.

My mind racing, I move towards the door. I pause outside and holding my breath I lean slightly forward and listen. Frustratingly the conversation has dried up and satisfied that I'm not going to get anything in the way of advance warning, I clear my throat and push the door open.

15.

A sea of faces meets me as I enter the room. Instantly I pass over nodded greetings, my gaze flitting eye to eye with Mum and Dad, three old grey haired women on the couch whom I vaguely recognise as being from the Women's Guild or something similar and finally onto the girl perched awkwardly on a stiff backed chair requisitioned from the dining room. I hold her gaze as she holds mine and gently but nervously she smiles.

"Craig you remember Heidi don't you?" my mum echoes in the background.

I pause for a second or two, my mind short-circuited but still holding her stare.

"Of course I remember Heidi." I reply and I feel myself break into a huge, winning smile.

Chapter 22
Endings and Beginnings

1.

"I don't understand. How did you find me? ... ehhhhh .... *Why* did you find me?"

Heidi and I have escaped to the kitchen on the premise that mum's big china tea pot needs immediate refilling and it's clearly a two person job. I have confusion etched across my face, corner to corner while Heidi for her part seems quietly amused.

"Simple really," she smiles beguilingly, fingering the round grey teabag in her hand, " When you're as mental a football fan as you clearly are then you can't stay hidden for long."

"How do you mean?" I ask finding myself more lost by the minute.

"Well, I Googled your name with 'Arthurston Rovers' and found a happy little rant you made on that web-site message-board. You know, *Sorry Mr Wrecker07, £17 does not give you carte-blanche to insult a player's appearance, disrespect his wife or question his sexual preferences.....*".

"A proper little Sherlock you are" I smile flirtatiously.

"Hardly, you wrote your address on it at the bottom. Was that some sort of Neanderthal challenge for the guy you were arguing with to come round for a football hooligan type of fight then?"

"God no!" I shudder, " I worried for about a week afterwards in case he did just that. " A pause then I bluster again, "I'm amazed you're here ....." another slight shake of the head , " emm ..... why?"

Heidi smiles and for the first time since she burst back into my life I get to take her in. Her hair seems a little blonder than I remember and a touch shorter, her smile just as warm. As she moves over to the kettle which just clicked off I guiltily steal an appreciative look at her petite form which is ably hidden under a strange blue chunky knit sweater with a peculiar splashed yellow pattern on the front. Below this yellow explosion a short tartan skirt shows off shapely legs in black woollen tights which I shamefully find it impossible not to follow all the way down to her low black suede boots. All in all around five foot six's worth of perfection and wonderment, fear, confusion and excitement – all rolled into one. My mind is still reeling.

"Because Mr Donald," she announces turning round from the now boiling kettle, "... you make quite an impression." Butterflies burst into my belly and I start to feel my face burn from the neck up.

"Don't be stupid." I eventually mumble, looking down at my fingers which seem to have found a life of their own drumming away to themselves on the kitchen table.

"No I mean it. Not many people would have put themselves through what you did when you came over last time. That took real guts."

I laugh slightly in admission. "So what about Jed 1?"

Heidi looks at me momentarily confused. "Oh yeh .... Jed", an instant of dawning, " Jed is .... no more." An expectant silence falls on us.

"I mean he's not dead or anything !" Heidi adds anxiously, " He just was .... an arse." She finishes off thoughtfully with a cheeky smile on her face. And it is then, quite sensationally, that it dawns on me – Its in the bag! This beautiful, funny, intelligent girl actually likes me and wants to be with me. I feel like jumping to my feet and shouting 'I am the Greatest!' in a Mohammed Ali type of way. Instead I smile back, my heart racing.

"Well that's ...... that's good" I conclude, the smile remaining.

Heidi rattles the small china tea-pot lid into place, lifts it gingerly and moves to the door.

"Can I ask you something?" I get to my feet and begin to follow her out.

"Sure."

"What's going on with the front of your pullover?" I point at the vivid yellow mess, smirking.

Heidi stops and turns round with mock indignation then laughs. "Gran knitted it for my Birthday, it's not the best is it? But she likes knitting God bless her and she likes daffodils. So, since you kindly ask, they're a bunch of Daffodils. And with that she heads into the hall towards the waiting living room.

"Daffodils.... " I reply nodding, ".... Of course they are ."

2.

I wake up with a start, my heart thumping and cold sweaty legs sticking on the mattress. Vague segments of a bad dream linger at the front of my mind. In it I was trapped in Morton's old pie stand at Cappielow. The one bizarrely shaped like a big plastic beaker of Kenco coffee. Outside, a gang of Partick Thistle fans were trying to get at me but I'd pulled down the hatch and they couldn't get in. So they had toppled the big cup over and suddenly I was rolling down a huge hill bouncing off the inside walls, thousands of little plastic stirring spatulas and sachets of poor quality brown sauce slapping off my face. As the cup came to a halt leaving me battered and bruised, brown tepid Bovril started spewing from a dispenser on the counter. In seconds I was up to my neck and then it was in my mouth. "ITS NOT VERY BEEFY!" I screamed before falling out the hatch and landing on an uncomfortable damp seat in what I instantly recognised as the sloping old stand at Berwick Rangers' Shielfield Park.

"EAT THESE CHEESEBURGERS!" shouted likable snooker ned Jimmy White brandishing two dripping rolls in one hand and his cue in the other.

"I CAN'T, I'LL DIE!" I screamed back. "EVEN THE ONIONS ARE BOGGIN' !" . Two patently half-cooked burgers were forced into my mouth, I gagged, then Gordon Ramsay appeared and dragged me over rows of seats up to the serving hatch in the middle of the dripping wet stand. A queue of over a hundred people snaking down to the distant sea-shore started shouting 'Oi we've been waiting for 3 days here. Get yerself tae the end!". Ramsay told them to fuck off and then ordered a pie and coke. A man resembling Ralf Feinnes in the English Patient then handed us, with hideously flaky-skinned fingers, a lump of lard and a half filled paper cup of flat brown liquid,

"Seven hundred pounds please" the English Patient slurped impassively.

"BUT YOU ONLY POURED THAT COKE FROM A 99P BOTTLE FROM THE SUPERMARKET!" I screamed

"You took all those spatulas" Fiennes said reasonably.

"NEVER MIND THAT, GET HIM ANOTHER FUCKING BURGER!" yelled Ramsay with a look of revulsion on his face. Another filled roll appeared in front of me which I took a mouthful of. I can remember shouting ' I can't eat any more or I'll be sick !'

"Eat it!" shouted Ramsay , "It cost me a mint and I may be rich but I'm not that rich.

"But if I'm sick, I'll miss the last game of the season ...." I panicked.

And that's when I woke up. Wide eyed, breathing heavily, on the verge of panic. And its *so* bright. Evidently I forgot to shut my curtains when I came in last night in yet another state of disrepair and three thick rays of sunshine are flooding into my room picking out millions of gently moving particles of dust in their wake.

Reality hits me hard and fast and my nightmare instantly fades. Today's the day. Home to Hearts - The final day of the season. Had you told me at the start of the season we'd have a chance on the last day to stay up I'd have said 'Bugger off we're aiming for a European spot' but hey, beggers can't be choosers, This'll have to do.

Stumbling over three shoes, a crumpled pair of black denims and a bent 'traffic merging from the left' road-sign, I turn on the TV where the usual kiddies stuff seems to have lost its slot to yet another one of those infernal cookery programmes. I immediately turn the volume down and collapse back into bed and briefly under the sheets . Peering out from the covers I stare numbly as big Ainsley Whatsisname slices a whole onion in a nano-second. 'Trick photography; I think dismissively. Real people (like me) would take a good five minutes to dice that bad boy what with getting all that stubborn, sticky, flaky brown skin the hell away from the vicinity and wiping our poor, streaming eyes. 'And why is he dressed to go to a nightclub?' I muse gently. I mean, he's making a Spanish Omelette for God's sake not heading for Stringfellows. Maybe that's where I'm going wrong. I make a mental note to try on Ted Baker's onion cutting range next time I'm in town.

Ten more minutes of vacant staring before *the* most pointless concept since TV was invented takes place – The cooking programme's 'tasting' section. What *honestly* is the point of a studio full of guests 'mmmmmmming' and nodding heartily over finished culinary gems. It doesn't matter! We can't taste it! Its like having a camera trained on Rob McLean commentating on a game over a wall, him full of joy and wonderment at the football he can see from his vantage point– us left looking at his sleepy, heavy-eyed expression and wondering if he's about to drop off. As I say – pointless. And just once I'd like someone to say 'I'm sorry Ainsley, it tastes like a cheesy belly-button' or better still see them projectile vomiting their 'nut-stuffed cockatoo in a Hollandaise sauce' across the studio catching the token Coronation Street star in the eye with a sprig of rocket, seconds before the Top Gear presenter's head swells up like an inflating bouncy-castle due to a previously undiagnosed nut-allergy.

Disappointingly none of this happens and the programme concludes with plentiful hamster cheeked grins and exaggerated stomach rubbing – Mmmmmm deeelicious Mr Smug TV Chef! The show has done a job of sorts though as my own food deprived belly gives a bubbly gurgle of appeal, I swing my legs back onto the floor, hoist myself vertical and stumble off in search of breakfast.

3.

Its perfectly simple. We have to win today and Partick Thistle must lose. Our goal difference is so much better than theirs ensuring that it won't be a factor in the final shakedown – the three points will take us onto the same tally as the Jags and we'll steal it by a thread. As Celtic have yawned their way to another disengaging championship, the league once more has all the hallmarks of a Jay-Lo concert – all eyes are on the bottom.

The morning papers are pretty consistent in their view that we're for the drop. Behind four pages of Old Firm transfer speculation, the Daily Record has the words 'Down and Out 'printed big, black and inky. Their synopsis of the match is littered with patronising comments such as 'Rovers have made many new friends' and 'a brave effort comes to an end'. The Sun has run a story under the headline ' Stark Reality' where they have our skinny striker virtually throwing in the towel via a few dubious quotes which he may or may not have said. The Daily Express has us 'regrouping for next year's promotion drive' while The Glasgow Herald reports that Dougie McBride is available for selection for today's game. Surprising that last one as Dougie left the club two years ago and now plays his football in Australia I believe. 'Par for the course' to use golfing vernacular.

Wilf Schnabbel provided the only crumb of comfort in our own Gazette a few days previously where, amidst predictable Schnabbledeegook like 'We are in the soup but I have a ladle' and ' Victory is a seven letter word' he came up with something at the end of the interview that I felt was rather profound; 'I have in my garden a flower that has grown through a crack in the path. It has little soil below and cement on its shoulders. And yet it blooms today and gives me hope."

Mr Schnabbel you are Keats stuck in a lift with a gang of limerick writers. Indeed it does - It blooms and gives me hope.

4.

Hope that spurs me onwards to the 'Big Game', so called because of its huge importance coupled with its tendency towards frivolous pursuit. I'm meeting the guys at the ground today. Dave has 'business to attend to' while Jonesy, the virtually penniless Jonesy I hasten, is meeting a pushy financial advisor who 'cold called' him earlier in the week to discuss his financial 'opportunities'. I almost wish I was there to see that meeting. To see the guy's face when he finds out that Jones's current portfolio consists of an overdraft, a framed print of a female tennis player scratching her bare arse and an aging stock of five small tins of Campbell's condensed mushroom soup.

Walking up the Brew in the clear air and sunshine I feel the age old burst of nerves and my mind leaps back involuntarily to my first really big game. The match in question, a second division promotion decider at Stenhousemuir , was I reckon almost twenty years ago to the day. Twenty years ? How can *anything* have happened so long ago and yet I can remember it so clearly. Wasn't World War 2 twenty years ago, didn't they invent the bikini twenty years ago. At worst shouldn't twenty year old memories be grainy snippets of the womb or possibly detached flashes of Bob Monkhouse on 'The Golden Shot'? Not lucid moments with depth and detail. Twenty years - It sounds bad in my head.

Because the details *are* all still there for me - The sunny day, the expectations, the bigger than usual travelling support meandering around, lost in tight residential streets unable to remember where the ground was. (Many torrid tales are still told of passing the same crossroads in Larbert four or five times each before finally stumbling over Ochilview Park a good quarter of an hour after kick-off). It was the day that the Rovers finally hauled themselves out of the damp, chained confines of Division 2 for the first time in living memory. It was also the day of Alfie Daft, the steward who didn't know what to do with our complimentary tickets.

Grampa had brought us over to the Land that Time Forgot in his old bottle green mini, hilariously wearing his 'car coat' and perforated leather 'driving gloves' as was the fashion of the time. He had wonderfully scored us complimentary tickets from the less-than-lucid former director Archie Bywater. Bywater was an eccentric old 'country' gent from another age completely. Famous locally for wearing garish woolly tartan trousers for fun, he would infrequently collect his Sunday papers from Brown's newsagents on the Brew astride his trusty steed, Bismark, a huge dapple-grey, pot bellied horse he had allegedly won in a high-stakes hand of rummy at a National Farmers Union Convention[24] in Peebles some years previous. Bywater and my Grampa were contemporaries and a number of my earlier visits to see the Rovers would conclude with an enthused meeting with Bywater whereby he and Grampa would discuss canny wingers, dependable full-backs and strong right-halves.

Its funny how things stay with you. My lasting memory as a wee boy of Archie Bywater was not his vivacious strides, nor was it his fairly evident wig or his propensity to call folks 'squire' irrespective of age, sex or standing. No, it was a conversation Grampa had with him outside the main entrance to Wilmot Park after some game or other that has now faded from memory. Actually the conversation wasn't really the issue at all. What grabbed me primarily about the episode was that Mr Bywater, as I respectfully called him, spent the best part of this animated discussion mining for hidden gold up his right nostril. Bad enough you may think but when I got home and found a green and red-streaked goo on my shoulder where Mr Bywater had clapped me enthusiastically and said "See you next time Squire, we'll make a player of you yet" (which he said to me every time he saw me), I knew there and then that the Vice Chairman of Arthurston Rovers, elected member of The Scottish League Management

---

24   Bywater held the position of NFU Tractor Convenor for an unprecedented 18 years and was honoured by the Executive in 1996 with the
'Massey-Ferguson Lifetime Achievement Award '. His consultation
paper entitled 'Driving slowly along trunk roads on Bank holidays' is
still used as blueprint for Scottish farmers today.

Committee and Honorary President of the Arthurston Area Rotary Club had deliberately 'relieved' his heavily snottered finger on the person of an unsuspecting seven year old. I felt confused and faintly violated. When I told my Grampa he simply chuckled and said "Be thankful his piles are on the mend." That confused me as well.

God bless Archie Bywater though - for all his strangeness and clatty-bastardness he *had* left us those comps that day and that was just perfect. There is, after all, no better feeling than going to the game with freebie tickets holding the notion, as you invariably do, that it doesn't matter how piss-poor the match is you're still ahead of the game with a bit of cash in your pocket for a fish supper on the way home and a couple of cans of lager for the football on the telly at night.

Those comps fair confused Alfie Daft though. It all started well enough when we presented the said briefs at the turnstile. A surly fellow sitting in the brick-lined shadows initially peered at them as if they were tickets for Verdi's La Traviata and we'd come to the wrong place, but eventually he scowled, grunted, and grudgingly clicked us through with his pre-industrial revolution cranking foot-peddle contraption. With good natured smiles we squeezed through the gap in the wall to find ourselves in a little cemented corner area between the Main-stand and the terracing behind the goals. The problems began when we immediately realised that because of a strategically placed wall we couldn't access the terracing where all the Rovers fans were housed. Grampa turned and called back to the turn-style man inquiring how we could get to the away support whereby an arm emerged from the gloom and pointed menacingly in the direction of a rotund steward of advancing years decked out in a crumpled grey suit, a brown pullover with visible remnants of pie crust hanging from it, and an oily looking red baseball cap with 'Yellowstone – Colorado' emblazoned over two jagged mountaintops on its front. A luminous orange bib strapped tightly over the suit jacket completed the outfit majestically leaving the dishevelled steward with all the look of someone in the process of being air-sea rescued.

So Grampa strolled up to Alfie Daft the steward who at this point was manfully engaged in howking at one of his huge cauliflower ears whilst staring intently at what looked like a beer mat in his hand. Having tapped him on the shoulder making him jump about three feet in the air, Grampa politely asked how we could transfer over to the terracing. Rapidly pulling himself together after the shock of being dragged from whatever beer-mat related world he had sunk into, Alfie looked us up and down, visibly inflated his not inconsiderable chest and gut outwards and said in a throaty Stirlingshire accent "Canny!"

Grampa looked at him confused and replied something to the tune of 'we only want to go over there' and pointed hopefully over to the red and white mass twenty yards away from us behind the goals. Holding up the complimentary ticket stubs he then explained why we had come in a different entrance from the rest of the away support.

"Canny dae it." The steward replied again with a forced sternness to his voice. When asked somewhat reasonably "Why not?" Alfie Daft seemed to shut down for a moment or two before the light in his eyes suddenly relit and he announced triumphantly; "Health and Safety!"

"How do you mean?" Grampa persisted pleasantly, the golden glow of free stadium entry clearly still contributing to his overall sense of wellbeing. At that point Alfie asked us to make our way to the stand as we were blocking the "thurryfare". Collectively swivelling round and staring behind us we immediately disconcerted a nearby old man (the only body within ten feet of us) to the point that he yelled "Whit?" before checking his fly and sidling off towards the pie stand in the corner.

Grampa at that point decided, I imagine, to cut his losses and with a sigh and a resigned tone asked the steward to let us out and we would pay to get in through the other turnstile.

"Canny dae that!" Alfie replied controversially shaking his head. At which point the beer-mat in his hand slipped out his grasp and fluttered to the ground at our feet. In a state of mild panic Alfie nearly fell over scrabbling around trying to catch the feisty card which was hopping around elusively on the breeze. After five or six swipes at what had now revealed itself as a mat advertising Colt 45 lager and bearing the definitive drinking instruction 'Never Bolt A Colt!', he caught the square piece of cardboard and struggled into an upright position with a pained expression on his face

"Let us out!"Grampa insisted more forcefully.

"Nuh - canny" Alfie replied irritated and slightly puffed, rubbing dirt of the corner of his rescued beer-mat. "Now cun ye make yurr way to the staun', yer blockin the thurryfare ken!"

After asking once more to be allowed to leave and once more being denied AND after Grampa issuing the challenge "If you're not going to charge us you need to let us go free!" a comment which was clearly lost on Alfie, my now irked relative pitched a curve-ball.

"If I go into that stand I'll start a fight !" he began spectacularly.

"Eh?" said the steward a horrified look spreading on his round, jowly face.

"That's right, I'm an away fan ..... and I *hate* Stenhousemuir!" Grampa added venomously. " And if I go in there I'm going to get all wound up and hit someone .... " He then proceeded to fumble around in his jacket pocket before awkwardly dragging out the contents and brandishing of all things, his glasses case in the steward's reddening face, " ..... with this!" he concluded threateningly.

I think there was a stand off at that point but I'm not sure. At that point I had dissolved in a combination of incredulity, anxiety and embarrassment ."I've done it before" Grampa growled quietly just to reinforce his position. And that, I think, is where the police wandered over.

"What seems to the trouble here?" the tallest cop in world asked in a tone mixed with boredom and ever so slight trepidation.

Quick as a flash Grampa was in there. Replacing his tartan lined martial arts weaponry into his jacket pocket he explained how we had the comps, were in the wrong area etc and were now being refused exit from the ground. Alfie made a few strangled exclamations of dissent but a cloud had drifted over his day in the sun and he knew it. To make matters worse for the steward a gentleman in a club tie and a brown checked sports jacket suddenly appeared on the cop's shoulder and demanded to know what was going on. Again the explanation was given only this time the steward remained silent.

"Alfie go over there and help Frank with the bottles of cola for the shop will you." The official barked. Alfie Daft, his power stripped in a Samsonian manner threw Grampa a final dirty look before shuffling off towards the pie stand. Taking only a few steps he turned round in instant remembrance and pointed at Grampa . "He was going to fight in the stand Mr Mackay!" Grampa shrugged and the official smiled apologetically, Alfie clearly thought about saying more but thought the better of it and sloped off still gripping his Colt 45 beer mat in his hand.

In a matter of seconds we were led out of the ground through a small door in the wall and given instructions to show our ripped tickets at the other turn-style and say the 'George Mackay said it was ok'. This worked like a charm and we took our places on the weed infested terracing moments before the Rovers ran on to the park to confirm their place in a bigger and better league.

When my Grampa went into his pocket and drew out a paper bag of midget gems, shook his head, and muttered 'Fucking stewards', it was the first time I ever heard him swear. When he absently picked out one of the small sweets , popped it in his mouth and discovered he was chewing on a black one it quickly became the second.

5.

Brown's Newsagent is still on the Brew, about three quarters of the way up on the left hand side of the steep cobbled street as you climb. Of course there *are* no buildings on the right, just a low brick wall between the pavement and the tumbling grass and gorse that falls steeply down to the back gardens of the old grey stone houses on Collection Row.

Coming out of the shop where I used to get my Matchbox cars and where I bought my first slinky (which quickly got bent and had to be replaced the next day) and into the bright sunshine, the contrast with the dank, musty, paper and ink smelling newsagents hurts my eyes. They burn momentarily in the light before I manage to fully focus on my surroundings. This side of the street is now busy with Hearts and Rovers shirts wending their way up the last section of terraced shops (the Second Wind as we call it) before the slope flattens out in the short lead up to Wilmot Park. I cross the road and start to stroll up the quieter pavement on the other side, munching away greedily at the crisps I've just bought.

I gladly make it to the top out breath at the effort of climbing the Brew with my mouth full and stop briefly to recover. Across the way at the stadium the Hearts fans are funnelling down the short length of Madelaine Street, past the turnstile queues of the TP Hughes stand on their right shoulder and the leafy play-park to their left. As the maroon crowd disappear one by one round the corner, heading purposefully to the away entrance, I dwell on three small boys chipping a ball to each other over the roundabout in the park. A Scotland top, a Rovers top and a Celtic top are being worn with pride by the small boys as they knock the ball about skilfully. Two out of three ain't bad I reflect as I turn my face to the warm sunshine.

Behind me now, the tinny sound of the Wilmot Park PA system drifts over forcing out an indistinguishable track (from Jimmy Bently's 'Hits of the 70's cassette no doubt) , down below me the town of Arthurston spreads itself towards the distant winding River Arr, and off in the distance, partially hidden by the romantically named Rainbow Woods, are the roofs and the church spire at Lingford. The view on a sunny day like this is inspirational. So much so that a few years back my mother, in a 'my life is slipping by and I need a new hobby to pay lip service to for a month' sort of way bought a canvass, paints and a folding chair and came up here to create a masterpiece. It took her three afternoons to produce what she Christened her 'New Life Project' in which time she contrived to drop her best brush down a drain, get hit by a salvo of half filled Irn Bru cans by a team of particularly vicious under-tens, and be propositioned indecently by a man who sounded a lot like Danny Rainbow . To the untrained eye the finished painting looked a lot like a Meat-feast Pizza, my mother however proclaimed it as the first step to a greatness that clearly was local to her own mind. Two weeks after that the legion of hardened brushes, three blank canvasses and enough acrylic paint to cover the Forth Railway Bridge twice (assuming you'd want to paint it 'Burnt Sienna') were under a tarpaulin sheet in the garage tucked in neatly beside the Linguaphone Spanish Course and the 'Introductory Macramé set' . Sadly there just wasn't enough time apparently for my mum to become the new Frida Kahlo *and* experiment with hair dye in order to achieve a shade she had been quite pleased with in the month that Charles and Diana were married. And the art world mourned.

A wave of nostalgia and hometown sentiment hits me and, for the first time in a while, I decide I've been relatively lucky with my lot. However before all this brewing contentment can catch too much of a hold I'm brought back to the moment with the sound of the teams being announced over the system.

Mumner mun	Ammy Homshon
Mumner hoo	Yerry Hidd
Mumner ree	Yonn Horry
Mumner hore	Iwin Fechnich
Mumner high	Maar Mirrh
Mumner Hix	Shoff Mahain
Mumner Heven	Mihee Henshhh
Mumner Aith	Momert Hrushh
Mumner Nigh	Hony Munhon
Mumner Hen	Haay Haarf
Mumner Huwewen	Wuff Winmohh

Cheers echo after each announcement and as I excitedly scuttle across the street I cant help worrying if tactically Hony Munhon should be in the team today. I'd heard his recurring ankle injury has recurred and worse, he is persisting with growing his hair into something fast resembling a mullet. I make a mental note to discuss my concerns with the guys when I get in. A glance at my watch tells me its a quarter to three. Fifteen minutes of freedom, of normality. Then it'll be something different.

6.

My breath deserts me as I emerge from the stand. The ground is packed beyond anything I expected. A healthy maroon and white army have travelled through from the capital, presumably to get away from the American and Japanese tourists, and are stretched in the sunshine the length of the pitch across from me. Elsewhere in the stadium, the whole of Arthurston would appear to be present, ready to bare witness to whatever story is about to be told. Left, under the red and white roof of the TP Hughes Stand, there's scarcely a space to be had. Behind the opposite goals, a good few hundred Rovers fans have spilled into the usually deserted lines of benches. Jaimie Dott's large three part flag , red-white-red with ARFC stamped boldly in black is draped loosely over the first four brown, parallel stretches of wooden beams. Over in the corner reaching up into the dark shadow of the tree is, a brightly striped police tape. Either there has been a Taggart type murrdurrrr over there or this is what passes as crowd segregation these days. Three policemen and two stewards are guarding the border crossing and despite the lack of anything resembling threatening behaviour in the vicinity, our guardians of peace and control look edgy.

Dave and Jonesy aren't here yet and - Crime of Crimes - there are people sitting in our season ticket seats. Two middle aged guys who look related by virtue of some hitherto illegal inter-family tryst. Both have tight cropped crew-cuts, receding hairlines and big fat guts peaking out from under stripy polo-shirts. At first they look like they aren't going to move. "Excuse me you're on our seats" I venture politely. Two pairs of close set eyes look at me confused and irritated in equal measures. "That's my season ticket seat" I repeat, instantly reminded of the times this routine has been played out when Rangers or Celtic come to visit. Despite our seats having 'Reserved' plastered on the backrest it seems persistently to be a claim that old firm and fair weather Rovers fans alike choose to disregard.

"Can ye not sit down there? " the nearest one says with an annoyed look nodding his head towards the front of the stand. Before I can answer though old Billy has leaned over from his seat behind and quietly growls in their earshot "Those are season tickets seats, you'll need to move." The vocal 'brother' looks ready to shoot something back however all the 'Associates' in the vicinity turn round or lean over and fix the interlopers with a threatening looks. God bless family. Reluctantly Ray and Billy-Bob hoist themselves to their feet and with beady eyes set to the ground shuffle along the row, past me and down the stairs to the front section of seats.

"Awright?" I ask generally, squeezing into my seat which to my disgust is disconcertingly 'pre-heated'.

"Fine son!" replies Billy cheerfully. His anchormen, Harry and Alistair nod cheerfully too. Alistair's normally red face is glowing like a Bordello window and not for the first time I wonder if today's the day that he ends up in A&E.

"Couple of arseholes those boys were," Billy confides in a low tone, "Made a crack about my cigar smoke." At which point he scans furtively in all directions before relighting a chubby half-finger of cigar and taking a luxurious draw on it.

"Aaaaahhh" he sighs contentedly, "So you think we're going to win son?"

"Hmmm not sure , Tony Bunton is ...."

"Course we are son!" Billy interrupts enthusiastically taking another big puff on his cigar causing the end to glow majestically

715

before lowering it back down between his knees and expelling the smoke surreptitiously from the side of his mouth.

"Teams like the Rovers are always win games like this. They've got some great tryers on that team. Maybe no' the best players, but real tryers. I canny say what'll happen at the Thistle game mind. That Motherwell are a bad lot and I could see them dropping a point or three."

Before I can answer Jonesy appears at the end of the row wearing last year's striped home top which is clearly a size too big for his skeletal frame. The greetings all begin again before Jonesy edges into his seat. He catches me staring at the flapping sleeves of his shirt and cheerfully informs me that he hasn't worn this top since Somerset Park last year. He rubs its material in between his thumb and third finger and adds "Just for good luck."

"How did you get on with your financial advisor?"

Jonesy laughs. "When he asked me where I wanted to be in the future I said 'the Premier League'. He seemed to lose heart after that."

Suddenly a roar goes up and the players appear from the tunnel and sprint onto the field. Everyone around us leaps to their feet applauding, yelling and shouting "C'mon the Rovers!'

"COME ON THE ROVERS!"

7.

"Where's Dave?" I ask Jonesy as Jimmy Bently once more runs down the teams and the players find their starting positions on the pitch, getting in a last minute mix of arm wind-milling, leg stretching and pleasant reflection on appearance bonuses.

"Running five minutes late!" he shouts back over the rising storm of encouragement for the Rovers who are shaping to kick off with Stark and Dinsmore once more on the centre spot.

"Where was he this morning?" I yell. Jonesy replies with a shrug and as the referee's whistle blows Ray Stark tips the ball to his team-mate and the match begins.

The Rovers are kicking from left to right in their home strips of red and white striped shirts, white shorts and white socks. Hearts in deference to the rules of the game are kicking in the opposite direction and are wearing Carmen Miranda fruit head-dresses and hand stencilled kaftans. Actually they're not but it would be pleasantly variant if they were.

We look jittery. In the first few minutes of play we have, under no pressure, kicked the ball out of the park three times and given away two stupid fouls in dangerous positions. Luckily Hearts have started without an edge and haven't put us under any pressure. The ball for the most part is bouncing around on the hard, sun-baked turf giving the action all the feel of frantic Saturday morning scuff around on a public park.

Dave's head pops into view at the top of the entrance stairs just in time to see Scott McLean hammered from behind on the half-way line by an errant Hearts tackle. The crowd leap to their feet in outrage, enjoying the venomous pointing and aggressive bellowing that the situation demands. By the time we are back in our seats and McLean is on his feet gingerly applying pressure to his injured ankle, I have hopped over one place to the left and Dave is in position between myself and Jonesy who looks wide eyed and on the verge of a panic attack.

"Seat's warm "he mutters, without a hint of pleasure, "Have I missed anything?"

"Nope, ball's like a hot potato." I reply, "A couple of poor Hearts free kicks and that's it. Where have you been then?" Dave looks a bit unsure then smiles nervously.

On the pitch Bunton takes our free kick playing a low ball forward into Mickey Hedge's feet. The wee man manages to knock the ball to the side before being unceremoniously dumped to the floor by another rash challenge. We are on our feet again this time excitement takes over as the ref gives the free kick at the edge of the box in good position.

"I've been at Linda's." Dave says sideways standing amidst the baying mass. "We had a long talk about where we are, what we want, that sort of thing." We both sit down again and I look expectantly at my friend.

Tony Bunton and Russ Dinsmore are over the ball, the Hearts keeper is organising his maroon wall which the referee is forcing back the required ten yard distance.

Dave clears his throat, "We're going to give things another shot." he says in a level tone not taking his eyes off the game.

Dinsmore hits the ball from standing and curls it into the top left corner. The keeper doesn't even move.

And the place erupts. "Waaaaaaaahhhhhhhhhhhhh!!!!!" I yell grabbing onto Dave and giving him a hug cum wrestle that nearly pulls us both over the seats and onto Jeff Singer and Parka Man in front of us. Jonesy for his part is staring at the roof, grabbing onto Dave's right shoulder absently as if to stop himself falling off the planet.

I look at Dave. "Brilliant!" I shout above the singing that has broken out along the length of the normally restrained Main Stand. For a second Dave looks blankly back at me then breaks into wide grin.

"Pie and a Bovril to celebrate?" he yells back

"I don't mind if I do" I reply cheerfully, "And don't forget the important things in life" I add. "Dave looks momentarily confused.

"Brown sauce with the pie and pepper in the Bovril!"

Dave smiles again "Ahhh no, we can't forget the important things in life." And with that he squeezes back out our row down the wooden steps and into the belly of Wilmot Park.

8.

The goal, coming after eight minutes, has wakened Hearts up and now alarmingly we cannot get the ball off them. Their main tactic would appear to be to feed their wide man over on the far side of the pitch who then rifles a fearsome dipping cross right down the throat of our keeper. As the clock hits 25 minutes its happened four or five times now and in view of how bad we are defensively in the air I can't see us riding our luck much longer.

Irrationally I wonder why Hearts don't just roll over. They have nothing to play for here. Surely they could just give us a break, lie down and give us the points we need

"What's got into Hearts?" says Jonesy as if reading my mind, "They're trying like bears." I'm about to reply when I sense a ripple of excitement behind me. Intelligible murmurs, give rise to scattered exclamations until someone from a couple rows back confirms 'Motherwell have scored!" An intangible wave of energy spreads almost instantaneously as other confirmations spread the word around the ground. The nuclear reaction funnels outwards and as someone screams "COME ON NOW ARTHURSTON!' a wall of noise builds up around three sides of the ground. Suddenly everything is going to plan.

On the pitch Hearts have the ball though. The hubbub on the 'terracings' seems to have hypnotised the Rovers players and we find ourselves momentarily off the pace. Surging through the middle come the Jam Tarts and suddenly its two on two. Ivan Pecnic steps out to meet the advancing midfielder and as he does so the ball is deftly slipped passed him. The Hearts forward has made a darting angled run beyond a transfixed Jerry Kidd and latches on to the threaded through ball. One touch of control, then another to push the ball nearer the goal and the striker unleashes an unstoppable drive low past Andy Thomson's diving body. The Hearts fans are on their feet, my head is in my hands. Until a loud cheer goes up around me that is. I look back up and a section of Hearts fans are screaming frantically at the far side linesman who is holding his flag up resolutely, indicating that the running striker, in his opinion, had been off-side when the ball was kicked.

"Did you think he was off-side?" I turn and ask Dave speculatively. Dave's bemused expression and shake of the head suggests not.

"Me neither." I agree. The Football Gods are most definitely with us.

9.

We reach half time relieved but with little else to cheer about bar the score. Hearts have been frustratingly dogged in their approach to winning this game and have hit the post and the bar, the latter a thirty yard wonder strike from their tall centre half that had everyone blowing through pursed lips. Moments before the break we lost Russ Dinsmore to a clear pull of his hamstring (a muscle I don't think I have possessed in either of my legs since the cross-country running module, Arthurston High, November '86). He was replaced to everyone's consternation by Ally Fairful who for yet another year has narrowly missed out on the Adidas Golden boot award, this season by a mere thirty four goals.

Today's half- time entertainment is a double treat. Firstly we have a keepy-uppy competition between a herd of young hopefuls who look as if they could do with more fresh air and less jam-doughnuts. The winner is a young lad abusively called Hoby with a hairdo like he'd been pulled through a wind-tunnel backwards and an arse the size of Uruguay. He scores a miraculous five by virtue of going over on his ankle on his fourth desperate kick, falling on his gargantuan bottom and the ball hitting him in the face on its return trip to Mother-Earth. A cheer goes up from the less charitable members of the crowd moments before club director Gordon Miller sashays on the park anxiously in his grey slip-ons, bravely holding his club blazer together at the waist, club tie wrapped around his neck like a noose. A quick check on the lad's well being and a covert nod to the groundsman to rake out any divots in the vicinity, he ushers the limping boy off the park repeatedly mouthing 'he's okay, he's okay' towards the gathered ensemble standing at the mouth of the players' tunnel.

As if that wasn't enough exhilaration, Jack Lees then walks round the ash at the side of the pitch with his tall 50/50 draw sign accompanied by a steam engine.

A steam engine.

Reasoning aside, God did that thing move slowly. The players were on the park lining up for the second half while the engine and a black-affronted Jack were just squeezing by the goals in front of the TP Hughes Stand. As its big shiny back wheel disappeared out the corner gate no one said anything. It was beyond comment.

10.

The May leaves shimmer in the breeze. From Madelaine's Tree a small brown helicopter seedling looses itself and flies away on the pockets of air, soaring to the sun then swinging downwards to earth and life. Downwards, twirling hypnotically over heads, falling and spinning past striped shirts, finally bouncing off white leather and coming to land beside four maroon socks, into the soil. Into the soil at the very moment a whistle blows and the stationery ball is first moved slightly then smacked forward with power and purpose – the second half is off and running.

The ball soars high in the air, quickly reaching full height before dropping down and down towards the Yellow jersey who, peddling backwards just makes the tip, fingers brushing the Mitre branding and sending it beyond the bar into the waiting crowd. A bad start by the home team straight from kick off is narrowly averted.

Its a spectacle. The men are fit. Fitter and stronger than we can ever comprehend. Machines almost. Moving with grace, power commitment and fearlessness. Crunching tackles rain at full-tilt sending bodies heavily to the ground. Foreheads meet leather with terrifying purpose. Pounding athletic runs are made, then made again, the smack of each shot and pass on the ball marking the passage of time. The crowd move and roar to their command. Inching forward on their seats. Eyes on the ball, to the heavens, to the feet. Wide, closed, anxious.

4.10

4.14

4.22

4.30

4.37

4.39

4.40

4.41

So my watch tells me.

Five minutes to go.

Just five.

Something on the pitch has changed though. There's fear in our play, in the eyes of our players. A sound half of control and self-belief and competitive instinct is rapidly dissolving in front of our eyes.

"Don't panic!" yells Jonesy. But we are panicking. Hearts attacks are coming in waves, like bombing runs in the war. Their upstanding supporters applaud madly as another corner is awarded, the third in the matter of a minute.

4.42

"Still one nil at Fir Park?" I turn and ask nervously behind me. Two heads nod and I look back to the game. The corner rips over and is nodded on at the front post by the waiting Hearts man. The ball streaks terrifyingly across the face of the goal and all sections of the crowd gasp as a flying diving header is narrowly missed at the other side by another maroon clad assassin . "Ooooooaaaaaahhhhhh" the crowd howl as Mark Bird slices the escaping ball out for a throw in, the danger not yet averted.

4.43

The ball is bouncing around the edge of the area just daring someone to rifle a shot at our goal. Amidst the melee it pops up just in front of the Hearts number seven. Just as he completes his wind up he is savagely pushed out of the way by a desperate

722

Tony Bunton. The referee blows immediately. Dave , Jonesy and everyone else look on in horror. A free kick - at the edge of the box.

4.44

The only comfort is the time it takes to book Bunton , get the wall back the required distance and for Wilf Schnabbel to substitute Robert Crush for Mickey Hedge. Hedge, when he gets the call to come off is conveniently standing closer to St Petersburg than the bench and takes an inordinate amount of time to cross the pitch limping slightly for good measure.

4.45

The fourth official holds up the electronic board above his head. It signifies 3 minutes in yellow dotted numbers and my stomach lurches. Four deliberate steps back and kick is taken. My leg jerks forward in unison with the strike, a ridiculous motion that thankfully no one notices. The ball whips low round the side of the wall and amidst the crowded box it momentarily slips out of sight. A roar goes up and my mouth drops open. Thomson is on the ground stretched out desperately to his left .... as the ball squirts back from either a leather glove or a white post. A mad pin-ball stramash ensues with what seems like every player on the park diving after the prize. The ball falls to a maroon shirt six or seven yards out. Head down, elegant technique, the Hearts man roasts a shot with everything he has ......

"Ohhhh n.....!" I start to scream but I'm stopped as a powerful, heaven-sent boot meets the shot with superhero force sending the ball shooting out the side of the pitch in front of the sun-baked Hearts fans. Robert Crush picks himself up from his last gasp sliding tackle and takes a 'high five' from a charged up Ivan Pecnic.

"Gowannnyafukkka!" I gargle in a state of near meltdown. Dave, clearly in his own world of pain, turns round and manages to look at me quizzically. I shrug and point him back to the game.

The ball is thrown back in quickly and Hearts come again. Another looping cross from the right only this time we are treated to sight that would stir the most impassioned heart. Andy Thomson, almost in slow motion charges out from his line, launches himself high into the air and grasps the ball in outstretched hands, easily a good foot above the nearest enemy head. He falls to the ground with an unceremonious thump but holds the ball safely to his chest under him. A triumphant cheer bursts the tension and as the keeper struggles to his feet, accepting back-slaps and hair rubs from surrounding team mates, we get to our feet too. To a man. A tidal wave of applause and yells of 'Cuuummm Onnnnnnnnnn yooooouuu Rovvverrrrrrrrs" rise around the ground. The noise is deafening and as Thomson rolls the ball out to Scott McLean who passes it calmly out right to Jerry Kidd, its only when Kidd lets the ball roll on and raises both his arms in the air that it becomes clear that the ref has blown his whistle.

McLean runs to bench then turns round punching the air. Amidst hugs and incoherent yelling I wheel round and shout "No change at Motherwell?" A couple of head shakes and I'm staring up at the old rafters in the roof, punching the air. "Yesss, Yessss!" I scream repeatedly.

11.

One voice behind me starts it all off. Simple and barely audible.

"Thistle have scored."

I pretend for a second I haven't caught it right but instantly I know I have. A few heads turn round. Most still singing, clapping and congratulating anyone in close proximity. On the pitch most of the players are in the centre circle dancing up and down held together in a chain-hug. Scott McLean is lying on his back looking at the sky. Wilf Schnabbel is gripping Robert Crush by the cheeks and shaking his head back and forward wildly.

"Nawww, nawww – it finished one nuthin'" another voice chips in reassuringly. But I hear it again, "One all at Fir Park"- the claim is spreading. Jonesy and Dave are bouncing up and down beside me, singing hysterically at the top of their voices when I catch the eye of Parka-man who is standing below me with a radio at his ear. He slowly lowers it to his side and gives me a life-sucking look. He then slumps onto his seat and slowly lowers his head in his hands.

All my nervous energy is suddenly spent and I too slump to my chair. Dave turns to me now aware something is wrong. He gives me a raised eyebrow.

"Thistle have equalised" I say dejectedly. And around the ground the clang of the big penny dropping is now forcing everyone into the stark realisation that its all over – we're down. The players too have apparently heard the news and the dancing has stopped. Five or six of them have collapsed on the turf looking at their boots. The rest are mulling around, shaking their heads, lost in their own reflections.

At least no one is crying. Like in those touching 'human' TV moments which have become so fashionable. Scenes of football fans greetin' their eyes out, slouched inconsolably in their bucket seats after what in reality is the least of disappointments. The Rovers fans are made of sterner stuff. A rallying cry of support goes up and the applause begins. Just a smattering at first but it soon builds into a crescendo of noise. The standing ovation continues as the players one by one lift their chins, stand in front of their fans and try like the rest of us, to conquer the disappointment of the day. Then, one by one with rueful smiles or grim countenances they trudge off the pitch and with nothing left to give, we, the fans, make our way to the doors.

12.

All things considered, the Sunday morning roll and sausage still tastes like heaven. And the mug of tea is one of those good ones that holds thirst quenching and life giving powers in equal measures. The warm sun is beating through the window onto the round, friendly, pine kitchen table casting its rays on the formidable bundle of newspapers and colour supplements spread in front of me.

For about the hundredth time I'm absorbing, contemplating and reflecting on all the disappointment that this 6cm square of newsprint represents. My eyes are lingering ruefully on the lower reaches of one league in particular;

Scottish Premier League

	Pld	W	L	D	GF	GA	PTS
Motherwell	38	7	17	14	36	55	35
Patrick Thistle	38	7	19	15	29	65	33
Arthurston Rovers	38	88	22	8	34	60	32

The important thing is that single, thin, black line drawn deliberately above my team's statistics. The line that separates the victors from the vanquished, the survivors from the corpses, from them and us. The line that has confirmed again and again, all morning long, that the long journey is over.

So sayonara Celtic, adios Aberdeen and catch-ya-later Killie. Its back to what we know and dare I say it , love. I sigh, fold the paper closed and, mug in hand, get up and move over to the kitchen window. Dad is outside standing, leaning on his big rusty early Bronze Age fork, staring balefully at the withered sapling in front of him. With a brief shake of the head he grasps the fork handle (not the four candles) and drives its prongs deep into the earth below the dead tree. Red faced and straining he hauls it up out the ground and swings a mass of roots, falling earth and dead wood into the waiting wheelie-bin. That done he takes one last sorrowful peek into the bin before resting back on the fork and wiping the sweat off his forehead. For a good thirty seconds he doesn't move, staring blindly at the hole he's made in front of him, then, as if awakening from a dream, he turns and disappears into the garage returning seconds later carrying another potted sapling ceremoniously in his hands.

In minutes the tree is expertly planted in its new home and Dad is scrambling back to his feet and with folded arms is admiring his handy work. I'm just about to move away when he looks over to the window and catches my eye. I smile and conjure up an impressed expression. Dad holds my gaze, smiles back, and after an instant of reflection, holds his hand up and beckons me to join him. Taking a final mouthful of tea I nod, put the cup down on the window-sill and walk out into the sunshine .

Epilogue.

Its not the worst thing in the world being back in the Scottish First Division. The passes go astray a bit more often, the insults thrown down from the stand are more easily heard, and we're thinking about chartering a light aircraft for some of the away trips but its all relative and its all much the same. Eleven men against eleven, the personalities , the hopes and the disappointments. Its still football after all. Wilf Schnabbel insists we will come straight back up again this year – he has instructed the players, according to the Arthurston Gazette to 'Just do it!'. And Raith Rovers momentously signed Ally Fairful for 'a nominal fee' during the summer transfer window which pleased us no end at the time but now has left us the unsatisfactory situation of having no one to shout at, a void we're anxious to fill.

And the world keeps spinning - for all of us. Jonesy is settled in his new job which he says feels more like being a double-glazing salesman than a banker. He has recently embarked on driving lessons and with personal safety in mind, I for one am heading down to Arthurston Central any day now to pick up a train timetable. Dave is back in the marital home and as part of Linda's terms of reconciliation, is visiting a marriage guidance counsellor once a week . "While the woman talks a lot of Bollocks she *has* got fabulous legs" he admitted recently over a lunchtime beer and steak-pie. And me? Well in the words of Bob Dylan, 'The times they are a changin'."

I moved out of my parents' in the Autumn and am renting a small upstairs flat above Ronnie Johnston's gift shop on the Main Street. It has peeling wallpaper of a design not seen since in the movie 'Shaft in Africa', a heating system that gets temperamental only when the outside temperature drops below zero, and a bathroom that smells of in between your toes – but its home. I still miss my Grampa, especially for our tea and chocolate biscuit chats but I've got someone new to boil the kettle for. Heidi and I are getting on great and she remains both amazed and impressed at my intricate knowledge of hardware and of how little time I spend in the toilet. Sandy is talking of retiring from the store and a piece of me is thinking of buying the business. And last week I had a conversation with Dad which lasted more than a minute, contained spontaneous laughter and finished with him patting me on the shoulder and saying 'Good on you son.' We are indeed living in strange times.

And of course Saturdays are still the Rovers. Because I am an Arthurston Rovers supporter. I had no choice in the beginning and I have none now. They represent my home town and therefore they are my team. If things go well I'll be there, if they don't, I'll still be there. And my friends will be there too because that's what its all about. Next year and the year after, and the year after that, the three of us will roll along to Wilmot Park and beyond. And when we're doddery old men we will be sat there, all in a row because we have a common purpose that brings us together and will do so until the day we die. We're all gloryhunting – and we know we are.

Lightning Source UK Ltd.
Milton Keynes UK
09 March 2010

151117UK00001B/2/P